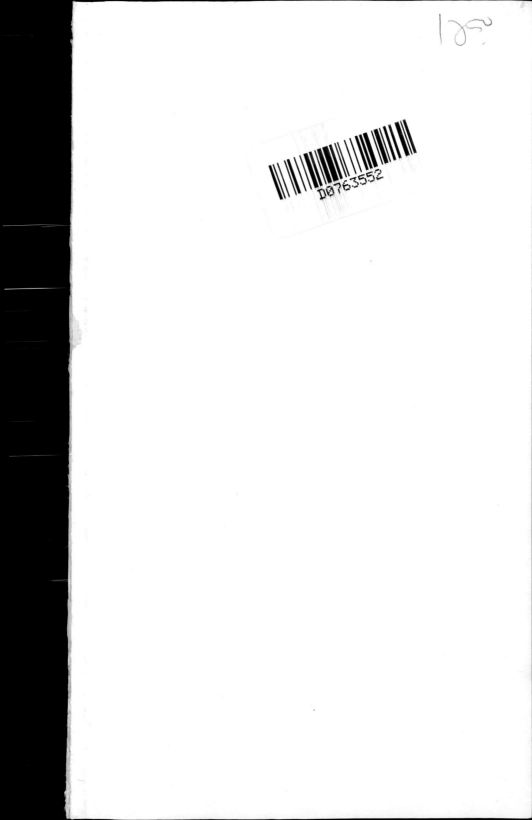

ART GUIDES

THE TREASURES of LUXOR and the VALLEY OF THE KINGS

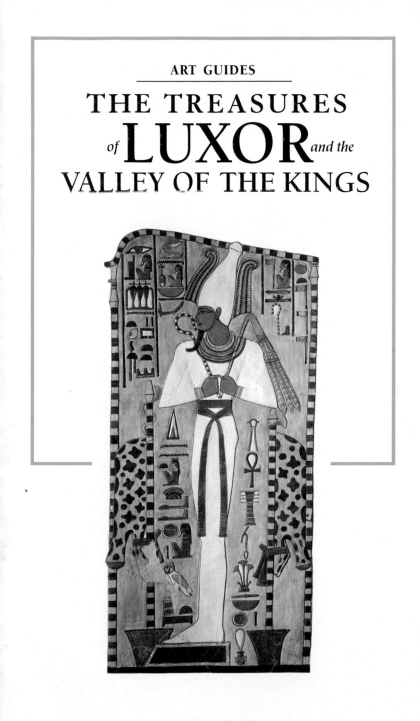

WHITE STAR PUBLISHERS

Authors

TEXT
Kent R. Weeks

EDITORIAL COORDINATION
Laura Accomazzo

GRAPHIC DESIGNERS
Patrizia Balocco Lovisetti
Paola Piacco

Via C. Sassone, 22/24
13100 Vercelli, Italy
www.whitestar.it

ISBN 88-544-0033-5

REPRINTS:
1 2 3 4 5 6 09 08 07 06 05

Printed in Italy
Color separation by Fotomec, Turin, Italy.

1 OSIRIS, GOD OF THE AFTERWORLD, FROM A PILLAR OF THE BURIAL CHAMBER OF NEFERTARI.

2-3 COLOSSAL STATUE OF RAMESES II FROM THE FIRST COURTYARD OF LUXOR TEMPLE.

CONTENTS

5
4
6

INTRODUCTION

So many guidebooks to Egypt are available today that another may seem unnecessary. But I hope that this one will serve a useful purpose: no other guidebook offers as much descriptive information on the tombs and temples of Thebes or such a large collection of photographs, maps, and plans. It is intended for visitors who wish to examine Theban monuments in detail, trace the development of their decorative programs, compare the works of different artisans, or try to better understand the purpose the monuments were meant to serve. It is also meant to be used after a visit to Thebes, as a reminder of sites visited and paintings enjoyed, and by armchair travelers who only dream of a visit.

The book is ordered monument by monument and along easily-followed itineraries within each of them. On the West Bank, sites are arranged first by type—temples, royal tombs, private tombs—then chronologically within the category. The monuments included are those that were open to the public early in 2004 and others likely to be opened within the next few years. Three exceptions to this are KV 17, the tomb of Sety I, KV 7, the tomb of Rameses II, and KV 5, the tomb of the sons of Rameses II. None of them is likely to be opened soon, but the three are of enough interest to justify inclusion. The Supreme Council for Antiquities is implementing a program of temporary tomb closures in the Valley of the Kings so that the tombs can recover from the pressures of tourism. It is possible that at any one time, one or two of the tombs described here will be inaccessible for periods of up to a year.

To avoid excessive repetition, cross-references in the text will lead the reader to explanatory details available elsewhere. For example, scenes on the walls of KV 9, the Valley of the Kings tomb of Rameses VI, are described at some length; when similar scenes occur in other tombs, instead of repeating that description, a reference to the KV 9 description is included.

A glossary of selected Egyptological terms is included, and a short bibliography, because this book is appearing in several different languages and a long list of references would be irrelevant in a field guidebook. Readers wishing further bibliographical information can easily find it on the internet by accessing such sites as http://www.theban-mappingproject.com, http://www.leidenuniv.nl/nino/aeb.html, or the websites of major university libraries. I have also avoided footnotes.
(I must, however, thank my colleague Rob Demarée for the translation quoted in the section on KV 2.)
The walls of corridors and chambers in tombs and temples are referred to as left, right, front, and rear. The left end of a wall is its left when you are facing it. Chamber designations in royal tombs are those used by the Theban Mapping Project.

Those in other tombs and in temples generally follow the *Topographical Bibliography* of B. Porter and R. Moss.

Ideally, a visitor to Thebes will have adequate time and stamina to visit everything described here. That, of course, is highly unlikely and a selection of monuments will have to be made. Of the nobles' tombs, one tomb from each of the five chronological divisions given here would provide a representative sample of New Kingdom private funerary art. But any visit should include Ramose, Rekhmire, Roy, Sennedjem, and Sennefer. Of the royal tombs, Thutmes III, Thutmes IV, or Amenhetep II should be on the list, as should Horemheb, Rameses III, and Rameses VI. In addition to Luxor Temple and the Karnak complex, one should see the temples of Madinat Habu, Merenptah, and Dayr al-Bahari. Dayr al-Madina and a hike over the hills are also to be recommended. The Luxor Museum of Ancient Art and the Karnak Open-Air Museum both deserve visits. And, of course, any time spent wandering through West Bank villages or the shopping streets of Luxor will be rewarded with scenes of beauty and vitality, new friendships, and reap scores of lasting memories. Markets in Luxor and on the West Bank (across the road from the temple of Sety I) are held early Tuesday mornings. Both are wonderful experiences, even if you are not in need of a tin cup or a donkey.

I must acknowledge my debt of thanks to Mark Linz at the American University in Cairo Press, John Swanson, Jill Kamil, Nicole Hansen, Francis Dzikowski, Walton Chan, Lamice Gabr, Ahmed Mahmoud Hassan and Magdy Abou Hamad Ali, and the staff of the Supreme Council for Antiquities in Luxor and Abbassiyah. And, of course, many thanks to Susan Weeks and the crew of the *Kingfisher.*

Kent Weeks

6 THE GOD PTAH, FROM THE TOMB OF NEFERTARI.

7 THE GODDESS HATHOR FROM THE TOMB OF HOREMHEB.

8 THE FIRST PYLON OF LUXOR TEMPLE WITH A COLOSSAL STATUE OF RAMESES II.

9 TOP VIEW OF THE BURIAL CHAMBER OF THE TOMB OF PASHEDU.

9 BOTTOM THE GOD SHU FROM THE TOMB OF KHAEMWASET.

12-13 NEFERTARI PRESENTING OFFERINGS, FROM THE QUEEN'S TOMB.

WEST VALLEY
VALLEY OF THE KINGS
DAYR AL-BAHARI

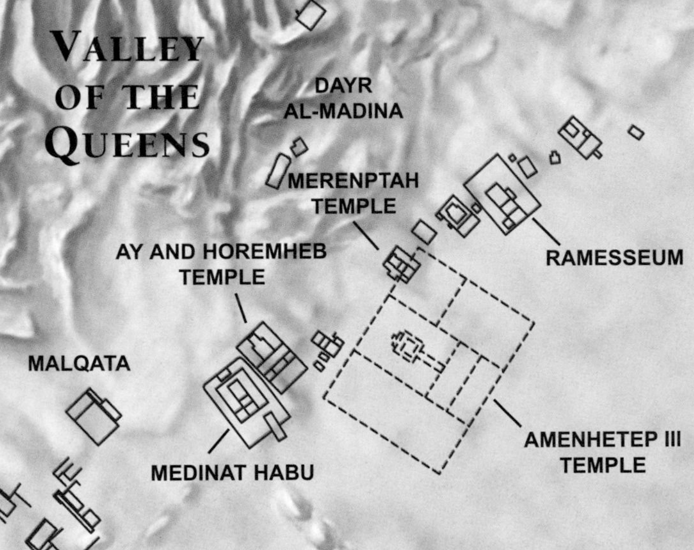

VALLEY OF THE QUEENS
DAYR AL-MADINA
MERENPTAH TEMPLE
AY AND HOREMHEB TEMPLE
RAMESSEUM
MALQATA
MEDINAT HABU
AMENHETEP III TEMPLE

0
1 km

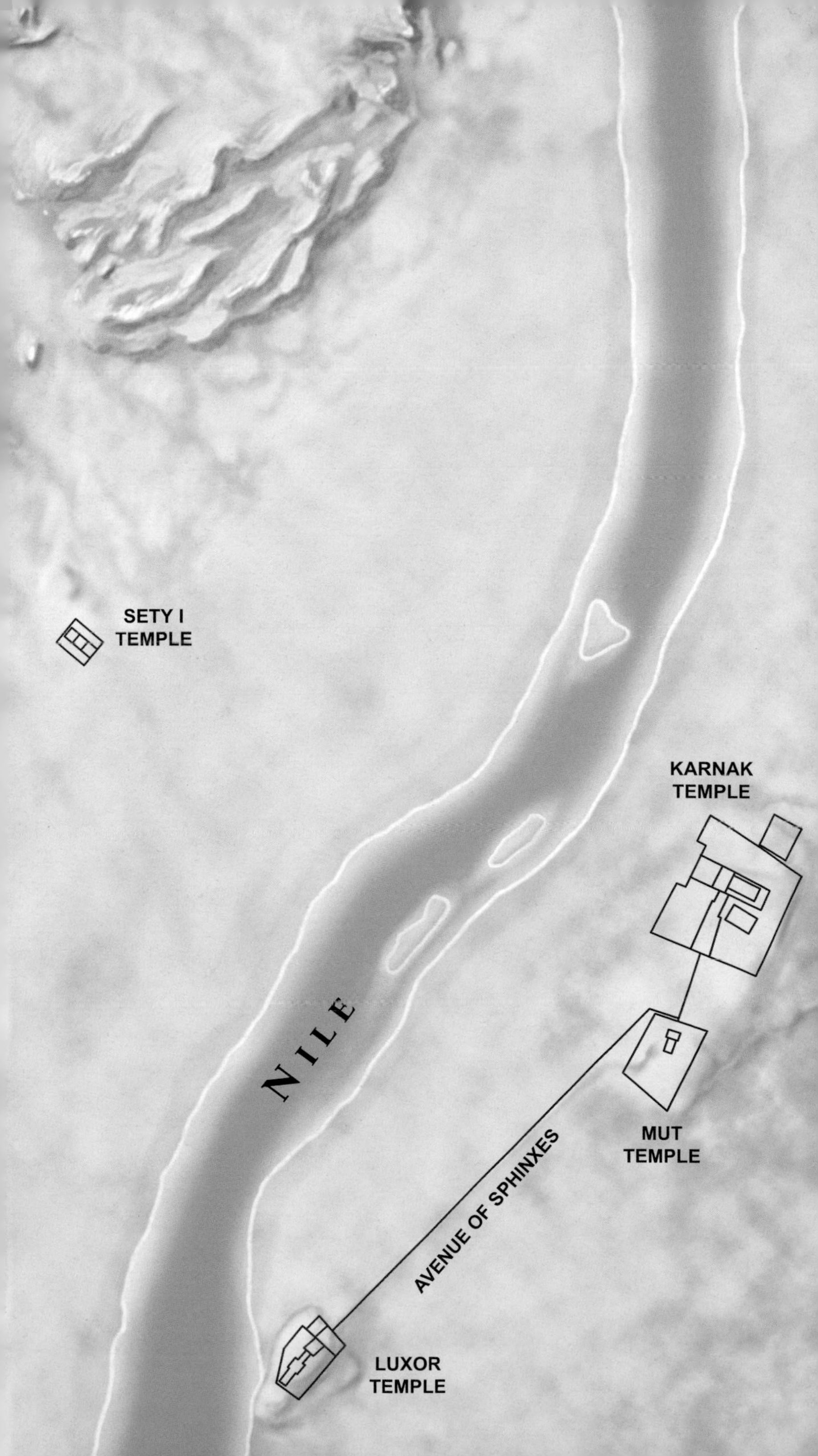
SETY I
TEMPLE
KARNAK
TEMPLE
NILE
MUT
TEMPLE
AVENUE OF SPHINXES
LUXOR
TEMPLE

GEOGRAPHY AND NATURAL HISTORY

Upper Egypt—the Nile Valley from Aswan at the First Cataract north to al-Lisht, near the entrance to the Fayyum—was divided in dynastic times into twenty-two administrative districts called *sepat* by ancient Egyptians and nomes by the Greeks. Nomes varied greatly in size, and their wealth depended upon how much agricultural land they possessed and what natural resources lay nearby. The first nome, at Aswan, for example, was rich in building stone and profited from bordering the gold lands of Nubia. The second and third nomes, whose capitals were at Edfu and Hierakonpolis, respectively, boasted agricultural land but little else. The fourth nome, headquartered at Thebes and named *Waset*, boasted rich farm land, mountains of fine limestone, and proximity to trade routes that led to oases in the Western Desert, gold mines and mineral deposits in the Eastern Desert, and wadis leading to the Red Sea.

But Thebes was not just rich in natural resources. What made Thebes the capital city of Egypt in the New Kingdom was its people: independent, spirited, militarily talented, and increasingly devoted to a local god called Amen, whose cult encouraged those attributes. Little more than a village of mudbrick huts in the Old Kingdom, by the New Kingdom Thebes had become the richest, most powerful city in the ancient world, home to the largest religious structures and most spectacular tombs and palaces ever built.

The banks of the River Nile at Thebes are broad, extending more than three kilometers to the east and west. Every year in summer, the Nile rose and overflowed its banks, covering the river valley with twenty to thirty centimeters (eight to twelve inches) of water for about six weeks in August and September. That water carried nutrient-rich silts that settled as the flood waters slowed, each year leaving behind another millimeter of fresh, rich soil and carrying away accumulated salts. As the waters receded, seed was sown broadcast across the freshly-irrigated fields and three to six months later crops were ready to harvest. Little wonder that ancient Greek visitors spoke in awe of this landscape and were convinced that the gods had blessed the Egyptians beyond all humankind. Nowhere in the ancient world did agriculture seem so easy as in Egypt.

The rich Nile floodplain produced abundant fruits and vegetables, but their variety was fairly limited. Emmer and barley were the principal grains and were used for making bread and beer. (For reasons still unclear, wheat did not appear until Graeco-Roman times.) Leeks, onions, and garlic were grown, as were lentils, chickpeas, fava beans, lettuce, and from the late New Kingdom, olives. Dates, figs, sycomore figs, pomegranates, various melons, sesame and safflower (for oil), and a few herbs and spices were raised. Grapes were made into several varieties of wine. (Red wine was the favorite drink of the Old Kingdom, white wine the favorite of the New Kingdom.) The only sweetener available was honey. Cattle were raised for milk and meat; sheep, goats, rabbits, and pigs were

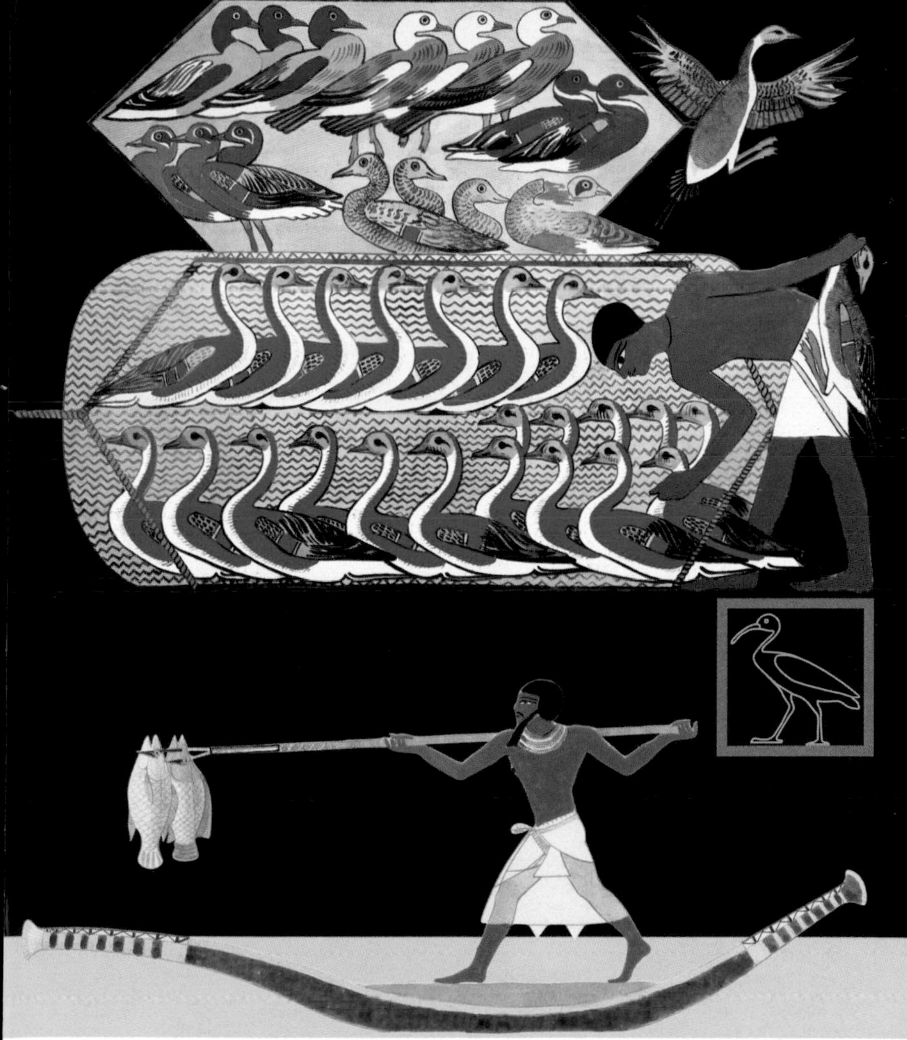

common, and the available fowl included ducks, geese, pigeons, and quail, but not chicken. Fishing and fowling, frequently depicted in tomb paintings, supplemented domesticated food sources. Flax was grown for the making of linen and gardens devoted to flowers were common at almost all social levels. Many foods that we take for granted, such as the potato, tomato, maize, citrus fruits, and sugar, were unknown and, indeed, would not be introduced into Egypt for several thousand years. Rice and water buffalo were unknown until about the fourteenth century A.D.

15 BIRD NETTING IN THE MARSH (TOP) AND AN EGYPTIAN FISHERMAN (BOTTOM). DRAWINGS BY IPPOLITO ROSELLINI FROM TOMBS IN BENI HASAN.

Agriculture came to Egypt from the ancient Near East around 5000 B.C., first appearing around the Fayyum, then moving southward, reaching the Theban area about a thousand years later. We know little about its subsequent development there until the New Kingdom. Then, Thebes provides us with a wonderful collection of texts and tomb paintings detailing many aspects of the agricultural cycle. For example, we have been able to track commodity prices through the Rameside period; the mechanics of land tenure and crop yields; and the shipping, storage, and redistribution of foodstuffs. Tomb paintings such as those in the tomb of Nakht (TT 52), show the techniques of ploughing, sowing, irrigating, harvesting, threshing, and storing of crops.

As long as the Nile flood was neither too low nor too high, crops grew in abundance, often producing sizeable surpluses. The summer flood pattern that typified dynastic times was established by about 12,000 B.C. But during the next millennia, "Wild Niles" flooded the valley with several meters of water in some years and barely a centimeter or two in others. In dynastic times, elaborate efforts were made to track and predict the Nile flood, and Nilometers were built at various places along the river to monitor its rise. Such information was crucial: several times in dynastic history floods were insufficient to grow adequate crops and the result was famine. At other times, high Niles wreaked havoc, destroying dikes, canals, and villages. In the reign of Rameses III, for example, a series of low Niles brought several years of social and economic chaos.

The annual deposition of Nile silts was heaviest along the banks of the river, less so as the waters moved

16 TOP FORCE-FEEDING LIVESTOCK. ALL DRAWINGS BY IPPOLITO ROSELLINI FROM TOMBS IN BENI HASAN.

16-17 PLOWING WITH OXEN. BEHIND THE PLOW, A FARMER SOWS THE FRESHLY TURNED LAND.

16 BOTTOM THE GRAIN HARVEST INCLUDED WINNOWING, MEASURING, TRANSPORTING, AND STORING IN SILOS.

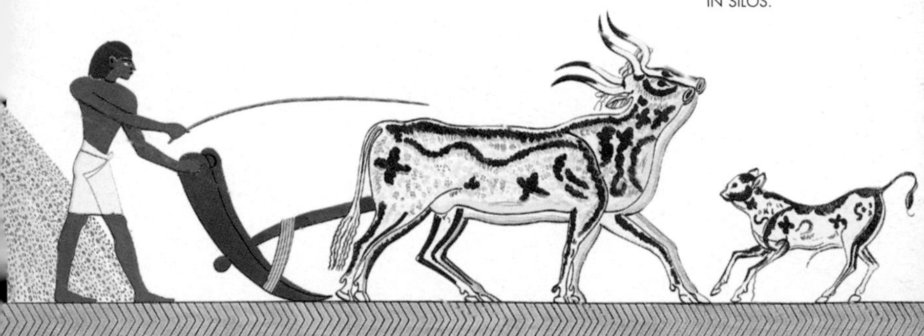

nearer to the desert edge. The result was that the Nile Valley gradually took on a convex cross-section. Levees along the river were the logical site for building settlements since the higher land there was usually safe from flooding and unsuitable for growing crops. Over time, however, as the mud-brick villages built here or on small mounds within the flood plain were abandoned or destroyed by high floods, settlements were eventually buried deep beneath layers of silt. That is why archaeologists even today know relatively little about the domestic architecture of ancient Egypt and so much about its funerary and religious architecture. Tombs, meant to last for eternity, were cut in stone in dry desert wadis where their preservation could be assured. Temples, built of stone but requiring regular accessibility, were erected on desert lands near the edge of the cultivation. They generally have survived, too, although their numerous outbuildings, usually constructed of mudbrick, have not.

Great limestone cliffs rose near the edge of the cultivable fields on the west bank at Thebes, and it was into those hills that both royal and private tombs were dug. But limestone was not used for the building of temples. They were constructed of sandstone which had to be dragged from quarries such as Jabal al-Silsila, 140 kilometers south. Granite from Aswan, basalt from the Red Sea Hills, and alabaster from the Western Desert were also transported to Thebes for the construction of doorways, lintels, obelisks, and statuary. The deserts were also a source of stone for jewelry and inlays, and produced turquoise, gold, jasper, galena, malachite, emerald, amethyst, and lapis lazuli, among others.

Egyptians were keen observers of their natural world and regularly depicted it in their tomb paintings. Lying in northeast Africa, at the crossroads of several different natural areas, Egypt has always been richly populated with many species of animals. It is largely from the meticulous paintings of nature we find in Theban private tombs that we can reconstruct the natural environment of New Kingdom Thebes in such detail. Egyptian artists, who presumably worked from a kind of artist's guidebook, took great pains to clearly represent species and even sub-species of plants and animals. For example, paintings of kingfishers carefully distinguished *Alcedo atthis* from *Ceryl rudis*. The special fea[illegible] of the White Pelica[illegible] drawn differently [illegible] those of a Dalma[illegible] Pelican. Such a[illegible] also to be see[illegible] representat[illegible] wild and [illegible] animals [illegible] and tre[illegible]

The Nile Valley today is still a beautiful and magical place, and one should take the time to enjoy its many attributes. Few things are quite as pleasant as sailing at sunrise along the west ank of the river. There, ecially in the autumn g the annual ward migration, of species of birds n, from herons s to bee-eaters It is not November ocks of a more e fields, searching for a place to spend the night.

Walking, or riding on horses, camels or donkeys through West Bank fields is equally rewarding, especially on cool winter afternoons. The crops are different today than in ancient times, of course, and sugar cane and wheat predominate, but the overall experience is nearly the same. All is quiet except for the call of a bird or the distant braying of a donkey; clean, fresh air carries the faint aroma of basil; tiny puffs of dust rise from a nearby path as an unattended donkey trots along the familiar route home. Palm trees and the tops of distant hills rise above the fields and wisps of smoke rise from village bread ovens. A stroll along the footpaths that crisscross the broad fields and lead to small mudbrick villages is an experience to be savored.

Much of the West Bank still retains a bucolic flavor, although new buildings of red brick and concrete, satellite dishes, tourist shops, and paved roads are springing up along the Nile and farther

18 TOP VARIOUS SPECIES OF BIRDS WERE PAINTED IN THE TOMBS.

18-19 THE NILE AND THE CITY OF LUXOR. LUXOR TEMPLE CAN BE SEEN AT THE LOWER RIGHT.

west at the desert edge. In another five or ten years, the character of the West Bank will have disappeared and one will have to travel outside Luxor's tourist zone to enjoy rural Egypt. Such changes have already overtaken the East Bank. Luxor today is a bustling, noisy city, filled with tourist hotels, gaudy bazaars, and coffee shops that blast pop music into crowded streets. Children shout, determined to sell cheap trinkets to tourists. Two statistics tell the story: thirty years ago, Luxor had two paved streets; today they are all paved. Twenty years ago, Luxor boasted only five taxis; today there are hundreds.

We know little about the layout of the Nile floodplain at Thebes in the New Kingdom. It is possible to trace the boundaries of several natural irrigation basins, but the location of villages, paths, and canals is largely conjectural. Among the few archaeological features known in the cultivation, the southernmost is Birkat Habu, a huge artificial harbor dug in the reign of Amenhetep III for the celebration of his first and second sed-festivals. To its north, also within the cultivation, lay that king's memorial temple, its first pylon fronted by the famous Colossi of Memnon. At the northern end of the Theban Necropolis lay an ancient village called Khefet-her-nebes and, adjacent to it, the memorial temple of Sety I. Artificial canals ra through the fields, connecting small harbo dug before the many memorial temples bu here.

20 TOP HOUSES OF QURNA, THE HILLSIDE ON THE WEST BANK WHERE NOBLES' TOMBS ARE LOCATED.

20 BOTTOM EGYPTIAN ART INCLUDED MANY REPRESENTATIONS OF THE COUNTRY'S FLORA AND FAUNA.

21 BALLOONS LIFT OFF AT SUNRISE FROM LUXOR'S WEST BANK DESERT.

The desert on the West Bank is another matter. Not only do we have the remains of ancient structures, we also have found an ancient papyrus that lists in geographical order the temples and houses that were built along the edge of the cultivation. From such data, we are able to divide the West Bank into several archaeological zones.

Adjacent to the cultivable land, a low, sand-covered strip of desert extends from the northern end of the necropolis to the southern. It varies in width from only a few meters (about 10 feet) to nearly three ilometers (1.8 miles). At e northern end lies an a called al-Tarif, site of ral hundred Old and le Kingdom tombs. To th, immediately adjacent to modern cultivation, lies a string of memorial temples, starting with that of Sety I and continuing southward with those of Amenhetep I and Ahmes-Nefertari, Hatshepsut, Thutmes III, Merenptah-Siptah, Amenhetep II, Rameses II, a son of Thutmes I, Thutmes IV, Merenptah, Rameses IV, Amenhetep son of Hapu, Thutmes II, Ay, Tutankhamen, Horemheb, and Rameses III. The Dynasty 18 palace of Amenhetep III is located at the southern end, and nearby stand the Ptolemaic temple at Qasr al-'Ajuz and the Roman temple at Dayr al-Shalwit, which mark the southern end of the Theban Necropolis.

Several small hills lie scattered within this low desert area, each of them pockmarked with the entrances to numerous small tombs known generally as the Tombs of the Nobles, or private tombs. A few date to the Old and Middle Kingdom but most are from the New Kingdom. They number in the hundreds, but only a few have been cleared or opened to the public. At the northern end of the necropolis is Dira' Abu al-Naja whose tombs are primarily of Rameside date. Near the road to Dayr al-Bahari stands al-'Asasif, housing about forty tombs, and al-Khokha, with about sixty. Shaykh 'Abd al-Qurna is a long, narrow hill with close to a hundred tombs. Qurnat Murai, beside the road into Dayr al-Madina, has seventeen.

Behind these small hills

stand the sheer cliffs of the Theban mountain. At their base stand several memorial temples, the best known of which are the three at Dayr al-Bahari belonging to Mentuhetep I, Thutmes III, and Hatshepsut.

Within the Theban hills proper, small wadis were used for the burials of Egypt's New Kingdom royal families and the workers responsible for digging and decorating their tombs. The workmen lived and were buried in Dayr al-Madina. To its south lies the Valley of the Queens and, between those two sites, the so-called Valley of the Dolmen. Several Coptic monasteries were also built in this area. The Valley of the Kings, actually two valleys, the East and the West, lies farther north and west, at the base of the highest point in the Theban hills, called al-Qurn or "The Horn." Many other areas on the West Bank are home to archaeological monuments, but most remain unstudied, unpublished, and inaccessible to tourists.

On the East Bank of the Nile lie the major temple complexes of Karnak and Luxor, as well as the ancient city of Thebes, now buried beneath the modern city of Luxor.

Most tourists to Thebes spend only one day on the East Bank and one day on the West Bank. But the sites here are so numerous and of such interest that, if at all possible, more time should be devoted to both sides of the Nile. At the very least, on the West Bank one should see tombs in the Valley of the Kings, a selection of the tombs of the nobles, Dayr al-Bahari, and Madinet Habu. The number of monuments to be visited in each of these areas can be extended to fill all available time, and to the list can be added the Valley of the Queens, Dayr al-Madina, the Ramesseum, and the temple of Sety I. On the East Bank, Karnak alone deserves a full day or, better, two mornings, and one should spend a couple of hours in Luxor Temple and the Luxor Museum of Ancient Art. A day spent walking through West Bank fields and villages, stopping often for tea and conversation, or hiking over the Theban Hills to admire the spectacular view, can all be high points of a visit here.

A HISTORY OF EGYPTOLOGICAL WORK AT THEBES

More than two thousand Greek and Latin graffiti carved on tombs in the Valley of the Kings indicate the interest of classical travelers in ancient Theban monuments two millennia ago. Even in dynastic times, the Egyptians themselves had showed a fascination with Theban history, and several kings boasted of conducting research and excavations in order to accurately restore ancient monuments.

In classical times, Diodorus Siculus described Thebes as a great city filled with "huge buildings, splendid temples, and other ornaments ... more opulent than the others in Egypt or anywhere else." Even then, Theban monuments were being carried back to Europe where they were admired for their size, beauty and mysterious hieroglyphs.

But surprisingly, all that interest in Thebes, even the knowledge of its location, disappeared from Europe for over fifteen hundred years. From the fourth to the eighteenth century, almost no mention is made of Thebes in European texts and there is no evidence that more than a handful of Europeans even visited the site. This may have been due in part to the inaccessibility of Upper Egypt for political or practical reasons.

It was not until 1726 that a French Jesuit, Claude Sicard, relocated and

correctly identified Thebes. Other travelers followed. A Danish engineer, Frederick Norden, drew sketches of Theban temples in the 1730s. At about the same time, an Englishman, Richard Pococke, drew a map of the Valley of the Kings and briefly described eighteen tombs he visited there. The accounts of Thebes published by these early travelers and the Egyptian objects that made their way into European collections once again fired the European imagination. Tourism, exploration, and collecting slowly began to revive.

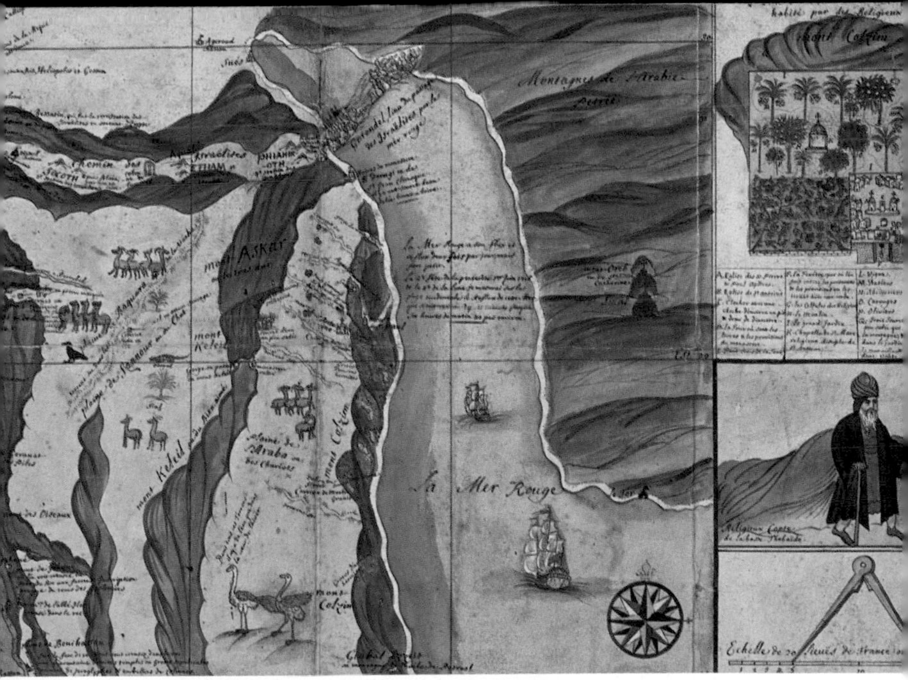

James Bruce, for example, visited in 1769 and explored the tomb of Rameses III in the Valley of the Kings. It became known as Bruce's Tomb after his publication of its scenes in 1790. Bruce also visited Madinat Habu and wrote a description of the techniques ancient artists had used to decorate its walls.

22 VIEW OF THE VALLEY OF THE KINGS BY R. POCOCKE IN 1738.

22-23 MAP OF EGYPT BY THE FRENCH JESUIT CLAUDE SICARD.

23 TOP THE COLOSSI OF MEMNON IN A PLATE BY F. NORDEN.

24 THE PTOLEMAIC TEMPLE AT DAYR AL-MADINA (ABOVE) AND DETAIL FROM THE TOMB OF RAMESES III (BELOW), FROM DESCRIPTION DE L'EGYPTE.

25 THE FRONTISPIECE OF THE SECOND EDITION OF THE DESCRIPTION DE L'EGYPTE SHOWING LARGELY FANCIFUL MONUMENTS.

By far the most significant early expedition to Thebes was that of Napoleon's army, which arrived in Egypt in 1799. The 130 scholars that accompanied the army were charged with making a detailed record of the country. One of the French scholars, Vivant Denon, described the awe his soldiers felt when they first saw Thebes: "At nine o'clock, in making a sharp turn round the point of a projecting chain of mountains, we discovered all at once the site of the ancient Thebes in its whole extent; this celebrated city, the size of which Homer has characterized by the single expression of 'with a hundred gates'... The whole army, suddenly and with one accord, stood in amazement at the sight of its scattered ruins, and clapped their hands with delight." Their work was published between 1809 and 1828. Called the *Description de l'Egypte,* one of its elephant folio volumes was devoted to drawings of Theban monuments and provided the first accurate record of Theban sites to appear in Europe. Hundreds of plates recorded architecture, relief decoration, and painting in tombs and temples, and accompanying volumes of text described what the scholars had seen. Even today, the *Description* can profitably be consulted by scholars because much of what it contains has vanished, victims of erosion, vandalism, and theft.

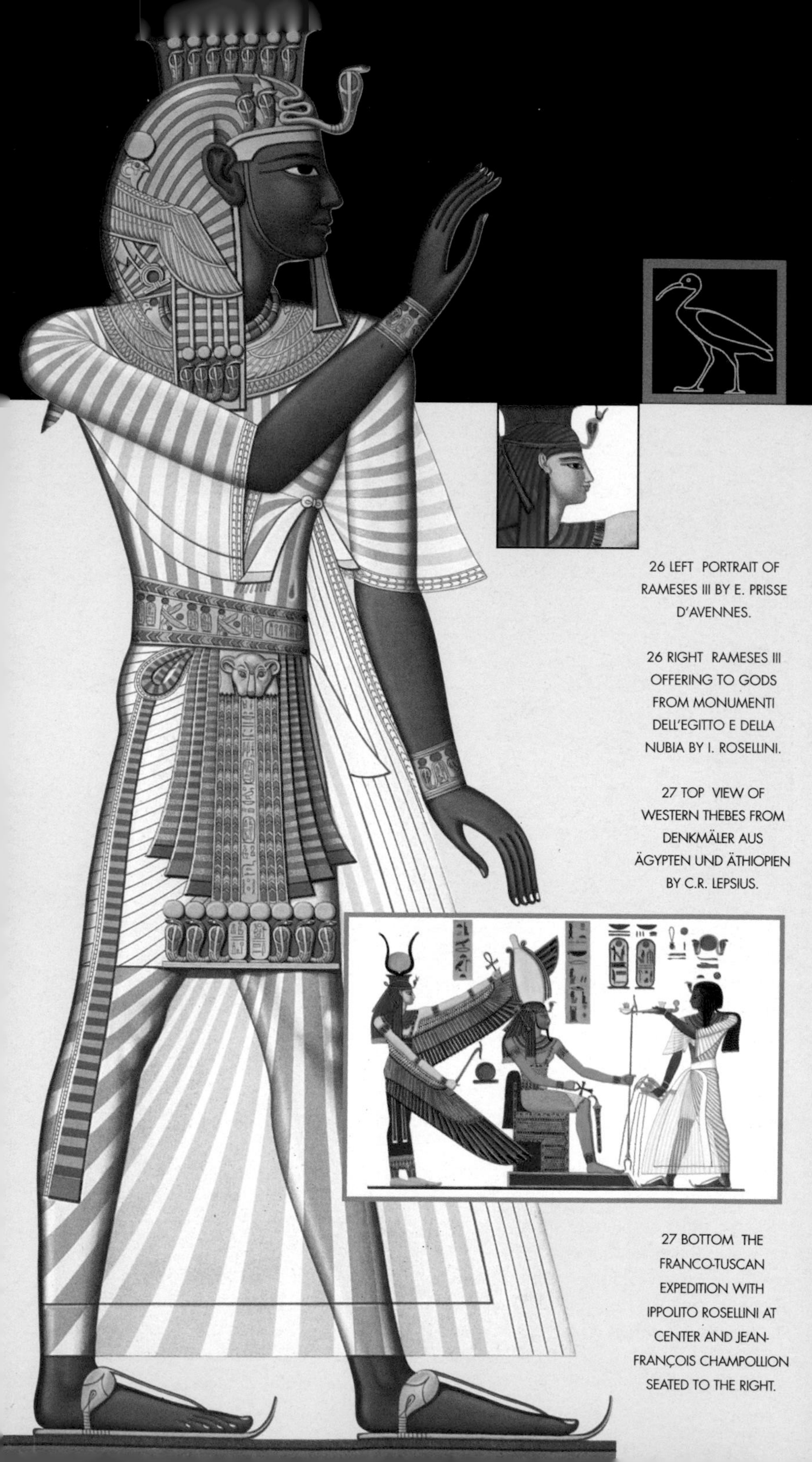

26 LEFT PORTRAIT OF RAMESES III BY E. PRISSE D'AVENNES.

26 RIGHT RAMESES III OFFERING TO GODS FROM MONUMENTI DELL'EGITTO E DELLA NUBIA BY I. ROSELLINI.

27 TOP VIEW OF WESTERN THEBES FROM DENKMÄLER AUS ÄGYPTEN UND ÄTHIOPIEN BY C.R. LEPSIUS.

27 BOTTOM THE FRANCO-TUSCAN EXPEDITION WITH IPPOLITO ROSELLINI AT CENTER AND JEAN-FRANÇOIS CHAMPOLLION SEATED TO THE RIGHT.

As interest in ancient Egypt grew in Europe among scholars, decorators, and collectors, other records of Theban monuments appeared. Jean-François Champollion, who had published the key to the decipherment of hieroglyphs in 1822, visited Thebes in 1828, accompanied by an Italian colleague, Ippolito Rosellini. They recorded scenes and inscriptions in the Valley of the Kings, Madinat Habu, the Ramesseum, and several nobles' tombs. Emile Prisse d'Avennes published a collection of elegant watercolors of tomb paintings in 1847. Other artists, too, painted Thebes: Alma Tadema (1836–1912), David Wilkie (1785–1841), Edward Lear (1812–1888), John Frederick Lewis (1805–1876), and most importantly, David Roberts (1796–1864). Some of them published very accurate paintings of Theban monuments, others produced scenes of ancient Theban life that were purely flights of fancy.

Of all the teams to record Thebes, the Prussian expedition of Carl Richard Lepsius was the most ambitious and the most accurate. Lepsius led an epigraphic expedition in 1842–1845. He spent much time at Thebes, and his publication, *Denkmäler aus Ägypten und Äthiopien* (1849–1859), immediately became an indispensable reference for scholars. Detailed and remarkably accurate, it still is a primary research tool.

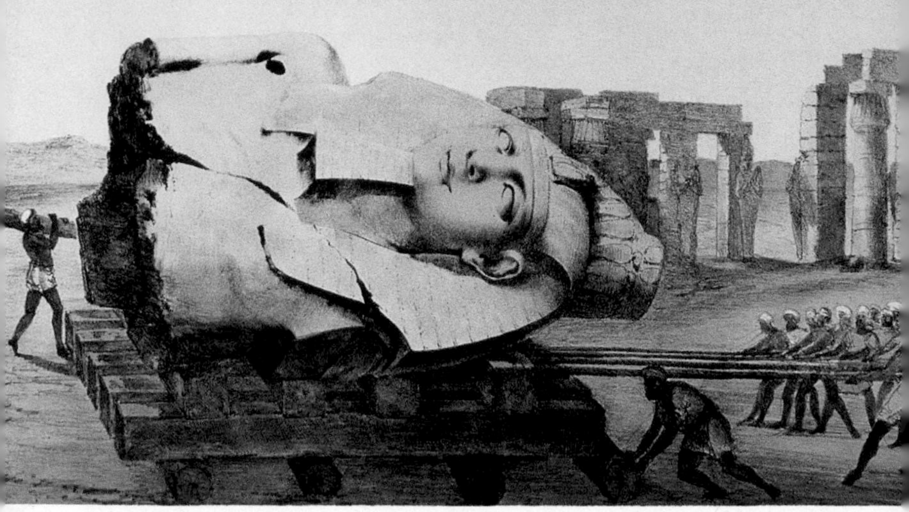

Giovanni Belzoni visited Thebes between 1816 and 1821. During the course of digging in the Valley of the Kings, he discovered six tombs, including those of Mentuherkhepshef, Ay, Rameses I, and Sety I. He also worked in the memorial temples of Amenhetep III and Rameses II (the Ramesseum) and carted off many objects to England, including several huge statues. Belzoni's techniques were primitive: "Every step I took, I crushed a mummy in some part or other," he wrote at one stage. But his London exhibition of impressions from walls of the tomb of Sety I was extremely popular and contributed greatly to ancient Egypt's popularity. So did the hugely successful book by Amelia Edwards, *A Thousand Miles up the Nile* (1877), a beautifully-written personal account of Egypt and its monuments.

The Englishman John Gardner Wilkinson worked at Thebes in 1824 and 1827–1828, recording with great skill scenes of daily life on the walls of nobles' tombs. The book he published, *The Manners and Customs of the Ancient Egyptians* (1837), is a tour de force that reconstructs

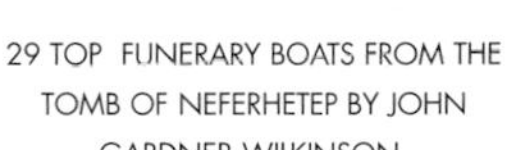

28 TOP, 28-29 AND 29 CENTER G.B. BELZONI (RIGHT) HAD THIS STATUE TRANSPORTED FROM THE RAMESSEUM TO THE BRITISH MUSEUM (LEFT). HE ALSO DISCOVERED THE TOMB OF SETY I (BELOW).

29 TOP FUNERARY BOATS FROM THE TOMB OF NEFERHETEP BY JOHN GARDNER WILKINSON.

in anthropological detail aspects of ancient life from kinship to cooking, chronology to costume. It was also Wilkinson who first established the numbering system still used today to identify tombs in the Valley of the Kings. Later, Norman (1875–1941) and Nina de Garis Davies continued this recording tradition, producing beautiful copies of private tomb paintings. (The originals are now displayed in the Metropolitan Museum of Art in New York). Meticulous and highly detailed epigraphic surveying was developed by the Oriental Institute of the University of Chicago and has been used by them at Thebes since 1924 to record inscriptions and scenes in the temples of Madinat Habu, Luxor, and other Theban monuments.

By late in the nineteenth century, photography was used to record Theban monuments, first by such famous photographers as Francis Frith and Maxime du Camp, later by the highly skilled photographers Felix Guillmant and Harry Burton. The latter was the photographer for Howard Carter's clearing of the tomb of Tutankhamen.

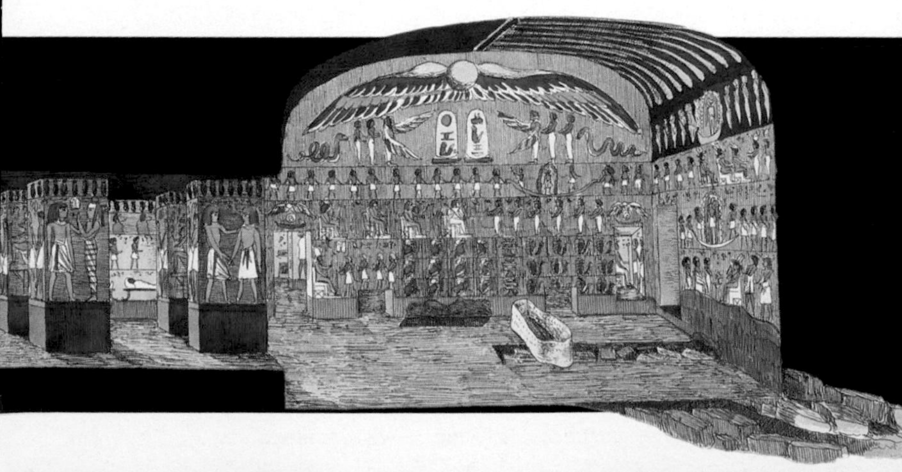

Early excavations of Theban sites were rarely more than the careless work of villagers or the hasty searches by Europeans for objects to install in Europe's many new museums. Richard Pococke complained of the cavalier treatment of the monuments by local villagers: "They are every day destroying these fine morsels of Egyptian Antiquity, and I saw some of the pillars being hewn into millstones." Champollion boasted that by shipping Theban monuments back to France he was performing a noble act: "One day you will have the pleasure of seeing some of the beautiful bas-reliefs of the tomb of Osirei [Sety I] in the French Museum. That will be the only way of saving them from imminent destruction and in carrying out this project I shall be acting as a real lover of antiquity, since I shall be taking them away only to preserve and not to sell." Other collectors included Henry Salt (1780–1827), whose collections formed the core of several of Europe's major museums, and Bernardino Drovetti (1775–1852), who collected for the Louvre and the museum in Turin.

These early collectors usually worked with the knowledge and permission of the Egyptian government. But by 1858 it was clear that greater control over Egypt's antiquities was necessary if the sites were to be protected. The Egyptian government, at the urging of Auguste Mariette, a French scholar, established a national museum and shortly thereafter, a national antiquities service. The export of antiquities was not banned by the new service (that

did not happen until the 1960s) but it was more strictly controlled, and attempts were made to guard and protect principal archaeological sites.

Over the next several decades, the new Antiquities Service employed several committed and talented people. Eugène Lefébure (1838–1908), for example, came to Egypt in 1881 after a career in the French Post Office. Consumed by an interest in Egyptology, he set out to record the texts in tombs in the Valley of the Kings. His two-volume publication, *Les Hypogées royaux de Thebes* (1888), was the first attempt to systematically record that famous site. A few years later, men like Victor Loret devoted several seasons to the excavation of tombs in the Valley of the Kings (in 1898–1899). Loret's excavation techniques were primitive by modern standards, but he and others added many more tombs to those already known in the Valley of the Kings.

Since the mid-nineteenth century, the quality of archaeological work at Thebes has been steadily improving. In the Valley of the Kings, for example, one can cite the work of Edward Ayrton, Arthur Weigall, and Howard Carter.

30 TOP THE ARCHAEOLOGISTS ARTHUR WEIGALL (LEFT) AND EDWARD AYRTON (RIGHT) IN FRONT OF THE TOMB OF RAMESES IV WITH THEODORE DAVIES, WHO FUNDED MANY EXPEDITIONS.

30 BOTTOM AN ARCHAEOLOGIST FROM THE ITALIAN EXPEDITION DIRECTED BY ERNESTO SCHIAPARELLI IN THE TOMB OF NEFERTARI.

30-31 THE MEMORIAL TEMPLE OF RAMESES III AT MEDINET HABU IN A PHOTOGRAPH BY AUGUSTE MARIETTE.

Carter (1874–1939), self-trained in England as an artist, had come to Egypt in 1892 to work with Flinders Petrie. Seven years later, he was appointed Chief Inspector of Antiquities in Upper Egypt and immediately began work in the Valley of the Kings. His artistic talents and insistence on meticulously recording what he uncovered set a high standard. They served him well when, after a sometimes tumultuous career in the Antiquities Service, Carter discovered the entrance to the tomb of Tutankhamen in 1922. It is arguably the most famous archaeological discovery ever made, and one that demanded almost infinite patience to clear and record.

The French have worked at Karnak almost continuously since 1899, the year part of the great Hypostyle Hall collapsed due to weakened foundations. They have undertaken excavation and publication as well as highly important engineering and conservation projects. The Open-Air Museum at Karnak, in which several important monuments have been reconstructed, is a tribute to their admirable work.There have been other excavators whose work has made significant contributions to our knowledge of ancientThebes. Ernesto Schiaparelli (1856–1928) excavated the workmen's village at Dayr al-Madina, bringing to light thousands of ostraka that tell us more about daily life in ancient Egypt than almost any other source. Uvo Hölscher excavated around the memorial temple of Rameses III at Madinat Habu in the 1930s, making it possible to trace in detail the history of the Madinat Habu complex. Herbert

Winlock and his colleagues from the Metropolitan Museum of Art in New York worked in the Dayr al-Bahari cirque from 1911 to 1932 on some of the most important excavations ever made at Thebes.

Visitors to the West Bank of Thebes today can still see the headquarters of these expeditions. Howard Carter's original house stands behind the offices of the antiquities inspectorate; his later house lies in a grove of trees at the north end of the necropolis. German House, reputedly burned down by the British at the start of World War I and again at the start of World War II, has been rebuilt west of the Ramesseum. The original Chicago House, headquarters of the University of Chicago, is now the Marsam Hotel, behind the memorial temple of Amenhetep III. (Its current headquarters are on the east bank of the Nile, in Luxor.) Metropolitan House, headquarters of the Metropolitan Museum of Art and later of the Polish Mission to Dayr al-Bahari stands before the memorial temple of Dayr al-Bahari. The home of Norman and Nina de Garis Davies lies about two hundred meters to its west. The house of the American businessman Theodore Davis, who funded many expeditions early in the twentieth century, lies near the start of the dirt track into the West Valley of the Kings, a satellite dish incongruously mounted beside the front door.

Today, there are many projects working at Thebes, but few are there to

excavate. Instead, they are projects to record, clear, stabilize, and conserve the fragile remains of its tombs and temples. Such measures are overdue and the need for them is rapidly increasing. Over eight thousand tourists visit the West Bank sites every day and that number is expected to rise to twenty-five thousand per day within a decade. The development of conservation measures and plans for site management are urgently needed if ancient Thebes is to survive. Egyptologists are finally aware of the serious threats to the monuments, and it is hoped that these new projects will ensure that ancient Thebes will survive for another five thousand years.

32 HOWARD CARTER (AT RIGHT) OPENS THE FOURTH GILDED SHRINE IN THE TOMB OF TUTANKHAMEN.

33 THE TOMB OF TUTANKHAMEN AT THE TIME OF ITS DISCOVERY. THE TOMB LIES IN THE WALLED PIT, LOWER RIGHT.

A BRIEF HISTORY OF THEBES

Human beings have lived at Thebes for at least half a million years. The first discovery of Paleolithic tools in Africa was made in the 1850s on the hillsides above the Valley of the Kings, and today hikers still find chert hand axes, scrapers, and drills lying about on the surface. Paleolithic weather was wetter than that of today, and wild grasses growing in now-arid valleys attracted rabbits, gazelle, ostriches, and other game, plentiful food for the bands of hunters and gatherers that lived here. The Paleolithic population in Upper Egypt was small and culturally conservative. Even after the coming of agriculture around 5000 BC, the hunting of small game and the gathering of wild plants continued to play a major role in Upper Egyptian culture.

Neolithic agricultural settlements lay scattered along the Nile, especially between Hierakonpolis in the south and Abydos in the north. For example, a few kilometers downstream from Thebes lay the large Neolithic village of Naqada, site of a sophisticated pre-literate culture. Examples of its beautiful pottery and stone crafts can be seen in the Luxor Museum of Ancient Art. Evidence of the Neolithic at Thebes itself is skimpy, probably because Nile silts now cover ancient sites. Equally rare are traces of the Early Dynastic (Dynasties 1–2) habitations.

The Egyptian Old Kingdom saw the development of pyramids at Giza, mastaba tombs at Saqqara, an increasingly sophisticated and codified system of writing and literature, and brilliant art, elaborate expression of religious beliefs, the growth of science, complex political and economic structures, and an expanding population. Together, these factors combined to make the Old Kingdom one the most impressive periods in

human history. But these developments mostly took place in a limited geographic area extending only about fifty kilometers (thirty miles) south of modern Cairo. Farther south only a few sites, like Elephantine and Abydos, shared these defining attributes of civilization. Thebes was apparently not one of them.

At this early date, the Fourth Egyptian Nome—the Theban Nome—boasted three principal villages. Armant, called Hermonthis by the Greeks, stood on the West Bank of the Nile, near the nome's southern border. It was the nome capital until about the Fourth Dynasty. On the East Bank two other villages were of importance: Tod, which lay in the south, and Medamud, in the north. Until the Middle Kingdom, the city of Thebes was little more than an inconsequential cluster of rude huts. The Theban Necropolis was in use, however: nomarchs were buried here from the Old Kingdom onward, probably because of the quality and accessibility of its limestone bedrock. We know of five nomarchs' tombs in the West Bank area of al-Khokha, and several others father north in al-Tarif. (None is open to the public.)

Toward the end of the Old Kingdom, the strong central authority of Egypt's capital city, Memphis, began to crumble due in part to the inertia and stagnation that had slowly come to characterize the long reign of Pepy II. As the court's authority declined, local nomarchs quickly moved to assume its powers, and by Dynasty 5, Egypt's central bureaucracy had been replaced by local dynasties that paid little attention to events beyond their borders. Their lack of a broad power base, coupled with a series of disastrously low Nile floods, resulted in the eventual collapse of these nomarchies, and Dynasties 7 and 8 were little more than a rapid succession of short-lived and competing rulers. Officials' tombs were no longer built near the king's pyramid complex in the Memphite nome. Instead, nomarchs chose to be buried at home, and provincial styles in art and architecture offer graphic evidence of the central government's demise.

34 LEFT DETAIL OF BIRDS FROM THE TOMB OF MENNA.

34 RIGHT AND 35 NILE GOD REPRESENTATIONS FROM THE TOMB OF RAMESES III, FROM MONUMENTI DELL'EGITTO E DELLA NUBIA BY IPPOLITO ROSELLINI.

36 LEFT OFFERING BEARER FROM THE TOMB OF MEKETRE, NOW IN THE EGYPTIAN MUSEUM, CAIRO.

36 RIGHT NEBHEPETRA MENTUHOTEP, FROM DAYR AL-BAHARI NOW IN THE EGYPTIAN MUSEUM, CAIRO.

37 SENUSRET I, IN THE LUXOR MUSEUM OF ANCIENT ART.

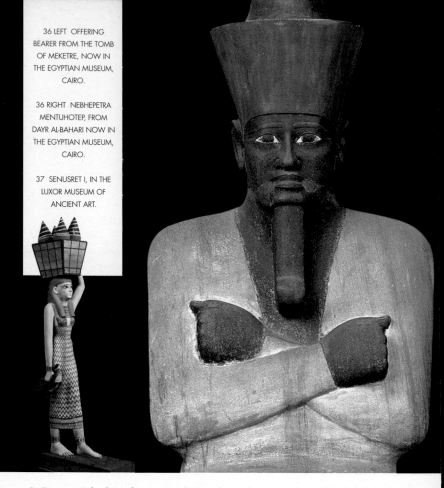

In Dynasty 9, leaders of Heracleopolis, a nome about 200 kilometers (120 miles) south of Memphis, declared themselves rulers of all Egypt and seized control of Memphis and the royal court. The major threat to the Heracleopolitans was the leadership of the Theban nome, who backed up their competing claim to authority with military forays against Heracleopolitan holdings. For fifty years, Theban rulers including Intef I, Intef II, Intef III, and the succeeding series of rulers named Mentuhetep devoted themselves to building Thebes and expanding its control over Egypt. Nebhepetra Mentuhetep I, for example, worked in Dynasty 11 to create a strong, Egypt-wide bureaucracy with its capital at Thebes. At first he called himself the Divine One of the White Crown, implying that he controlled Upper Egypt, and then Uniter of the Two Lands, meaning that he ruled all of Egypt. At Dayr al-Bahari, he built a mortuary temple and tomb of new design that served as the inspiration for Queen Hatshepsut's memorial temple five hundred years later. Scenes in his temple provide early evidence that the Thebans were elevating to prominence a little-known local god, Amen, who would soon surpass the nome's principal deity, Montu, in wealth and power.

One of Mentuhetep's successors was responsible for an unfinished temple-tomb complex in a small cirque half way between Dayr al-Bahari and Dayr al-Madina. Court officials of the time, most notably Meketre, built tombs nearby.

Meketre's tomb contained a number of elegant wooden models of daily life that are among the treasures of the Egyptian Museum in Cairo and the Metropolitan Museum of Art in New York.

Mentuhetep III was an apparently illegitimate ruler quickly succeeded by his vizier, Amenemhet, the son of a priest from Elephantine. He claimed the throne as Amenemhet I, first king of Dynasty 12, and immediately moved his court from Thebes to a site thirty kilometers (eighteen miles) south of Memphis called Itj-tawy, the modern al-Lisht. Thebes continued to be a principal religious center—the Temple of Amen at Karnak had been enlarged by each of the Dynasty 11 kings—but Itj-tawy remained Egypt's administrative capital for the remainder of Dynasty 12.

Amenemhet I's successors continued to enhance Egypt's economic well-being and contributed to the growing prominence of the priesthood of Amen. His son, Senusret I, paid tribute to Amen by building at Karnak, and his White Chapel, now in Karnak's Open-Air Museum, is one of ancient Egypt's most beautiful buildings. Amenemhet II expanded foreign trade and military activities in both Nubia and in western Asia, and his successor, Senusret II, created extensive agriculture lands in the Fayyum. Senusret III cut a channel through the Nile's First Cataract to speed economic and military expeditions south into Nubia, and Amenemhet III expanded trade even further. Much of this new wealth went to Thebes and its temples.

Amenemhet I called himself a "Repeater of Births," that is, the founder of a renaissance, and it is certainly true that he and his successors brought about a remarkable revival of Egyptian culture and society. Agricultural expansion put thousands of hectares of new lands under cultivation. This produce, as well as significant increases in foreign trade and tribute, brought immense wealth to Egypt. The results were dramatic: literature thrived in Dynasty 12 and there were great advances in the sciences. Arts and crafts, especially sculpture and architecture, achieved new aesthetic heights. Dynasty 12 lasted two hundred years and was one of the richest and most creative periods in Egyptian history. But it ended with the death of Amenemhet IV, who lacked a male heir and who was therefore succeeded by his sister, Sobekneferu, perhaps the first woman in ancient Egypt to be crowned ruler. She ruled for just three years before western Asiatic tribes collectively known as the Hyksos, "Rulers of Foreign Lands," seized control of Lower Egypt. Their occupation marked the beginning of what Egyptologists call the Second Intermediate Period.

The Hyksos had been moving gradually into Egypt for over a century, not at first as conquerors, but as servants and settlers. As their numbers grew, they took control of large tracts of agricultural land and sought to establish their own government in the Delta. As they pushed farther south, the Theban nome under Seqenenra Tao II declared war against them. He was killed in the ensuing battle and succeeded as king by his son, Kames. At first, Kames controlled only Upper Egypt from Elephantine to Cusae, a town near modern Asyut. But he quickly pushed northward into the Delta, and successfully attacked Avaris (Tall al-Daba'a), the Hyksos capital near the site of the modern Suez Canal.The Hyksos brought many new innovations with them into Egypt, including new techniques of pottery making, bronze working, and weaving. In warfare, they introduced the composite bow, more efficient swords and daggers, and most importantly, the horse and war chariot. These presented a formidable challenge to the Egyptian army, but the Egyptians persevered and slowly gained ground. Kames continued to pound at their armies, and after his death, his brother and successor, Ahmes, pushed to final victory. His military success against the Hyksos was coupled with the rapid reconquest of Nubia and its gold mines, and the invasion of Sinai, southern Palestine, and Crete. Ahmes was lauded as the founder of Dynasty 18, and because of his reputation as a military leader, he was deified and worshipped at Thebes well into the Rameside period.

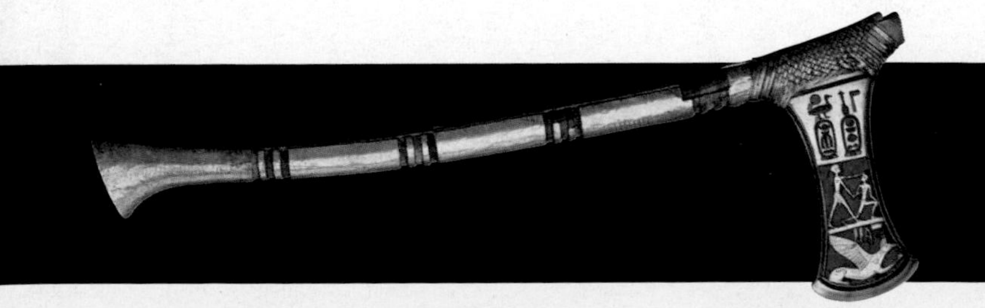

38 TOP SPHINX OF AMENEMHET III, EGYPTIAN MUSEUM, CAIRO.

38 CENTER BRACELET OF QUEEN AHHOTEP, MOTHER OF KAMES AND AHMES, EGYPTIAN MUSEUM, CAIRO.

38 BOTTOM AND 39 AHMES'S DAGGER AND CEREMONIAL AXE, EGYPTIAN MUSEUM, CAIRO.

40 HEAD OF HATSHEPSUT FROM DAYR AL-BAHARI TEMPLE, EGYPTIAN MUSEUM, CAIRO.

41 LEFT AMENHETEP II WITH THE THEBAN GODDESS MERETSEGER, FROM THE TEMPLE OF KARNAK EGYPTIAN MUSEUM, CAIRO.

41 RIGHT STANDING STATUE OF THUTMES III FROM THE CACHETTE OF KARNAK, EGYPTIAN MUSEUM, CAIRO.

After Ahmes's death, his son, Amenhetep I, rapidly consolidated his father's political and military gains. The skillful administration established by the new king led later generations to declare him patron deity of the Theban Necropolis. Amenhetep I's tomb is thought to be the first royal tomb to be built apart from its memorial temple. Thutmes I married Amenhetep I's younger sister and succeded him as king. The new king's military campaigns in western Asia and Nubia were so successful that Egypt extended its control into foreign lands over 1,600 kilometers (1,000 miles) up the Nile and 1,500 kilometers (900 miles) east to the banks of the Euphrates River. The royal architect, Ineni, continued in office and supervised the king's substantial building activity at Karnak and the construction of his tomb, perhaps the first tomb to be cut in the Valley of the Kings. New theological texts appeared during the king's reign, including the *Imydwat* and the Litany of Ra, and the god Osiris assumed an increasingly prominent role in Egyptian theology.

The older sons of Thutmes I predeceased their father and the throne fell to his third son, Thutmes II. One of the new king's first acts was to make his half-sister, Hatshepsut, his chief royal wife. It was a decision that would have far-reaching consequences. Thutmes III, the son of a minor wife of Thutmes II, was only six or seven years old when his father died. Because of his youth, Hatshepsut was appointed regent. Within two years, however, she had herself crowned king of Upper and Lower Egypt in an elaborate ceremony described in her memorial temple at Dayr al-Bahari. Texts there proclaimed that she had been born of the gods, and ignoring the reign of Thutmes II, claimed that she was the direct and legitimate heir of her father, Thutmes I. Thutmes III continued to be referred to as if he and Hatshepsut ruled jointly, but for all intents and purposes, Hatshepsut had pushed him into the background and taken control of the country. Apparently one of her principal advisors was her architect, Senenmut, who had served as the tutor of her daughter, and who called himself "the greatest of the great in all the land." Before his death in the seventeenth year of her reign, he had overseen the building of her memorial temple at Dayr al-Bahari, arguably one of ancient Egypt's most beautiful monuments, and made extensive additions to the Temple of Amen at Karnak.

When Hatshepsut died after twenty years on the throne, Thutmes III finally became sole ruler of Egypt. One Egyptologist called him "a Napoleonic little man"—he stood only 157 cm (five feet two inches) tall—and militarily his reign was one of Egypt's most energetic. Over sixteen campaigns in western Asia alone restored lands lost during the more pacific years of Hatshepsut, and in Nubia he solidified Egyptian control as far south as the Fourth Cataract. Memphis was the administrative and military capital of the country during his reign, but Thebes continued to receive special attention as its religious center. The king ordered major construction at Thebes, and his additions to the Temple of Amen at Karnak are among the most extensive ever built there. His tomb, KV 34, is elaborately and beautifully decorated. The tombs of his officials (that of Rekhmire is a good example) are among the finest in the Theban Necropolis, filled with scenes that proudly display tribute from Egypt's growing empire.

Amenhetep II and Thutmes IV continued this military tradition and both led expeditions into Nubia and Syria. They were great supporters of art and architecture, built extensively at Karnak, and dug impressive tombs in the Valley of the Kings.

Amenhetep III, son of Thutmes IV, came to the throne while still a child and arguably contributed more to the growth of Thebes than any other king in Dynasty 18. Although he led many expeditions abroad, Amenhetep III is best known for his work at home. There was a deliberate emphasis on the past, and archaizing styles resulted in many changes in the plans and decoration of tombs and temples. He ordered substantial additions to the temple of Amen in Karnak, including the Third and Tenth Pylons, and to the Temple of Mut. He built a great palace, Malqata, on the Theban West Bank and beside it dug a huge harbor nearly 2 kilometers (1.2 miles) long and 1 kilometer (0.6 miles) wide, used for religious celebrations. He dug a superbly cut and decorated tomb in the West Valley of the Kings (soon to be opened to tourists). But his most impressive monument must surely be his memorial temple, Kawm al-Haitan, on the West Bank, the largest memorial temple ever built. The Colossi of Memnon that stand at its entrance are among the largest monolithic statues ever carved. Amenhetep III and his queen, Tiy, were deeply involved in theological and political discussions which gave increasing emphasis to the solar cult and the divine nature of kingship, and they laid the foundation for the traumatic religious changes wrought by their son, Amenhetep IV.

42 STATUE OF AMENHETEP III, LUXOR MUSEUM OF ANCIENT ART.

43 COLOSSAL STATUE OF AMENHETEP III, QUEEN TIY, AND DAUGHTERS, ORIGINALLY IN HIS MEMORIAL TEMPLE, EGYPTIAN MUSEUM, CAIRO.

Amenhetep IV, who changed his name to Akhenaten in the fifth year of his reign and moved his capital from Thebes to the new city of Akhetaten (Tall al-Amarna), introduced profound changes in Egypt's art, architecture, written language, and especially, religion. Temples to traditional gods were closed; the writing of the word 'god' in the plural was forbidden; aspects of the solar cult were combined and worshiped as the Aten, the solar disk. The king and his family were also given unusual divine status. Thebes suffered because of the temple closures and the move to Akhetaten, and few monuments were built at Thebes after. An exception is an enormous temple to the Aten he built east of the Temple of Amen at Karnak, blocks from which can be seen today in the Luxor Museum of Ancient Art. Equally important for art historians is the beautifully decorated tomb of the vizier, Ramose, begun under Amenhetep III and continued under Amenhetep IV/Akhenaten.

Akhenaten may have been succeeded by a certain Smenkhkara, but we do not know with certainty who this person was or for how long he (or she) might have ruled. The next successor was Tutankhamen, perhaps the adolescent son of Amenhetep IV/Akhenaten, whose tomb in the Valley of the Kings housed the most spectacular collection of objects ever found in Egypt. Its discovery in 1922 guaranteed that Tutankhamen would become the best-known king in all Egyptian history, even though his reign was short, his activities unremarkable, and his Theban building projects few in number (at Luxor Temple, for example).

Tutankhamen's regent, Ay, became ruler when the boy-king died. We know little about him except that he is shown on the wall of Tutankhamen's burial chamber performing the king's Opening of the Mouth ritual, and he was buried in a tomb (perhaps originally intended for Tutankhamen) in the West Valley of the Kings.

Ay in turn was succeeded by a general of the army, Horemheb, the first ruler in over fifty years to build extensively at Thebes. He added to the Temple of Amen at Karnak, often re-using blocks taken from the temple of Akhenaten. His tomb in the Valley of the Kings is one of its most impressive. Horemheb was the last king to use Thebes as an administrative capital, and he boasted about how he had reformed the bureaucracy there by appointing not simply men of high rank "to judge the citizens of every town," but men "of perfect speech and good character."

44 TALATAT BLOCK WITH AKHENATEN ADORING THE SUN, FROM KARNAK TEMPLE, LUXOR MUSEUM OF ANCIENT ART.

45 LEFT COLOSSAL HEAD OF AKHENATEN, FROM KARNAK TEMPLE, LUXOR MUSEUM OF ANCIENT ART.

45 RIGHT DETAIL OF COLOSSAL STATUE OF TUTANKHAMEN, EGYPTIAN MUSEUM, CAIRO.

Horemheb's deputy, the army officer Paramessu, succeeded him and took the name Rameses I. He ruled from the Delta town of Tanis, leaving Thebes to continue as a religious center but not as a secular capital. Rameses I is often considered the first king of Dynasty 19. The kings of this new dynasty took names compounded with those of the Lower Egyptian gods Ra, Seth, and Ptah, not with the names of Upper Egyptian gods Amen and Thoth that had been prominent in royal names of Dynasty 18.

The son of Rameses I, Sety I, conducted several military campaigns in western Asia. As a matter of convenience he too resided in the Eastern Delta, but he devoted substantial wealth to religious buildings at Thebes. His memorial temple on the West Bank and his tomb in the Valley of the Kings became models of design that were highly praised and emulated by later kings. His additions to the Temple of Amen at Karnak, especially the Hypostyle Hall and the decoration of its outer north wall, are among the finest examples of art and architecture to be found in Egypt. Sety I also established the Valley of the Queens as a royal necropolis, and his mother was buried in the first tomb to be dug there. His successor, Rameses II, continued military activity on a grand scale, although there is good reason to believe that he greatly exaggerated his prowess as a military commander. Indeed, many Egyptologists consider some of his boasts to be outright lies. But as a builder, there is no doubt that Rameses II excelled. He may have emphasized quantity over quality, but his monuments were intended to impress and in that they succeed brilliantly. In Nubia, he ordered the carving of two gigantic temples at Abu Simbel. At Thebes, he ordered a huge and spectacular tomb for his wife, Nefertari. He completed work on the Hypostyle Hall at Karnak; added to Luxor Temple; built for himself a glorious memorial temple, the Ramesseum; and finally carved two huge tombs in the Valley of the Kings, one for himself and another, the largest tomb in the valley, for several of his many sons. His reign of sixty-seven years is ancient Egypt's second longest, and the king lived well into his eighties at a time when the average Egyptian male died before forty-five.

It was his thirteenth son, Merenptah, probably already well into his fifties, who finally succeeded Rameses II. The new king resided at Memphis and undertook several military campaigns in Nubia and in western Asia against the Sea Peoples, Libyans, and Sardinians. At Thebes, he is best known for his tomb in the Valley of the Kings and his memorial temple, which reused hundreds of statues and blocks from structures nearby. The Israel Stela, in which the name of that people is mentioned for the first time in an Egyptian text, was written during his reign and installed in his memorial temple. Some claim that Merenptah was the pharaoh of the biblical Exodus, but there is no evidence for this.

47 TOP COLOSSAL HEAD OF RAMESES II IN THE FIRST COURTYARD OF LUXOR TEMPLE.

47 BOTTOM CARTOUCHES AND CEILING DECORATION FROM THE TOMB OF SETY I, REPRODUCED BY G.B. BELZONI.

Sety II, a son of Merenptah, was crowned king after the brief reign of a usurper, a Viceroy of Nubia named Messui (who changed his name to Amenmeses) who gained control of Upper Egypt. But the supporters of Sety II easily thwarted the attempted take-over and Sety II ruled for about six years. His tomb is open to the public; that of Amenmeses, KV 10, is currently under excavation.

When Sety II died, his son Siptah was still a child and Sety II's wife, QueenTausert, served as the young boy's regent. When Siptah unexpectedly died, she then served as sole ruler for two years, supported by the chancellor Bay, a Syrian who wielded great power in the Egyptian court and who was rewarded with a tomb in the Valley of the Kings (KV 14; closed to tourists). She was succeeded by Setnakht, a man of unknown origin who, unusually, usurped and enlarged her tomb.

The only significant New Kingdom ruler after the death of Merenptah was Rameses III, son of Setnakht. Rameses III modeled his reign after that of Rameses II; he named his sons after the sons of Rameses II; and he built a memorial temple, Madinat Habu, that followed the plan of the Ramesseum. He erected a shrine in the First Court of the Temple of Amen at Karnak and began work on the Temple of Khonsu, again following the style of Rameses II. But the similarities between the two kings' reigns are superficial. Unlike Rameses II, Rameses III faced serious economic problems: early in his reign commodity prices quintupled and workmen from Dayr al-Madina, complaining that they had not been paid for months, went on strike. Charges of corruption were successfully leveled against important court bureaucrats. Rameses IV, the king's son and successor, later compiled a list of the donations he claims his father made to Egypt's many temples, perhaps an attempt to counter arguments that Rameses III was an uncaring monarch who had ignored the needs of his subjects. But there is little doubt that Rameses III's inefficient and increasingly corrupt reign was a major cause of the troubles Egypt was facing.

One of Rameses III's minor wives, Tiy, even conspired with priests and officials to murder the king and have her son installed on the throne. Rameses III was already seriously ill, and the plotters were determined to name his successor. But the conspiracy was discovered, Tiy and the others were tried, found guilty, and forced to commit suicide. Rameses III died before the trial ended and his rightful heir, Rameses IV, ascended to the throne.

The remaining eight Ramesside rulers of Dynasty 20 witnessed the decline of ancient Thebes. Marauders stalked travelers in Upper Egypt, civil wars brought chaos to Thebes, and bureaucratic corruption was rampant. Even thefts in the Valley of the Kings were tolerated for a time because the loot they produced helped to offset rising inflation and economic depression. At the beginning of Dynasty 20, a Nile flood of such severity hit Thebes that three thousand men were needed to repair damage to Luxor Temple. By its end, more corruption scandals so rocked Thebes that a sixty-six day trial resulted in the cancellation of the Opet Festival, one of the country's most important religious ceremonies. Still, Ramesside rulers continued to be buried in the Valley of the Kings and some of their tombs are large and of considerable interest. The tomb of Rameses IX, for example, is elaborately decorated with a prodigious number of religious texts. Priests of Dynasty 21 oversaw the safeguarding of royal mummies, taking them from their plundered tombs in the Valley of the Kings and hiding them in caches elsewhere (in DB 320 and KV 35).

49 BOTTOM DETAIL OF STANDING STATUE OF RAMESES III FROM KARNAK TEMPLE, EGYPTIAN MUSEUM, CAIRO.

49 RIGHT RELIEF DEPICTING RAMESES III IN THE FIRST COURTYARD OF HIS MEMORIAL TEMPLE AT MADINAT HABU.

During the reign of Rameses IV, the administrators of the Theban priesthoods had become hereditary appointments whose growing authority posed a serious threat to the king. When the last Ramesside king, Rameses XI, died, most of Egypt was ruled from the Delta site of Tanis. Thebes, in contrast, was controlled by the High Priest of Amen at Karnak and his extended family. The rulers of Dynasty 22 gradually took control of the Temple of Amen at Karnak and appointed their relatives as High Priests of Amen, thereby taking control of Upper Egypt. In Dynasty 23, the Divine Adoratrice of Amen at Thebes became the nome's principal authority, a situation that continued until Egypt was made a part of the Persian Empire in Dynasty 27. The wealth of the priesthood of Amen can be seen in the enormous size of the tombs some of them built in the Theban Necropolis. The Dynasty 25 and 26 tombs of Montuemhat (TT 34) and Pedamenophis (TT 33) in al-'Assasif, for example, are labyrinthine collections of subterranean corridors and chambers.The end of dynastic history saw a brief revival of indigenous Egyptian authority in Dynasty 30, but it was short-lived. Alexander the Great conquered Egypt in 332 BC, adopting Egyptian customs and adding to monuments at Karnak, Luxor Temple, Dayr al-Madina, and other sites in the Theban nome. Subsequent rulers brought about agricultural reforms that greatly increased productivity and allowed Egypt's Late Dynastic population of about four million to double by early Roman times. Building activity continued at Thebes during the Graeco-Roman period. But the city's great distance from Alexandria assured that it increasingly

50 LEFT RAMESES VI OFFERING WINE FROM A SCENE IN HIS TOMB.

50-51 RAMESES IX OFFERING TO THE SUN GOD, HERE DEPICTED AS A RAM-HEADED MAN.

51 RAMESES VI, STATUE FOUND IN KARNAK, EGYPTIAN MUSEUM, CAIRO.

became a backwater, and frequent feuds between local villagers and their foreign occupiers meant that Upper Egypt did not benefit from reforms as much as the Delta. Thebes, 'The Model for Every City' no longer played a significant role in Egyptian arts or politics. With the coming of Christianity, numerous monasteries, convents, and churches were built in Thebes and their remains can still be seen on the West Bank at Dira' Abu al-Naja, Dayr al-Madina, and elsewhere. (See also the examples of arts and crafts from this period in the Luxor Museum of Ancient Art). The coming of Islam may have initially had less of an economic effect because Thebes lay south of Wadi Hammamat and Wadi Qena, two of the four principal routes of pilgrims to Mecca and traders to the Red Sea and Indian Ocean (the other two lay further north). Indeed, it was not until the coming of European tourists in the nineteenth and more especially in the late twentieth century that Thebes again rose to be an economic and cultural power in Egyptian society.

CHRONOLOGY

Dynasty "0"	c. 3050 BC

◆

EARLY DYNASTIC PERIOD

Dynasty 1	3000–2800
Dynasty 2	2800–2670

◆

OLD KINGDOM

Dynasty 3	2670–2600
Dynasty 4	
Snefru	2600–2571
Khufu	2571–2548
Radjedef	2548–2540
Khafra	2540–2514
Menkaura	2510–2491
Shepseskaf	2491–2487
Dynasty 5	
Userkaf	2487–2480
Sahura	2480–2468
Neferirkara	2468–2449
Niuserra	2443–2419
Menkauhor	2419–2411
Djedkara Isesi	2411–2378
Unis	2378–2348
Dynasty 6	
Teti	2348–2320
Userkara	
Pepy I	2316–2284
Merenra I	2284–2270
Pepy II	2270–2205
Merenra II	
Nitocris (?)	

◆

FIRST INTERMEDIATE PERIOD

Dynasties 7–8	2198–2160
Dynasties 9–10	2160–1980
Dynasty 11	
Intef I	2081–2065
Intef II	2065–2016
Intef III	2016–2008
Nebhepetra Mentuhetep I	2008–1957
Sankhkara Mentuhetep II	1957–1945
Nebtawyra Mentuhetep III	1945–1938

◆

MIDDLE KINGDOM

Dynasty 12 (overlapping dates indicate co-regencies)	
Amenemhet I	1938–1909
Senusret I	1919–1875
Amenemhet II	1877–1843
Senusret II	1845–1837
Senusret III	1837–1818
Amenemhet III	1818–1773
Amenemhet IV	1773–1763
Sobekneferu	1763–1759

◆

SECOND INTERMEDIATE PERIOD

Dynasty 13	
Many short-lived rulers	1759–1630
Dynasty 14	
Many short-lived rulers	1700–1630
Dynasty 15–16	
(The Hyksos)	1630–1522
Dynasty 17	
(Theban)	
Intef V	c. 1630
Senakhtenra Tao I	c. 1570
Seqenenra Tao II	c. 1560/1550
Kames	1543–1539

◆

NEW KINGDOM

Dynasty 18	
Ahmes	1539–1514
Amenhetep I	1514–1493
Thutmes I	1493–1482
Thutmes II	1482–1479
Hatshepsut	1479–1458
Thutmes III	1479–1426
Amenhetep II	1426–1400
Thutmes IV	1400–1390
Amenhetep III	1390–1353

Amenhetep IV/	
Akhenaten	1353–1336
Smenkhkara	1336–1333
Tutankhamen	1333–1323
Ay	1323–1319
Horemheb	1319–1292
Dynasty 19	
Rameses I	1292–1290
Sety I	1290–1279
Rameses II	1279–1213
Merenptah	1213–1203
Sety II	1203–1196
Amenmeses -	
Siptah	1196–1190
Tausert	1190–1188
Dynasty 20	
Setnakht	1188–1186
Rameses III	1186–1155
Rameses IV	1155–1148
Rameses V	1148–1143
Rameses VI	1143–1135
Rameses VII	1135–1129
Rameses VIII	1129–1127
Rameses IX	1127–1108
Rameses X	1108–1104
Rameses XI	1104–1075

◆

THIRD INTERMEDIATE PERIOD

Dynasty 21	
Smendes	1075–1044
Amenemnisu	1044–1040
Psusennes I	1040–990
Amenemope	993–984
Siamun	978–960
Psusennes II	960–945
Dynasty 22	
Sheshonk	945–924
Osorkon I	924–889
Takelot I	889–874
Osorkon II	874–850
Takelot II	850–825
Sheshonk III	825–773
Pami	773–767
Sheshonk V	767–730
Osorkon IV	730–715?
Dynasty 23	
Pedubaste	818–793
Sheshonk IV	793–787
Osorkon III	787–759
Takelot III	764–757
Rudjamon	757–754
Iupet	754–715?
Dynasty 24	725–712
Dynasty 25	
Nubian	712–664
Assyrian Conquest	671–664

◆

LATE PERIOD

Dynasty 26	
Saite	
Necho I	672–664
Psammetichus I	664–610
Necho II	610–595
Psammetichus II	595–589
Apries	589–570
Amasis	570–526
Psammetichus III	526–525
Dynasty 27	
Persian Period	525–404
Dynasty 28	404–399
Dynasty 29	399–380
Dynasty 30	
Nectanebo I	380–362
Teos	362–360
Nectanebo II	360–343
Second Persian Period	343–332
Macedonians	332–305
Ptolemaic Period	305–30
Roman and Byzantine Periods	30 BC–AD 642

◆

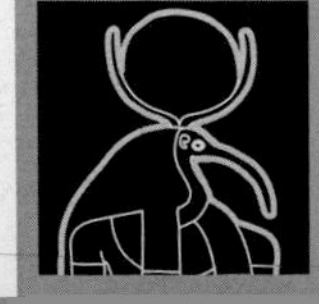

EGYPTIAN RELIGION AND RELIGIOUS FESTIVALS

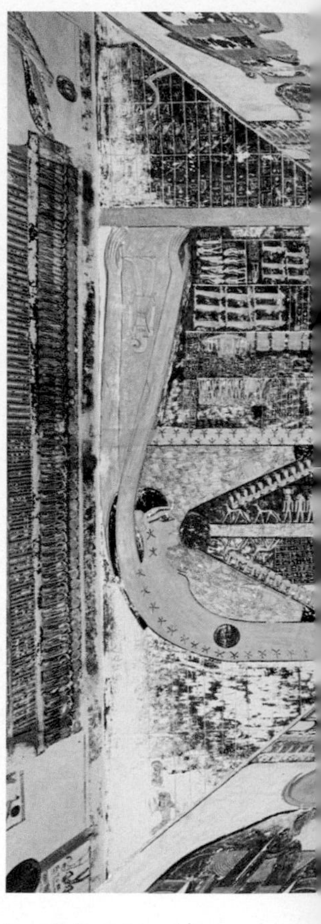

The universe of the ancient Egyptians had three parts: earth, heaven, and the underworld. The earth was a flat disk with Egypt at its center, surrounded by foreign lands and deserts, the whole enclosed by a vast primeval ocean called Nun. It was in this sea, on a small mound, that the creation of the gods took place. It occurred when the god Atum ("He who is self-created") spat (or, according to other legends, masturbated) and thereby created Shu, god of air and sunlight, and Tefnut, goddess of moisture. They in turn gave birth to Geb, god of the earthly disk that grew from the primeval mound, and Nut, goddess of the heavens. Geb and Nut were the parents of Osiris, Isis, Seth, and Nephthys. They in turn bore other gods.

Around the edge of the earth four great poles supported a huge heavenly dome to which the sun, moon, and stars were attached and on which various cosmic deities made their homes. In another version, the heavenly dome was the body of Nut, who hovered protectively over the earth.

Below the earth lay the netherworld, the realm of the dead and home to Osiris. It was here that living beings went after death to be judged and to spend boat protected by other deities, but the bark was also threatened by evil creatures such as the snake Apophis, who sought to destroy the sun. The journey was also said to be made through the body of journey. Texts like the Book of Gates, the *Imydwat*, and the Book of Caverns provided spells that would defeat the sun's enemies, and it was a principal task of Egypt's many gods to assist in this treacherous voyage.

eternity. The netherworld was a place very much like earth, although it was fraught with dangers.

These dangers were especially serious for solar deities like Ra. Each evening, the sun set on the western horizon and began a twelve-hour-long journey through the darkness of the netherworld. The journey could be made on a great the goddess Nut, who swallowed the sun at sunset and gave birth to it at dawn. But however it was made, if the journey was unsuccessful, the sun would fail to rise at dawn and life on earth would end. Much of the decoration on the walls of royal tombs in the Valley of the Kings was devoted to ensuring the success of this nightly

54 THE GODDESS NUT PREPARES TO SWALLOW THE SOLAR DISK, FROM THE BURIAL CHAMBER OF THE TOMB OF RAMESES VI.

54-55 THE BOOKS OF THE DAY AND NIGHT, FROM THE CEILING OF THE FIRST PILLARED ROOM OF THE TOMB OF RAMESES VI, IS DOMINATED BY NUT.

The gods of ancient Egypt were sometimes shown in animal form, sometimes in human form, and frequently as a combination of the two. In the Litany of Ra, the sun god appeared in seventy-five different forms, sometimes male, sometimes female, with the heads of many different creatures. The gods shared many anatomical features with humans, but they were taller. Texts claim that Osiris stood 4.7 meters (over 15 feet) tall and Horus stood 4 meters (13 feet). This may explain why, according to the Greek traveler Diodorus Siculus (90–21 BC), Egyptian priests kept precise records of the height of their kings as an indication of their divinity.

Despite their strange appearance, ancient texts tell us that the gods displayed very human behavior. They were born, they married and had children, celebrated birthdays, felt emotions, had friends and enemies, even wrote letters to each other. Their bodily functions were the same as ours: they wept, bled, defecated, sweated, and vomited. They fell ill, grew old, and eventually died. Ra, for example, died each evening at sunset and was reborn at dawn. Some gods seem almost like comic superheroes: they could be burned, beheaded, or cut into pieces, but then they could restore themselves or be restored by other gods and return to the world of the living, again and again.

Egyptians claimed that the number of gods was infinite; we know the names of several hundred. Perhaps to help make sense of so many, priests arranged them into communities, enneads (usually groups of nine, like that of Atum described above), families, and triads (e.g.,the Theban Triad of Amen, his wife Mut, and their son Khonsu). Like human families, these various divine groups shared festivals together, pursued mutual interests, and argued with other groups.

During the New Kingdom, the Theban Triad was the most powerful group of deities in Egypt, and Amen, especially in his syncretized form of Amen-Ra, was rightly called the "king of the gods." Although he is first mentioned in the Old Kingdom and began his rise to prominence in the Middle Kingdom, it was during Dynasties 18–20 that Amen gained a position of pre-eminence among the gods. His name means "The Hidden One," but the huge temples built for him by armies of dedicated priests were anything but hidden. Amen came close to being a monotheistic deity, and for a time, he was the wealthiest and most powerful force in all of Egypt.

56 BOTTOM RAMESES II OFFERING TO THE THEBAN TRIAD (AMEN, MUT AND KHONSU) FOLLOWED BY MA'AT, FROM LUXOR TEMPLE.

56-57 DEIFIED RAMESES II SITS BETWEEN AMEN-RA AND MUT, FROM MONUMENTI DELL'EGITTO E DELLA NUBIA BY I. ROSELLINI.

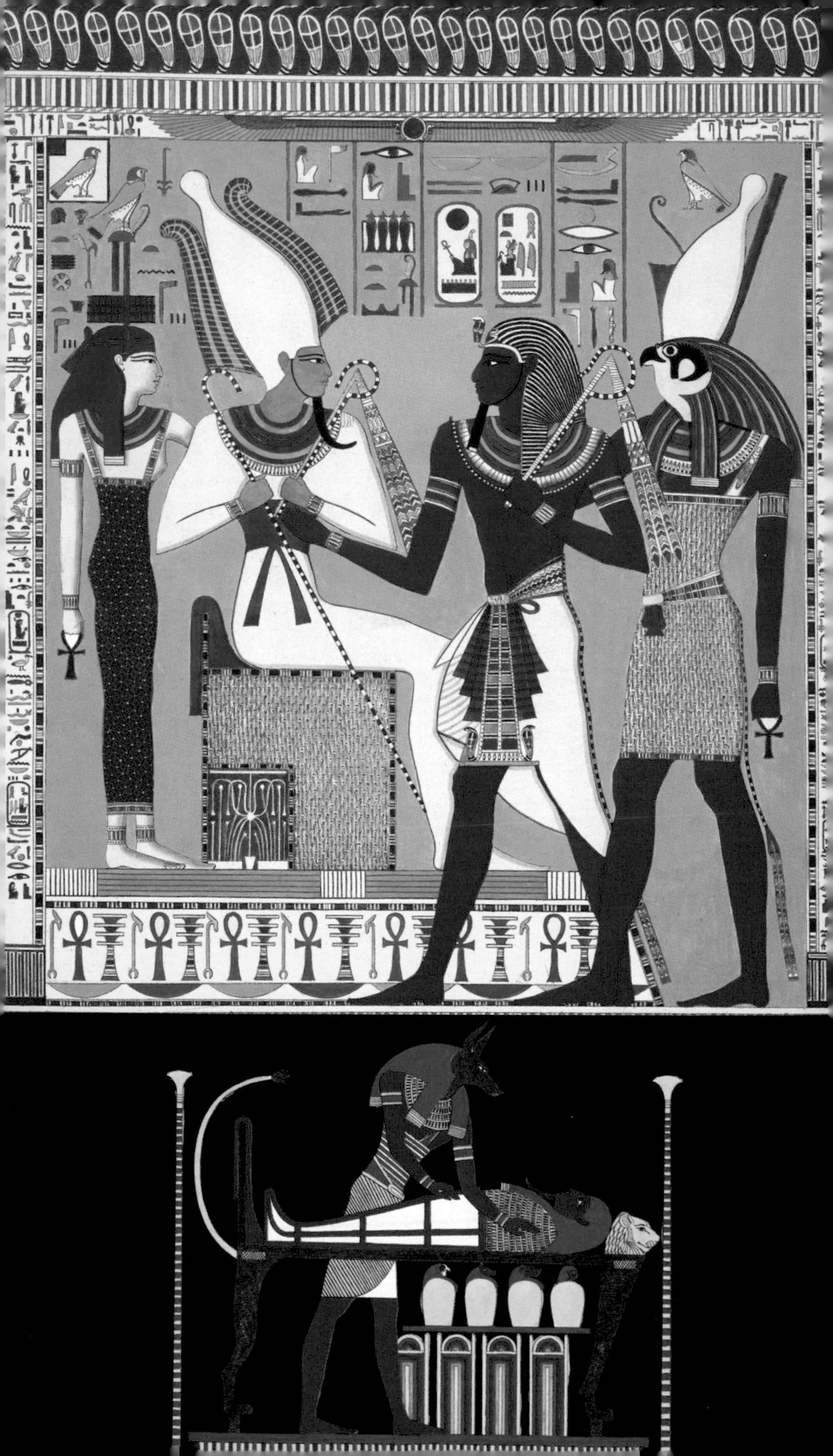

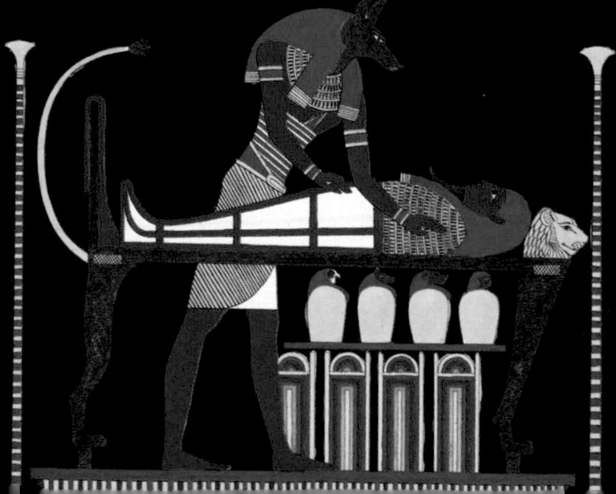

What Egyptologists sometimes call "minor" or "personal" gods were responsible for the homely needs of human beings. Bes or Taweret, for example, could be asked by a peasant woman for protection during pregnancy or help curing a sick child. Other gods could be approached for marital advice or good crops. But the principal "state" gods tackled more serious duties: they were responsible for ensuring that the sun would rise and set, the moon wax and wane, the Nile rise and fall, and that Ma'at would triumph over chaos and discord. Our life and death was in their hands. These were the gods for whom great temples were built and who were worshipped and offered to by great armies of priests. These were deities so powerful, so awesome that, until well into the New Kingdom, ordinary mortals had no direct access to them.

This had not always been the case. The origin of humankind is dealt with only cursorily in Egyptian texts: we are said to have come from the tears of the creator-god, a play on the words: *remi* means "to weep," *remitj* means "humankind." We were separate from the gods and lived apart from them, but at one time early in the history of the cosmos, men and gods had lived together on earth. Then, because of humankind's annoying behavior, the gods decided to leave earth and take up residence in the heavens. Of course, we humans immediately regretted the resulting loss of divine help and we pleaded for it to continue. In a moment of compassion, the gods designated one of their number, Horus, to serve as an intermediary between man and gods. He was the "living Horus" and he resided on earth in the body of the king. The king's position between gods and man might be likened to the constriction in an hourglass whose upper part was the realm of gods, its lower part the realm of man. Any communication between the two parts had to flow through the constriction, i.e., through the king. It was he who made known to the gods the needs of humankind, and to humankind the wishes of the gods.

Given such an arrangement, the death of a king was a supremely threatening event because it severed this line of communication upon which all life depended. This is why such care was taken by means of elaborate rituals and careful burial of the dead king to ensure that he would journey safely to the netherworld where he joined the gods as Osiris. It also explains why the coronation of his rightful successor, the next king, was so carefully orchestrated: the ceremony had to ensure that the new king could replace his father as living Horus, intercessor between man and gods. And if the transition from the dead king to his living successor were upset in any way, humankind would suffer terrible consequences.

The precise orientation of temples (their foundations were often surveyed by priests at night so the temple axis could be aligned with Ursa Major), the careful design of royal tombs, the care taken in carving religious texts and scenes, and the elaborate process of mummification—all are the result of this concern with maintaining communication between man and god. Offerings had to be precisely prepared and arranged, prayers had to be spoken without error, and even the smallest acts of ritual had to be performed according to exacting ritual or the gods might turn their backs on humankind.

58 TOP SETY BROUGHT BEFORE OSIRIS BY HORUS. BEHIND IS THE GODDESS OF THE WEST, FROM MONUMENTI DELL'EGITTO E DELLA NUBIA BY I. ROSELLINI.

58 BOTTOM ANUBIS TENDING THE MUMMY OF TAUSERT, FROM MONUMENTI DELL'EGITTO E DELLA NUBIA BY I. ROSELLINI.

Two annual ceremonies in Thebes were devoted to reaffirming the relationship between the king and the gods, between the three parts of the Egyptian cosmos. Like nearly all Egyptian religious festivals, they involved processions. It was such processions that

helped to determine the location of tombs and temples in Thebes and dictated their plan.

During the Opet Festival, a celebration held in the second month of the Nile flood, priests carried barks with the statues of Amen-Ra, his wife, and son from their home at Karnak to Luxor Temple. The festival's purpose was to reaffirm the close ties between Amen-Ra and the king, the living embodiment of Horus on earth.

Musicians, dancers, acrobats, and others accompanied chanting priests as thousands of commoners looked on. In Dynasty 18, this celebration grew from eleven days to twenty-seven, an indication of the festival's increasing importance.

The Beautiful Feast of the Valley was a festival of regeneration and re-creation, a reaffirmation of the ties between the living and the dead. About eight months after the Opet Festival, statues of Amen-Ra and former kings were carried in grand processions from Karnak across the Nile, then along canals cut through the valley floodplain to the royal memorial temples, stopping at each in turn on their way to an ancient shrine of Hathor in the Dayr al-Bahari cirque. Later in the New Kingdom the procession continued by canal to Madinat Habu, then eastward to the Nile, to Luxor Temple on the east bank, and finally back to Karnak.

Theban families, decked out in their finest clothes, took picnics and bouquets of flowers and visited local cemeteries, honoring their ancestors, just as the living king honored both his mortal and divine predecessors. Scores of other ceremonies were performed as well, and most Egyptian temples were beehives of activity, with processions, prayers, and offerings conducted several times each day. If the gods for whom these acts were undertaken seem strange to us, if Egyptian religious beliefs seem at odds with our own, it is well to remember that the Egyptians' goals were little different from those humankind has sought for millennia: they were attempts to give meaning and purpose to our transitory existence on earth and to explain the otherwise inexplicable phenomena of the eternal and transitory, of good and evil, of life and death. We may not agree with the paths the Egyptians trod, but we can hardly fault the passion with which they explored these profound and frightening questions.

61 BOTTOM DETAIL OF RELIEF WITH THE SACRED BARK OF AMEN-RA, FROM KARNAK TEMPLE.

60-61 PROCESSION OF THE BEAUTIFUL FEAST OF THE VALLEY, FROM KARNAK TEMPLE.

1

MONUMENTS OF THE EAST BANK

THE TEMPLES AT KARNAK

THE HISTORY

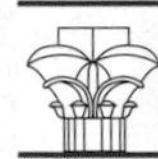

Karnak is a difficult site to understand. Jean-Francois Champollion, the Frenchman who first deciphered Egyptian hieroglyphs, described it as "so vast and so grandiose" that the Egyptians must have designed it for "men one hundred feet tall." Not only is Karnak huge—the complex covers over two square kilometers (1.6 square miles)—but it is the result of almost constant building activity that began over 4700 years ago and continues even today. The Temple of Amen-Ra, Karnak's principal building, is the largest religious structure ever built. It was the god's home on earth, and around it lay the homes of his relatives—his wife, Mut, and their son, Khonsu. Their temples, too, are enormous. Successive kings renewed, repaired, and enlarged these residences much as generations of a family might remodel their ancestral home to accommodate changing needs and tastes.

The earliest structures found at Karnak date to the Middle Kingdom. But there are references to building activity as early as Dynasty 3, and archaeological evidence shows that the site was inhabited thousands of years before that, in prehistoric times. In the New Kingdom, each king in turn seems to have vied with his predecessors to build a bigger monument here. Kings tore down earlier buildings and used the stones to construct new ones. For example, Amenhetep III built a pylon with stones he took from over a dozen earlier structures. Kings often remodeled a predecessor's building, then erased and redecorated its walls, replacing the earlier king's name with their own. Egyptologists find it difficult to track the history of all this activity.

Egypt's New Kingdom rulers were exuberant builders and they spent fortunes adding to Karnak's size and complexity—and to its wealth. Its priesthood was one of the richest in Egypt. New Kingdom records show that the priests of the Temple of Amen owned over 81,000 slaves and servants, 421,000 head of cattle, 691,000 acres of agricultural land, 83 ships, 46 shipyards, and 65 cities. In the reign of Rameses III alone, the temple received gifts that included 31,833 kilograms of gold, 997,805 kilograms of silver, 2,395,120 kilograms of copper, 3722 bolts of cloth, 880,000 bushels of wheat, 289,530 ducks and geese, and untold quantities of oil, wine, fruits, and vegetables. For economic as well as religious reasons, Amen truly was "King of the Gods."

Over two hundred large structures have been found at Karnak. Undoubtedly, there are hundreds more. Some are simple mudbrick buildings that have nearly vanished; some are elegant structures built of fine

65 COLOSSAL GRANITE STATUE OF RAMESES II BY THE ENTRANCE TO THE HYPOSTYLE HALL.

alabaster; others are enormous monuments of sandstone and granite with walls 15 meters (49 feet) thick that stand 50 meters (164 feet) high. By the late New Kingdom, Karnak had become so crowded that new structures were built wherever space permitted and older buildings were often demolished to accommodate them. Clearly, there never was a master plan for the site.

Many of Karnak's monuments are poorly preserved. Wind and water erosion have taken their toll, and earthquakes, like that in 27 BC, caused damage so great that engineers are still working to repair it. Curiously, the huge walls, pylons, and columns at Karnak were erected on the flimsiest of foundations, often nothing more than shallow trenches filled with pea gravel. Rising groundwater so weakened the foundations of some buildings that they simply collapsed. That happened in October 1899, when columns in the Hypostyle Hall toppled with a crash heard for miles around. Many parts of Karnak were razed by later rulers (Ptolemy IX is a prime example of such a vandal), or used by early Christians as houses, stables, and monasteries, or damaged in local riots and wars. Over the last two millennia, tourists have scrawled their names on decorated walls and hacked out pieces of relief. Treasure hunters have dug for *objets d'art,* in the process destroying much of the site. Yet, hundreds of hectares of Karnak still remain unexplored and many structures are known only from bits of stone jutting through dirt and weeds or found re-used in later buildings.

For all these reasons,

66-67 KARNAK, THE CENTRAL ENCLOSURE SEEN FROM THE SOUTH.

Karnak remains a bewildering architectural puzzle. It began as a few small shrines scattered about the present site, then grew outward from them like overlapping ripples on a pond. If you walk for ten minutes in any direction among its ruins you will encounter buildings from nearly every period of Egypt's history in no predictable chronological order.

Karnak can be divided into four areas. To the north, a large enclosure is home to a temple for the god Montu, another enclosure is dedicated to the goddess Ma'at, and there are numerous smaller buildings of stone and mudbrick. The Montu temple may have been connected by an avenue of sphinxes to a much earlier temple for that god at Medamud, a site five kilometers (three miles) farther north. To the east, Amenhetep IV/Akhenaten built a huge open-air temple complex dedicated to his solar deity, the Aten. To the south, another enclosure wall surrounds a temple to the goddess Mut and smaller temples for Amenhetep III and Rameses III. (None of these areas is open to tourists.)

The fourth area is the largest and most important. Called the Central Enclosure, this is the area visited by tourists, and the one to which Egyptologists have paid the most attention. Here lies the great Temple of Amen-Ra, King of the Gods. That building alone stretches 375 meters (1220 feet) front to back and covers over 25 hectares (61 acres). The Central Enclosure covers 100 hectares (247 acres) and, in addition to the Temple of Amen, encompasses temples to Ptah, Khonsu, Osiris, Opet, and others.

Surrounding the four temple areas, buried under several meters of Nile silt, the remains of ancient Thebes extend outward in a huge urban sprawl that probably covers thousands of hectares. Even in the New Kingdom, Thebes had a population of over 50,000 people and this ancient city is still virtually unexplored by archaeologists.

The ancient Egyptians called Karnak *Ipet Sout,* Most Esteemed of Places, although originally that term referred only to a small part of the Temple of Amen, not to the entire complex. Some scholars suggest that the first part of the name, *Ipet,* with the definite article *ta*, was pronounced something like "taype," and Greek visitors heard it as Thebes, the name of a Greek city with which they were familiar. The Egyptians called the city *Waset.* Karnak is the Arabic name of the adjacent modern village. The word may mean "fortified settlement," a description suggested to early Moslem visitors by the huge mud brick wall surrounding the Central Enclosure, but its etymology remains unclear.

The enclosure wall defines a rectangular area 500 meters (1640 feet) deep and 550 meters (1,790 feet) wide, and stands over 12 meters (39 feet) high and 8 meters (26 feet) thick. Its courses of mudbrick were not laid horizontally. Instead, they undulate like waves of water. That was intentional; it was meant to mimic waves in the great primeval sea that Egyptians believed had covered the earth before the creation of life. Priests claimed that the land enclosed within this wall—the temple of Amen-Ra—was an island on which the act of original creation took place. Large parts of the enclosure wall were rebuilt by the Antiquities Department about sixty years ago, when an admission fee was first levied at the site and access had to be controlled, and the undulating pattern of the mudbrick courses was retained in the new additions.

Four monumental gateways and several minor ones pierce the enclosure wall. Decades ago, tourists entered the Central Enclosure through its southern gate. But the principal gate lies in the western wall, in the First Pylon of the Temple of Amen-Ra. It was closed until only a few decades ago because it was farther from the hotels of Luxor where tourists stayed and because, being close to the Nile, it was impassable during the annual inundation.

Today, in the absence of the annual flood, one approaches the temple from the Nile, entering into a large, ugly parking lot. Curio shops stand on the left (north); the headquarters of the French archaeological mission lies to the south. The road from the parking area to the temple lies directly atop the route taken by ancient priests, but their journey was made by boat along a canal dug from the Nile to a T-shaped basin beside a stone landing quay. The Karnak ticket office lies in the southeast corner of the parking lot, about a hundred meters (three hundred feet) west of Karnak itself. The Sound and Light (Son et Lumière) ticket office is adjacent.

LEGEND

1 *AVENUE OF SPHINXES*
2 *FIRST PYLON*
3 *FIRST COURT*
4 *SHRINE OF SETY II*
5 *SHRINE OF RAMESES III*
6 *BUBASTITE PORTAL*
7 *SECOND PYLON*
8 *OPEN-AIR MUSEUM*
9 *HYPOSTYLE HALL*
10 *THIRD PYLON*

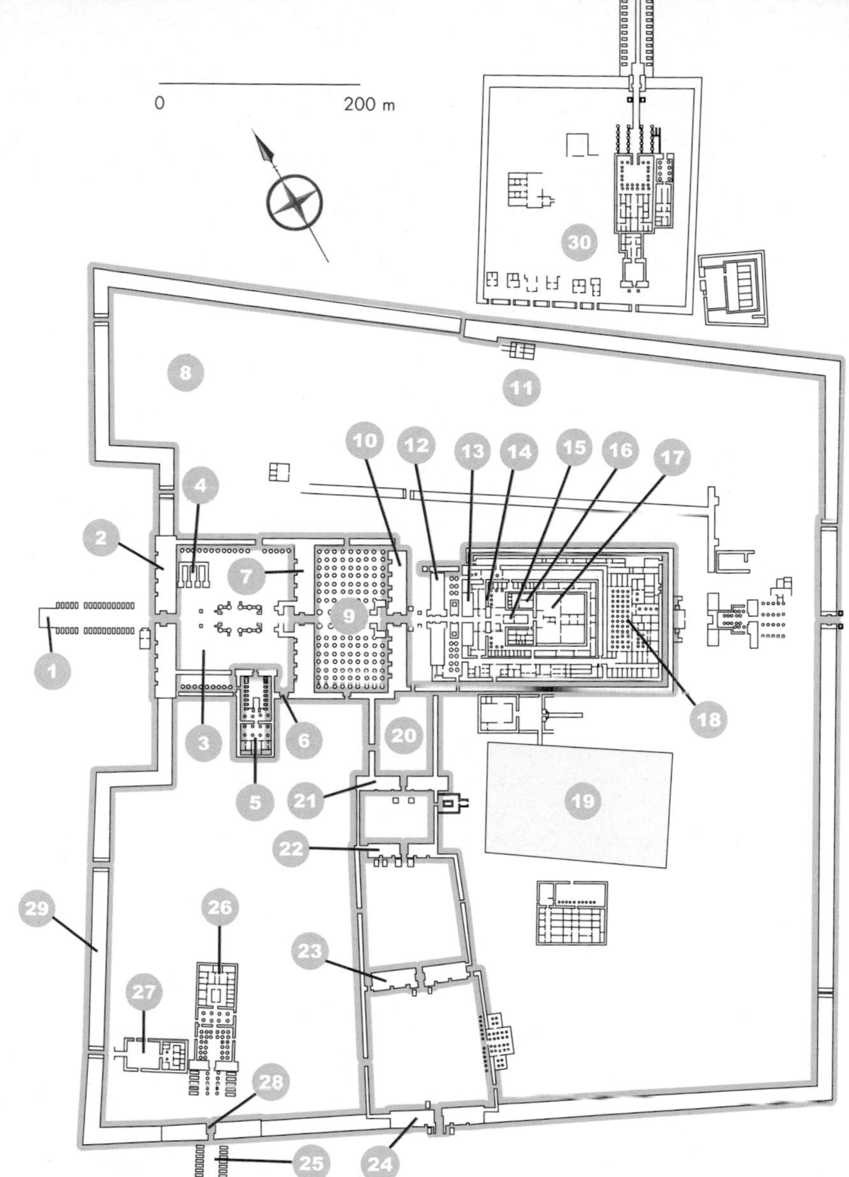

11 *TEMPLE OF PTAH*
12 *FOURTH PYLON*
13 *FIFTH PYLON*
14 *SIXTH PYLON*
15 *SHRINE OF PHILIP ARRHIDAEUS*
16 *SHRINE OF HATSHEPSUT*
17 *MIDDLE KINGDOM COURT*
18 *AKH-MENOU, TEMPLE OF THUTMES III*
19 *SACRED LAKE*
20 *COUR DE LA CACHETTE*
21 *SEVENTH PYLON*
22 *EIGHTH PYLON*
23 *NINTH PYLON*
24 *TENTH PYLON*
25 *AVENUE OF SPHINXES*
26 *TEMPLE OF KHONSU*
27 *TEMPLE OF OSIRIS AND OPET*
28 *GATEWAY OF PTOLEMY III EUERGETES*
29 *CENTRAL ENCLOSURE*
30 *TEMPLE OF MONTU*

VISIT

◆ THE QUAY ◆

The Quay of Amen is the landing stage where the great boats bearing statues of Amen and his entourage docked on festival occasions. It is a sandstone platform, 13 by 15 meters, reached today by a wooden bridge that crosses the eastern end of the ancient T-shaped basin. Two four-meter (13 feet) high obelisks once stood at the northeast and southeast corners of the platform and one of them, carved for Sety II (Dynasty 19), stands there today. A granite pedestal in the center of the quay was used during ceremonies to hold a model bark bearing the god's statue. When the lower part of the quay was recently cleared, texts of the Third Intermediate Period were found that recorded the heights of annual Nile floods. The highest flood occurred in the sixth year of the reign of Taharqa (684 BC) and flooded the Hypostyle Hall in the Temple of Amen with 84 centimeters (33 inches) of water. Such floods continued until a drainage canal was dug around Karnak in 1925.

Southeast of the quay (slightly to its right) near the First Pylon stands a chapel of Acoris, a king of Dynasty 29. It is one of several way stations where priests carrying statues of the god could pause for prayers during processions to and from the Temple of Amen. The statues were brought forth from their temple sanctuaries in gilded shrines on model boats borne on the shoulders of priests. From the quay they were sent off on great barges on ceremonial visits to various Upper Egyptian temples. Two such boats were called *Merit-Amen* and *Userhet* and were made of cedar wood, decorated with sheets of gold and elaborately woven fabrics. Musicians and dancers performed age-old rituals and offering bearers carried inlaid boxes filled with gold and jewels and finest linen. Priests, dignitaries, and local villagers watched in awe as the statue of the god passed by. Before the First Pylon was built, these processions would have passed through an area in front of the First Pylon filled with lush gardens and ponds of papyrus and lotus flowers. We have paintings of these gardens in several private tombs at Thebes (for example in TT 49, the tomb of Neferhetep from the end of Dynasty 18, and TT 161, the tomb of Nakht from the reign of Amenhetep III). From these sources, we know that royal palaces were built north of the quay and were surrounded by gardens of date palms and pomegranate

trees. Vegetables and flowers grew in profusion, many of them used in offerings made to the god. On the east side of the quay, a ramp slopes down to an avenue of sphinxes called the Way of Offerings, which leads to the First Pylon. The figures are criosphinxes, bodies of lions with the heads of rams, symbols of the god Amen. Small figures of King Rameses II in the pose of Osiris stand between their paws. It was once thought the sphinxes were the work of Rameses II, but in fact they were carved for Amenhetep III and Thutmes IV in Dynasty 18 and installed at Luxor Temple. They were usurped by Rameses II and moved here only later. Forty criosphinxes line the avenue today, but before the First Pylon was erected, when the Avenue of Sphinxes extended to the Second Pylon, there were 124. After the First Pylon was built, 84 sphinxes were moved alongside the walls of the First Court. They were to have been taken to another site, but that did not happen and so they stand here even today.

◆ THE FIRST PYLON ◆

In spite of its rough-cut stones and lack of decoration, the unfinished First Pylon is an impressive introduction to the Temple of Amen. It was planned by Sheshonk I (Dynasty 22) to be an exact copy of the Second Pylon; actual building did not begin until the reign of Nectanebo I (Dynasty 30). The pylon stands 113 meters (370 feet) long, 15 meters (49 feet) thick, and 40 meters (142 feet) high. Eight large windows were cut into each of its two towers and below them, four niches held flagpoles that towered at least 46 meters (165 feet) high and carried long, colored linen banners. In the center of the pylon stands a doorway 19 meters (62 feet) high, 7.5 meters (24 feet) wide, and 5 meters (16 feet) deep. In antiquity, wooden doors were fitted here, covered with sheets of gold or bronze with beaten relief decoration. The adjacent walls still show traces of a fire that destroyed the doors early in the Ptolemaic Period. High up on the right (south) jamb, scholars accompanying Napoleon's expedition in 1799 inscribed the latitude and longitude of "Carnac," Luxor, and other Egyptian sites. The height of the inscription above the modern ground level shows how much debris covered the pylon when it was seen by those Europeans two centuries ago.

70 AND 70-71 AN AVENUE OF CRIOSPHINXES (LIONS WITH HEADS OF RAMS) LEADS TO THE FIRST PYLON.

◆ THE FIRST COURT ◆

The gate in the First Pylon was built during the Dynasty 30 reign of Nectanebo and has served as the formal entrance to the Temple of Amen for the last 2300 years. It leads into the First Court, 100 meters (325 feet) wide and 82 meters (267 feet) deep. Prior to the construction of the First Pylon, this was a large open area with several buildings. Two of them remain: a small shrine of Sety II in the northwest corner of the court, and a shrine of Rameses III in the southeast corner. When the First Court was built, the two shrines were incorporated into the new plan.

The idea of enclosing the area in front of the Second Pylon had been around for some time before it was finally acted upon, and took several centuries to complete.

Our tour of the court starts at the shrine of Sety II, immediately left of the entry gate. The shrine, called the August Temple of Millions of Years, is a simply-constructed and hastily-decorated structure. It was dedicated to the Theban Triad and served as another of the many buildings used as rest stops during processions of sacred barks. Statues of Sety II stood between the doors to the three corridor-like rooms. The room in the center was dedicated to Amen, depicted in human form on the left wall and as a ram-headed deity on the right. The room on the left was dedicated to Mut, that on the right to Khonsu. On the chamber walls Sety II offers to each deity.

In the center of the First Court, two rows of five columns once formed part of a large kiosk built by Taharqa in Dynasty 25 and restored in the Ptolemaic Period. Only one of the original columns still stands; the five on the left (north) were partially reconstructed in the last century. These huge columns with open papyrus capitals stood nearly 19 meters (62 feet) high and were joined by a thin wall of stone in the reign of Ptolemy IV. The roof—if the shrine was roofed—presumably was built of wood because the space between the rows of columns, 14 meters (45 feet), could not have been spanned by stones. (One scholar has also suggested that the columns were not supports for a ceiling but pedestals for statues; that seems unlikely.) A large

block of alabaster in the center of the structure served as a resting-place for sacred barks during ceremonial processions.

One of the most interesting features in the First Court is a huge mudbrick construction ramp whose remains abut the eastern face of the south tower of the First Pylon. It consisted of a series of mudbrick walls built at right angles to the pylon, the spaces between them filled with rubble. (A ramp built against the north tower, now gone, was more carefully built entirely of well-laid brick.) Blocks of stone for the pylon's construction were dragged up these ramps using rollers or sledges and ropes. When Napoleon's expedition visited here, several sandstone blocks still sat on the ramp where they had been left by workmen 2600 years earlier.

The ramp should have been removed when the pylon was completed but, as the unfinished face of the pylon attests, it never was.

A similar ramp can be seen in wall paintings in the tomb of Rekhmire.

The row of columns along the court's southern wall offers further evidence of ancient building techniques.

The drums of the column nearest the First Pylon were not dressed or decorated. Typically, that work would have proceeded from the top down after the rough-cut drums had been set in place and as the construction ramp was removed.

72-73 AERIAL VIEW OF THE FIRST COURT, WITH THE SHRINE OF RAMESES III BOTTOM RIGHT.

72 CENTER THE SHRINE OF SETY II, AT THE LEFT OF THE ENTRANCE OF THE FIRST PYLON.

72 BOTTOM MUDBRICK RAMP AGAINST THE FIRST PYLON, IN THE FIRST COURTYARD.

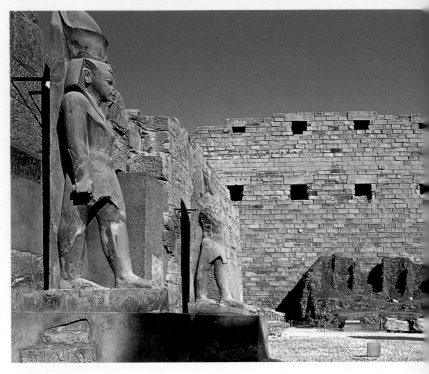

◆ THE SHRINE OF RAMESES III ◆

The shrine in the southeastern (right rear) corner of the First Court is one of the best-preserved architectural features at Karnak. Rameses III based its plan on his memorial temple at Madinat Habu on the West Bank at Thebes. The small shrine/temple seems out of place here because it was built before the First Court was enclosed. It juts through the enclosure wall and now seems awkwardly placed.

Until 1896, the shrine was almost completely buried under debris whose depth can be judged from the heavy staining on the walls. The shrine was decorated in the squat, heavy-handed style characteristic of most of Rameses III's monuments, but it is well preserved largely because it was buried, and unlike many larger temples, its ground plan is easy to understand.

Two statues of Rameses III stand before the shrine's first pylon. Nearby texts describe a great double leaf door of acacia wood plated with bronze that closed the doorway.

The king wears the double crown of Upper and Lower Egypt on the face of the left (east) tower of the pylon and the crown of Lower Egypt on the right (west). His pose is a typical one, standing before Amen with a mace in one hand, grasping foreign captives with the other. Amen holds forward a sword of victory. The names of towns and countries in Nubia and western Asia from which the captives came were written nearby, but they are now destroyed.

The west outer wall of the shrine shows the procession of barks from Karnak to Luxor Temple during the Opet Festival. This is also the subject of scenes in the colonnade of Luxor Temple.

Inside the temple a small peristyle court has a

and beyond that, three doorways lead into chambers for Amen (in the center), Mut (on the left), and Khonsu (on the right). Each has at least one side chamber.

Imagine an ancient procession entering this temple. It is early morning, already hot, and the

priests, the king, selected royal family members—and they come to welcome the god's statue and pray for a safe journey. To witness a ceremony in such a place must have been a profoundly moving experience.

Rameses III's shrine is an excellent example of a traditional New Kingdom temple. All the standard features are present. The temple façade is a pylon whose tall towers resemble mountains on the horizon, with a valley between them, behind which the sun rises and sets. The temple is bilaterally symmetrical along a single axis. Stone ramps in each gateway raise the floor of each chamber higher than its predecessor and the ceilings become lower, their dimensions smaller. The procession from an open, sunlit environment into increasingly more restricted, dark, silent, and claustrophobic rooms reinforces the impression that one has entered a sacred place.

colonnade of eight pillars on its east and west sides. Mummiform figures of the king as Osiris stand before the pillars, stocky figures carved with little concern for proportions or detail. The backs of the pillars show various deities. On the left (east) wall of the court, the bark of Amen is carried in procession by priests; on the right (west) wall, they carry ithyphallic statues of Amen; on the inside face of the pylon, Amen delivers blessings for a long life to Rameses III.

At the southern end of the court a ramp leads to a vestibule (the pronaos) with four Osirid pillars and four columns. Behind it stands an eight-columned hypostyle hall

sunlight is intense. Senior priests carry on their shoulders a wooden bark with a gilded shrine holding a statue of the god. They have come from deep within the Temple of Amen and will pause here for prayers before continuing to the quay. Outside, the sunlight emphasizes the brilliant red, blue, yellow, and blindingly white paint on the temple walls. The procession moves slowly into the increasingly cool, dark chambers, and the priests pause to let their eyes adjust to the dim light. In the holy of holies at the rear of the temple, where the god's statue is to be placed, the shrine is completely dark and silent. Only a few people are permitted here—senior

74-75 TWO STATUES OF RAMESES III STAND BEFORE THE SHRINE'S FIRST PYLON.

74 BOTTOM THE PERISTYLE COURT OF THE SHRINE HAS MUMMIFORM FIGURES OF THE KING AS OSIRIS.

75 RAMESES III OFFERING TO AMEN IN THE SHRINE.

◆ THE BUBASTITE PORTAL ◆

Between the shrine of Rameses III and the Second Pylon stands a gate known to Egyptologists as the Bubastite Portal. It takes its name from the Delta town of Bubastis, capital city of the Dynasty 22 kings who built it. The stones for the gate came from a quarry south of Thebes at Jabal as-Silsila and an inscription there tells that King Sheshonk I instructed his overseer of works, Horemsaf, to undertake the building project: "His Majesty gave stipulations for building a very great pylon...in order to brighten Thebes; erecting its double doors of myriads of cubits in height, in order to make a jubilee court for the house of his father, Amen-Ra, king of the gods; and to surround it with a colonnade." At the top of the east wall of the gate King Osorkon I receives from Amen-Ra a sword and palm branches symbolizing long life. Below, the god Khnum offers an *ankh*-sign (the symbol of life), and the king is suckled by the goddess Hathor. On the west wall, Takelot II and his son, a High Priest of Amen, stand before the god. Through the Bubastite Portal to the left, on the southern end of the Second Pylon, King Sheshonk I—the Pharaoh Shishak of the Bible—commemorates his victory over Rehoboam, son of Solomon, king of Judah, when Egypt attacked Solomon's temple in Dynasty 22. The quality of carving is only fair (and best seen in mid-morning light), but the scenes have historical interest. In one, Amen-Ra stands with a sword in his hand and announces the conquest of 156 villages in Judah and Palestine. Each town is named in crenellated ovals surmounted by human heads. The battle is described in 2 Chronicles (12:2–3) and in 1 Kings (14:25–26): "In the fifth year of King Rehoboam, Shishak king of Egypt came up against Jerusalem; he took away the treasures of the house of the Lord and the treasures of the king's house; he took away everything. He also took away all the shields of gold which Solomon had made...."

To the right (east), on the southern outer wall of the Hypostyle Hall, Rameses II carved military scenes in imitation of his father's on the north side of the hall.

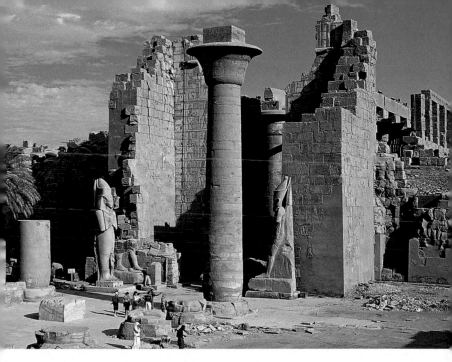

◆ THE SECOND PYLON ◆

Begun by Horemheb, continued by Rameses I and Rameses II, and finally added to in the Ptolemaic Period, the Second Pylon was built partly of blocks taken from earlier structures built east of the Temple of Amen by Amenhetep IV/Akhenaten. The pylon was called Illuminating Waset, or, less commonly, Amen Rejoices. Large holes cut into the lower part of the pylon were made by archaeologists looking for earlier re-used blocks in its interior. A red granite statue of Rameses II, usurped by several later kings, stands in front of the north (left) side of the Second Pylon's gateway. His daughter Bint-anta is shown at much smaller scale standing between his feet. Two other statues of Rameses II, one now destroyed, flanked the gateway. The gateway itself is thirty meters (ninety-eight feet) tall and was restored by Ptolemy VIII.

Before the gateway proper, a small vestibule was begun in Dynasty 18 by King Horemheb and completed by Rameses II. Scenes in the vestibule show Rameses II before Amen smiting the enemies of Egypt. On the south wall, sacred barks of the Theban Triad bear cartouches of Rameses II and III. On the doorjambs, Rameses II offers to the gods.

76 PRINCESS BINT-ANTA, DAUGHTER OF RAMESES II, IS PORTRAYED BETWEEN THE FEET OF THE COLOSSAL STATUE OF THE KING.

76-77 IN FRONT OF THE SECOND PYLON STAND COLOSSAL STATUES OF RAMESES II.

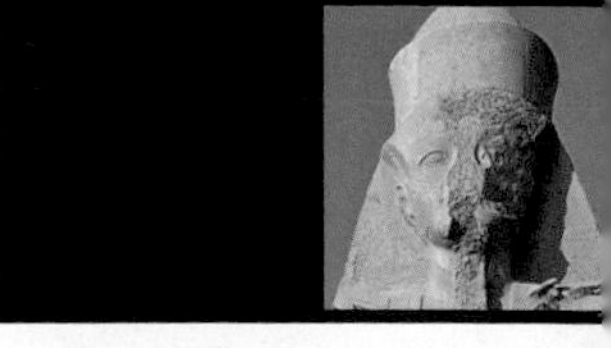

77 BOTTOM THE RED GRANITE STATUE OF RAMESES II, WEARING ROYAL REGALIA.

78 134 SANDSTONE COLUMNS SUPPORT THE CEILING OF THE HYPOSTYLE HALL.

78-79 AERIAL VIEW OF THE 'FOREST OF COLUMNS' OF THE HYPOSTYLE HALL.

At this point in the tour you have two choices of itinerary. If you wish to visit the Open-Air Museum (which deserves a visit), walk northward (to your left as you face the Second Pylon) and exit the First Court through the door in its north wall.

The museum entrance lies directly in front of you, a few meters along a paved pathway. (Toilets are located nearby.) If you chose not to visit the museum, then proceed eastward through the Second Pylon and enter the Hypostyle Hall.

◆THE HYPOSTYLE HALL ◆

No part of the Temple of Amen is more famous or impressive than this huge pillared hall, one of the largest religious structures ever built. Neither photographs nor raw statistics give a true impression of its size and beauty—or in the eyes of some travelers, its clunkiness. One visitor waxed enthusiastic: "The Pyramids are more stupendous. The Colosseum covers more ground. The Parthenon is more beautiful. Yet in nobility of conception, in vastness of detail, in majesty of the highest order, the Hall of Pillars exceeds them every one." But another remarked that "the columns are far too numerous. The size which strikes us is not the grandeur of strength, but the bulkiness of disease." Perhaps the Hypostyle Hall was over-engineered with too many large columns placed too close together, but there can be no doubt that it inspires

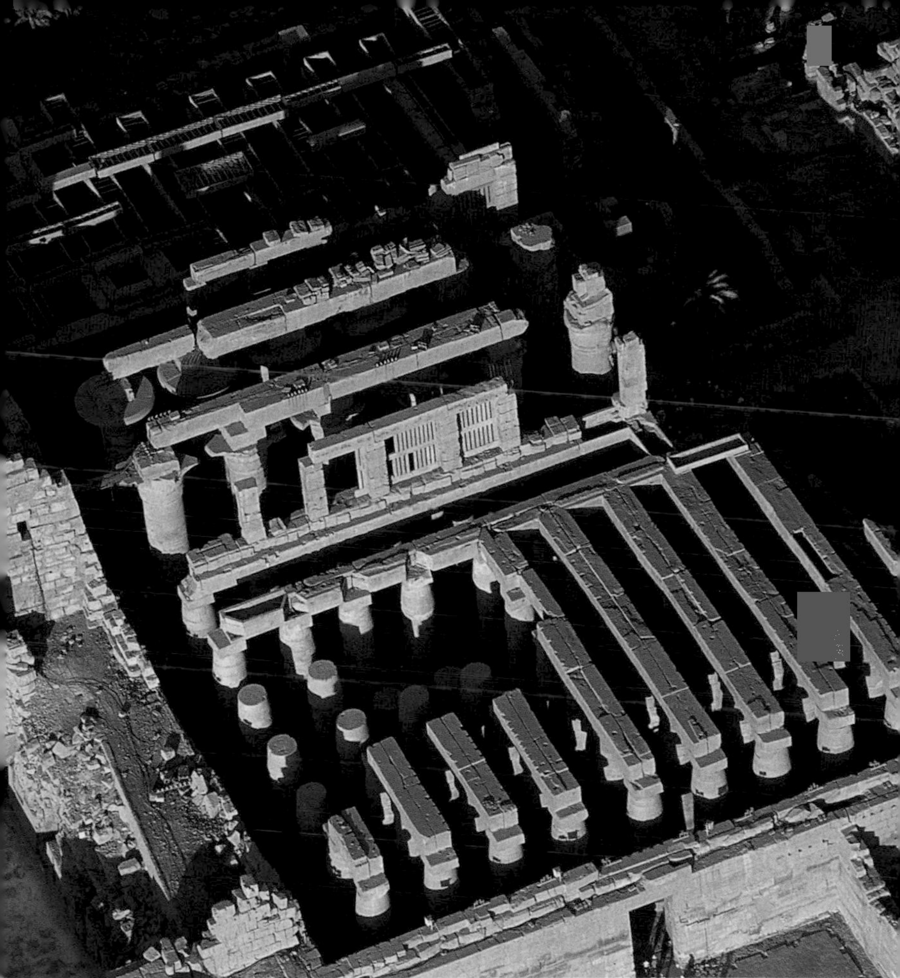

overwhelming awe.

Ironically, this vast forest of columns, larger than any other such hall on earth, was intended to symbolize the most prosaic of features, a papyrus swamp like the thousands that lined the banks of the Nile. Each year, such thickets flooded during the inundation and the Hypostyle Hall was built so that it too would be covered with shallow Nile water in summer. The hall represented the swampland surrounding a primeval mound on which Egyptians believed life was first created. Originally, in Dynasty 18, only two rows of six huge columns stood here.

They are the ones we see today on the central east-west axis of the hall. Immediately to their north and south, two walls defined a colonnade similar to that in Luxor Temple. It was only later, in Dynasty 19, that these walls were moved farther out and the Hypostyle Hall we know today created by adding another 122 columns.

When first seen by Europeans, parts of the Hypostyle Hall were already in a disastrous state. The situation was made even worse in October 1899, when foundations weakened by ground water caused columns to topple and walls to collapse. Thanks to French archaeologists and engineers who have been working here for nearly a century, this splendid monument is being restored to its original condition.

The Hypostyle Hall is 103 meters (335 feet) wide, 53 meters (172 feet) deep, and covers 5,500 square meters (58,000 square feet). Its ceiling is supported by 134 sandstone columns. Six columns on each side of the main east-west axis have open papyrus flower capitals and stand 23 meters (75 feet) tall. They are 10 meters (32 feet) in circumference, built of stone drums, each 1 meter (3 feet) high and 2 meters (6.5 feet) in diameter. One hundred and twenty-two other columns stand in four groups, two on each side of the hall's north-south and east-west axes. They have closed papyrus flower capitals and are 15 meters (49 feet) tall, 8.4 meters (27 feet) in circumference. The difference in height between the two central rows of columns and the others in the hall—a difference of about 10 meters (33 feet)—allowed clerestory lighting to be installed along the main axis. Some of the huge sandstone grills in the windows are still in place. This design meant that the main axis of the hall was brightly lit, but away from the axis the hall became increasingly dark. Statues were placed throughout the hall and must have appeared as eerie presences in the dim light. Three such statues stand today near the main axis.

The Hypostyle Hall was apparently envisioned by Rameses I, but it was built by Sety I and Rameses II. Cartouches in the northern half of the hall are Sety I's, in the southern half, Rameses II's. The names of Rameses I, III, IV, and VI are also present. The cartouches and royal titles of these kings constitute the principal inscriptions on the columns.

There is a clear difference in the quality of workmanship in the two halves of the hall: Sety I's artisans produced delicately carved raised relief, and there are many examples of figures that were recut several times before the artisan achieved what he considered proper proportions. (Look, for example, at the face of Sety I at the north end of the west wall.) In contrast, Rameses II's decoration was hastily done, often in sunk relief; there was little modeling or attention to detail.

Many reliefs still retain traces of paint, and it is worth spending time wandering through this forest of columns, admiring the architecture and decoration. If you are lucky enough to be in the hall alone, the silence and the sense of grandeur make it a truly impressive experience.

On the left as you enter the hall stands a huge statue of Rameses II and Amen. On the right, a slab of alabaster lies on the floor (below what was originally a large stela), carved with figures of Nubian and Asiatic enemies of Egypt, collectively known as the Nine Bows.

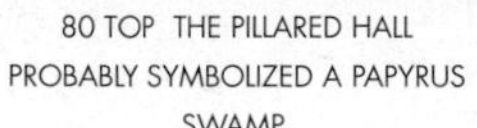

80 TOP THE PILLARED HALL PROBABLY SYMBOLIZED A PAPYRUS SWAMP.

80 BOTTOM AND 81 MANY RELIEFS OF THE HYPOSTYLE HALL STILL RETAIN TRACES OF THE ORIGINAL PAINT.

82 HIGH QUALITY RELIEF CHARACTERIZE THE HYPOSTYLE HALL IN THE NORTH HALF DECORATED FOR SETY I.

82-83 RAMESES II KNEELS CLOSE TO A PERSEA TREE BEFORE AMEN-RA.

83 BOTTOM LEFT RAMESES II BURNS INCENSE BEFORE THE SACRED BARK OF AMEN.

83 BOTTOM RIGHT MA'AT AND THOTH IN PROCESSION.

The scenes in the hall all have religious themes intended for a limited audience of priests. They show the king offering to deities, the processions of the sacred barks, and various temple rituals. For example, north (left) of the gate in the Second Pylon, Sety I and Hathor greet Amen and Mut. Farther along, Rameses I adores eight deities. On the north wall of the hall (left of the door), priests in full regalia carry an elaborate sacred bark of Amen on their shoulders and Sety I greets the Theban Triad. Traces of paint can still be seen here and indicate how brilliantly decorated (even how garish) the walls originally must have been. This wall has on it some of the finest carving to be found at Karnak. The bark, smaller than the actual river-going barges used in festival processions but still large enough to require twenty men to lift it, has the head of the god Amen carved bow and stern. To the left (east), a stunning raised relief figure of Sety I presents a bouquet of papyri. His mouth and nose are finely carved, his cheeks delicately modeled, his wig and broad collar drawn in great detail.

On the right (east) side of the door, Thoth stands and writes the king's names on the leaves of a persea tree *(Mimusops schimperi)*. Sety I kneels beneath it. Compare the workmanship here with that in a similar scene carved for Rameses II on the hall's southern wall. The Sety I scene has considerably more appeal.

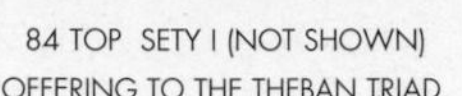

84 TOP SETY I (NOT SHOWN) OFFERING TO THE THEBAN TRIAD.

84-85 VIEW OF THE OUTER NORTH WALL OF THE HYPOSTYLE HALL.

84 BOTTOM ASIATIC PRISONERS OF WAR BEING LED INTO EGYPT.

◆ THE OUTER WALLS OF THE HYPOSTYLE HALL ◆

To us, scenes on the inner walls of the Hypostyle Hall often appear cryptic, filled with untranslatable details of strange ceremonies. This part of the temple was intended for the initiated, for priests and royalty who already knew the iconography and understood what it meant.

The outer walls, however, served another purpose. They could be seen by low-level priests and by minor temple employees, perhaps even by commoners allowed to visit parts of the temple enclosure on certain festival days. The subject matter on the exterior walls is not religious but in a sense propagandistic. The scenes emphasize the virility and military prowess of the king: he leads his army into war, wages great and always successful battles, returns in glory to Egypt, and donates the booty he has gathered and the prisoners he has captured to the Temple of Amen-Ra. Lengthy texts laud the king's powers, describe his daring exploits, and catalog the towns he has captured. Since over ninety-nine percent of the Egyptian population was illiterate, such reliefs would certainly have impressed upon them the awesome power of gods and their king, just as paintings in medieval churches showed illiterate viewers the torments of hell and the joys of true belief. There was also a desire to contrast the disorder and chaos that existed beyond the temple enclosure with the peace and harmony that reigned within the "dwelling-place of the gods," and to show how great a role the king played in keeping discord at bay and maintaining the order called Ma'at.

The best such scenes of royal power are the battle scenes carved for Sety I on the north outer wall of the Hypostyle Hall. Few traces of paint are preserved, but the bare stone carving emphasizes the technical skill of artisans who created what are some of

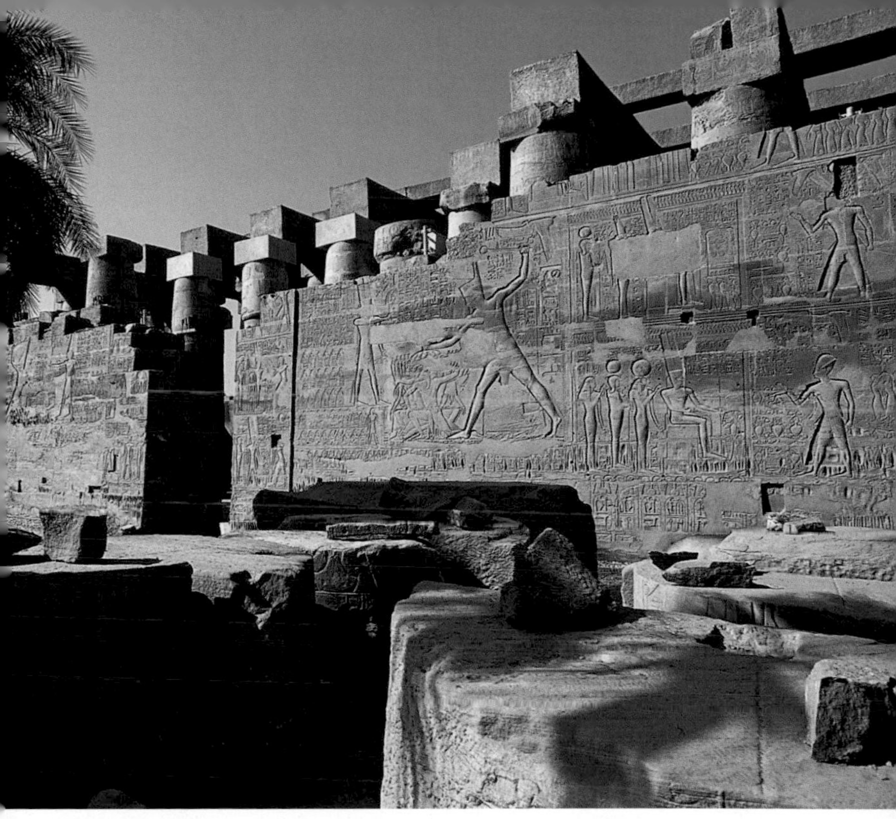

the most detailed and elegant examples of monumental art to be found in Egypt. Because the scenes were cut in subtle and delicately modeled raised relief, they are best seen in brilliant, raking light. Ideally, they should be visited early on a crisp winter morning, when the sun is low in the sky, but any early morning visit will be worth the trip.

This wall originally stood over 25 meters (81 feet) high and extended over 30 meters (98 feet) on each side of a central door. There are over a thousand square meters (about eleven thousand square feet) of decoration.

To see the battle scenes, walk north through the Hypostyle Hall, exit through the door in the middle of the wall, and turn to the right. The left (east) half of the wall recounts the king's battles in Syria and Palestine. At the far end, the king drives forward in his war chariot firing arrows at enemy soldiers. Many men already lie dead or dying on the battlefield. Egypt's border with Asia is shown in the center of the wall, marked by a long, narrow pond called the Water of Cutting.

It was located in the ancient border town of Tharu, near the modern Suez Canal. The pond teems with crocodiles. A small bridge runs across it, between two small buildings that are perhaps the offices of border guards. The building on the left (east) side is of Asiatic design; that on the right (west) is purely Egyptian. On the east side of the lake, Sety I drives bound captives across the Sinai Peninsula toward the border. On the west side, in Egypt itself, crowds of priests from the Temple of Amen chant and play musical instruments as they excitedly await the arrival of the prisoners. The captives grimace in pain as they are driven forward. Note the contrast between the discord and confusion on the Asiatic side of the pond and the well-organized, well-mannered Egyptians on the west.

86 TOP ENEMY SOLDIERS BEING ROUTED BY EGYPT'S CAVALRY.

86 BOTTOM SETY I ON HIS CHARIOT, FIGHTING ENEMIES.

87 SETY I PRESENTING PRISONERS BEFORE AMEN-RA.

Above the scene, Sety I described the moment: "The heart of his majesty was glad because of it. As for the good god, he rejoices to begin battle, he is delighted to enter into it, his heart is satisfied at seeing blood, he cuts off the heads of the rebellious-hearted, he loves an hour of battle more than a day of rejoicing. His majesty slays them one at a time. He leaves not a limb among them, and he that escapes his hand as a living captive is carried off to Egypt."

To the right, a colossal standing figure of the king wields a mace and grasps prisoners by the hair. When the light is good, the meticulous details of these beautifully carved faces spring to life. Their race and nationality—Libyan, Syrian, and Nubian—are shown in immediately recognizable detail and so too is their despair.

The name Amen means "The Hidden One," and when lower classes of priests and commoners were allowed into this part of the temple compound the god's image had to be concealed from the eyes of the impure.

Just below and to the right of the monumental figure of Sety I, near the wall's central doorway, several small figures of the god Amen were carved about 1.5 meters (4.5 feet) above the ground. Each is no more than 40 centimeters (16 inches) tall. Four small holes were drilled near the shoulders and feet of each of the gods' images. Into these holes wooden dowels were inserted and a woven mat or a piece of linen attached to hide the figure of the god from view. Similar but larger dowel holes can be seen around the colossal figures of the god on this wall.

On the right (west) half of the Sety I wall, the king battles Libyans and Hittites. One of the most beautifully executed of these scenes can be seen in the uppermost register at the far right end of the wall, just before the torus molding that marks the corner of the Second Pylon. Egyptian war chariots race

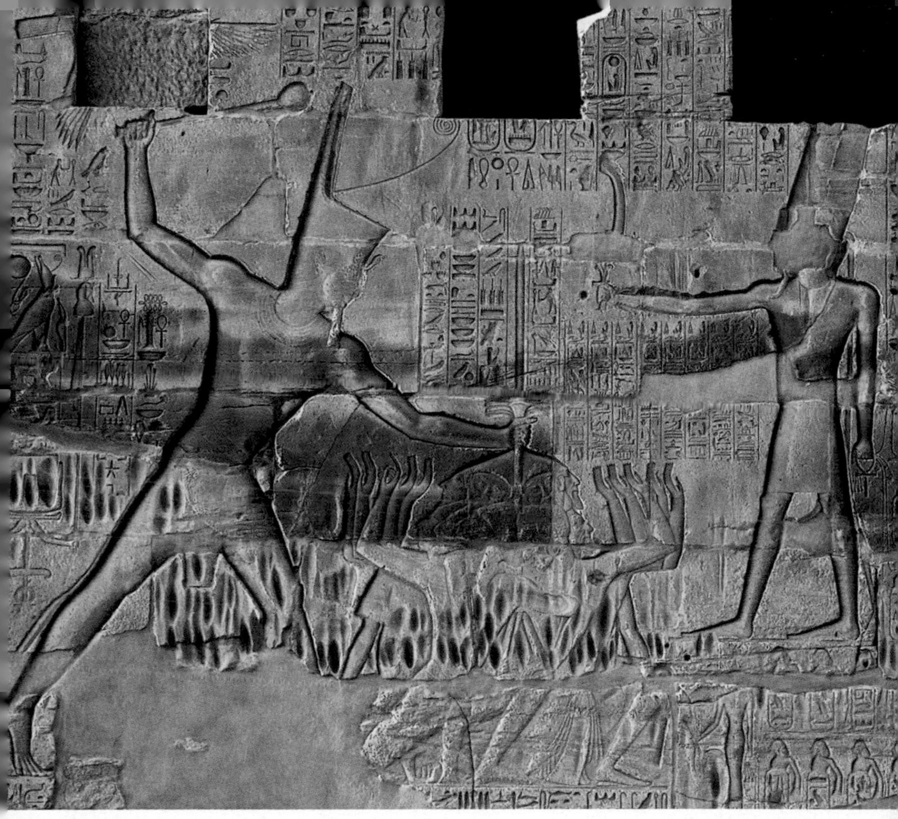

at full speed across the desert toward the site of Qadesh, a fortification in the land of Amor. A tower stands on a hill and soldiers fall from its battlements, killed by pharaoh's arrows. The dead and wounded lay scattered across the battlefield. The scene is vivid: one can imagine the dust, the noise, the blood, the sweat, and the shaking earth as the Egyptian cavalry pounds forward. Below the fortification, the hillside is forested and terrified enemies try to hide among the trees. In a departure from the standard practice of drawing faces in profile, here the artist has shown the enemies' faces frontally with their hands on their head in a pose that emphasizes their look of utter despair. A frightened herdsman tries to drive his cattle out of harm's way behind the hill. He turns in panic as the Egyptian chariotry gallops nearer and raises an arm in self-defense. It is a futile gesture. In another moment, he too will be butchered and his cattle taken.

In the register below this scene, a small male figure stands to the right of a large, east-facing war chariot of Sety I. There are five other representations of this figure on the Sety wall, and in each case ancient artisans plastered over the original carved figure and replaced it with a figure of Rameses II. For many years, Egyptologists believed this was evidence that Rameses II had an elder brother who was the rightful heir to Sety I's throne and who Rameses II murdered in order to have himself declared king. In fact, we now know that the original figure was that of a Fan Bearer and Troop Leader named Mehy (short for Horemheb or Amenemheb), a close confidant of the king. Removing Mehy's figure and replacing it with Rameses II's was not the result of palace intrigue by an evil prince but simply a declaration that Rameses II had reached his majority and was now the heir apparent.

◆ THE THIRD PYLON AND THE COURT ◆

The Third Pylon, which now forms the rear wall of the Hypostyle Hall, was built by Amenhetep III in part from blocks taken from earlier buildings. Archaeologists removed these blocks from the pylon's core and found that many came from a shrine of Senusret I, others from a shrine of Hatshepsut and over twelve other buildings. The Senusret I and Hatshepsut shrines have been reconstructed in the Open-Air Museum.

The pylon is in poor condition. On the rear (east) face of the right (south) tower an extensive list records tribute received by Amenhetep III from Asiatic countries, but the text is damaged and difficult to read. More interesting are scenes on the outer face of the left (north) tower. They show Amenhetep III sailing the Nile on Amen-Ra's huge bark during the important Opet Festival and the Beautiful Festival of the Valley. The barks fill the entire north half of the north tower's east face; they are magnificent boats over 130 cubits (about 68 meters, 221 feet) long. Amenhetep III was so proud that he described one on a stela erected in his memorial temple on the West Bank: "I made another monument for him who begat me, Amen-Ra, lord of Thebes, who established me upon his throne, making for him a great barge for the 'Beginning-of-the-River' (named): Amen-Ra-in-the-Sacred-Barge, of new cedar which his majesty cut in the countries of God's Land. It

88 OBELISKS OF THUTMES I (LEFT) AND HATSHEPSUT. BETWEEN THEM LIES THE FOURTH PYLON. IN THE BACKGROUND STANDS THE TEMPLE OF PTAH.

was dragged over the mountains of Retenu by the princes of all countries. It was made very wide and large...adorned with silver, wrought with gold throughout, the great shrine of electrum so that it fills the land with its brightness."

Thutmes I created a small open court between the Third and Fourth Pylons. It is little more than a patch of dirt and modern paving stones today, but in antiquity it housed four massive obelisks, two each for Thutmes I and Thutmes III. Only the bases of three obelisks remain, but the fourth, for Thutmes I, still stands. It is a monolithic block of granite 22 meters (72 feet) tall, 1.8 meters (6 feet) square, and weighs over 140 tons. The obelisk was quarried near the First Cataract at Aswan and transported down the Nile on a huge barge. How such blocks were moved, and, more remarkably, how they were erected with such precision, are matters still debated by scholars. Thutmes I's name appears on each side of the obelisk; Rameses IV added his own names later.

◆ A DETOUR TO THE TEMPLE OF PTAH ◆

From the courtyard between pylons three and four, one can walk north about 100 hundred meters (325 feet) along a dusty path through a field filled with inscribed blocks to the northern limit of the Central Enclosure. Here stands the Temple of Ptah, one of Egypt's principal creator gods. With his consort, the lion-headed goddess Sekhmet, Ptah played an important role in the coronation of the king.

His temple is well designed, attractively located, and worth a visit. Thutmes III described it in a text carved in the monument's central shrine: "I made it as a monument to my father Ptah...erecting for him the House of Ptah anew of fine white sandstone, doors of new cedar of the best of the terraces. It is more beautiful than it was before....My majesty found this temple built of mudbrick and wooden columns, and its doorway of wood, beginning to go to ruin....I overlaid for him [Ptah] his great seat with electrum of the best of the countries. All vessels were of gold and silver, and every splendid, costly stone, clothing of fine linen, white linen, ointments of divine ingredients, to perform his pleasing ceremonies at the feasts of the beginnings of the seasons, which occur in this temple..." The temple was built on the foundations of an earlier structure and then further enlarged in the Late Period and Ptolemaic times. Five, mostly Ptolemaic, pylons were built along the temple's east-west axis and decorated by various Ptolemaic kings (and by Shabaka of Dynasty 26). They lead to the original (Sixth) Pylon of Thutmes III, rebuilt by Rameses III. That pylon precedes a vestibule housing three offering tables. The table on the right (south) was cut by Amenemhet I in the Middle Kingdom and moved here by Thutmes III. Three sanctuaries lie beyond: shrines to Ptah on the left (north) and center, a shrine to Hathor on the right (south). In the center shrine, Thutmes III offers to Ptah and Amen.

A statue of Sekhmet in the right-hand chamber is dramatically lit at certain times of day by a beam of light that streams in through a small opening in the ceiling. It is worth spending a few moments in this chamber to appreciate the statue's dramatic setting. The Sekhmet statue has a beautifully modeled woman's body but the head of a lion, and it so frightened local villagers a century ago they claimed it was a monster that came to life on moonless nights and wandered village lanes devouring small children. Villagers were known to attack the statue with clubs and stones.

90 TOP AND BOTTOM RIGHT FRAGMENT OF HATSHEPSUT'S GRANITE OBELISK.

90 BOTTOM LEFT THE TRANSVERSE HALL BUILT BY THUTMES I.

90 BOTTOM CENTER COLOSSAL STATUES OF THUTMES I PORTRAYED AS OSIRIS.

91 THE OBELISK OF QUEEN HATSHEPSUT BETWEEN PYLONS FOUR AND FIVE.

◆ FROM THE FOURTH PYLON TO THE SIXTH ◆

The Fourth Pylon was built by Thutmes I, repaired by Thutmes IV, and altered by Sety II, Ptolemy VIII, and Alexander the Great. Behind it, Thutmes I built a transverse hall (sometimes called a hypostyle hall or a colonnade). Huge statues of the king in the costume and pose of Osiris stand before the east walls of the north and south towers. Originally, the hall had a wooden roof supported by wooden columns. Wood was a precious commodity in ancient Egypt, and pieces of the size used here would have been especially valuable donations to the temple. Thutmes III later replaced the wood with fourteen stone columns and a stone roof.

The granite obelisk here is one of a pair erected by Hatshepsut in the sixteenth year of her reign. The other was broken up and scattered about Karnak. One piece, with scenes of the queen's coronation, lies at the northwestern corner of the Sacred Lake. (No traces remain of two other obelisks Hatshepsut erected at Karnak.) The standing obelisk is 30 meters (97 feet) tall, 2.6 meters (8.5 feet) square, and weighs 323 tons. It was sheathed in electrum, a mixture of silver and gold. Hatshepsut and her engineers were proud of these huge monuments and the story of the work involved is recounted in scenes and texts in Hatshepsut's temple at Dayr al-Bahri and in inscriptions on the obelisks themselves.

With obvious pride the queen explained why she ordered such a massive project to be undertaken. On the standing obelisk's base she wrote: "I have done this with a loving heart for my father Amen...There was no sleep for me because of his temple...I was sitting in the palace and I remembered the one who created me; my heart directed me to make for him two obelisks of electrum, so that their pyramidions might mingle with the sky amid the august pillared hall between the great pylons of [Thutmes I]...They are each of one block of enduring granite without joint or flaw therein. My Majesty began work on them in regnal year 15, second month of winter, day 1, continuing until year 16, fourth month of summer, day 30, making 7 months in cutting them from the mountain....Let not anyone who hears this say it is boasting that I have said, but rather say, 'How like her it is, she who is truthful to her father.'" After Hatshepsut's death, Thutmes III had the obelisks walled up in a futile attempt to obliterate her memory. He only succeeded in protecting them from damage.

92 TOP THE AREA BETWEEN THE FIFTH AND THE SIXTH PYLONS.

92 BOTTOM THE PAPYRUS, SYMBOL OF LOWER EGYPT, IS CARVED ON A RED GRANITE HERALDIC PILLAR.

93 A STATUE OF AMEN FROM THE REIGN OF TUTANKHAMEN.

Little remains of the Fifth Pylon. It was also the work of Thutmes I, with alterations made by Thutmes III and Amenhetep III. In the reign of Thutmes III, the pylon served as the entrance to another transverse hall. That hall is badly ruined today, but in antiquity it contained twenty sixteen-sided columns and a row of Osirid statues along its eastern face. A statue of Amenhetep III sits before the left pylon tower. Two columned courts lie on the north and south.

The Sixth Pylon was built by Thutmes III and its west face was inscribed with the names of 120 Syrian towns (on the left) and Nubian towns (on the right) conquered by his army. The gate is of red granite.

Small chambers flanking the vestibule immediately east of the Sixth Pylon are known as the Hall of Records of Thutmes III. Two huge heraldic pillars stand on the north side of the temple axis, one carved with a lotus flower, the symbol of Upper Egypt, the other with a papyrus, symbol of Lower Egypt. The red granite is of excellent quality and the workmanship unsurpassed. Remains of statues of the god Amen and the goddess Amenet, carved in the reign of Tutankhamen and usurped by Horemheb, stand nearby. Amen's face is especially well modeled. Texts recounting events in the reign of Thutmes III are carved on the walls and continue into other parts of the building that surround the pink granite shrine of Philip Arrhidaeus a few meters to the east. In the Second Hall of Records, south of the shrine, these texts describe the king's military activities and show him offering to Amen-Ra.

◆ SHRINES OF PHILIP ARRHIDAEUS AND HATSHEPSUT ◆

The half-brother of Alexander the Great, Philip Arrhidaeus ruled Egypt from 323 to 317 BC. Like many non-Egyptians who assumed control of the country, Philip adopted Egyptian costume, titles, and religious beliefs. Philip was chosen to lead Egypt by Greek military officers who considered him the least threatening of a bad lot of candidates. He was dim-witted, epileptic, and the illegitimate son of Philip II of Macedonia and a dancing girl. Until the army had him murdered after six years of rule, military officers or his wife, his first cousin, Eurydice, made most of the government's decisions.

Among those was the decision to build in the Karnak complex. The choice of location for Philip's shrine was no accident: it was set in the very heart of the Temple of Amen, precisely on its main axis, adjacent to the earliest part of the temple, the Middle Kingdom court. Few sites were more central to temple ceremonies. The shrine of Thutmes III that stood here was torn down and replaced with Philip's shrine. The earlier shrine may have been damaged by Assyrian or Persian invaders three centuries earlier, and Philip claimed that he found it "fallen into ruin." His shrine, of identical plan to the shrine it replaced, was made of pink granite with carved figures painted yellow. It was 18 meters (58 feet) long, 6 meters (20 feet) wide, and divided into two rooms, the first for offerings, the second for the sacred bark. Some of the most interesting and best-preserved scenes were carved on the outer face of the right (south) wall: there are four registers, the uppermost of which documents Philip's ritual purification, coronation, and enthronement before Amen.

It is worth walking counterclockwise around the shrine of Philip Arrhidaeus to its northwest corner. North of the shrine, a large relief scene shows Thutmes III dedicating offerings to Amen. Immediately in front of the king, two obelisks that he erected at Karnak are shown standing in front of the Seventh Pylon. Below the scene, sixty-seven columns of text describe in detail the king's military campaigns in western Asia.

A doorway through the western end of this north wall leads to a chamber decorated with beautifully painted reliefs of Hatshepsut, Thoth, and Horus. The figures of the god Amen and the well-painted hieroglyphs are masterfully sculpted, but the figures of the queen were erased by Thutmes III, who replaced them with figures of himself.

◆ THE MIDDLE KINGDOM COURT ◆

East of the shrine of Philip Arrhidaeus is the earliest part of the Temple of Amen yet known, a large open court recently covered over with gravel and stones. Senusret I built a shrine here in Dynasty 12. Recent excavations have revealed traces of its foundation walls and trenches. Attempts were made to rebuild this Middle Kingdom temple in the fourth and fifth centuries BC but were never completed.

94 TOP THE MIDDLE KINGDOM COURT WITH THE SHRINE OF PHILIP ARRHIDAEUS (CENTER) AND THE AKH-MENOU (BOTTOM).

94 BOTTOM AND 95 RELIEFS FROM THE SHRINE OF PHILIP ARRHIDAEUS.

◆ THE AKH-MENOU - TEMPLE OF THUTMES III ◆

Most of the construction surrounding the Middle Kingdom court was the work of Thutmosid rulers. Nearest the court are pylons and enclosure walls of Thutmes I and Thutmes II; a few meters beyond them stand buildings of Thutmes III. The most elaborate of Thutmes III's monuments is the large and unusual structure immediately east of the Middle Kingdom Court, in ancient times called *Akh-Menou*, Brilliant of Monuments, and today called his Festival Hall. The ceremonies conducted here were closely associated with the king's *Sed*-festival, and the building's architecture and decoration reflect this emphasis.

Thutmes III boasted how he carefully prepared the ground before beginning work on the monument: he "exorcised its evil, removed the debris which had mounted to the town quarter," and began his construction anew because he "would not work upon the monument of another."

Its western wall is broken and many tourists enter the *Akh-Menou* along the east-west axis of the Temple of Amen. But the proper entrance is located in the southeast corner of the Middle Kingdom Court, behind two sixteen-sided columns and a pair of Osirid statues. Another sixteen-sided column stands in the small foyer just beyond the door. To the right, a corridor leads to nine small chambers used as storerooms for ritual equipment and priestly costumes. The contents of each chamber are shown in the reliefs carved on their walls: one held bread, another held vases, a third wine, and so on. The corridor's long north wall is decorated with scenes of the king's *Sed*-festivals.

Turning left (north) from the foyer, one enters the vast Festival Hall, 44 meters (143 feet) wide and 16 meters (52 feet) deep. Two rows of ten columns support the high roof of the central aisle. These columns are unique in Egyptian architecture. Each tapers toward the base and is topped with an oddly-shaped capital. The columns are painted red, the color of wood, and are said to imitate tent poles, either those used in the king's battlefield tent, or more likely, in tents used during the celebration of *Sed*-festivals. These are surrounded by 32 pillars, shorter than the central columns, to permit

96-97 VIEW OF THE AKH-MENOU, THE FESTIVAL HALL OF THUTMES III.

97 THIS OSIRIS STATUE STANDS BEFORE THE ENTRANCE OF THE TEMPLE OF THUTMES III.

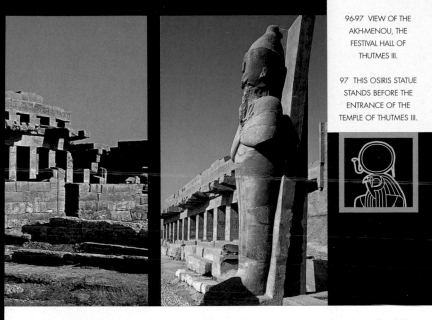

clerestory lighting. Texts and figures on the columns depict the king with various gods, nearly all of them erased by followers of Akhenaten in Dynasty 18 or by Christian priests who used the Festival Hall as a church. Traces of an elaborately painted Christian saint can be seen at the top of the column in the second row, fourth from the southern end. (On one column, the first in the second row, the misspelled name "Champoleon" is a weak nineteenth century joke.)

The column bases along the hall's central axis have been cut to make the space between them nearly a meter wider. This was done after the hall was completed, apparently when priests introduced a new and wider bark than the one used in earlier processions. Until part of the bases had been cut away, there was concern that priests carrying the sacred bark might stumble and drop the statue of the god.

Chapels at the north end of the hall include scenes of royal statues brought to the temple (center chapel, west wall) and offerings to various deities (west chapel, east wall). The left (west) chapel houses a huge, damaged statue of the king with Amen and Mut. A small doorway immediately at the left leads to a corridor with a scene of the king offering to an ithyphallic Amen. In the northeast corner of the hall, a stone staircase leads to a room that held a clepsydra, a pot with a hole through which water drained at a constant rate that was used to measure the passage of time. Such information was important for determining when liturgical services should be performed.

Explorers in the nineteenth century discovered an important stone inscription known as the Karnak King List in the southwest corner of the hall. Written in the reign of Thutmes III, it lists sixty-one kings starting with Snefru of the Old Kingdom. It is not a complete table of Egypt's rulers but a selection of those who had played especially important roles in the history of Thebes, and whose lineage demonstrated the legitimacy of Thutmes III's royal line. The blocks inscribed with the King List were dismantled one dark night in spring 1843 by a Frenchman, Emile Prisse d'Avennes, who smuggled them out of Egypt in boxes labeled "natural history specimens." They are in the Musée du Louvre in Paris.

Farther east, just south (right) of the main axis, small rooms of Thutmes III were usurped in Ptolemaic times and decorated with several well-painted scenes of Alexander the Great.

The most interesting room in the *Akh Menou* is the so-called Botanical Garden, which lies immediately north of the main temple axis east of the hall at the end of the temple. A set of modern wooden stairs climb over a badly damaged wall into a rectangular chamber with four papyriform columns down its midline.

The walls of the Botanical Garden are carved in very low raised relief best seen in raking early morning light. The room's south and north walls (15 meters or 49 feet long) and east and west end walls (6 meters or 20 feet wide) display remarkable drawings of plants and animals that Thutmes III claims he collected on military campaigns in foreign countries, especially in Syria, in regnal year 25. He writes, "I swear, as Ra (loves me), as my father, Amen, favors me, all these things happened in truth—I have not written fiction about that which really happened to my majesty." Thutmes III apparently realized that he might be accused of making it all up, that the drawings might raise a few eyebrows.

For decades, the drawings defied explanation and many scholars insisted that they were flights of royal fancy. Recently, however, the figures have been identified. It was discovered that the artist was not always depicting whole organisms, but *parts* of plants and animals. There are representations of rare birds, animals, flowers, and trees from Asia and East Africa that had never before been seen in Egypt. But also there are drawings of the internal organs of animals, small parts of exotic flowers, deformed creatures, and genetic sports. They include strange seeds, misshapen gourds, and cattle with three horns or two tails. In the words of one scholar, the Botanical Garden is a "cabinet of curiosities."

Why did Thutmes III collect such oddities and devote a part of the *Akh-Menou* to their description? Perhaps it was a way of acknowledging the enlargement of Amen's

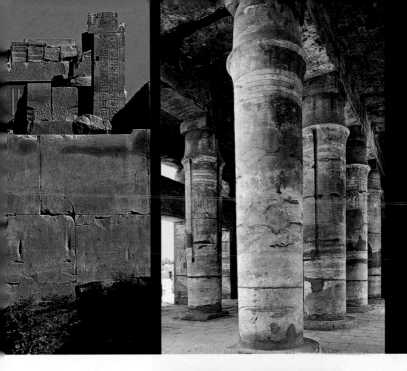

domain. As Egypt conquered more and more of western Asia and northeast Africa, they proclaimed that as Egypt's frontiers were expanding, so were Amen's. Amen was the creator of things Egyptians had never before imagined and the acknowledgement of this was recognition of the god's growing power. Amen was no longer a local *Egyptian* god but a universal god whose powers extended far beyond Egypt's borders. Such a view would have had major theological implications at a time when most cultures accepted that the power of their gods was limited to the people who made offerings to them and to the land in which their temples were built.

99 TOP THE PAINTED COLUMNS OF THE FESTIVAL HALL.

99 BOTTOM STONE STAIRCASE IN THE NORTHEAST CORNER OF THE FESTIVAL HALL.

98-99 VIEW OF THE SOUTH WALL OF THE TEMPLE.

◆ THE EASTERN PART OF THE COMPLEX AND THE SACRED LAKE ◆

Leaving the Botanical Garden from its northeast corner, a wooden ramp leads over the broken wall of the *Akh-Menou* and into the easternmost part of the Central Enclosure, behind the Temple of Amen. The exterior walls, built by Thutmes III, were mostly decorated by Rameses II.

The Chapel of the Hearing Ear was constructed by Thutmes III in the eastern wall of the Temple of Amen and alabaster statues of the king and a goddess sit inside it. Here, ordinary people came to petition the god, seeking cures for medical or social problems. Not having undergone ritual purification and therefore barred from entering the main part of the temple, this was as close as a commoner could get to the god's abode. Rameses II also built a temple here for similar purposes, and he usurped the six Osirid statues that stand nearby.

Farther east, still largely unexcavated and covered with brush, two temples were built by Thutmes IV and Rameses II. Thutmes IV also re-erected here an obelisk originally commissioned by his grandfather, Thutmes III. It stood 33 meters (107 feet) tall and in AD 357 was removed to the Circus Maximus in Rome. In AD 1567 it was transferred to the Piazza San Giovanni in Laterano. Rameses II built a temple in this area that extended east to the enclosure's undulating mudbrick wall. The monumental gateway there (19 meters, 62 feet tall) was built by Nectanebo I in Dynasty 30. Beyond the eastern wall of the Central Enclosure lie the partially excavated remains of a huge temple erected by Amenhetep IV/Akhenaten.

South of the Thutmes III temple, past walls heavily decorated with scenes of Rameses II offering to various deities, lies Karnak's Sacred Lake, in its present form the work of Taharqa (Dynasty 26). It measures 200 by 117 meters (650 by 380 feet). The lake is filled with seeping ground water and for much of the year is a dirty and smelly algae color, in spite of recent attempts to clean and aerate it. Locals call it the Saltwater Lake. Recent tests indicate that it contains an extremely high level of the parasite that causes schistosomiasis (Bilharzia) and one should avoid any contact with the water. Three thousand years ago, temple priests also avoided the lake, but not because it was polluted. Religious regulations demanded that they use fresh, flowing water for their daily ablutions, but they did row small sacred barks across the lake's surface on festival days. A modern Luxor folktale predicts that gilded barks rowed by solid gold statues will one day sail on the Sacred Lake—after the last liar and thief have been banished from Egypt. In the southern wall of the lake a stone-lined tunnel, one meter square, leads to a small stone building that served as home to a flock of geese raised by temple priests. Geese were symbols of Amen, and each morning these representatives of the god were driven through the tunnel to spend the day swimming in the lake's sacred waters. Thutmes III wrote, "My majesty formed for him [Amen] flocks of geese, to fill the Sacred Lake, for the offerings of every day. Behold, my majesty gave to him two fattened geese each day, as fixed dues, for my father Amen." From the late New Kingdom onward, priests of Amen lived to the east and south of the lake Several of their houses, some with household goods and priestly accessories still lying on their floors, were uncovered in the 1970s when Sound and Light (Son et Lumière) built its bleachers there. In this religious community within the sacred enclosure, away from the impurities of normal life, priests led a segregated existence, praying, meditating, and performing the tasks necessary for proper temple operations. Inscriptions on walls of the village and its gates reminded the clergy of the importance of sound moral behavior and ritual purification.

100-101 THE SACRED LAKE IS 200 BY 117 METERS (650 BY 380 FEET).

101 TOP THE WALLS NORTH OF THE SACRED LAKE ARE DECORATED WITH SCENES OF RAMESES II OFFERING TO GODS.

101 BOTTOM GEESE – SYMBOLS OF RA – WERE RAISED BY TEMPLE PRIESTS AT KARNAK.

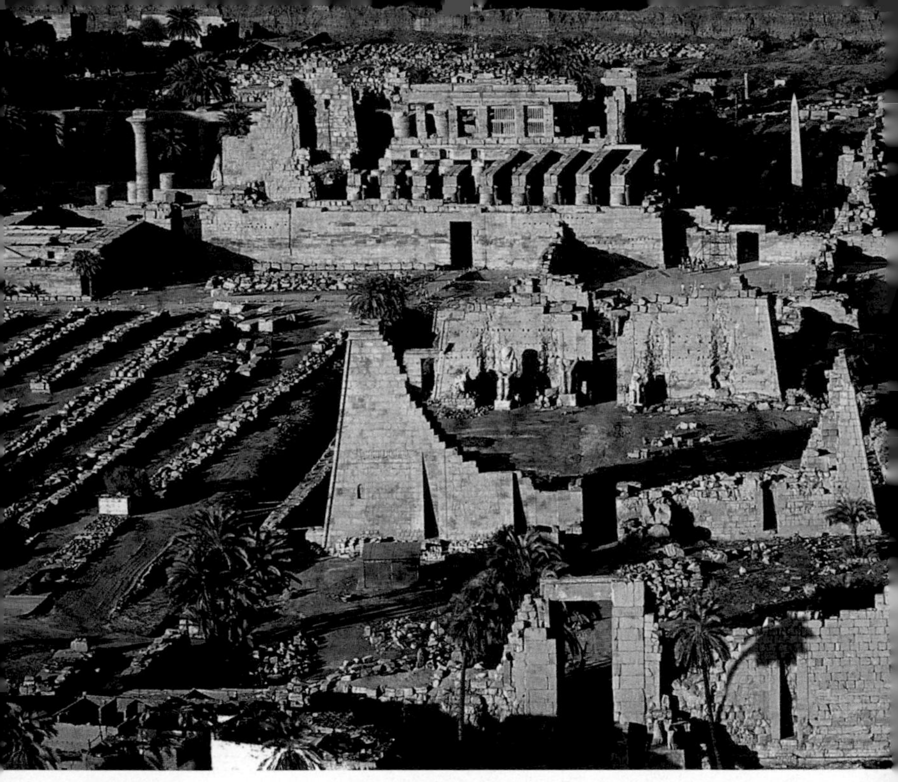

At the northwestern corner of the Sacred Lake, a refreshment stand sells soft drinks and postcards. Immediately to its west, a large granite pedestal topped by a huge stone scarab, a model of the dung beetle representing Atum-Khepri, a form of the sun-god, is the only remaining scarab of four that Amenhetep III installed in his memorial temple on the West Bank. It was brought here in Dynasty 25 by Taharqa, whose temple to the sun-god lies immediately to the north. (Do not believe tour guides who will tell you with a straight face that ancient Egyptian women walked seven times around this scarab to become pregnant. There is no proof of this.) A few meters to the north lies the top of one of the Hatshepsut obelisks that stood between the Fourth and Fifth Pylons. The scenes on this fragment show the queen's coronation.

◆ THE NORTH-SOUTH TEMPLE AXIS ◆

A few meters west of the scarab and obelisk, a small doorway leads through a north-south wall into a courtyard that marks the start of the Temple of Amen's second building axis. That axis runs at roughly a right angle to the axis of the First through Sixth Pylons. It extends from the Seventh Pylon through the Tenth and on to the Temple of Mut. The new axis was actually established by Queen Hatshepsut when she erected the Eighth Pylon, one of the earliest pylons to be built at Karnak. Earlier New Kingdom temples and shrines already stood in the area when Hatshepsut ordered work here, and the new axis was intended to provide a processional connection between them, the Temple of Amen, and the Temple of Mut. Shortly after ascending the throne, Thutmes III built a Seventh Pylon in front of the Eighth.

The courtyard created between the Seventh Pylon and the Great Hypostyle Hall is known by Egyptologists as the Cour de la Cachette. It was the place where ancient priests

make way for the scores of new statues and shrines constantly being produced in temple workshops. (These workshops were overseen by such officials as Neferrenpet, whose Theban tomb, TT 178, contains scenes of the many crafts projects they undertook.)

Between 1902 and 1909, the French archaeologist Georges Legrain cleared a huge pit that had been dug in the Cour de la Cachette in the Ptolemaic Period. Using thirty-two shadufs—local Egyptian water-lifting devices with a bucket on a counter-balanced pole—he was able to dig 14 meters (46 feet) into the ancient buried temple paraphernalia they no longer required, a repository similar to what in other religions is called a "favissa" or a "genizah." Such house cleanings may have taken place regularly as old statues and furniture were discarded to pit before ground water forced him to stop. In the pit, Legrain uncovered 780 larger-than-life-size stone statues, 17,000 bronze statuettes, and hundreds of architectural fragments that had been buried here by temple priests around 300 BC. It is one of the largest caches of statuary ever discovered. The objects are now in the Egyptian Museum, Cairo. Legrain could not recover all of the statues buried here, and undoubtedly many more will one day be found.

102-103 THE TENTH, NINTH AND EIGHTH PYLONS APPEAR IN THIS AERIAL PHOTOGRAPH LOOKING NORTH.

103 TOP LION WITH A SOLAR DISK CARVED ON THE SEVENTH PYLON.

103 BOTTOM A STONE SCARAB (RIGHT) LOCATED AT THE NORTHWESTERN CORNER OF THE SACRED LAKE.

The north wall of the First Court, which is also the south wall of the Great Hypostyle Hall, was decorated for Rameses II in the hasty manner typical of his reign, but its texts have considerable historical interest. They include a copy of the peace treaty Egypt signed with the Hittite ruler, Hatusilis III, in regnal year 21. Among its clauses, it declares that, "The Great Ruler of Hatti shall never trespass against the land of Egypt, to take anything from it. And [Rameses II], the Great Ruler of Egypt, shall never trespass against the land [of Hatti, to take anything from it.]" Then it quaintly states that the signing of the treaty was witnessed by "thousands of gods, male and female," and by "the mountains and the rivers of the land of Egypt; the sky, the earth, the great sea, the winds, and the clouds." The lawyers had thought of everything.

The Seventh Pylon has seven statues in front of it: four of Thutmes III (at left), two of Second Intermediate Period kings (on the right),

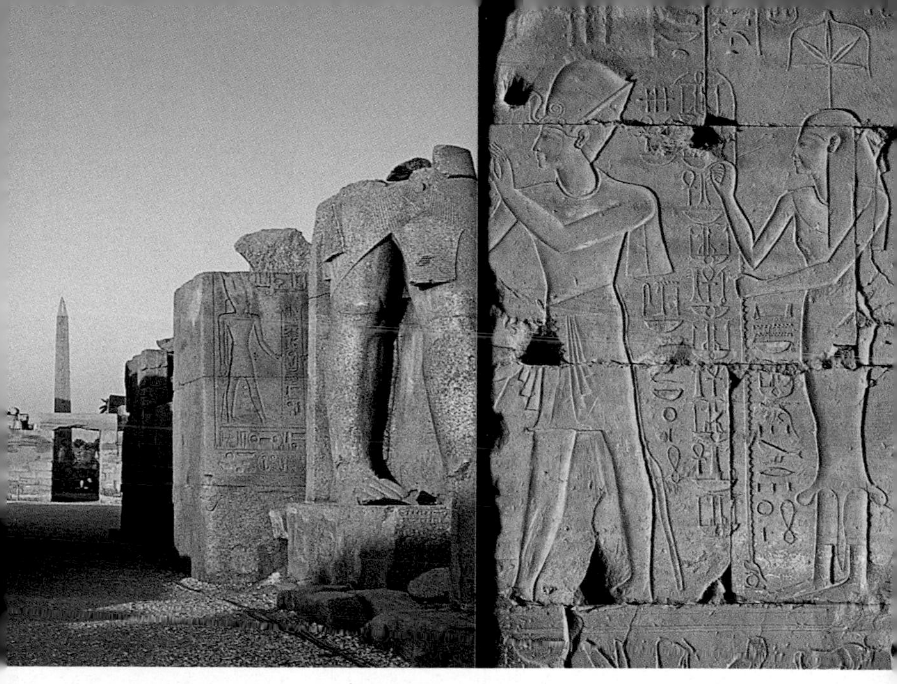

and one of Amenhetep II. They are not in their original positions. There is also a fragment of an obelisk carved for Thutmes III; its twin, which originally stood before the pylon's west (right) tower, is now in Istanbul. Between the Seventh and Eighth Pylons, in the left (east) wall of the Second Court, an alabaster shrine was built by Thutmes III.

Hatshepsut's Eighth Pylon is carved with a text written by her, but which she falsely attributed to Thutmes I, that offers a justification for her ascendancy to the throne of Egypt. The pylon was re-inscribed by Thutmes III, defaced by Amenhetep IV/ Akhenaten, and restored by Sety I. On the north face of its left (east) tower, Sety I offers to the gods. In an earlier scene here, Thutmes II walked forward with the lion-headed goddess Werethekau and the goddess Hathor. On the right (west) tower, Sety I walks with the falcon-headed god Montu and priests who carry a sacred bark. On the rear (south) face of the pylon, Amenhetep II grasps foreign captives in the presence of Amen. It is rare that such prisoners are depicted standing, as they are here, instead of kneeling.

On the Ninth Pylon, Horemheb is shown in procession with a sacred bark. The Ninth Pylon is currently being restored after sixty thousand blocks, taken by Horemheb from buildings of Amenhetep IV, (Akhenaten) and used as fill, were removed by archaeologists.

A *Sed*-festival temple for Amenhetep II was built on the left (east) side of the Fourth Court between the Ninth and Tenth Pylons, and scenes of Rameses II and Horemheb cover its walls and the faces of the pylons. Sety I undertook extensive restoration in this part of the Central Enclosure. Beyond the Tenth Pylon, an avenue of ram-headed sphinxes continues to the Temple of Mut.

104-105 THE SEVENTH PYLON, WITH REMAINS OF COLOSSAL STATUES IN FRONT.

104 CENTER AND 105 RIGHT RELIEFS FROM THE SEVENTH PYLON SHOWING PHARAOH OFFERING TO GODS.

104 BOTTOM FOUR SEATED COLOSSAL STATUES STAND IN FRONT OF THE EIGHTH PYLON.

◆ THE TEMPLE OF KHONSU ◆

The Temple of Khonsu, moon god and third member of the Theban Triad, lies in the southwestern corner of the Central Enclosure. One walks from the Hypostyle Hall of the Temple of Amen south along a stone path through a great field of decorated temple blocks that await re-installation in various Karnak monuments. A spectacularly old and gnarled tamarisk tree stands just east of the temple. It has figured in artists' paintings of the area for well over a century and offers a delightful spot to take a brief rest.

The Temple of Khonsu lies immediately north of the monumental gateway built by Ptolemy III Euergetes, called the Bab al-Amara. The gate stands 21 meters (68 feet) high and is one of the best-decorated examples of Ptolemaic architecture to be found at Thebes. A text on the gate mentions that a law court, A Site for Giving Ma'at, stood just outside it in Ptolemaic times. The gate also leads to the avenue of sphinxes, perhaps established by Amenhetep III but here built by Nectanebo I in Dynasty 30, which extends nearly three kilometers (1.8 miles) southward to Luxor Temple. At this end of the avenue, the sphinxes are in poor condition; they have served for centuries as playthings for nearby village children. A shorter row of sphinxes and pillars extends inside the enclosure from the gateway to the temple.

Like the Shrine of Rameses III in the Great Court of the Temple of Amen and his West Bank temple at Madinat Habu, the Temple of Khonsu is also a well-preserved monument with its walls and ceiling still intact. All of these monuments were in large part the work of Rameses III, although the Temple of Khonsu probably was begun in Dynasty 18 by Amenhetep III, then enlarged and extensively decorated by later rulers, especially Rameside rulers, Herihor (the High Priest of Amen), and Pinedjem.

The last two were responsible for building the temple pylon and its peristyle court.

The Temple of Khonsu is an important monument for Egyptologists because it is one of the few that makes contemporary reference to the serious changes Egypt underwent at the end of the New Kingdom. Rameses XI was the last king of Dynasty 20 and his reign witnessed the collapse of Egypt's fortunes. Foreign relations were at a low, trade was non-existent, and the government was faced with economic depression and civil war. Rameses XI, who resided in the north, could barely control Lower Egypt. Upper Egypt was in the hands of the High Priest of Amen, a former military officer named Herihor, who had adopted several senior titles including that of vizier. Herihor proclaimed that he was re-establishing "divine rule" in Thebes and would restore Egypt's former glory.

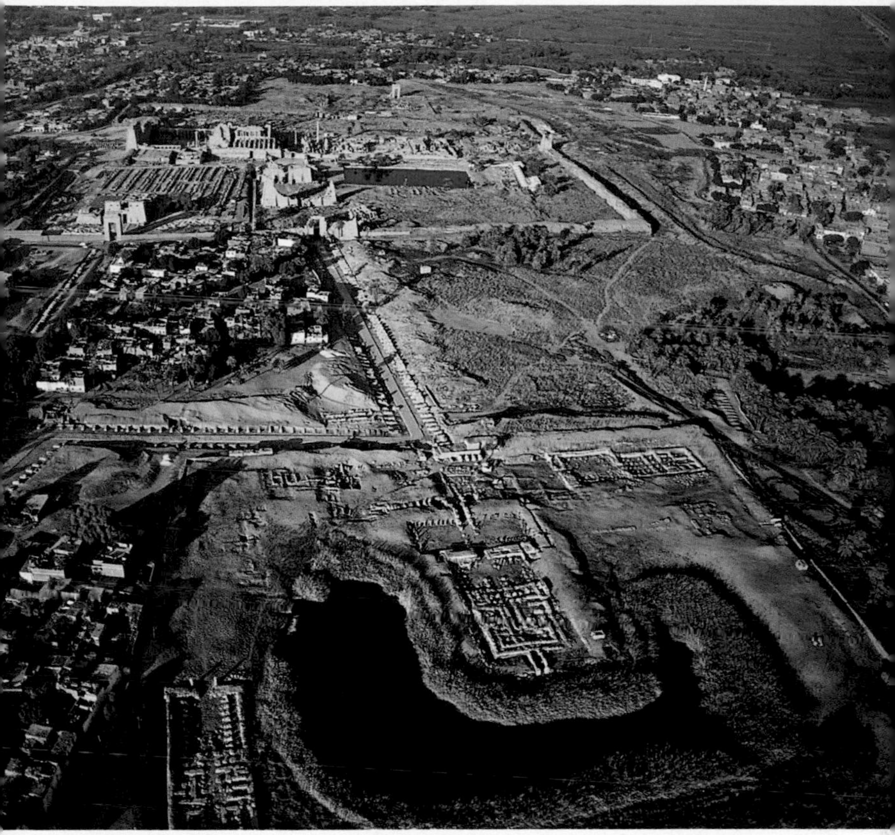

Khonsu, in his form as Khonsu-in-Thebes-Neferhetep was an especially popular deity at this time, perhaps more popular even than Amen, and Herihor chose Khonsu's temple as the place in which to commemorate this change in administration. Here, Herihor confidently represented himself at the same size as Rameses XI and wore costumes usually restricted to the king. With the wealth and backing of the priesthood of Amen, Herihor had in fact become the ruler of Upper Egypt.

106 THE TEMPLE OF KHONSU IN THIS AEREIAL VIEW IS IN THE FOREGROUND.

106-107 THE AVENUE OF SPHINXES LEADS FROM KHONSU TEMPLE TO LUXOR. ANOTHER AVENUE LEADS TO MUT TEMPLE, BEFORE A U-SHAPED GATE.

107 BOTTOM THE GATEWAY OF PTOLEMY III EUERGETES.

The temple's first pylon is 17 meters (55 feet) high, 32 meters (104 feet) wide, and 10 meters (33 feet) thick. Its face is carved with scenes of Pinedjem I of Dynasty 21 and his wife Henuttawi, offering to Amen, Mut, and Khonsu. In later scenes on the jambs of the doorway, Alexander the Great offers to the triad.

The peristyle court has double rows of columns on three sides. It was the Dynasty 21 work of Herihor, who is shown with the goddess Hathor offering to the Theban Triad on the right (east) wall. To the right of this scene the Temple of Khonsu itself is shown, and one can identify the façade of the first pylon with flagpoles standing in its four niches. Other offering scenes can be seen on the rear wall of the portico. Beyond the peristyle court, a doorway inscribed with the name of Ptolemy IV leads to the hypostyle hall. It has eight columns with papyrus capitals standing over 7 meters (22 feet) tall, each carved with figures of Ramses XI and Herihor. As usual in such halls, the four columns along the main axis are higher than those on the sides. A statue of Khonsu in the form of a baboon has been placed here. The sacred bark of the god was housed in the next chamber, originally made by Amenhetep II and then usurped by Rameses IV. Its walls are decorated with scenes of Rameses IV and various deities. Holes in the floor may have held posts that supported a woven reed mat hiding an altar or shrine from view.

Chapels on either side of this sanctuary have well-preserved color in scenes that show the king and various deities. One of the most interesting scenes, in the right (eastern) chapel, includes a rare figure of an ithyphallic lion-god on the left (west) wall. Most lion deities were female. Behind the sanctuary, a small chamber for the god Khonsu has four sixteen-sided columns and reliefs that show Rameses III in some scenes, the Roman Emperor Augustus Caesar in others. To its northeast, another chamber is decorated with figures of the dead Osiris, lying on his bier with Isis and Nephthys in attendance.

◆ TEMPLE OF OSIRIS AND OPET ◆

Immediately west of the Temple of Khonsu stands the small Temple of Osiris and Opet. Opet was a hippopotamus goddess of childbirth whom Egyptians considered to be Osiris's mother. Ptolemaic Egyptian religious beliefs held that when Amen died he took the form of Osiris, entered the body of his mother, Opet-Nut, and was reborn as Khonsu.

Thus, the birthplace of Khonsu stood adjacent to Khonsu's temple. The Ptolemaic Opet temple follows an unusual plan. It stands on a 2 meter (6.5 foot) high platform with a cavetto cornice along its top edge. This podium represents the primordial mound of creation, but also provides space for a pair of chambers cut below the temple floor that served as a crypt and chapel for Osiris.

Surrounding a two-columned hall, nine small, dark chambers have well-cut texts and scenes of Ptolemy II in adoration before Opet, Osiris, Horus, and other deities.

108 LEFT RELIEFS FROM THE TEMPLE OF KHONSU.

108 RIGHT THE HYPOSTYLE HALL OF THE TEMPLE OF KHONSU.

109 TOP THE FIRST PYLON OF THE TEMPLE OF KHONSU.

109 BOTTOM INNER HALL OF THE TEMPLE OF KHONSU.

THE OPEN-AIR MUSEUM

VISIT

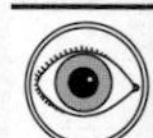

When archaeologists working at Karnak have found stones from earlier buildings re-used in later walls and pylons, they have removed and catalogued the blocks and stored them in open fields within the central enclosure. A few decades ago, a number of these blocks were gathered together and the buildings from which they came were reconstructed. They were placed in what is now called the Open-Air Museum in the northwest corner of the Karnak's central enclosure.

The Open-Air Museum is a lovely and tranquil place, filled with mature trees, stone footpaths, and some of the most beautiful monuments ever to come from the Temple of Amen. The number of monuments displayed here is growing rapidly: in 1999, there were only three structures and a small collection of statues and loose blocks; today, there are four way-stations, several huge temple walls, storage chambers, statues, and hundreds of blocks from still-unreconstructed and many other buildings. These monuments are of such interest that the museum should be visited by every tourist who comes to Thebes.

◆ THE WHITE CHAPEL OF SENUSRET I ◆

In the autumn of 1927, French archaeologists working to restore the Third Pylon of the Temple of Amen found a large, beautifully inscribed limestone architrave reused in the pylon's interior fill. Over the next ten years, hundreds more inscribed blocks were uncovered, all from the same Middle Kingdom building of Senusret I. Egyptologist Pierre Lacau and architect Henri Chevrier began in 1937 to reconstruct the building, which they called the White Chapel. It was the first monument to be installed in the Open-Air Museum. Originally, it probably stood on the west side of the Middle Kingdom courtyard. That courtyard was called "The High Lookout of Senusret I," and the shrine itself was called "The Throne of Horus." It was built by Senusret I for the celebration of his first *Sed*-Festival.

At the time of its discovery, the White Chapel was unique. No examples of such a building had ever come to light. Thanks to almost perfect preservation, it was possible to rebuild what many consider the finest example of relief carving to come down from the Middle Kingdom.

The White Chapel was but one of the many way stations erected at Karnak, small buildings where priests could set down the divine bark and the god's statue while they briefly rested and recited prayers during the many religious processions that took place each year.

It is a small monument: 6.75 meters (22 feet) square, with ramp and stairway combinations at either end that lead to the chapel floor, 1.8 (nearly 6 feet) meters above ground. The shrine has four rows of four pillars each 2.5 meters

(7.5 feet) tall, supporting architraves and a cornice above. There are waterspouts to collect the rare rain that falls on the roof, water that was used in purification ceremonies. The plan and section of the building are simple and even a bit heavy. But this is more than made up for by the relief carving that covers nearly every vertical surface. It is certainly the most elaborately decorated of all the chapels at Karnak.

On the pillars, Senusret I stands with Amen, sometimes shown in his ithyphallic form, and with other gods and goddesses including Anubis, Thoth, Ptah, Horus, Atum, Montu and Amenet. The accompanying texts give titles and epithets of the king and deities. The detail in these figures is truly astonishing: kilts and unusual capes are meticulously pleated; every bead in a necklace or collar is carefully delineated. The hieroglyphs are even more elaborate: the feathers of a bird's wing; the musculature of a bull; the curls on the *hr*-sign (a human head); the twisted strands in a rope cartouche; the transparent wings of a bee; the pattern of a woven basket—all are shown with the minutest attention to detail. There is very little paint preserved, but each hieroglyph is a fully formed work of art, a tiny masterpiece cut in finest limestone.

But the inscriptions are of more than just aesthetic interest. There is a list of nomes, the ancient administrative districts into which Egypt was divided, on the outer walls, carved in a series of rectangles just below the shrine's windows. On the right (north) side are the nomes of Lower Egypt, on the left (south) those of Upper Egypt. For example, at the right (east) end of the south wall appears the name *Ta-Sety,* the first nome of Upper Egypt, called Elephantine or Aswan. Below its name another rectangle gives the name of the nome's principal deity, in this case Horus. Below that, a string of numbers indicates the length of the nome's Nile shoreline, in this case, 10 *itru,* 2 *kha,* 7 *setjat,* which is 112.061 kilometers. (One *itru* is 10.5 kilometers; *kha* and *setjat* are fractions thereof.) At the left (east) end of the north wall, a rectangle encloses the name of the first Lower Egyptian nome, Memphis, *inbu hedj,* which extends 4 *itru,* 1 *kha,* or 42.523 kilometers along the Nile. Twenty-two Upper Egyptian and fourteen Lower Egyptian nomes are listed. Also on the outer north wall of the chapel, flood levels at several sites along the Nile are given in cubits. This is extremely important information for reconstructing the geography and politics of ancient Egypt.

110 DETAILS FROM THE WHITE CHAPEL OF SENUSRET I.

111 LEFT THE WHITE CHAPEL OF SENUSRET I.

111 RIGHT PILLAR OF THE WHITE CHAPEL OF SENUSRET I WITH THE KING BEFORE AMEN.

◆THE ALABASTER SHRINE OF AMENHETEP I ◆

Amenhetep I erected several buildings in and around the Middle Kingdom Court, several of which were dismantled and used as fill in the Third Pylon and to create the court before the Seventh Pylon. One of these, from the Third Pylon, is a remarkable alabaster bark-shrine, recently reconstructed in the Open-Air Museum. Called the *Menmenu*, it originally stood in the Middle Kingdom precinct as a repository for the sacred bark of Amen. Amenhetep I said that, "Never since the first primeval time of the earth has the like of this been made in the land." Its name was found in an inscription in the Red Chapel of Queen Hatshepsut, which now stands nearby. The shrine was the work of a prominent architect of the early New Kingdom, Ineni, who also was responsible for many works of Amenhetep I's successor, Thutmes I.

Amenhetep I's shrine measures only 9 meters (29 feet) long and consists of a single chamber, built of huge blocks of alabaster. Alabaster was a valuable material rarely found in such large pieces. The alabaster, probably from the Hatnub quarries, has mottled shades of caramel and honey running through it, and is pockmarked with pits, gashes, and impurities that give it the appearance of pulled taffy. These imperfections so overpower the delicate relief that the carved figures completely disappear in all but the sharpest raking light. Originally, the scenes must have been painted, for that is the only way the figures could have been easily seen. But painting the surface would have concealed the fact that the shrine was built of such costly material. Why use blocks of precious alabaster if it could not be seen? Perhaps the magical and religious associations of alabaster were more important than its ostentatious display.

Scenes on the outer north wall of the Menmenu show Amenhetep I mystically joined with the god Amen, dedicating offerings of food, oils, and water as part of his coronation ceremony. The outer face of the south wall is decorated with figures of Thutmes I, and some scholars think this proves that the shrine was built late in the reign of Amenhetep I as a joint venture with his successor. The interior faces of the two walls show Amenhetep I and Amen standing before offerings and a divine bark.

◆ THE RED CHAPEL OF QUEEN HATSHEPSUT ◆

This large and elegant building was re-erected in 2000, making it one of the most recent additions to the museum, although the recovery of blocks in 1898 makes it one of the first to have been discovered. Like all the shrines here, the building goes by several names and descriptive terms: Chapelle Rouge, Red Chapel shrine, bark-shrine, chapel or way station. Like the others, the Red Chapel functioned as a temporary resting-place for divine barks during religious processions. The monument, found re-used in the Third Pylon, bore the cartouches of Thutmes III and Hatshepsut. Originally, it may have stood near the shrine of Philip Arrhidaeus, west of

the Middle Kingdom court. It is larger than the other shrines, 15 meters (50 feet) long and 5.77 meters (18.5 feet) tall.

The shrine is a fascinating piece of architecture. It is built of red quartzite on a base of black granite that is inscribed with lists of Upper and Lower Egyptian nomes. There is a torus molding at each corner and a cornice across the top. The courses of stone are laid horizontally with vertical joints between the blocks. Each register is one block in height, and there are six registers on the exterior wall, seven on the interior. Each block is of a slightly different length so that it can accommodate a single scene or part of a scene. This must mean that each block was custom-cut and decorated at the quarry, then installed in a predetermined place in the structure. This implies that its builders had a detailed architectural plan for the monument.

The floor of the shrine has several channels cut into it to direct the flow of water used in ceremonies of purification.

112 LEFT THE ALABASTER SHRINE OF AMENHETEP I.

112 RIGHT AND 113 RELIEFS FROM THE RED CHAPEL OF QUEEN HATSHEPSUT.

THE TEMPLE OF LUXOR

THE HISTORY

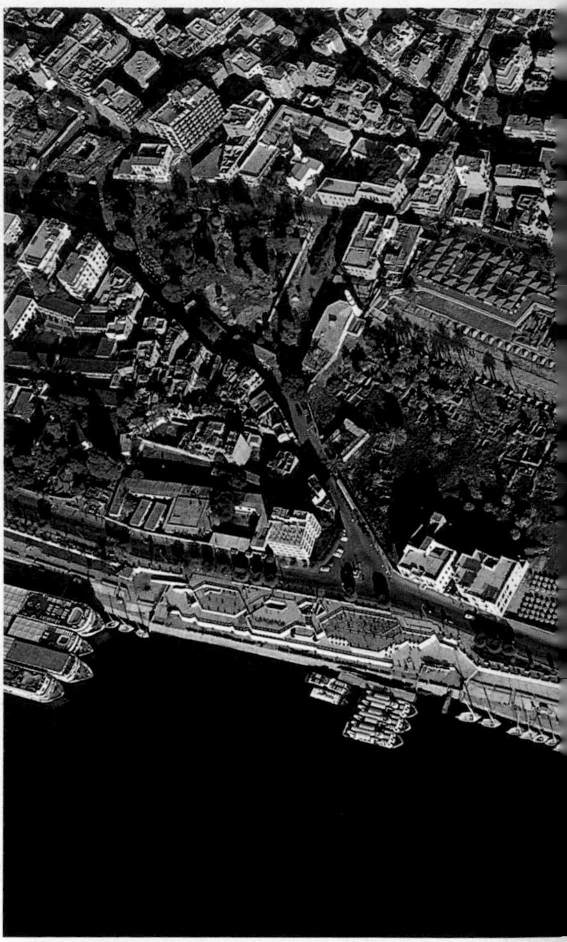

In ancient times, religious processions moved between the Karnak Temple complex and Luxor Temple along a 2.5–kilometer-long paved Avenue of Sphinxes. The causeway was lined with a thousand larger-than-life-size ram-headed sphinxes backed by gardens and pools. Six bark shrines, similar to those now in Karnak's Open-Air Museum, were built at intervals along its length, structures in which priests carrying the statue of Amen from the one temple to the other could pause for rest and ceremonies. The northernmost of these shrines lay just outside the Bab al-Amara at Karnak; the southernmost lay in the First Court of Luxor Temple.

Early in the New Kingdom, before the Avenue of Sphinxes was built, a water-filled canal apparently ran here and sacred barks sailed on it between Karnak and Luxor. By the later New Kingdom, however, as lunar-dated festivals progressed through the calendar and began to fall outside the season of the annual flood, there was too little water to float the barks and the canal was filled in and paved over. Henceforth, processions moved overland or on the Nile.

114 TOP, 115 TOP AND BOTTOM DETAILS FROM A COLOSSAL STATUE OF RAMESES II IN THE GREAT COURT.

114-115 THE TEMPLE OF LUXOR.

116-117 THE AVENUE OF THE SPHINXES EXTENDS NORTH FROM LUXOR TEMPLE TO THE TEMPLE OF KHONSU AT KARNAK.

The Avenue of the Sphinxes was begun in the New Kingdom, but took its final form only in the 30th Dynasty reign of Nectanebo I. Only a few short stretches of the Avenue of Sphinxes have been excavated. The best-preserved of them extends a few hundred meters northward in front of the Luxor Temple, and about thirty-five sphinxes are exposed on each side of a paved roadway. Trees and broad strips of grass line the avenue, flowers bloom in season, and the noise of the nearby town is thankfully muted. It is worth walking along the processional way to admire the ancient construction and to enjoy the fine view it offers of the temple's First Pylon.

In antiquity, an extensive complex of buildings surrounded Luxor temple. The city of Thebes was a warren of narrow streets that wound between markets, workshops, animal pens, and mud brick houses ranging from hovels to villas. The French novelist Gustave Flaubert described the temple compound as it appeared in the nineteenth century: "The houses are built among the capitals of columns; chickens and pigeons perch and nest in great (stone) lotus leaves; walls of bare brick or mud form the divisions between houses; dogs run barking along the walls." Thebes outside the temple enclosure probably looked very similar 2,500 years earlier. Some of the houses Flaubert saw were torn down in 1885. But, except for a small area of the Roman Period city west of the Avenue of the Sphinxes, most of the ancient urban buildings still lie beneath modern Luxor. It is unlikely they will be excavated any time soon because of the costs involved.

Today, Luxor temple is surrounded by a modern city that caters to thousands of tourists and a rapidly growing local population. The city poses problems for the temple. The novelist William Golding visited Luxor Temple and wrote, "There was about the building that ineffable air of having outstayed any welcome the town was prepared to give it and of only waiting for the arrival of the removal men." Modern buildings, which means those erected during the past two centuries, have intruded into the ancient monuments, and the city's deteriorating infrastructure has resulted in water and sewage seeping westward into the temple compound, seriously damaging its foundations. The pressures continue. Recently, the Amenhetep III Courtyard had to be dismantled and a concrete pad poured beneath its columns to

prevent their imminent collapse. The success of this work is uncertain. Carved stone walls have been so adversely affected by rising groundwater that decorated surfaces have already crumbled away. The mud brick walls of the temple's ancillary structures have fared even worse: many have simply vanished. A burst water main in 2001 did serious damage to the Roman remains at the southern end of the site. Work to protect the temple area continues today and will likely continue long into the future. There has been talk of exposing the entire length of the Avenue of the Sphinxes, clearing the ancient city around Luxor Temple and making the area an open-air museum. But that would cut the modern city of Luxor in half and require turning the highly valuable land between the causeway and the Nile into a park or pedestrian mall. Because of costs and politics and uncertain conservation requirements, the proposal is unlikely to be implemented any time soon.

West of the temple compound, a main street, the Corniche, separates the temple from the Nile. It is lined with rows of benches beneath small shade trees where young Egyptians sit and talk in the cool evening. South of the temple stand the ugly New Winter Palace Hotel and a slowly decaying shopping mall filled with curio shops and cloth merchants. To the northwest, built atop the Roman village, two dilapidated 19th century houses, one of them the headquarters of Egypt's National Democratic Party, slowly crumble away. The Brooke Animal Hospital, the city jail, the fire department, and a pottery dealer lie behind it, built directly atop the ancient town. To the east, Luxor's bustling business district is filled with street vendors, grocers, restaurants, department stores, and a thriving McDonald's. The smells of spices and grilling fish waft through the air. The shouts of men selling sweet dates, fresh juices, tins of mackerel, and a bewildering array of cheap housewares compete with shouting tour guides, honking buses, and the sirens of VIP motorcades. The market streets of Luxor are fascinating (the major weekly market is on Tuesday mornings) and well worth exploring. But to get the flavor of Luxor Temple free from modern intrusions, it is necessary to go deep inside it, where ancient stone walls block views of the modern buildings and shut out the din of the city. It is even better to visit in the evening, when the walls are illuminated and the temple is engulfed by surrounding darkness.

VISIT

Visitors to the temple today enter from the Corniche on the west. There was an entrance very near here in ancient times, too, and below street level on the edge of the Nile one can see the stones of the landing quay built to receive sacred barks and other vessels that arrived and departed the temple on festival days.

A stone path leads eastward from the entrance across an open area recently cleared of many inscribed stone blocks, alongside remains of the Roman fort, Roman temples and, farther south, a Christian church. A broad stairway leads to a courtyard built by Nectanebo I between the First Pylon and the Avenue of the Sphinxes. Several monuments were built here during the Roman Period. Nearly all of them are destroyed, but an interesting small chapel still stands in the northwest corner, built by Hadrian and dedicated to Serapis early in the second century AD. This is just one of the major building projects the Romans undertook in the Luxor compound when they converted the entire area into a fortified garrison about 250 AD. Luxor Temple itself lay at the center of this defensive complex and served as a temple to Roman emperors who saw themselves as the divine inheritors of Egyptian kingship. In fact, the name Luxor comes from the Arabic *al-Uksur,* meaning "fortification," which in turn derived from the Latin word "castrum," the word for a fortification. The temple was also called the "Temple of Amen of the Opet," "Amenemopet," or "The Southern Sanctuary."

Like the temples at Karnak, Luxor Temple has undergone numerous changes and additions over the past three millennia. Undoubtedly, an earlier Middle Kingdom temple once stood on the site, perhaps even an Old Kingdom temple before that. There is certainly evidence that Queen Hatshepsut built here in the 18th Dynasty. But the earliest structures visible today were erected by Amenhetep III, and he and Rameses II were responsible for most of the temple's huge colonnades and courts. Later, substantial redecorating was undertaken by Ptolemaic and Roman rulers, Christian priests, and Moslem sheikhs. The architectural history of Luxor Temple is less complex than that of the monuments at Karnak, but we are again forced to work our way backward through time as we enter the temple and explore its many parts.

118 DETAIL ON THE THRONE OF A COLOSSAL STATUE OF RAMESES II IN THE GREAT COURT, WITH THE NILE-GODS BINDING TOGETHER THE TWO LANDS OF EGYPT.

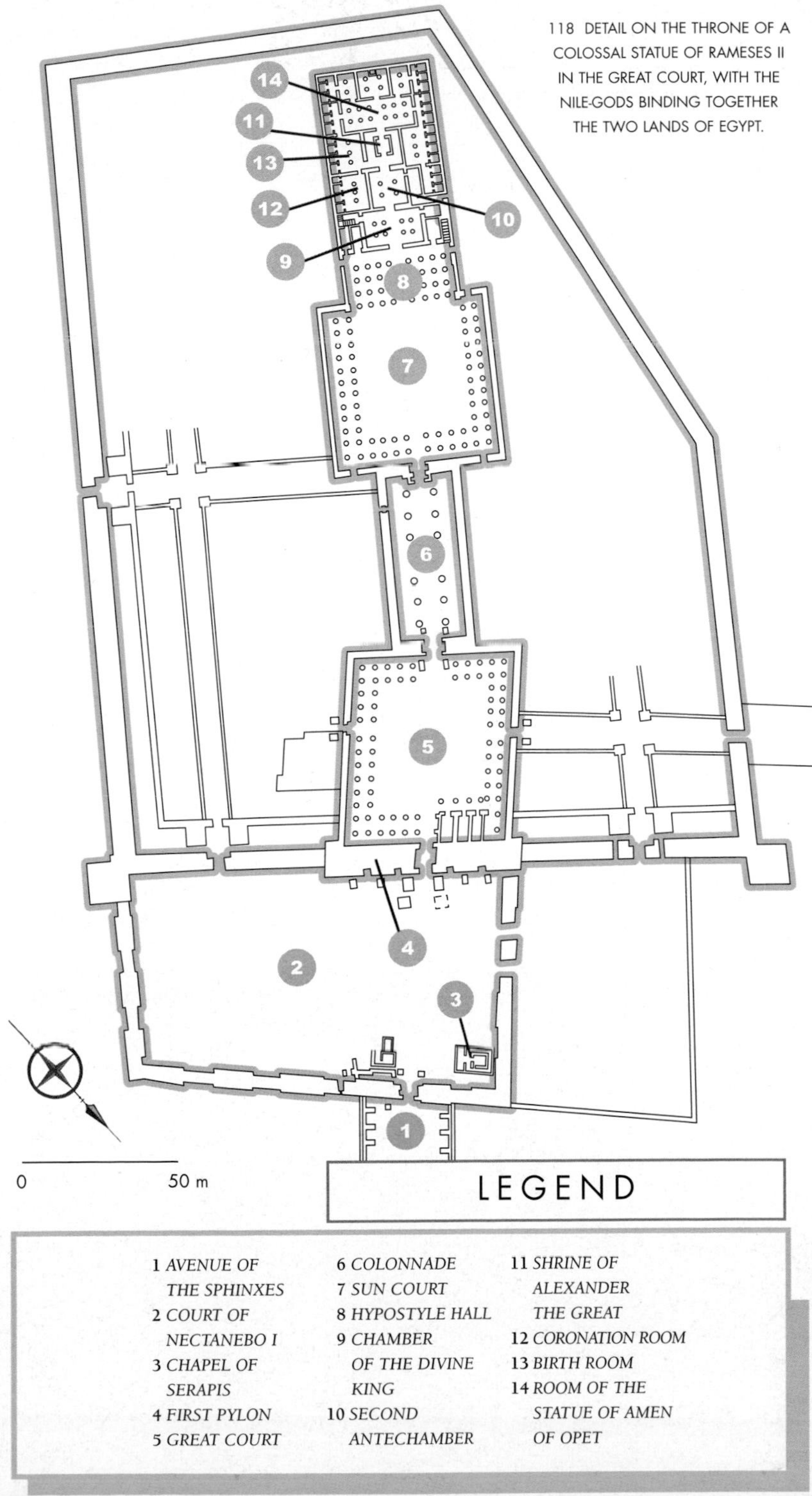

Throughout its long history, Luxor Temple served as the dwelling-place of an ithyphallic form of the god Amen closely associated with ideas of fertility and rejuvenation. Each year, a statue of Amen of Karnak was carried in a procession to Luxor Temple to greet Amen of the Opet, Amenemopet, in a ceremony called "The Beautiful Festival of the Opet." The ceremony was one of the most important in Egypt's religious calendar. The procession between the temples and the ceremonies held at Luxor are shown on the outer walls of the shrine/temple of Rameses III in the Great Court at Karnak and on the walls of Amenhetep III's Colonnade at Luxor Temple. Among its several functions, the festival was meant to reaffirm the authority of the king, his ties to the royal ancestors, and his bonds to the gods. It was a ceremony of royal rejuvenation and a reassertion of the gods' power over Egypt. The festival was celebrated in the second month of summer, during the annual inundation of the Nile.

This ancient Luxor tradition of processions and festivals has survived. The modern Festival of Abu-el-Haggag has retained, in modified form, many ancient festival activities. Abu-el-Haggag was a venerated Moslem sheikh whose mosque and tomb lie within the temple compound and who is said to have brought Islam to Luxor eight centuries ago. To celebrate Abu-al-Haggag, each year in the Moslem month of Shaban, Luxor is transformed into a three-day-long carnival. Fruits and nuts are sold on the streets, minstrels and magicians perform, horses race up and down the Corniche, men dress as women, and women wear their fanciest clothes. At the height of the partying, thousands of people watch as a model bark filled with gaily dressed children is paraded through town on a horse-drawn wagon from Luxor Temple toward Karnak. Children scream, women ululate, men chant as the bark passes by. It is a different century, a different religion, a different culture, but the Festival of Abu-el-Haggag continues the traditional forms of the Festival of Opet.

120 THE WEST WALL OF THE GREAT COLONNADE: PROCESSION OF "THE BEAUTIFUL FESTIVAL OF THE OPET."

121 ALEXANDER THE GREAT OFFERING TO THE ITHYPHALLIC FORM OF AMEN.

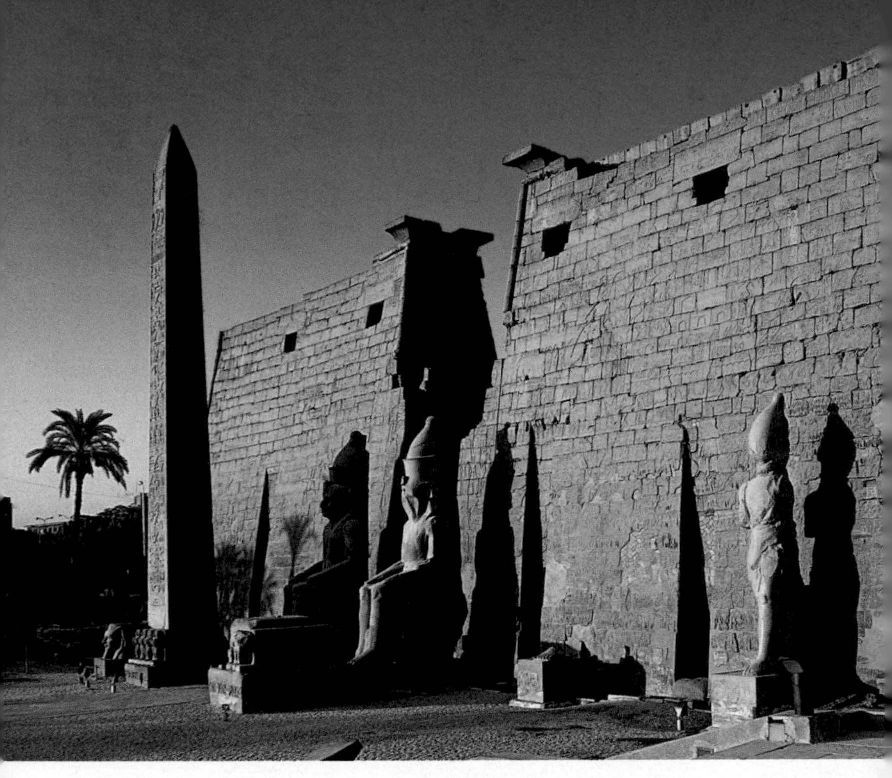

◆ THE FIRST PYLON ◆

The earliest part of Luxor Temple consists of the assemblage of chambers at its southern end. The buildings at the northern end are later, and include substantial structures built in the 19th Dynasty by Rameses II. Those additions, consisting most prominently of the First Pylon and Great Court, form the entrance of the temple today. In front of the First Pylon, Rameses II erected two red granite obelisks. The one still standing here is 25 meters (82 feet) tall and weighs 254 tons; the other, removed in 1835 to the Place de la Concorde in Paris, stands 22.5 meters (73 feet) tall and weighs 227 tons. Each was erected on a base with four baboons carved on its face.

The story is told that Josephine bade farewell to Napoleon with the words, "While in Egypt, if you go to Thebes, do send me a little obelisk." After several years of negotiations, the French received permission to do just that. Both Luxor Temple obelisks were originally to have been shipped to Paris, but the work was judged too costly, and the French elected to ship only the better-preserved of the two. The west (right) obelisk was loaded onto a great barge and sailed to Alexandria, then on to France.

It arrived in Paris in October, 1833, and its re-erection was witnessed by the king and queen and 200,000 onlookers. The Place de la Concorde is an especially impressive place because of the obelisk that now stands proudly in its center but, as one observer has remarked, Luxor Temple now resembles an elephant with one tusk missing. In 1846, in a gesture of thanks for being given the obelisk, the French king sent an elaborate clock to Egypt, where it was installed at the Citadel in Cairo, in the courtyard before the Mosque of Mohammed Ali. It is still there. It has never worked.

Next to the Luxor obelisks, two seated statues of the king, seven meters (23 feet) tall, flanked the gate between the pylon's two towers. There are also

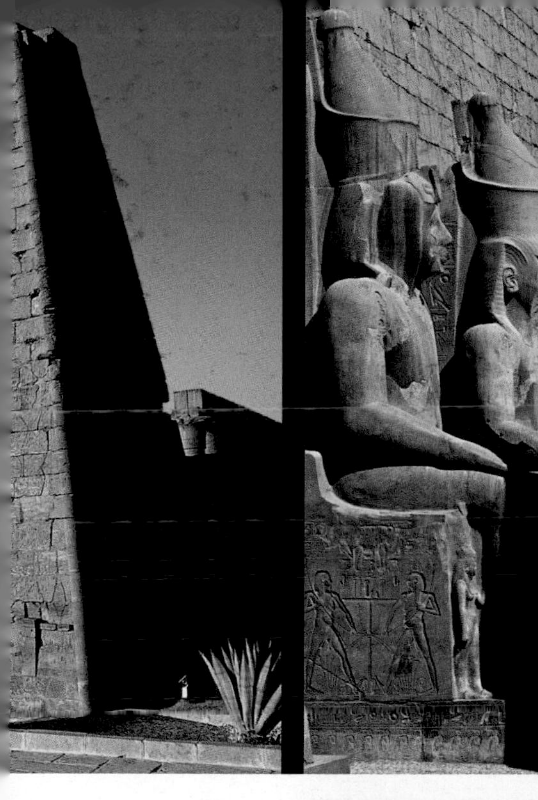

traces of four striding statues of the king (one of them now in the Louvre). The seated statue on the east (left) shows a princess and Queen Nefertari, carved at much smaller scale, next to the king's legs. On both statues, the sides of the king's throne are decorated with figures of Nile-gods binding together the Two Lands of Egypt. The towers of the First Pylon stand 24 meters (78 feet) high and 65 meters (211 feet) wide. The façade is carved in sunk relief with scenes of Rameses II's battle against the Hittites at Kadesh, fought in the fifth year of his reign. Many scenes in many temples depict this event. Unfortunately, the façade of the pylon has been badly eroded and this record of the event is difficult to see. On the west (right) tower, the king holds a conference on tactics with his princes and advisors. Nearby, he drives a war chariot into battle. On the east (left) tower, the battle rages, and dead and dying enemies lie strewn across the field. On the jambs of the gateway, Rameses II stands with various gods.

122-123 THE FIRST PYLON, BUILT IN THE 19TH DYNASTY BY RAMESES II.

123 TOP TWO SEATED STATUES OF RAMESES II FLANK THE ENTRANCE OF THE FIRST PYLON.

123 BOTTOM RELIEF FROM THE FIRST PYLON DEPICTING RAMESES II IN HIS WAR CHARIOT.

◆THE GREAT COURT◆

Immediately behind the First Pylon, the Great Court measures 57 meters (185 feet) deep and 51 meters (166 feet) wide. This is a peristyle court, with a double row of 74 columns around its four sides supporting a narrow roof around its perimeter. The northeastern (left front) quadrant of the court is unexcavated; a deep layer of debris and the remains of an early Christian church lie beneath the

mosque and tomb of Abu-el-Haggag. The minaret of this mosque was erected in the 13th century, and the mosque is so important a monument in its own right that it is unlikely this area will ever be cleared to its dynastic levels.

The walls of the court are decorated with scenes of the king censing, making offerings with chanting priests, and of Thoth recording gifts. The most interesting scenes are on walls in the southwest (right rear) corner of the court. Here, on the west (right) wall, a collection of beautifully garlanded bulls is led to the temple for sacrifice. Walking in the procession before them, on the south (rear) wall, seventeen sons of Rameses II approach the temple. Their names and titles are given beside each figure, and the sons appear in birth order, the oldest (Amenherkhepshef) standing first at left. Before them is a finely drawn representation of the First Pylon of Luxor Temple that shows it with flags flying, obelisks and statues clearly and accurately depicted.

In the southeast (left rear) corner of the court, an imposing statue of Rameses II and Queen Nefertari is one of several originally carved for Amenhetep III and usurped by Rameses II. This one shows the king powerfully and confidently striding forward, the ideal well-muscled and perennially youthful ruler. Equally well-carved seated statues of the king flank the door into the next room. In the northwest (right front) corner of the court stands a small Triple-Shrine of the Theban Triad, Amen, Mut, and Khonsu. Originally built by Hatshepsut and usurped by

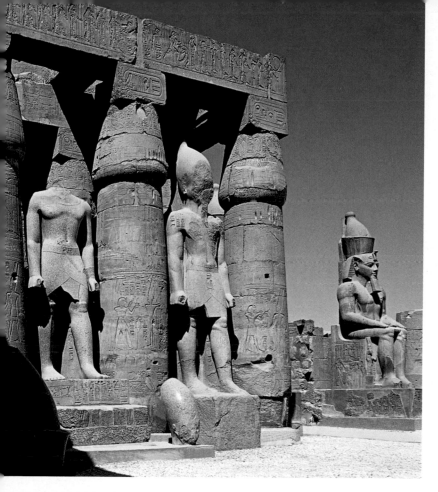

Thutmes III and then by Rameses II, four graceful papyrus-columns stand on its portico. The three shrines belong (left to right) to Mut, Amen, and Khonsu. In each, the king kneels before the god. Scenes of sacred barks cover the walls. The building was the southernmost of the bark shrines used in processions between Karnak and Luxor temples and played an important role in the ceremony. It may originally have stood in a more central position near the entrance of the temple, then moved here by Rameses II.

124 AERIAL VIEW OF THE GREAT COURT WITH THE MOSQUE OF ABU-EL-HAGGAG.

124-125 COLOSSAL STATUES STAND BETWEEN THE COLUMNS OF THE GREAT COURT.

125 BOTTOM PROCESSION OF SONS OF RAMESES II FROM A RELIEF IN THE GREAT COURT.

◆ THE COLONNADE ◆

This is one of the most impressive spaces in any Egyptian monument. Built by Amenhetep III to be the grand entrance to the Temple of Amen of the Opet, the Colonnade was the third stage in the king's elaborate building plan. It chronologically precedes the Great Court but follows it geographically. The two rows of columns he erected may have been intended as the main axis of what was to become a great hypostyle hall, similar to that at Karnak. If so, that work was never finished. Only the Colonnade was completed after the death of Amenhetep III by Tutankhamen, Ay, and Horemheb.

The axis of the Colonnade and chambers south of it is noticeably different than the axis of the Ramesside additions that precede it. The change was made necessary when Rameses II sought physically to join Luxor Temple by causeway to the Temple of Khonsu in Karnak, which had a different axial alignment.

The Colonnade has fourteen columns with open papyrus capitals that supported a roof 21 meters (68 feet) above the ground. The room is narrow, only ten meters (32 feet) wide and 26 meters (85 feet) long. Originally, its walls rose to the full height of the roof, and the only light came from small clerestory windows cut at ceiling level.

It is difficult now to appreciate just how impressive this room must have been, because the walls are preserved only a few meters high. But to have walked into this dark and forbidding colonnade in antiquity, passing from the open and brightly-lit courtyard into a dimly-lit space proportioned like a great European cathedral must have been an awe-inspiring experience. The scenes in the Colonnade are the best sources available for the study of the Opet Festival, one of the most important religious ceremonies in the New Kingdom. They include details of the processions from Karnak to Luxor and return. Their "compositional unity" and carefully-followed sequential ordering indicate that they had been laid out according to a single, comprehensive master plan drawn up before actual work began. This "cartoon" was prepared by artisans of Amenhetep III—men like Hor and Suty, "Overseer of Works of Amen in the Southern Opet"—working with the senior priests responsible for the Opet

126 THE COLONNADE, BUILT BY AMENHETEP III, HAS TWO ROWS OF 7 COLUMNS EACH.

127 LEFT STATUE OF AMENHETEP III WITH HIS WIFE IN THE COLONNADE.

127 RIGHT RELIEF DEPICTING TUTANKHAMEN, FROM THE NORTHWEST WALL OF THE COLONNADE.

Festival. Their design survived Amenhetep III and the Amarna Period, and was acted upon later by artisans of Tutankhamen and Ay. Thus, the scenes represent a decorative scheme that had been laid out before the Amarna Period but only realized two decades later when post-Amarna artists tried to restore earlier traditions. Later, under Seti I, further additions were made to the decoration. These are easy to distinguish from the earlier work by the greater height of the raised relief and the more meticulous modeling of figures.

The Opet scenes can be divided into twelve parts: five scenes on the west wall deal with the procession from Karnak to Luxor and initial ceremonies in Luxor Temple; five others, on the east wall, treat further festivities in Luxor Temple and the return to Karnak. In addition, there are scenes on the northern and southern end walls. In the northwest (right front) corner of the Colonnade, the procession begins with the king, Tutankhamen, greeting the gods at Karnak. He then makes offerings to the barks of the Theban Triad and joins the procession of those boats from their shrines to the Nile. Flags fly from staffs before Karnak's Third Pylon. From Karnak, the barks are towed south against the river's current by men on shore and by rowboats, then carried by priests from the quay and placed in bark shrines in the First Court. On the south end wall, the king greets Amen, Mut, and Amenet in Luxor Temple.

The Colonnade reliefs are difficult to see in diffuse light, and it is best to concentrate on the parts of the walls that are exposed to raking sunlight or, in the evening, on the parts that are floodlit. In such light, wonderful details emerge: one can admire the finely modeled faces and detailed costumes of priests and officials, the minutiae of the nautical rigging and hardware, the agile movements of young acrobats, the gestures of musicians with elaborate drums, lutes, and sistra.

Only the lowest registers on these walls have been preserved, but Egyptologists have identified hundreds of stone blocks from the upper parts of the walls that now lie about the perimeter of Luxor Temple. They are working to reconstruct, on paper at least, the subject-matter of those upper scenes.

◆ THE SUN COURT ◆

South of the Colonnade stands the beautifully-proportioned Sun Court of Amenhetep III. It is a peristyle court measuring 45 meters (146 feet) deep and 51 meters (166 feet) wide with a double row of sixty papyrus-bundle columns on three sides. The walls of the court are poorly preserved, but traces of scenes showing Amenhetep III and Amen, and others with Alexander the Great, can still be seen on the east (left) side.

In recent decades, ceremonies have continued to be performed in this court. They have included a "crossed-oar ceremony" that preceded Nile races between rowing crews from Oxford, Cambridge, Harvard, Yale, Cairo, and Cairo Police. Children from Luxor dressed in pharaonic costume scattered flower petals before the oarsmen. Rock concerts were held here, too, until officials began to worry about the effects of vibrations on the columns.

In 1989, workmen sweeping the unpaved floor of the court exposed a large, filled-in hole found to contain twenty-six statues buried in Roman times by priests anxious to devote more temple space to statues of their emperors than to those of ancient Egyptian kings. The perfectly preserved statues, some of them among the finest examples known of Egyptian sculpture, are now in the Luxor Museum of Art.

◆ HYPOSTYLE HALL - SANCTUARY - OTHER CHAMBERS ◆

Beyond the Sun Court lie the rooms of the original Opet Temple. This area has a complicated plan and contains twenty-three chambers and twenty-seven small chapels. All were built atop a socle, a low stone platform that served as an architectural model of the primeval mound of creation.

The Hypostyle Hall is damaged, but thirty-two papyrus-bundle columns stand inside, some inscribed with the names of their usurpers, Rameses IV and VI. The east (left) wall of the hall is decorated with scenes of the king offering milk, ointments, birds, and fish to Amen and Amenet, and other scenes of the king and his *ka* driving calves and consecrating boxes of cloth. In the southeast (left rear) corner of the Hypostyle Hall stand two small, rectangular chapels for Khonsu (far left) and Mut, and in the southwest (right rear) corner there is a second chapel for Khonsu and a staircase leading to the temple roof.

Along the main temple axis south of the Hypostyle Hall, low steps lead up to a room originally with eight columns, whose bases can be seen in the floor.

128 TOP LEFT AND BOTTOM THE SUN COURT PRESENTS 60 PAPYRUS-BUNDLE COLUMNS.

128 TOP RIGHT THE HYPOSTYLE HALL HAS 32 PAPYRUS-BUNDLE COLUMNS.

129 LUXOR TEMPLE WITH THE SUN COURT (CENTER), THE HYPOSTYLE HALL, AND THE SANCTUARY (FOREGROUND).

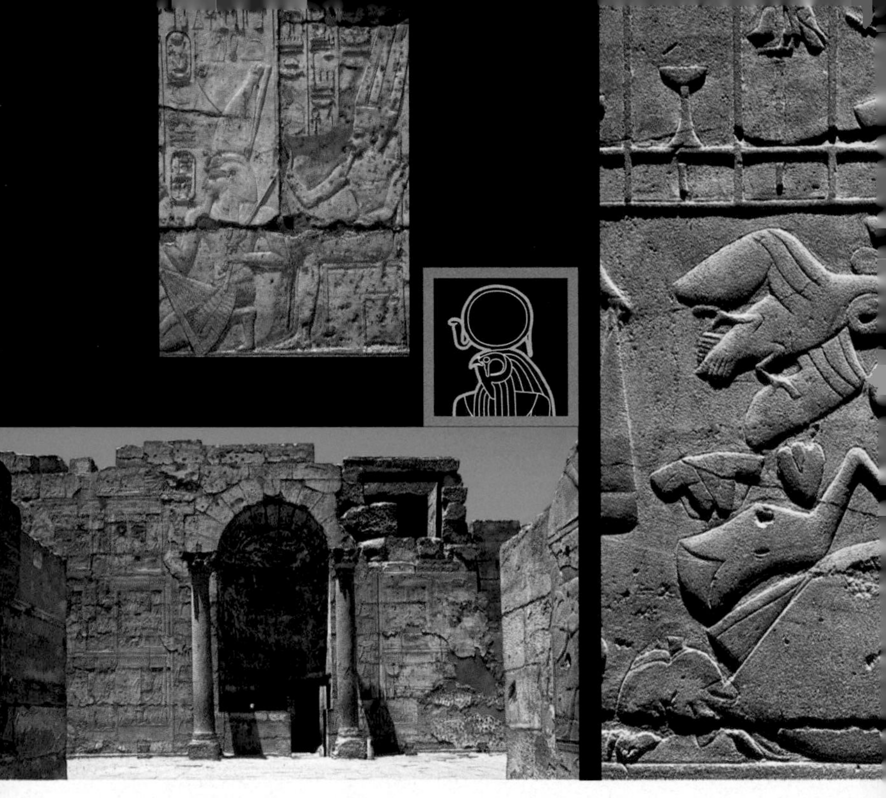

Called the First Antechamber, or, more properly, the "Chamber of the Divine King," it served as a bark shrine but was converted to a chapel for the Roman imperial cult. Scenes of Amenhetep III and Amen were covered over with plaster and painted with scenes of Roman officials. However, Amenhetep III and Amen-Ra can still be seen on the south (rear) wall, where the plaster has fallen away. Also on this wall, an apse with flanking columns was built in what had been a doorway and painted with standing figures of Diocletian and Maximillian and two Caesars. (The doorway through the apse was cut by the Antiquities Department in the 1950s.) The long-held belief that this room served as a Christian church is no longer accepted. Indeed, it is here that Christians were forcibly made to declare their allegiance to the Roman god-emperor.

A four-pillared Second Antechamber, called the "Offering Vestibule," lies beyond the apse, and here the principal temple offerings were made to Amen. On the walls, Amenhetep III drives cattle to the temple to be slaughtered before the god, and the king offers flowers and vases and incense.

The "Bark Shrine of Amen-Ra" lies immediately behind the vestibule, inside what is sometimes called the Third Antechamber. Scenes show Amenhetep III or Alexander the Great standing before figures of the ithyphallic Amen. Originally, four pillars defined the spot where the sacred bark of Amen of Karnak was placed during the Opet Festival, but these were replaced by an inner shrine in the time of Alexander the Great. (Above the doorway into this antechamber a small

room was built into the wall just large enough to accommodate a man. Some scholars believe that a priest concealed himself here during religious ceremonies and acted as the voice of Amen when priests asked questions of the god. Others, less cynical of Egyptian religion, think it was a secret store for ceremonial objects.

To the east (left), a doorway leads into two rooms: the first is called the "Coronation Room," the second the "Birth Room." In the latter, scenes showing the divine birth of Amenhetep III is depicted on the west wall of the chamber and are to be read right to left, bottom to top. At bottom left, the god Khnum fashions Amenhetep III and his ka on a potter's wheel. Small chapels line the eastern walls of these rooms and held either statues of deities or temple furniture.

South of the shrine, a series of four pillared halls, the first and largest of which, with twelve columns, served as the room in which the statue of Amen of Opet resided. The doorway into this suite of rooms is not original. In dynastic times, this was in effect a separate temple-within-a-temple, and its entrance was through the west wall. In each room, scenes show the king offering to Amen—bread, milk, wine, meats, and a score of other foods. This is the temple's "holy of holies," the most sacred part of the temple complex.

130 TOP DETAIL FROM THE CENTRAL WALL OF THE SHRINE OF ALEXANDER THE GREAT.

130 BOTTOM THE THIRD ANTECHAMBER OR SHRINE OF ALEXANDER THE GREAT.

130-131 OFFERING SCENE FROM THE THIRD ANTECHAMBER.

Let us put all this together. The Temple of Luxor was above all meant to serve the Opet Festival; the various architectural and decorative changes it underwent were made as priests sought to perform this service more effectively. Recently, Egyptologists have studied the reliefs and inscriptions in Karnak and Luxor temples and have reconstructed the Opet Festival's procession from the one temple to the other. Here is how they think the ceremony went.

Early in the morning of the first day, the king, high priest, and many others gathered in Karnak's *Akn-Menou* and walked to the sanctuary of the sacred bark of Amen-Ra. Carrying the bark, they proceeded into the Hypostyle Hall, then south along the north-south temple axis through pylons 7 and 8 to Khonsu Temple where Khonsu's bark and representatives of his priesthood joined the group. They then continued on to the Mut Temple where her bark and representatives of her priesthood joined the procession. By now a large group, the procession moved south along the Avenue of the Sphinxes, stopping at the six way-stations en route. At each of these stops, prayers would have been said and offerings made. Along the way, crowds of locals lined the avenue, chanting and cheering, perhaps throwing flowers. Musicians and dancers, acrobats and colorfully attired offering bearers gave a festive air to the procession.

Once through the First Pylon of Luxor Temple, however, the audience would have been more select and the mood more subdued. The first stop was at the Triple Shrine in the First Court of Luxor Temple. After ceremonies here, the priests moved through the Processional

132 TOP PRIESTS BEAR ONE OF THE DIVINE BARKS FOR THE OPET FESTIVAL.

132 BOTTOM SOLDIERS IN THE OPET FESTIVAL PROCESSION.

133 TOP ATTENDANTS BRING PAPYRUS FLOWERS, GEESE, AND BULLS FOR THE OPET FESTIVAL.

133 BOTTOM MUSICIANS, PERCUSSIONISTS, AND HAND-CLAPPERS, IN THE OPET RELIEFS.

Colonnade, whose walls depict this very ceremony, and into the Sun Court, where a large group of invited citizens were permitted to witness parts of the service. The procession then entered the southern "core" of the temple. In the "Chamber of the Divine King," the pharaoh underwent a purification ceremony in which he was crowned and blessed by Amen-Ra. The group then moved into the "Central Bark Sanctuary," for more prayers and sacrifices. Turning left, they entered the "Coronation Room," and the "Birth Room," whose walls are decorated with scenes of the king's divine birth, his coronation, and his Sed-festivals. At the climax of the service, the group moved to the very rear of the temple, the "Sanctuary of the Southern Opet," where final prayers and offerings were made. From here, the procession retraced its steps back through the temple and returned to Karnak by boat along the Nile. The entire festival took about eleven days.

Rather than retracing one's steps, one can exit the temple by one of the doors in the western wall at the back of the building and walk through the remains of the priests' quarters. The outer west wall of the temple is decorated with extensive scenes that recount Rameses II's military compaigns in western Asia, especially the Battle of Qadesh.

LUXOR MUSEUM OF ANCIENT ART

Opened in 1975, this small museum on the Nile Corniche holds one of the finest collections of Egyptian sculpture in the world, in a building whose layout and lighting show the objects to their best advantage. Open in the morning from 9 to 1 o'clock and again in the evening from 4 to 9 (in winter) and 5 to 10 (in summer) it is a perfect place to spend a relaxing and rewarding hour or two. About three hundred objects are on display, many from the Theban nome, illustrating every period from predynastic to medieval Islam. Among my personal favorites are the following objects, listed in order of their current position in the museum.

Luxor catalogue entry 5: This head of the cow goddess Mehit-Weret, a form of Hathor, was found in the tomb of Tutankhamen. Made of wood, copper, lapis lazuli, and gilt, it captures perfectly the grace and dignity of the animal and the divine nature of the goddess who welcomed the dead into the netherworld.

Luxor catalogue entry 34: A red granite head of Senusret III wearing the double crown of Upper and Lower Egypt is a stunning example of the realism that characterized royal sculpture in Dynasty 12. This is a man of regal bearing whose heavy eyelids, wrinkled upper lip are meant to emphasize the thoughtfulness and authority with which the king bore the heavy duties of his office.

Luxor catalogue entry 3: This granite block statue belonged to Yamu-nedkeh, royal herald of Thutmes III. It is easy to see the inspiration for statues of this type: look today in any Upper Egyptian village at men seated on the ground with their jallabiyas pulled tightly over legs drawn up under their chin, hands crossed over their knees. The face is that of a serene and self-confident man.

134 TOP DETAIL ON THE SANDSTONE WALL BUILT BY AKHENATEN, UPPER LEVEL OF THE MUSEUM.

134 BOTTOM GRANITE HEAD OF SENUSRET III.

135 TOP HEAD OF MEHIT-WERET FROM THE TOMB OF TUTANKHAMEN.

135 BOTTOM THE FAÇADE AND A GALLERY OF THE MUSEUM.

Luxor catalogue entry 43: This 2.3 meter (5 feet) tall limestone stela from Karnak's Amen Temple recounts the Dynasty 17 king Kames's raid against the Hyksos. The Hyksos attempted the conquest of Egypt in the Second Intermediate Period. Kames described one of his army's attacks on thet enemy: "As lions are with their prey, so were my army with their servants, their cattle, their milk, fat, and honey." When he returned to Thebes, Kames claimed that "every face was bright, the land was in affluence, the river bank was excited and Thebes was in festival." The small figure shown in the lower left corner is Neshy, whom Kames commanded to carve the stela and to erect it in the temple.

Luxor catalogue entry 140: A limestone relief showing Thutmes III wearing the *atef*-crown. It is a superbly painted and well-preserved example of the magnificent reliefs that once filled the king's memorial temple at Dayr al-Bahari. One hopes that some day the thousands of other pieces of this stunning work, now kept in a storeroom on the site, will be put on display.

Luxor catalogue entry 139: A limestone relief of a god from the memorial temple of Thutmes III at Dayr al-Bahari and another example of the stunning relief from this temple. This piece, showing the god Amen-Min, was defaced in the reign of Akhenaten and then very successfully restored during the reign of Horemheb.

Luxor catalogue entry 2: Arguably one of the finest examples of Egyptian artisans' mastery of difficult material, this superbly modeled greywacke statue shows the king Thutmes III striding forth to magically participate in temple ceremonies at Karnak. This is one of the most important pieces of sculpture in the museum.

Luxor catalogue entry 155: This calcite statue of Amenhetep III and the crocodile god Sobek stands over 2.5 meters (8 feet) tall. This monolithic statue is one of the most awe-inspiring ever found in Egypt: Sobek, wearing the *atef*-crown, sits protectively beside the king, offering him an *ankh*-sign. The statue was usurped by Rameses II, whose names appear in texts on its back.

Luxor catalogue entry 149: A limestone stela of the High Priest, Pia, shows him worshipping Sobek and the goddess Mistress of the Breeze before an *ima*-tree. The stela was commissioned by Pia's son, who is seen in the upper register and who, in the text below, prays that the god will favor him.

136 TOP LEFT AND 137 MAIN GALLERY OF THE LUXOR MUSEUM, FEATURING A CALCITE STATUE OF AMENHETEP III AND SOBEK.

136 BOTTOM LEFT DETAIL OF THE LIMESTONE RELIEF DEPICTING AMEN-MIN.

136 RIGHT SCHIST STATUE OF KING THUTMES III.

On the upper level of the museum, the following pieces deserve special mention:

Luxor catalogue entry 183: An Old Kingdom relief of Unas-ankh taken from his tomb on the West Bank (TT 413) and one of the few examples of Old Kingdom art from the Theban Necropolis. It is worth comparing the proportions of the human figures on this piece with reliefs from the later New Kingdom. Unas-ankh was the Governor of Upper Egypt in Dynasty 6.

Luxor catalogue entries 159–164: These examples of Neolithic pottery (dating to a period called Naqada II) are good examples of predynastic pottery decorated with red-brown paint on a buff background and of the often earlier black-topped red ware.

Luxor catalogue entry 4: A fine example of a scribal statue, this granite piece shows one of the most important officials in the reign of Amenhetep III, the king's Director of Royal Works, Amenhetep son of Hapu, responsible for carving and erecting the Colossi of Memnon. Amenhetep sits, reading a papyrus scroll that is unrolled in his lap. The folds on his abdomen mark him as a successful man of late middle age.

Luxor catalogue entry 223: This sandstone wall comes from a temple at Karnak built by Amenhetep IV/ Akhenaten. It consists of 283 blocks, called *talatat*.

These were found re-used as fill in the Ninth Pylon of the Temple of Amen. The blocks show scenes of temple workmen in storehouses, craft shops, and a brewery. It is worth spending time admiring the details: geese eating grain from a jar, men hungrily gnawing loaves of bread, cattle force fed before slaughter.

The scenes and figures are characteristic of the early Amarna style.

138 GRANITE STATUE OF AMENHETEP, SON OF HAPU.

139 TOP AND BOTTOM LEFT TWO SHABTIES AND ONE BARK FROM THE TREASURE OF THE TOMB OF TUTANKHAMEN.

139 BOTTOM RIGHT SANDSTONE WALL (LEFT) FROM A TEMPLE AT KARNAK OF AKHENATEN (AMENHETEP IV).

In 1989, cleaning in the northwest corner of the great court in Luxor Temple revealed a cache of twenty-six statues, and several are now on display in the lower level of the museum. They are well-preserved. Note the diorite statue of Horemheb kneeling before Atum. Note also the diorite statue of Horemheb standing before a seated figure of Amen.

In 2004, several new galleries were added to the Luxor Museum. The collections emphasize the military history of the New Kingdom. The quality of display and the selection of objects are first-rate.

140 TOP GODDESS HATHOR (LEFT) AND AMEN-RA PROTECTING HOREMHEB (RIGHT).

140 BOTTOM LOWER LEVER ROOM WITH THE STATUES FOUND IN THE CACHE OF THE GREAT COURT IN LUXOR TEMPLE.

141 GODDESS IUNTET (LEFT) AND DETAIL OF THE GROUP WITH HOREMHEB KNEELING IN FRONT OF ATUM (IN THE IMAGE).

MUSEUM OF MUMMIFICATION

This one room museum opened in Luxor in 1998. Its entrance is on the Nile Corniche, a few hundred meters north of Luxor Temple, across the street from the Mina Palace Hotel and down a steep flight of stairs toward the Nile. (Wheelchair access can be found at the north end of the building.) It is open daily from 9 to 1 a.m. and from 4 to 9 p.m. The collection will not teach one about the process of mummification, but it has several interesting objects.

A small vitrine holds possible mummification tools—copper tweezers, needles, and a razor. Another holds dishes of substances used in the mummification process: natron, sawdust, various ointments, resins, and linen bandages. Four canopic jars that belonged to Wahibra Menneferu, a royal son of Dynasty 26, occupy another case, and there are faience *shabti*-statuettes, a boat model, and amulets. Most of the mummies in the museum are of animals: there is a mummified ram, wrapped in gilded cartonnage, and the mummies of a cat, a goose, a Nile fish, a newborn crocodile (a big mature one), an ibis and a baboon. But the most interesting items are from the burial near Dayr al-Bahari of a High Priest of Amen and General of the Army, Masaharti, of Dynasty 21. His mummy is on display, but it is the wooden coffins and coffin lids that held the mummy that are worth a careful look.

2
MEMORIAL TEMPLES

2 INTRODUCTION

144-145 THE WEST BANK LOOKING SOUTHWEST. DAYR AL-BAHARI LIES AT THE END OF THE PAVED ROAD, UPPER RIGHT.

Egyptologists often distinguish two types of ancient Egyptian temples: cult temples and memorial temples. Cult temples are those, such as the Temple of Amen at Karnak, dedicated to the worship of a deity or group of deities. They are sometimes described as the earthly home of a divinity. Memorial temples, less accurately also called mortuary temples, together with the royal tomb, are considered to be a part of a king's funerary complex. But the distinction between cult and memorial temples is less clear-cut than this. Memorial temples, for example, played more than just a role in funerary ceremonies. They do involve kingship and mortuary practices, but they also had a principal role in the Beautiful Festival of the Valley, an annual reaffirmation of the union between living and dead, between kings and gods. They also contained chapels not only for the king but for Amen and the solar cult. Moreover, they played a significant role in the economy of the state.

In New Kingdom Thebes, a temple's location and plan was inspired by its role in religious processions. The religious year at Thebes was an almost constant round of parades from one part of a temple to another or from one temple to others. Statues of kings and gods were carried in shrines on the shoulders of priests along grand sphinx-lined avenues or on boats up and down the Nile. During the Opet Festival, held every year during the Nile inundation, the king and Amen-Ra moved from Karnak to Luxor Temple for ceremonies to reaffirm the divinity of the king. Five months earlier, during the Beautiful Festival of the Valley, statues of king and god were carried from Karnak across the Nile to visit each memorial temple in turn, finally reaching the Dayr al-Bahari cirque, an area that for millennia had been sacred to the goddess Hathor. Canals connected the West Bank temples to each other and to the Nile, and by the late New Kingdom extended from the Sety I temple in the north to that of Rameses III at Madinat Habu in the south.

Unlike the memorial or mortuary temples of earlier times, those built in New Kingdom Thebes were separated from the royal tomb, often by distances of several kilometers. The reason for this was functional. Tombs had to be cut in a secure area, away from destructive ground water. Temples had to be accessible during festival processions that often moved by boat. Thus, kings were buried in the Valley of the Kings several kilometers into the Western Desert, while memorial temples were built along the edge of the cultivation, where canals could be dug.

All Theban temples shared features in common, including a bilaterally symmetrical plan laid out along a single (often east-west) axis, with pylons that defined the monument's

increasingly sacred interior spaces. As one walks into a temple, one moves from open-air courtyards to chambers of increasing darkness, from large spaces to smaller ones, from rooms with high ceilings to rooms with low ceilings and raised floors. Such architecture was meant to emphasize the increasing sacredness as one moved toward the shrine where the statue of the god was housed.

Most memorial temples were built of sandstone. Their surrounding buildings were of mudbrick and included priests' quarters, administrative offices, a small royal palace, outbuildings, and huge granaries and storerooms. The latter were used to store the great amounts of produce collected by the temple priesthood as rents and taxes. The storerooms in the memorial temple of Rameses II, the Ramesseum, for example, could hold over sixteen million liters of grain, enough to feed twenty thousand people for an entire year. Assuming that the temple levied a rent calculated at 30% of a field's yield, priests in the Ramesseum alone would have had the right to tax over 400 square kilometers (150 square miles) of fields to collect such an amount. In addition, the temple received a portion of other crops, as well as cattle, sheep, goats, fish, beer, wine, oils, quarried stones, ores, minerals, cloth, wood, tribute and booty from foreign lands. Clearly, such temples played major roles in the redistributive economy of Egypt. Like other ancient Egyptian monuments, the plans of temples changed over time depending on current theological views, available raw materials, and the state of the economy.

Over thirty temples were built on the West Bank at Thebes, but today most are little more than jagged stones jutting through alabaster factory parking lots and rubbish heaps. One day these monuments, too, will be cleaned and protected. Many still contain decorated blocks whose texts could make important contributions to the history of ancient Thebes. In the meantime, seven West Bank temple complexes are open to tourists. Each is well worth a visit. Queen Hatshepsut's temple at Dayr al-Bahari is the earliest of the temples

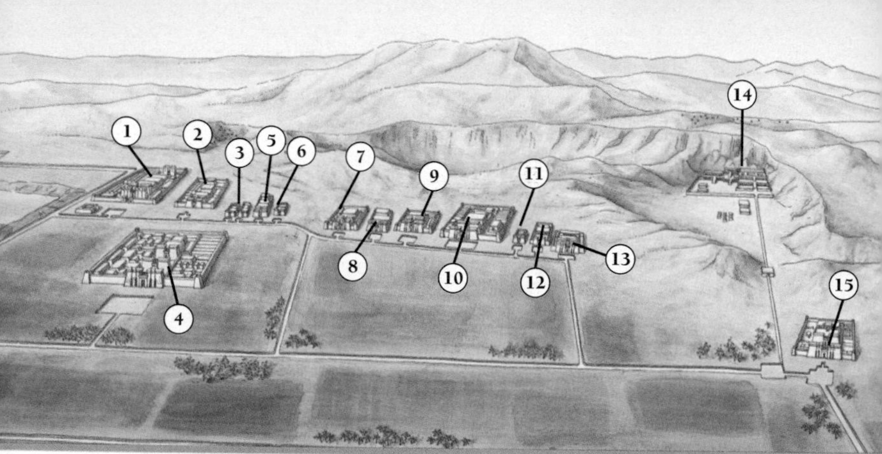

now open and certainly one of the most beautiful. It is seen to best advantage from the low wall lying a few hundred meters to its east near the parking lot; from here its relationship to the surrounding cliffs is most apparent. The elegant carvings on its walls, unfortunately, are very difficult to see because no raking light is available to bring out the relief.

The temple of Amenhetep III and the Colossi of Memnon are a brief stop on everyone's tour of Thebes. Excavations currently underway at the western end of the temple complex are bringing many new features to light. If time permits, a walk along the adjacent roadway to see the newly-exposed statues and column bases is worthwhile.

The Ramesseum, memorial temple of Rameses II, is justly famous for the fallen statue that inspired Shelley's poem "Ozymandias." Battle reliefs on the second pylon and scenes of the king's many sons in the temple interior are worth study, and it is interesting to wander through the many mudbrick outbuildings, some of them only recently cleared, that served as storerooms and offices of the priests.

Behind the Amenhetep III temple sits the newly-opened temple of Merenptah. Parts have been reconstructed as an open air museum, and significant pieces of statuary are on display in three small storerooms on the site. The sculpture is fascinating and well worth a visit.

Madinat Habu boasts the best-preserved West Bank temples, including the huge

LEGEND

1 *TEMPLE OF RAMESES III AT MADINET HABU*
2 *TEMPLE OF AY-HOREMHEB*
3 *TEMPLE OF THUTMES II*
4 *TEMPLE OF AMENHETEP III AND COLOSSI OF MEMNON*
5 *TEMPLE OF AMENHETEP SON OF HAPU*
6 *TEMPLE OF THUTMES II*
7 *TEMPLE OF MERENPTAH*
8 *TEMPLE OF TAUSERT*
9 *TEMPLE OF THUTMES IV*
10 *RAMESSEUM, TEMPLE OF RAMESES II*
11 *TEMPLE OF AMENHETEP II*
12 *TEMPLE OF SIPTAH*
13 *TEMPLE OF THUTMES III*
14 *TEMPLES OF MENTUHOTEP, THUTMES III, HATSHEPSUT AT DAYR AL-BAHARI*
15 *TEMPLE OF SETY I*

memorial temple of Rameses III. Its beautifully carved and painted walls, especially in the northwest corners of the first three courtyards, are astonishingly well-preserved.

The royal palace and the surrounding village also deserve a visit.

At Dayr al-Madina, a small but well-preserved Ptolemaic cult temple at the north end of the village provides a good example of the art and architecture of that later period. The temple of Sety I, at the northern end of the necropolis, inspired the design of the temples of Rameses II and Rameses III. Recent excavations within its enclosure walls have uncovered several interesting architectural features. Unfortunately, some of them were badly damaged during a torrential 1994 rainstorm and flood.

146-147 FROM LEFT, THE MEMORIAL TEMPLES OF MERENPTAH, RAMESES II AND HATSHEPSUT.

2

THE DAYR AL-BAHARI CIRQUE

THE TEMPLE OF QUEEN HATSHEPSUT

THE HISTORY

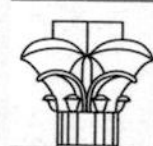

One of the most memorable panoramas in Thebes is the approach to the memorial temple of Queen Hatshepsut. Turning west beside a small mosque, a paved road leads in a straight line to a dramatic expanse of rugged limestone cliffs that rises over three hundred meters (nearly one thousand feet) above the desert plain. Water-worn for millions of years and buffeted for millennia by hot winds, the cliffs have eroded into an intricate pattern of cracks and crevices and deep vertical fissures. The fractures are in deep shade, the bedrock blinding in the intense sunlight. They create a façade that captures the eye and holds it. Only slowly does one realize that at the base of the cliff stands a low, wide monument of even more breathtaking beauty. This broad, perfectly proportioned building rises in low terraces to meet the jagged cliffs. Rhythmic patterns of light and shade give its façade military rigor and geometric formality, a stark contrast to the rugged mountain behind. But together, the mountain and the temple form a perfect marriage: each enhances the other.

True, the modern paved road is ugly, certainly less attractive than the original stone causeway along which priests carried statues of gods and kings. One would also wish away the huge asphalt parking lot filled with tour buses and gaudy kiosks thoughtlessly built before it. Nevertheless, even these cannot diminish the overwhelming beauty of this masterpiece. Traffic and curio sellers notwithstanding, one sees this temple and stands in awe. European visitors first saw Queen Hatshepsut's memorial temple in a very ruined state at the end of the eighteenth century. Originally buried beneath tons of debris, it has undergone almost continuous excavation and restoration since the end of the nineteenth century. But it was not until the 1920s that enough clearing had been done that visitors could appreciate the temple's beauty. When Howard Carter (who later went on to discover the tomb of Tutankhamen) published the first paintings of its decoration at the end of the nineteenth century, Europeans were stunned. Before then, the temple had rated only a few lines in most guidebooks; since then, it has become one of the most-visited and most-admired monuments in Egypt.

148 OSIRID STATUES FROM THE TEMPLE OF HATSHEPSUT.

149 TOP HEAD OF HATSHEPSUT, NOW IN THE CAIRO MUSEUM.

149 BOTTOM VIEW OF THE DAYR AL-BAHARI COMPLEX.

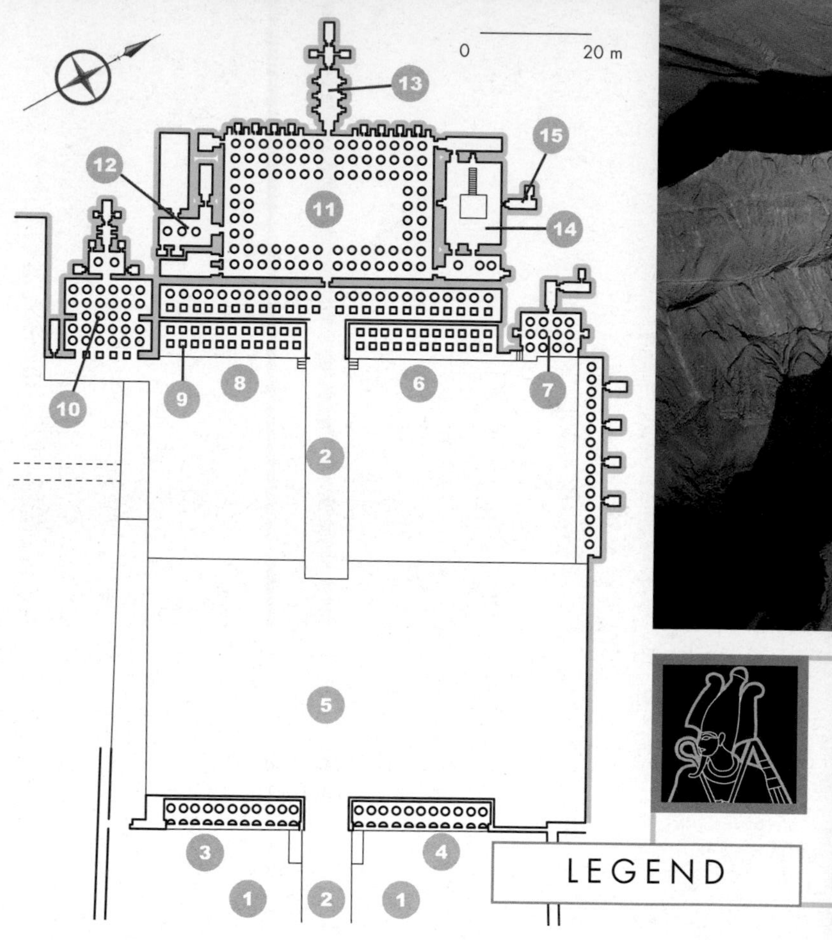

The design of the temple may seem dramatically different from other New Kingdom temples. However, it was meant to function as a memorial temple and therefore shares all such temples' components and plan: its gates, pillars, columns, Osirid statues, sphinxes, gardens, rising central axis, and tripartite plan are standard features. What makes Hatshepsut's temple unique is the way these features fit together to take advantage of their natural setting.

The temple's design was obviously influenced by the Dynasty 11 temple of Nebhepetra-Mentuhetep a few meters to the south. It too used ramps, colonnades, and terraces. But Hatshepsut's temple was not a copy of her predecessor's structure, in spite of comments to that effect by detractors. To the contrary, one Egyptologist referred to the earlier temple as a "lost opportunity" and described Hatshepsut's as "the only possible solution to the problem presented by a most attractive, but also most difficult, site."

Hatshepsut's architect, Senenmut, may have found inspiration in the earlier Mentuhetep monument—the idea of using a series of terraces is an obvious borrowing—but he went far beyond it, creating a work of art by "divining that only long horizontal lines could live in the presence of the overwhelming vertical lines of the background."

The building site was certainly chosen in part because of the formidable cliffs behind it. But there were other reasons, too. The god Amen was given

151 THE DAYR AL-BAHARI CIRQUE AND THE VALLEY OF THE KINGS BEHIND.

1 *FIRST COURT*
2 *RAMP*
3 *LOWER COLONNADE SOUTH*
4 *LOWER COLONNADE NORTH*
5 *SECOND COURTYARD*
6 *MIDDLE COLONNADE NORTH*
7 *THE ANUBIS SHRINE*
8 *MIDDLE COLONNADE SOUTH*
9 *PUNT RELIEFS*
10 *HATHOR SHRINE*
11 *UPPER TERRACE*
12 *CHAPELS FOR ROYAL WORSHIP*
13 *CHAPEL OF AMEN AND ROYAL FAMILY*
14 *COURTYARD OF RA-HARAKHTY*
15 *UPPER CHAPEL OF ANUBIS*

special prominence in the temple and that is why it was built almost exactly in the same axial line as the Temple of Amen at Karnak. Indeed, if you extend the principal axis of Hatshepsut's temple five kilometers (three miles) east to Karnak, it runs within one hundred meters (three hundred feet) of the axis of the Temple of Amen-Ra.There had been a shrine to Hathor at Dayr al-Bahari for centuries before Hatshepsut ordered that her own temple be built there. A shrine to Hathor stood in the Nebhepetra-Mentuhetep Temple immediately south, and Hatshepsut built her own Hathor shrine as close to it as possible. Amenhetep I erected a substantial temple with a shrine to Hathor on what later became the Hatshepsut Temple's middle terrace. Indeed, so important was this area to the cult of Hathor and its associated Beautiful Festival of the Valley—an annual festival formerly of minor importance but given great emphasis by Hatshepsut—that Hatshepsut deliberately sited her temple here so that it would become the principal West Bank destination of the festival's processions. It is also no coincidence that KV 20, the tomb attributed to Hatshepsut, was dug in the Valley of the Kings behind the temple. If her tomb had been dug along a straight axis, as some believe was the original idea, its burial chamber could have lain directly beneath the temple. But poor quality bedrock forced workmen to follow a corkscrew-like course in a vain search for better stone, and the burial chamber was finally located deeper and to the southwest.

The ancient Egyptians called the temple *Djeser-djeseru,* "Most Holy of Holies." Originally, a causeway connected it to a canal dug along the edge of the cultivation. The valley temple there was never completed, but the causeway leading from it was, and it measured 13 meters (40 feet) wide, 400 meters (1,200 feet) long. It was lined with statues and sphinxes that probably stood as close together as those leading to Luxor Temple. They were not inconsequential sculptures: the red granite sphinxes were over 3 meters (nearly 10 feet) long and each weighed seven and a half tons. Indeed, Hatshepsut's program of statuary set a record for quantity and size not equaled until the reign of Amenhetep III. Statues of Hatshepsut in the pose of Osiris, for example, were erected at either end of the upper and lower terraces, before each of the upper terrace's twenty-four pillars, in each of ten niches in the upper hall, and in the four corners of the upper sanctuary. A Coptic monastery, Dayr Apa Phoibamon, was built in the northwest part of the temple's upper terrace and flourished in the seventh and eighth centuries AD. It was one of the largest monasteries in Upper Egypt and survived remarkably well for over a millennium until it was dismantled by Egyptologists early in the twentieth century. The monastery is the reason that *Djeser-djerseru* came to be called Dayr al-Bahari, meaning "The Northern Monastery" in Arabic. Its construction did substantial damage to the upper terrace, and archaeologists have worked for over a century to restore it, a task that is still not completed.

Once you have run the

152-153 OSIRID STATUES FROM THE MIDDLE COLONNADE.

153 THE ARCHITECT SENENMUT HOLDING HATSHPESUT'S DAUGHTER, NEFERURA, NOW IN THE CAIRO MUSEUM.

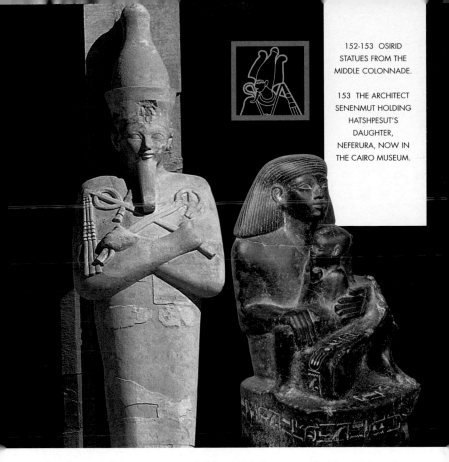

gauntlet of curio sellers and taxi drivers and passed through the security gate, walk slowly and take time to savor the splendor of the Dayr al-Bahari cirque and the temple's place within it. Way stations used in the many processions that came here every year stood along the avenue. North and south of the axis lay gardens, orchards, and ponds. Small planting holes can still be seen in parts of the temple compound and the original ancient tree roots are still visible. Near the bottom of the first ramp, two small T-shaped ponds surrounded by such holes have been outlined by their excavators. They once contained tamarisk, sycomore fig, and persea trees, as well as rare species brought back from the African land of Punt.

VISIT

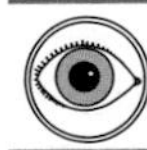

Before ascending the first ramp to the middle terrace, spend some time in the two colonnades on either side. That on the left especially has some interesting and important reliefs. But be forewarned: recently the Supreme Council of Antiquities installed iron rails at the front of each colonnade to keep tourists several meters from the walls. It is now extremely difficult to see the decoration. Patience, imagination, and a keen eye are needed. The temple is best viewed early in the morning when the sun is low in the sky. Later in the day, the reliefs are all but invisible. Another reason to avoid an afternoon visit is that Dayr al-Bahari holds the record as one of the hottest places on our planet (a temperature of 55 degrees Celsius was recorded recently).

◆ LOWER COLONNADE SOUTH: TRANSPORTING OBELISKS ◆

These fascinating reliefs (to the left of the ramp), unfortunately in poor condition, tell how Hatshepsut's architects and engineers brought two huge obelisks from quarries in Aswan to Thebes. The cutting, transport, and installation of these huge monoliths were major projects: each weighed 186 tons.

The obelisks are shown at the left (south) end of the wall, drawn as if they were placed end-to-end on a huge ship. However, marine historians believe that they actually were placed side-by-side and consider the drawing an artistic device to emphasize the vast size of the load. If correct, then the ship carrying them would have been 95 meters (309 feet) long with a beam of 32 meters (104 feet), a draft of 3 meters, and a deck that stood 9.5 meters (31 feet) above the water line. The boat was built of wood from sycomore fig trees, a wood impervious to water but difficult to work, hard to find in large pieces, and very heavy. Naval historians calculate that the ship weighed 2500 tons and had a displacement of 7300 tons. This huge vessel was towed downstream from Aswan to Thebes by thirty smaller ships, each manned by thirty-two oarsmen.

What a job! To cut these gigantic granite blocks out of the bedrock of the Aswan quarries, drag them across a rugged landscape of boulders to a canal extending eastward to the Nile, and then maneuver them onto a huge ship required not only brute strength but also meticulous planning. One slip and the stones would have cracked and years of work ruined. Just ensuring that the load was properly balanced, not listing even slightly to port or starboard, must have been a nightmarish undertaking.

Scheduling was critical, too. Loading had to take place in winter when the Nile was at its lowest. Then one had to wait for the summer flood to free the boat from the shore. After sailing 220 kilometers (132 miles) downstream, the ship would moor in a canal near Karnak at high Nile and then wait months for

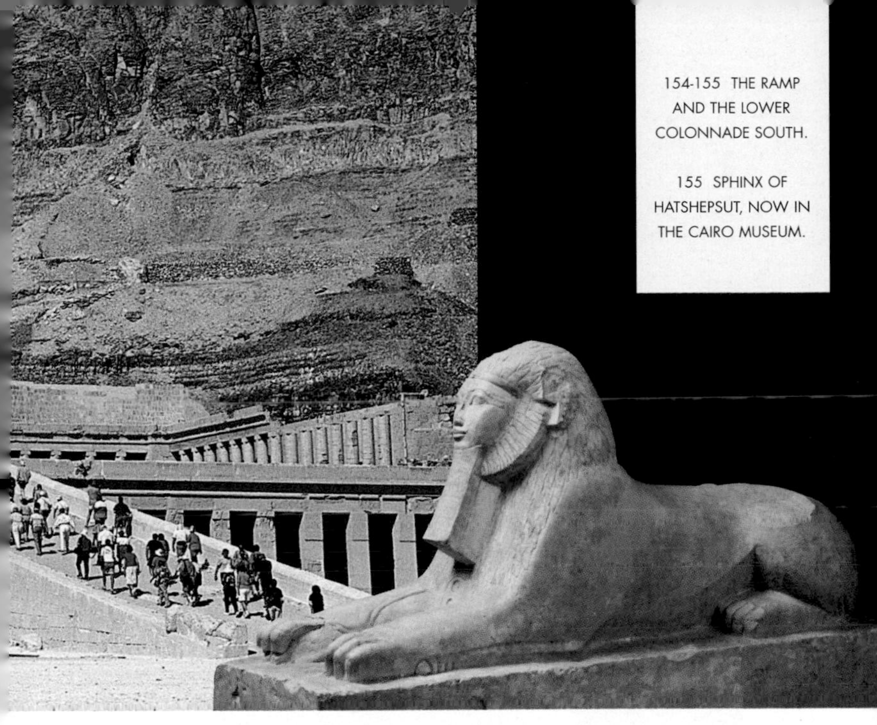

154-155 THE RAMP AND THE LOWER COLONNADE SOUTH.

155 SPHINX OF HATSHEPSUT, NOW IN THE CAIRO MUSEUM.

another low Nile before unloading. Once ashore, the obelisks were dragged across the floodplain into the Temple of Amen. A gigantic ramp was built, the monoliths dragged up it and carefully lowered into a sand-filled hole at the top. The sand was slowly removed until the obelisks gently settled onto stone pedestals. This was done with such precision that the obelisks were almost precisely vertical, within one or two millimeters parallel to the sides of the base.

Infantry, archers, and priests are shown lining the shore as the obelisks sailed past. At Karnak Temple, dancers and musicians playing horns and drums heralded the obelisks' arrival. This was indeed a project worth boasting about, and Hatshepsut and her officials were obviously proud of the accomplishment. The accompanying text describes many of the obstacles her engineers overcame and tells us that it was only Hatshepsut's great love of her divine father, the god Amen, that made this effort possible. (See also the description of the obelisks in the Temple of Amen at Karnak.)

◆ LOWER COLONNADE - NORTH: FOWLING ◆

This wall is badly damaged but there is such a wonderful scene of bird netting at the right (north) end that a brief visit should be made. A mythological scene shows gods in the Nile Delta pulling a net filled with scores of birds. Ducks are shown in great number, but there are other species as well. Note particularly the superbly drawn grey heron *(Ardea cinera)* with a fish in its beak standing at the right. It is arguably one of the most realistic ornithological drawings in Egyptian art. There is also a well-preserved representation of Hatshepsut as a sphinx trampling the enemies of Egypt.

The ramp leading to the middle terrace has balustrades ending at the bottom with lion-heads. These are symbols of the horizon and are meant to protect the higher levels of the temple from this world's chaos and confusion. Although they are clearly leonine, their human face resembles the face one sees in the statuary of Queen Hatshepsut.

◆MIDDLE COLONNADE - NORTH: THE QUEEN'S BIRTH◆

Behind two rows of eleven pillars, scenes show the divine birth of Queen Hatshepsut. The reliefs are difficult to see, for they were deliberately defaced after Hatshepsut's death. Moreover, the original relief carving was shallow and the absence of strong raking light in the colonnade renders them nearly invisible; recently installed barriers prevent close examination. But they are of great importance, for they were meant to offer theological proof that Hatshepsut was entitled to ascend the throne as king. They proclaim that Amen-Ra was her divine father and Thutmes I her secular one. Such scenes were later elaborated upon in reliefs carved for Amenhetep III in the southern chambers of Luxor Temple, but the ones here are the first known examples.

Hatshepsut's mother, Queen Ahmes, appears in two scenes. In one she sits on a couch and is offered an *ankh* sign, the hieroglyph for "life," by Amen-Ra. This is a tactful way of saying that she was being impregnated by the god. The accompanying text poetically describes what happened:

"Then came the glorious god Amen himself, lord of the thrones of both lands,

When he had taken the form of her husband,

They found her resting in the beauty of the palace.

She awoke at the perfume of the god and laughed in the face of his majesty.

Enflamed with love, he hastened toward her,

He had lost his heart to her. She could behold him in the shape of a god,

When he had come near to her, she exulted at the sight of his beauty.

His love entered all her limbs, the palace was filled with the sweet perfumes of the god, all of them from the land of incense, Punt.

The majesty of this god did to her all that he wished. She gladdened him with herself and kissed him."

In another scene, Ahmes appears before the frog-headed goddess Heket and the ram-headed god Khnum, both associated with childbirth. She is clearly pregnant and they lead

her to the birthing chamber where, in the presence of many divine witnesses, she gives birth to Hatshepsut. Amen-Ra stands nearby and affirms that he is Hatshepsut's father. In a stunningly immodest text, Hatshepsut's personality and youthful growth are described: "Her majesty became more important than anything else. What was within her was godlike; her manner was godlike; godlike was everything she did; her spirit was godlike.

Her majesty became a beautiful maiden...She is a woman of distinguished appearance."

The queen's coronation is shown at the top of the wall, where she stands in the presence of her father Thutmes I and the gods Amen and Ra-Harakhty in ceremonies of purification.

◆MIDDLE COLONNADE - NORTH: THE ANUBIS SHRINE ◆

A small vestibule to the right (north) of the birth scenes contains some of the best-preserved painted reliefs to be found at Thebes. Figures of Hatshepsut have been defaced, but figures of Thutmes III, the god Anubis, and especially the piles of food offerings before him are as bright and fresh as the day they were first painted. On the left (south) wall of the vestibule, Queen Hatshepsut appears in a small recess with deities. To the left, the queen is with Anubis, to the right, with Nekhbet and Ra-Harakhty. The names of the queen are written between them. Above the doorway, the queen offers water to Osiris. On the right (north) wall there is another recess with Thutmes III offering wine to Sokar above it, and on the right, the queen and Anubis before a dog's head that represents the god of the dead. Behind the vestibule, three small chambers, currently closed to the public, contain well-preserved scenes of the queen and various deities, especially Anubis.

The right (north) wall of the middle colonnade, lined with fifteen sixteen-sided columns, was originally intended to have four statue niches dedicated to various deities, but work on this part of the temple was never completed and the undecorated niches were covered over in modern times.

156 TOP THE MIDDLE COLONNADE NORTH IN FOREGROUND.

156 BOTTOM PAINTED RELIEF FROM THE QUEEN'S BIRTH SCENE.

157 LEFT THUTMES III MAKES OFFERINGS IN THE SHRINE OF ANUBIS.

157 RIGHT PAINTED RELIEF OF FOOD OFFERINGS FROM THE ANUBIS SHRINE.

◆ MIDDLE COLONNADE - SOUTH: THE PUNT RELIEFS ◆

The Egyptians are rightly admired for producing some of the ancient world's most accurate and sensitive drawings of plants and animals. From the Old Kingdom onward, scenes of papyrus thickets, animal husbandry, bird netting, fishing, and hunting—virtually every aspect of the natural world—captured details that only long and careful observation could have made possible. Egyptians were endlessly fascinated by nature, and Egyptian artisans were intent on depicting it accurately.

In the New Kingdom, two walls show this particularly well and, curiously, both depict scenes of foreign lands. The more recent is the "Botanical Garden" of Thutmes III, in the *Akh-Menou,* the king's festival hall in the Temple of Amen at Karnak. The earlier, by about twenty-five years, is Queen Hatshepsut's maritime expedition to the land of Punt, depicted here.

The great American Egyptologist James Henry Breasted called the Punt reliefs "undoubtedly the most interesting series of reliefs in Egypt." That is hardly an exaggeration. The scenes form an ancient ethnographic, biological, and geographical record showing how the Egyptians tried to make sense of this strange country and fit it into their view of the world. They depicted what in Punt struck them as odd, humorous, or especially characteristic. Egyptian art frequently included representations of foreign people or foreign animals, but nowhere else do whole scenes give such attention to foreign architecture, foreign activities, and foreign landscapes. The Punt reliefs do that, precisely and uniquely. Apparently, the Egyptians were so impressed by the unusual plants and animals they found that they made detailed records on the spot and used their notes when they undertook the temple decoration. This may reflect a realization that their world had grown, and that Egypt's gods had extended their authority and become gods whose powers extended far beyond the Nile Valley.

Hatshepsut's expedition to Punt set out in the eighth year of her reign. Hers was not the first reference to Punt—one mention may date as early as Dynasty 4—nor was it the last. But Hatshepsut's is the most complete, and certainly one of the most charming.

Egyptologists think that Punt was located in the Horn of Africa, in modern Somalia or Eritrea. This is based on three observations: Punt was accessible to overland expeditions from Egypt, because earlier Egyptian texts make reference to such journeys; it was also accessible by sea, as the Punt reliefs attest; and its flora, fauna, and architecture, as shown in the Punt reliefs, are consistent with what one would find on the Red Sea coast of Africa, not in the Mediterranean, Western Asia, Arabia, or Europe.

For example, the aquatic scene across the bottom of

158 LEFT TWO PUNTITE MEN WITH A DONKEY, RELIEF NOW IN CAIRO MUSEUM.

158 RIGHT PUNT CHIEFTAIN PEREHU AND HIS WIFE ITY, KNOWN AS QUEEN OF PUNT.

159 THE MIDDLE COLONNADE WITH THE PUNT RELIEFS.

the wall indicates that Punt must be in East Africa. There are turtles, parrot-fish, scorpion-fish, soldier-fish, trigger-fish, wrasse, squid, and spiny lobster among the saltwater species, and tilapia, catfish, and turtles among the freshwater species. All the saltwater species are common to the Red Sea and the Indian Ocean, while the freshwater species are known in East Africa but not in the Arabian Peninsula. (A recent suggestion that Punt lay east of the Gulf of Aqaba is not widely accepted.)

The Punt reliefs can be divided into several sections, each illustrating a different stage of the expedition. The lower registers on the left (south) end wall show the landscape of Punt and the reception of the Egyptians by local officials.

The houses of Punt are beehive-shaped grass huts, mounted on stilts to protect them from damaging floods, wild animals or insects, or perhaps to keep them cool in summer. A ladder gives access to the living platform. Several such houses are scattered throughout a grove of dom- and date-palms. Long- and short-horned cattle graze nearby. Birds flutter in the trees; a dog sits before its master's hut. More exotic animals can also be seen: a giraffe, a panther, primates, and what may be a rhinoceros. The Egyptian army has pitched tents "in the myrrh-terraces of Punt on the side of the sea," and the king's messenger is presenting jewelry, beads, daggers, and metal axes in exchange for the raw materials of Punt that they will load onto their ships. Egyptian traders had visited Punt before. We know this from several different sources. Yet the Puntite officials express surprise at seeing them. Above the scene they ask, "Why have you come here into this land, which the people [of Egypt] know not? Did you come down upon the ways of heaven, or did you sail upon the waters, upon the sea of God's-Land?" No answer is recorded. Among the Puntite officials their chief, Perehu, stands with his morbidly obese wife, Ity, known to Egyptologists as the Queen of Punt. Originally, they were also accompanied by two sons and a daughter as obese as her mother, but these figures have been destroyed. Singled out for special mention, and perhaps intended as a wry comment on the size of queen, is "the donkey which carried his wife." A plaster cast has replaced the original carving of the Queen of Punt, which is now on display in the Egyptian Museum, Cairo. Medical historians have written numerous articles about the cause of the queen's obesity, but none of the diagnoses they have proposed (most commonly elephantiasis or steatopygy) is widely accepted. In contrast to the women, Puntite men seem almost Egyptian in their physique, facial features, and costume. Even their skin is the red color of Egyptian males, not the black of Nubians.

In the upper registers, Egyptian sailors load their ships with incense and other raw materials. The cargo includes "all goodly fragrant woods of God's-Land, heaps of myrrh resin, with fresh myrrh trees, with ebony and pure ivory...with cinnamon wood, *khesyt*-wood, with *ihmut*-incense, *sonter*-incense, eye cosmetic, with apes, monkeys, dogs, and with skins of the southern panther, with natives and their children. Never was brought the like of this for any king since the beginning." The men strain as they lift the heavy bundles into the holds. Men carry carefully bundled myrrh trees and one of them cries, "Watch your feet! Behold! The load is very heavy!" A couple of men remark that the trees are to be planted at Dayr al-Bahari, and their mates seem excited at the prospect of bringing such delights back to the Theban court. Around the corner, at the left (south) end of the rear (west) wall, the Egyptian fleet is shown in the lower registers arriving in Punt and, at right, returning to Egypt. Once the ships have returned to Thebes their cargo is weighed and measured by Horus and a Nubian god, Dedun. "Thoth records them in writing, Sefkhet counts the numbers. Her majesty herself is acting with her two hands, the best of myrrh is upon all her limbs, her fragrance is divine dew, her odor is mingled with Punt, her skin is gilded with electrum, shining as to the stars in the midst of the festival hall, before the whole land." Further right, Hatshepsut announces the success of the voyage and offers its cargo to Amen. The incense-trees are shown already thriving in the gardens of Amen's temple at Karnak.There were five ships in Hatshepsut's fleet (five are shown arriving, five departing). The drawings of the ships are detailed and have been carefully studied by marine historians, who consider them among the best nautical representations from the New Kingdom. They calculate that the boats were about 25 meters (81 feet) long and narrow, perhaps with only a 7-meter (23-foot) beam and a 2-meter (6-foot) draft, designed to cut quickly through the dangerous waters of the Red Sea. Prevailing winds on the Red Sea generally blow from north to south from June through September and from south to north from November through March. The rest of the year, they are unpredictable. The sailors would have had to row into the wind for a fair part of the journey. The alternative, tacking, could have added another 800 kilometers (480 miles) to the already 1500 kilometer (900 mile) long journey. Assuming that the boats sailed eight or nine hours a day, stopping in inlets and coves along the way, and assuming that they could sail or be rowed at about 5 kilometers (3 miles) an hour, the one-way trip would have taken between forty and

fifty days. Perhaps they spent three or four months in Punt negotiating, assembling, and loading their cargo. There may also have been marching time ashore, for we know from other documents that it rained in Punt, and that suggests that the country may have lay in the interior. Unless the Puntites had prepared in advance for the Egyptians' arrival and assembled their goods at one seaside location, the Egyptians may have had to hike into the highlands to collect the raw materials they wanted. How long, then, did the trip take? Consider this: the boats were probably constructed at Coptos (modern Qift) at the mouth of the Wadi Hammamat 50 kilometers (30 miles) north of Thebes. They were taken apart and they and their cargo carried overland in donkey caravans 200 kilometers (120 miles) through the Eastern Desert and the Red Sea hills to the port of Qusayr. There they were reassembled. That arduous, hot and dusty journey through rugged desert terrain probably took two months. Sailing south to Punt took another six to eight weeks. Allow at least three months in Punt, then three months to sail back to Qusayr. From there, the crew traveled overland to the Nile, then on to Thebes. This would have taken another two months. The total elapsed time would have been nearly a year.

The logistics of such an expedition were complex. Each of the five ships had places for thirty oarsmen and there would have been a back-up crew plus laborers, officials, scribes, and translators—say 250–300 men in all. They would have had to leave Qusayr with enough provisions and fresh water for the journey. On the return, they would have to carry an equal supply of food and water plus the cargo from Punt. Little wonder that Hatshepsut devoted an entire wall of her temple to its story.

160 DETAILS OF THE PUNT RELIEFS SHOWING AN EGYPTIAN BOAT.

161 TOP SCENE OF SAILORS LOADING THEIR SHIP WITH GOODS FROM PUNT.

161 BOTTOM MEN CARRYING LIVING TREES TO THEIR SHIP.

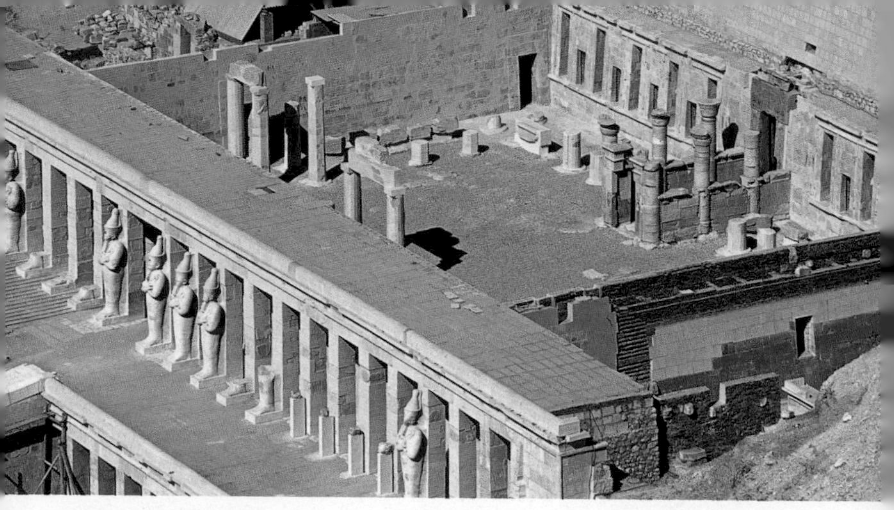

◆ MIDDLE TERRACE - SOUTH: THE HATHOR SHRINE ◆

To the left (south) of the Punt colonnade stands a shrine dedicated to Hathor, perhaps the most important goddess worshipped in the Dayr al-Bahari area. Her pride of place among goddesses at Thebes was underscored by the fact her shrine could be accessed by means of its own ramp from the lower terrace. The shrine has two halls, now badly destroyed, the first with eight pillars and eight sixteen-sided columns, the second with sixteen sixteen-sided columns. Each has a Hathor-headed capital showing the goddess with a human head and bovine ears and a sistrum on her head. Two engaging reliefs on the rear (west) wall show figures of Hathor as a cow licking the royal hand. The text reads: "To kiss the hand, to lick the divine flesh; to endow the king with life and purity." Adjacent to this, another figure of Hatshepsut holds an oar and a carpenter's square. Hatshepsut kneels and drinks from the udder of a Hathor-cow, as the goddess boasts, "I have suckled your Majesty with my breasts. I have filled you with my intelligence, with my water of life and happiness. I am your mother, who formed your limbs and created your beauties." On the right (north) wall there is a particularly well carved and painted figure of Hathor as a cow with horns and a sun disk on her head, and a major naval procession and military parade.

Beyond the pillared halls, a three-room chapel was cut into the mountainside. It is currently closed to the public. But peer through the doorway to see the brightly-painted and well-preserved scenes of Hatshepsut and Thutmes III before various deities. Not visible, unfortunately, is a small figure of the queen's architect Senenmut, who some believe was her lover, carved behind the door.

◆ UPPER TERRACE ◆

After a quarter-century of restoration work by a joint Polish-Egyptian mission, the upper terrace has recently been re-opened to the public. Architecturally, it is the most spectacular part of Queen Hatshepsut's temple; its smooth and well-carved columns and walls stand in sharp contrast to the rugged cliffs that loom so dramatically behind it. Twenty-four colossal Osirid statues front the pillars on either side of a huge granite doorway at the top of the ramp. The statues were originally painted and would have been visible from a distance. Their long beards would have been blue, their throats and faces red, with black and white eyes and blue eyebrows. The various items that they wore or held were red, blue, and yellow. Behind, on the right wall, are scenes of the queen's coronation in which she is

162 AERIAL VIEW OF THE UPPER TERRACE.

163 LEFT RELIEF FROM THE HATHOR SHRINE.

163 RIGHT HATHOR COLUMN FROM THE HATHOR SHRINE.

escorted by the gods, the crowns of Upper and Lower Egypt placed on her head. The central door, with huge and elaborate door boltholes and hinge sockets, leads into a great columned hall. Two rows (three in the front) of seventy-two thirteen-sided columns surround it. Kneeling statues of Hatshepsut once lined the axis of the courtyard. Its walls are decorated with festival scenes. On the north side of the front (east) wall and the entire right (north) wall, the scenes are of the Beautiful Feast of the Valley. Hatshepsut, Thutmes II, and Thutmes III are shown in a great procession from Karnak across the Nile into this very sanctuary. The Opet Festival is shown in the other half of the court and again, the procession of boats on the Nile is elaborate and impressive.

On the right (north) side of the court a series of rooms (now closed) are devoted to the solar cult of Ra-Harakhty and to Anubis. On the left (south) side a complex of rooms (also closed) was used for the royal cult of Hatshepsut and Thutmes I. In the rear (west) wall of the court a series of niches, eight large ones, ten small, once held statues of the queen in the pose of Osiris and statues of Thutmes III. In the northwest corner is a small hall of Amen and in the southwest, a chamber decorated with scenes of Amen-Ra and the queen. There is considerable evidence of archaizing in many of the reliefs in the side chambers of the upper terrace and many iconographic details are copies of Old Kingdom originals. Such archaizing helped to reinforce their potency during religious ceremonies that the text claims originated in the time of the gods. There are also cryptographic inscriptions here, religious texts considered so sacred that they had to be encoded to protect their power from prying eyes. Such texts can be seen, for example, in the shrine of Ra-Harakhty.

In the center of the rear wall, a great granite doorway leads into three chambers (now closed) decorated with scenes showing the queen and Amen laying out the boundaries of her temple. In the Ptolemaic period, this shrine was converted to a sanatorium dedicated to the deified Amenhetep son of Hapu, the Dynasty 18 architect responsible for works of Amenhetep III. As a god, he was considered a healer, and pilgrims came to this spot to pray their ailments would be cured. Priests apparently hid inside the shrine, speaking as the voice of the god to the afflicted, offering solace and advice. Several graffiti in the shrine indicate that there were many satisfied visitors, although one or two considered their visit a waste of time, calling the priests' comments a hoax.

THE TEMPLE OF NEBHEPETRA-MENTUHETEP

About five hundred years before Senenmut began planning the construction of Hatshepsut's temple at Dayr al-Bahari, another architect was working on a combined temple and burial place for the Dynasty 11 ruler Nebhepetra-Mentuhetep. His monument lies only a few meters south of Hatshepsut's and was excavated by several British and American missions between 1859 and 1931 and extensively studied by a German mission in the 1970s. Like Hatshepsut's temple, Mentuhetep's building was reached by a long avenue, lined with statues, two of which are still standing in place, and a ramp that leads up to a low terrace. Colonnades on either side of the ramp and on the terrace above continue around to the north and south sides of the building.

Unlike Hatshepsut's temple, Mentuhetep's is small. It was topped by a mastaba or by a mound (but probably not by a pyramid, as was once thought). And unlike Hatshepsut's temple, Mentuhetep's was used both as a temple dedicated to the king and to Hathor, and as the royal burial-place. Behind the mastaba or mound atop the temple, a large columned courtyard has eighty octagonal pillars. In the floor is the entrance to a 150 meter-long corridor leading westward to his burial chamber cut deep in the limestone cliffs.

Mentuhetep's monument is closed

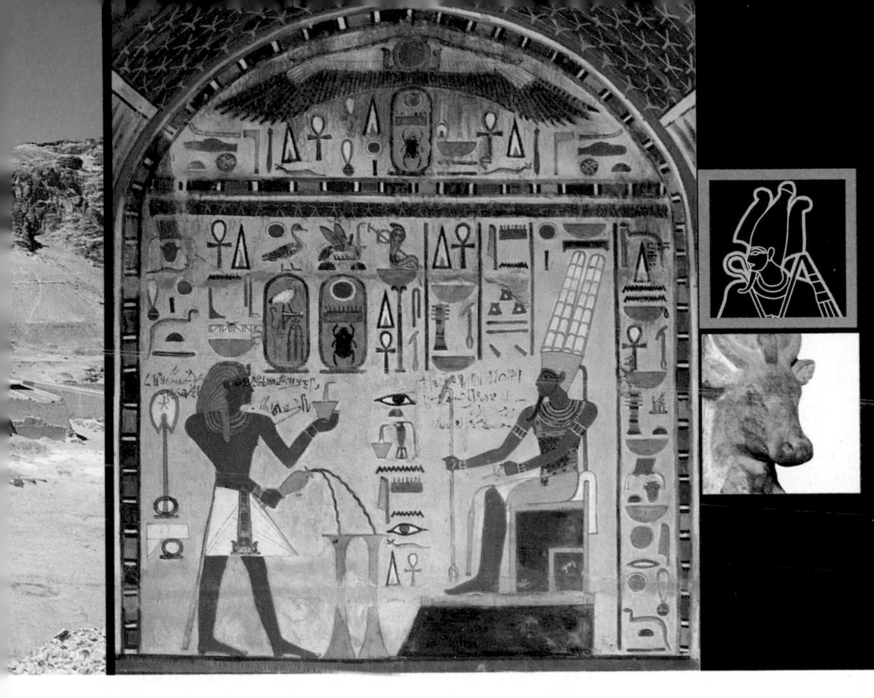

THE TEMPLE OF THUTMES III

to visitors today but a good view can be had from the open court in front of it that once was filled with trees, flowers, and statuary. There is a depression in the courtyard into which Howard Carter's horse is said to have fallen. At its base, a corridor leads to a chamber under the temple in which excavators found an unusual red, black, and white statue of Mentuhetep (now in the Cairo Museum).

This badly-destroyed temple was not discovered until the 1960s. It had suffered from frequent rock falls from the hills above, and lay buried beneath rubble for nearly three millennia. It lies above and behind the temples of Hatshepsut and Mentuhetep and shares design features with both. Pilgrims coming to pay homage to the goddess Hathor wrote numerous graffiti on its walls. The area is closed to tourists, and for structural reasons probably will remain closed. But one hopes that the collection of stunningly beautiful carved and painted relief blocks recovered in Polish and Egyptian excavations and now stored at Dayr al-Bahari will one day be put on display. A few of these blocks, together with pieces from Mentuhetep's temple, can be seen in the Luxor Museum of Ancient Art.

164 TOP THE TEMPLE OF MENTUHETEP.

164 BOTTOM COLONNADE ON THE MENTUHETEP TERRACE.

165 LEFT WALL PAINTINGS FROM THE TEMPLE OF THUTMES III NOW IN CAIRO MUSEUM.

165 RIGHT HATHOR'S STATUE FROM THE TEMPLE OF THUTMES III, DETAIL, NOW IN CAIRO MUSEUM.

2

MEMORIAL TEMPLE OF AMENHETEP III AND THE COLOSSI OF MEMNON

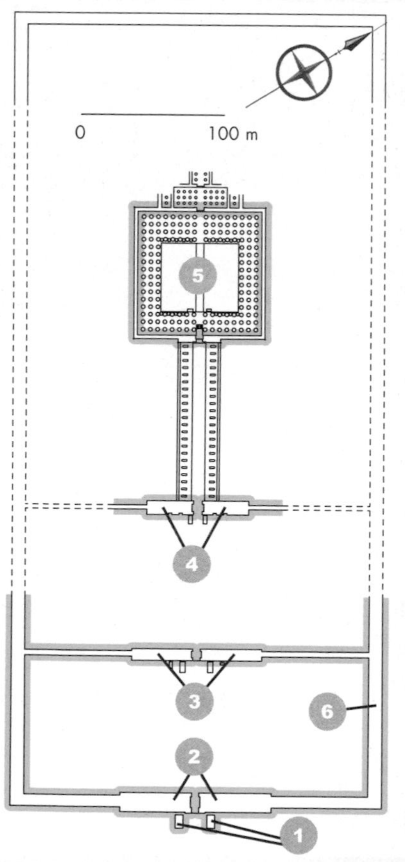

THE HISTORY

The memorial temple of Amenhetep III, known in Arabic as "Kawm al-Haitan," the "Mound of the Walls," was the largest temple ever built in Egypt. When completed, it included a massive array of pylons, chambers, walls, and statues that covered an area of over 385,000 square meters (4,200,000 square feet). The temple's main axis stretches nearly a kilometer from its first pylon westward to its rear wall. It was 550 meters wide, extending from near the Rameseum southward to the temple of Madinat Habu and Malqata, Amenhetep III's vast palace.

Unfortunately, the temple

LEGEND

1 *COLOSSI OF MEMNON*
2 *FIRST PYLON*
3 *SECOND PYLON*
4 *THIRD PYLON*
5 *SOLAR COURTYARD*
6 *ENCLOSURE WALL*

166 RELIEF FROM THE SIDE OF ONE THRONE WITH THE NILE GOD.

166-167 VIEW OF THE AREA OF THE MEMORIAL TEMPLE OF AMENHETEP III AND THE COLOSSI OF MEMNON.

167 RIGHT QUEEN'S STATUE AT THE FEET OF A COLOSSUS.

was built largely of mud brick and lay in the Nile floodplain where it was subject to the annual inundation. When it was abandoned and regular maintenance ceased, its brick walls dissolved and the stones were taken away and used by later kings in the construction of their own memorial temples. As a result, little of the huge complex is visible. Indeed, for most visitors, the two huge statues of Amenhetep III, known as the Colossi of Memnon, stand in isolation, and most visitors have no idea that the statues were but a small part of a gigantic temple complex.

The statues are truly spectacular: each is cut from a single block of stone that stood over 20 meters (65 feet) tall and weighed a 1,000 tons. When their crowns were still intact and their bases fully exposed, they stood even taller.

They were carved in beautiful orthoquartzite, one of the hardest stones known and extremely difficult to carve, brought by boat from quarries near Heliopolis, seven hundred kilometers (420 miles) to the north or from a quarry to the south–no one is yet sure. The choice of stone, Egyptologists believe, was due to the association of its red color with the solar cult. Transporting the statues was one of the many major projects supervised by Amenhetep, son of Hapu, the brilliant official of Amenhetep III whose impressive career led to his eventual deification. The "Chief Sculptor of the Great Monument of the King in the Red Mountain," named Men, was responsible for carving them.

The northern (right) colossus shows Amenhetep III seated on a throne, the arms of which are carved Nile gods binding together a lotus and papyrus, symbols of Upper and Lower Egypt. Beside the king, at much smaller scale, stands his mother, Mutemwia. On the southern colossus, the king is shown with figures of Queen Tiy and an unnamed daughter.

The northern colossus was especially popular with ancient Greek and Roman travelers. In 27 BC, an earthquake cracked the statue, and for the next two hundred years it emitted an eerie whistling noise each morning as the sun rose and the temperature and humidity changed. Greek travelers claimed that this sound was the cry of Memnon, a mythical African warrior slain by Achilles in the Trojan War, to Eos, his mother and goddess of the dawn. To hear the statue cry was said to bring good fortune, and it quickly made the colossi a major tourist destination. Both colossi are covered with hundreds of Greek and Latin graffiti left by grateful visitors. The statue stopped its singing in AD 199, when Septimus Severus filled the cracks in an attempt to renew the statue's appearance.

VISIT

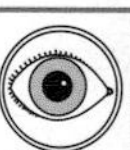

Visitors rarely do more at Kawm al-Haitan than stand in the awkwardly-located parking lot trying to photograph the colossi through a sea of tourists and tour buses. But there is more to see than just the two famous statues, and it is worth walking around the open field that defines the site. The colossi stood before the temple's mud-brick first pylon. Originally, two other quartzite colossi stood before the second pylon and two alabaster colossi stood farther west before a third pylon. One of these

huge statues fell in antiquity and has lain here for millennia, buried in silt. In 2001, a German expedition began work to re-erect it, although groundwater is making that work extremely difficult.

Amenhetep III was inordinately fond of sculpture. Egyptologists estimate that this temple alone had thousands of statues installed within it. Over 730 statues of Sekhmet were placed here, one seated and one standing Sekhmet for every day of the year, and these were only a small part of the hundreds of statues erected for other deities. Indeed, Amenhetep III's memorial temple boasted the largest program of statuary ever undertaken in ancient Egypt. Its variety and quality is hinted at by a sphinx with the body of a crocodile that still stands on the site, by the 8–meter tall (26 feet) statues of the king posed as Osiris that once stood in the temple compound, and by the many statues usurped by Merenptah now displayed in the open-air museum in his memorial temple, immediately behind that of Amenhetep III.

The king described his statuary on a great stela found west of his temple in 1896. The temple, he wrote, "is extended with royal statues of granite, of quartzite and of precious stones, fashioned to last forever. They are higher than the rising of the heavens; their rays are in men's faces like the rising sun...." On another stela, still standing at the western end of the temple, the king boasted that "when [the statues] are seen in their place, there is great rejoicing because of their size." The king described the temple itself as "an everlasting fortress of sandstone, embellished with gold throughout, its floors shining with silver and all its doorways with electrum." Even admitting that such texts are filled with hyperbole, archaeological evidence confirms that this must have been one of the most awe-inspiring buildings in the ancient world.

At the western end of the site, recent excavations have exposed more of the temple, including a huge hypostyle hall. Preceding the hall lies a great solar court, and east of that a series of colonnades and courtyards. Typical of ancient Egyptian building practice, the huge columns were built directly on Nile silt with no attempt to lay a foundation. Little wonder they soon collapsed.

168 GREAT STELA FROM THE INNER COURT AND DETAIL.

169 THE TWO HUGE STATUES OF AMENHETEP III, KNOWN AS THE COLOSSI OF MEMNON.

2 MEMORIAL TEMPLE OF SETY I

THE HISTORY

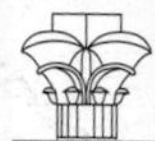

The memorial temple of Sety I, called The Domain of Amen in the West of Thebes, lies at the northern end of the Theban Necropolis, directly across the Nile from the Temple of Karnak. The location is lovely; there is a fine view of a large palm grove and the Theban Hills from atop the temple enclosure walls. The temple is very well preserved and was a favorite subject of nineteenth century watercolorists.

The name of the Sety I temple is nearly identical

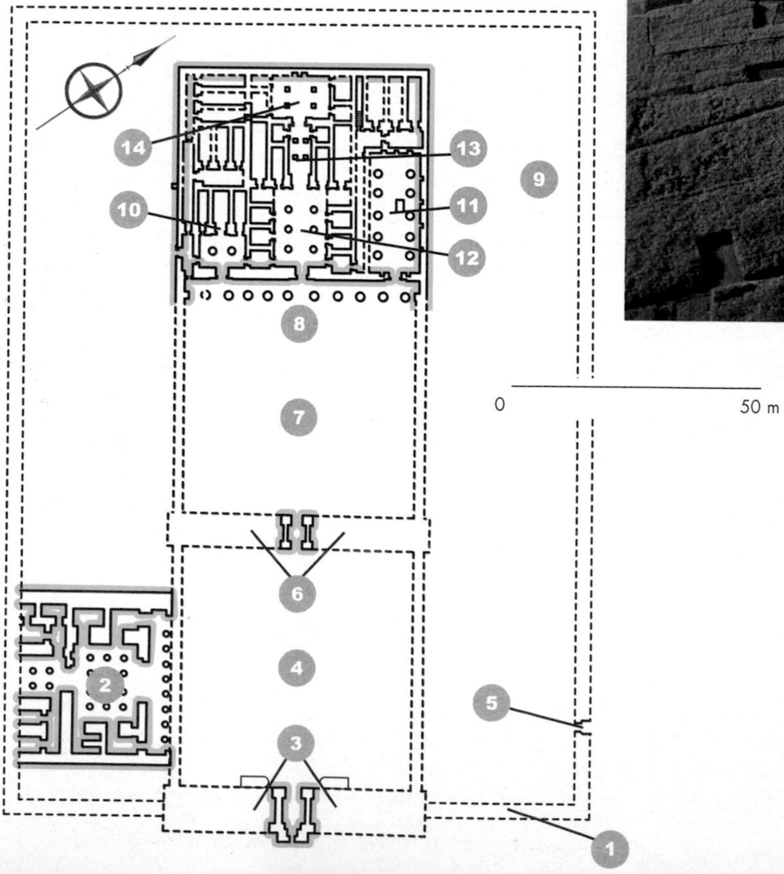

to that of the Hypostyle Hall at Karnak, and the two sites were linked both physically and functionally by their ceremonial roles in major festivals. In antiquity, a canal led here from the river, and during the Beautiful Festival of the Valley and other festivals, processions of sacred barks sailed here from the Temple of Amen at Karnak and then continued in other West Bank memorial temples.

The temple of Sety I, sometimes called the Qurna Temple, was where nineteenth century tourists began their West Bank tour. (More precisely, travelers started from here in the summer and

LEGEND

1 *ENCLOSURE WALL*
2 *ROYAL PALACE*
3 *FIRST PYLON*
4 *FIRST COURT*
5 *NORTH ENTRANCE*
6 *SECOND PYLON*
7 *SECOND COURT*
8 *PORTICO*
9 *MAGAZINES*
10 *RAMESES I SUITE*
11 *SUN COURT*
12 *HYPOSTYLE HALL*
13 *SANCTUARY OF AMEN-RA*
14 *FOUR PILLARED HALL*

170-171 THE MEMORIAL TEMPLE OF SETY I AND THE VILLAGE OF QURNA.

171 BOTTOM RELIEF DETAIL WITH SETY I AND KHONSU.

autumn months, when the annual flood made impassable the route from the Nile west to the Colossi of Memnon.) A century ago, the Nile flowed several kilometers farther west than it does today, and tourists moored their boats near the temple beside a huge sycomore fig tree and a water wheel that soon became famous landmarks mentioned in every tourist guidebook. The sycomore tree has disappeared, but pieces of the water wheel still stand in the garden of the Abdel Kassem Hotel and Alabaster Factory three hundred meters east of the temple.

In dynastic times, this area was called *Hefet-her-nebes,* a phrase meaning that it lay "in front of its lord," the Temple of Amen at Karnak. Three thousand years ago, there was a large village of the same name immediately north of the temple. There is still a village there today, called Naj' Junayna, and it is the site of a lively Tuesday morning market. It is great fun to visit: noisy and colorful, a dusty field that covers several hectares is filled with people who gossip, drink sticky sweet tea, quarrel over prices, and sell vegetables, hardware, sandals, sheep, and goats.

Farther north, a large First Intermediate Period and Middle Kingdom cemetery called al-Tarif is surrounded by modern village houses. Beyond it lies New Thebes, a recently-built settlement where families who lived in and around the Qurna tombs have been relocated.

The temple of Sety I was badly damaged in November 1994, when torrential rains in the nearby Theban hills sent floodwaters cascading through desert wadis. The storm dumped thousands of liters of water into *Hefet-her-nebes.* The floodwaters rose to over 1 meter (3 feet) deep and poured into the temple compound at 20 kilometers (12 miles) an hour. They broke the enclosure wall, flooded storerooms, destroyed limestone statues and stelae, and left tons of silt, sand, and stone in their wake. Several people in nearby villages were injured and many homes were destroyed. The temple's mudbrick walls were washed away, but fortunately its stone walls emerged relatively intact and their decoration was undamaged.

VISIT

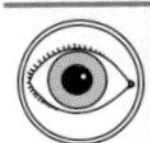

Today, Sety I's temple seems a small structure, but it originally extended 160 meters (520 feet) from pylon to rear wall. One enters the temple through a small door in the northeast corner of the enclosure wall and proceeds into the First Courtyard. The First Pylon stood to the left (east) and the remains of sphinxes and inscribed blocks, badly damaged by the flood, stand along the temple's main axis. Originally the pylon measured 69 meters (224 feet) wide and 24 meters (78 feet) high. Directly ahead, on the south side of a courtyard known as the Festival Court of the Subjects, the remains of the king's palace have recently been cleared. On the north side of a large hypostyle hall with twelve pillars, a broad set of steps leads up to the Window of Appearance from which the king observed ceremonies and processions in the courtyard. The palace is similar in plan to the better-preserved palaces of Rameses II at the Ramesseum and Rameses III at Madinat Habu; it is the earliest example of a palace built within a memorial temple. There are numerous stelae, inscribed temple blocks, and damaged sphinxes in the courtyard. Originally, the temple causeway was lined with dozens of large sphinxes and the whole area was filled with outbuildings and orchards of persea trees.

The Second Pylon originally cut in half what now looks like a single courtyard. The pylon itself has vanished, but its position is marked by a low mudbrick wall and a gate. It was small, not more than 7 meters (23 feet) high.

172 LEFT WALL RELIEF WITH DETAIL OF AMEN BARK.

172 RIGHT TWO VOTIVE STELAE OF SETY I IN THE FIRST COURT.

172-173 RELIEF IN THE FIRST COURT WITH THE KING OFFERING.

The west facade of the temple was laid out as a portico with a row of ten papyrus-bundle columns. Texts on the architrave were written by Sety I's son, Rameses II, who describes how he completed work on the temple after his father's death. On the wall behind, scenes include personifications of Upper Egypt on the left (south) side and of Lower Egypt on the right (north). Above them on the left, priests carry the sacred bark of Amen into the temple and the king makes offerings of incense.

Three doorways lead through this wall into three separate parts of the temple. This tripartite plan is typical of most memorial temples on the West Bank: the center rear part of the temple is devoted to the cult of Amen; the left to the king and his ancestors; and the right side to the solar cult.

The doorway in the center leads into the Hypostyle Hall, with six columns and three small chapels on each side that are dedicated to the Theban Triad (Amen, Mut, and Khonsu). The carving on the walls was begun by Sety I and completed by Rameses II. It is easy to identify who did what: the work of Sety I's craftsmen is of fine quality; that of Rameses II's is hastily done and heavy-handed. Scenes show one or the other of the two kings offering to various deities, including Thoth, Osiris, Amen, Mut, Ptah, and Sekhmet.

Chambers in the rear part of the temple are devoted to the Beautiful Festival of the Valley and the god Amen. Behind the hall and a small vestibule, five doorways lead into rooms that housed the sacred barks of Amen (in the center), Mut (on the left, south), and Khonsu (on the right, north). At the far ends, two other chambers served purposes unknown to us. The central shrine for Amen is particularly well decorated with scenes of the elaborately furnished sacred bark being offered to by the king.

Behind the central shrine stands a room with four pillars decorated with scenes of the king and various gods. To the rear (west), a false door (now gone) gave the *ka* of the king access to the netherworld.

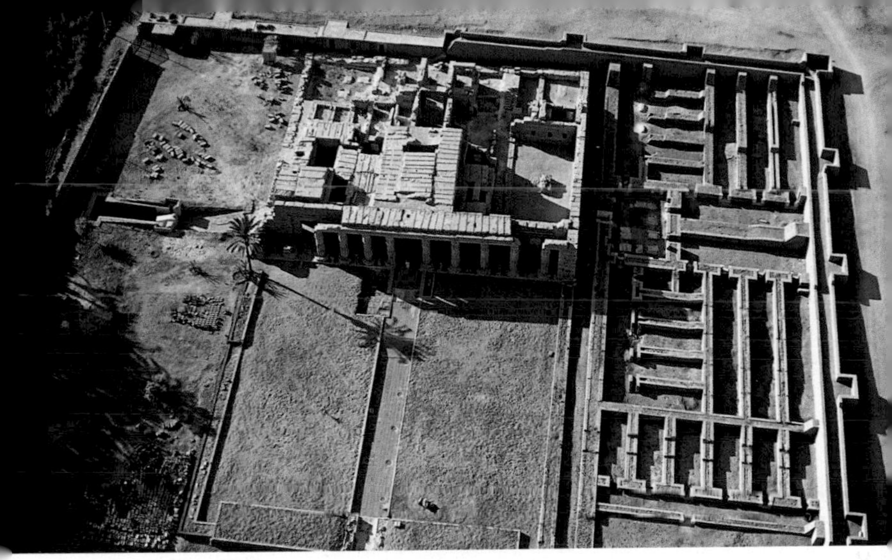

The doorway at the left (south) end of the portico leads to a room with two columns. Behind them stand three small chapels. These were dedicated to Rameses I by his son Sety I in an act of filial piety done because Rameses I reigned only briefly and had no memorial temple of his own. Rameses I, Sety I, and Rameses II are all shown here in scenes before Amen. A double false door for Rameses I was carved on the rear (west) wall of his chapel

The doorway at the right (north) end of the portico leads into a damaged court dedicated to the solar cult.

Storerooms built of mudbrick lie between the temple and the right (north) enclosure wall. This is the first time that storerooms were included as part of a memorial temple. Earlier, foodstuffs would have been shipped to temples from the storerooms at Karnak. A small well was dug on the left (south) side of the temple and has been partially cleared.

174 TOP TWO COLUMNS OF THE HYPOSTYLE HALL.

174 BOTTOM THE PAPYRUS-BUNDLE COLUMNS OF THE PORTICO.

175 TOP AERIAL VIEW OF THE TEMPLE WITH THE MAGAZINES ON THE RIGHT.

175 BOTTOM INSIDE THE TEMPLE.

2

THE RAMESSEUM, MEMORIAL TEMPLE OF RAMESES II

THE HISTORY

"Of all the Theban ruins," wrote the nineteenth century Englishwoman Amelia Edwards, "the Ramesseum is the most cheerful. Drenched in sunshine, the warm limestone of which it is built seems to have mellowed and turned golden with time. No walls enclose it. No towering pylons overshadow it. It stands high, and the air circulates freely...There are not many Egyptian ruins in which one can talk and be merry..." The Ramesseum has changed since Ms. Edwards wrote those words but it is still a lovely monument. Rameses II called his temple "The Temple of Millions of Years of User-Ma'at-Ra United with Thebes in the Estates of Amen West of Thebes," and it was known to classical visitors as the Memnonium or the Tomb of Ozymandias, and to modern tourists as the Ramesseum, a name coined by Jean-François Champollion, the man who deciphered hieroglyphs. It was built immediately north of the temple of Amenhetep III, at the edge of the cultivation, beside a ceremonial canal that extended from the temple of Sety I south to Madinat Habu. Its construction was supervised by two of the king's pre-eminent building officials, Penra and Amenemonet, and the work continued from the beginning of his reign until regnal year 22.

VISIT

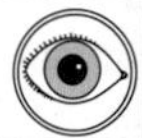

The entrance to the temple today is through a narrow doorway in the northeast corner of the enclosure wall. A path leads south past mudbrick storerooms into the Second Court, and one should turn left (east) there and proceed across a small grassy field to the First Pylon. Several innovations in temple design were introduced at the Ramesseum. The most impressive is the use of sandstone instead of mud brick for the huge First Pylon, 67 meters (220 feet) wide and originally about 24 meters (78 feet) high. The pylon is badly damaged, in part because it was built in the flood plain on weak foundations, but traces of decoration can still be seen in late afternoon light on its inner (west) face. Like many other monuments of Rameses II, the scenes deal with a military campaign against the Hittites in his fifth regnal year. On the left (north) tower, one can see a dozen Syrian fortresses. Near them, the Egyptians are encamped and soldiers lounge about, drinking, talking, and wrestling with each other. Freight wagons filled with baggage approach the camp, donkeys graze nearby, and the king is shown in council with his sons and advisors. Here, all appears calm. But on the right (south) tower, the Battle of Kadesh rages and Egypt's enemies flee in panic from Rameses II and his army.

177 TOP CORONATION SCENE WITH RAMESES II, AMEN-RA AND MUT.

177 BOTTOM DETAIL OF AN OSIRIS COLUMN.

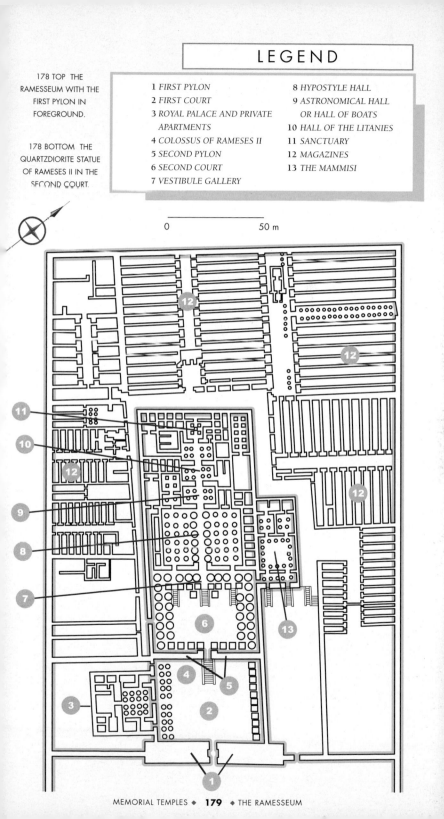

178 TOP THE RAMESSEUM WITH THE FIRST PYLON IN FOREGROUND.

178 BOTTOM THE QUARTZDIORITE STATUE OF RAMESES II IN THE SECOND COURT.

LEGEND

1 *FIRST PYLON*
2 *FIRST COURT*
3 *ROYAL PALACE AND PRIVATE APARTMENTS*
4 *COLOSSUS OF RAMESES II*
5 *SECOND PYLON*
6 *SECOND COURT*
7 *VESTIBULE GALLERY*
8 *HYPOSTYLE HALL*
9 *ASTRONOMICAL HALL OR HALL OF BOATS*
10 *HALL OF THE LITANIES*
11 *SANCTUARY*
12 *MAGAZINES*
13 *THE MAMMISI*

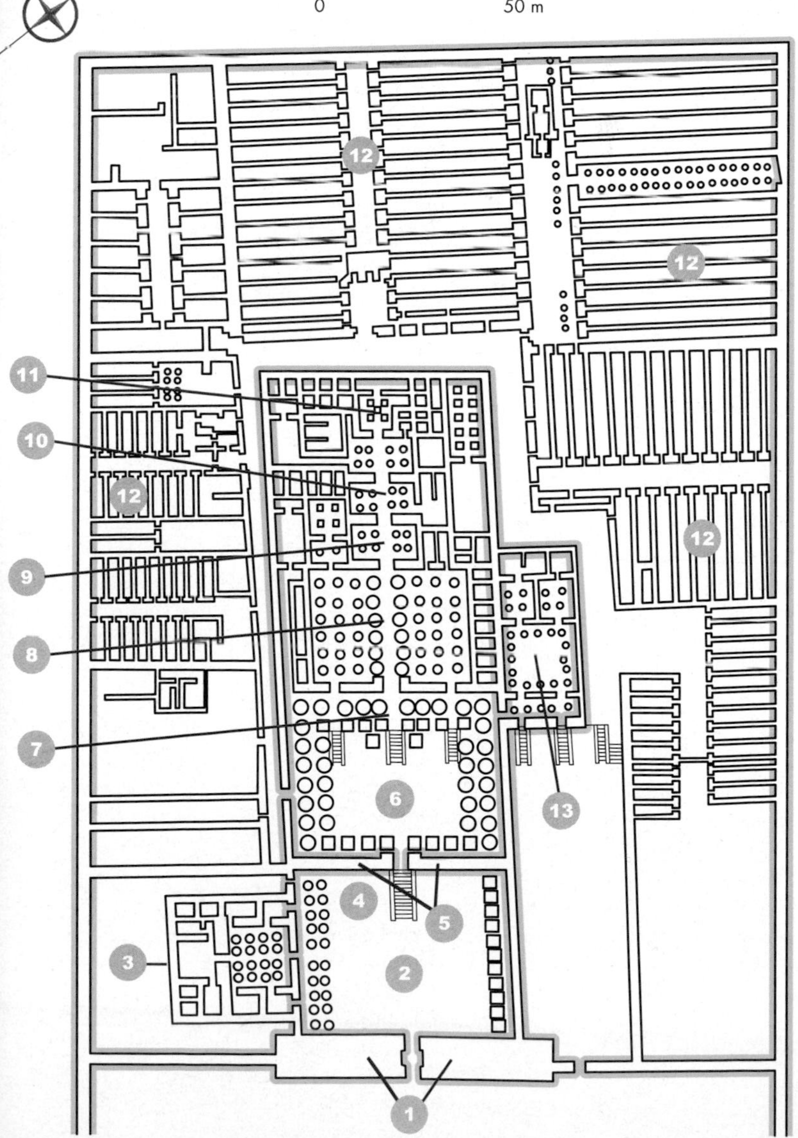

◆ THE FIRST COURT ◆

Between the First and Second Pylons, an attractive open space is covered with wild grass, and home to a beautiful tamarisk tree and several species of birds. On the south side of the court there once stood a double row of columns, and behind them, a doorway that led into the king's palace. The plan of the palace is very similar to that at the memorial temple of Sety I and to the first version of the palace of Rameses III at Madinat Habu. Behind the palace lie the remains of recently excavated kitchens, bakeries, and a slaughter-house that served the needs of the temple priesthood and the royal family. On the west side of the court, next to what remains of the Second Pylon, the colossal statue of the deified Rameses II, one of the most famous statues in all Egypt, has fallen in the dirt. Originally 17.5 meters (57 feet) high (not including its base), this seated figure of the king weighed over one thousand tons, and is the largest monolithic statue ever sculpted. It is so large that one ear is more than a meter (3 feet) long and the shoulders are over 7 meters (23 feet) broad. It is made of granite. Whether this statue was one of a pair intended to stand before the Second Pylon or whether it stood alone is not known; there is no physical evidence of a second statue. It is also unclear if Rameses II commissioned the statue especially for installation here, or if it had originally been ordered by Amenhetep III for *his* temple, then usurped and moved by Rameses II. Exactly when the statue collapsed is also unknown, but we do know that it was standing when Diodorus Siculus visited the site in the first century AD. It may have fallen because of quarrying activity around its base. (See more below.)

180 TOP THE FEET OF THE COLOSSAL STATUE OF RAMESES II.

180 BOTTOM THE FIRST COURT AND, BEHIND, THE FIRST PYLON.

180-181 THE REMAINS OF THE COLOSSAL STATUE IN THE FIRST COURT (FOREGROUND) AND THE SECOND COURT AND THE HYPOSTYLE HALL.

◆ THE SECOND PYLON ◆

The Second Pylon has fared even worse than the first, and only part of its north tower remains today. It was built on bedrock nearly two meters (6 feet) higher than the floor of the First Court and was reached from that court by a staircase cut in its western face. Around the Second Court, a portico stands with rows of Osirid pillars on the east and west sides and columns on the west, north and south.

The western face of the Second Pylon behind this portico is carved with further scenes of the king's military campaigns in western Asia. It is a brilliant depiction of the chaos of battle, a huge canvas covered with figures of terrified horses and dead and dying soldiers. The Hittite infantry is trampled beneath the king's cavalry, and men throw themselves into the Orontes River in vain attempts to escape. One of their leaders has nearly drowned in the river, and his men hold him upside down and pound his chest, attempting artificial respiration. Paint is still preserved on the wall and the light blue Orontes meanders across the scene, its shores covered with Egyptian and Hittite cavalry, archers, and spear-carriers. At the far right, a remarkably-drawn crowd of over a hundred soldiers watches the battle. The group is so densely packed together that only the soldiers' heads can be seen, and their intense stares and furrowed brows register shock as they focus on the grisly scene before them. The scene may be unique in Egyptian art.

In contrast to these scenes of mayhem, the upper register shows harvest festivals for the god Min. Birds are being released into the air, each with a small piece of papyrus hanging around its neck that bears an announcement of the king's coronation. These "carrier-pigeons" were meant to spread the good news around the world.

◆ THE SECOND COURT ◆

The Second Court is paved with large stone blocks but its walls, columns, and pillars are largely destroyed. On the western side of the court, three broad, low staircases lead to a portico and a hypostyle hall. The portico is fronted by ten Osirid pillars and ten columns. On the wall behind, the king is led into the temple by Atum and Montu, and at the right he kneels before the Theban Triad. In other scenes the king offers to Ptah and to Min. Below, a line of royal sons walk in the procession.

The central staircase was flanked by two huge statues of Rameses II.

The upper part of one statue was carted away by Giovanni Belzoni in 1816 and sold to the British Museum. Its arrival in

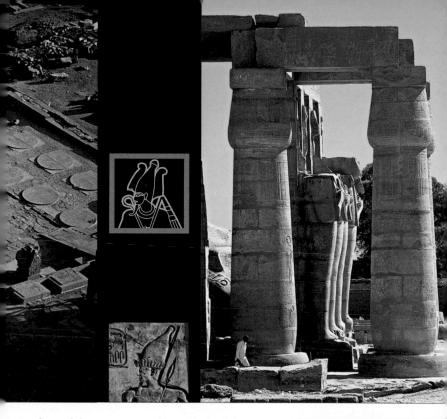

London and the publication of Belzoni's Egyptian activities inspired Percy Bysse Shelley to pen his famous poem, "Ozymandias," a reference to the fallen colossus in the gateway of the Second Pylon. (The name "Ozymandias" is a Greek rendering of one of Rameses II's names, User-Ma'at-Ra.) *"I met a traveler from an antique land Who said: Two vast and trunkless legs of stone Stand in the desert...Near them, on the sand, Half sunk, a shattered visage lies, whose frown,*

And wrinkled lip, and sneer of cold command

Tell that its sculptor well those passions read

Which yet survive, stamped on these lifeless things, The hand that mocked them, and the heart that fed. And on the pedestal these words appear: 'My name is Ozymandias, King of Kings: Look on my works, ye Mighty, and despair!'

Nothing beside remains. Round the decay

Of that colossal wreck, boundless and bare,

The lone and level sands stretch far away."

Seventeen centuries before Shelley, Diodorus Siculus had wrongly claimed to have seen an inscription on the fallen statue that read: "I am Ozymandias, king of kings; if any would know how great I am, and where I lie, let him excel me in any of my works."

182-183 AERIAL VIEW OF THE SECOND COURT.

182 BOTTOM THE VESTIBULE GALLERY WITH THE LOWER SECTION OF THE STATUE OF RAMESES II (UPPER PART IN THE BRITISH MUSEUM).

183 TOP LEFT RAMESES II WEARING THE DOUBLE CROWN.

183 TOP RIGHT THE COLONNADE OF THE SECOND COURT.

183 BOTTOM RAMESES II IN FRONT OF AMEN-RA, MUT AND KHONSU.

◆ HYPOSTYLE HALL ◆

Three doorways behind the portico each lead into a grand hypostyle hall with forty-eight sandstone columns. The central two rows of six are taller than the others to accommodate clerestory lighting. On each column, Rameses II makes offerings to the gods. On the front (east) wall, the king in his war chariot leads an attack on a Hittite fort at Dapur. Soldiers using ladders scale the fort's walls and quickly overcome its guardians. Scenes like this have given military historians a wealth of detail about ancient military tactics. On the rear (west) wall, below scenes of the king standing before Amen and Mut, a long procession of royal princes and one princess marches

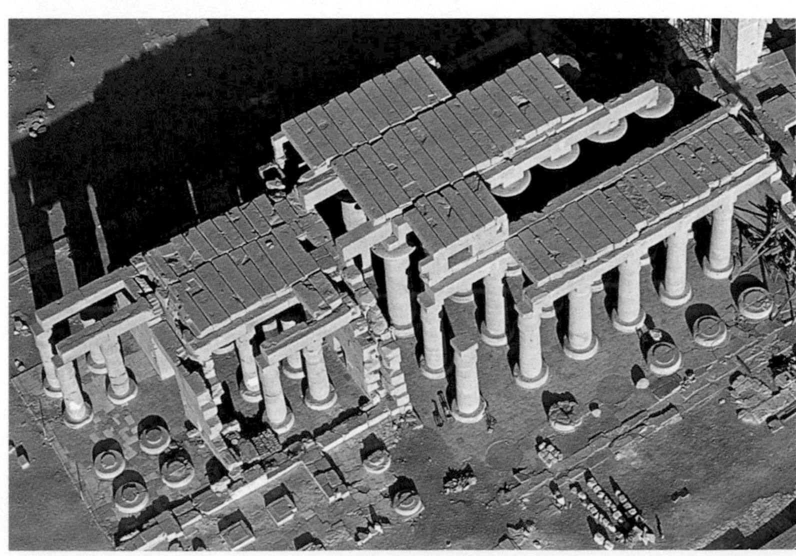

forward, nineteen figures on the left (south) side, twenty-three on the right (north) side. The princes are shown in birth order, as they are in other processions that Rameses II had carved in a score of temples in Egypt and Nubia.

West of the Hypostyle Hall, a doorway leads into the Astronomical Hall. Eight columns support a ceiling decorated with scenes that show constellations and the thirty-six groups of stars, called "decans," into which the Egyptians divided the night sky. On the front (east) wall priests carry the sacred barks of Amen, Mut, Khonsu, Ahmes-Nefertari, and Rameses II. On the rear (west), Rameses II and Atum are seated beside a persea tree. At right, the goddess Sefkhet-'Abwy stands with the god Thoth, writing the king's name on leaves of the tree. (The eighteenth century Danish traveler Frederick Norden believed this was a drawing of Adam and Eve beside the Tree of Knowledge.) Beyond the Astronomical Hall, in the so-called Hall of Litanies, the king makes offerings to Ptah and Ra-Harakhty. The rooms at the rear of the temple are badly damaged.

184-185 RAMESES II IN HIS CHARIOT ATTACKS A HITTITE FORT AT DAPUR, RELIEF IN THE HYPOSTYLE HALL.

184 BOTTOM THE HYPOSTYLE HALL SEEN FROM ABOVE.

185 TOP RAMESES II SEATED BESIDE A PERSEA TREE; THE GOD WRITES HIS NAME ON ITS LEAVES.

185 BOTTOM THE COLUMNS OF THE HYPOSTYLE HALL STILL RETAIN MUCH ORIGINAL COLORS.

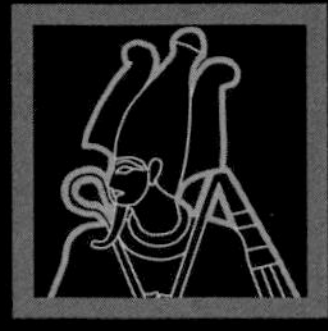

◆ OUTBUILDINGS ◆

Around the perimeter of the temple a series of remarkably well-preserved vaulted mudbrick chambers were used as storerooms for the agricultural surpluses and foreign tribute the temple amassed and redistributed. These storerooms are described in an inscription on an architrave in the Hypostyle Hall: "...He has caused that his temple may be like Thebes, it being supplied with every good thing, the granaries reaching the sky, an august treasury with silver, gold, royal linen and every kind of real gemstone, which was brought for him by the King of Upper and Lower Egypt..." Administrative offices and workshops were also located here.

On the north side of the temple lie the scanty remains of a small chapel originally built by Sety I. Some believe that the presence of this earlier temple was the reason Rameses II chose this site for his own monument. Later it became a *mammisi* (birth-house) honoring Tuy, mother of Rameses II, and his wife, Nefertari.

A colossal statue of Tuy stood in its courtyard.

Not long after the end of the New Kingdom the Ramesseum was stripped of its wealth by hungry and unruly citizens, and its buildings were used as quarries for the construction of other monuments.

Tombs for major and minor court officials were cut into the bedrock beneath it, small shrines built from its stones, and eventually a Christian church built within the ruins.

186 TOP THE MUDBRICK ENCLOSURE WALLS OF THE MEMORIAL TEMPLE OF RAMESES II ARE DOMINATED BY AL-QURN.

186 BOTTOM LEFT AND 187 BOTTOM THE RAMESSEUM IS SURROUNDED BY MANY MUDBRICK BUILDINGS, INCLUDING MAGAZINES.

186 BOTTOM RIGHT IN THIS DETAIL ARE CLEARLY VISIBLE THE STRUCTURES OF THE BUILDINGS (COLUMNS AND WALLS) SURROUNDING THE RAMESSEUM.

187 TOP SOME VAULTED MUDBRICK CHAMBERS OF THE STOREROOMS ARE STILL WELL PRESERVED.

2

THE MEMORIAL TEMPLE OF MERENPTAH

THE HISTORY

Merenptah's memorial temple, which lies almost directly behind that of Amenhetep III, was little more than a scattering of fallen stones and mounds of rubble a few years ago. It had been partially cleared by Flinders Petrie early in the 1890s. But the dedicated work of the Swiss Institute over the last several decades has transformed the site into a fascinating open-air museum in which one can trace the temple's original plan and see examples of its statuary and wall reliefs. The temple, opened to the public only since 2003, should be on everyone's list of West Bank sites to visit.

The principal attraction of Merenptah's temple is not its architecture but its sculpture. The king had a number of pieces carved especially for this monument, but he also unashamedly took many pieces from the nearby temple of Amenhetep III, added his name to their inscriptions, and installed them here. The site is therefore a very important source of information for the study of Amenhetep III's monument as well.

Before entering the temple proper, it is a good idea to walk behind the ticket office into the small museum. Here, a series of texts describe the history of the temple and archaeological work there, and exhibits of ostraca, pottery, and minor arts show the results of recent excavations. There are virtually no labels in the temple itself, so this museum provides the background to understand the temple plan.

While in the museum, note the limestone heads of Anubis jackals, carved several times larger than life. They came originally from the temple of Amenhetep III. Egyptian art, unlike that in many other ancient Near Eastern cultures, has always seemed to me non-threatening, even friendly. But these heads of Anubis are frightening, malicious creatures, the kind of animals that could give a child nightmares. Their fearsome appearance seems completely out of place in an ancient Egyptian monument. It is largely the use of red paint on the eyes and nostrils that makes them seem so feral. Other statues are to be seen in a magazine inside the temple, behind the Sacred Lake.

Merenptah's temple has a standard plan, similar to that of the Ramesseum but only about half its size.

189 THE TEMPLE OF MERENPTAH IS IN CENTER FOREGROUND AT THE EDGE OF THE CULTIVATION.

LEGEND

1 *FIRST PYLON*
2 *FORECOURT*
3 *PALACE*
4 *SECOND PYLON*
5 *SECOND COURT*
6 *TWELVE COLUMN HYPOSTYLE HALL*
7 *EIGHT COLUMN HYPOSTYLE HALL*
8 *SANCTUARY*
9 *CHAPEL OF OSIRIS*
10 *CHAPEL OF THE SOLAR CULT*
11 *MAGAZINES*
12 *TREASURY*
13 *SACRED LAKE*

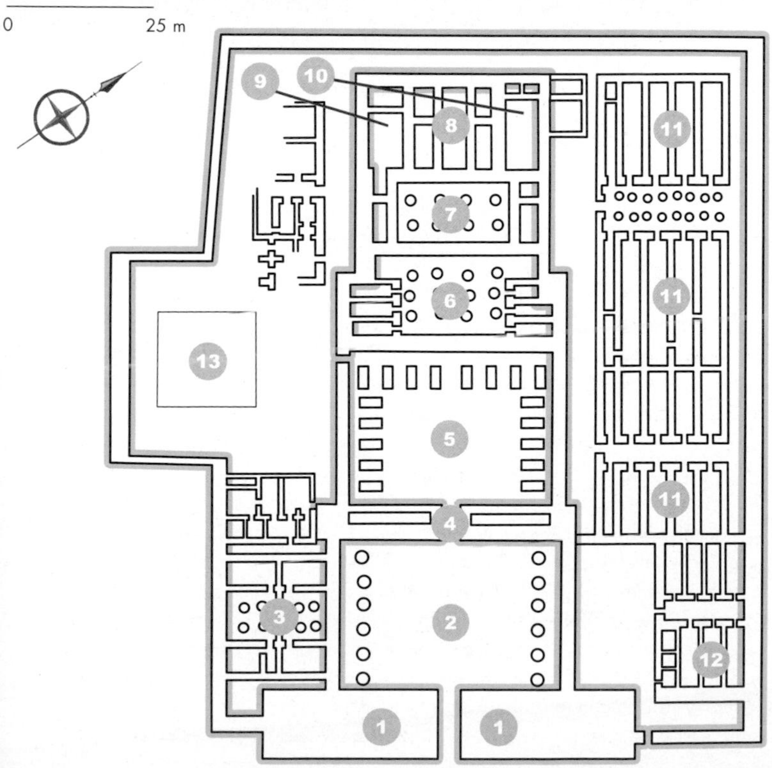

0 25 m

1
1
2
3
4
5
6
7
8
9
10
11
11
11
12
13

VISIT

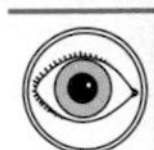

Only a few courses remain of the First Pylon, which originally stood over 10 meters (32 feet) tall; its outer face is decorated with scenes of the king, Amen, and a goddess, while its inner face depicts the king, Amen, and another god. Beyond the pylon, one enters a forecourt with a row of papyriform columns on the north and south sides. Statues of the king stood on the north side. In the southeast corner, a replica of the so-called Israel Stela, discovered here by Flinders Petrie, is carved with an inscription giving the only mention of "Israel" in an Egyptian text. "Israel is devastated," it reads, "her seed is no more. Palestine has become a widow for Egypt." The name can be seen in the second line of text from the bottom. It begins with two reed leaves and ends about eight characters later with drawings of a seated man and woman.

On the south side of the forecourt, behind the columns, a window of appearance joined the forecourt and the palace behind it. It was here that Merenptah would have stood and watched processions of the bark of Amen during the Beautiful Festival of the Valley and other ceremonies. The palace was constructed first as a mudbrick building, then slightly enlarged and rebuilt in stone.

The second pylon leads to a second court with porticos taken from Amenhetep III's temple

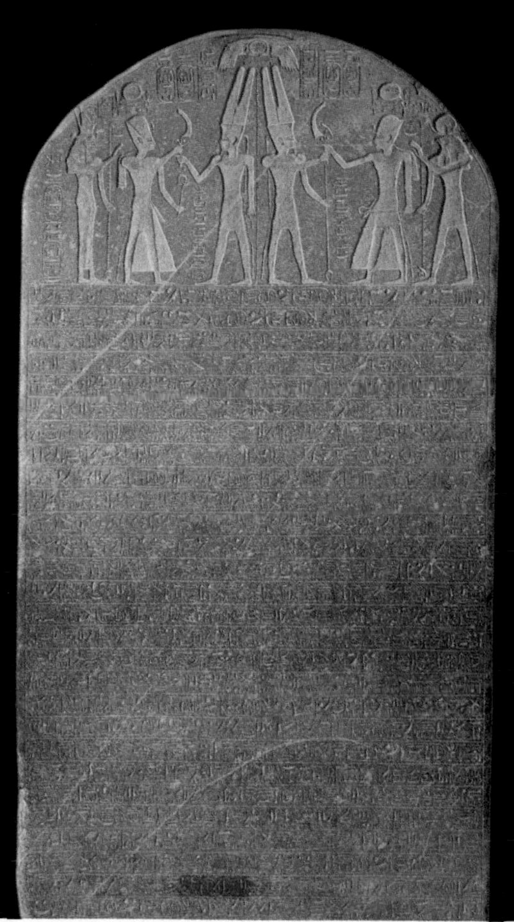

190 GRANODIORITE BUST OF MERENPTAH FOUND IN HIS MEMORIAL TEMPLE, NOW IN THE CAIRO MUSEUM.

191 THE SO-CALLED ISRAEL STELA FOUND IN MERENPTAH'S MEMORIAL TEMPLE, NOW IN THE CAIRO MUSEUM. A COPY HAS BEEN ERECTED AT THE SITE.

showing the king in Osirid pose before the pilasters. The Osirid figures alternated with three colossal crystalline limestone statues of Amenhetep III, usurped by Merenptah. There is a dyad of Amen and the king, and a triad of Osiris, the king, and Hathor/Isis. Fragments of statues of the royal couple, Amenhetep III and Queen Tiy, wearing elegant and very complex costumes, were found in the foundations of the temple.

Beyond the second court stand two hypostyle halls, the first with twelve columns, the second with eight. Behind that lies the holy of holies, a chapel to Osiris (to the south), and a chapel to the solar cult (to the north).

A series of mudbrick magazines stands to the north of the temple. In the northwest corner, beside the first pylon, a group of rooms form what is called the "treasury". Nearby, a slaughterhouse was built in which cattle were killed to be given as offerings in temple ceremonies. On the south side of the temple, south and east of the palace, one can make out a small sacred lake, priests' quarters, and a complex of workshops.

Within the Merenptah temple, the Swiss built two semi-subterranean display rooms that hold several superbly painted examples of wall decoration. Some pieces are displayed upside down, as they were originally placed when re-used in the temple.

East of the sacred lake, heads and other body parts of colossal sphinxes are displayed in a large storeroom. Several are similar to the sculptures in the museum at the temple entrance. One is a huge jackal head of the god Anubis that stood 6.5 meters (21 feet) long. A figure of Amenhetep III stands beneath its jaws. Fragments of a dozen other jackal figures, each 5 meters (16 feet) long, also with a royal figure beneath their snouts, are displayed here, and there are smaller sphinxes and statues as well.

MADINAT HABU

0 100 m

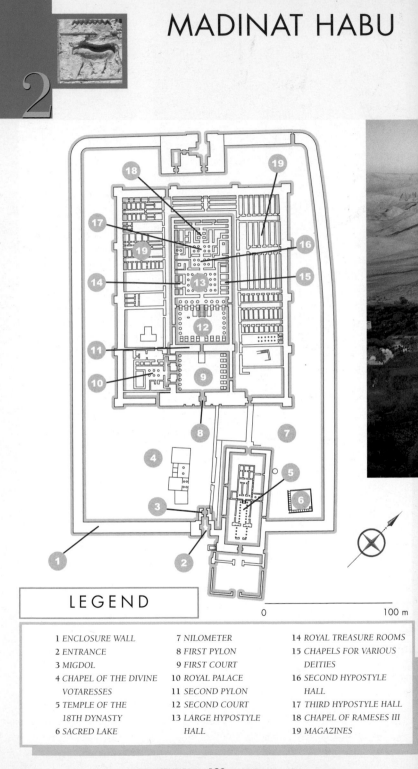

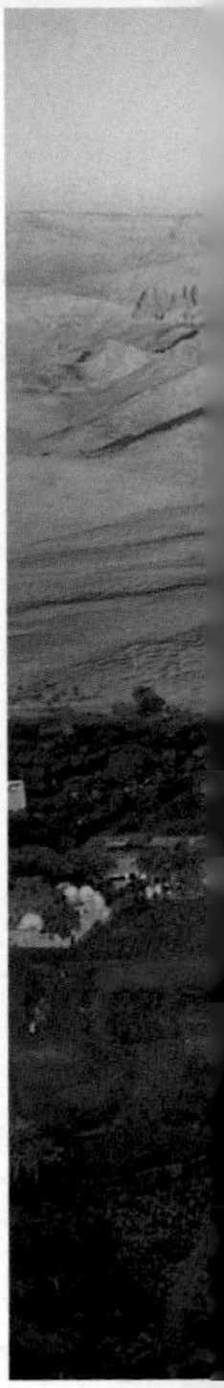

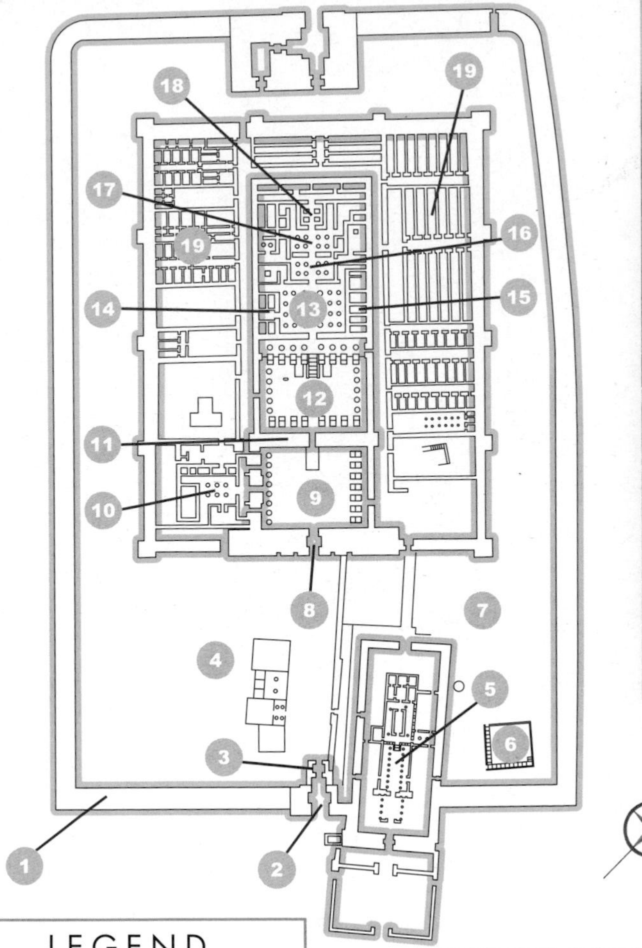

LEGEND

1 ENCLOSURE WALL
2 ENTRANCE
3 MIGDOL
4 CHAPEL OF THE DIVINE VOTARESSES
5 TEMPLE OF THE 18TH DYNASTY
6 SACRED LAKE
7 NILOMETER
8 FIRST PYLON
9 FIRST COURT
10 ROYAL PALACE
11 SECOND PYLON
12 SECOND COURT
13 LARGE HYPOSTYLE HALL
14 ROYAL TREASURE ROOMS
15 CHAPELS FOR VARIOUS DEITIES
16 SECOND HYPOSTYLE HALL
17 THIRD HYPOSTYLE HALL
18 CHAPEL OF RAMESES III
19 MAGAZINES

193 THE MEDINAT HABU COMPLEX AT DAWN. VIEW TO THE WEST.

THE HISTORY

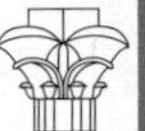

Madinat Habu is one of Egypt's best preserved and most interesting temples. Unfortunately, most tourists arrive here at the end of a long morning of sightseeing and rarely get more than a quick peek at this fascinating monument. The temple deserves better. It is one of the few monuments in Egypt to convey the emotional impact that religious art and architecture must have had for the ancient Egyptians.

The site of Madinat Habu lies at the southern end of the Theban Necropolis and is surrounded by a thick wall, 210 x 315 meters (682 x 1024 feet) that defines a 66,150 square meters (698,000 square feet) enclosure.

Its name is Arabic and means "The City of Habu," perhaps a reference to the great Dynasty 18 architect, Amenhetep, son of Hapu, whose memorial temple lies 300 meters (1,000 feet) to the north. Another suggestion is that it derived from the word *hebu,* the ancient name for the ibis, symbol of the god Thoth, who has a Ptolemaic Period temple a few hundred meters to the south. In earlier times, the site was called Djeme, after a nearby town.

Djeme may come from a word meaning "troops" or "young men," and a play on that word, *tchau-muwe,* meaning "fathers and mothers," was the name of a temple predating the Dynasty 18 monument in Madinat Habu's forecourt.

194 LEFT THE PYLON OF PTOLEMY VIII RIGHT OF THE HIGH GATE.

194 RIGHT THE KING SMITING ENEMIES, FROM THE ENTRANCE TO TH COLONNADE OF THE SMALL TEMPLE.

195 AERIAL VIEW OF THE HIGH GATE AND THE MIGDOL.

VISIT

The Madinat Habu enclosure is home to several monuments, but by far the best known and most studied is the memorial temple of Rameses III. It is also one of the best-preserved temples in Egypt. It was known in ancient Egypt as the Mansion of Millions of Years of the King of Upper and Lower Egypt User-Ma'at-Ra-Mery-Amen in the Estate of Amen on the West of Thebes.

The temple of Rameses III is one of the few temples in Egypt to be completely excavated and published. Since 1924, the Oriental Institute of the University of Chicago has worked here, excavating and mapping the site from 1924 to 1937 and recording its scenes and inscriptions from 1924 onward. Because large parts of its ceiling have been preserved, its justly famous decoration was protected from wind and rain and still displays much of its original paint, giving visitors a taste of what the temple originally looked like, with bright, vividly colored—even gaudy—scenes of religious ceremonies and historical events. Two gates pierced the Habu enclosure walls. On the west side, at the rear of the temple, a stone gate that is now blocked was used by temple employees, delivery men, and minor officials. The gate on the east side was the grand processional entrance, and it is the one used by tourists today. In antiquity, two canals met before the gate: one ran west from the Nile, another south along the edge of the cultivation from the temple of Sety I. They joined in a T-shaped harbor beside a great stone quay. It was here that ceremonial barks made their final stop on the West Bank during the Beautiful Festival of the Valley, bringing priests and members of the royal family and divine statues in procession for ceremonies before sailing to Luxor Temple on the East Bank.

The quay and canal today lie beneath a modern

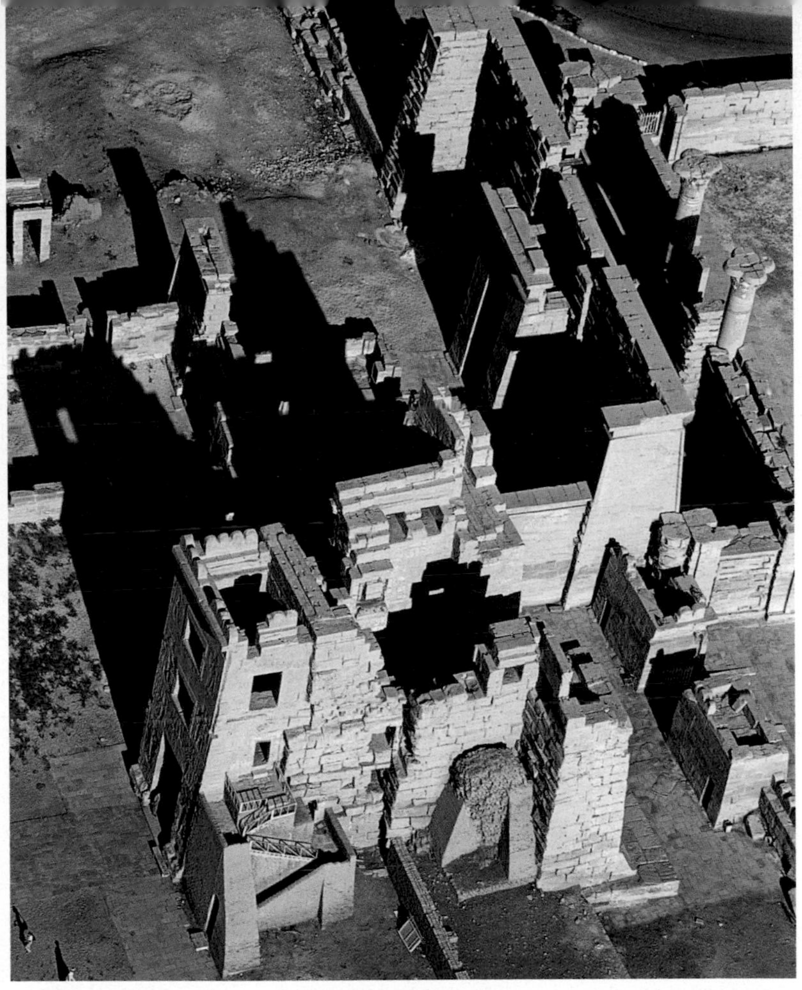

asphalt road. Traces of stone buildings that once lined the canal can be seen in a nineteenth century watercolor by David Roberts, but they have since vanished beneath the rapidly-expanding modern village of Kawm Lulah and a cluster of small coffee shops and backpacker hotels. From the quay west to the temple enclosure, a stone pathway leads to a doorway called the Syrian Gate, modeled after a *migdol,* a western Asiatic fortification. It is also called the High Gate.

◆ THE HIGH GATE ◆

The High Gate leads through two walls that surround the Madinat Habu complex. There is a stone wall with western Asiatic crenellations on its parapets and a mudbrick wall that originally stood 19 meters (60 feet) high and ten meters (33 feet) thick. On either side of the entrance, where tickets are collected and security checks are conducted today, two stone lodges were built for the ancient temple gatekeepers. It is not clear why a foreign military structure would serve as the model for an Egyptian temple enclosure. Temples were divine enclosures that needed to be protected from the forces of an unruly and treacherous world, but at Madinat Habu the term "fortification" seems to have been taken more literally. Some Egyptologists believe that the gate and walls were intended to protect the temple from attacks by an unhappy populace. Certainly, a serious decline in Egypt's economic fortunes is suggested in texts from the reign of Rameses III.

196 LEFT WINDOW OF A ROOM BUILT WITHIN THE HIGH GATE.

196 RIGHT THE MIGDOL SEEN FROM THE NORTHWEST.

196-197 VIEW OF THE ENTRANCE (LEFT) AND PTOLEMAIC BUILDINGS.

For example, in the king's twenty-ninth regnal year unpaid workmen marched from the Valley of the Kings to demand food: "We have been hungry for eighteen days this month," they cried. "We have come here by reason of hunger and thirst; we have no clothes, we have no ointment, we have no fish....Send word to Pharaoh, our good lord, and write to the vizier, our superior, in order that the means of living be provided for us." They got their rations. In the reign of Rameses XI insurrectionists again came to the temple, this time destroying the wooden doors of the High Gate when they were rebuffed.

The gate itself stands 22 meters (71 feet) high. It is decorated with relief carvings of Rameses III smiting enemies in the presence of Ra-Harakhty. There are bound captives from Syria, Sardinia, Palestine, and other Mediterranean and western Asiatic countries on the right, Nubians and Libyans in the presence of Amen-Ra on the left. The faces of the captives on the left wall are especially well carved, and in early morning raking sunlight, show beautiful detail and modeling.

The walls of the gate show a feature characteristic of Rameses III's work at Madinat Habu: along the bottom of the wall, huge hieroglyphs are deeply cut into the sandstone blocks. They give royal names and titles and were carved as if the king was trying to ensure that they could never be erased. The rest of the texts and scenes on the wall are of normal size and depth. Elsewhere in the temple, even more dramatic cutting can be seen, and the deep hieroglyphs serve today as nesting places for owls and sparrows whose droppings pose serious problems to preservation.

Above the entrance, small rooms were built within the gate. Access is by means of a modern staircase left (south) of the entrance. (The rooms currently are not open to visitors, but some of their decorated walls can be glimpsed through the windows.) The rooms were used during royal visits to the temple by women of the king's harem. Reliefs in them show the king surrounded by beautiful young women who hold flowers, play musical instruments, and make affectionate gestures to the king.

But not all the women of the harem were the sweet, innocent young things their lord might have wished for. A papyrus from the time relates how one of Rameses III's minor wives, Tiy, conspired with officials of the harem to have the king murdered and her son, Pentwere, crowned in his place. The conspiracy was discovered, Tiy and the others were arrested, tortured until they confessed, then killed or forced to commit suicide. Rameses III himself died before the proceedings were complete, but whether his death was from natural causes or because he had been poisoned is not known. Apparently, much of the planning for the king's murder took place in these very rooms. (An architectural note: the doors into the harem rooms were designed to be locked from the outside, not from the inside.)

Two seated statues of the goddess Sekhmet flank the court between the gate's twin towers. High up on the walls beside and behind them, shelves carved with the heards of captives were cut to hold royal statues. Scenes show Rameses III offering to Seth, Nut, Atum, Montu, Ma'at, Thoth, and other deities. In other scenes, the king offers bound captives to Amen. They include Libyans, whose faces are drawn frontally to show more dramatically the terror they feel in the presence of Egypt's all-powerful ruler and omnipotent god. Figures here originally had hair, eyes, and beards inlaid with blue faience plaques. Holes were drilled into the wall from which screens or veils could be hung to shroud the figures of the gods.

197 BOTTOM ONE OF THE TWO STATUES OF SEKHMET THAT FLANK THE COURT BETWEEN THE GATE'S TWIN TOWERS.

◆ FORECOURT ◆

West of the High Gate is a huge Forecourt, 200 meters (650 feet) wide, 60 meters (200 feet) deep. Today, the area seems barren, but in antiquity a large array of buildings filled the space. The royal stables stood south of the gate, near the barracks where the king's bodyguards lived. The smells of trees, flowers, vineyards, and pools of lotus flowers wafted from nearby gardens.

Immediately left (south) of the forecourt's east-west axis stand the Chapels of the Divine Votaresses.

◆ THE CHAPELS OF THE DIVINE VOTARESSES ◆

These four small chapels were each built for a God's Wife of Amen, princesses designated by kings in the Late Period as administrators of the cult of Amen. Nearest to the High Gate is the chapel of Amenirdis I (Dynasty 25), called The Vineyard of Anubis. In the center of her four-columned hall a black granite offering table is decorated with loaves of bread, jugs of wine, and cooked fowl. On the walls are lists of the foodstuffs and other offerings required in the next life. A vaulted shrine was built within a larger room behind the columned hall, and it is worth walking through the narrow passage that surrounds it. The light in the passageway comes only from a few small holes in the high ceiling, and the dimness and silence give an impression of what it might have been like to visit here three millennia ago.

The first of the other three shrines belonged to Nitoctris, a daughter of Psammetichus I (Dynasty 26). The second is for Shepenwepet II, the third for Mehitenweskhet, the mother of Nitocris. The bodies of the princesses were buried in small crypts below their chapel floors. Above the doors of the chapels, texts appeal to visitors to pray for the princesses and make offerings to their souls. If visitors do not, the texts threaten, the princesses will "cause them to be sick and their wives to be afflicted." In late antiquity, these buildings became revered places of pilgrimage, but eventually they too were plundered.

◆ THE SMALL DYNASTY 18 TEMPLE ◆

North of these chapels stand the remains of a stone gate built by Nectanebo I (Dynasty 30) as part of a mudbrick wall that has since disappeared. Behind it, to the north, a small chapel was built in Dynasty 18. It is the oldest monument still standing in the Madinat Habu compound. Begun in the reigns of Hatshepsut and Thutmes III, it was defaced by Amenhetep IV/ Akhenaten, then restored by Horemheb, Sety I, and of course, by Rameses III, who decorated its outer walls. Additions were also made in Graeco-Roman times.

The temple lies atop even earlier structures. Traces

198 THE MIGDOL AND THE CHAPEL OF THE DIVINE VOTARESSES ON THE RIGHT.

199 LEFT STONE GATE BUILT BY NECTANEBO II.

199 RIGHT THE TEMPLE OF DYNASTY 18 SEEN FROM THE SACRED LAKE.

have been found of a building from the Middle Kingdom that may have been dedicated to four male and four female deities, the Ogdoad, associated with Egyptian creation myths and the god Amen. For many centuries, from the Middle Kingdom to Graeco-Roman times, the site of the temple was called the Mound of Djeme, and was the scene of religious services that included processions of sacred barks made every ten days to bring the statue of Amen from Luxor Temple to Madinat Habu. In antiquity, this procession entered the small temple from the east, through a portico and columned hall leading to a central bark shrine. Today, one usually enters through a side door in the southern wall into a corridor between the bark shrine on the right (east) and a series of six small chambers on the left (west). These chambers are decorated with scenes of Thutmes III taking part in rituals and purification ceremonies. A huge black granite statue of Thutmes III and Amen, both seated, was found beneath the floor of the central room. The statue is now undergoing restoration by the Oriental Institute of the University of Chicago, who are also cleaning and recording the texts and scenes on the temple walls.

Scenes on the outer walls of the bark shrine deal with the founding of the temple. They are well done and well preserved. On the north side, Thutmes III and the goddess Sefkhet-'abwy "stretch the cord," laying out the temple's plan on the ground, marking its foundation trenches with limestone chips, and digging those trenches with a hoe. In the Late Period and again in Graeco-Roman times, the temple was significantly enlarged: forecourts, porticos, walls, and pylons were added to the east in front of the original Dynasty 18 structure. Two slender columns, 13.4 meters (44 feet) tall, with paint still preserved on their elaborate capitals, grace the entrance of this new addition that was built by Ptolemy VIII. The painted cornice of the front pylon is especially well done.

A small sacred lake lies north of the Dynasty 18 temple. To its west, a Nilometer is marked by a doorway bearing the name of Nectanebo II (Dynasty 30). Until the 1970s, when the Antiquities Department rebuilt the walls around the perimeter of Madinat Habu, village women would come here on Friday mornings and walk seven times around the sacred lake, reciting prayers in hopes of becoming pregnant or avoiding illness. The women perhaps were also responsible for gouges cut into the outer walls of the memorial temple. These were made to gather bits of stone, which were then ground and drunk in potions to cure illness or ensure the birth of a male child.

200 TOP VIEW OF THE FIRST PYLON.

200 BOTTOM DETAIL OF THE FIRST PYLON WITH NAMES OF DEFEATED ENEMIES.

201 TOP RAMESES III SMITING ENEMIES BEFORE AMEN-RA. SOUTH TOWER OF THE FIRST PYLON.

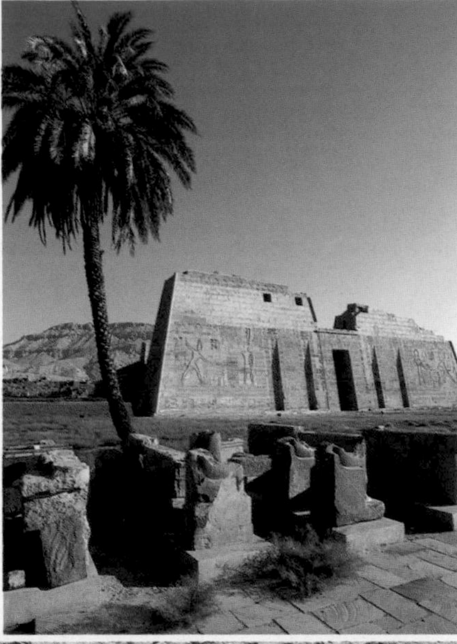

201 BOTTOM LEFT THE ENTRANCE OF THE FIRST PYLON.

201 BOTTOM RIGHT THE HUGE FIGURE OF RAMESES III CARVED ON THE NORTH TOWER OF THE FIRST PYLON.

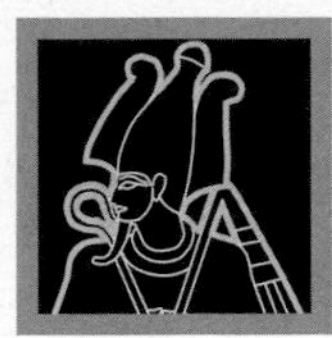

◆ THE MEMORIAL TEMPLE OF RAMESES III ◆

Rameses III regularly copied the works of Rameses II, and the plan of his memorial temple was closely modeled after the Ramesseum. It is much better preserved, however, and visiting Madinat Habu before visiting the Ramesseum helps one better appreciate both monuments.

It is occasionally remarked that Madinat Habu's construction and decoration is of poor quality, that its large and deeply cut hieroglyphs are "grotesque" and "tasteless." One prominent architectural historian described its columns as "gigantic sausages." Even the eminent American Egyptologist, James Henry Breasted, expressed disappointment that this monument had survived so well preserved instead of the more aesthetically-pleasing temples of Dynasty 18. In spite of such statements, there is much in Madinat Habu to appreciate, in part because its colors are better preserved than in any other temple at Thebes except Queen Hatshepsut's at Dayr al-Bahari.

◆ THE FIRST PYLON ◆

The First Pylon stands 27 meters (88 feet) high and 65 meters (211 feet) long. Its two towers are decorated with huge figures of Rameses III smiting prisoners before Ra-Harakhty on the right (north) tower and Amen-Ra on the left (south). Amen holds a sword of victory. Below and behind the gods appear the names of Egypt's defeated enemies. Between the flagstaff niches on the north tower a lengthy text recounts the king's victory over Libya in his twelfth regnal year. On the south tower, Ptah offers long life and victory to the king. There is a stela carved on each side of the central door. The stela on the right is a record of a speech given by Rameses III urging his subjects to remain loyal to him. This seems a highly unusual request and an indication of trouble in Egyptian society.

◆ THE FIRST COURT ◆

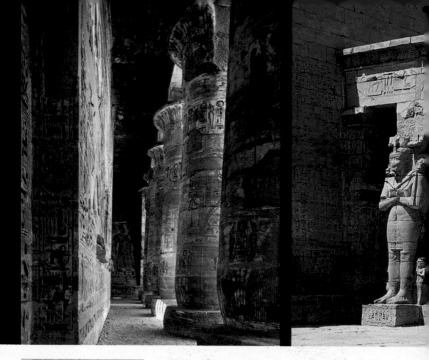

The doorway in the first pylon leads to the First Court, a colonnaded open area 48 x 35 meters (156 x 114 feet). This was not only the forecourt of Rameses III's temple, but of his palace as well. The palace lies beyond the left (south) wall and its location perhaps explains why the forecourt was asymmetrically fitted with seven Osirid pillars on the right (north) side, and eight columns with open papyrus capitals on the left (south).

On the back of the first pylon, the eastern wall of the forecourt, military scenes continue those carved on the pylon's outer face. On the south tower, Rameses III leads Egypt's army and a regiment of Sardinians into a fierce battle against the Libyans. On the north tower, scribes dump basketsful of hands and penises that had been hacked off Libyan soldiers killed in battle. This was how enemy dead were counted so that army units could be commensurately rewarded for their deeds, in effect an early bookkeeping system. The penises are uncircumcised, setting the Libyan soldiers apart from Egyptians for whom circumcision was a near-universal practice.

On the rear (west) wall of the first court, that is, on the face of the second pylon, Rameses III offers prisoners of war to Amen-Ra and Mut. These are captured Sea Peoples, an Indo-European enemy of Egypt from Western Asia. Their capture is also recounted in scenes on the temple's outer north wall. A text describes the king's military campaign in his eighth regnal year. Other battles are shown in elaborate scenes on the north wall, behind the

pillared colonnade, and include an attack on a fortified Amorite building in Syria. The north wall also shows offerings for the daily rituals that were performed in this court. In the upper register, incense is offered and the shrine housing the statue of the god is opened to receive food and clothing.

The south wall of the first court was also the façade of the king's palace. In addition to scenes of the king smiting Egypt's enemies, he is shown on this wall leading processions of officials and family members. At the west end of the wall, he visits the royal stables (the real ones lay just west of the first pylon), where crowds applaud him and dance in his presence.

A central window of appearances was cut into the wall from which the king and senior officials could watch from the palace the preparation of ritual offerings in the courtyard. (The preparations are shown on the north wall of the first court.) In the lower register, on either side of the window, wrestlers engage in stylized combat, flipping their opponents over their shoulders, throwing them to the ground, grabbing them in headlocks and other holds. Most pairs pit an Egyptian against a foreign opponent. The wrestlers shout to each other: "Woe to you, enemy!" "My lord is with me and against you!" or "Watch it! Pharaoh is present!" The audience enthusiastically hurls insults and encouragement. Wrestling was a regular part of temple festivities from at least the Old Kingdom onward and many such scenes are known from Egypt.

202 TOP THE SOUTH COLONNADE OF THE FIRST COURT.

202 BOTTOM LEFT THE FIRST PYLON SEEN FROM THE FIRST COURT.

202 BOTTOM RIGHT WRESTLERS PERFORM IN RELIGIOUS CEREMONIES.

202-203 THE NORTH COLONNADE OF THE FIRST COURT.

203 BOTTOM A SCRIBE DUMPS BASKETSFUL OF PHALLUSES OF ENEMIES, FROM THE NORTH TOWER.

◆ THE SECOND COURT ◆

The painted reliefs in the second court have special importance. They reflect its function as the site of several major festivals, and they trace the stages of religious processions involved in the festivals. Military scenes are not completely lacking, but most of the walls are devoted to festivals of the ithyphallic god, Min, and a guardian of the underworld, Ptah-Sokar. The scenes are detailed and meticulously choreographed. They are also remarkably lively, filled with dancing, singing, clapping, and eating—activities that show Egyptians having a good time even in the serious business of appeasing the gods.

The second court measures 38 meters (125 feet) deep and 42 meters (138 feet) wide. On the left and right (north and south) sides, the roof of the narrow colonnade is supported by columns with closed capitals. The east and west sides have Osirid pillars. On the rear (west) side a row of columns stand behind the pillars, and both pillars and columns stand on a wide ledge. Scenes on the pillars and columns show Rameses III offering to various gods. A part of this court was damaged in early Christian times when it was converted to a church.

The festival of Min appears on the right (north) wall and the rear (west) face of the second pylon's right (north) tower. The festival was a brief one, lasting just one day in mid-February. Scenes outlining the ceremony begin in the northwest corner of the court. Because of its leeward setting and the well-preserved ceiling of the colonnade, the original paint here has remained bright and fresh for over three thousand years. Many tourists are convinced that it has been recently retouched, but that is not the case. The scenes are some of the most impressive at Thebes, well worth a close look and a photograph, especially in mid-morning sunlight.

204 VIEW OF THE SECOND COURT WITH OSIRIS COLUMNS.

204-205 AERIAL VIEW SHOWING ROOFING OF THE PORTICOES OF THE SECOND COURT.

205 BOTTOM COLUMNS
AND PORTICOES OF THE
SECOND COURT.

Royal princes carry their father on a throne in an elaborate palanquin, protected by two figures of the goddess Ma'at. Senior court officials are joined by musicians, dancers, soldiers, and priests as the procession moves west along the main axis toward a chapel of Min. A statue of Min precedes the king (it can be seen at the eastern end of the north wall). It is not hidden in a closed shrine but stands on a palanquin covered with an elaborate red cloth. The priests who carry the image on their shoulders are hidden by the cloth and only the tops of their heads, their feet, and ankles are visible. Rows of priests march before Min and with small statues of Rameses III's ancestors. As the king cuts grain with a curved sickle and flocks of birds are released into the air, he is said to be reborn.

The left (south) wall and the rear (west) face of the second pylon's left (south) tower depicts the festival of Ptah-Sokar, which lasted for ten days in mid-September. Only the last five days of the festival are shown in the scenes here. Starting at the right (west) end of the court's left wall, the king makes offerings to the hawk-headed Sokar-Osiris and three other deities. Farther left (east), a statue of Sokar is placed in a bark shrine and prayers are made to the god by the king and priests. The bark is then carried out and around the perimeter of the temple. Priests carry a palanquin bearing a lotus flower, the symbol of Nefertum, a son of Ptah who is associated with the powers of the sun. On the east wall, Sokar and several other deities are greeted by joyful priests and an audience of clapping, chanting citizens.

◆ THE PORTICO ◆

The terrace at the west side (rear) of the Second Court is decorated with scenes of Rameses III offering to various deities and taking part in the rituals of his coronation. Of particular importance is the procession of royal sons and daughters. Unlike the processions of princes and princesses in the Ramesseum, on which these scenes were modeled, no names were written beside the figures. The ancient scribe left the spaces blank. Apparently the names that can be seen today were added later by the princes themselves when they became Rameside rulers, notably Rameses IV, VI, VII, and VIII. Some Egyptologists think this is because Rameses III died before he could issue instructions as to which son's names were to be included. Each of the princes stands before a deeply cut cartouche of his father. The first four sons wear more elaborate costumes than the others and have a uraeus on their foreheads, probably because they were first in the line of royal succession.

206 AND 207 BOTTOM PAINTED RELIEFS OF THE SECOND COURT WALLS ARE PARTICULARY WELL PRESERVED.

207 TOP THE PORTICO ON THE WEST SIDE OF THE SECOND COURT IS DECORATED WITH PAINTED RELIEFS SHOWING RAMESES III.

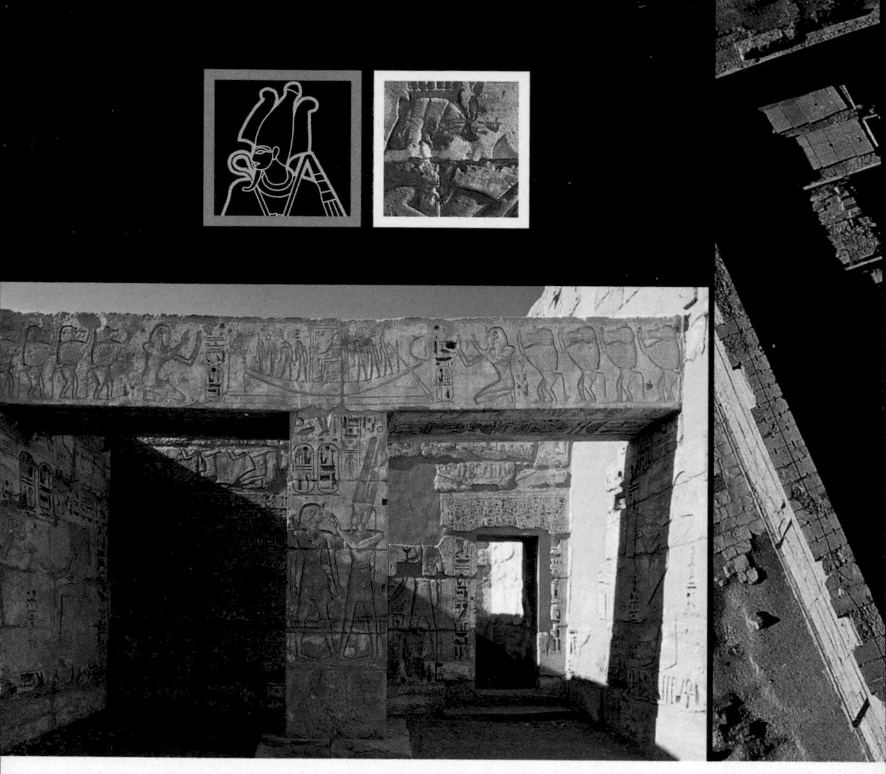

◆ FIRST HYPOSTYLE HALL ◆

From the portico to the rear (west) wall of the temple, only the lower courses of central stone walls and columns in the central rooms are preserved. The upper courses were removed by later builders who used the temple as a quarry. But the extensive damage allows one to see how closely spaced and heavy its columns were, and how claustrophobic the hypostyle halls must have seemed. The 52 side chambers at the rear of the temple, on the other hand, are still in good condition. From their decoration we can infer what functions they served. These rooms were off limits to all but upper levels of the priesthood, for it was here that gods and goddesses took up residence on festival days. The sanctity of these rooms deep within the sanctuary was emphasized by their architectural features: raised floors, lowered ceilings, small size, and increasing darkness. A huge double leaf door that hung in the gateway behind the hypostyle hall was closed and sealed except when priests came to make offerings. Along the bottom of its doorjambs, small holes held dowels to which thin sheets of beaten copper were attached.

The first hypostyle hall follows a standard plan with eight large columns along the east-west axis and sixteen smaller ones to the left and right, an arrangement that permitted the installation of clerestory lighting. The columns are deeply incised, and their hieroglyphs and figures still show traces of brightly colored plaster filler. The side chambers on the north and south sides of the hall are well preserved and worth a visit. The six on the north (right) are chapels dedicated to different deities. Moving from east to west (front to back), the first has scenes of Rameses III, a queen, and several royal children. The second was dedicated to Ptah, the third to the sacred ceremonial equipment of Thoth, Isis, Wepwawet, and other deities.

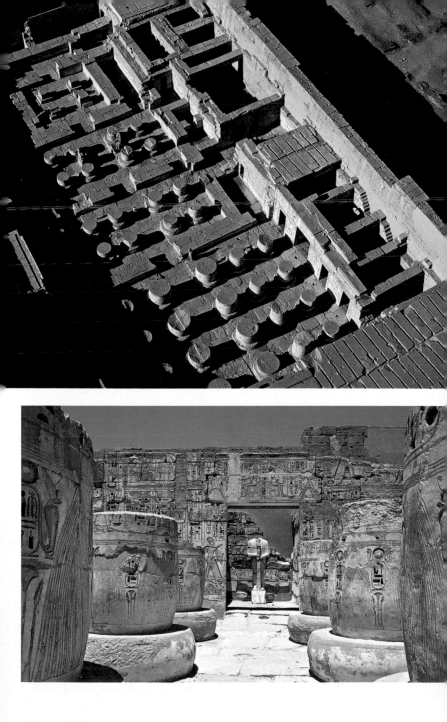

208 TOP RELIEF WITH A QUEEN PLAYING SISTRA.

208 BOTTOM SIDE CHAMBERS OF THE HYPOSTYLE HALL.

208-209 AERIAL VIEW OF THE THREE HYPOSTYLE HALLS AND THE CHAPEL OF RAMESES III.

209 BOTTOM THE FIRST HYPOSTYLE HALL WITH A STATUE OF PTAH IN THE BACKGROUND.

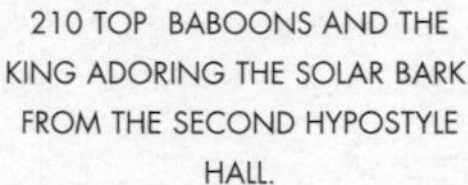

210 TOP BABOONS AND THE KING ADORING THE SOLAR BARK. FROM THE SECOND HYPOSTYLE HALL.

210 BOTTOM RAMESES III ADORES THE GOD HAPI.

210-211 STATUES FROM THE TEMPLE OF AMENHETEP III REUSED BY RAMESES III IN THE THIRD HYPOSTYLE HALL.

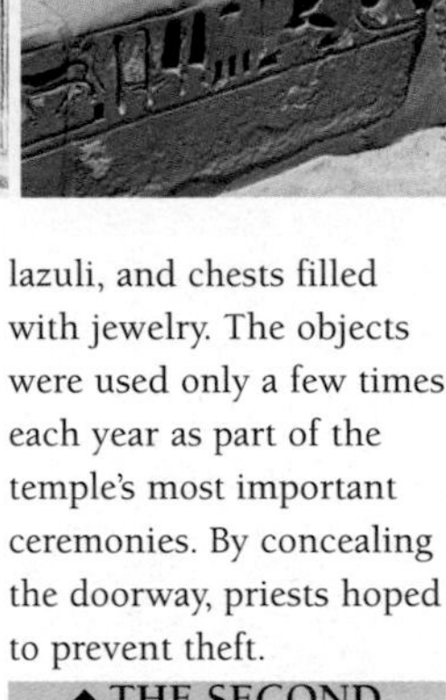

The fourth housed a bark of Sokar that was used in ceremonies shown in scenes in the second court. A fragmentary alabaster statue of Ptah stands here today. The fifth chapel, which includes a room with a single pillar and a small side chamber is decorated with scenes of butchering, and of the king offering cuts of meat to various gods. The actual butchering was probably not performed here—the rooms are too small and there is no drain in the floor—but piles of cooked meat may have been ritually offered up to the gods. The sixth chapel, in the northwestern corner of the hall, served as a room for the sacred bark of Rameses III.

A suite of five small rooms is entered through a doorway in the southeastern (front left) corner of the first hypostyle hall. At first glance, the door appears to have been cut after the hall's south wall was decorated: figures of prisoners are cut through and partly missing. But in fact, the cutting was original, and a deliberate ruse. Most of the year, this opening was plastered over and painted to look like a part of the solid stone wall. The reason was that the suite served as the storeroom for the temple's large collection of religious objects. Inside, the king and Amen-Ra are shown examining mounds of gold, silver, copper, lapis lazuli, and chests filled with jewelry. The objects were used only a few times each year as part of the temple's most important ceremonies. By concealing the doorway, priests hoped to prevent theft.

◆ THE SECOND AND THIRD HYPOSTYLE HALLS ◆

There is little of interest in these two damaged rooms, but chambers on their right (north) and left (south) sides contain well-preserved reliefs.

On the right (north) side of the second hypostyle hall, a small rectangular vestibule is decorated with scenes of the king and Ra-Harakhty. A larger chamber, entered through a door in the vestibule's left (west) wall, is partly

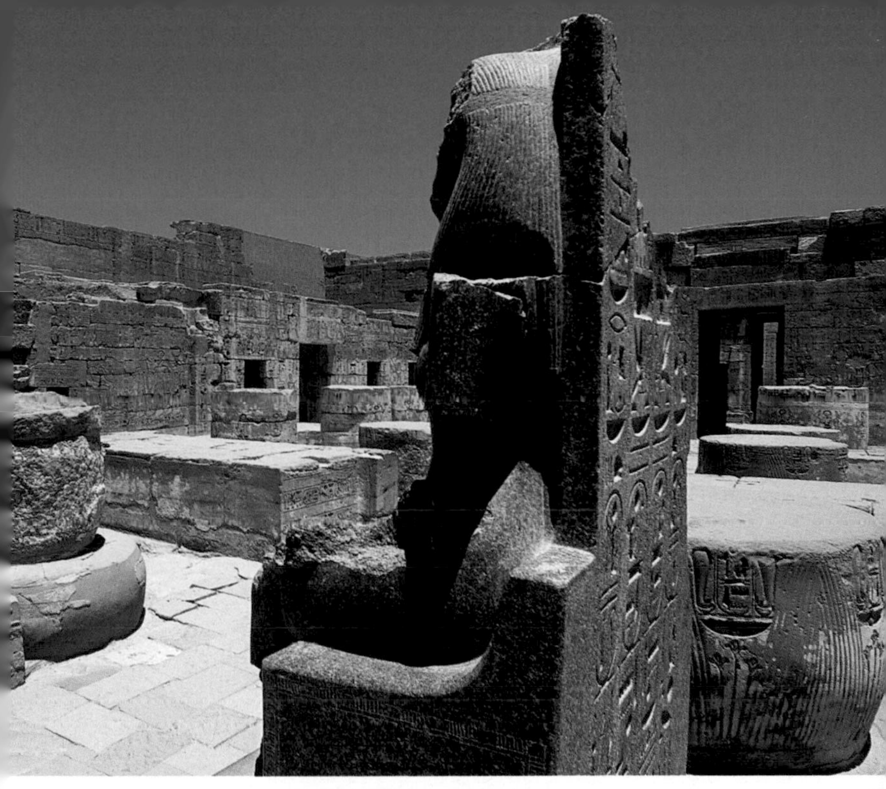

open to the sky and scenes on its architrave show the bark of the sun being adored by lines of baboons whose cries were thought to announce the dawn. Other scenes deal with the sun's journey through the heavens and with sunset. A small staircase leads from the vestibule to the roof, and traces of decoration suggest that numerous small shrines were erected there to local Egyptian deities. Directly on the left (south) side of the second hypostyle hall, a larger suite of eight rooms was devoted to the king's reception by Osiris in the afterlife. In the first on the left (east), the king receives offerings from Thoth and a priest and performs the Opening of the Mouth ritual. Thoth writes the king's name on the leaves of a persea tree. In a chamber to the west with two columns along its midline, the king offers to Ptah, Amen-Ra, Sekhmet, Nefertum, Isis, Ptah-Sokar-Osiris, and Horus. In the small chambers beyond, thin shafts of sunlight stream through small apertures in the ceilings. On one wall, sunlight illuminates a fine copy of a vignette from chapter 110 of the Book of the Dead, in which the king tills the fields of Iaru in the afterlife, harvests grain, and presents it to a seated Nile god. Elsewhere in these rooms, the king describes his work in the fields: "I know the lakes of the fields of offerings in which I am. I am strong therein. I am glorified therein. I exist therein. I plough therein. I reap therein. I beget therein. I remember...I am alive!" In the innermost chamber, a vignette from Book of the Dead chapter 148 depicts a procession of seven "celestial cows" and a bull, associated both with the sun god and Osiris.

Chambers at the rear of the temple include a third hypostyle hall, but they are poorly preserved and sparsely decorated. We will ignore them and retrace our steps to the entrance and turn right (south) to examine the exterior walls of the temple and the buildings that surround it.

◆ WITHIN THE TEMPLE ENCLOSURE ◆

The exterior rear wall of the south tower of the first pylon is carved with a dramatic scene of Rameses III standing in a war chariot drawn by two majestic horses. He is a confident charioteer: his right leg is nonchalantly draped over the side of the chariot and his foot rests on the pole. The king is racing into Nile marshlands, hunting wild bulls, his long spear poised for the kill. Two bulls already lay dead in the papyrus thicket and a third crumples slowly to the ground. Fish and birds flee in panic as soldiers armed with bows race forward, following their king into the fray. In the scene above, the king hunts antelope and wild asses. Egyptian kings routinely boasted about their prowess as hunters, especially of lions and bulls, and such traditional and highly stylized scenes were routinely included in temple relief to demonstrate their control over the chaotic forces of nature. Immediately south of the temple stand the remains of a brick palace where Rameses III held court when at Madinat Habu. Actually, two palaces were built here, one atop the other. It is the second that has been partially restored and its walls topped with a protective course of fired brick and cement. Evidence of the first palace can still be seen on the southern outer wall of the temple; there are traces of barrel vaults, walls, and holes cut into the stone. The plan of the second palace, modeled after that of Rameses II at the Ramesseum, includes a series of ceremonial rooms between the window of appearances in the south temple wall and the king's audience hall. Inscriptions adjacent to the window of appearances state that the king came here "to see his father, Amen" during such ceremonies as the Opet Festival and the Beautiful Festival of the Valley. It was through the doorways in this temple wall that Rameses III entered the palace, carried on a sedan chair into the audience hall, a rectangular room with four columns and a stone dais for the royal throne. To its immediate

212 SOLDIERS MARCHING WITH THEIR KING. RELIEF FROM THE BACK OF THE FIRST PYLON, SOUTH TOWER.

213 TOP RAMESES III SHOOTS AN ARROW (ABOVE) AND HUNTS BULLS IN THE MARSH.

213 BOTTOM DETAIL OF FISH AND BIRDS IN THE NILE MARSHLANDS.

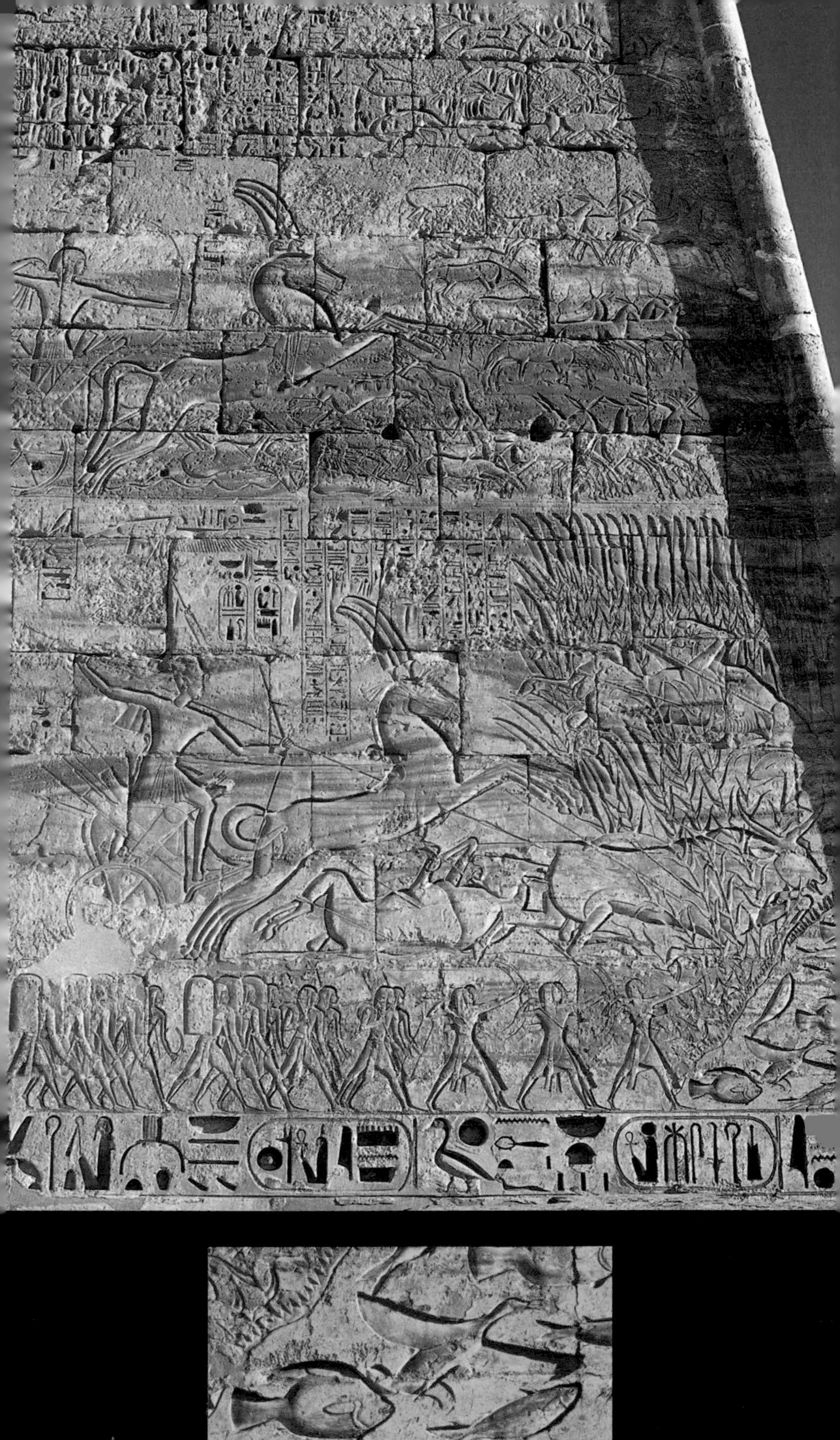

214 ROWS OF CAPTIVES CARVED ON THE EXTERIOR OF THE SECOND PYLON.

214-215 AND 215 BOTTOM PALACE OF RAMESES III ON THE SOUTH SIDE OF HIS MEMORIAL TEMPLE.

right (west) there is a toilet for His Majesty's comfort.

The south outer wall of the temple is covered with one of the longest inscriptions known from ancient Egypt. It was based on a similar text inscribed on the walls of the Ramesseum and is called the Madinat Habu Calendar. The text lists many of the ceremonies that were performed here each year. Entries give the name of the festival, its dates and duration, and details of the kinds of offerings that are to be made. In one festival, for example, each kind of bread to be offered up is named, the type and quantity of flour to be used is given, and the size and shape of the loaves and the number of loaves to be baked are described. Servants bearing baskets of offerings on their heads march in procession below the inscription.

The area between the palace and the western mudbrick enclosure wall is filled with the remains of temple offices and priestly residences. These continue around the corner, between the temple and the enclosure's western gate. In the southwestern corner four stone columns that formed part of the residence of the Dynasty 21 scribe Butehamen are still standing. He was one of the officials at the end of the New Kingdom who was responsible for supervising the cutting of tombs in the Valley of the Kings. Butehamen and other artisans from Dayr al-Medina moved into the Madinat Habu compound when economic conditions had deteriorated to the point that bands of marauders were attacking and robbing people in the workmen's village. The craftsmen, fearing for their safety, moved within the temple walls for protection.

The west wall of the temple is covered with scenes of military campaigns against the Kushites, a people who lived in Nubia south of the First Cataract, and against the Libyans in the west. The Libyan battles continue on the temple's north outer wall (at its west end), where battles against the Sea People are also shown (at the east).

The Libyans and the Sea People joined forces against Egypt during the reign of Rameses III. For a quarter-century, they posed a serious threat to its northern and western borders. In the fifth year of the king's reign, his army lashed out in the attacks documented in these scenes. These battles temporarily quashed the enemy, but Rameses III was forced to attack again in his eighth year and these battles, too, which finally brought the Sea People to their knees, are shown in detail.

Of particular interest is the naval battle fought off the coast of western Asia. It is one of the earliest naval battles ever depicted. Some of the enemy's boats have capsized and bodies of dead sailors float in the churning waters. An Egyptian craft with a duck-headed prow makes ready to draw alongside an enemy craft and a sailor in the crow's nest lobs stones at it with a slingshot. In the second court, where other scenes depict the battle with the Sea Peoples, Rameses III described how he cleverly led the Sea Peoples to defeat: "A net was prepared for them, to ensnare them. As they entered secretly in the mouth of the harbor, they fell into it, being caught in their place."

Between the temple and the northern enclosure wall there is a confusing hodge-podge of Roman and Christian buildings from the ancient town of Djeme. Numerous carved blocks from a Christian church lie scattered about the area.

2

THE VILLAGE OF DAYR AL-MADINA

216 TOP OSTRAKON FOUND AT DAYR AL-MADINA, NOW IN THE CAIRO MUSEUM.

217 THE VILLAGE (FOREGROUND) AND THE PTOLEMAIC TEMPLE.

THE HISTORY

During the reign of Rameses III, a scribe inventoried the houses that stood along the edge of the cultivation on the West Bank. It offers a fascinating glimpse of what the ancient West Bank might then have looked like and of the inhabitants that resided there. For example, between two of the memorial temples built here stood the homes of "a slave, a woman, a Sardinian mercenary, a priest, the retainer of a Sardinian mercenary, a goat herd, a quartermaster, a stable-master, a tenant-farmer, and a soldier." There were also "coppersmiths, embalmers, cattle-branders, beekeepers, sailors, scribes of the law-court, and various foreigners: Sea Peoples, Libyans, Syrians, and the teher-chariot-warriors, who may have been Hittites." Like the villages in Upper Egypt today, hovels lay beside great houses, and lowly peasants lived next door to wealthy officials. There is no evidence of urban planning. But a kilometer to the southwest lay a well planned and neatly constructed village of mud and stone where the men responsible for cutting and decorating the tombs of Egypt's New Kingdom pharaohs lived with their families. It was a small village called in Egyptian, *Pa Demi*, The Village, or *Ta Set Ma'at*, The Place of Truth. Today, it goes by its Arabic name, Dayr al-Madina, The Monastery of the City. For five hundred years, Dayr al-Madina was a thriving community of architects, stone masons, draftsmen, artists, carpenters, goldsmiths, and other craftsmen. After it was abandoned at the end of the New Kingdom, only a scattering of people came here, mostly to visit a small temple nearby or to use some of its buildings for storage. In the Ptolemaic period, a small temple to Hathor was constructed north of the site. It was later converted to a Christian church and a monastery (whence the Arabic name). But gradually, Dayr al-Madina disappeared beneath blowing sand and lay forgotten for nearly two millennia.

Not until the nineteenth century did anyone realize that Dayr al-Madina was a site rich in antiquities. From 1815 to World War II, excavations, mostly illegal, recovered thousands of objects from Dayr al-Madina. Few of them were great works of art or valuable pieces of gold or silver. Most, in fact, were nothing but small sherds of limestone on which ancient scribes had written memos or practiced their drawing skills. These limestone chips, called ostraca, are the ancient equivalent of Post-It notes, and most of their texts dealt with the mundane affairs of everyday life. For an Egyptologist, these documents are treasures more valuable than gold. They allow us to visit the three-thousand-year-old world of these artisans and peer over their shoulders as they worked and played. There are marriage contracts, letters, receipts, love

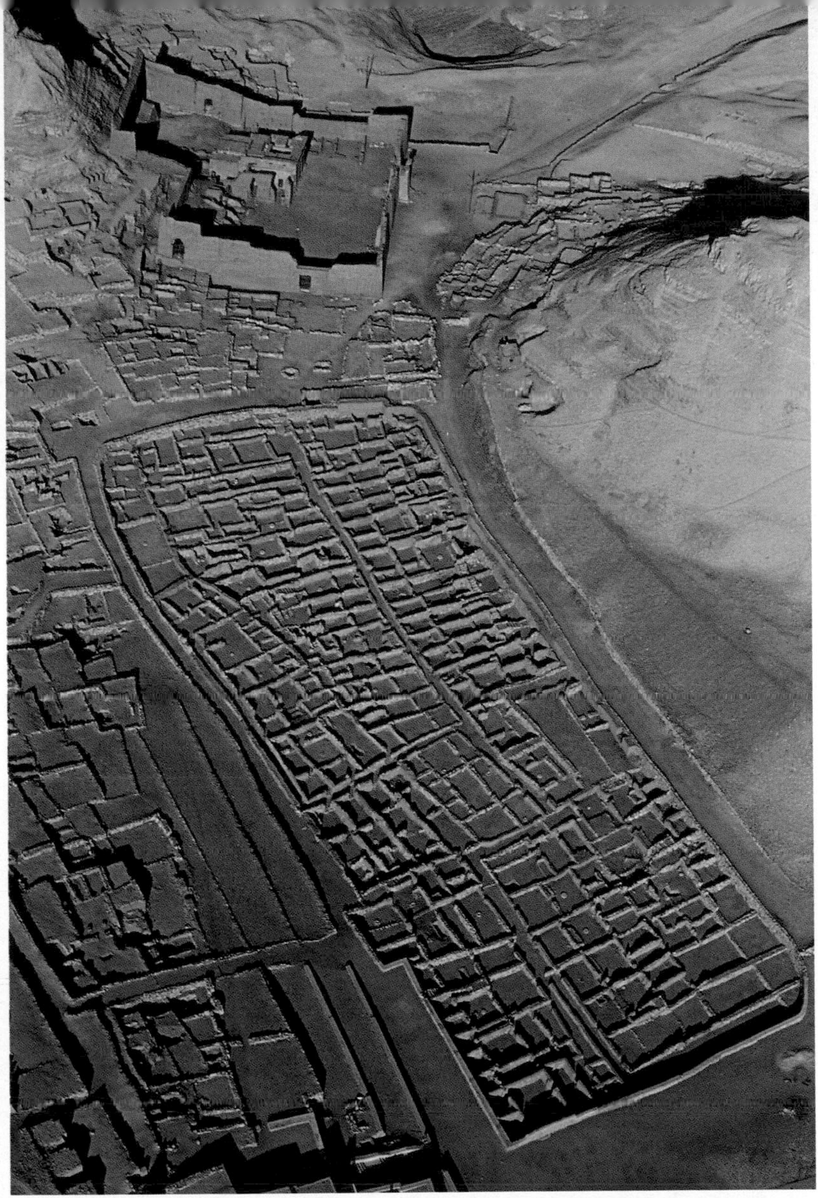

notes, angry complaints, inventories—thousands of documents that describe in often intimate detail the lives of the people who lived here.

During much of its history, about fifty families lived at Dayr al-Madina (the number fluctuated from about forty to over a hundred) and in some cases we can trace the history of a house by a single family for a dozen generations or more. Today, we can identify seventy houses, each built of stone and mud brick in a walled town complex that covered about 5,100 square meters (53,500 square feet). There was only one entrance into the compound and it was regularly guarded, not so much to isolate the workmen as to protect the valuable materials with which they worked.

Each house covered about 70 square meters (750 square feet) and followed a fairly standard plan.

VISIT

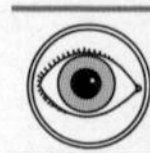

Typical is the home of the workman Sennedjem, who lived during the reigns of Sety I and Rameses II. His house lies in the southwestern corner of the village, at the edge of the modern parking lot, a few meters in front of a flight of steps leading to his tomb (TT 1). Its entrance lies at the end of a long corridor paralleling the principal north-south path through the village. A doorway leads into a small foyer off which lie three storerooms, probably intended for tools, clothing, and other bric-a-brac of life, and maybe also used as servants' quarters. One room had pots set into the floor for grain storage. To its west, a well-built door with a stone lintel led into a rectangular reception hall with a mudbrick bench standing against the south wall. Beyond lay another reception room with a (now-missing) palm trunk column on a limestone base in its center, supporting the (now-missing) roof. A low bench along the eastern wall served as a bed or a seat, and two stelae were set into the wall above it. We know from goods placed in Sennedjem's tomb that the furniture here included small stools and chairs, beds, boxes, chests and tables, most of it purely utilitarian, but well-made and nicely decorated. A flight of steps led to the roof. Accommodations at Dayr al-Madina were spartan, the houses small. Sennedjem, his wife Iyneferti, and their several sons and daughters probably spent a good part of their time on the roof or outside the house, talking with friends and colleagues. The menfolk, of course, worked much of the day, so most of the time the village belonged to women, children, and the elderly. Compared to the homes of most Egyptians, Dayr al-Madina offered comfortable accommodations and attractive ones. The walls of the houses were painted white and they had small, red doors. The floors were plastered. Brightly-colored textiles adorned the furniture and stelae and amulets hung from the walls. At the back of the house lay the kitchen and small room, including a cellar for food storage. There was no money used in

LEGEND

1 *ENTRANCE*
2 *CORRIDOR*
3 *FOYER*
4A, B, C *STOREROOMS*
5 *RECTANGULAR RECEPTION HALL*
6 *SECOND RECEPTION HALL*
7 *STAIRS TO ROOF*
8 *KITCHEN*
9 *SMALL STOREROOM*
10 *CELLAR*

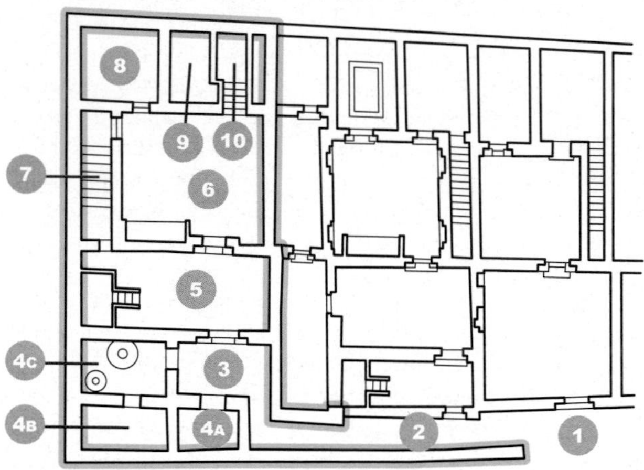

219 THE BRICK WALLS OF THE HOUSES OF THE VILLAGE.

ancient Egypt, and the government paid the workmen in kind. Sennedjem's cellar and storerooms would have housed these monthly payments of grain (for making bread), barley (for making beer), dried fish, vegetables (such as beans, garlic, onions, and lettuce), fruits (such as pomegranates, grapes, dates, and figs), fuel for the bread oven, and water. On special occasions, there were also baskets of dates, sweet cakes, honey, wine, and spices (cumin, coriander, and dill), salt, various cooking oils, meat, and fowl. Some of these foods came raw, others ready-made, and they came in large quantities. We have records of a family receiving a payment that included several hundred loaves of bread and many liters of beer. There were also regular deliveries of cloth and clothing, furniture, cooking utensils, and lamps. Wood cutters, water carriers, fishermen, gardeners, washermen, potters, and delivery men were employed full time to serve the needs of the Dayr al-Madina craftsmen. Peer over the walls of Sennedjem's house and look inside. It is not difficult to imagine the evenings that he spent in these rooms, playing games with his family, telling stories, dressing for a special festival. One can imagine him sitting in the columned hall, talking to fellow workmen about the next day's schedule. One can see him walking into the kitchen to prepare a snack of bread and spices and climbing to the roof, sitting quietly, eating beneath the stars.When Sennedjem left home each morning for work in the Valley of the Kings, he and his colleagues hiked over the hill along a path still used by tourists today. The trip takes under an hour, the return trip, because it is mostly downhill, slightly less. If the workmen chose not to return to their village at the end of the day, perhaps because of the heat, a family argument, or pressures of work, they could stay the night in one of the small stone huts built at the top of the hill. Here, the workmen could enjoy "the sweet breath of the north wind," sitting together at dusk, talking, carving amulets and shabtis, drinking bowls of thick beer their wives had carried up from the village.

Digging a royal tomb must have been generally unpleasant work. Limestone is a relatively soft material and not difficult to carve. But when shattered, its razor sharp edges can easily cut even tough skin and it produces thick dust that makes breathing and seeing difficult. Maintaining the correct axial alignment of tomb chambers, ensuring that room corners were squared and walls vertical took patience and skill. But the craftsmen did it extremely well, even in this uncomfortable environment, using nothing more than a plumb bob, a piece of string, and a carpenter's square.

Cutting the limestone was done using copper chisels and wooden mallets, chert hand-axes, and sandstone abrasives. Such simple tools could be repaired and re-sharpened as needed, and although simple, they worked well. Lighting the dark tomb interior was done using bowls of vegetable oil in which a wick was floated and lit. The wicks were of standard thickness and length and the rate at which they burned provided a measure of the work day. Salt was added to the oil to prevent it from smoking.

220 PTOLEMAIC TEMPLE AT DAYR AL-MADINA.

220-221 THE PRONAOS WALLS ARE COVERED WITH RELIEFS SHOWING THE KING OFFERING TO VARIOUS DEITIES.

◆ PTOLEMAIC TEMPLE ◆

At the northern end of the village, a number of small temples were built in the New Kingdom. Some of these were replaced in Ptolemaic times, and indeed, there is a well-preserved example of a temple from that period still standing. It was begun during the reign of Ptolemy IV Philopater and work on it continued for the next sixty years, under Ptolemy VI Philometer and Ptolemy VIII Euergetes II. It was built over several earlier small temples, perhaps similar to the still-visible remains immediately north, where there is a temple of Amenhetep I, a Hathor shrine of Sety I, and a temple to the Theban Triad built by Rameses II.

The Ptolemaic temple was dedicated to the goddesses Hathor and Ma'at. It is a small building lying within a mud brick enclosure wall within which there are also tiny New Kingdom chapels erected by Dayr al-Madina's occupants and dozens of Greek, demotic and Coptic Christian graffiti that cover its outer walls.

Within the enclosure we enter a vestibule which has two papyrus columns. A low flight of steps leads into the pronaos, defined by a pair of columns, pillars, and curtain walls. Figures on the columns show Amenhetep, son of Hapu, and Imhotep, both architects who were deified after their death. Amenhetep, son of Hapu, may have built an earlier temple on this site. The curtain wall is covered with reliefs showing the king offering to various deities. In the rear wall of the pronaos are three doorways and above them seven Hathor heads.

The three doorways each leads into a long, narrow chapel. The chapel on the left is dedicated to Amen-Sokar-Osiris and has well-carved reliefs whose subject is the judgment of the dead.

Judgment scenes such as this are not common in temple decoration, and more often are found in tombs or on papyrus scrolls.

The limbs of Ptolemaic relief figures often look like overstuffed sausages, but these are carved with greater restraint, and are well proportioned and modeled.

Dog-headed genii and figures of Ptolemy IV can be seen in the doorway. On the left wall, Ma'at leads a figure of the deceased king toward the hall of judgment. Above him, forty-two judges sit ready to render their decision on his fate. Anubis and Horus weigh the heart of the deceased on a balance against the feather of Ma'at, and ibis-headed Thoth stands nearby, recording the result. A lion-hippopotamus-crocodile figure called Ammit sits nearby, ready to devour the heart of the unjust. At the far right, Osiris sits on his throne. On the rear wall, the king, Ptolemy IV Philopater, offers to Osiris and Isis. On the right wall, a bark of Sokar-Osiris stands on a pedestal, and to its right, Ptolemy VI offers to Anubis and Min.

The Ptolemies were enamored of Egyptian hieroglyphs and religious motifs and delighted in taking simple iconographic elements and making them complex. For example, look at the lintel above the door as you leave this chapel, where four-headed rams and ram-headed scarabs have been depicted.

The central chapel was dedicated by Ptolemy IV to Hathor and she receives offerings from Ptolemy IV, his sister Arsinoe, and Ptolemy VII, who continued the decoration.

The right chapel was for Amen-Ra-Osiris, and its reliefs show the king before various deities, including Hathor, Isis, Nephthys, Horus, Anubis, Mut, Amen, and others.

Leaving the Ptolemaic temple enclosure, turn left (north) to a strange feature known as the Great Pit. Great it is: over 50 meters (164 feet) deep and 30 meters (98 feet) wide, it is thought to have been an attempt to dig a well so that Dayr al-Madina could have a convenient supply of water. Why such a massive excavation would have been necessary has never been explained. Water was available only a few hundred meters away in the agricultural land and could easily be transported by donkey. The search for water was not successful. Archaeologists who dug here found that work had been abandoned and the hole filled with tons of sand and pots herds.

2 A WALK OVER THE HILLS

Footpaths connect the sites on the West Bank and many are the same ones taken by ancient craftsmen on their way to work or by priests and guards who made tours of inspection of the temples and tombs. Several routes climb over the Theban Hills and offer outstanding views of the monuments and the emerald green Nile Valley. None of the paths is particularly difficult—they are uphill walks rather than hikes—and most can be made in less than two hours. From October through April the weather is usually balmy, and what ancient Egyptians called "the sweet breath of the north wind" blows refreshingly across the hillsides. On clear days, it is possible to see 40 kilometers (25 miles) or more, to the Red Sea Hills in the east, and to towns north and south along the Nile.

The shortest and easiest of the walks is between the Valley of the Queens and Dayr al-Madina (and should be made in that direction, not the reverse, because there are fewer hills to climb). Leaving the gate at the Valley of the Queens entrance and turning left (north), a narrow path leads northeast across gently rising desert to a low hill. Into its northern slope, a series of chapels have been cut. One was dedicated in the New Kingdom to the goddess Meretseger, "She who loves silence," the goddess of the Theban Hills. Another was cut for the god Ptah. This is the Valley of the Dolmen, and there are also several fine stelae from the reign of Rameses III cut into the bedrock. Stone walls surround an irregular courtyard in front of them, and nearby there are traces of small stone huts, also of Rameside date. From here, the path continues on to Dayr al-Madina.

The most beautiful walk is that from the Valley of the Kings to Dayr al-Madina. The first few hundred meters of the trail are steep, but then the path begins to level off and rises gently to the top of the hill. From there, it is downhill the rest of the way to Dayr al-Madina. It is much easier to walk the path in this direction than to start at Dayr al-Madina. Start beside KV 17, the tomb of Sety I where the path is marked. During the first part of the walk, you will climb about 100 meters (325 feet) and then skirt the western and southern ends of the Valley of the Kings. From here, the path offers excellent views of the valley. At the valley's southernmost limit, above KV 34, the tomb of Thutmes III, you will see the remains of a small stone hut where necropolis guards stood watch in the late New Kingdom. You can follow the edge of the cliffs surrounding the valley to the west and north from here, walking along the lower slope of the pyramid-shaped summit, known as al-Qurn in Arabic, meaning "the horn." On your left you will pass several dozen small stone shrines, each about the size and shape of a shoe box, in which workmen from Dayr al-Madina placed tiny statuettes, stelae, and perhaps candles. They knelt here, facing al-Qurn, and prayed to Meretseger, the mountain's goddess.

222 TOP WORKER FROM THE TOMB OF REKHMIRE.

223 THE WHITE PATHS LEAD FROM DAYR AL-MADINA (BOTTOM OF THE PHOTO) TO THE VALLEY OF THE KINGS (TOP CENTER).

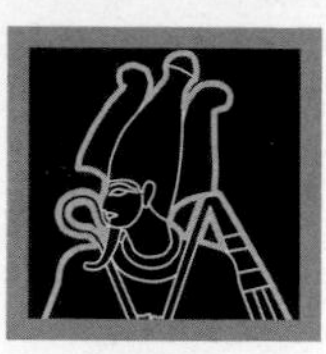

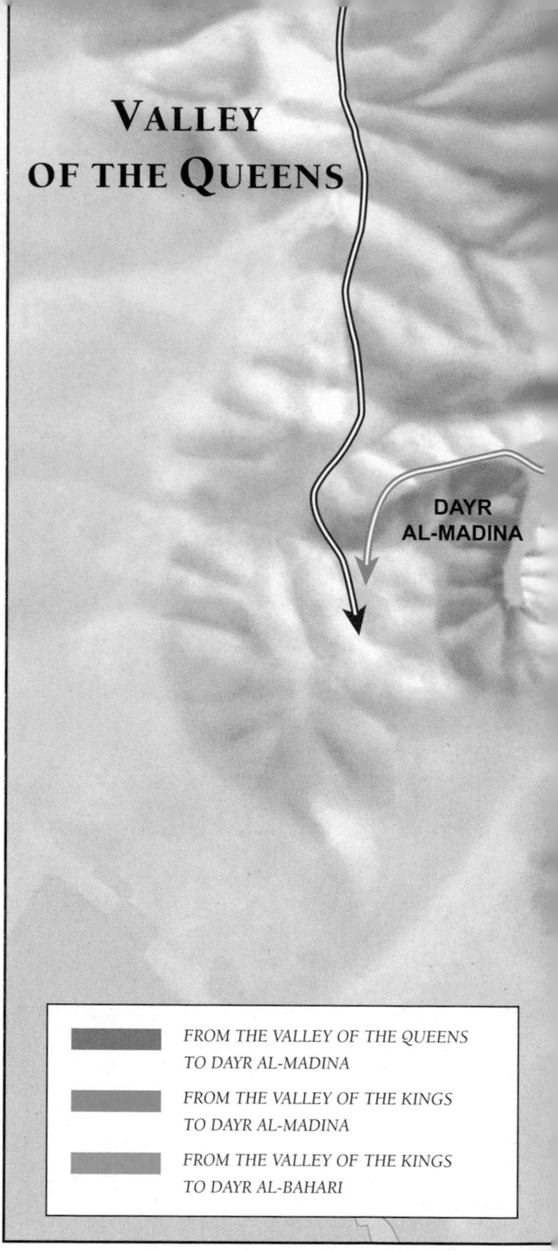

VALLEY OF THE QUEENS

DAYR AL-MADINA

FROM THE VALLEY OF THE QUEENS TO DAYR AL-MADINA

FROM THE VALLEY OF THE KINGS TO DAYR AL-MADINA

FROM THE VALLEY OF THE KINGS TO DAYR AL-BAHARI

This path will take you around the edge of the valley past another guard's hut, and you will return to the valley floor near the tomb of Rameses II.

If you continue southward up the hill past Thutmes III's tomb, you will reach the base of a steep cliff that defines al-Qurn. On your right, you will pass a wide drainage field carved by torrential rain-generated floods and defined by a surface deposit of dark stone debris. Across it lies KV 39, thought by some to be the tomb of Thutmes I, the first tomb dug in or near the Valley of the Kings.

At the top of the footpath, a village of stone huts was built for workmen digging and decorating tombs in the Valley of the Kings. This apparently was where they chose to spend nights instead of walking back to their homes in Dayr al-Madina. The ground around the huts is littered with ancient pottery and stone tools. Thirty-million-year-old fossil clamshells lie about, some the size of a fingernail, others the size of a fist, reminders of a time when this area lay beneath the sea.

The view of the Nile Valley from here is breathtaking. The Tombs of the Nobles, dozens of memorial temples, the green fields, and brown villages of the West Bank are all laid out at one's feet. Beyond them lie the Nile, the city of Luxor, and the Red Sea Hills.

From the hilltop, the path continues southward, almost entirely downhill. There are one or two short stretches where you may have to use your hands for balance while clambering along the narrow path, but the route is neither difficult nor dangerous. The path eventually forks and will

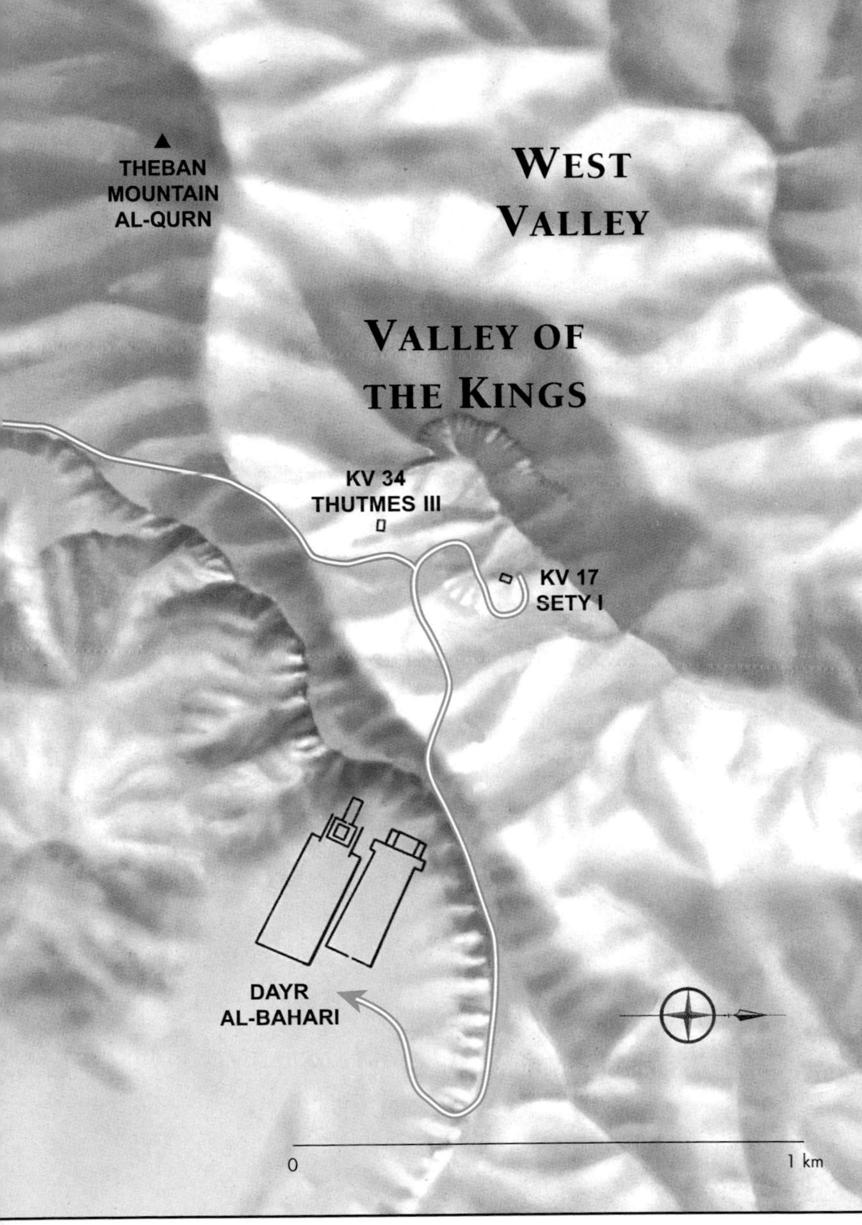

lead either to the shrines of Meretseger and Ptah (see the walk described above) or to the village of Dayr al-Madina, where ice cold water and soft drinks are available beside the tomb of Sennedjem. One also can continue another kilometer southward to Madinat Habu where there are several small cafes.

An alternative trip over the hill also begins at the tomb of Sety I, but instead of walking up the hill and to the south, you walk upward to the first fork in the path and turn left (east). This path will then circle the east side of the valley and take you to the hill directly above Dayr al-Bahari. The path then descends north of the temple of Queen Hatshepsut, past tombs of Dynasty 11, and ends at the Dayr al-Bahari parking lot.

3

THE VALLEY OF THE KINGS

INTRODUCTION

3

It was called The Great, Noble Necropolis of Millions of Years of Pharaoh, and for five hundred years it was the burial place of Egypt's New Kingdom rulers. Sixty-two tombs and twenty unfinished pits have been found here, seven of them in the large West Valley of the Kings, the rest in the East Valley of the Kings. It is the East Valley that is visited by most tourists.

The Valley of the Kings was chosen as the royal burial place for several reasons. The quality of its limestone bedrock is generally good: solid, strong, and at least in some areas, relatively free of cracks and fractures. The valley was convenient: a long wadi, along which a funeral procession could move, meanders from the northern end of the Theban Necropolis westward to the Valley of the Kings; footpaths provided easy access over the hills to areas to the south and east. It was easily protected: steep cliffs surround it and guard huts built above them provided 360 degree coverage. The large mountain at the southern end of the Valley of the Kings, al-Qurn or "Horn," looks from the valley—and only from the valley—rather like a pyramid, a form associated with solar deities who play so great a role in the iconography of royal tombs.

Tombs in both the West and East Valley follow a common numbering system that was first established in 1827 by John Gardner Wilkinson. Wilkinson numbered the twenty-one tombs accessible in his day from the entrance of the valley southward and from west to east. Since then, tombs have been added to the list in the order of their discovery. KV 62, the tomb of Tutankhamen, is the most recent.

No two royal tombs in the Valley of the Kings are precisely alike. As priests developed differing explanations about the nature of the sun's journey through the night sky and the king's journey to the netherworld, tomb plans changed to reflect their itineraries. The earliest Dynasty 18 tombs were cut at the base of sheer cliffs, deliberately sited at points

where rainfall might send water and debris cascading down to cover their entrances. They are relatively small and their plan incorporates an axis that makes one or two right-angle turns to the left. Later Dynasty 18 and early Dynasty 19 tombs are

228-229 THE VALLEY OF THE KINGS DOMINATED BY THE PYRAMID SHAPED MOUNTAIN CALLED AL-QURN.

not associated with any particular topographical features. Their plan incorporates a single 90–degree turn to the left and a "well shaft" in chamber E. A third type of royal tomb is significantly larger than either of the previous types. A series of long, wide corridors extend along a single axis (or an axis that makes a short jog to the left about halfway along its length) to the burial chamber. Such tombs lie at the base of the valley's more gently sloping hills.

However much they differed from one another during the New Kingdom, tombs in the Valley of the Kings also showed many similarities. This can be seen, for example, in the functions served by the chambers and corridors that each tomb possessed.

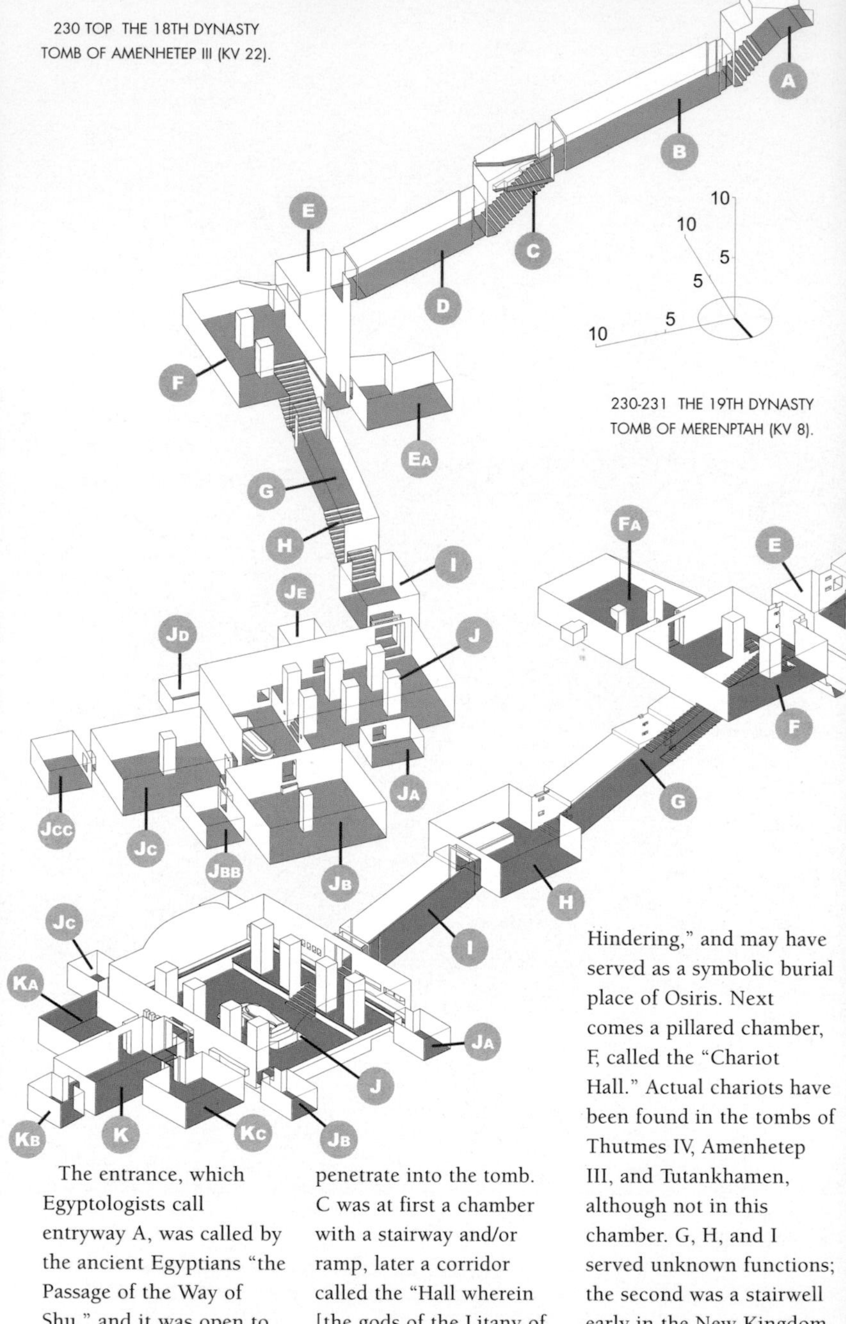

230 TOP THE 18TH DYNASTY TOMB OF AMENHETEP III (KV 22).

230-231 THE 19TH DYNASTY TOMB OF MERENPTAH (KV 8).

The entrance, which Egyptologists call entryway A, was called by the ancient Egyptians "the Passage of the Way of Shu," and it was open to the sky until the middle of Dynasty 18 and partially covered thereafter. Corridor B, the "Passage of Ra," usually marked the farthest sunlight could penetrate into the tomb. C was at first a chamber with a stairway and/or ramp, later a corridor called the "Hall wherein [the gods of the Litany of Ra] reside." D, was simply the second passage. A small, square chamber, chamber E, often with a deep well cut into its floor, was called the "Hall of Hindering," and may have served as a symbolic burial place of Osiris. Next comes a pillared chamber, F, called the "Chariot Hall." Actual chariots have been found in the tombs of Thutmes IV, Amenhetep III, and Tutankhamen, although not in this chamber. G, H, and I served unknown functions; the second was a stairwell early in the New Kingdom, later a corridor, while I was a chamber that later became a corridor. The burial chamber, J, was called the "Hall in which One Rests," "The House of

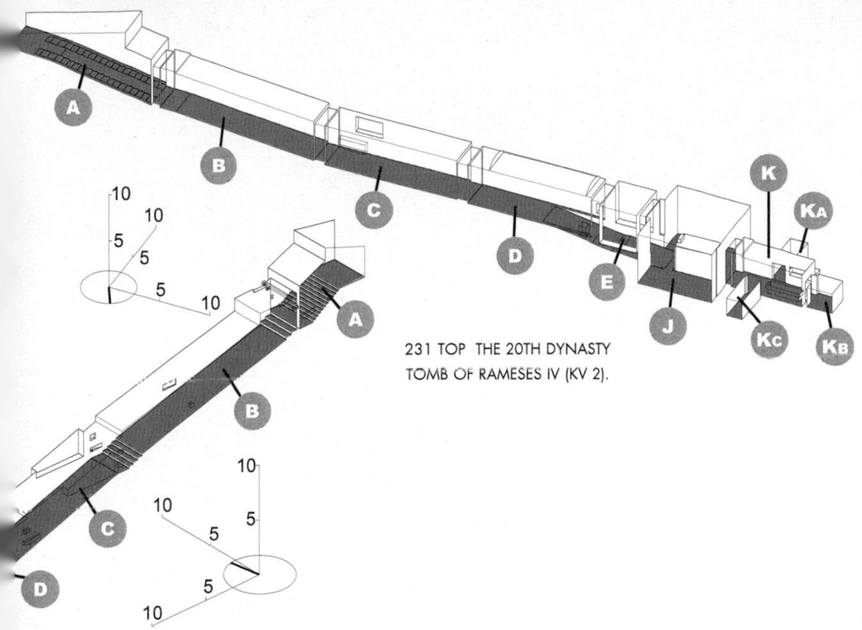

231 TOP THE 20TH DYNASTY TOMB OF RAMESES IV (KV 2).

Gold," or "The Hidden Chamber." Its shape changed during the New Kingdom, and sometimes is oval and sometimes rectangular, sometimes with pillars and sometimes without. Usually, a series of small side chambers were used for the interment of funerary offerings and furniture. In seven royal tombs, rooms or corridors lie beyond J. These are designated by Egyptologists as K and L.

Royal tombs in the Valley of the Kings were decorated with religious texts including the Book of Gates, the *Imydwat*, the Litany of Ra, and others, accompanied by numerous vignettes and scenes. Like the plan of the tombs, the decorative programs also changed through time. Tombs in the Valley of the Kings are perhaps the first in ancient Egypt to have scenes depicting gods and goddesses on their walls.

The selection of a site for a royal tomb was a major decision, probably taken by priests and senior workmen from Dayr al-Madina. Once chosen, ceremonies were performed to sanctify the site and small pits were dug and filled with miniature tools and religious symbols. These "foundation deposits" have been found associated with nine tombs in the valley, but it is likely that future excavations will reveal that most if not all royal tombs had them.

The workmen who dug the royal tombs were divided into two work teams, a "left gang" and a "right gang" of about ten men each, supervised by a foreman. Using simple metal chisels, wooden mallets, and chert hand axes, they cut through the soft limestone bedrock at a fairly rapid rate. The men worked eight hour days for ten days, then enjoyed a two-day "weekend." As the quarrymen dug further into the hillside, other specialists followed behind, checking that the walls were vertical, their corners cut at 90 degrees, and smoothing their surfaces. Either plasterers came next or scribes, outlining the scenes and texts to be carved and painted. (For further details see the tomb of Horemheb). Carving and decorating a royal tomb, even a large one, was a major undertaking but not a particularly time-consuming one. Even with a small labor force working on a tomb, it may have taken only a few years to complete.

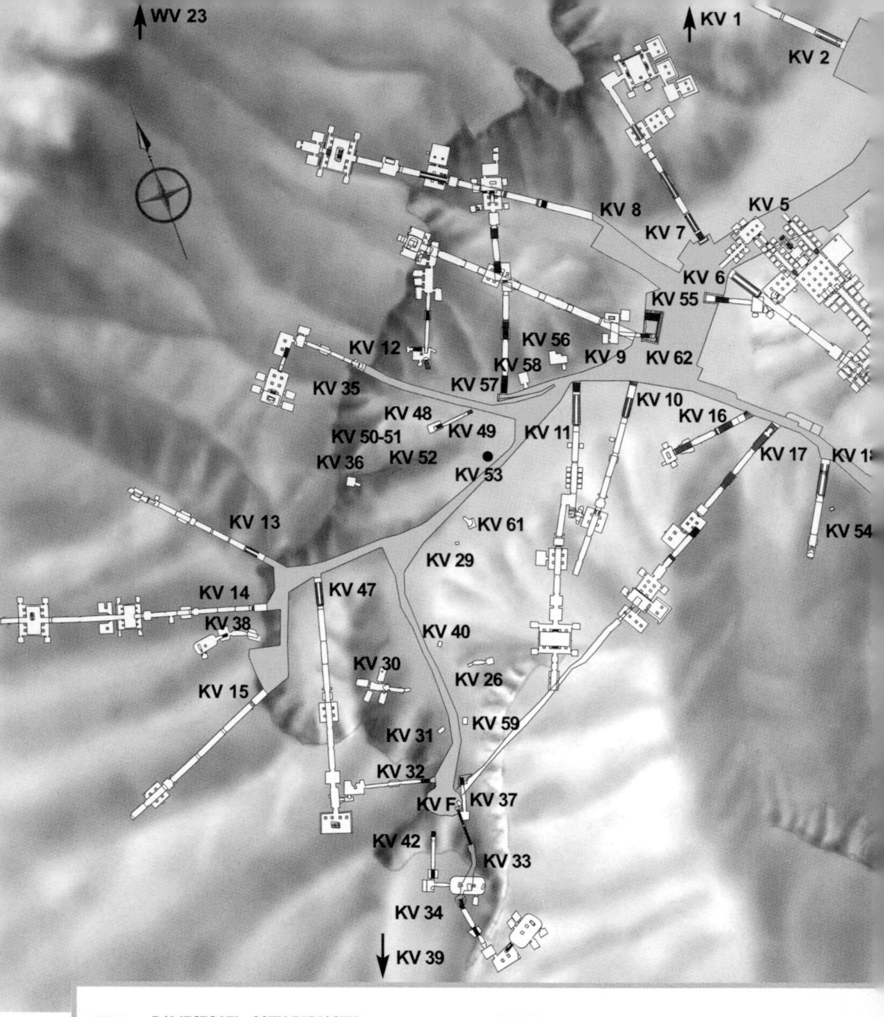

KV 1 RAMESES VII - 20TH DYNASTY
KV 2 RAMESES IV - 20TH DYNASTY
KV 3 CA. RAMESES III - 20TH DYNASTY
KV 4 RAMESES XI - 20TH DYNASTY
KV 5 SONS OF RAMESES II - 19TH DYNASTY
KV 6 RAMESES IX - 20TH DYNASTY
KV 7 RAMESES II - 19TH DYNASTY
KV 8 MERENPTAH - 19TH DYNASTY
KV 9 RAMESES V/VI - 20TH DYNASTY
KV 10 AMENMESES - 19TH DYNASTY
KV 11 RAMESES III - 20TH DYNASTY
KV 12 UNKNOWN - 18TH DYNASTY
KV 13 BAY - 19TH DYNASTY
KV 14 TAUSERT/SETNAKHT - 19TH-20TH DYNASTY
KV 15 SETY II - 19TH DYNASTY
KV 16 RAMESES I - 18TH DYNASTY
KV 17 SETY I - 19TH DYNASTY
KV 18 RAMESES X - 20TH DYNASTY
KV 19 MENTUHERKHEPSHEF - 20TH DYNASTY
KV 20 HATSHEPSUT - 18TH DYNASTY
KV 21 TWO QUEENS - 18TH DYNASTY
WV 22 AMENHETEP III - 18TH DYNASTY
WV 23 AY - 18TH DYNASTY
WV 24 UNKNOWN - 18TH DYNASTY
WV 25 AKHENATEN (?) - 18TH DYNASTY
KV 26 UNKNOWN - 18TH DYNASTY
KV 27 UNKNOWN - 18TH DYNASTY
KV 28 UNKNOWN - 18TH DYNASTY
KV 29 UNKNOWN - 18TH DYNASTY
KV 30 UNKNOWN - 18TH DYNASTY
KV 31 UNKNOWN - 18TH DYNASTY
KV 32 UNKNOWN - 18TH DYNASTY

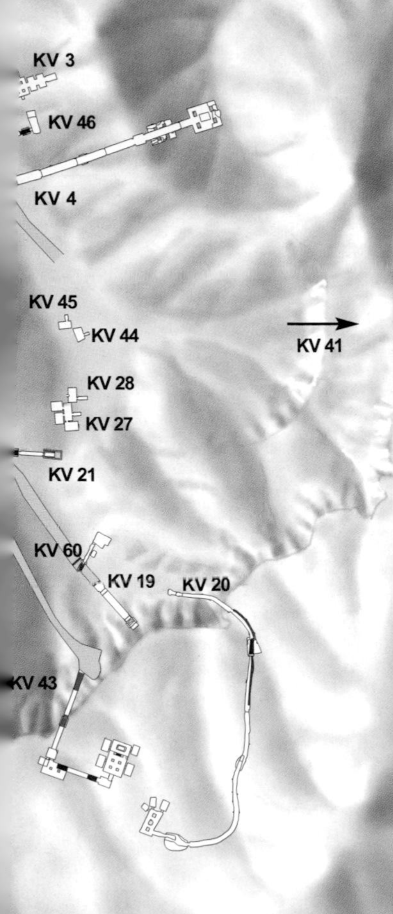

233 TOP THE HIGHER PATH LEADS TO THE TOMB OF AMENHETEP II (KV 35), THE LOWER TO THE TOMBS AT THE END OF THE VALLEY.

233 BOTTOM THE MAIN PATH IN THE VALLEY OF THE KINGS. IN BACKGROUND IS AL-QURN.

LEGEND

KV 33	*CA. THUTMES III - 18TH DYNASTY*
KV 34	*THUTMES III - 18TH DYNASTY*
KV 35	*AMENHETEP II - 18TH DYNASTY*
KV 36	*MAIHERPERI - 18TH DYNASTY*
KV 37	*CA. THUTMES III - 18TH DYNASTY*
KV 38	*THUTMES I - 18TH DYNASTY*
KV 39	*UNKNOWN - 18TH DYNASTY*
KV 40	*UNKNOWN - 18TH DYNASTY*
KV 41	*UNKNOWN - 18TH DYNASTY*
KV 42	*UNKNOWN - 18TH DYNASTY*
KV 43	*THUTMES IV - 18TH DYNASTY*
KV 44	*UNKNOWN - 18TH DYNASTY*
KV 45	*USERHET - 18TH DYNASTY*
KV 46	*YUYA AND TUYA - 18TH DYNASTY*
KV 47	*SIPTAH - 19TH DYNASTY*
KV 48	*AMENEMOPET - 18TH DYNASTY*
KV 49	*UNKNOWN - 18TH DYNASTY*
KV 50	*ANIMALS - 18TH DYNASTY*
KV 51	*ANIMALS - 18TH DYNASTY*
KV 52	*ANIMALS - 18TH DYNASTY*
KV 53	*UNKNOWN - 18TH DYNASTY*
KV 54	*UNKNOWN - 18TH DYNASTY*
KV 55	*AMARNA CACHE - 18TH DYNASTY*
KV 56	*UNKNOWN - 18TH DYNASTY*
KV 57	*HOREMHEB - 18TH DYNASTY*
KV 58	*UNKNOWN - 18TH DYNASTY*
KV 59	*UNKNOWN - 18TH DYNASTY*
KV 60	*TWO WORKMEN - 18TH DYNASTY*
KV 61	*UNKNOWN - 18TH DYNASTY*
KV 62	*TUTANKHAMEN - 18TH DYNASTY*
KV A	*UNKNOWN - 18TH DYNASTY*
KV F	*UNKNOWN - 18TH DYNASTY*

3

KV 34: THE TOMB OF THUTMES III

THE HISTORY

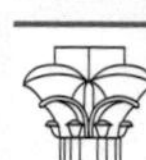

KV 34 is the earliest of the Dynasty 18 tombs in the Valley of the Kings that are currently open to the public. It is therefore a good first stop on a tour tracing the development of royal tomb architecture. Earlier tombs include those of Thutmes I (possibly KV 38), Hatshepsut (KV 20), Ahmes, and Amenhetep I. The locations of the last two are not known; the first two are closed to visitors.

All of these early tombs have either a set of curving corridors or a floor plan in which the axis makes a right angle turn at the chamber preceding the burial chamber. These are carry-overs from Middle Kingdom plans and, like all features of royal tombs from the Middle and New Kingdoms, architectural reflections of the path the deceased was thought to take from this life to the next. Only a few chambers in these early tombs were decorated. Many walls were not even smoothed or plastered. Usually, the decorated rooms included the well chamber and the burial chamber, but even they were often incompletely done. The decoration consisted largely of texts and scenes from the *Imydwat,* the "Book of That Which is in the Netherworld," also called the "Book of the Secret Chamber." It gives an hour-by-hour description of the nighttime journey of the sun through the Netherworld. This emphasis on the *Imydwat* did not diminish until the end of Dynasty 18.

The tomb of Thutmes III lies in a narrow cut in the bedrock cliffs high above the floor of the Valley of the Kings. It is an unusual location (only KV 20, Hatshepsut's tomb, is even vaguely similar) and an impressive one. In ancient times, access to the tomb was by means of a path at the top of the cliff or via a mudbrick staircase built up from the Valley floor to the edge of the cut. That staircase was removed after the king's funeral and replaced only a few decades ago by a steel staircase rising over twenty meters above the Valley floor. (Climbing this open-work staircase is not recommended for the acrophobic.) From the top of the stairs, one walks 20 meters (60 feet) along a narrow, natural cleft in the bedrock to the tomb's entrance. It is a dramatic approach and the view of the Valley of the Kings from here is impressive. Steps and a ramp cut into the bedrock run steeply downward from the tomb entrance, descending through unplastered, undecorated corridors to chamber E, a square room known as the well. It is about 7 meters (21 feet) deep. This is the first example of a well in a tomb in the Valley of the Kings, and Egyptologists have offered several explanations for its presence. One is that it was meant to thwart tomb robbers. Upon entering the tomb, thieves would encounter the deep well and see that the wall beyond it was sealed with stone and plaster. They would assume that the tomb was unfinished and contained nothing worth stealing and they would leave. If this is correct, the ruse never worked. Thieves

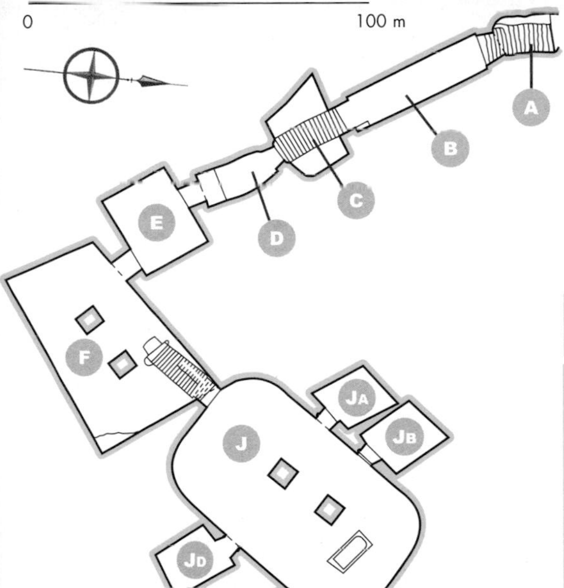

234 TOP DETAIL OF THE DECORATION OF THE BURIAL CHAMBER.

235 LEFT THE PILLARED HALL F.

235 RIGHT A STEEP STONE AND IRON STAIRCASE LEADS TO THE TOMB.

LEGEND

A *ENTRANCE*
B *FIRST CORRIDOR*
C *STAIRWELL*
D *SECOND CORRIDOR*
E *WELL CHAMBER*
F *PILLARED CHAMBER*
J *BURIAL CHAMBER*
JA, B, C, D *SIDE CHAMBERS*

seemed to know from the outset that tombs continued beyond the well chamber. Another theory is that the well was intended to trap floodwaters from torrential rainstorms and prevent water from reaching the burial chamber and damaging the mummy and funerary equipment. This explanation, too, is unconvincing A third explanation is that the shaft was the symbolic burial place of the god Osiris, the quintessential god of the afterlife. In some tombs, KV 35 for example, well shafts had chambers cut at their base, a feature that lends support to this theory and seems to invalidate the first two.

VISIT

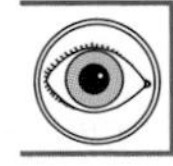

The **WELL CHAMBER** here has a decorated ceiling with yellow stars on a blue background and a *khekher*-frieze painted along the top of the walls. Beyond the well shaft, **CHAMBER F** is a quadrilateral room with

two off-center, undecorated pillars. The walls are elaborately painted with the names of the 741 deities who appear in the *Imydwat.*

A steep staircase in the left front corner of the room leads through the floor into the burial chamber.

The **BURIAL CHAMBER** is large, about 14.6 meters (46 feet) by 8.5 meters (28 feet), and has an oval plan. Its shape may have been intended to represent a cartouche in which royal names were written. The walls of the chamber are covered with scenes and texts from the *Imydwat.* They are drawn in black and red ink on a light yellow background, painted to mimic text on a roll of papyrus. The hieroglyphs and figures are done in a cursive style like that used on papyri, written with rapid, minimalist brush strokes that produce stick-like, almost comic-book-style scenes. Although simple, they are admirable examples of the artist's talent.

The *Imydwat* is divided into twelve hours, the first to fourth on the chamber's front wall, fifth and sixth on the right wall, seventh and eighth on the left, ninth to twelfth on the rear. [For more detailed descriptions, see the tomb of Rameses VI. See also another version of the text in the tomb of Amenhetep II.] The first hour starts at the entrance to the netherworld, at the Gate Which Swallows All. It describes the netherworld's inhabitants and continues the list of 741 deities given in chamber F. In the second and third hours, the netherworld's fertile farmlands are described, and evil beings are overcome by knife-wielding figures. The fourth hour takes us to the desert land of *Ro-Setau,* the Land of Sokar Who Is Upon His Sand, a place of snakes, barred doors, and darkness. Here and in the fifth hour, male and female figures tow the solar bark through blackness and thirst. In the sixth hour, the sun, in the form of a scarab beetle, reaches midnight in the depths of the netherworld. Ra and Osiris join together and the living king brings his dead ancestors back to life. In the seventh hour, the snake-god Apophis tries to blot out the sun, but he is

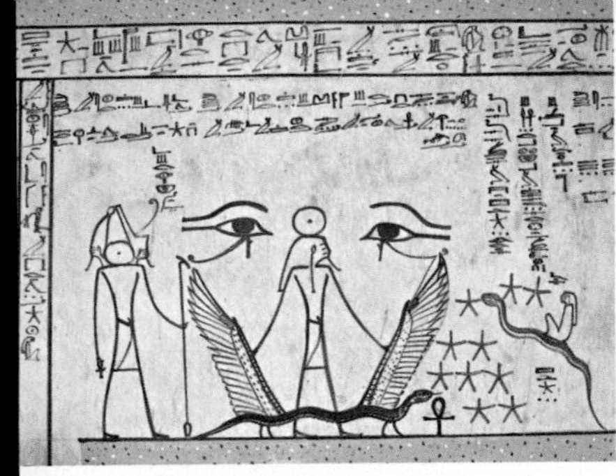

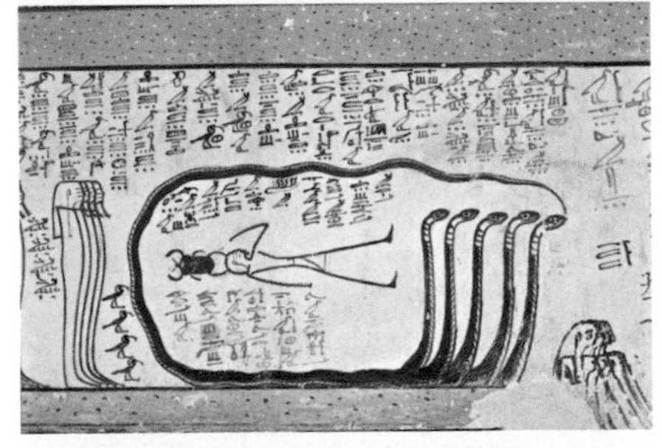

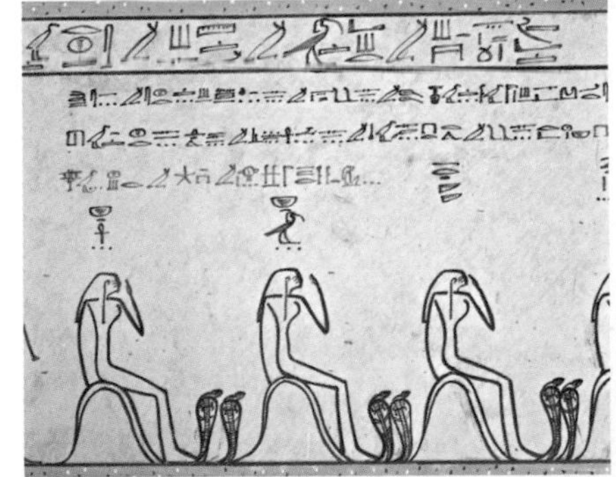

defeated by Isis, Seth, and Serqet; Osiris triumphs over his enemies. In the eighth and ninth hours, Ra opens the doors of five caverns and provides clothing for the worthy dead. In the tenth, a rectangular pool is shown, filled with the floating bodies of those who have died by drowning. They are considered especially blessed, and although a normal funeral is not possible, Horus carries them safely into the netherworld. In the eleventh hour, preparations are made for sunrise. In the twelfth hour, twelve men and thirteen women pull the bark of the blessed dead into daylight, and the sun, shown as a beetle, joins Shu, the god of air, at the start of another day.

236 VIEW OF THUTMES III'S BURIAL CHAMBER.

237 DETAILS FROM THE WALL PAINTINGS IN THE BURIAL CHAMBER OF THUTMES III WITH SECTIONS OF THE IMYDWAT.

238 AND 239 TOP THE CARTOUCHE-SHAPED QUARTZITE SARCOPHAGUS STILL IN THE BURIAL CHAMBER.

239 CENTER DETAIL FROM THE SARCOPHAGUS SHOWING TWO WEDJAT EYES.

239 BOTTOM LEFT IMYDWAT DETAIL OF THE SOLAR BARK FROM A PILLAR OF THE BURIAL CHAMBER.

239 BOTTOM RIGHT THUTMES III SUCKLED BY ISIS AS TREE GODDESS, FROM THE LEFT SIDE OF THE FIRST PILLAR IN THE BURIAL CHAMBER.

Four small **SIDE CHAMBERS** lie off the burial chamber; each was used for the storage of funerary equipment.

Several faces of the two pillars in the burial chamber were decorated with scenes and texts from The Litany of Ra, a text that praises the sun god and associates him with the pharaoh. On the left side of the first pillar is a justly famous scene of Thutmes III being suckled by Isis, shown as a tree goddess. The economy of lines is impressive.

The breast of Isis emerges from the branches of the sycomore tree *(Ficus sycomorus)* and she holds it toward the king. A larger second figure of the king stands at left, watching himself being suckled. This lovely scene has unfortunately suffered in recent years from thoughtless tourists and guides who have poked at the drawing.

The beautiful cartouche-shaped, quartzite sarcophagus still sits in the burial chamber. It is actually cut from yellow quartzite but was painted red to mimic red granite, a considerably more valuable stone. Its sides are decorated with figures of the king and various deities.

KV 34 was discovered in 1898 and cleared by Victor Loret, then director of the Antiquities Service. The tomb had been robbed in antiquity, a brutal attack on its contents made by thieves who tossed things about and smashed what they did not cart away. Apparently, the thieves carried many of the objects they found to KV 4, at the entrance to the Valley of the Kings, where they could sort through them at leisure. Clearing of KV 4 in 1978 revealed a number of pieces with Thutmes III's name on them.

The mummy of Thutmes III was taken from the tomb in antiquity and reburied in TT 320, the cache of royal mummies near Dayr al-Bahari.

3

KV 35: THE TOMB OF AMENHETEP II

THE HISTORY

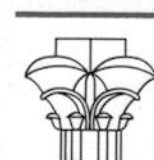

KV 35 is one of the most beautiful and impressive tombs in the Valley of the Kings. It lies at the base of a sheer cliff nearly 30 meters (100 feet) high, about 150 meters (500 feet) west of the tomb of Tutankhamen. It was deliberately cut below a "waterfall" over which flood waters would have poured whenever rain fell on the hills above. Such floods would have carried tons of stone and sand, burying the tomb entrance under increasingly deeper debris. It was an ingenious way to conceal a tomb entrance and was a recurring feature of early Dynasty 18 tombs. Recently, the tomb entrance was roofed over to prevent future flood damage like that which occurred in 1994 when rain entered the tomb. Before the roof was built, the tomb entrance was well concealed and a principal reason why it was chosen by priests in the tenth century BC as a place to hide New Kingdom royal mummies from thieves. In the two side chambers off the right side of the burial chamber, Loret found the mummies of Thutmes IV, Amenhetep III, Merenptah, Sety II, Siptah, Setnakht, Rameses IV, Rameses V, and Rameses VI. These were removed to the Egyptian

240 TOP DETAIL OF THE THIRD CORRIDOR.

240-241 THE UNDECORATED PILLARED CHAMBER F.

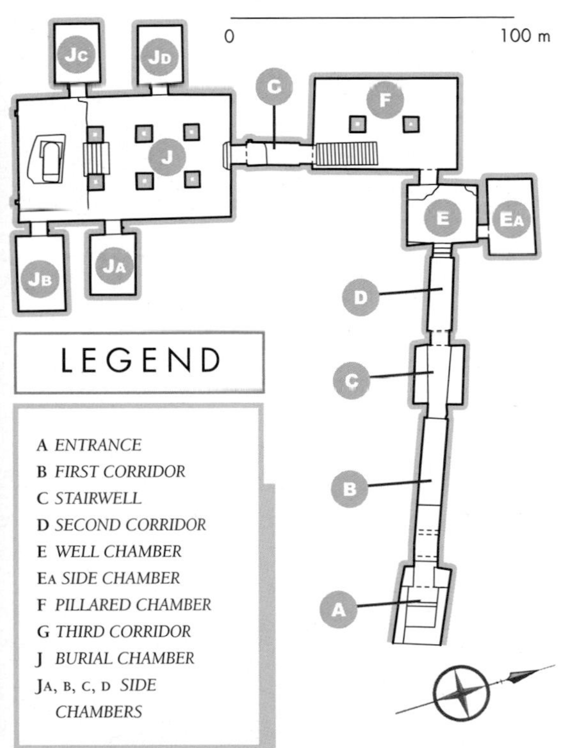

LEGEND

A *ENTRANCE*
B *FIRST CORRIDOR*
C *STAIRWELL*
D *SECOND CORRIDOR*
E *WELL CHAMBER*
EA *SIDE CHAMBER*
F *PILLARED CHAMBER*
G *THIRD CORRIDOR*
J *BURIAL CHAMBER*
JA, B, C, D *SIDE CHAMBERS*

Museum, Cairo. The mummy of Amenhetep II was found in his sarcophagus in the burial chamber and was shipped to Cairo in 1928. KV 35 was found by Victor Loret in 1898, only a month after he had discovered KV 34, the tomb of Thutmes III, but neither tomb was published until 1932. KV 35 immediately became a must-see tomb in the valley because of its fine quality workmanship and beautiful decoration.

VISIT

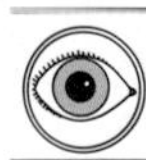

The basic plan of KV 35 follows that of KV 34 (Thutmes III), but with the enhancement of some elements and the addition of others. A steep set of entry stairs leads to a sloping corridor, then to a second set of stairs, a second corridor, and a well chamber. Here, the **WELL SHAFT** is about 6.5 meters (21 feet) deep and has a small, rectangular chamber cut at the bottom. The presence of such a chamber suggests that the well was more likely a symbolic tomb for the god Osiris than a device to trap rainwater or thwart thieves. A **TWO-COLUMNED CHAMBER** lies beyond. As in KV 34, a steep stairway was cut through its floor in the left front corner. These steps lead to a third sloping corridor, and beyond it, the burial chamber.

It is the **BURIAL CHAMBER** that shows the greatest departure from the earlier plan of KV 34. Both burial chambers are about the same size—KV 34's is 380 cubic meters (13420 cubic feet), KV 35's is 408 cubic meters (14410 cubic feet)—but here the burial chamber is rectangular with square corners. Six pillars support the ceiling in the front 10 meters (33 feet) of the room. The floor in the rear 5 meters (16.5 feet) was cut 1.5 (5 feet) meters lower than the rest of the hall, in effect dividing the chamber into two unequal areas. Steps along the chamber's main axis lead from one level to the other.

Amenhetep II's yellow quartzite sarcophagus lies in the lower level. Like the sarcophagus of Thutmes III, it was painted to simulate granite. Four small, rectangular holes are cut in the lower section of the burial chamber, two in the rear wall, one each in the rear face of the last pair of pillars. Thus, they surround the sarcophagus. These are called magical brick niches and were intended to house small mudbricks on which part of spell 151 from the Book of the Dead was incised or painted and which were accompanied by the figure of a mummy or a jackal or the hieroglyph meaning "to endure." A part of the text reads, "I have come as your protection, and my protection will be about you forever."

Only the burial chamber of KV 35 is decorated, but the quality of the drawing makes it one of the finest examples of New Kingdom mortuary art. The walls of the chamber are covered with a complete version of the *Imydwat* (as in KV 34) written in red and black ink. Only the sky on the ceiling and occasional bodies of water in some of the scenes have blue paint, and only the *kheker*-frieze along top of the wall and the vertical bands in the corners have color. The background color is meant to suggest papyrus.

242 TOP THE BURIAL CHAMBER WITH THE SARCOPHAGUS.

242 BOTTOM THE CEILING OF THE BURIAL CHAMBER BETWEEN FOUR OF THE SIX COLUMNS.

243 DETAILS OF THE YELLOW QUARTZITE SARCOPHAGUS, PAINTED RED TO SIMULATE RED GRANITE.

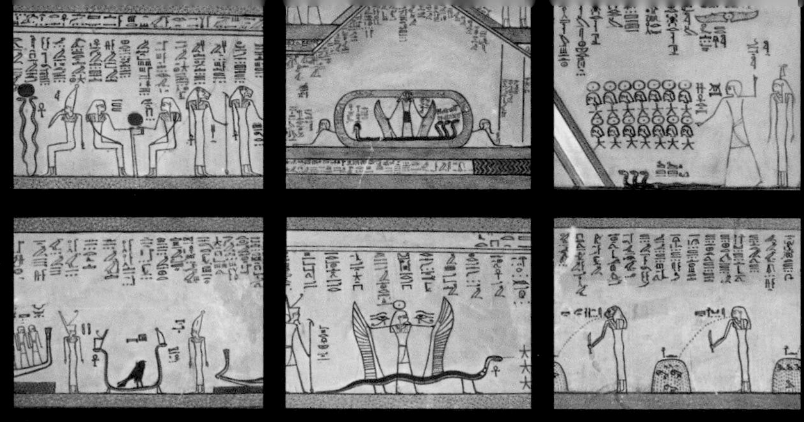

The brush strokes used for these schematic stick figures and cursive hieroglyphs were made with great confidence. In many royal tombs, senior artists have made corrections and alterations to the drawings by junior artisans; spellings of words are corrected or the proportions of figures changed. There is no such editing here, partly because of the cursive nature of the figures, but also because the artists' skill made it unnecessary. The seventh hour of the *Imydwat* is shown on the front wall. In the upper register, Osiris sits on his throne protected by a huge snake, watching as a god with the ears of a cat beheads the enemies of Osiris. Below, Isis stands in the prow of a boat as the evil Apophis-serpent is rendered harmless by knives and ropes. (Another version can be seen in the tomb of Thutmes III.) An interesting scene from the tenth hour of the *Imydwat* was painted on the left wall in the upper level of the chamber. In the lowest of three registers, a rectangular body of water, painted blue with the wavy lines of the water hieroglyph, represents Nun, the primeval ocean. Floating in it are twelve men who have died by drowning. In Egypt, where drowning in the Nile was common and where the body might never be found or might be eaten by a crocodile and deprived of proper burial, the fate of the person's soul posed a serious problem. The solution was provided by Horus, who stands on the shore to the left of the water and calls out to the drowned men, promising to lead them into the afterlife. In the register above, spearmen stand guard as the sun god travels through the heavens in his sacred bark.

The faces of the six pillars show the king with one of several deities, each of whom offers him an *ankh*-sign, representing life. Again, the work is of outstanding quality. Here, instead of using a papyrus-colored background, the black-lined figures were painted against contrasting bone-white. The figures were drawn by a supremely confident artist using a minimal number of lines and a limited palette. They are not the stick-like figures seen on the chamber's walls. Instead, they are well-proportioned outlines with little interior detail or modeling but with attention to the details of the costumes. Colors appear in only a few elements of the scenes: a gold headdress, a broad collar inlaid with black, red, yellow, and blue, and a red solar disk. Above each scene, the hieroglyph for "sky" is painted blue and covered with five-pointed stars. The scene is surrounded by a band of yellow, red, and blue rectangles.

Three deities are represented on the twenty-four faces of the six pillars: ten figures of the king with Hathor (she is the only goddess depicted), eight with Osiris, and six with Anubis. It is they who will protect the king in the next life. The accompanying hieroglyphs give simply the name of the king and of the god with whom he stands, and sometimes the phrase, "Beloved of Osiris."

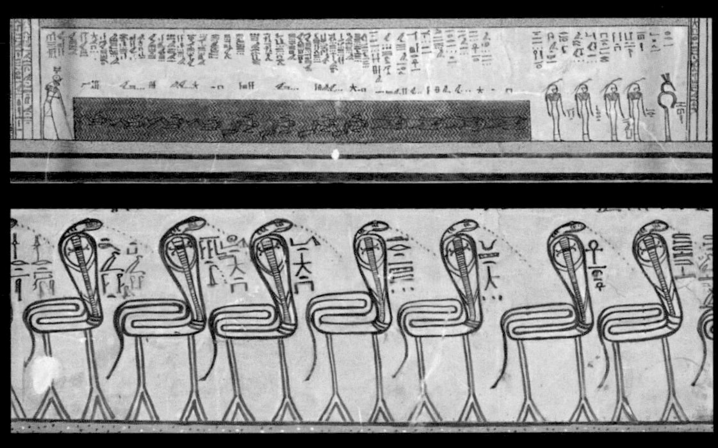

244 AND 245 BOTTOM DETAILS FROM THE BURIAL CHAMBER'S WALLS WITH SCENES FROM THE IMYDWAT.

245 TOP ON EACH SIDE OF EACH PILLAR OF THE BURIAL CHAMBER AMENHETEP STANDS WITH A DEITY.

245 CENTER FROM THE IMYDWAT, BLUE IS NUN, THE PRIMEVAL OCEAN, IN WHICH TWELVE MEN ARE FLOATING.

3

KV 43: THE TOMB OF THUTMES IV

The tombs of Thutmes III (KV 34), Amenhetep II (KV 35), and Thutmes IV (KV 43) lie at the extreme southern, western, and eastern limits of the Valley of the Kings respectively, about as far from each other as it is possible to be and still lie within the valley. The three sites may have been chosen because they boast sheer cliffs with "waterfalls" at the top. The tombs were cut at the base of the cliffs, where fissures and cracks in the bedrock would conceal their entrance from a casual viewer. Debris washed over the waterfall during a torrential rain would further hide the entrance. Later tombs were dug in quite different localities because changes in funerary beliefs meant that the first part of a tomb had to remain accessible after interment for further services by priests.

The tomb of Thutmes IV is generally similar to that of Amenhetep II, but it has a second right-angle turn in the axis just before the burial chamber, and the distribution of its decoration is different.

The tomb is especially well cut in good quality limestone bedrock. The tomb was entered in 1903 by Howard Carter. He found numerous objects inside and two collections of foundation deposits placed in small pits cut just outside the tomb entrance.

The only decoration in KV 43 is on the walls of the well chamber and the chamber preceding the burial chamber. The former consists of scenes of Thutmes IV being given an *ankh* sign by Osiris, Anubis, and Hathor. Unlike similar scenes in the tomb of Amenhetep II (KV 35), these are well painted, not just outlined. Hathor, for example, wears an elaborately patterned dress, a different pattern in each of her three representations. The headdresses and costumes of other figures are equally well done.

Inside the tomb, a rope used by ancient thieves still lay in the first pillared chamber, tied around one of the pillars and hanging into the preceding well shaft. Apparently, several robberies had taken place here in antiquity, and during the reign of Horemheb a court official was commanded to inspect the tomb and reseal it. The official responsible, Maya, left a beautifully calligraphic record of his tour on the right (south) wall of the chamber just before the burial chamber:

"Year 8...His Majesty commanded that the fan-bearer on the king's

right hand, the royal scribe, overseer of the treasury, overseer of

works in the palace of eternity and leader of the festival of Amen in

Karnak, Maya, son of the noble Iawy, born of the lady of the house

Weret, be charged to renew the burial of king

LEGEND

A *ENTRANCE*
B *FIRST CORRIDOR*
C *STAIRWELL*
D *SECOND CORRIDOR*
E *WELL CHAMBER*
EA *SIDE CHAMBER*
F *PILLARED CHAMBER*
G *THIRD CORRIDOR*
H *STAIRWELL*
I *ANTECHAMBER*
J *BURIAL CHAMBER*
JA, B, C, D *SIDE CHAMBERS*

[Thutmes IV], true of voice, in the noble mansion upon the west of Thebes." The decoration on three walls of this chamber is similarly painted to what was found in the well chamber and includes the same deities. This is the first tomb in the Valley of the Kings to have such scenes.

The burial chamber, like that in KV 35, was cut on two levels with six pillars on the upper level and a central staircase leading to the lower. There is no decoration in the burial chamber, only a red-painted quartzite sarcophagus at the far end of the chamber. It is decorated with finely carved hieroglyphs. Four magical brick niches are cut in the lower part of the chamber, one on each of its walls, a fourth in the rear face of the left pillar. Four side chambers, two cut into the side walls of the upper level, two into the side walls of the lower, were closed by wooden doors in ancient times and contained food offerings and various funerary objects. The way in which the tomb was quarried, together with the small number of decorated walls, suggests that Thutmes IV had been buried in haste.

246 TOP DETAIL OF THE CALLIGRAPHIC RECORD OF MAYA, OFFICAL RESPONSIBLE OF THE TOMB.

247 TOP DECORATION FROM THE WELL CHAMBER WITH THUTMES IV RECEIVING AN ANKH SIGN FROM VARIOUS GODS.

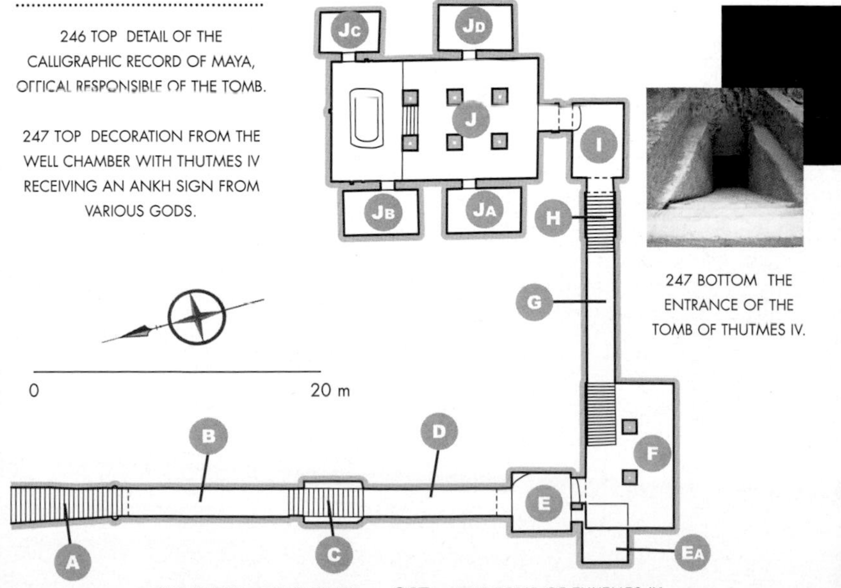

247 BOTTOM THE ENTRANCE OF THE TOMB OF THUTMES IV.

3

KV 62: THE TOMB OF TUTANKHAMEN

THE HISTORY

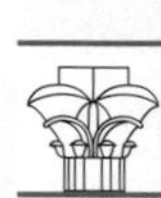

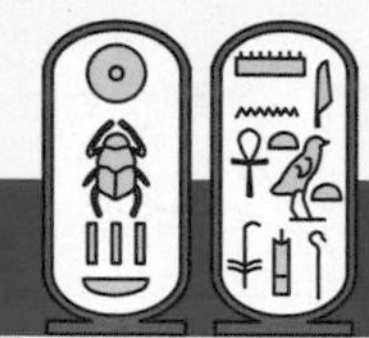

Ironically, the smallest of the royal tombs in the Valley of the Kings is also the most famous. From the day its discovery was announced in November 1922, the tomb of Tutankhamen has captured the world's imagination, inspiring more bad films and novels and youthful dreams of an archaeological career than perhaps any other archaeological discovery. The reason is simple: treasure. Small though it may be, KV 62 was packed with thousands of beautifully crafted objects, many of them solid gold. Little wonder the world was awestruck when news and photographs of the discovery were published. Tutankhamen's tomb is not the only Egyptian tomb to be found nearly intact (the tomb of Yuya and Tuya in the Valley of the Kings and that of Hetepheres at Giza are two examples), but no other find comes even close to the quality and quantity of contents in KV 62.

It seems likely that Tutankhamen was buried in KV 62 because he died unexpectedly, still a teenager. If a tomb had even been begun for him at such a young age, the work was not far enough along for it to be used. The way in which the funerary objects were crammed into the tomb suggests a burial done in considerable haste. But a recent claim that Tutankhamen was murdered by court officials and his burial done quickly to hide evidence of the crime is not widely accepted.

Almost immediately after it had been sealed, the tomb was robbed, not once but at least twice, perhaps by some of the guards assigned to protect it. Both robberies were quickly discovered. Eight gold rings were found

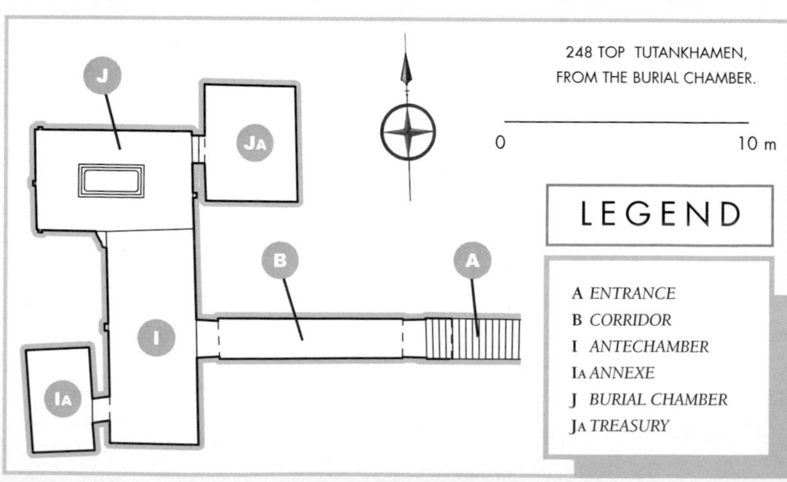

248 TOP TUTANKHAMEN, FROM THE BURIAL CHAMBER.

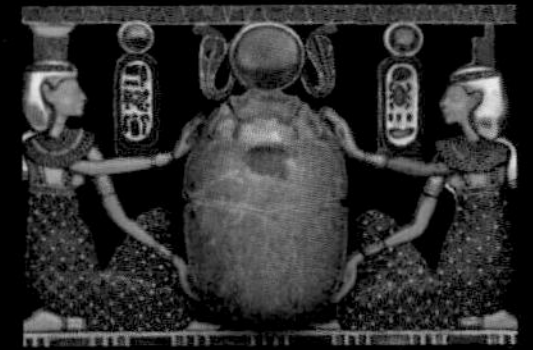

by Carter lying on the floor of the Treasury, wrapped in a piece of cloth as part of the goods the thieves were planning to haul away. Apparently they were thrown back into the chamber when the thieves were apprehended. There is ample evidence for these ancient thefts. But there is no evidence to support recent claims by several hack writers that Carter and Carnarvon had found KV 62 long before 1922 and were systematically plundering it until nearly caught and then, in a panic, staged its "discovery."

Tutankhamen's treasure, now displayed in the Egyptian Museum in Cairo, is breathtakingly beautiful, and visitors coming to the Valley of the Kings often expect the tomb to be equally impressive. It is not. The tomb consists of four small chambers covering only 110 square meters (1184 square feet). It is claustrophobic and virtually empty. But a lovely quartzite sarcophagus still stands in the burial chamber, inside it the outer coffin and the mummy of young Tutankhamen. Only the walls of the burial chamber were decorated, very simply, with few figures and little text. The rest of the walls are bare.

249 TOP PECTORAL OF TUTANKHAMEN FOUND IN THE TOMB, NOW IN THE CAIRO MUSEUM.

249 BOTTOM THE BURIAL CHAMBER WITH THE RED QUARTZITE SARCOPHAGUS.

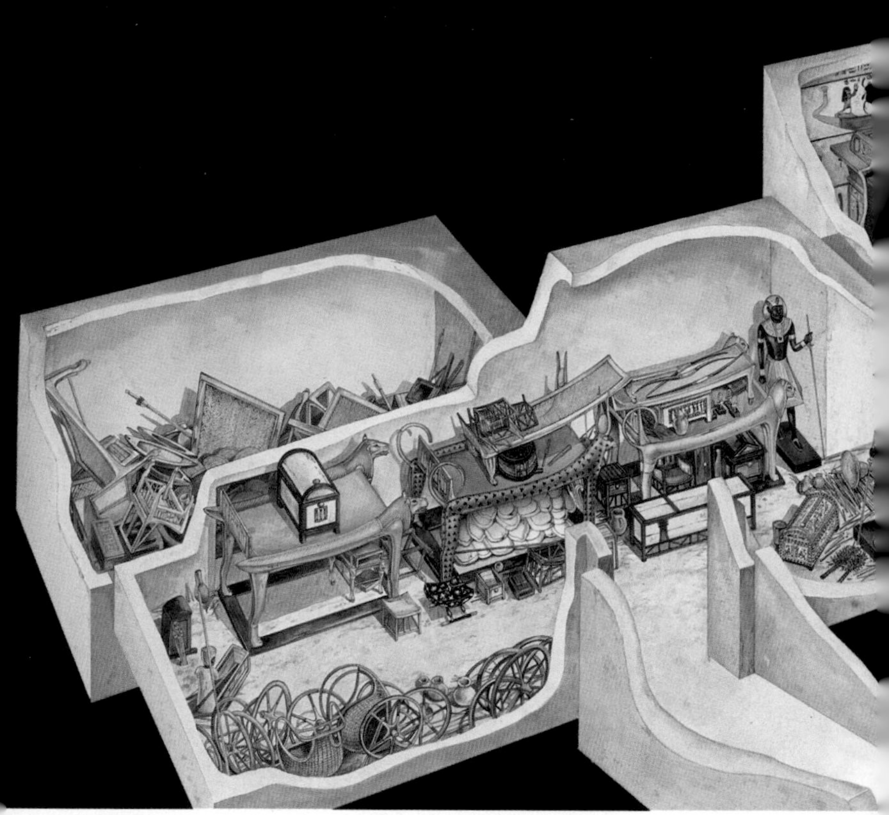

The entrance staircase to KV 62 was discovered by Howard Carter's workmen on 4 November 1922, and the next day they exposed the now-famous sixteen steps that led down to a tomb entrance closed with mud and stone and stamped over thirty centuries earlier with seals of the necropolis guards.

Carter cabled his English benefactor news of the discovery and impatiently awaited Lord Carvarnon's arrival before breaking through this doorway on 24 November. "At first I could see nothing," Carter later wrote, "the hot air escaping from the chamber causing the candle flame to flicker, but presently, as my eyes grew accustomed to the light, details of the room within emerged slowly from the mist, strange animals, statues, and gold—everywhere the glint of gold." It took ten years of painstaking work to photograph, record, remove, and conserve the more than three thousand objects found inside, and still today many of them remain unpublished.

VISIT

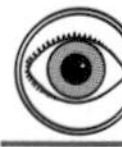

The tomb has an unusual plan, different from other royal tombs and the small nobles' tombs at Thebes. But if the entrance staircase that leads to what Carter called the Antechamber were moved around to the Antechamber's left end, the resulting tomb plan would not be too different from standard Dynasty 18 royal tombs: a staircase and corridor leading to a burial chamber with a side chamber.

An **ENTRANCE CORRIDOR** lies at the bottom of the sixteen steps, 8 meters (27 feet) long and 1.7 meters (6 feet) wide. When Carter entered this corridor it was filled with rubble. But originally it had been used as another store room until necropolis guards discovered that the tomb had been robbed. The contents of the corridor were then moved to another site, KV 54. They included large jars, dockets, bags of natron, bandages, and

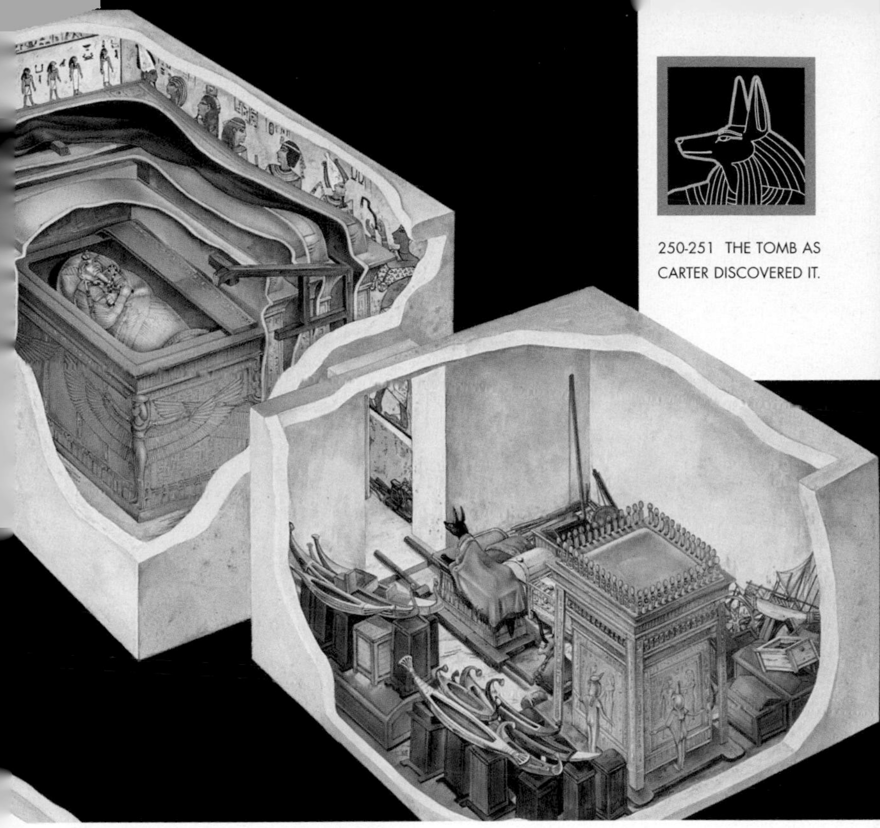

250-251 THE TOMB AS CARTER DISCOVERED IT.

flowers—materials apparently used for the embalming of the young king. After re-burying the objects, necropolis guards filled the corridor with debris as a further means of thwarting future tomb robberies. KV 54, the embalming cache, was found and excavated in 1907.

The first chamber beyond the corridor, the **ANTECHAMBER,** measures 7.9 meters (26 feet) by 3.6 meters (12 feet) and is 2.8 meters (9 feet) high. Into this relatively small space Tutankhamen's priests had crammed huge beds, war chariots, chairs, stools, elaborately inlaid and painted boxes, alabaster jars, mummified ducks, and gilded statues that stood guard at the entrance along the right (north) wall.

At the left side of the rear wall of the Antechamber a small, low door leads into what Carter called the **ANNEXE** (4.4 meters or 14 feet long and 2.6 meters or 9 feet wide). Its floor lies about a meter (3 feet) below that of the Antechamber, but its ceiling is lower, too (2.6 meters or 8 feet). Into this room priests had packed foods and unguents, bottles of wine, jars of oils, baskets of fruits and vegetables, and there were pieces of clothing, jewelry, and furniture.

The floor of the **BURIAL CHAMBER** is also about a meter below that of the Antechamber and measures 6.4 meters (21 feet) long by 4 meters (13 feet) wide. It is 3.7 meters (12 feet) high. Four gilded shrines that nearly filled the room nested one inside the other and held the quartzite sarcophagus inside which were two gilded coffins holding a third, of solid gold, in which lay Tutankhamen's mummy.

East of the burial chamber lay the Treasury, 4.8 meters (16 feet) by 3.8 meters (12 feet) and 2.3 meters (8 feet) high. It was filled with a gilded canopic shrine, boats, shabti-statuettes, boxes filled with figures of gods and goddesses, a large statue of a recumbent Anubis jackal, and two mummified fetuses that may have been Tutankhamen's unborn children.

The only decoration in KV 62 is on the walls of the Burial Chamber and it bears some similarities to KV 23, the tomb of Ay. On the left (west) wall twelve baboons, each in its own rectangle, kneel beneath the night bark of the sun god in its form as Khepri, the scarab beetle, preceded by three male and two female deities. This is a scene from the first hour of the *Imydwat*.

On the rear (north) wall, king Ay stands before the royal mummy, wearing the elaborate panther-skin costume of a *sem*-priest, performing the Opening of the Mouth ritual. Between the two figures, a low table is piled with various instruments needed for its performance and five small bowls of incense. At left, Tutankhamen, wearing an elaborately folded kilt, stands before the goddess Nut in whose hands are hieroglyphs representing water. Farther left, Tutankhamen (in the middle) and his *ka* stand before Osiris.

Like all of the decoration in KV 62, the figures here are rather hastily done and ill-proportioned. The figure of Ay and, to a lesser extent, one of the figures of Tutankhamen, shows the influences of Amarna art. Note their sagging stomachs, for example, the thin limbs, long fingers, and slightly prognathous chins. The artist has managed to show genuine affection in the way the hands of the king and of Osiris reach out to touch and embrace each other.

On the right (east) wall of the chamber, the funeral procession is led by twelve senior court officials, similarly dressed but two of them without wigs. They pull on a rope tied to the sled on which the mummy of Tutankhamen lies in an elaborate shrine guarded by two small figures of Isis and Nephthys.

On the front wall of the burial chamber, not visible to tourists today, the king is welcomed into

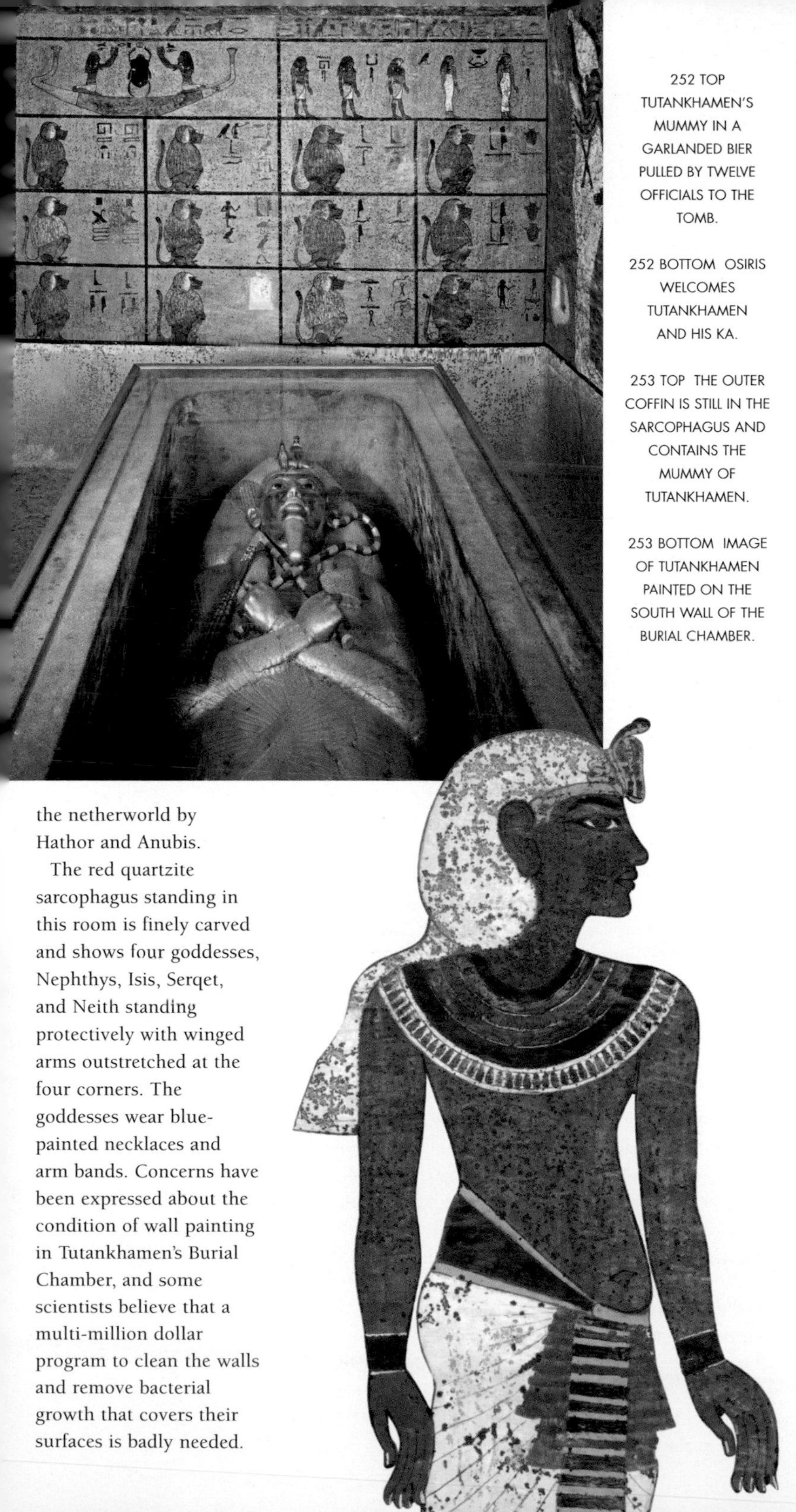

252 TOP TUTANKHAMEN'S MUMMY IN A GARLANDED BIER PULLED BY TWELVE OFFICIALS TO THE TOMB.

252 BOTTOM OSIRIS WELCOMES TUTANKHAMEN AND HIS KA.

253 TOP THE OUTER COFFIN IS STILL IN THE SARCOPHAGUS AND CONTAINS THE MUMMY OF TUTANKHAMEN.

253 BOTTOM IMAGE OF TUTANKHAMEN PAINTED ON THE SOUTH WALL OF THE BURIAL CHAMBER.

the netherworld by Hathor and Anubis.

The red quartzite sarcophagus standing in this room is finely carved and shows four goddesses, Nephthys, Isis, Serqet, and Neith standing protectively with winged arms outstretched at the four corners. The goddesses wear blue-painted necklaces and arm bands. Concerns have been expressed about the condition of wall painting in Tutankhamen's Burial Chamber, and some scientists believe that a multi-million dollar program to clean the walls and remove bacterial growth that covers their surfaces is badly needed.

3

WV 23: THE TOMB OF AY

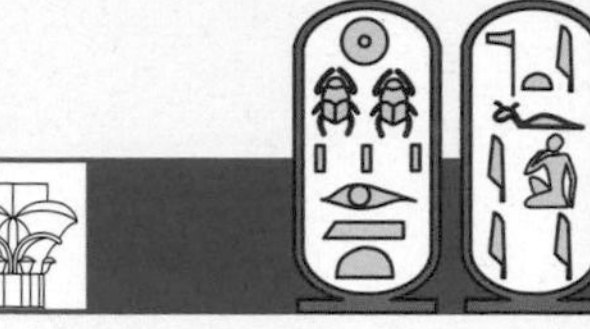

THE HISTORY

One of the most enjoyable parts of a visit to WV 23 is the long approach leading to it. There are two Valleys of the Kings, the East Valley, whose 58 tombs are the ones to which nearly all tourists flock, and the much larger West Valley, with just four (known) tombs, only one of which is open and which only a few tourists visit. That is just as well: the West Valley of the Kings is the perfect place for a solitary stroll. It is a huge wadi, a desert canyon over 2 kilometers (1.2 miles) long, defined by steep slopes and rugged cliffs that rise several hundred meters above the narrow floor. It boasts astonishingly beautiful, rugged desert scenery at its very best, but its most remarkable attribute is its silence. This was the home of Meretseger, a local Egyptian goddess whose name meant "She Who Loves Silence," and it is clear why she chose to make these hills her home. If you explore the West Valley on foot—and it is worth making a leisurely trip from the rest house to WV 23 on foot—stop frequently to enjoy a silence so profound that you can hear the beating wings of raptors in the azure sky above. The silence, the clean, clear air, and the play of sun and shade on limestone cliffs make this valley a magical place.

Following the dirt track that meanders from the rest house and parking lot through the valley, you will pass a stone house built nearly a century ago by the American benefactor Theodore Davis as his field headquarters, and a small stone hut where the guard with the key to WV 23 resides. Farther on, a narrow trail leads to the tomb of Amenhetep III. It has only recently been cleaned and is not yet open to the public. To the right of the track, a complex of low stone walls are the remains of a small village built for a Hollywood film about the Valley of the Kings called *Sphinx*. Fragments of plaster columns and wall carvings from the movie set still litter the ground.

WV 23 lies at the far end of the West Valley, a few meters from two other small, undecorated tombs, WV 24 and 25. A nearby electrical generator provides light for the tomb and sadly, breaks the spell of the silent valley. (It is best to have the guard turn the generator on just as you enter the tomb and turn it off immediately after you leave it.)

The tomb was first explored in 1816 by Giovanni Belzoni, but it was not until the 1970s that a thorough clearing and study was undertaken. Those excavations found evidence that the tomb had been sealed in antiquity with mudbrick and plaster over the gate before chamber E, proof that the burial chamber had been used in antiquity. But for whom? There is no doubt that the ultimate occupant of the tomb was Ay, the royal successor of Tutankhamen and Smenkhkare. But Egyptologists believe that the tomb may originally have been dug for Amenhetep IV/Akhenaten, Tutankhamen, Smenkhkare, or some combination of these three rulers.

A steep set of stairs leads to two long, wide corridors, an intervening staircase, and the small chamber E. None of these chambers is decorated. The chamber beyond, burial chamber J, was originally meant to be pillared. It is unclear why the tomb's plan was changed.

The tomb of Ay owes its plan to the design of royal tombs at Tall al-Amarna rather than to earlier Dynasty 18 royal tombs.

254 TOP THE KA OF AY, FROM THE BURIAL CHAMBER.

255 TOP THE BURIAL CHAMBER OF AY.

255 BOTTOM DETAIL OF TEXT ON THE LEFT WALL OF THE BURIAL CHAMBER.

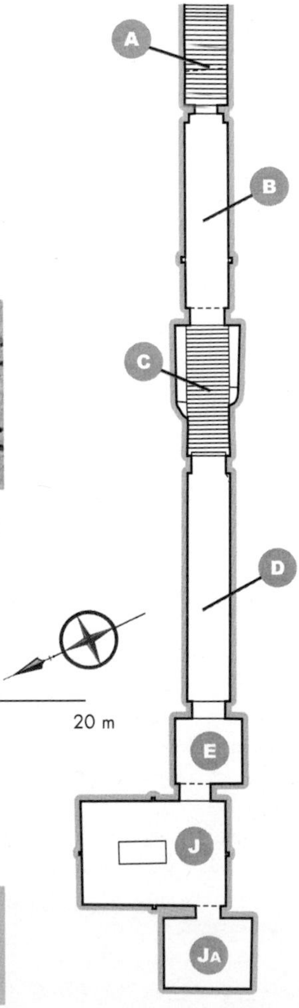

0 20 m

LEGEND

A *ENTRANCE*
B *FIRST CORRIDOR*
C *STAIRWELL*
D *SECOND CORRIDOR*
E *WELL CHAMBER*
J *BURIAL CHAMBER*
JA *SIDE CHAMBER*

VISIT

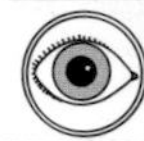

The tomb is similar to KV 62, the tomb of Tutankhamen, and some Egyptologists believe that the same artist was responsible for the two. In both, only the burial chamber was decorated. Unfortunately, many of the scenes in WV 23 have been damaged, some by ancient Egyptians bent on destroying any vestiges of the Amarna Period—the cartouches and faces of the king are nearly all defaced—others by thieves and vandals. Recently, the burial chamber was cleaned by the Egyptian Supreme Council of Antiquities, and pine flooring, fluorescent lights, and an electric fan installed in the chamber. It has more the appearance of a provincial art gallery than a royal tomb, but it is the decorated walls that one has come to see, and they are well worth a look.

On the left wall of the chamber, in the upper register, the goddess Nephthys stands between two solar barks. That on the left carries two standards topped with falcons. On the right, the other carries the nine deities of the Ennead. From right to left, these are: Ra-Harakhty, Atum, Shu, Tefnut, Geb, Nut, Osiris, Isis, and Horus. Below, columns of text are from chapters 130 and 144 of the Book of the Dead, dealing with giving eternal life to the soul of the deceased and with the gates in the netherworld.

On the rear wall, a fine representation of the Four Sons of Horus was painted directly above a low gate leading to side chamber Ja, thought to be the storeroom for canopic jars. Canopic jar stoppers were usually carved in the form of the heads of those four deities. Seated at left, wearing the crown of Upper Egypt and carrying flails, are Duamutef and Qebehsenuef; at right, sit Imsety and Hapi, wearing the crowns of Lower Egypt. Between them an elaborately-painted offering table is piled high with foodstuffs. To the right, Ay and his ka greet Hathor, Nut, and Osiris.

On the right wall, the scenes come from the first hour of the *Imydwat*. In the upper register, a scarab beetle, the daytime form of the sun god, comes forth in his sacred bark. Below, baboons express the world's delight at the reappearance of the sun.

The front wall of the chamber is particularly interesting because its scenes are ones generally found only in private tombs; they are unique in this royal setting. Ay and his wife stand in a small reed skiff sailing through a marsh along the edge of the Nile, and the queen reaches out to pull papyri from the water. At left, the king wields a throwing stick and a dozen ducks rise from the marshes, trying to escape. The birds are very formally positioned and their number, twelve, reminds us again of the hours of night and day. At right, there was a scene of the king harpooning a hippopotamus, but the wall here has been so badly destroyed that nothing is visible today.

The beautiful granite sarcophagus in the center of the chamber was found broken by thieves and removed to the Egyptian Museum, Cairo about a century ago for restoration. It was returned to the tomb in the 1990s. Scenes on the box are from the Book of the Dead and show the goddesses Neith, Serqet, Isis, and Nephthys, as well as a winged solar disk.

The small square holes in each wall of the burial chamber are niches in which magical bricks bearing inscriptions were placed to protect the mummy.

256 THE FOUR SONS OF HORUS, FROM THE REAR WALL OF THE BURIAL CHAMBER.

257 TOP SACRED BABOONS FROM THE NORTH WALL OF THE BURIAL CHAMBER.

257 CENTER NEPHTHYS IN FRONT OF A SOLAR BARK, FROM THE LEFT WALL OF THE BURIAL CHAMBER.

257 BOTTOM A FLIGHT OF DUCKS FROM THE EAST WALL OF THE BURIAL CHAMBER.

3

KV 57: THE TOMB OF HOREMHEB

THE HISTORY

KV 57 was discovered in February 1908 by the British archaeologist, Edward Ayrton, whose project was funded by the American industrialist, Theodore Davis.The tomb is one of the largest and most beautiful in the Valley of the Kings. Upon its discovery Davis confidently proclaimed that "the Valley of the Tombs is now exhausted." How wrong he was! Only fourteen years later, Howard Carter discovered the tomb of Tutankhamen.

The tomb of Horemheb is remarkably well preserved, and its decoration is some of the most important in the Valley of the Kings. Architecturally, it marks a transition between earlier tombs, whose axes made a right-angle turn, and the straight-line, single-axis tombs of the later New Kingdom. The axis of Horemheb's tomb makes a jog in chamber F, shifting about 2.5 meters (8 feet) to the left. That is about the same as the change in axis in the tomb of Sety I, which moves left 2.9 meters (9.4 feet). The tomb is 128 meters (416 feet) long and covers over 473 square meters (5028 square feet). KV 57 was damaged during a rainstorm in the Valley of the Kings in 1996 and has since been closed for repairs. Plans call for it to be reopened soon.

The tomb was sealed in antiquity. The rear wall of well chamber E had been closed with stone and mudbrick, traces of which can still be seen in the lower left and right corners of the gate. The stairway in chamber F, at the start of the "jogged axis," was sealed with stone blocks, and the gates into chamber I and into burial chamber J were closed with wooden doors. Thieves had breached all these barriers in antiquity. The funerary equipment they left behind included a number of small wooden figures of gods, an alabaster canopic chest, miniature embalming beds, garlands of flowers, human bones, jewelry, and some of the tools used for digging and decorating the tomb. The sarcophagus in the burial chamber was the most impressive piece thieves left behind, a beautifully carved box and lid, 2.7 meters (9 feet) long and 1.5 meters (6 feet) wide.

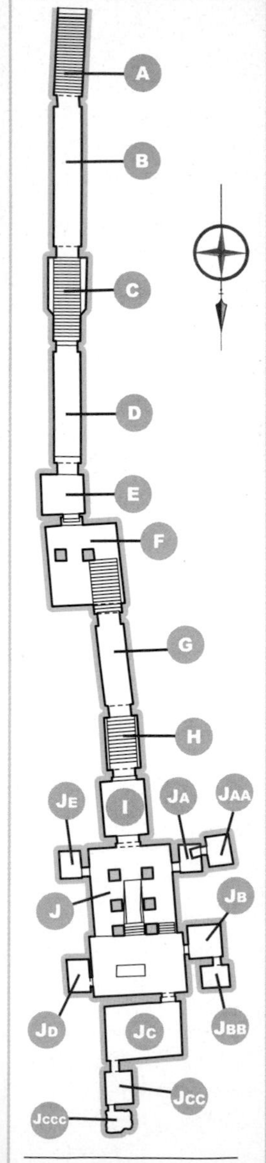

258 TOP DETAIL OF CARVED AND PAINTED TEXTS.

259 VIEW OF THE WELL CHAMBER E.

LEGEND

A *ENTRANCE*
B *FIRST CORRIDOR*
C *STAIRWELL*
D *SECOND CORRIDOR*
E *WELL CHAMBER*
F *PILLARED CHAMBER*
G *THIRD CORRIDOR*
H *STAIRWELL*
I *ANTECHAMBER*
J *BURIAL CHAMBER*
JA, AA, B, BB, C, CC, CCC, D, E *SIDE CHAMBERS*

VISIT

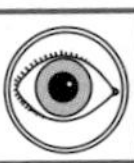

The first four corridors of the tomb were never decorated, but they are interesting nevertheless. Walking down the alternating ramps and steps in **CORRIDORS A THROUGH D** one can admire the limestone bedrock and embedded layers of chert through which the tomb was cut. It is some of the best stone to be found in the Valley of the Kings.

WELL CHAMBER E is the first decorated part of KV 57, and its four walls are covered with finely carved figures painted on a blue-grey background. Well shafts like this were intended to thwart thieves, some say, or to block flood waters. But Ayrton reported seeing a small chamber cut at the bottom of the shaft, a feature that would argue against these explanations. Instead, the shaft may have served as a symbolic burial place of Osiris. Debris still fills its lower part and the chamber has not been seen in recent times.

260 PAINTING FROM THE WELL CHAMBER WITH OSIRIS, ANUBIS AND HORUS.

260-261 HOREMHEB OFFERING TO VARIOUS GODS, FROM THE LEFT WALL OF THE WELL CHAMBER.

261 BOTTOM DETAILS FROM THE LEFT WALL OF THE WELL CHAMBER: ISIS ON THE LEFT, HORUS ON THE RIGHT.

Horemheb's tomb was the first royal tomb decorated in painted raised relief instead of simply painted on flat, plastered surfaces. Some Egyptologists have claimed that this new and unfamiliar technique slowed the work so dramatically that the tomb had to be left unfinished. That seems unlikely: artisans were perfectly aware of how to carve relief. More likely, work on the tomb had started late in the king's twelve-year reign and was not yet finished at the time of his death.

The carved and painted figures in well chamber E are beautifully executed, the colors as bright as the day they were first applied. The layout of the scenes creates a simply ordered but harmonious and pleasing picture. Notice the details of Horemheb's costume, the finely modeled ears of the goddesses, and the elaborate headdress of the falcon-headed god.

The dresses of the goddesses are among the most elaborate woven cloth patterns to be seen in any Egyptian tomb.

The hieroglyphs too, are perfectly proportioned and detailed: note the feathers of the geese, the frontally drawn human face, and the woven patterns of reed mats and baskets.

Scenes in well chamber E show the king with various deities. Horemheb is the first king depicted actively praying and offering to the gods. Earlier scenes showed the king statically posed with a deity.

On the front wall, Horemheb stands with Horus and Hathor.

An Anubis jackal sits atop a shrine. On the left wall, he is with Horus, Isis, Hathor, and Osiris. On the right wall, he offers to Hathor, Osiris, Horus, and Isis, and on the rear wall, he stands with Horus, Anubis, and others before the god Osiris, who is seated on his throne.

Across the top of all four walls, a *khekher* frieze has been painted in a simple but brightly-colored style.

CHAMBER F follows; it is a small two-pillared chamber in which the central axis of the tomb jogs to the left. This is a transitional tomb plan, an intermediate stage between the right angle turns of earlier royal tombs and the single straight axis of later ones. The pit in which the following stairs were cut was originally sealed with limestone blocks. The next two rooms, alternating stairways and corridors, are again undecorated.

CHAMBER I, however, is decorated with scenes similar to those in well chamber E. On the front wall, Horemheb stands with figures of Hathor and Horus on the left, and Hathor only on the right. Unlike other figures in this tomb, which are attractively done, the figure of Hathor is oddly proportioned: her head is much too large for her body, her shoulders much too broad. She affectionately cradles the king's elbow in one hand and rests her other hand on his shoulder. On the left wall, the king stands with Anubis, offers wine to Isis and Hathor, and greets Horus and Osiris. On the right wall, he is with Anubis, Isis, Horus, Hathor, and Osiris. On the rear wall, he is shown with Ptah and Nefertum. There is also a *djed*-pillar and an Isis knot on the rear wall. A *khekher* frieze can be seen at the top of all four walls; the ceiling is covered with stars. Ma'at stands in the entrance to the burial chamber.

Horemheb's **BURIAL CHAMBER** has two parts. At the front is a six-pillared section, the floor of which lies at the same level as the preceding chamber. At its rear, two sets of stairs, the center one preceded by a ramp, descend into a slightly lower, rectangular section with a flat ceiling. Each part of the burial chamber has a single, small side-chamber on its right side and double side chambers on its left. The second room of the two on the left side of the chamber's first part lies below the first side chamber, an unusual if not unique feature in a royal tomb. The left-hand chamber at the rear of chamber J has an especially fine figure of Osiris on its rear wall, painted directly on roughly cut, unsmoothed stone, giving the figure a rumpled and slightly disconcerting appearance. There are three other side chambers, cut one behind the other, beyond the burial chamber's rear wall. Such chambers were used as storerooms for funerary furniture and offerings of food and drink.

262-263 DECORATION OF THE WEST WALL OF THE ANTECHAMBER: HOREMHEB STANDS BEFORE ANUBIS, ISIS, HORUS AND OSIRIS.

263 BOTTOM SCENES FROM THE BOOK OF GATES IN THE BURIAL CHAMBER.

The sarcophagus of Horemheb is a beautifully carved box and lid made of red granite and decorated with sunk relief that was painted yellow. At each corner, a goddess with wings outstretched protectively encircles the king's mummy. At front left is the goddess Serqet, at front right the goddess Nephthys; Isis and Neith are on the back corners. Figures on the front-facing side of the box are the deities Duamutef, Anubis, and Imsety; on the rear-facing side, Hapy, Anubis, and Qebehsenuef.

It is the decoration in Horemheb's burial chamber that makes this tomb an essential part of a tourist's itinerary. The workmanship is very good quality, although the decoration was never finished. Because work was abandoned at different stages, we are able to trace the progress of the ancient artisans as they carved and painted the tomb. Let us first describe the subject-matter of the decoration in the burial chamber and then look more closely at the artisan's techniques.

KV 57 is the first royal tomb to have scenes from the Book of Gates on the walls of the burial chamber. In earlier royal tombs that is where the *Imydwat,* "The Book of That Which Is in the Netherworld" was placed. The name "Book of Gates" refers to the gates that defined each of the twelve hours of the night, and the text describes the journey of the sun, accompanied by the king, through the night sky. In KV 57, the text is incomplete. On the front wall of the burial chamber, the Book of Gates' second hour appears; on the left wall, we find a continuation of the second hour as well as the fourth and fifth hours; on the right wall, the third and sixth hours; and on the rear wall more of the sixth hour.

The second hour shows the blessed dead in the upper register with the sacred bark being towed into the presence of seven deities. Only the god standing in the bark shrine is carved; all other figures here are painted. Below, the four "exhausted ones" and twenty bound men are being taken away. "Ra has judged you and your false testimonies are to you," the text reads in part, "your evil grumblings are to you, bad is the judgment of my father to you."

In the third hour, mummies are being revived and the sun god is towed in the Bark of the Earth, with bulls at either end. It is borne by eight mummies. The snake at the bottom is Apophis, archenemy of the sun god, overcome by Atum and other deities. At right, as in the other scenes from the Book of Gates, the gate, shown as an open door, accompanies the scene. It is watched over by

264-265 THE JUDGEMENT OF THE DEAD.

265 TOP CARVED SCENE IN THE BURIAL CHAMBER.

265 BOTTOM THE RED GRANITE SARCOPHAGUS.

a snake, drawn vertically, which will open the gate only for the bark of the sun god.

The bodies of water in the fourth hour are the Lake of Life and the Lake of Uraei, guarded by jackals and uraeus figures. In the middle register, the solar bark is towed before nine rooms, each with a recumbent mummy called a "divine follower of Osiris." At right, figures representing the twelve hours of the night stand on either side of a great snake whose coils are meant to suggest the passage of time. Horus stands at far left in the lower register with eleven deities and a uraeus facing a shrine of Osiris. Enemies of the gods are condemned by four "captains of the furnaces" to pits of eternal fire.

In the fifth hour, snakes again represent the passing of time. Figures of Nubians, Libyans, Asiatics, and Egyptians are included; all will be cared for in the afterlife.

Preceding the sixth hour, a scene of the judgment of the dead was drawn on the rear wall of Horemheb's burial chamber. Osiris sits on a throne placed on a dais before a balance. Nine of the blessed dead climb the stairs toward him. A pig, symbol of the god Seth and associated with evil, stands in a small boat and is being attacked by monkeys, protectors of the sun god, carrying sticks. The sixth hour is the midpoint of the sun's nocturnal journey and at this critical point, men armed with pronged sticks stand guard against the sun's enemy, Apophis. So significant was this scene in Egyptian religious belief that the texts accompanying it are written cryptographically. Only the few priests who were familiar with the code could read them.

An especially fine scene from the sixth hour at the right end of the lower right wall shows four men pulling a bark with a figure of Ra standing in a shrine.

These scenes are complex and highly symbolic, and there is much about them we do not fully understand. They deal with some of the most important events Egyptians could have imagined: the safe, nighttime passage of the sun through the netherworld, and its reappearance in the morning; the journey of the deceased king as he accompanies the sun; and the relations between humankind, the king, and the gods.

All living beings depended on the successful performance of these activities, and the artisans, priests, and scribes who drew them and the accompanying texts must have been under some pressure to "get it right" when they decorated the tomb. Such concern for accuracy can be seen in Horemheb's burial chamber.

266 TOP VARIOUS STAGES OF DRAWINGS AND RELIEFS, WITH RED AND BLACK INK OUTLINES.

266 BOTTOM DETAILS OF PAINTED RELIEFS FROM VARIOUS CHAMBERS.

267 SOME OF HOREMHEB'S TOMB SCENES WERE ONLY PAINTED, NOT CARVED, LIKE THIS SCENE OF THE BARK OF RA.

After the burial chamber had been roughly cut, masons smoothed its walls. Presumably using papyrus copies of the Book of Gates as their guide, the artisans first outlined the text and scenes on the walls in red ink. A senior scribe then reviewed their work, making initial corrections in red ink, final versions in black ink. These corrections could simply change the proportions of figures to make them more aesthetically pleasing, or they could correct errors of spelling or iconography that could negate the effectiveness of the text. There are numerous examples of such corrections. After the outlines had been revised, the background surrounding the figures would have been cut away, leaving them standing out as if they had been stamped by a cookie cutter. The figures would then have been given interior details and modeling. Interestingly, although there are many examples of incompletely carved scenes, painted scenes are almost always either completely painted or not painted at all. A rare exception is the unfinished gray background behind the line of men on the front corner of the left wall

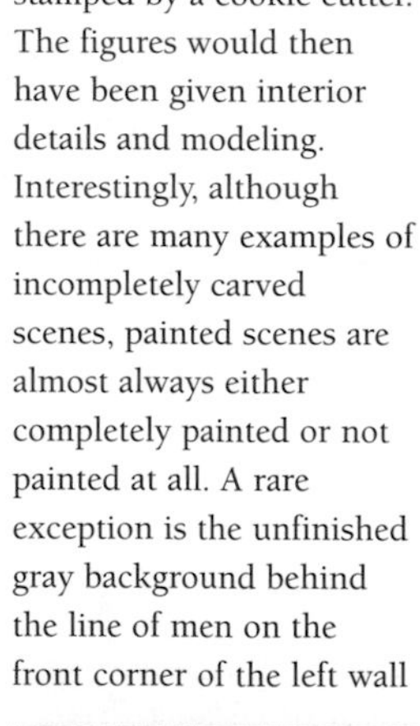

in the lower part of the burial chamber. It is worth looking carefully at the carved and painted figures in the burial chamber; the workmanship is of good quality, the details sometimes exceptionally well drawn. But there are also figures that seem slapdash: on the right side of the front wall in the upper, pillared section of the burial chamber, a finely executed figure of Ra-Harakhty stands in a shrine with two sloppily painted men sharing the bark.

An example of the stages of work can be seen on the left wall in the pillared front part of the burial chamber. The scene, from the fourth hour of the Book of Gates, shows the god Ra standing in his bark. Only the god has been carved; the other figures are painted outlines. The figure standing behind him was redrawn several times, twice in red ink, once in black, and with each correction, its size was reduced. The proportions of many surrounding hieroglyphs were changed or their placement adjusted, sometimes several times. On the gate at left, the outlined figures seem to have been carved almost at random; carved hieroglyphs are surrounded by uncarved neighbors. The glyphs have been cut in outline only and there is no interior detail or modeling. The *khekher* frieze underwent a number of revisions, and the red-line corrections show at least three changes in position and size. The final, black-line version, however, is done with the certainty and confidence only a senior artisan could have brought to the task. The scene of the judgment hall on the rear wall is drawn in outline, but a scarab beetle, a mask of Anubis, and the throne, beard, and *ankh*-sign of Osiris are painted solid black.

It would have been difficult working underground to remember which was the north, south, east, or west wall of a chamber, but that information was important because scenes had to be properly located and oriented. Therefore, in each corner of the burial chamber and on each wall, a scribe has written in black ink the hieroglyphic word indicating the appropriate cardinal direction.

KV 16: THE TOMB OF RAMESES I

THE HISTORY

Rameses I came to the throne after a career in the army under Horemheb. Members of his court apparently did not expect him to rule very long—he was already quite old—and they carved for him a small tomb that satisfied only the barest requirements of a royal funeral, a tomb that could be completed quickly. They were prescient: Rameses I died only sixteen months after being crowned. Hasty changes had to be made to the already-abbreviated tomb plan: what might have become a corridor became instead the burial chamber, and the unusually wide niches in corridor C were left unfinished. The tomb is the smallest royal tomb in the Valley of the Kings, smaller even than that of Tutankhamen. Even so, it is clear that the original tomb plan owed much to that of Horemheb (KV 57). This is especially clear in its decorative style and the use of grayish-blue as the background color for scenes and texts.

Some believe that the same artists were responsible for both tombs. Only burial chamber J and a small niche beyond (side chamber JB) were decorated.

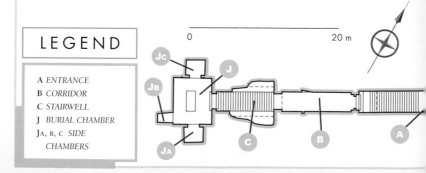

LEGEND

A *ENTRANCE*
B *CORRIDOR*
C *STAIRWELL*
J *BURIAL CHAMBER*
JA, B, C *SIDE CHAMBERS*

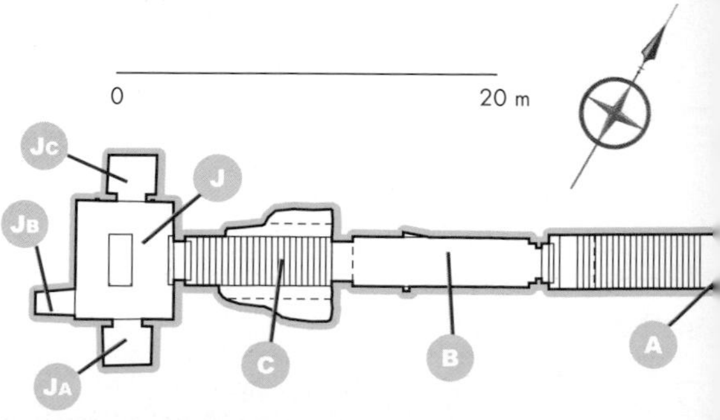

0 — 20 m

Jc
J
JB
C
B
A
JA

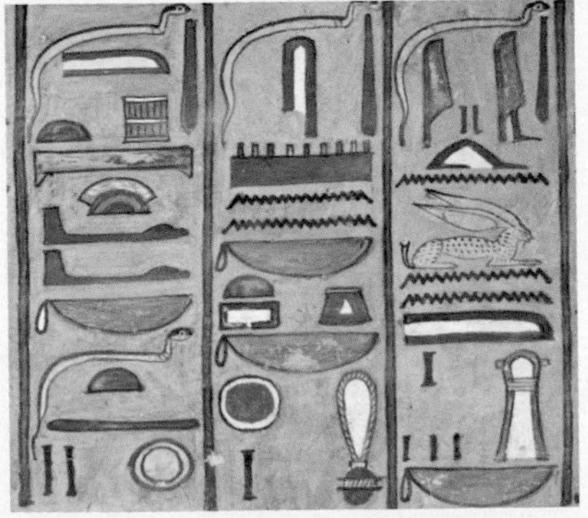

268 TOP RAMESES I, FROM THE BURIAL CHAMBER.

268-269 BACK WALL OF THE BURIAL CHAMBER WITH ATUM-RA-KHEPRI AND OSIRIS ON THRONES.

269 TOP THE RED GRANITE SARCOPHAGUS IN THE BURIAL CHAMBER.

269 BOTTOM DETAIL OF TEXTS IN THE BURIAL CHAMBER.

270 TOP, 271 TOP AND BOTTOM LEFT RAMESES I WITH NEFERTUM AND MA'AT; PTAH; HORUS AND ANUBIS.

270 CENTER THE BOOK OF THE GATES FROM THE BURIAL CHAMBER.

270 BOTTOM PROCESSION, FROM THE RIGHT WALL.

271 BOTTOM CENTER AND RIGHT BARK WITH SUN GOD; OSIRIS IN A SHRINE.

VISIT

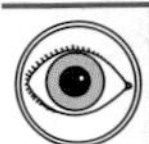

On the left wall of the **BURIAL CHAMBER**, the fourth hour of the Book of Gates begins with a representation of the gate in the left corner, protected by a vertically drawn snake. The solar bark is towed toward nine shrines in which nine mummies lie, awaiting resurrection by the sun god. Below, a huge multi-coiled snake represents the passage of time, watched over by twelve goddesses who represent the twelve hours of the night.

A single register on the rear wall includes nicely painted figures of Atum-Ra-Khepri—a human god with the head of a scarab beetle—and Osiris, seated on thrones that face in opposite directions. A *Iwnmutef* priest stands before Osiris, preparing to receive Rameses I, who is being led before the god by Horus, Atum, and Neith. Atum-Ra-Khepri receives another figure of Rameses I, very finely dressed, who presents the god with four caskets of cloth. To the right, above the entrance to side chamber JB, a kneeling figure of Rameses I is joined by the Souls of Pe (Buto) and Nekhen (Hierakonpolis) in adoration of Osiris.

A well-drawn bark carrying a ram-headed figure of the sun god is painted on the right wall against a white background. The shrine in which he stands is protected by a snake called Mehen, and by the gods Sia and Heqa. The scene comes from the third hour of the Book of Gates. The bark is about to travel through the long tube-like feature at left. In the register below, the evil snake Apophis poses a potential threat to the sun god but is restrained by Atum and nine other deities.

On the front wall, the goddess Ma'at greets the king as he enters his tomb. Behind her, the king stands with the gods Ptah and lotus-crowned Nefertum.

The red granite sarcophagus was painted red. Yellow figures with their details in black are of the Four Sons of Horus, Anubis, Thoth, Isis, and Nephthys. There is a lovely scene in the small niche in the rear wall of the chamber showing Osiris standing in a shrine, his feet on a snake, protected by Anubis and the uraeus-cobra.

3

KV 17: THE TOMB OF SETY I

THE HISTORY

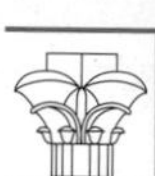

In 1821, huge crowds in London and Paris attended an exhibition of paintings copied from the tomb of Sety I. That tomb, which had been discovered four years earlier, received an enthusiastic reception in Europe. Indeed, except for the 1922 discovery of the tomb of Tutankhamen and the 1995 discovery of KV 5, no tomb in the Valley of the Kings was ever more in the public eye. It is not difficult to understand why: the tomb was huge, completely decorated, beautifully preserved, and its discoverer, Giovanni Belzoni, published a captivating account of his work there. KV 17 was the first tomb in the Valley of the Kings to be completely decorated; every wall and pillar from the entrance onward is covered with scenes from the Book of Gates, the *Imydwat*, the Litany of Ra, the Book of the Heavenly Cow, and the Opening of the Mouth ritual. The work was finely done, with elaborate details in costumes and hairstyles, and the scenes are among the best-preserved in the valley. Or rather, they were.

Belzoni and other visitors not only made water color copies of the walls but took squeezes, pressing wet paper against the relief carving, letting it dry, then pulling the three-dimensional copy off the walls. Naturally, this damaged the paint. Belzoni also cleared the tomb entrance and removed natural barriers to flooding. When a torrential rain hit the valley shortly after the tomb was opened, floodwaters poured into the first several chambers and did serious harm. A few years later, several pieces of wall decoration were hacked out and taken to Europe—by Jean-François Champollion and Ippolito Rosellini. Many other visitors followed suit.

Clearing of the long passageway that had been cut deep below the floor of the burial chamber, an operation first attempted a century ago and restarted in the 1950s by the descendents of a well-known tomb robber, created serious structural problems in the tomb that required adding brickwork and steel to correct. More projects have had to be undertaken in the last few decades to keep parts of the tomb from collapsing. Recently, the tomb was closed to visitors in order to make extensive conservation studies, but these have not been completed and no plans have yet been made to start the needed work. As a result, KV 17 is likely to remain closed for the foreseeable future.

272 TOP AND 273 TOP RELIEFS OF IWNMUTEF PRIESTS.

272-273 ISIS WITH SPREAD WINGS.

CORRIDOR B A steep staircase leads down to the entrance of the tomb into corridor B. The walls of the corridor are decorated with the Litany of Ra, with a figure of the king standing before Ra-Harakhty on the left wall, followed by the "title page" of this text, shown here for the first time in a royal tomb. This is followed by the text itself, along with seventy-five invocations of the sun god. The text continues on the right wall. The ceiling is decorated with birds whose heads are alternately vultures and snakes.

CHAMBER C or **STAIRWELL** A large staircase was cut in the floor of stairwell C and

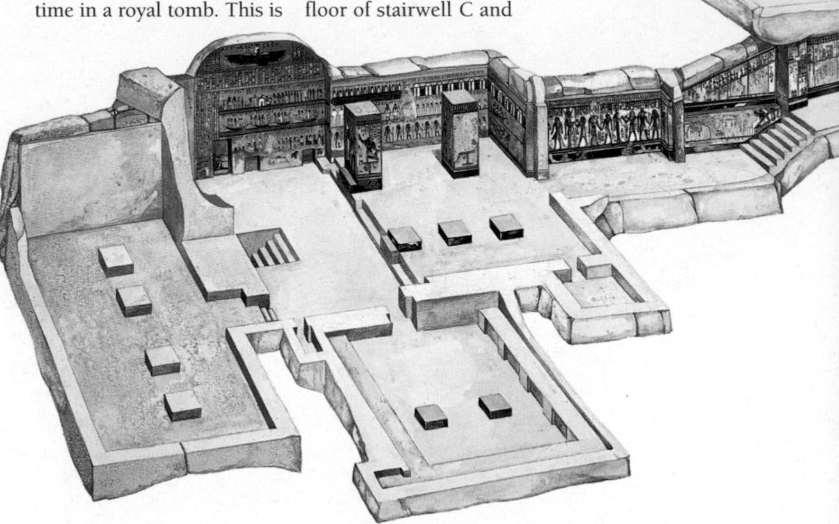

LEGEND

A *ENTRANCE*
B *FIRST CORRIDOR*
C *STAIRWELL*
D *SECOND CORRIDOR*
E *WELL CHAMBER*
F *PILLARED CHAMBER*
FA *SIDE CHAMBER*
G *THIRD CORRIDOR*
H *FOURTH CORRIDOR*
I *ANTECHAMBER*
J *BURIAL CHAMBER*
JA, B, C, D *SIDE CHAMBERS*
K *CORRIDOR*

274-275 DRAWING OF THE NORTH SIDE OF THE TOMB.

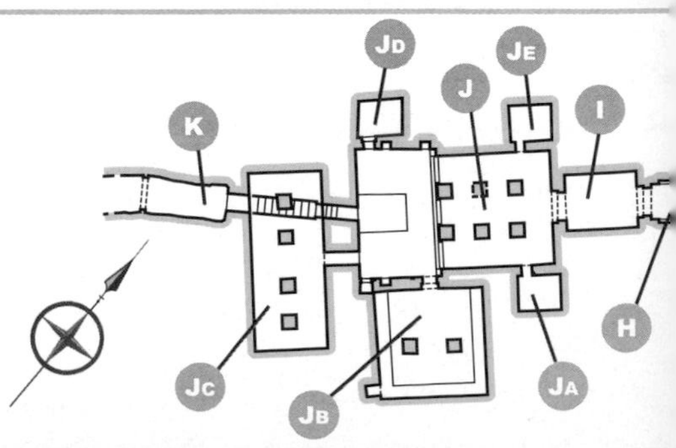

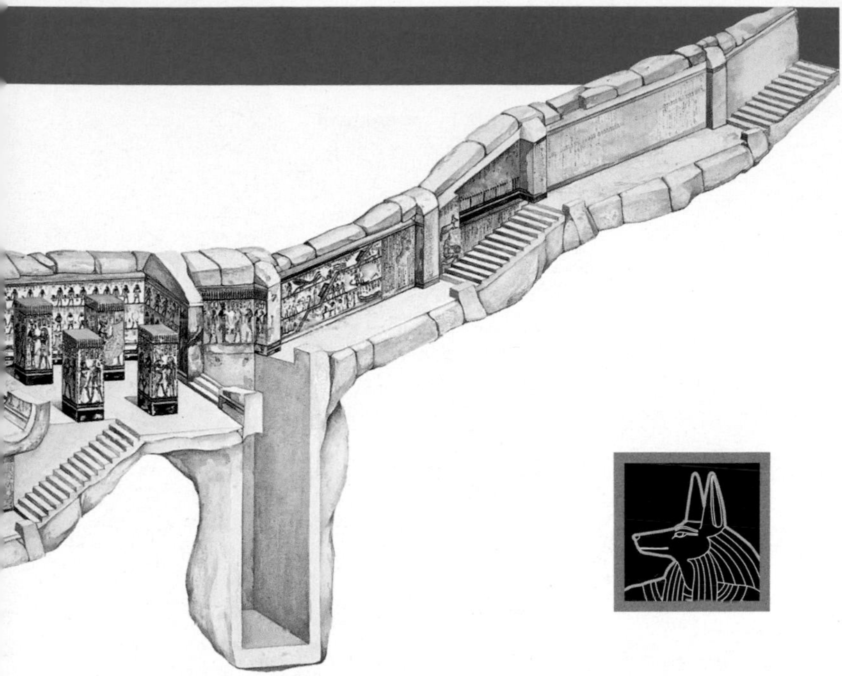

large recesses were cut in the walls above it. The Litany of Ra continues, followed by the last part of the third hour of the *Imydwat*. Beyond the recesses, a figure of Isis kneels below a reclining Anubis jackal on the left wall. Nephthys is similarly posed on the right. Above the rear door is a figure of Ma'at and the cartouches of Sety I. In **CORRIDOR D**, the fourth hour of the *Imydwat* appears on the right wall, the fifth hour on the left. Black ink outlines mark the location of uncut recesses. Much on these walls has been badly damaged, but when Belzoni first visited the tomb they were in almost pristine condition.

CHAMBER E, with a well shaft, 6.7 meters (22 feet) deep, is decorated at the top on the left side with a single row of figures showing the king being led by Harsiese before Isis, offering wine to Hathor, and standing before Osiris and the Mistress of the West. In the right half of the chamber, a seated figure of Osiris is followed by Anubis and Harsiese and other scenes similar to those on the left. The rear wall of the chamber originally was blocked with stone and brick, then covered with plaster and painted, apparently in an attempt to thwart tomb robbers.

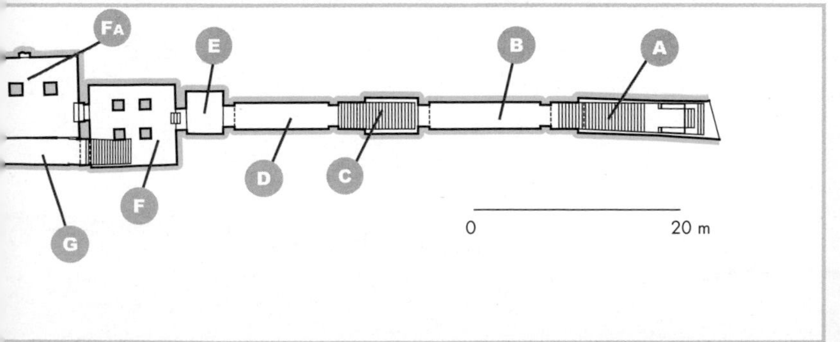

276-277, 277 BOTTOM LEFT AND RIGHT THE FOUR PILLARED ROOM, ON EACH FACE OF EACH PILLAR SETY I STANDS WITH A DEITY.

276 TOP MUMMIES ON A SNAKE-SHAPED BIER, FROM THE BOOK OF THE GATES.

276 BOTTOM SETY I STANDS BEFORE OSIRIS, FOLLOWED BY HORUS, FROM THE REAR WALL.

277 BOTTOM CENTER THE SNAKE APOPHIS, FROM THE BOOK OF THE GATES.

Beyond the well shaft, **CHAMBER F** is a four-pillared chamber whose walls are decorated with the fifth hour (on the left) and the sixth hour (on the right) of the Book of Gates. In the lower register, the souls of the dead are united with their mummies, and these lie on a long snake-shaped bed. In the upper register, divine guardians keep the snake Apophis from doing harm to the sun god. At the left front corner of the chamber is a damaged scene that, a century ago, was well-preserved and one of the most-admired scenes in the tomb, frequently copied and commented upon. It shows a row of western Asiatics, Nubians, Libyans, and Egyptians, dressed in traditional costume and wearing traditional hairstyles. The white background on these side walls contrasts with the rear wall where, against a yellow background, Sety is led by Horus before a figure of Osiris who is seated before Hathor. A small section of this scene has recently been cleaned as a test by conservators and reveals how affected the pigments have been by dust and humidity over the last three millennia.

Moving clockwise around pillar 1 (front left), we see the king standing before Ptah and embraced by Harsiese, then Anubis, then the Mistress of the West. On pillar 2 (rear left), the king is embraced by Ra-Harakhty, Shu, Serqet, and Isis. Pillar 3 (front right) shows the king before a god, then Hathor, Harsiese, and Anubis. Finally, pillar 4 (rear right) shows the king with Atum, Nephthys, Neith, and Ptah-Sokar.

Side **CHAMBER FA**, the two-pillared chamber beyond, has a lower floor than chamber F and was decorated only with figures and texts outlined in black ink. It is not clear why these walls were not painted like all other scenes in the tomb. Some have suggested that the chamber's unfinished state, the jog in the tomb axis, and the possibility of hiding the succeeding staircase combined to provide yet another way of convincing tomb robbers they had reached a dead end. The scenes are taken from the ninth, tenth, and eleventh hours of the *Imydwat*. The skill of the artist is impressive: lines are drawn with long and confident strokes. Note on the left wall the figures of those who have died by drowning and therefore require special assistance to enter into the netherworld. On the pillars the king is shown with Nefertum, Ra-Harakhty, Ma'at, and Atum; and with Ma'at, Osiris, Hathor, and Sokar-Osiris.

A decorated staircase leads down to **CORRIDORS G AND H**. Its scenes are taken from the Opening of the Mouth ritual and show priests performing the ceremonies. They are dressed in the leopard skin costumes of *Iwnmutef* priests and stand before royal statues. Great care was taken in the painting of the leopard skin and the leopard-head-shaped clasp. Note also the unusual way the priest holds the paw of the leopard in his left hand. This is one of the best-drawn representations of the Opening of the Mouth ceremony to be found in the Valley of the Kings, but much was destroyed by nineteenth century visitors who hacked pieces away for shipment to European collections. **CHAMBER I**, the chamber preceding the burial chamber, was called the Hall of Beauties by Belzoni because of its finely painted figures of the king and various gods. Unfortunately, the squeezes made by nineteenth century visitors seriously damaged the paint and stained the walls. What one sees today is a mere shadow of what once had been a masterpiece. Nevertheless, the quality of the relief carving can still be admired, especially details of faces and hieroglyphs. On the left side of the chamber, the king is shown seven times, embraced by Hathor, standing before Anubis, offering to Isis, standing before Harsiese, offering to Hathor, standing before Osiris, and with Ptah. The right side is similar, except at the far end, where the king stands before Nefertum.

278-279 RIGHT WALL OF ANTECHAMBER I, OR HALL OF BEAUTIES.

279 CENTER FROM CORRIDOR H, RITUAL SACRIFICE FOR THE OPENING OF THE MOUTH CERIMONY.

279 BOTTOM TWO-PILLARED CHAMBER FA DECORATED ONLY IN BLACK INK.

Sety's Burial **CHAMBER J** has two sections, a front part with six pillars and a rear part with a lowered floor on which the sarcophagus originally sat beneath a dramatic vaulted ceiling. The pillars are damaged: one of them is missing; others were cut up and removed to museums in Europe. Originally, all of them showed the king with various gods, including *Iwnmutef*, Ptah-Sokar, Geb, Osiris, Khepri, Thoth, Harsiese, Shu, Ra-Harakhty, Anubis, and the souls of Pe and Nekhen. The latter three are arranged along the main tomb axis. The walls in the upper, pillared section contain texts and scenes from the Book of Gates, the second and fifth hours on the left side, the third on the right.

On the side walls of the lower, vaulted part of the chamber, winged figures of Isis and Nephthys kneel, flanked by cartouches of Sety I. The *Imydwat* begins with the first hour on the left wall in both a long and an abbreviated version. The second hour can be seen on the rear wall, the third on the right.

The **VAULTED CEILING** is one of the most impressive in the Valley of the Kings. It deals with astronomical subjects, many of them obscure. A hippopotamus and a crocodile near the midline of the ceiling are constellations the Egyptians located in the northern sky.

280 TOP THE SIX PILLARED BURIAL CHAMBER.

280-281 THE SOLAR BARK, SOUTH SIDE OF THE BURIAL CHAMBER.

281 TOP LEFT SOUTH SIDE OF THE LOWER PART OF THE BURIAL CHAMBER.

281 TOP RIGHT SETY I WITH OSIRIS ON A PILLAR OF THE BURIAL CHAMBER.

281 BOTTOM DETAIL OF THE ASTRONOMICAL CEILING.

SIDE CHAMBERS off both the upper and lower parts of the burial chamber are decorated with the fourth hour of the Book of Gates. The Book of the Heavenly Cow is in the first right-hand chamber. The left rear chamber has two pillars painted with figures of Osiris, and extensive wall decoration that includes the seventh through ninth hours of the *Imydwat*.

In the lower part of chamber J, a square pit was dug in the floor, and into its rear wall quarrymen cut a small doorway. It leads into a narrow, well-carved tunnel extending at least 100 meters (325 feet) at a steep downward angle into the bedrock. When Belzoni entered the tomb, the tunnel was completely filled with dense debris. It still has been only partly excavated, so its ultimate destination is unknown. Some have expressed the hope that burial chamber J is not really the burial place of Sety I but a false chamber meant to fool tomb robbers. The tunnel, they claim, leads to the real burial place deep inside the mountain, and is still filled with treasure. This seems unlikely. Most Egyptologists argue that the tunnel was intended to join the burial of Sety I to ground water, and was similar to what Sety I had done in the Osireion at Abydos, where the "burial" of Osiris was symbolically joined to the primeval waters of creation.

282 TOP THE LEFT REAR CHAMBER JB WITH TWO PILLARS.

282 BOTTOM, 283 CENTER AND BOTTOM DETAILS OF WALL DECORATION IN CHAMBER JB.

283 TOP SETY I EMBRACES AN UNUSUAL REPRESENTATION OF OSIRIS, FROM A COLUMN IN CHAMBER JB.

3

KV 7: THE TOMB OF RAMESES II

At least ten archaeologists and explorers have tried their hand at clearing the tomb of Rameses II; all but the most recent quickly abandoned the work. We know that the tomb was open in antiquity, but it has suffered since, hit by a series of torrential floods that washed tons of debris into the tomb's chambers, doing serious damage to walls and pillars. Richard Pococke was here in 1737, the Napoleonic expedition in 1799, and Henry Salt around 1817. In 1913, Harry Burton described the tomb as being in "a very bad state....It was necessary to pull down a great deal of the ceiling." Since 1993, French Egyptologist Christian LeBlanc has been working here, and his reports regularly announce important discoveries.

It is unlikely that KV 7 will be opened to the public any time soon. There are still thousands of cubit meters of debris to clear away and substantial structural engineering to be done. It is a pity: Egyptologists fortunate enough to visit the tomb are invariably impressed as they walk down long corridors still half-full of debris. The descent is made in total darkness, only a torch offering a dim light, and dust that fills one's nostrils also muffles their footsteps. Stepping into the vast burial chamber, the thin light of the torches reveals piles of debris lying in a great void created when the pillars supporting the vaulted ceiling collapsed thousands of years ago.

As befits a king with the power and longevity of Rameses II, KV 7 is one of the largest tombs in the Valley. It covers 686 square meters (7384 square feet), extends 168 meters (551 feet) into the hillside, and was one of the first tombs to be dug near the entrance to the Valley of the Kings. That area is prone to serious flooding (as the tomb damage attests), but perhaps the large hillside here seemed the best site to accommodate so large a tomb. Its plan reverts to the right-angled layout of Dynasty 18 royal tombs, and its decorative program is like that of KV 17, the tomb of Sety I. There also were changes: KV 7 is the first royal tomb to have the jambs and lintel of the entrance gate decorated, and the reveals of the gate are carved with figures of the goddess Ma'at.

Excavations have revealed only a few objects in the tomb, probably because it was heavily robbed in antiquity. We know, for example, that thieves broke in during the twenty-ninth regnal year of Rameses III, and undoubtedly there were many other robberies as well.

The tomb was extensively decorated, in both raised and painted relief and in painted plaster, but few of its damaged walls have been exposed for study. As in the tomb of Sety I, corridor B was decorated with the Litany of Ra. Texts in corridor C are from chapter 151 of the Book of the Dead. The Book of What is in the Netherworld (*Imydwat*), follows in corridor D and well chamber E. Then follow scenes and texts dealing with the Opening of the Mouth ritual. In chamber I, where the tomb's axis makes a right angle turn to the north, the rear wall is

JA
JB
JC
JD
JDD
JDDD
JE
JF
J
I
H
G
F
FA
FAA
E
D
C
B
A
0
20 m
LEGEND
A ENTRANCE
B FIRST CORRIDOR
C STAIRWELL
D SECOND CORRIDOR
E WELL CHAMBER
F PILLARED CHAMBER
FA, AA SIDE CHAMBERS
G THIRD CORRIDOR
H FOURTH CORRIDOR
I ANTECHAMBER
J BURIAL CHAMBER
JA, B, C, D, DD, DDD, E, F
SIDE CHAMBERS

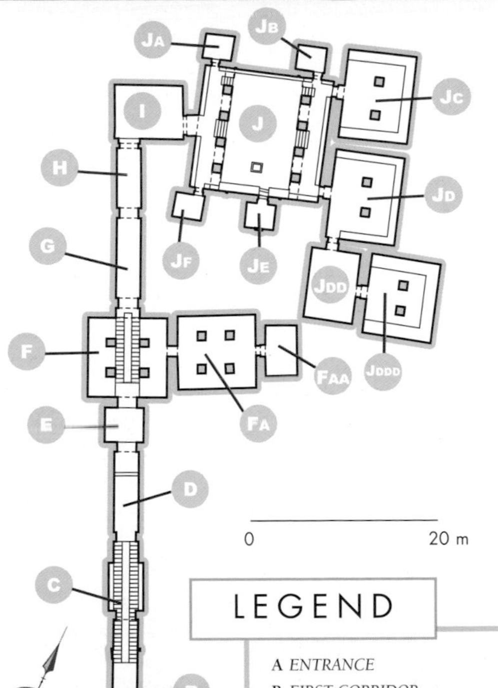

covered with the Negative Confession, chapter 125 of the Book of the Dead. In burial chamber J and its several side chambers, we return to the *Imydwat* and the Book of Gates. The Book of the Heavenly Cow, which also is to be seen in a side chamber in the tomb of Sety I, can also be seen in side chamber JF.

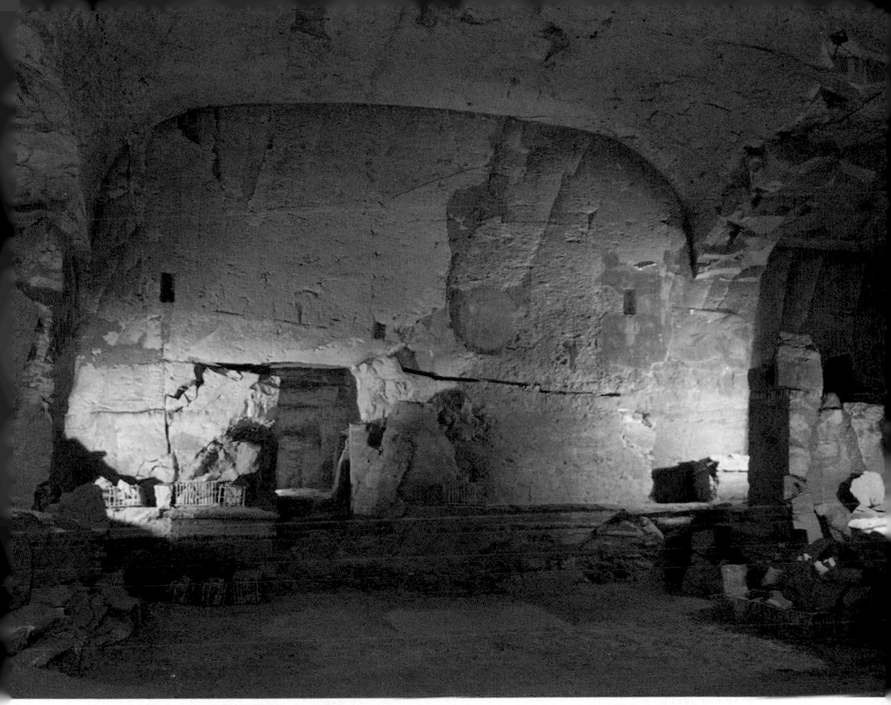

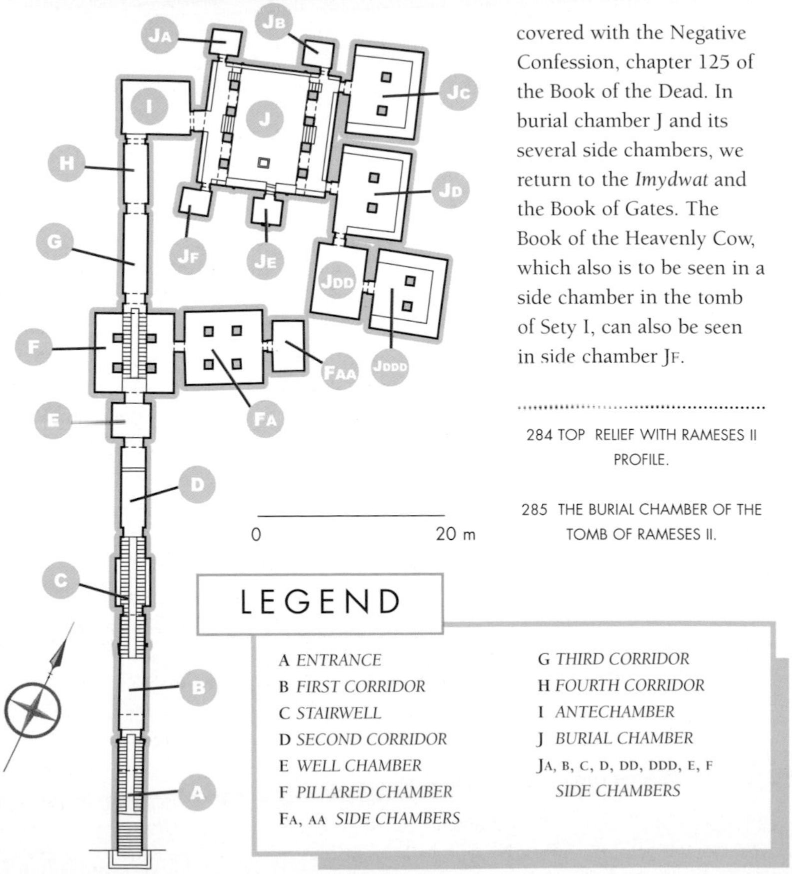

284 TOP RELIEF WITH RAMESES II PROFILE.

285 THE BURIAL CHAMBER OF THE TOMB OF RAMESES II.

KV 5: THE TOMB OF THE SONS OF RAMESES II

In 1987, the Theban Mapping Project relocated a tomb near the entrance of the Valley of the Kings that had been "lost" for nearly a century. Called KV 5, it was the fifth tomb south of the valley's entrance to be numbered by John Gardner Wilkinson in his 1827 survey of the royal tombs. The tomb was first mentioned in modern times in 1825 by the Englishman James Burton. Burton dug a narrow channel through the densely packed debris that filled the tomb (debris washed in during heavy rains to which the valley is occasionally subjected) and managed to crawl about 25 meters (80 feet) beyond its entrance. But in the eight chambers into which he was able to slither, he saw no decoration or objects, and decided that KV 5 was uninteresting, simply a debris-packed-hole in the ground. A century later, Howard Carter also decided the tomb was of no value and dumped debris from his nearby excavations atop its entrance.

But shortly after it relocated KV 5 and began to clean the debris from its first chamber, the Theban Mapping Project discovered that the tomb was decorated with important scenes and texts that revealed it had been the burial place of several sons of Rameses II. During the next several years, excavations found decoration on every wall and pillar they cleared. In February 1995, while digging along the back wall of chamber 3, a huge sixteen-pillared hall, the Theban Mapping Project uncovered a doorway that led into a series of long corridors. Extending deep into the hillside, more than fifty side chambers extended to their left and right. KV 5 suddenly had become the largest tomb ever found in the Valley of the Kings and one of the largest in all Egypt. It was a tomb unique in plan and in its function as a mausoleum for several members of the royal family.

Clearing has continued, and by 2004 the Theban Mapping Project had found over 130 corridors and chambers in KV 5, and many more are certain to be exposed in the future. The hugely complicated plan of the tomb reveals features that were dug on several different levels, in many different directions, providing multiple burial suites for at least six sons of Rameses II. Hundreds of thousands of potsherds, thousands of broken objects, animal bones, and human remains have been found in the debris. Some were washed into the tomb, some were found *in situ*. On the walls are the names and titles of Rameses II and his sons; scenes of the king presenting sons to deities in the netherworld; and copies of religious texts such as the Book of the Dead's Negative Confession (chapter 125).

The debris choking KV 5 is so densely packed and the process of ensuring structural stability so time consuming, that by 2003 only two dozen of the tomb's many chambers had been cleared.

It will take many more years of work before KV 5 can be opened to the public. In the meantime, regular updates on these ongoing excavations are made available on the Internet at http://www.thebanmapping-project.com.

286 TOP PAINTED RELIEF WITH THE PROFILE OF RAMESES II.

287 KENT WEEKS AND ASSISTANT WORK CLEARING THE 16-PILLARED HALL.

0 20 m

LEGEND

A *ENTRANCE*
1 *CHAMBER 1*
2 *CHAMBER 2*
3 *16-PILLARED CHAMBER*
4 *6-PILLARED CHAMBER*
5 *PILLARED CHAMBER*
6 *CHAMBER 6*
7 *CORRIDOR*
8 *CHAMBER 8*
9 *CHAMBER 9*
10 *CORRIDOR*
11 *CORRIDOR*
12 *CORRIDOR*
13 *CORRIDOR*
14 *PILLARED CHAMBER*
15 *CHAMBER 15*
16 *CORRIDOR*
17 *CHAMBER 17*
18 *CHAMBER 18*
19 *CHAMBER 19*
20 *CORRIDOR*

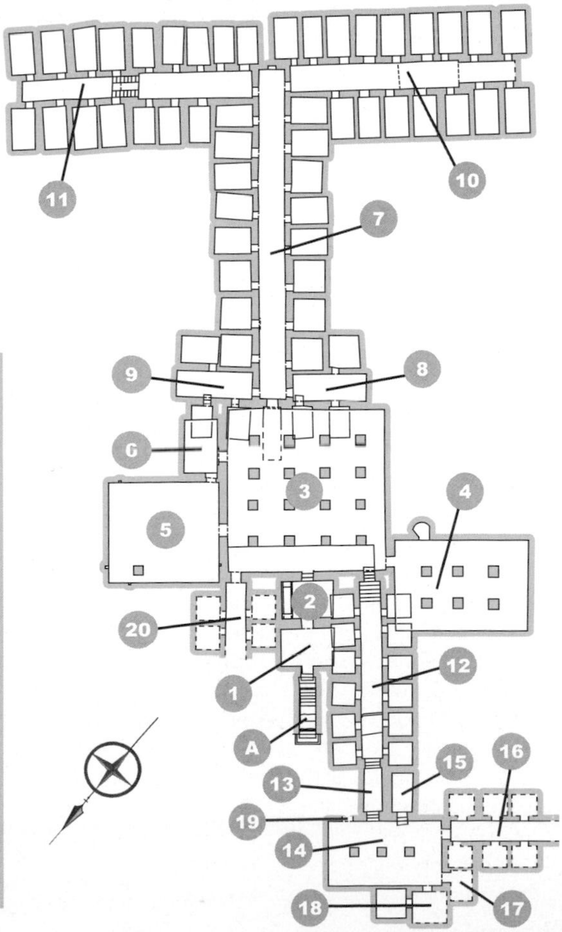

3

KV 8: THE TOMB OF MERNEPTAH

THE HISTORY

Occupying 2472 cubic meters (87,300 cubic feet), the tomb of Merneptah is the second largest in the Valley of the Kings, exceeded only by KV 5. The first half of this 135–meter (439 feet) long tomb has been accessible since antiquity—there are 121 Greek and Latin graffiti on the walls of its first six chambers. The rear half, however, was excavated only in 1903 by Howard Carter, and the burial chamber was not excavated until 1987. The four side chambers off the burial chamber still have not been freed of flood-borne silts and stone chippings. Merneptah was an old man when he ascended the throne after the long rule of his father, Rameses II, and he ruled for only about ten years. But work on his tomb was completed before his death, and only the rearmost chambers beyond the burial chamber were left roughly cut and undecorated.

KV 8 exhibits several interesting architectural features. It has a straight axis, slightly sloping corridors, and lacks the jog at midpoint that characterized the tombs of Horemheb and Sety I, or the right-angle turn in the tomb of Rameses II. Most interesting, however, is what some Egyptologists regard as evidence of a major construction error. Plans for the king's burial called for three huge granite sarcophagi and a fourth of calcite to be nested within each other in the burial chamber. When the largest of them arrived in the Valley of the Kings, it was discovered that it was too wide to fit through the gates of the tomb, even though the gates are among the widest in the valley. (The largest sarcophagus lid measures 2.13 meters wide; the gates average about 2.12 meters.) Apparently, the architects or quarrymen had made a serious blunder. Their solution was simple: the existing gates were cut away, even though they had already been decorated, the sarcophagi were dragged into the burial chamber, and then the gates were rebuilt using sandstone blocks. These blocks have mostly disappeared (a few lie in side chamber FA), and the scarred walls are glaring evidence of the embarrassing error.

The decoration of the tomb is traditional, similar to that in the tombs of Merneptah's father, Rameses II, and his grandfather, Sety I. The workmanship is generally good and the paint, unfortunately damaged by floods, still shows traces of fine, bright blue-green, yellow, and red pigments.

VISIT

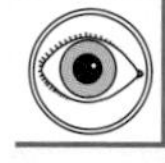

The **FIRST CORRIDOR, CORRIDOR B**, is decorated with a lengthy copy of the Litany of Ra. It begins on the left (south) wall with a well-carved scene of the king before Ra-Harakhty and the "title page" of the Litany that shows a sun disk enclosing a scarab and Ra-Harakhty with a serpent and a crocodile nearby. The ceiling decoration, a repetitive pattern of vultures, is brightly painted.

CORRIDOR C has large recesses at the front top of its side walls containing texts that continue the Litany of Ra. Below them are the second

and third hours of the *Imydwat* and, farther on, more of the third hour and part of the fourth. At the end of the corridor, scenes of Anubis jackals lie above figures of Isis (on the left wall) and Nephthys (on the right), together with a text from Chapter 151 of the Book of the Dead. It deals with important aspects of the king's funeral.

288 TOP DETAIL OF CEILING DECORATION.

289 LEFT MERNEPTAH BEFORE RA HARAKHTY IN THE FIRST CORRIDOR.

289 RIGHT THE BEGINNING OF THE LITANY OF RA: A SCARAB AND RA-HARAKHTY ENCLOSED IN A SUN DISK.

LEGEND

A *ENTRANCE*
B *FIRST CORRIDOR*
C *SECOND CORRIDOR*
D *THIRD CORRIDOR*
E *WELL CHAMBER*
F *PILLARED CHAMBER*
FA, AA *SIDE CHAMBERS*
G *FOURTH CORRIDOR*
H *SARCOPHAGUS CHAMBER*
I *FIFTH CORRIDOR*
J *BURIAL CHAMBER*
JA, B, C, D *SIDE CHAMBERS*
K *REAR CHAMBER*
KA, B, C, *SIDE CHAMBERS*

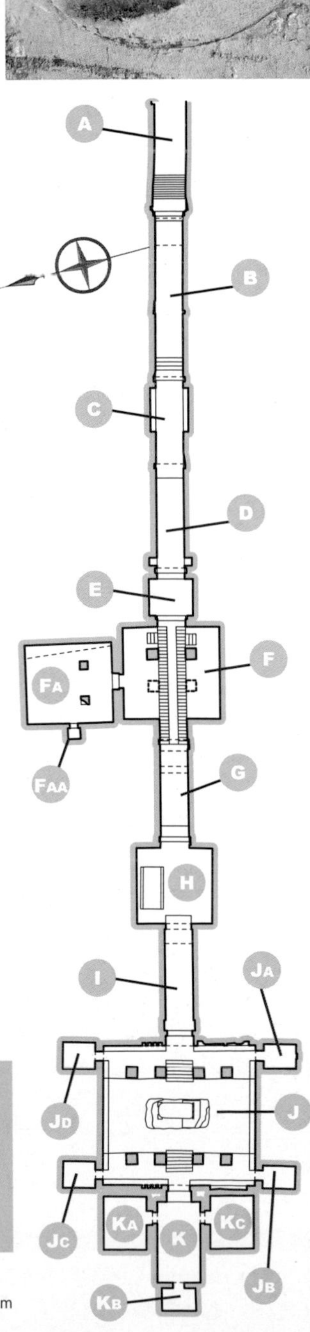

0 20 m

The *Imydwat* continues into **CORRIDOR D** with hours four (on the left wall) and five (on the right).

The well shaft, **CHAMBER E**, has never been completely cleared. The upper part of its walls shows figures: on the front wall of the chamber, Merneptah stands on the left of the door, Osiris on the right. On the rear wall, Anubis is on the left, the king as *Iwnmutef* on the right. On the left wall there are nicely painted standing figures of Imsety, Duamutef, Anubis, Khery-Baqef, Isis, and Neith. On the right, Hapy is followed by Qebehesnuef, Anubis, Nephthys, and Serqet.

Originally, **CHAMBER F** had four pillars but two were removed before its walls were decorated. A gate into a side chamber was cut through the right (north) chamber wall after the scenes there had been carved. The side chamber has two pillars and a small shrine to Osiris cut into its left (west) wall. The chamber is closed today, used as a storeroom for fragments of sarcophagi. A finely painted double scene of the king offering to Osiris on the rear (west) wall of chamber F and the fourth, fifth, and sixth hours of the Book of Gates cover the other walls. The pillars have been badly damaged and recently repaired, but one can identify scenes of the king offering to Osiris, Ptah, and Horus on the left pillar, Osiris, Ra-Harakhty, Ptah and Anubis on the right.

CORRIDOR G is also badly damaged, but originally had scenes of the Opening of the Mouth ritual on its walls. On the left wall, the king is seated before an offering table with two priests performing funeral ceremonies.

290 THE PILLARED CHAMBER F WITH DAMAGED PAINTINGS.

291 TOP MERNEPTAH OFFERING TO OSIRIS, FROM THE PILLARED CHAMBER.

291 CENTER AND BOTTOM DETAILS FROM THE BOOK OF GATES, ON THE REAR WALL OF THE PILLARED CHAMBER.

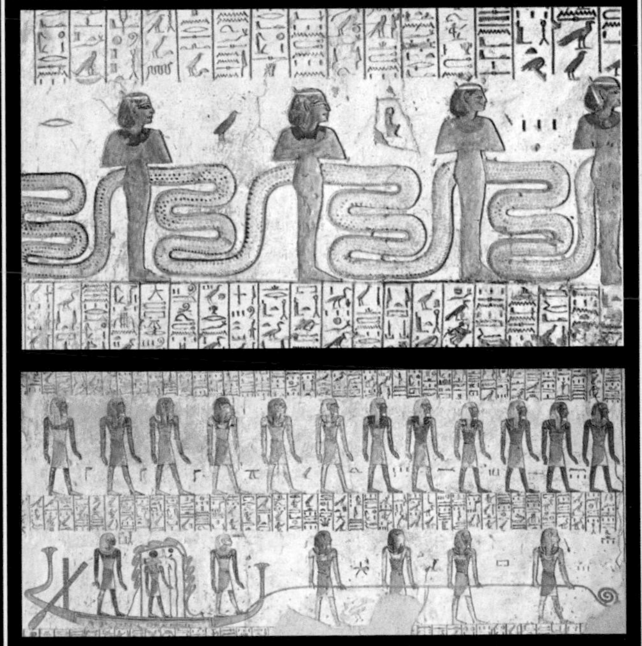

292 TOP DETAIL OF THE LID OF MERNEPTAH'S SARCOPHAGUS IN THE BURIAL CHAMBER.

292 BOTTOM THE ANTHROPOID SARCOPHAGUS IN THE CENTER OF THE BURIAL CHAMBER.

293 TOP LEFT THE SARCOPHAGUS LID IN CHAMBER H.

293 TOP RIGHT TWO DETAILS FROM THE BOOK OF THE CAVERNS ON THE RIGHT WALL OF THE BURIAL CHAMBER.

The sarcophagus lid that sits on the right side of **CHAMBER H** was left here in antiquity when priests dismantled Merneptah's sarcophagi and transported some of them to the Delta site of Tanis for the burial of Psusennes I in Dynasty 21. The walls of the chamber are decorated with scenes and texts from chapter 125 of the Book of the Dead, the Negative Confession. It begins on the front wall, then continues across the left wall and onto the rear.

Almost nothing remains of the decoration in **CORRIDOR I.**

The large **BURIAL CHAMBER** must originally have been a spectacularly well-decorated room, but much has disappeared because of flooding. Two rows of four pillars each stand before and after the lowered central floor where an anthropoid sarcophagus lid remains. (Look on its underside for a lovely figure of the goddess Nut.) The chamber's front wall is decorated with the ninth hour of the Book of Gates. On the left and rear walls are the twelfth hour of the Book of Gates and excerpts from the Book of the Earth; on the right wall is the Book of Caverns and more of the Book of the Earth. The king stands with various deities on the sides of the now-destroyed pillars. Only the barest traces remain of the elaborate astronomical scenes painted on the chamber's vaulted ceiling.

293 BOTTOM THE CARTOUCHE OF MERNEPTAH.

KV 15: THE TOMB OF SETY II

THE HISTORY

Lying in the southwestern corner of the Valley, Sety II's tomb was dug only a few meters away from the tomb of his wife Tausert, KV 14. The tomb has been open since antiquity, as Greek and Latin graffiti show, and it was visited by Europeans from the 18th century on. The tomb was cleared in the early 20th century by Howard Carter, but there still remain questions about the history of its cutting, decoration, and use.
KV 15 was damaged by heavy rains in 1994 and a cement porch has been erected over the tomb's entrance. The fine quality relief carving and painting in the first corridor is followed by hastily applied painted decoration in the rest of the tomb.

VISIT

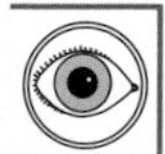

The tomb plan is simple and abbreviated because it was never finished. What should have been a corridor beyond pillared chamber F was hastily converted into the burial chamber.

Sety II was the eldest son of Merenptah, but a row over the royal succession and a temporary usurpation of the throne by Amenmeses made his reign a confusing and brief one. Many other problems, political and economic, plagued the court for the next dozen years. In such an environment, it is not surprising that planning for the king's burial was an unpredictable undertaking.

CORRIDOR B Figures of Ma'at kneeling on a basket decorate the thicknesses of the gate leading into the corridor. A recess cut into the beginning of the left wall after it had been decorated may have been intended as gate into a side chamber, but work was abandoned. Scenes on the left wall show Sety II offering to Ra-Harakhty and Nefertum. The workmanship is of excellent quality; note, for example, the costume of the king. Farther on, the opening scene of the Litany of Ra is followed by columns of its text. These continue on the right wall. The ceiling is decorated with brightly colored panels showing vultures with wings spread. The nicely cut and painted text abruptly stops before the end of corridor B, replaced by hieroglyphs written in red ink but not cut.

CORRIDOR C Red ink decoration continues into the next corridor and one can see hasty corrections to spelling and palaeography made by ancient scribes. At the beginning of the corridor, Sety II offers a small figure of Ma'at to Ra-Harakhty on the left wall and incense to Sokar on the right. Both walls are decorated with more of the Litany of Ra. In the upper register on each wall, the seventy-four forms of the sun god are shown, and beyond, the second and third hours of the *Imydwat*. On the ceiling, a sun disk with the ram-headed *ba*-bird of Ra is

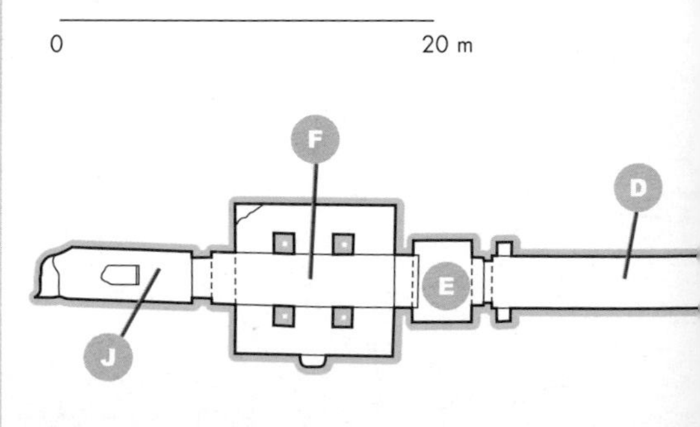

flanked by figures of Isis and Nephthys.

CORRIDOR D Again, in unfinished red ink outline we see the fourth hour (left wall) and fifth hour (right wall) of the *Imydwat*.

CHAMBER E No well shaft was dug here but the upper parts of the walls are decorated with images of divine statues, rather crudely drawn in red ink outline, and then filled with thick yellow ochre. One shows a statue of the king atop a feline in a shrine; another shows the king on a small reed boat holding a harpoon. Royal cartouches appear in faint blue paint.

CHAMBER F This four-pillared chamber with a central descent is decorated with the Book of Gates. The fifth hour is on the front and left walls, the sixth hour on the front, rear, and right walls. A double scene of the king offering to Osiris appears at the center of the rear wall. Only red and yellow pigments were used on the walls. On the pillars, green was added to scenes of the king with many gods. Figures of Ptah on the front faces of the first two pillars are more elaborately drawn than the other scenes here: the god stands in a shrine whose woven basketry walls are hastily but successfully detailed.

CHAMBER J Originally meant to be another corridor, chamber J was adapted as a burial chamber with almost no alteration to its plan. The roughly cut walls were heavily plastered and crudely painted with scenes of the sixth hour of the Book of Gates on the left and right walls and with figures of deities. Scenes of Anubis jackals atop shrines and of Osiris, both standard scenes from the sixth hour, are included. The ceiling is painted with a large and unusual figure of Nut. Sety II's sarcophagus, of red granite, lies broken on the floor.

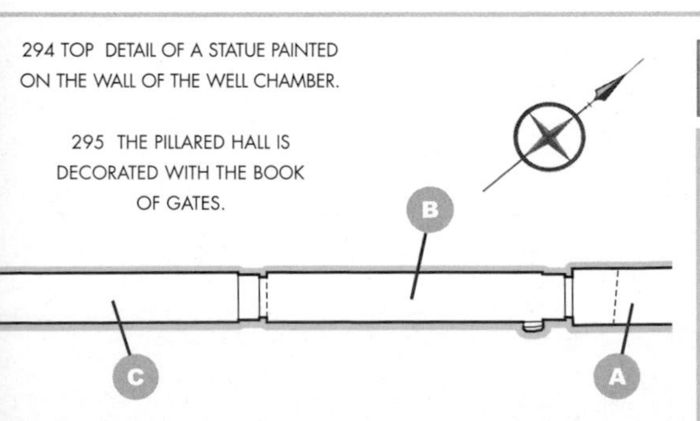

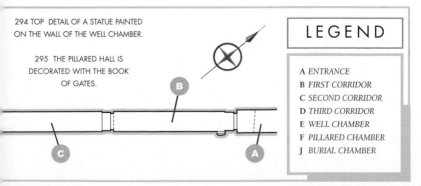

294 TOP DETAIL OF A STATUE PAINTED ON THE WALL OF THE WELL CHAMBER.

295 THE PILLARED HALL IS DECORATED WITH THE BOOK OF GATES.

LEGEND

A *ENTRANCE*
B *FIRST CORRIDOR*
C *SECOND CORRIDOR*
D *THIRD CORRIDOR*
E *WELL CHAMBER*
F *PILLARED CHAMBER*
J *BURIAL CHAMBER*

KV 47: THE TOMB OF SIPTAH

THE HISTORY

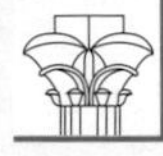

KV 47 is the burial place of Siptah, the son of Sety II, and a concubine, Tiaa. The tomb, 125 meters (406 feet) long, is like that of Sety II (KV 15), but with additional corridors in its back parts and no side chambers off the burial chamber. The tomb has a somewhat confusing history: at the end of Dynasty 19, after Siptah's burial, the king's cartouches were erased, then later restored in blue paint. The tomb was re-used in the Third Intermediate Period. Several attempts at excavation were made in 1905, 1912, and 1916 but they were thwarted because poor quality bedrock posed structural problems.

Only recently has further excavation been attempted.

VISIT

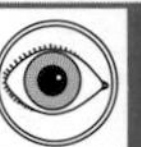

CORRIDOR B Stepping through a gate below a lintel with a brightly painted solar disk, and between figures of the goddess Ma'at seated on a basket, one enters a 15 meter (49 foot) long corridor whose walls are covered with finely executed texts and scenes. At the beginning of the left wall, Siptah stands with Ra-Harakhty, their figures painted against a yellow background. The remainder of the wall has a white background. First comes the standard opening scene of the Litany of Ra, and then the text of the Litany, which continues on the right wall. All of the Litany except the cartouches is done in painted sunk relief.

CORRIDOR C The Litany of Ra continues on both walls of this corridor with seventy-four figures, manifestations of the solar deity, standing in a long row at the top of the wall. At the end of each wall are scenes from chapter 151 of the Book of the Dead. Anubis stands beside a mummy lying on a bed with lion's heads and paws. Above, the Anubis jackal is flanked by figures of Isis and Nephthys.

CORRIDOR D Virtually all of the decoration in this chamber has gone. Originally, the walls were covered with scenes and texts from the fourth and fifth hours of the *Imydwat*.

On the right thickness of the gate leading into chamber E, at the top of the column of text, note a very finely drawn bull, in red and black, that stands with its head lowered as if preparing to charge.

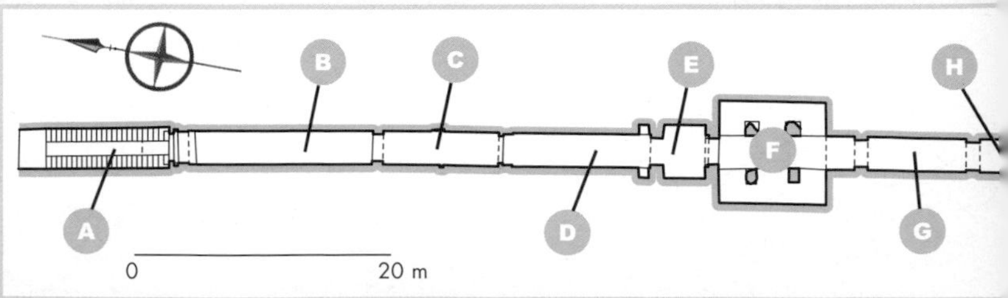

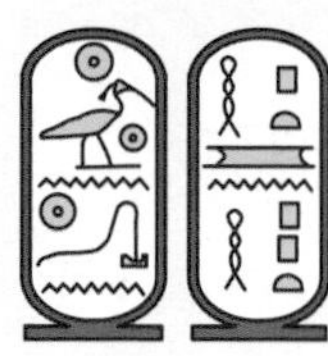

CHAMBER E AND BEYOND The remainder of the tomb has almost no preserved decoration. The poor quality of the stone, its irregular carving, and the dim lighting that has recently been installed here give the impression of walking down a mineshaft or into the dungeon of a decaying castle. In pillared **CHAMBER F** there are traces of red ink in the middle of the right wall outlining what was intended to have been a gate into a side chamber, but it was never cut. In the short corridor immediately before the burial chamber, a small side passage, perhaps intended to lead into a side chamber or to be a part of the burial chamber, broke into another tomb, KV 32, and work was therefore abandoned.

Siptah's red granite sarcophagus still stands in the burial chamber. His mummy, which shows that he suffered from poliomyelitis or clubfoot, was found in the cache of mummies uncovered in 1898 in the tomb of Amenhetep II.

296 TOP AND 297 BOTTOM THE ANTHROPOID SARCOPHAGUS OF SIPTAH.

297 TOP SIPTAH IN FRONT OF RA-HARAKHTY, FROM THE FIRST CORRIDOR.

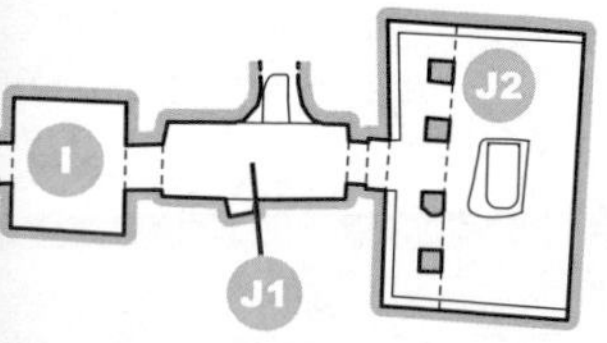

LEGEND

A *ENTRANCE*
B *FIRST CORRIDOR*
C *SECOND CORRIDOR*
D *THIRD CORRIDOR*
E *WELL CHAMBER*
F *PILLARED CHAMBER*
G *FOURTH CORRIDOR*
H *FIFTH CORRIDOR*
I *ANTECHAMBER*
J1 *SIXTH CORRIDOR*
J2 *BURIAL CHAMBER*

KV 14: THE TOMB OF TAUSERT AND SETNAKHT

THE HISTORY

The ancient history of KV 14 is confusing, and even today, Egyptologists argue about its many changes. Originally, in Dynasty 19, the tomb had been carved for king Sety II and his wife, Tausert. Sety II may actually have been buried in the tomb, in chamber J1. After Sety II's death, the throne was taken by a younger son, Siptah, and Tausert (his mother) acted as the boy's regent. Young Siptah had a club foot, suggesting that he may have suffered from poliomyelitis. He died six years later and was buried in KV 47. Tausert then declared herself sole ruler of Egypt. Her claim was not recognized, and almost immediately she was deposed—how we do not know—and a certain Setnakht was crowned in her place. (Where Tausert's mummy was buried we do not know, either; some think she was interred in KV 13.) Setnakht was to be buried in KV 11. But his son, the future Rameses III, intervened and ordered that the body instead be buried in KV 14. The extensive decoration in KV 14, begun by Sety II, then by Siptah, then by Tausert, was changed again, and Setnakht's names now replaced the earlier ones. Figures of Tausert were plastered over, hidden beneath Setnakht's painted cartouches. Many walls were left untouched, however, and the work you see in KV 14 is therefore largely that of Tausert.

VISIT

CORRIDOR B The names of the royal figures on the left wall of the corridor were changed in the course of KV 14's early history, but the scenes remained the same and are standard ones of life-size, paired figures of the deceased and deities. On the left wall, offerings of vases are made to Ra-Harakhty, of food to Anubis, and of a figure of Ma'at to Isis. A figure of Setnakht, carved over one of Tausert, stands before Horus and receives an *ankh*-sign, representing life, from Nefertum. On the right wall, a royal figure stands before Ptah, who is in an elaborate shrine, followed by the goddess Ma'at. A second figure offers to Geb, a third to Ra-Harakhty, Hathor, and Nephthys.

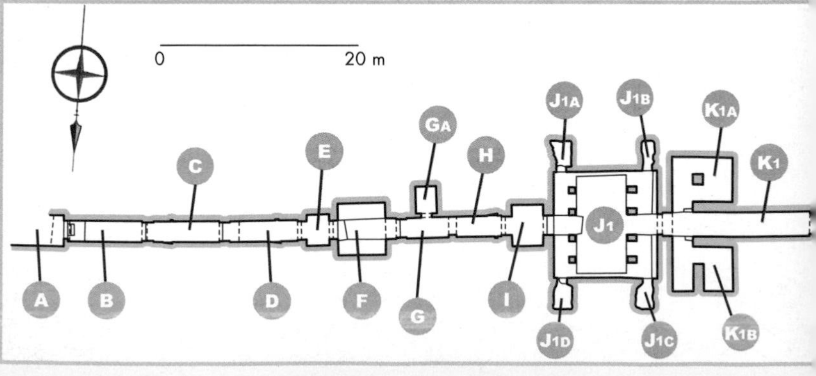

There is little color remaining in these scenes but they are generally in better condition than the salt-damaged reliefs that follow in corridor C. The carving is good, the lines spare and straightforward.

CORRIDOR C The scenes here are badly damaged but it is still possible to make out a copy of chapter 145 of the Book of the Dead at the beginning of both the left and right walls. Beyond, on the left wall, Sety II is purified by a figure of Anubis that almost seems to be smiling. On the right, Sety II offers to three knife-wielding guardians who stand before the gates of the netherworld that they protect. The rectangular holes in the middle of the left and right walls held thick wooden beams around which a rope would have been run to control the descent of a stone sarcophagus into the tomb.

Kneeling figures of the goddess Meretseger can be seen on the thicknesses of the gate between corridors C and D and on several subsequent gates as well. They were nicely painted, especially the basket on which the goddess kneels, but all are damaged.

CORRIDOR D Good quality painting can be seen in a few areas of well-preserved relief. The costumes of the deceased are nicely done. The texts on both walls are a continuation of chapter 145 of the Book of the Dead.

298 TOP GODDESS MA'AT NEXT TO THE DOOR BETWEEN SECOND AND THIRD CORRIDOR.

299 THE THIRD CORRIDOR WITH VARIOUS DEITIES.

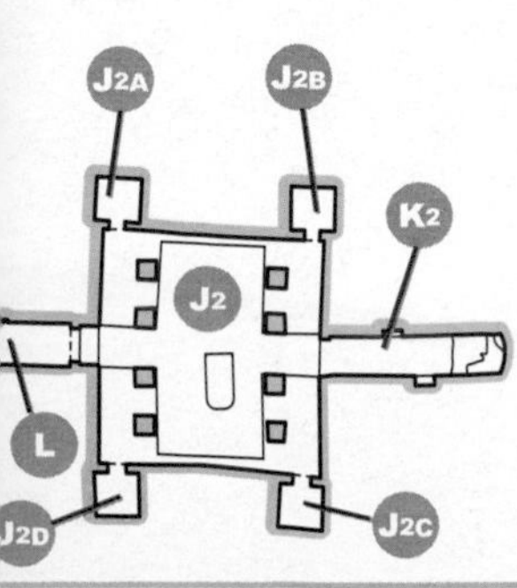

LEGEND

A *ENTRANCE*
B *FIRST CORRIDOR*
C *SECOND CORRIDOR*
D *THIRD CORRIDOR*
E *WELL CHAMBER*
F *UPPER CHAMBER*
G *FOURTH CORRIDOR*
GA *SIDE CHAMBER*
H *FIFTH CORRIDOR*
I *ANTECHAMBER*
J1 *ORIGINAL BURIAL CHAMBER OF TAUSERT*
J1A, 1B, 1C, 1D *SIDE CHAMBERS*
K1 *SIXTH CORRIDOR*
K1A, 1B *SIDE CHAMBERS*
L *SEVENTH CORRIDOR*
J2 *BURIAL CHAMBER OF TAUSERT WITH SETNAKHT'S SARCOPHAGUS*
J2A, 2B, 2C, 2D *SIDE CHAMBERS*
K2 *EIGTHTH CORRIDOR*

CHAMBER E There is no well shaft cut in this chamber but the walls were extensively decorated. On the front wall, Osiris stands on each side of the doorway. On the left wall stand figures of Imsety, Anubis, Duamutef, and Isis. On the rear wall, Horus *Iwnmutef* appears on either side of the doorway. Two Sons of Horus stand before Horus Iunmutef on the left (south) side. There are small figures atop a small alabaster table. On the right wall, also facing outward, stand Hapy, Anubis, Qebehsenuef, and Nephthys. All of the gods in this chamber are similarly dressed.

CHAMBER F No pillars were cut in this chamber but there is a central descent through its floor. Texts on both walls are from chapter 146 of the Book of the Dead. The strange-looking guardians on the side walls (three on the right, two on the left)—with heads of birds, a bearded lion, a cobra and a two-headed man—are guardians of the gates of the House of Osiris. The deceased must speak their names in order to pass through. On the rear wall is a double scene of the deceased before Osiris. Originally, there was a figure of Tausert here, being led to Osiris by Anubis and Horus. Her figure was later erased and replaced by a cartouche of Setnakht.

CORRIDOR G The Opening of the Mouth ritual is the subject of the decoration here, scenes one through five on the left wall, six through twelve on the right. In a small **SIDE CHAMBER (GA)** cut at the beginning of the left wall, chapter 151 of the Book of the Dead includes a finely-painted vignette on the rear wall showing Anubis tending a mummy flanked by Isis and Nephthys. Canopic jars and canopic chests stand beneath the bed. On the left and right walls are figures of two sons of Horus, Anubis, two goddesses, and the deceased. This small chamber is a feature found only in KV 14.

CORRIDOR H The Opening of the Mouth continues on the side walls of the chamber, sections thirteen through twenty on the left, twenty-one through twenty-six on the right. Scenes illustrating the text are arranged across the top of the wall.

CHAMBER I A very nicely drawn offering table was painted in the left half of the chamber to replace a figure of Tausert. Thoth and Ra-Harakhty are shown, as well as Ptah, who stands in his customary shrine protected by the goddess Ma'at. In the right half, the figures include Osiris, Isis, Nephthys, Horus, Geb, and Ptah again protected by Ma'at. Figures of the deceased were replaced by blue-painted cartouches of Setnakht.

300 TOP ISIS AND NEPHTHYS PROTECTING OSIRIS SITTING ON THE THRONE, FROM THE ANTECHAMBER.

300 BOTTOM PAINTINGS FROM CHAMBER F WITH TAUSERT (ERASED) LED BY ANUBIS AND HORUS TO OSIRIS.

301 VARIOUS DEITIES FROM THE ANTECHAMBER, FROM LEFT: GEB, HORUS, ISIS AND NEPHTHYS, RA-HARAKHTY, MA'AT AND THOTH.

302-303 VAULTED BURIAL CHAMBER J1.

302 BOTTOM THE NINTH HOUR OF THE BOOK OF GATES, FROM THE SOUTH WALL OF THE BURIAL CHAMBER J1.

303 THE BOOK OF THE CAVERNS ON THE RIGHT WALL OF THE BURIAL CHAMBER J1.

CHAMBER J1 This vaulted burial chamber is divided into three sections by two rows of pillars and differences in floor level. The right wall and the left end of the front wall are well-decorated with the ninth hour of the Book of Gates. A long, rectangular pool is filled with figures of those who have died by drowning. Scenes from the Book of the Earth occupy the upper part of the left and right wall. Excerpts from the sixth division of the Book of Caverns are carved on the right wall. The badly damaged ceiling still shows faint traces of astronomical subjects with decans. The rear was never decorated. Note the pieces of funerary furniture, chests, pots, and mirrors painted below the cornice and pillars. The deceased and various gods appear on the sides of the eight pillars, thirty-two figures of which many on the front face or the right side are drawn only in black and red ink.

CORRIDORS K1, K1A, K1B, L, J2 AND K2 Nearly all the decoration in the rear part of KV 14 was carved but not painted and much of it is in very poor condition. Originally, one would have seen here parts of the *Imydwat* and the Book of Gates. The sarcophagus of Setnakht that sits in burial chamber J2 is 3.25 meters (10.66 feet) long, decorated with scenes of the Book of the Earth and various deities. J2 is substantially larger than the preceding burial chamber, J1: the latter occupies 474 cubic meters (16,740 cubic feet), the former 790 cubic meters (27,900 cubic feet).

KV 11: THE TOMB OF RAMESES III

THE HISTORY

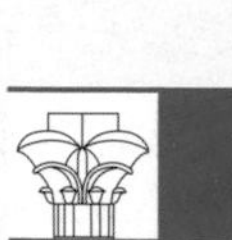

The entrance of KV 11 may have been accessible in late antiquity, but the absence of Greek or Latin graffiti inside the tomb suggests that it was choked with debris until late in the eighteenth century. Then, at least its front chambers were visited by European travelers, including James Bruce, who saw the tomb in 1769 and in 1790 published a highly imaginative drawing of the harpist depicted on the wall of side chamber Cd. His drawing struck a popular chord in Britain and KV 11 came to be called Bruce's Tomb, or the Tomb of the Harper, and grew to be one of the best-known monuments in the Valley of the Kings. Yet, in spite of its fame, most of the tomb was cleared only late in the nineteenth century.

VISIT

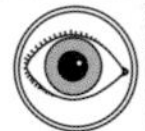

Today, the tomb of Rameses III is one of the most-visited in the valley, and as a result it can be cramped and hot when tourists crowd its corridors, as they do in mid-morning hours on Sundays and Fridays (when the Nile cruise boats from Aswan arrive in Luxor, and buses bring day-trippers from the Red Sea). If you can endure the crowds, there are some fascinating reliefs and paintings to be seen.

The first part of the tomb, from its entrance through corridor D1, was the work of Setnakht, first king of Dynasty 20. But when workmen inadvertently broke into neighboring tomb KV 10 (the tomb of Amenmeses), perhaps at about the same time that Setnakht had died, work was abandoned, and the king was buried in KV 14 instead. Some time later, Setnakht's son Rameses III resumed work on KV 11 and took it over as his own burial place. His workmen shifted the tomb's axis about 2 meters (7 feet) west in order to avoid KV 10 and continued digging into the mountain. The result was one of the longest tombs in the valley: KV 11 extends 188.11 meters (611 feet) from entrance to end. Only KV 20, the tomb of Hatshepsut, is longer: 210 meters (682 feet). Rameses III also added a series of small side chambers off the tomb's first two corridors, features found nowhere else. The nineteenth century English scholar, John Gardner Wilkinson, claimed that beneath each of the floors in these chambers lay a pit in which Rameses III had buried court officials. This remarkable statement has never been fully checked out, but when the Theban Mapping Project surveyed the tomb in 1983, it examined the floors of several side chambers and found no evidence of pits. More likely, the side chambers served as small storerooms for funerary paraphernalia and grave goods.

ENTRANCE Today, the tomb is approached by an L-shaped pair of stairs. Only the lower ramp-step combination is original; the upper stairs were added in 2003, to protect the tomb from flooding.

The usual sun disk, with a scarab and Ra-Harakhty cut within it, is carved above the gate.

Uniquely, the side walls of the entrance have beautifully carved cow-headed pilasters.

304 DETAIL FROM A SIDE CHAMBER OF THE SECOND CORRIDOR.

305 RAMESES III STANDS BEFORE RA-HARAKHTY, FROM THE FIRST CORRIDOR.

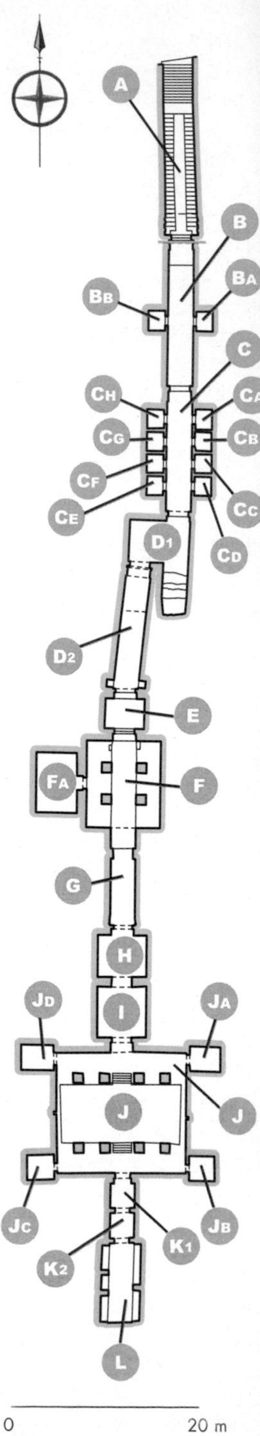

LEGEND

A *ENTRANCE*
B *FIRST CORRIDOR*
BA, B *SIDE CHAMBERS*
C *SECOND CORRIDOR*
CA-H *SIDE CHAMBERS*
D1 *THIRD CORRIDOR*
D2 *FOURTH CORRIDOR*
E *WELL CHAMBER*
F *PILLARED CHAMBER*
FA *SIDE CHAMBER*
G *FIFTH CORRIDOR*
H *ANTECHAMBER*
I *ANTECHAMBER*
J *BURIAL CHAMBER*
JA, B, C, D *SIDE CHAMBERS*
K1, 2 *REAR CHAMBERS*
L *REAR CHAMBER*

CORRIDOR B On the left (east) wall, the king stands before Ra-Harakhty. Beyond, the opening scene—the "title page"—of the Litany of Ra is followed by its text, which extends the length of this wall and continues onto the right. These scenes were done for Setnakht. On each side of the corridor, near its midpoint, two low gates lead into small chambers. These were cut and decorated for Rameses III. In the side chamber on the left, designated BA on the plan, two registers depict scenes of daily life: bakers, brewers, butchers, cooks, and leatherworkers ply their trades. Such scenes are unique in a royal tomb. Their figures are drawn in the ill-proportioned and hasty style that can also be seen in late New Kingdom private tombs. On the other side of the corridor, a second such side chamber, BB, has texts from the Litany of Ra on its front wall. On the other walls are twelve sailboats, each with elaborately patterned square sails.

CORRIDOR C and its **SIDE CHAMBERS**

The Litany of Ra continues on the walls of this corridor and in a band of text that decorates its ceiling. Across the top of the left and right walls are the seventy-four manifestations of the sun god. Chapter 151 of the Book of the Dead appears near the end of the walls, as do figures of Anubis and Isis (on the left wall) and Anubis and Nephthys (on the right).

There are eight side chambers cut into the sides of this long corridor, each decorated with unusual and often unique scenes. Many contain allusions to the Book of the Dead, but others have no obvious religious connection. I will describe the chambers from left to right, front to back. (In most cases, I omit descriptions of the front walls of the chambers, which cannot be seen by tourists because of the wooden rails and sheets of glass that have been installed in the corridor.) First on the left is **CHAMBER CA**. In the upper register there are seated personifications of the Nile flood and harvest (Hapy, Neperret, and Renenutet). Below them, in a badly damaged register, Nile gods make offerings to cobra deities. Across the corridor, in **CH**, rows of standards representing various divinities stand on the left and right walls. Well drawn weapons and arrow quivers cover the rear wall. In **CB**, the second side chamber on the left, processions of Nile gods fill the lower register. Above them, nome gods and goddesses carry offerings including nicely painted ducks and flowers and platters piled high with notched sycomore figs.

CG has leopard and other skins, sledges, and boxes on its left wall. Note the care the artist took to show the grain of the wood. He even included occasional knots and other imperfections on its surface. Throw sticks, bows, shields, and vases, some of Aegean design, stand in rows on the rear wall. The right wall is painted with ten ivory tusks and rows of vases.

In **CC**, the third side chamber on the left, two registers are filled with cows, bulls, and sacred oars. All are mentioned in chapter 148 of the Book of the Dead. One of the cattle is referred to as "the much beloved, red of hair," another "the bull, husband of the cows." The oars are called the Steering Oars of the Sky. Across from this, in **CF**, three registers depict the Fields of Iaru mentioned in chapter 110 of the Book of the Dead. People are sowing grain, ploughing with cattle, and reaping. Others sail across the Lake of Offerings. Much here is unfortunately destroyed. The last chamber on the left, **CD**, gives the names of Rameses III and shows him with harpists (one on each side wall) before Onuris-Shu and Ra-Harakhty (left side) and Shu and Atum (on the right). These are the famous harpists that James Bruce copied in the eighteenth century. Finally, **CE** has finely-drawn but damaged figures of Osiris, seated and wearing elaborate red-and-white checked costumes.

306 THE PAINTINGS IN THE TOMB CORRIDORS ARE PROTECTED BY GLASS.

307 NILE GODS AND GODDESSES CARRY FOOD OFFERINGS, FROM THE SIDE CHAMBER CB.

CORRIDOR D1 It was at this point that Setnakht's quarrymen broke through into the tomb of Amenmeses and abandoned their work. The hole that resulted can still be seen. This is not the only instance in the Valley of the Kings where tombs collided (KV 9 and KV 47 are two other examples), and the fact that this occurred suggests that there was no masterplan of the Valley of the Kings, and the memory of where earlier tombs lay was short-lived. When Rameses III decided to complete KV 11 as his burial place it was at this point that he moved the tomb axis west before continuing to dig new corridors southward. On the left (east) wall of the space thus created, Rameses III stands wearing the crown of Lower Egypt offering incense to the god Atum and, farther on, to Ptah. On the front wall, the standing king offers incense before a seated figure of Ptah-Sokar-Osiris. He holds three elaborate vessels and allows their contents to spill out onto the low platform on which the god sits. On the right (west) wall, the king offers a small statuette of Ma'at to Osiris and a libation to Anubis.

CORRIDOR D2 Note how the floor rises slightly here and the corridor angles slightly to the left, indications that the quarrymen were unsure just how close they might still be to the tomb of Amenmeses. Both the left and right walls of the corridor are decorated with texts from the *Imydwat*; the fourth hour is on the left wall, the fifth on the right. Note midway along the left wall the snake-shaped boat and, farther on, a huge snake with four legs and three heads. On the right wall, a boat bearing Ra-Harakhty and eight other figures is being towed through the underworld.

CHAMBER E The well chamber has images of several deities along the upper part of its walls. In the chamber's left half stand Osiris, Imsety, Anubis, Duamutef, Isis, and Iunmutef. In the right half stand Osiris, Hapy, Qebehsenuef, Nephthys, Serqet, and Iunmutef.

CHAMBER F This four-pillared chamber is decorated with the Book of Gates, the fifth hour in the left (east) half of the chamber, the sixth hour in the right (west). On the rear wall, a typical double scene shows the king offering to Osiris. Rameses III offers to various gods on each face of the four pillars: to Ptah (right face of left front pillar), Ra-Harakhty (rear face of front left pillar), Khepri (left face of the right front pillar), Atum (on the rear face of the right front pillar), Thoth (right face of left rear pillar), Geb (rear face of left rear pillar), Shepsy (left face of right rear pillar), and Nefertum (rear face of right rear pillar).

CORRIDORS AND CHAMBERS G, H, I, J, SIDE CHAMBERS JA-D, K, AND L None of these chambers is well enough preserved to merit detailed description. They originally contained scenes and texts from the Opening of the Mouth ritual, Book of the Dead chapter 148, the Book of the Heavenly Cow, and the fifth hour of the Book of Gates. The corridors are worth a glance, however, if one is interested in the geology of the Valley of the Kings and wants to see how poor—and sometimes dangerous—the bedrock in the valley could be.

308 RAMESES III IN THE ACT OF OFFERING INCENSE TO ATUM (LEFT) AND PTAH, THIRD CORRIDOR.

309 TOP LEFT THE BURIAL CHAMBER.

309 TOP RIGHT RAMESES III OFFERING AN IMAGE OF MA'AT, FROM THE SIDE CHAMBER FA.

309 BOTTOM RAMESES III OFFERING INCENSE AND LIBATION FROM THE THIRD CORRIDOR.

SIDE CHAMBER FA has scenes typical of KV 11's brightly painted decoration. On the front wall, Rameses III is led by Thoth and Horus (on the left side) and offers Ma'at to Osiris (on the right). The other walls show the seventh hour of the Book of Gates and include nice vignettes of men wielding sickles or standing beside trees, ensuring continued provisions in the afterlife.

On the rear wall, enemies of the solar god are bound to black Anubis-headed "stakes of Geb," so they cannot threaten the deity.

3

KV 19: THE TOMB OF MENTUHERKHEPSHEF

Mentuherkhepshef was a son of Rameses IX. Except for the sons of Rameses II who were buried in KV 5, he was the only prince to be buried in a decorated tomb in the Valley of the Kings. The tomb was discovered in 1817 by Giovanni Belzoni, on the eastern side of the valley. It lies below the tomb of Queen Hatshepsut (KV 20) and directly above New Kingdom tomb KV 60, whose entrance in the entryway of KV 19 is now covered by a sheet of plywood.

KV 19 was perhaps intended for Rameses Setherkhepshef, who was to be crowned as Rameses VIII (and whose burial site has never been found), then taken over by Mentuherkhepshef. The tomb was never finished and what should have been **CORRIDOR C** was converted into burial chamber J. A burial pit was cut into the floor and would have been covered over with stone slabs. Only **CORRIDOR B** is decorated, but the quality of work is excellent, enhanced by the uncluttered white background on which the figures were painted. The subject matter is similar to that in the tombs of royal sons in the Valley of the Queens, although here there are no representations of the prince's father.

At the beginning of the corridor, a single-leaf door is painted on each wall and on each is a now-damaged hieratic text. On the left, it is Book of the Dead chapter 139; on the right, it is Book of the Dead chapter 123. These are variations of a Spell for Entering the Great Mansion. On the left wall of the corridor, seven scenes separated by columns of text show Mentuherkhepshef adoring or making offerings to Osiris, Ptah Ta-tjenen, Khonsu, Bastet, Imsety, Qebehsenuef, and Amen-Ra. On the right wall, he stands before Ptah, Thoth, Banebdjed, Hapy, Duamutef, Meretseger, and Sekhmet. Notice the finely detailed costumes of the deities. The figure of Thoth (second on the right) wears a belt whose buckle bears the cartouche of Rameses IX.

Had it been completed, KV 19 might have been a substantial tomb. Its corridors and gates are among the widest in the Valley of the Kings. But its unfinished state offers visitors an excellent opportunity to see how ancient quarrymen worked. Beyond the burial pit, for example, the stone has been cut from the top down to produce a series of steps or terraces, surfaces on which workmen could stand as they dug their way forward.

310 BOTTOM MENTUHERKHEPSHEF OFFERING TO AMEN-RA, FROM THE LEFT WALL OF THE FIRST CORRIDOR.

311 TOP SEKHMET RECEIVING OFFERINGS FROM MENTUHERKHEPSHEF, FROM THE RIGHT WALL OF THE FIRST CORRIDOR.

A
B
C
LEGEND
A ENTRANCE
B FIRST CORRIDOR
C SECOND CORRIDOR
0

KV 2: THE TOMB OF RAMESES IV

THE HISTORY

When Rameses IV died after ruling for seven years, work on his tomb, KV 2, had to be cut short for his unexpectedly early burial. A chamber originally cut as a four-pillared chamber was re-cut as the burial chamber. The king apparently chose not to follow earlier New Kingdom tradition, creating for himself a tomb larger than his predecessors', but he did enlarge several of its component parts. The corridors in KV 2, for example, are wider and higher than earlier tombs, and so are the gates.

The tomb is one of the few architectural monuments from ancient Egypt for which we have a contemporaneous plan. A papyrus now in the Egyptian Museum, Turin, shows the plan of five tomb chambers and gives their measurements. For example, the papyrus states that corridor D was exactly 9 ubits long. A cubit is 0.523 ters, so this is the ivalent of 4.709 meters. heban Mapping Project measured corridor D d it to be 4.710 5.5 feet) long. difference of a few millimeters, hardly enough to worry about. But we do not know whether the Turin papyrus was the plan from which the engineers worked when cutting the tomb, or an after-the-fact drawing for use in dedication ceremonies.

KV 2 has been open since antiquity: there are over seven hundred Greek and Latin graffiti on the tomb's walls, and over fifty written in Coptic. Because of its convenient location near the entrance to the Valley of the Kings and its nearly horizontal floor, the tomb was frequently used as a hotel and rest stop by tourists until the early twentieth century. The tomb was cleared of debris by Edward Ayrton in 1905–1906 and again by Howard Carter in 1920. Many nineteenth century visitors wrote admiringly about its extensive decoration. The tomb is 89 meters (290 feet) long and covers 305 square meters (3800 square feet). A modern courtyard has been leveled in front of the tomb in an area where nine foundation deposits—an unusually large number—

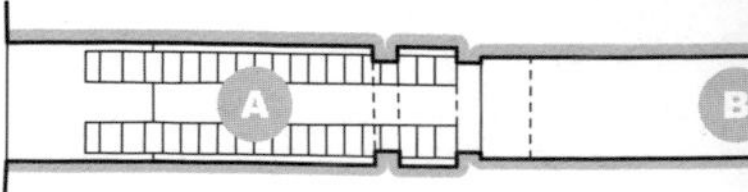

312 TOP DETAIL OF THE FOURTH HOUR OF THE BOOK OF GATES FROM THE RIGHT WALL OF THE BURIAL CHAMBER.

312-313 THE BOOK OF NUT, FROM THE CEILING OF THE BURIAL CHAMBER.

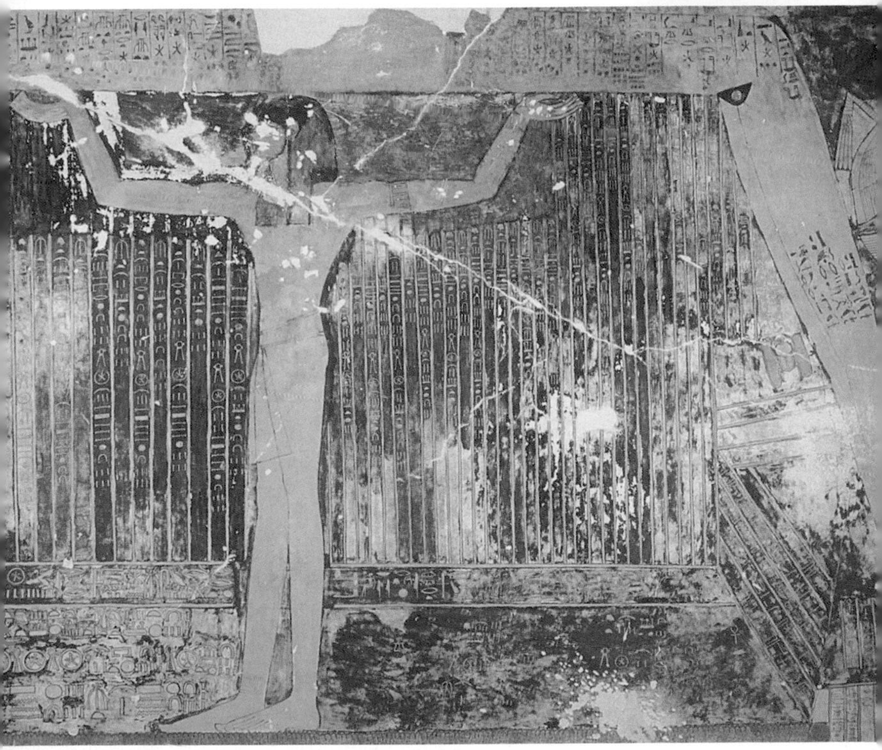

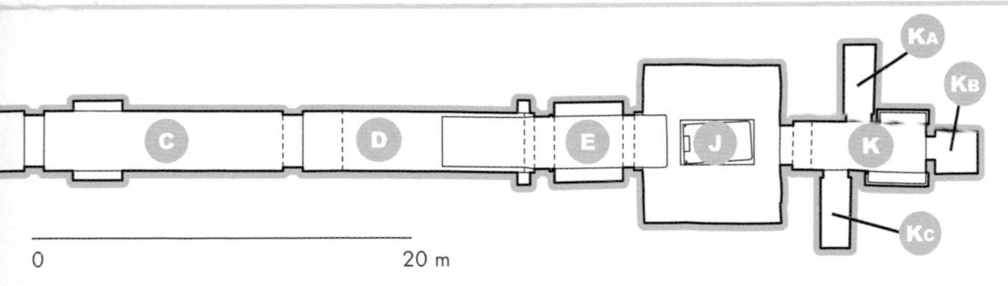

were discovered by early excavators. They contained the usual array of pottery and tools and were surrounded by a variety of other objects apparently tossed out of the tomb by later occupants. Early Copts built several small huts nearby.

LEGEND

A *ENTRANCE*
B *FIRST CORRIDOR*
C *SECOND CORRIDOR*
D *THIRD CORRIDOR*
E *WELL CHAMBER*
J *BURIAL CHAMBER*
K *FOURTH CORRIDOR*
KA, B, C *SIDE CHAMBERS*

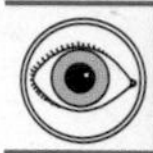

On the left wall of **CORRIDOR B**, the king stands before Ra-Harakhty. To their right begins an elaborate copy of the Litany of Ra, which fills the rest of the left wall and continues across the right wall of the corridor. It fills 120 columns of text cut in sunk relief that praise the sun god. It is appropriate that such a hymn to the sun should appear in the one part of the tomb that early morning sunlight could reach. On the ceiling, vultures alternate with falcons, scarabs, and the king's names.

Many graffiti, some scratched, others written in reddish-brown paint, cover the walls. An elaborate cross was painted on the left wall between the legs of the king. A graffito, at the beginning of the right wall, shows two crudely painted saints standing below a Coptic text. A monk called Jacob wrote the text over a thousand years ago. He described himself as a man unfit for the company of his brothers: "May anyone who enters here be merciful and pray for me. And may God take away from me the temptation of Satan....I am the miserable one...the very miserable and poor...the sinner more than the whole world." (I thank Rob Demarree for this translation.) Many other graffiti cover the walls of KV 2 and include the names of several nineteenth century visitors.

CORRIDOR C has over 150 columns of text that continue the Litany of Ra on its left and right walls. Above, some of the seventy-four different forms of the god Ra are depicted. Niches cut in the front end of each wall also show forms of the sun god. A frieze at the top of the wall gives elaborately painted names and titles of the king. On the ceiling, solar disks contain the *ba* of the sun god Ra, flanked by Isis and Nephthys, who are shown as kites. There are also various forms of the god Ra. The next, **CORRIDOR D**, is painted with the first and second divisions of the Book of Caverns. Ovals represent the sarcophagi of the blessed dead and the lower register shows bound figures of decapitated evildoers awaiting their fate. The ceiling is vaulted and is decorated with star patterns and names of the king. Above the rear gate appear winged uraei and cartouches of the king.

A ramp that begins in corridor D leads through chamber E. **CHAMBER E** was originally intended as a well chamber, but it was converted to an antechamber when the following pillared chamber became the tomb's burial site. It is decorated with seventy-four columns of text from the Book of the Dead, including chapters 123, 124, and 127. These texts tell the deceased what to say when questioned in the Hall of Judgment. Chapter 125, the Negative Confession, follows them. The cartouches of the king are highlighted in yellow paint. On the ceiling, three bands of texts with the names of the king stretch across a pattern of yellow stars on a blue background.

BURIAL CHAMBER J was converted when the king died unexpectedly. It is slightly larger than many earlier burial chambers (61 meters or 657 feet square, 5.2 meters or 17 feet high). It was decorated in sunk relief with a yellow background for the scenes, and a white background for the texts. The opening scene and first and second

hours of the Book of Gates begin to the left of the door and continue clockwise around the room. In addition, excerpts from the sixth through ninth hours of the *Imydwat* appear in a frieze text that extends across all the walls of the chamber.

The most appealing decoration in the chamber, however, is on the high ceiling. It is a flat ceiling, not vaulted, that is divided into two halves by figures of the goddess Nut stretching across it. In the left half, the figure of Nut is supported by the god Shu and the accompanying text is taken from the Book of Nut. The Book of Nut describes the path taken by the sun in its daily journey through the sky and deals with the distant regions of the universe where the sun never shines, and with migratory birds. On the right half of the ceiling, the Book of the Night starts at the second hour and stops at the fourth hour because of space limitations. It describes the journey of the sun from the moment when Nut swallows it at sunset to when she gives birth to it the next morning.

The huge sarcophagus that still stands in the tomb is 3.5 meters (7 feet) long, carved of red granite with a lid decorated with representations of human-headed uraei and snakes flanking the Osirid king. On the sarcophagus box are scenes from the Book of the Earth.

Beyond the burial chamber a narrow **CORRIDOR, K**, is painted, not carved, with the first part of the Book of Caverns. Recesses show figures of gods and assorted offerings. On the rear wall, a solar bark hovers above the god Aker, shown as a mound of earth flanked by two sphinxes. **SIDE CHAMBERS** show mummiform figures of the king and in the badly damaged rear side chamber there are depictions of funerary furniture, canopic jars, and goddesses who make a gesture of greeting known as *nini*.

315 LEFT THE SARCOPHAGUS WITH THE BOOK OF THE EARTH.

315 RIGHT CORRIDOR K DECORATED WITH STAR PATTERN NAMES OF RAMESES IV, THE BO OF CAVERNS, AND THE BOC OF THE EARTH.

3

KV 9: THE TOMB OF RAMESES VI

THE HISTORY

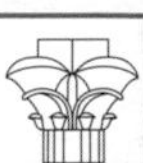

The Tomb of Rameses VI is one of the most impressive ombs in the Valley of the ings. Its wide corridors and h ceilings give it a much claustrophobic feel than many earlier tombs, and its decoration, painted in vivid colors against a crisp, white background, is bright and almost spring-like. Admittedly, the hieroglyphs lack the subtlety and elegance of some earlier tombs, but the overall effect is stunning, and the subject-matter is of great interest. The texts include versions of the Book of Gates,

Book of Caverns, and the Book of the Heavens, several in uniquely complete forms. There is a significant emphasis on the sun-god Ra in these texts, and the decoration gives special attention to astronomical subjects, too. The relatively short-lived Book of the Earth appears for the first time, in the large and spectacularly decorated burial chamber.

KV 9 was begun by Rameses V and completed by Rameses VI. Unusually, both kings were buried here, as we learn from a contemporary ostracon, although only the sarcophagus of Rameses VI remains. Both kings' mummies were moved to the royal cache in KV 35 in year 9 of Rameses IX.

KV 9 was robbed a few decades after it was sealed, probably just before the mummies were removed, and it has stood open since then, its carved and painted walls covered with nearly a thousand Greek, Latin, and Coptic graffiti left by a hundred generations of travelers who used the tomb as a hermitage, hotel, and dining room. Because of the importance and completeness of its decoration, we will devote considerable space to its description and refer back to it frequently in our descriptions of other royal tombs. Our survey of KV 9 is necessarily descriptive and visitors interested in magico-religious meaning of the scenes on its walls are encouraged to read the recent works of Eric Hornung and Jan Asmann.

Roman travelers called KV 9 the Tomb of Memnon because the cartouche with Rameses VI's prenomen looked to them like that of Amenhetep III which they had seen carved on the Colossi of Memnon. Nineteenth century French travelers called it the Tomb of Metempsychosis. (The word means the "transmigration of souls from one human or animal body to another," a phenomenon suggested by scenes on the tomb's walls.)

316 TOP DETAIL FROM THE NORTH WALL OF THE BURIAL CHAMBER.

317 BOTTOM DETAIL FROM THE SECOND HOUR OF THE IMYDWAT.

316-317 RAMESES VI OFFERS AN IMAGE OF MA'AT TO AMEN-RA, FROM A PILLAR OF THE BURIAL CHAMBER.

KV 9 is one of the six largest tombs in the Valley of the Kings, 117 meters (380 feet) long, covering 510 square meters (5,490 square feet). It was begun by Rameses V, whose workmen cut and perhaps decorated the first six chambers, and then usurped and enlarged by Rameses VI. The tomb was cleaned in 1888 and published in 1954. It is one of the few tombs in the Valley of the Kings to be completely recorded.

KV 9's program of decoration begins with complete copies of the Book of Gates on the left (south) walls of the first five chambers and the Book of Caverns on the right (north) walls. The former deals with the nighttime journey of the sun through the Netherworld, the judgement of the dead, and the realms of the Evil Ones and the blessed. The latter describes the caverns above which the sun travels on this journey, and Ra's relationship with Osiris, how he cares for him, protects him, and is united with him. The king, who accompanies the sun god into the Netherworld, is given instructions on how to pass safely through the gates, which are guarded by demons, and how to overcome the many obstacles the Evil Ones have thrown in his path. We shall describe the decoration chamber by chamber, moving between the two walls and the ceiling.

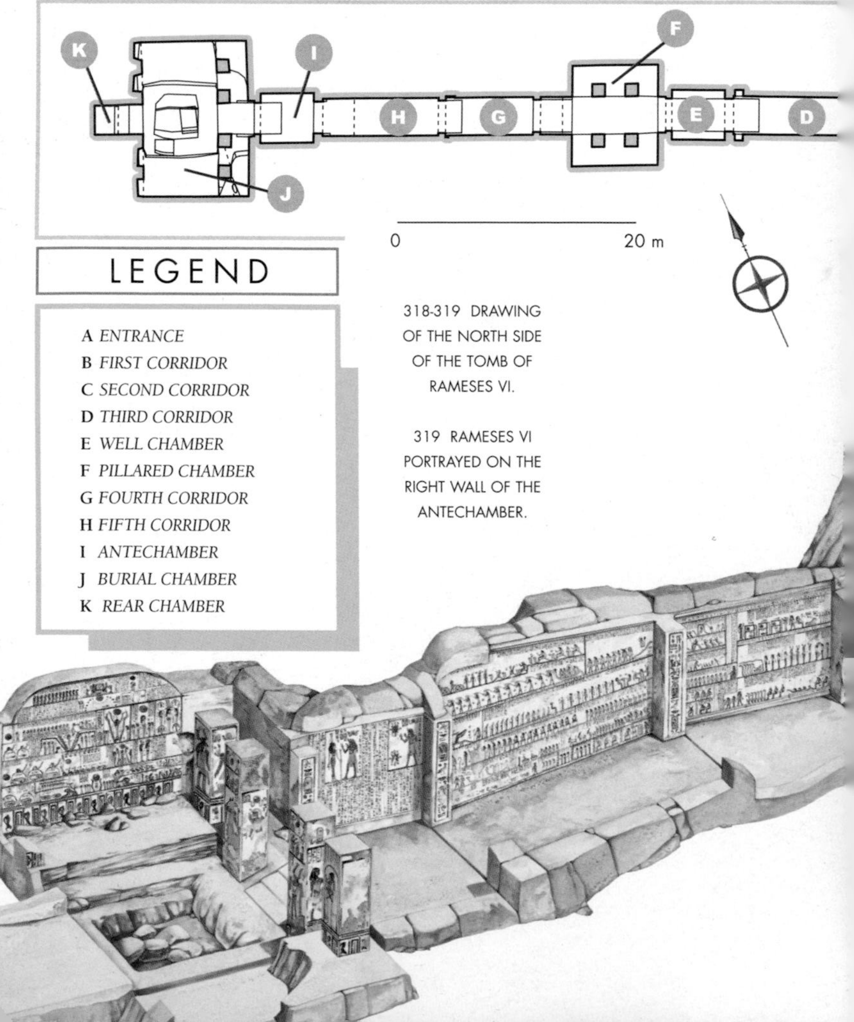

318-319 DRAWING OF THE NORTH SIDE OF THE TOMB OF RAMESES VI.

319 RAMESES VI PORTRAYED ON THE RIGHT WALL OF THE ANTECHAMBER.

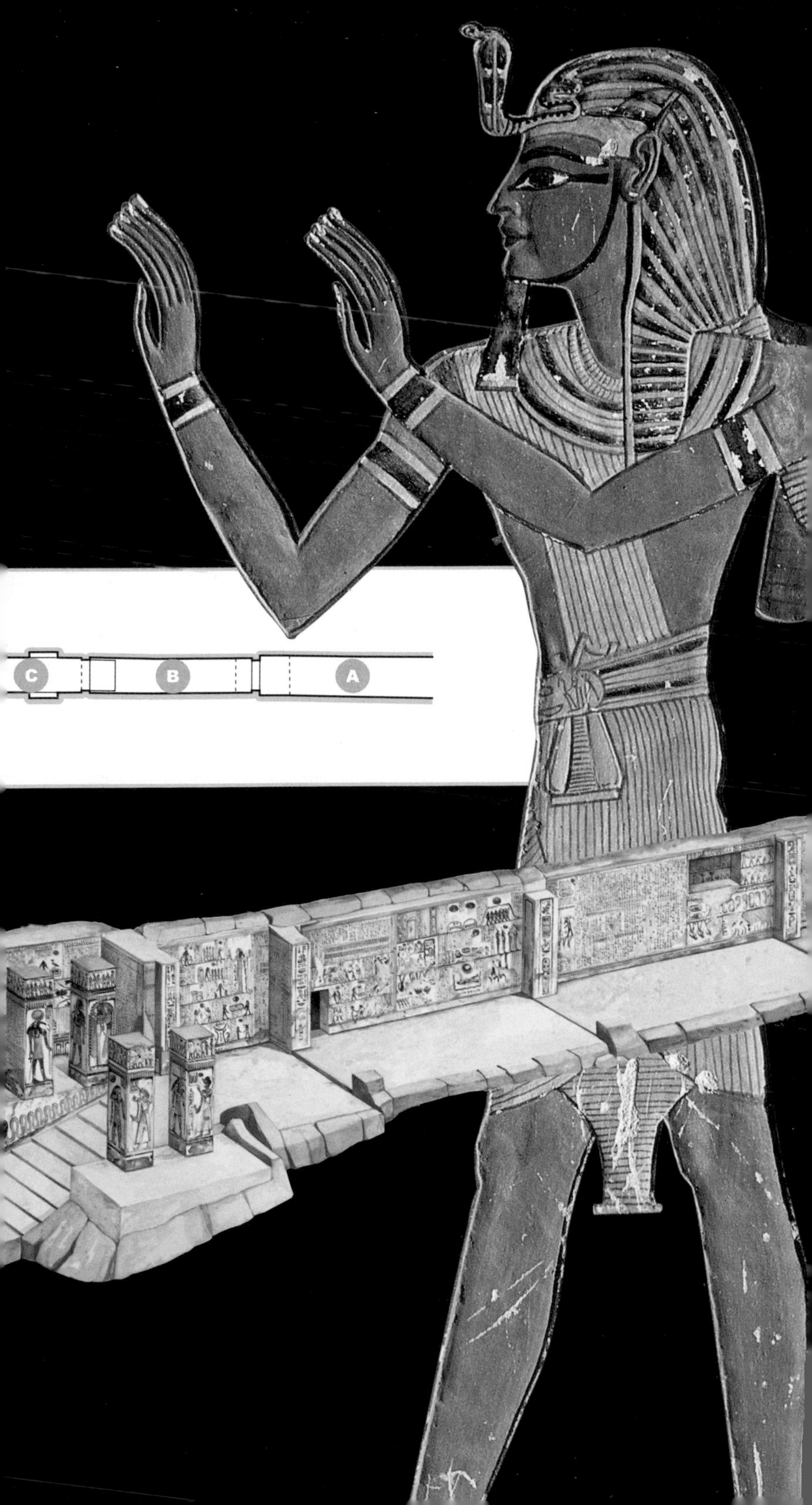
C
B
A

CORRIDOR B Above the gate into the first corridor (Corridor A lies outside the tomb's entrance), the sun god is invoked three times in a single artistic device: Isis and Nephthys kneel before a sun disk that encloses a scarab beetle (associated with the sun-god), and a figure of the ram-headed solar deity, Ra. This is an appropriate overture to the sun's journey into the night.

CORRIDOR B, LEFT (SOUTH) WALL is decorated with scenes from the first three chapters of the Book of Gates. At the front end of the wall, the king strides into the tomb. Originally, the king shown was Rameses V, but the figure was recut as Rameses VI and the crown was changed, the positions of the arms were altered, and the face was remodeled to look younger and thinner. The king stands before the gods Ra-Harakhty and Osiris. Behind them, in three registers, a solar bark sails between two mountains (one of them upside down) on the western horizon. Twelve Gods of the West stand nearby. Figures kneel before staffs. One figure has an Anubis head, and is called the Neck of Ra, another has a ram's head, and is called the Head of Ra. At right, the solar bark has passed through the Second Gate that is guarded by a great snake called The Guardian of the Desert. The wall beyond is divided into three registers: the middle represents the Nile; the upper and lower registers the east and west banks of the river. Four gods tow the bark on which the god Ra stands, protected by a coiled snake called The Enveloper. At top, twenty-four men stand in a long row. The first twelve are Worshippers of Ra, the next twelve the Just Who Are In The Netherworld. In the lower register, Atum leans on a staff watching the damned, four figures called The Tired Ones and twenty naked men with bound arms, described as liars and blasphemers. The Third Gate, called The One with Sharp Flames, is also guarded by a serpent. Beyond it, twelve mummies, the Holy Ones of the Netherworld, stand with a serpent above their heads. To their right, twelve gods emerge from the Netherworld's Lake of Fire. In the middle register, a bark carrying the sun-god Ra is pulled by four gods towards a long tube with bull's heads and standing bulls at each end. This is the Bark of the Earth, and it is supported by eight gods with seven other deities seated atop it. The bark will travel through this tube and emerge before the Fourth Gate. More gods fill the lower register.

321 RAMESES VI OFFERS INCENSE TO RA-HARAKHTY AND OSIRIS, FROM THE RIGHT WALL OF CORRIDOR B.

CORRIDOR B, RIGHT (NORTH) WALL is decorated with texts and scenes from the Book of Caverns. Like the Book of Gates on the south wall, the Book of Caverns continues through the first five chambers of KV 9. The first division begins at the eastern end of the wall with Rameses VI offering incense to Ra-Harakhty and Osiris. To the left of a solar disk, a ram-headed figure of Ra extends his hand into the middle of five registers, preparing to venture into the Netherworld and challenge the enemies of Osiris. "I am Ra," the god proclaims, "I enter the twilight shadow. Welcome me with open arms." The six units into which the journey is divided are each shown in three registers. In the top register, three

serpents are followed by nine cobras and a row of bull-headed gods with human bodies who guard the entrance to the Netherworld. In the second register, nine oval coffins (some have called them protective cocoons) hold figures of deities, some lying face down, some facing up, one standing upright. Beyond, nine jackal-headed gods bow slightly before them. These "great silent ones" act "like dogs who dig around in garbage and lap up corruption and filth." They are the gods who protect the souls of the dead. Behind, a male and a female deity hold solar disks. In the middle register, ten male and one female figure walk forward toward the god, bowing in obeisance. Behind them, four gods stand in ovals protected by serpents, and Osiris stands in a shrine also protected by a snake. He is followed by four more coffins with goddesses. Nine goddesses stand on baskets in the fourth register, followed by nine gods in ovals and four figures standing over cauldrons of burning flesh. Finally, in the bottom, the subject is the torture of the damned. In this chamber, three snakes stand guard over sixteen Evil Ones, enemies of Osiris who have been condemned to the Place of Annihilation. The first eight have been beheaded. Ra proclaims, "O you who ought to be decapitated, enemies of Osiris whose heads have been cut off, behold me: I pass above you, I regard you as no longer existing!"

Extensive texts follow these scenes explaining the role they play, as Ra and the king pass into the Netherworld. For example, the text referring to the nine cobras in the upper register reads in part: "O Ennead of Uraei whose flames from their mouths are to burn the enemies of Osiris, make the gesture of submission, withdraw your arm: Behold, I enter into the fair West to care for Osiris, to greet those who are in him. I set his enemies in their place of execution, I command those who are in his following, I illumine the darkness of the mysterious chamber for King [Rameses VI]." The enemies of Osiris, called those "who spread evil in the Hidden World," are in the bottom register.

CORRIDOR B, CEILING

The scenes here are badly damaged; it is better to pass them by and concentrate on the better-preserved ceilings farther inside the tomb.

323 DETAIL OF THE RIGHT WALL OF CORRIDOR D.

CORRIDOR C, LEFT (SOUTH) WALL Scenes here are similar to those after the Third Gate, but after the Fourth Gate, called the Mistress of Food, the gods change. Twelve jackals, gods, and cobras appear in a large niche, walking on the shores of small lakes. In the middle register, a bark is towed toward nine mummiform gods "who are in their coffins," soon to be revived by the sun god. Two groups of six goddesses stand at the edge of triangular bodies of water in the Netherworld flanking a monstrous serpent that represents the passing of time. Horus stands at left in the lower register, gazing over the heads of eleven gods toward a cobra guarding the shrine of Osiris. Twelve more gods approach the shrine and four men bend forward before "pits of fire" into which the Evil Ones are to be thrown.

Two main registers, each divided into three sub-registers, occupy the remainder of corridor C's left wall. The upper registers are devoted to the Fifth Hour and part of the Sixth Hour of the Book of Gates and to scenes in the Judgment Hall; the lower registers include the last part of the Sixth Hour. The Fifth Gate is called She Who Acts. The topmost register is filled with twenty-eight standing gods. Twelve of them hold a rope used to survey fields in the Netherworld, preparing to allocate farmland to the newly-arrived dead. Coiled ropes and coiled serpents suggest the passage of time, and the word for "lifetime" appears with them in the lower register. In the middle register, the bark of Ra is pulled by nine men with hidden arms, called "those who carry the moving one." These men apparently were responsible for disemboweling bodies during the mummification process and were considered an untouchable caste. In the lower register on the upper part of the wall, Horus leans on his staff, observing the four groups into which Egyptians divided humankind: Egyptians, Asiatics, Nubians, and Libyans. Foreigners, too, the scenes indicate, will be judged by Osiris.

At the right (west) end of the corridor, a representation of the Judgment Hall of Osiris has been inserted into the Book of Gates. (Another, particularly fine, copy of this scene, drawn only in black ink outline, can be seen in the burial chamber of the tomb of Horemheb, KV 57.) Osiris is seated on a throne before nine "justified dead" who ascend steps before him. A beam balance in the form of a mummy stands on the dais. Four upside-down gazelle heads (The Roarers) and, at top right, a figure of Anubis appear above Osiris. Below, two monkeys with sticks drive away a pig, the potent symbol of evil. These scenes occur near the halfway point of the sun's nighttime journey, the darkest and deepest point on its path through the Netherworld. So important is this scene that senior priests wrote the accompanying texts cryptographically, the code supposedly known only to a chosen few.

The Sixth Hour, whose gate is called The Mistress of Duration, occupies the lower half of the wall. Twelve gods with forked sticks follow twelve gods holding a serpent with twelve human heads on its body. The snake is Apophis, the enemy of Ra, and the gods are the ones who "repulse Apophis in the sky while on their way to the Netherworld." The heads are those of men Apophis has swallowed. Because twenty-four gods have successfully challenged Apophis, these men can now emerge from the snake's belly and proceed into the afterlife. Their heads have emerged from the body of the snake. Twelve men hold a double twisted rope tied to a standing mummy. Again,

the twisted rope symbolizes the passage of time. In the middle register, the bark of Ra is preceded by twelve men with hidden arms. In the lowest register, a god stands before twelve mummies (The Sleepy Ones) laid out on biers with a huge snake. Twelve other gods walk toward a circular pit of fire with a cobra coiled inside it. The appearance of men, gods and souls in units of twelve is, of course, a reference to the twelve hours of the night through which the sun god passes on his bark.

CORRIDOR C, RIGHT (NORTH) WALL The second division of the Book of Caverns follows in five registers. In the upper register, an upright snake is followed by four Serpent Guardians of the Gate and twelve gods, Lords of Manifestations, lying in coffins, restored to life for only an instant each night as the light of Ra passes over them: "Behold, I shine upon you while your faces are turned toward me." Four of them have the heads of catfish, eight the heads of mice. Seven goddesses, each given a different epithet, lie in coffins. Ra speaks to them: "If you conduct my soul towards my bodies, I will guide your souls toward the coffins which contain your corpses. I will give light to you and disperse your darkness."In the second register, part of which is carved within a large niche, nine mourners pull their hair, wailing and crying. Twelve mummiform gods stand before a mouse-headed deity called The Eyeless One, a form of Osiris. In the third register, the ram-headed god at right watches as five men stand before him in adoration. Behind them, on the side and rear walls of a niche—itself symbolizing a coffin—others stand before a sun disk housed in a chest. Sun disks alternate with ram headed poles and *user* staffs. Horus stands in the fourth register before twelve figures of Osiris in coffins and gods of the divine judgment hall

Finally, in register five, knife-wielding, bearded demons stand ready to torture four bound and decapitated bodies whose heads lie neatly stacked before them. Four more enemies and eight upside-down enemies follow. The last four upside-down figures of the damned have had their hearts ripped out and placed between their feet. They are described as "the bloody ones with torn-out hearts in the Place of Annihilation," and are said to vomit forth their own excrement.

324 DRAWING OF THE RIGHT WALL OF CORRIDOR D.

325 RAMESES VI AS OSIRIS PROTECTED BY FOUR SNAKES, FROM THE RIGHT WALL OF CORRIDOR D.

CORRIDOR D, LEFT (SOUTH) WALL The Seventh Hour of the Book of Gates continues here, although the gate itself (The Seat of Her Lord) was drawn at the end of Chamber B. In the top of three registers, twelve of the Blessed Dead carry baskets of grain on their heads; twelve more carry Ma'at feathers. In the middle register, a solar bark with Ra-Harakhty and a protective snake is pulled by four men toward a large figure of a god and seven poles with jackal heads called the Stakes of Geb. To these poles are tied fourteen Evil Ones. Each group is confronted by the figure of a god, and each is identified as the enemy of that god. In the lower register, a large figure, the Lord of Joy, stands before twelve deities tending grain and seven figures holding sickles. "Take your sickles," the text reads, "Reap your grain; I have granted you a portion of the plants. You have given me satisfaction..."

In the eighth hour, beyond a gate called the Brilliant One, twelve gods hold a coiled rope with human and hawk heads on it, and twelve others carry a snake. The first group is said to "carry the rope and create the mysteries," the second to "carry the coiled serpent rope and create the hours." In the middle register, the sacred bark is towed in a procession led by twelve gods with scepters and four mummies called the Fighting Faces. In the lower register, a god leans on a staff gazing toward twelve Perfect Spirits lying on beds and twelve members of "the council who judge."

NICHE At the bottom of the left wall in corridor D, a small niche is decorated with a part of the Book of the Heavenly Cow, which deals with mankind's short-lived but serious rebellion against Ra. More complete copies of this text can be found in the tombs of Sety I and Rameses II, as well as on one of the shrines of Tutankhamen.

CORRIDOR D, RIGHT (NORTH) WALL The third division of the Book of Caverns is laid out differently than the first two. Here in three registers, the text accompanies each of fifteen scenes instead of appearing in a block after them. From top right, Rameses VI as Osiris lies in an oval protected by two snakes. Seven gods with catfish-like heads are associated with Aker and stand beneath a snake called Nehebkau, in whom all sacred energy is joined. Ram-headed mummies lie within two mounds, about to be united with solar disks. Three deities appear in oval sarcophagi. Osiris stands in a shrine protected by four serpents. Eight deities stand in ovals. They took a vow never to lie down but to assist Osiris throughout all eternity. In the second register, Ra as a ram-headed god faces four mummiform Osiris figures. Double-headed Aker, representing the earth, is joined by three forms of Osiris and four goddesses, and above, by a scarab beetle and a reclining figure of Geb. He lies protectively

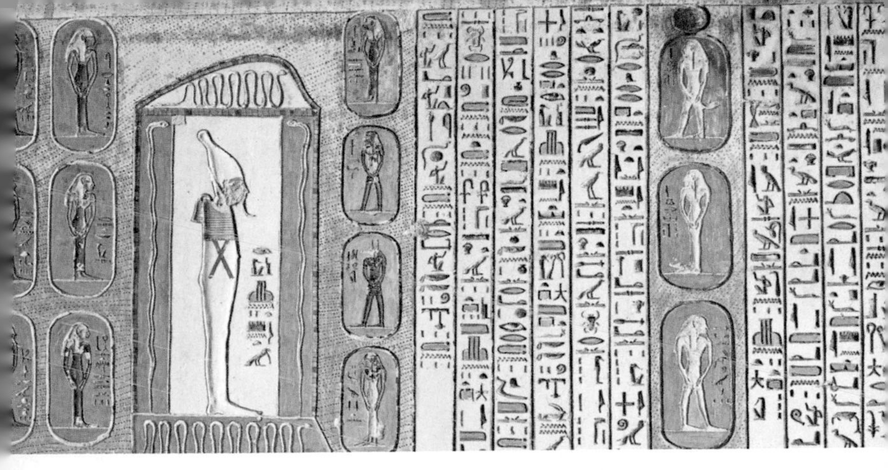

above one of the bodies of Osiris. At left, three ovals—one with Osiris and two with the head and eye of the sun—are surrounded by an ouroboros (a snake that swallows its own tail) and four bowing figures. A crocodile-headed form of Osiris stands on a snake, adored by two standing gods, one of whom pulls Osiris's beard.

In the third register, male and female figures appear upside down. Four of the male figures have been decapitated. "You are the enemies of Osiris," the sun god states, "Those enemies who have no soul, you will not see my rays." Unusually, they are accompanied by eight small figures of dead souls, condemned to the Place of Annihilation. In the middle of the register, an ithyphallic Osiris, encircled by a snake, lies beneath a solar disk and the figure of Aker.

The Fourth Division includes a snake and a ram-headed god to the left of a sun disk. The scene deals with the rebirth of Osiris and Ra and is similar to the beginning of the first division, but more elaborate. A lengthy text to Ra occupies the upper half of the wall. Below it are three registers. In the uppermost, Osiris looks as if he is being tossed into the air. In fact, the text reads "the two goddesses [Isis and Nephthys] lift up thy body, O Osiris" This is the first step in his resurrection. Farther left, jackal-headed Anubis and hawk-headed Horus stand in adoration of his renewed body and bathe and clothe him. In the third scene, a god called the Bull of the West stands before a mongoose that represents his son, Horus-Mekhentienirty, and a heart flanked by solar disks, both in ovals. They are meant to symbolize the start of an act of creation.

In the middle register, a ram-headed god, Ra, stands before three guards of the Netherworld. Next, Horus stands before two ovals with Osiris and a snake called the Terrible Face. In the third scene, Anubis bows before Osiris.

In the lower register, four bound men called "the blood-stained, the weepers," stand upside-down before a god called the Cat from Whom There Is No Escape, a form of the god Ra. In the middle scene, a goddess called the Annihilator holds hands with the lion-headed One Who Destroys, standing over a guardian of the damned. The accompanying text is blood-curdling: "O, you who come out of annihilated corpses, you are those who are annihilated in obscurity and blood, who live on what their hearts abhor. I have so ordered your bodies that you may come forth covered with your rottenness, but you will not come out of the putrefaction (which envelops you)." In other words, the Evil Ones will never be regenerated but will continue to rot away forever. At left, upside-down figures of the Mutilated Ones, the Miserable Ones, are met by a man called Annihilating Face.

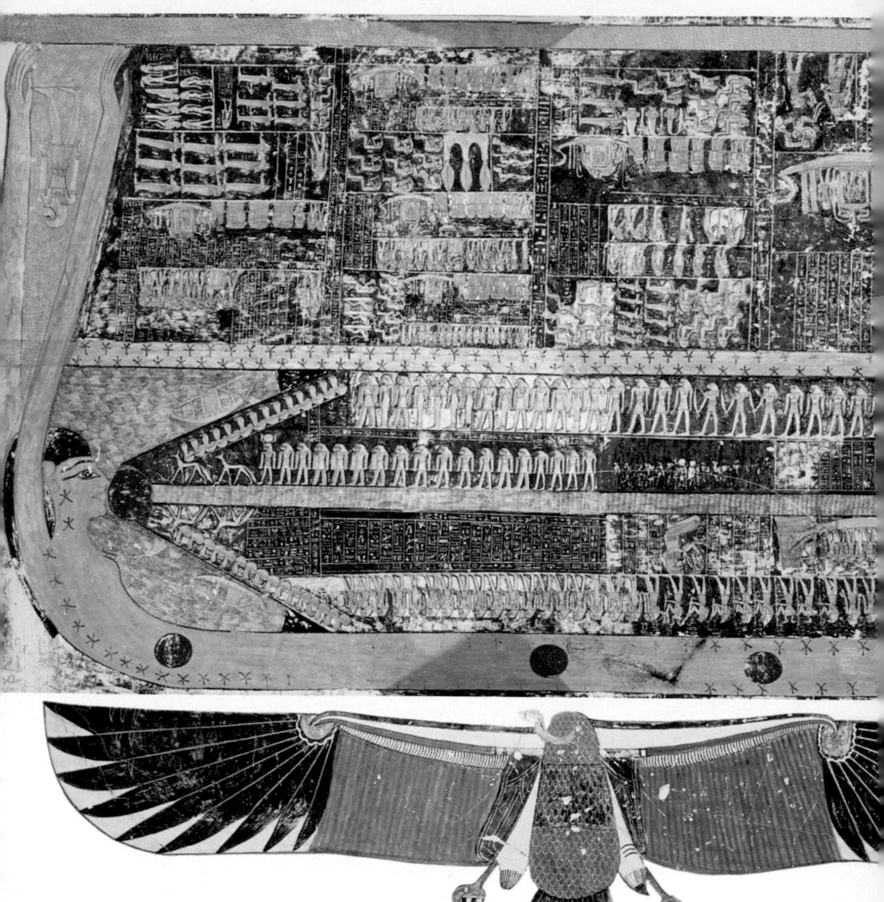

CORRIDOR C, D, E, F CEILINGS These ceilings are elaborately painted with two major astronomical texts, The Book of the Day and The Book of the Night. In the first, the sun god is shown as a falcon and the text describes his journey from sunrise, when he is born to the goddess Nut, to sunset, when she swallows him and he begins his nighttime journey through her body. In the second, he is shown as a ram, and the text relates his nighttime journey through the Netherworld. The body of the goddess Nut extends the entire length of these scenes, from the eastern end of corridor D into chamber F. The text closest to her body (between her and a band of stars) is the Book of the Day; the Book of the Night lies below the band. At the beginning of corridor D, Nut has given birth to the sun god. Isis and Nephthys kneel before the pregnant goddess, shown with the sun god in her abdomen, ready to assist in the birth. Above, the newborn solar disk is protected by a winged scarab. The figures of the goddesses are supported by a figure of Shu, who stands in a solar bark. Below, surrounded by water, are two other barks, the Bark of the Night and the Bark of the Day. Isis and Nephthys transfer the solar disk from one boat to the other. The body of water narrows to a river and flows westward across the ceiling. This is the path of the journey the sun will make during the day. Rows of gods fill the upper and lower registers. In the middle register, four apes

326-327 CEILING OF THE PILLARED CHAMBER.

326 BOTTOM WINGED GODDESS AT THE ENTRANCE OF THE PILLARED CHAMBER.

hail the rising sun. They are followed by nine barks. Deities thrust knives into the water to kill the Apophis serpent, enemy of the sun god. The procession culminates in a scene in which the sun is delivered to Nut. She will now swallow it at the start of its nighttime journey.

The Book of the Night records the twelve-hour-long journey of the sun through the body of the sky goddess. The scenes read from chamber F back to the beginning of corridor D. They begin with figures of the Spirits, the Nobles, and the Dead. At the end of the nighttime journey, there is an altar that supports a scarab from which water pours onto the hieroglyph for "heaven." Farther left stand figures of Isis and Nephthys, who pass the sun god from one to the other in preparation for a repeat of its daytime journey.

Between the side walls and pillars in chamber F smaller astronomical scenes include representations of constellations and decan lists.

CHAMBER E, LEFT (SOUTH) WALL The ninth hour of the Book of Gates fills nearly the entire wall, laid out in two sets of three registers each. Both gates for the ninth and tenth hours stand at the end of the wall. In the upper register, nine human-headed *ba*-birds with arms stand before a god holding a staff. Behind them, twelve gods in human form walk forward, identified as "those who lead the souls to the green growth in the Island of Flames." The second register includes a version of a well-known scene. The elaborately-drawn bark of Ra is pulled toward "He Who Is in the Abyss" a god who stands beside a great rectangle of water in which sixteen male figures are floating. These are the bodies of those who have died by drowning.

327 NUT HOLDS RA-HARAKHTY AND A SOLAR DISK, RIGHT WALL OF THE WELL CHAMBER.

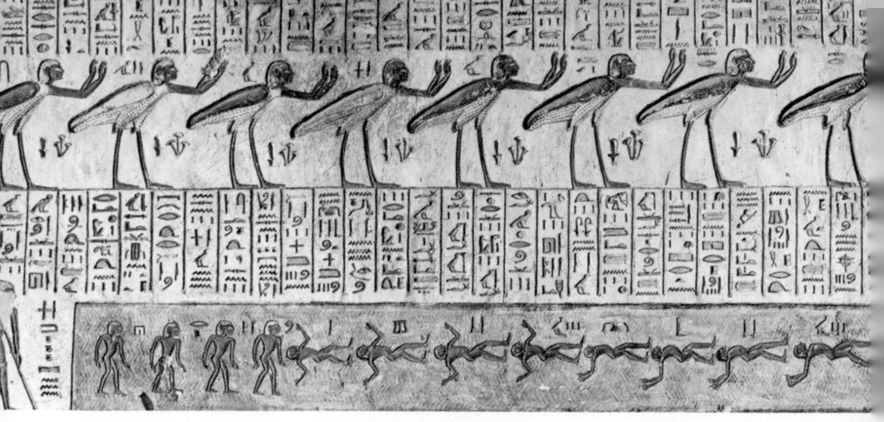

Because their bodies have been lost, they cannot be mummified or take part in funerary ceremonies, and therefore they require special assistance to enter the afterlife. The text reads in part: "Let your heads come forth, O drowned ones. May your arms move, O you who are under the water. Stretch out your legs, O you who swim. (Let) breath be for your nostrils, you who crouch in the waters. You who have dominion over your waters, you shall be content in your coolness, you shall move toward the primeval flood...[you] shall not perish." In the third register—the last of the ninth hour—Horus stands with his staff at the left end of the wall. He is observing twelve bound enemies who march toward a fire-breathing snake holding seven mummies in its coils. These are Evildoers who have their arms bound in several painful ways. They are the enemies of Osiris, a the text tells them that they are doomed "to be decapitated—you shall not exist! Your souls shall be annihilated and shall not live because of what you have done to my father Osiris." The serpent, the Fiery One, is instructed: "Open your mouth! Expand your jaws and belch forth the flames among the enemies of my father; burn their bodies, consume their souls!" The tenth hour of the Book of Gates appears on the lower half of this wall in three registers. In the upper register (fourth down from the ceiling), four headless gods wearing crowns of Upper Egypt raise a post topped with a crowned human head. The double-headed lion, Aker, god of earth, supports a two-headed figure with the faces of Horus and Seth. To his right, four more headless figures wear the crown of Lower Egypt and erect a post. Farther right, a six-headed, eight-legged snake called the Walker is held by a male figure. Another serpent lies at right, its two heads wearing the crown of Upper Egypt. The snake is called the Runner of the Earth, and carries nine human figures on its back. These two serpents are enemies of Apophis and help to protect the sun god. Beyond, two gods swing nets used to protect Ra: "Their magic is on the nets and inside the nets that are in their hands."

In the second register (fifth from the ceiling), the sun's bark is preceded by twelve more net-swinging deities, four with human heads, four with the heads of apes, one with a double-headed snake, one with a vulture head, and four human-headed females. Four men with spears precede them, holding a rope tied to a god called the Old One, (an earth god) who emerges from the Netherworld, prepared to kill the evil Apophis should he attempt to hinder Ra's bark on its journey into the Netherworld. A snake and a crocodile with a snake-like tail stand at right.

In the lowest register, a two-headed, two-legged serpent and two cobras are bound by ropes held by gods with heads of ibises, hawks, rams, and human beings. Above the serpent stands a falcon, Horus of the Netherworld.

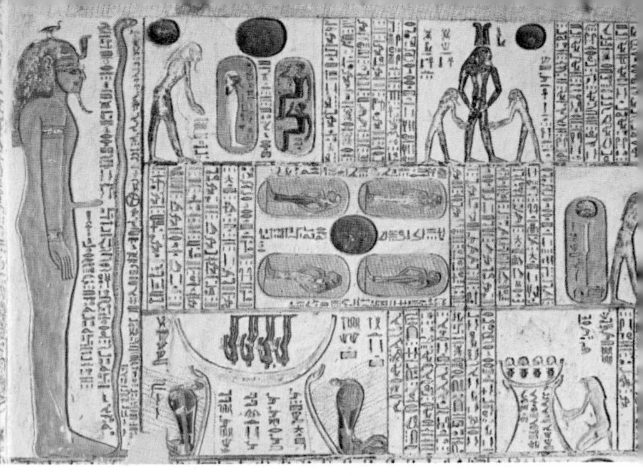

In **CHAMBER E, RIGHT (NORTH) WALL**, the resurrection of Osiris continues in the fifth division of the Book of Caverns. At top right, a large figure of the sky goddess Nut holds Ra-Harakhty and a solar disk in her upraised hands. She is flanked by human-headed serpents, crocodiles (representing the forces of the underworld), and the upside-down figures of a scarab, a ram, a god, and a child, each with a solar disk, each representing different stages in the life of the sun. The child, for example, is called "he who still has an umbilical cord." At the opposite end of the wall, an ithyphallic figure of Osiris stands with a *ba*-bird on his head and a protective snake before him. These two figures, which represent heaven and earth, flank three registers of text and scenes that recount the sun's journey toward the dawn. Two snakes flank Nut and represent enemies of Ra.

In the top register, at right, Osiris stands beneath a sun disk, his arms raised in adoration before a figure of Ra-Harakhty that is held in Nut's hand. Behind him stand four human-headed snakes, thwarted in their attempt to prevent the sunrise. In the center scene, the gods Atum and Khepri support Ptah-tjenen, the Exalted Earth. At left, a god stands in adoration before two ovals. In one stands a mummy called the One Who Is the Appearance of Osiris. In the other sit two children, the Child of Ra, and the Essence of Ra.In the second register, Anubis stands before four hawk-headed mummiform figures, manifestations of Horus. The oval behind Anubis holds the Rod of Power of Atum, "which created the Netherworld and brought forth the realm of the dead." At left, four goddesses "in their coffins" surround a sun disk.

In the third register, a goddess, nameless in this scene but in others called the Butcher, holds two staffs to which bound enemies are tied. In the center, two arms emerge from the Netherworld holding a huge cauldron filled with the hearts and heads of the Evil Ones, ready to be devoured by flames. Another cauldron holds four headless bodies called the Enemies of Ra.

Below the figure of Nut, in a fourth register, an oval coffin held by two gods is filled with hieroglyphs meaning "flesh" and referring to the body parts of both Ra and Osiris. The head of a ram (symbol of the god Ra) is flanked by Osiris and Horus adoring a sun disk. In the fifth register, the god Ra greets the goddess Tayet, called the Weaver, who will help to restore the god's body A huge cauldron, held by arms rising from the Netherworld, is filled with upside-down symbols of flesh, souls, and shadows.

328-329 NINTH HOUR OF THE BOOK OF THE GATES, DETAIL, LEFT WALL OF THE WELL CHAMBER.

329 ITHYPHALLIC FIGURE OF OSIRIS IN FRONT OF TEXT AND SCENES RECOUNTING THE SUN'S JOURNEY, RIGHT WALL OF THE WELL CHAMBER.

CHAMBER F is a four-pillared chamber that was the last part of KV 9 to be worked on by quarrymen of Rameses V. The eleventh hour of the Book of Gates is carved on the Left (South) Wall. Its gate, the Holy One, is shown in corridor E. In the upper register, eight gods armed with knives and sticks move towards Apophis. Four of the gods have human heads, and four have multiple heads of snakes. Apophis, shown as a huge snake, is bound by a long rope held by sixteen gods who stand on his body, and by a huge fist (the Body of He Who is Hidden) that rises from the Netherworld. Farther right, the rope is held by four snakes. Five figures of the Helpless Ones emerge from the chain and guard it.

In the middle register, the sun's bark continues on its journey preceded by four standing gods, another four holding stars, and four seated gods, some with animal heads. Before them, a large boat carries the frontally-drawn face of the god Ra. The boat seems to be sailing in the wrong direction: all other boats in these scenes move to the right, while this one is towed to the left. This is not an error: one Egyptologist suggests that it refers to the reversal of time alluded to in the *Imydwat* (see the tomb of Sety I). At right, a winged serpent is followed by a man holding a lamp, a human-headed serpent, four adoring women, and a double-headed figure of Seth-Horus with six cobras standing atop two bows.

In the lower register, twelve divine oarsmen come forward with twelve goddesses representing time,

preparing to deliver the sacred bark out of the Netherworld and back into daylight. The goddesses are referred to as "the hours who tow [the bark]." They "take hold of the *Nefert*-rope in order to tow Ra in Nut," preceded by four gods with scepters and heads of various shapes. All advance toward the Eye of Ra. Beyond the twelfth gate, called the Mysterious Entrance, the Twelfth Hour describes preparations for the morning rebirth of the sun. In the upper register, gods carry solar disks, the blazing light, in their hands, following behind other gods carrying stars. They are accompanied by twelve gods and eight goddesses seated on serpents. A crocodile-headed god precedes them.

In the middle register, the solar bark follows nine gods armed with knives and sticks, and moves toward Apophis who has been chained to five staples to keep him from hindering the sunrise. The rising sun is being enthusiastically announced by four baboons. In the lower register, gods and goddesses wear different crowns and headdresses symbolizing the power and authority of the god. The sun now emerges through a double leaf door, guarded by Isis and Nephthys, and into the day. In one large, final scene, the goddess Nun lifts the solar bark from the Netherworld. Above the bark, a scarab beetle rolls the sun toward Nut, goddess of the sky, who will watch its journey through the daytime sky. At sunset, the sun will be returned to Nut, when the cycle from light to dark, day to night, begins again.

330 DRAWING OF THE RIGHT WALL OF THE WELL CHAMBER AND THE PILLARED CHAMBER F.

330-331 VIEW OF THE PILLARED CHAMBER F.

332 LEFT WALL OF THE SLOPING DESCENT OF THE PILLARED CHAMBER.

333 LEFT RAMESES VI OFFERING, FROM THE SOUTH FACE OF THE SOUTH-WEST PILLAR.

333 RIGHT DRAWING OF THE RIGHT WALL OF CORRIDOR G.

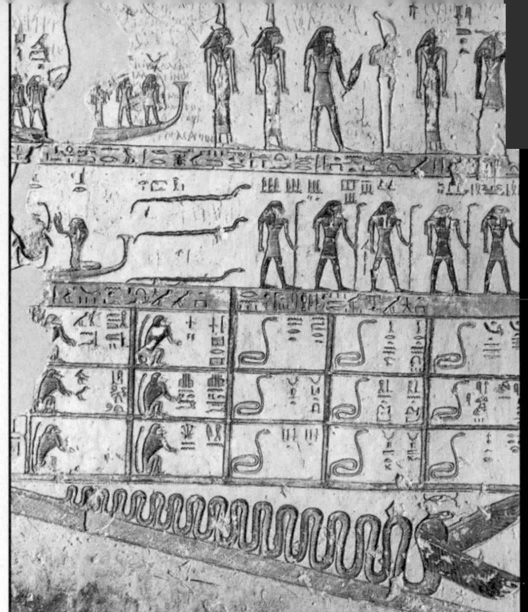

CHAMBER F, RIGHT (NORTH) WALL A lengthy text appears after the fifth division of the Book of Caverns, written in a repetitive, rhythmic style reminiscent of poetry. The sixth division follows, setting the stage for the reappearance of the sun at dawn. In the upper register, at right, Anubis protects two deities lying in coffins surmounted by their *ba*-birds. At left, Anubis stands before the sarcophagus of Ra, inside which are a ram, the head of a falcon, and a solar disk, all symbols of the sun god. It is flanked by two other coffins in which stand goddesses called Senet and the Engulfer and hieroglyphs denoting "flesh." The next scene is actually the final scene of the division. The forepart of the solar bark can be seen in the middle sub-register, pulled from the Netherworld into the day by twelve gods with the heads of humans, rams, and falcons. On board are symbols of the sun god: a ram with a sun disk on his horns, a scarab, and a bird. They move out of the Netherworld toward a large scarab and seated sun-child, between dark and watery triangles representing the Mountains of the East.

In the middle register four gods stand ready to greet the morning sun as it is pushed by a scarab beetle and emerges between two mountains. These symbols of the sun god are enclosed by a serpent that wraps its coils around him. But the text announces that the gods "have enchanted the serpent. We have cut off the soul of him who coils round you." The scene is flanked by human figures and the hieroglyphs for "flesh" in oval sarcophagi. At left, Osiris-Orion stands in adoration before a hill topped with a ram head and housing a serpent-enemy. A second figure stands before an oval, rising from the earth, with a deity who wears a feather headdress. In the third register, women with knives have killed four bound and decapitated men whose heads lie at their feet and whose hearts have been ripped out. The men are "The Putrescent Ones, great of putrescence... covered with the blood of the chastised ones, the beheaded ones, of the enemies lying on their sides, of those who perish having been killed, with shadows covered with blood." At right, two female Anubis figures stand beside four bound women called "the evil ones, the gory ones." A god and a goddess stand beside four bound and decapitated men.

On the rear wall, a double scene shows Rameses VI censing and libating before Osiris.

CHAMBER F, PILLARS Because of space limitations, parts of the Book of Caverns

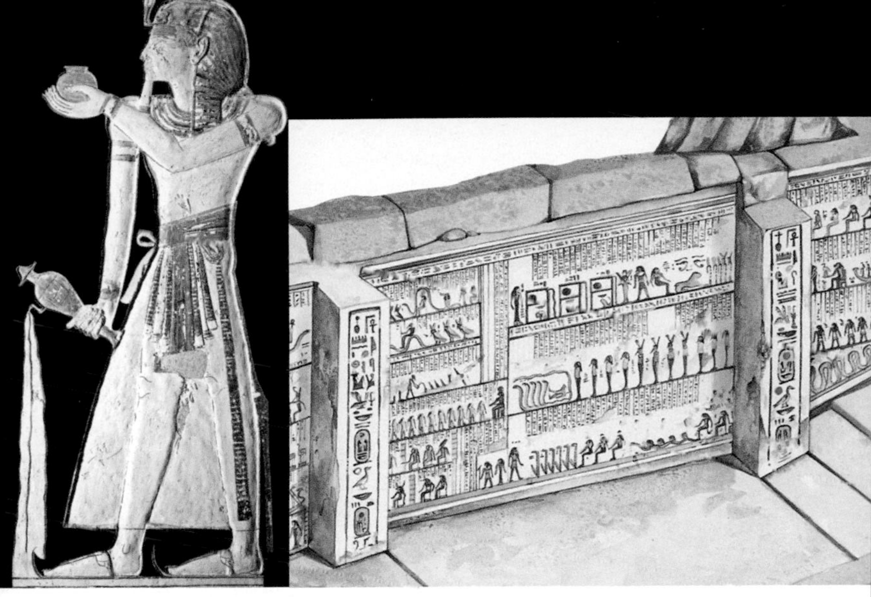

were carved on the faces of several pillars. A reclining god, a scarab, and a ram head appear in two oval sarcophagi flanked by two goddesses. Below, a bowing divinity with a staff stands atop a hill that houses a bound, decapitated man. At left, two ovals with hawk-headed gods called the Tramplers, stand below a sun disk. At the bottom of the pillar, Osiris, flanked by a snake, emerges from the earth. On either side, two upside-down male figures sink into it. At the top left of the pillar, four decapitated figures lie in oval sarcophagi below a solar disk. Other pillars show Rameses VI with Khonsu, Amen-Ra, Meretseger, Ptah-Sokar-Osiris, Ra-Harakhty, Ptah, and Thoth.

CORRIDOR G Beyond the four-pillared chamber F, KV 9 is decorated with texts and scenes from the *Imydwat*, the Book of What is in the Netherworld, also called the Book of the Hidden Chamber. The book describes in twelve hours or sections the journey of the sun god and the pharaoh through the Netherworld. It quotes the speeches of the god and describes creatures encountered during the trip. The most complete version of the *Imydwat* is that in the tomb of Sety I, which lacks only the twelfth hour. The version here also lacks the final hour, and the text is also abbreviated and sometimes jumbled. Nevertheless, we shall describe the Rameses VI version in some detail since Sety I's tomb is likely to remain inaccessible to tourists for some time.

The text begins on the left wall of the ramp leading from chamber F to corridor G. It occupies four registers. In the upper, forty-two squares contain figures of nine baboons, twelve goddesses, three crocodile-headed gods, three with jackal heads, three with human heads, and twelve more standing goddesses. Each deity is named; for example, the crocodile-headed gods are The One Who Passes Through the Netherworld, the Bull, and Powerful Face.

In the second register, a solar bark carries eight sailors, two goddesses, and the ram-headed sun god. Before the boat stand two figures of Ma'at and other deities including Osiris. Four personified stelae represent the power and knowledge of the sun god. The third register shows another bark with a scarab (a form of the sun-god) being adored by two figures and preceded by snakes, gods and goddesses, and a staff with horns and serpents. At the bottom of the wall, baboons, serpents, gods and goddesses occupy forty-two squares, as in the upper register. A long text follows in which the sun god directs the gods of the Netherworld to aid him in his journey. The second hour of the *Imydwat* shows the beginning of the journey across a body of water called Wernes. In the upper register, a row of goddesses advances toward a lion, a stela, a pair of crooks, a figure with the heads of both Horus and Seth, and two seated gods. At right, six seated gods with animal heads wield knives with which to repel the enemies of the sun god.

In the middle register a great barge carrying the sun god and other deities is preceded by four barges with prows of cobra heads, crowns, or gods. The second boat carries a crocodile, the third boat a symbol of the goddess Hathor, the fourth a Ma'at feather and a solar disk. Figures in the lower register include four running gods bearing the hieroglyph for "years." They include The Carrier, The Opener of Time, and The Guardian of Time. Standing gods carry symbols of time or stars. A figure of Osiris stands in the midst of other gods. At right, standing figures of the blessed dead hold stalks of wheat or wear them in their hair. These are farmers in the Netherworld who have been presented farmland by the god.

In the third hour, at the bottom of the wall, the journey continues across the Waters of Osiris. In the upper register, a baboon seated on a small sandy island and another baboon in a shrine are preceded by striding figures of gods and goddesses. In the middle register, the solar bark (with no figure) is preceded by three other boats, each with a different prow. In the lower register, two groups of seated Osiris figures, one group wearing the crown of Upper Egypt, the other wearing the crown of Lower Egypt, are separated by five ibis-headed men wielding knives. In the tomb of Thutmes III these scenes are followed by a lengthy text. That text does not occur here.

CORRIDOR H, LEFT WALL The fourth hour moves from a watery world to one of desert. This is Rosetau, and the sloping pathways "the sacred roads of the Imhat Necropolis, the hidden gates which are in the earth of Sokar, he on his sand." This is a place of snakes, and even the solar bark (in the middle register) becomes a snake-filled boat (in the lower register) as it is towed across the barren landscape. The boat's journey is an arduous and complex one, down ramps and across desert, confronted by sealed doors and serpents whose legs and wings are meant to emphasize the cleverness and unpredictability of their movements. Osiris stands in the middle register to aid the sun god and the king, and Horus and Sokar protectively hold the eye of the sun god between them. At the bottom right in the lower register, fourteen stars and heads with solar disks announce the successful passage of the solar bark through these barriers. (A finely-drawn "hieratic" version of the fourth hour can be seen in the tomb of Thutmes III.)

The fifth hour includes a complex series of scenes. In the upper register, a small mound represents the grave of Osiris, protected by two birds representing Isis and Nephthys. The sun-as-scarab emerges from the underside of this mound, joining with seven men and seven women to pull the tow-rope attached to the solar bark. The bark will continue (in the lower register) through the Netherworld, represented here by an oval cave with Sokar standing inside. Two sphinx-like figures of Aker flanking it. To its right four gods sit and look backward, with crowns, a ram head, or a feather on their knees. (Again, see the tomb of Thutmes III for another example of this scene.)

334 BOTTOM DETAIL FROM THE RIGHT SIDE OF CORRIDOR H.

335 DRAWING OF THE RIGHT WALL OF CORRIDOR H.

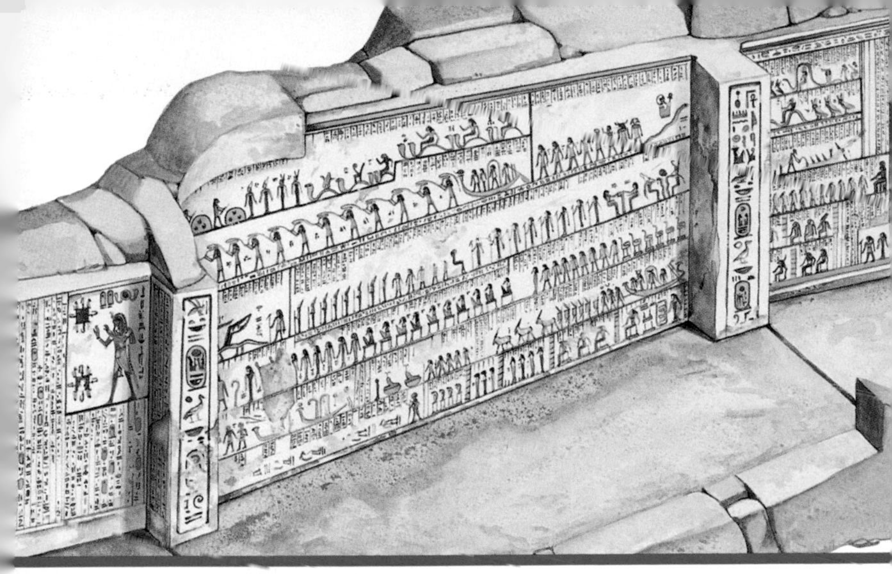

On the **RIGHT WALL OF THE RAMP AND CORRIDOR G**, the sixth hour shows the solar bark sailing in the primeval waters of Nun at the very deepest point in the Netherworld. In the upper register, nine deities are drawn in a semi-seated pose suggesting the process of resurrection. Nine crowned crooks with knives precede them, faced by a lion surmounted by *wedjat*-eyes. The lion, representing both the sun god and Osiris, is called the Bull with the Thunderous Voice. At right, three chests containing solar disks and the hind part of a lion, a wing, or a human head, are partly open and serpents spit into it. These scenes allude to the unification of the sun god with his *ba* and his subsequent rebirth. In the middle register, the solar bark is preceded by Thoth, a goddess, and sixteen mummiform deities called the Kings of Upper Egypt and the Kings of Lower Egypt who will witness the god's resurrection. At right, the sun god wears a scarab on his head and is surrounded by a five-headed snake. Sobek and Nun flank the lower register showing a serpent with the heads of the Four Sons of Horus emerging from its body, fourteen gods and goddesses, and nine fire-spitting serpents with knives. In the upper four registers on the right wall, the seventh division shows the solar deity being reborn, as the forces of evil, especially the serpent Apophis, are prevented from attacking him. In the upper register, a cat-headed demon had decapitated enemies of Osiris. At right stand three *ba*-birds of the god. In the middle register, the solar bark sails forth toward a snake, said to be 433 cubits (over 200 meters, 610 feet) long, which has been rendered impotent by the many knives thrust through its body. At right stand four boxes, "the mysterious forms of the Netherworld, the chests with mysterious heads," named Atum, Khepri, Ra, and Osiris. In the lower register, the sun god sits on his throne with a scepter and an *ankh*-sign in his hand facing personifications of stars. At right, a crocodile sits on a sand bar with the head of Osiris, searching for any missing parts of the body of the sun god.

CORRIDORS G AND H, RIGHT SIDE The eighth hour shows five caverns in both the upper and lower registers, each closed by a single-leaf wooden door. In each cavern, three gods sit on the hieroglyph sign for cloth. Each is here to receive clothing for the afterlife. The deities cry out to the sun god from the caverns, but to human ears the sounds are "like the cry of male cats" "the sound of a bank falling into the flood," "the lowing of mating bulls," or "a nest full of birds."

336 RAMESES VI BEFORE MA'AT, FROM THE RIGHT WALL OF THE ANTECHAMBER.

In the middle register, the solar bark continues its journey towed by eight men. It is accompanied by an entourage of nine hieroglyphs meaning "followers" and four rams of the Exalted Earth, each wearing a different crown.

The ninth hour occupies the second and third registers (counting from the bottom of the right wall) in corridor H. Much of it is a continuation of the eighth hour in which gods seated on the cloth hieroglyph prepare to be dressed in the afterlife. Other figures carry stalks of wheat as provisions in the afterlife. The solar bark sails in this scene instead of being towed. It is preceded by twelve gods carrying oars. At right, three deities on baskets are associated with the outfitting of the dead. They are called Tiut at the Head of the Netherworld, the One of the Necropolis in the Netherworld, and the Lady of Gifts in the Netherworld. The tenth hour can be found in the registers above and to the left of the ninth hour. In the upper, a god holding a scepter is preceded by a scarab and goddesses holding the solar disk. At right, Sekhmet in several forms and other deities surround a seated figure of Thoth who holds the solar eye in his hand. These scenes here are intended to protect the sacred eye. In the middle register, the solar bark, again sailing and not being towed, it is protected by armed guards. Osiris appears as a falcon-headed snake, Sokar as a falcon standing on a serpent. Those who have died by drowning are shown in the lower register tended by Horus, who will assure them passage to the Netherworld.

In the eleventh hour, the sun god prepares to be reborn and to rise on the eastern horizon at daybreak. This hour occupies the upper two registers on the right wall, and the left end of the third register. In the upper register, a double-headed god, The One Provided with a Face, stands behind a winged serpent next to a god with a solar disk on its head. Beside him are two *wedjat* eyes. Ten stars and a god on the back of another serpent follow. Then come twelve gods, some with animal heads, some with no arms, and four goddesses seated on two-headed serpents. These goddesses breathe fire and bring "the rebellion and storm that appear in the Netherworld." The solar bark sails toward dawn in the middle register, preceded by a huge snake called the World-Encircler in whose coils sunrise will take place. Snakes representing Isis and Nephthys carry the crowns of Upper and Lower Egypt on their backs to Sais where they will be greeted by four figures of the goddess Neith. Great pits of fire can be seen in the lower register, tended by goddesses who oversee the immolation of those who might threaten the sun god. The scene is watched over by Horus (at left). The twelfth hour is shown neither in the tomb of Rameses VI nor Sety I, but it is found in the tombs of Thutmes III and Amenhetep II and depicts the rebirth of the sun at daybreak. Two dozen deities pull the solar boat through the body of a serpent. The solar deity appears (at right) as a scarab beetle, flying into the waiting arms of the goddess Shu. With the coming of the twelfth hour, the long nighttime journey is over, the gods rejoice, and, in the lower right corner of the scene, Osiris, in his form as a mummy, now sleeps until the cycle is repeated.

CORRIDOR H, CEILING Goddesses carrying huge cauldrons on their heads appear at the beginning of registers one and three. These cauldrons are filled with stars, birds, or disks. Four bulls' heads appear in each corner of these small scenes, accompanied by a gazelle head. Next, three double shrines or mounds are shown holding strange-looking mummiform figures, two of them with two heads, two others with hands in place of heads. These are followed by nine figures with disks instead of heads or nine figures with stars on their heads and disks at their feet.

In the middle register, a ram head and a scarab emerge from a solar disk. At right, the ram-headed solar deity stands on a boat whose prow and stern are human heads and hands. The boat floats on stars enclosed by a large serpent. Seven men with disks instead of heads stand in adoration at right, followed by two pair of gods with women's heads and bodies between them.

Farther on, in the sloping part of the corridor, a disk and crescent are flanked by four gods and four hearts. In the register below, a boat in the form of a human body carries a god with two ram's heads and four arms. Other heads emerge from his body.

Above the gate leading into chamber I, a mountain supports human figures with disks instead of heads and serpents emerging from their feet. Between them, four serpents emerge from a large solar disk to spit flames at four captives, either bound or shot by arrows. Some Egyptologists suggest that this scene was added after workmen had broken through into the overlying tomb KV 12, in hopes of warding off any evil consequences of this accident.

CHAMBER I This room has a relatively low ceiling, made necessary by the presence of KV 12, a neighboring tomb that lies only about 50 centimeters above. Ancient engineers apparently discovered this when they broke through the overlying floor of KV 12 while carving the ceiling of corridor H.

The decoration in this small room reads counterclockwise and begins immediately left of the entrance. In the right half of the room, Chapters 126, 129, and 127 of the Book of the Dead appear in long columns. In the top right corner of the side wall, the king is shown in adoration before two square pools of water each flanked by four baboons and four lamps. The king asks the baboons for assistance entering the Netherworld and the baboons agree. At left, another scene shows the king before the goddess Ma'at. On the right rear wall, the king stands below with two of his names in cartouches. The text deals with the king's speeches to the guardians of the caverns in the Netherworld.

The left half of the chamber quotes Chapters 124 and 125 of the Book of the Dead and is to be read from the back of the room to the front. Chapter 125 is the famous Negative Confession, in which the king lists the sins he did not commit during his lifetime. For example, he boasts that he was not greedy, did not kill, cheat, steal offerings to the gods, exaggerate, argue or slander.

On the **CEILING**, the king stands with various deities in the barks of the day (left) and the night (right) beneath a winged sun disk and beside a column of cartouches with his names and epithets. This register is separated from that beyond by a long strip of water representing the celestial river. Note the woman harvesting papyrus at the far right. Below the band of water, a second scene shows a reclining figure of Osiris rising from a lion-headed bier under an elaborate canopy to receive an *ankh*-sign by the now-destroyed figure of his son Horus.

CHAMBER J Rameses VI's burial chamber is not the largest in the Valley of the Kings but it is one of the most impressive because of its extensive decoration. The chamber covers only 118.5 square meters (1,276 square feet) but it has over 300 square meters (3,230 square feet) of wall surface, all of it carved and painted on a stark white background with vivid reds, blues, and yellows that stand in dramatic contrast to the more somber mustard-on-black astronomical ceiling.

The result is unique in the Valley of the Kings. The complex scenes are from a text whose original name is unknown but which Egyptologists call the Book of the Earth, the Book of Aker, or The Creation of the Sun Disk. It is a text rarely found outside the royal burial chambers of the tombs in the Valley of the Kings. Originally, the chamber was to be larger: a row of four columns across the front should have been matched by four columns across the rear. These were never cut; instead, four pilasters were carved and only a central doorway extended further into the hillside (into chamber K). Indeed, two of the front pillars (numbers 1 and 4) were left unfinished as well, perhaps due to the quality of stone encountered in the chamber's front corners. The pit in the floor atop which the stone sarcophagus sat was also to have been bigger, and the huge fragments of the destroyed sarcophagus overwhelm the space and make the room seem crowded.

The Book of the Earth is basically an elaboration of chapter eleven of the Book of Gates, in which the solar bark prepares to emerge at dawn from the Netherworld and return back to the earth. The scenes depict the Netherworld in great detail and move from the left (south) wall to the back wall, then the right (north) wall, then to the pillars.

338 THE BURIAL CHAMBER WITH FRAGMENTS OF THE SARCOPHAGUS.

339 TOP DETAIL FROM THE NORTH COLUMN IN THE BURIAL CHAMBER.

339 CENTER THE REAR CHAMBER, OR CHAMBER K.

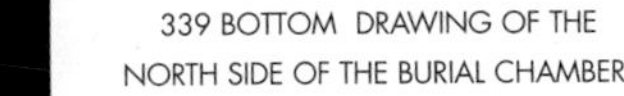

339 BOTTOM DRAWING OF THE NORTH SIDE OF THE BURIAL CHAMBER.

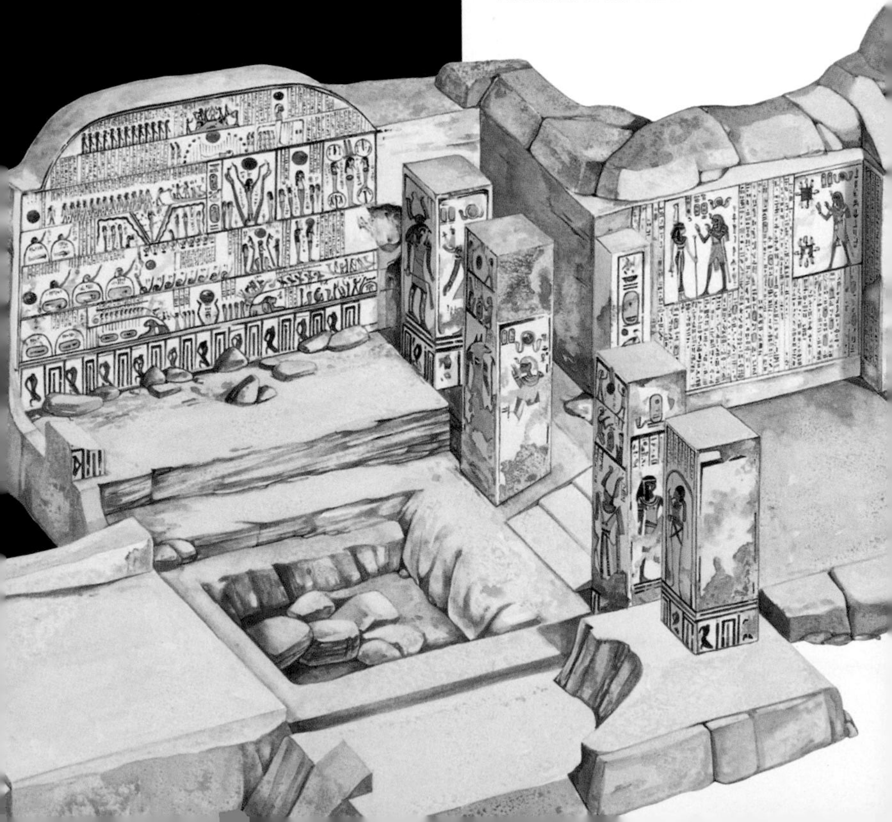

340 A SCARAB EMERGES FROM A SUN DISK, LEFT WALL OF THE BURIAL CHAMBER.

340-341 THE LEFT WALL OF THE BURIAL CHAMBER.

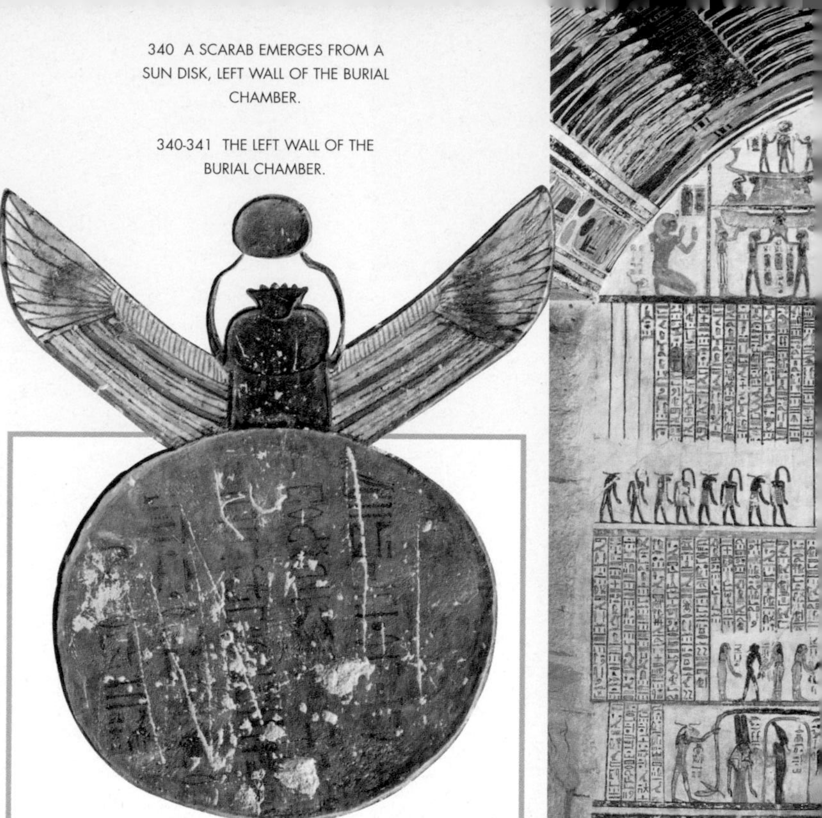

LEFT (SOUTH) WALL In the upper register, at right, Osiris stands in a shrine protected by three serpents and receives adulation from figures of his *ba* who stand on small mounds of earth. Below him a small casket containing the god's mummy is watched over by Anubis and a goddess called the Mysterious One. On either side of the shrine, gods raise huge cauldrons above their heads. The blood of the god's enemies streams into the pots. Bound and headless captives kneel below. In the center of the register, two pair of arms support a huge solar disk surmounted by a mummiform sun god and flanked by fire-spitting cobras. The figures are surrounded by twelve disks and twelve stars. At the left, The Mysterious One holds symbols of the sun in her hands and each symbol is watched over by a human-headed snake. Left of these figures, a complex scene shows the solar bark resting on a figure of Aker, depicted as a two-headed sphinx. On board the boat stand Khepri, the sun god, and Thoth. Beneath, a winged scarab and sun disk are held by two men. Behind them stand the goddesses Isis and Nephthys. At far right in the second register, Horus emerges from the corpse of Osiris. Even though he is dead, Osiris is still able to procreate: "Horus came from the seed of his father when he was already putrid," a text claims. At left, seven deities stand frontally within seven mounds. Then, Horus is shown coming forth from the body of Osiris. The accompanying text announces that, "This Great God is like this in his egg which is in the Netherworld. Horus comes out of the body of his father, and praises him who has procreated him while the two goddesses (Isis and Nephthys) join his body."

In another scene to the left, two mummified ram-headed gods called "The Roarer" and "Seny" lie beneath two mounds while

two gods raise up the *ba* of Osiris.

At the right end of the sub-register below, a sun disk is held in "The Arms of the Abyss" emerging from the Netherworld as a ram-headed god observes three gods adoring a sun disk from which the head of Hathor emerges. This scene and the next refer to the rebirth of the sun god at dawn. In the next scene, a scarab comes forth from the disk. It is flanked by two cobras with arms and four shrines holding deities including Osiris (top left, called "The Bull of the West"). In the next picture, gods stand or bow down in five ovals while, to their left, four ram-headed gods alternate with four gods whose heads are lamp wicks called, appropriately, "The Burning Ones."

In the third register, a ram-headed god stands amidst fifteen small shrines housing various gods and a scarab emerges from a large sun disk. To their left, four gods called by such names as "The Slasher," carry the bloody decapitated bodies of the gods' enemies. Further left, four enemies with fire on their heads are being bound by goddesses called "The Fiery One," and "She Who Scorches." The men are being burned alive because "This Great God makes them suffer."

In the sub-register below, the heads of the decapitated enemies are being boiled up in huge cauldrons heated by fire-breathing heads in "The Place of Annihilation." Gods with knives supervise the deed while two goddesses protect a large heart. "The Place of Annihilation" is represented in the next scene by a woman lying in a coffin. She is called "The Body of Annihilation" and six deities stand beside her in shrines, praying. Finally, ram-headed gods hold a snake above a shrine for Osiris. The head of the snake is being severed by a large knife. Standing beside the shrine are the corpses of two deities, Geb and Tatenen, emerging from the Netherworld.

REAR WALL On the left side of the back wall of the burial chamber, a ram-headed deity stands in the top register observing *ba*-birds at prayer. One of them stands above a scarab beetle that emerges from a serpent followed by Atum and Shu. Below, the ram-headed god stands before the sun god and other deities greeting Horus as he emerges from a within another pair of arms that hold scepters. Behind stand four mummies with *ba*-birds and two barks that carry the mummified Osiris and Horus. Large ovals represent the burial mounds of the sun disk and gods with the hieroglyphs for "flesh." Below them, gods pray among figures of *ba*-birds and a hieroglyph meaning "shadow."

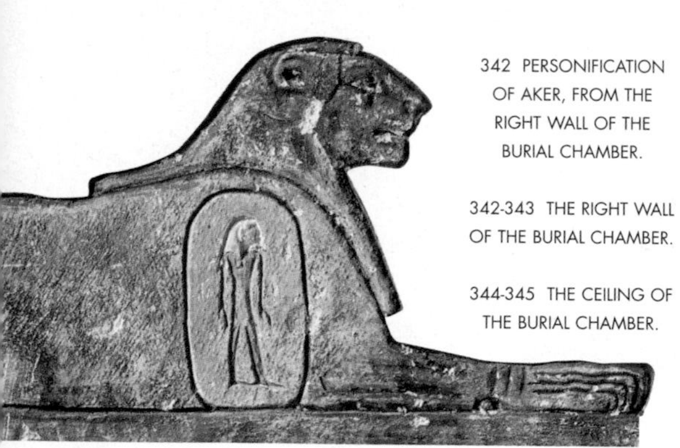

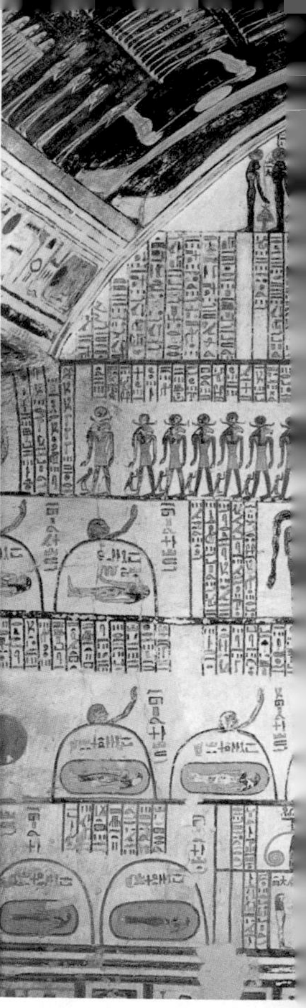

342 PERSONIFICATION OF AKER, FROM THE RIGHT WALL OF THE BURIAL CHAMBER.

342-343 THE RIGHT WALL OF THE BURIAL CHAMBER.

344-345 THE CEILING OF THE BURIAL CHAMBER.

solar disk. In the third register, gods stand before "the mooring posts in the mysterious abode."

On the right side, four ovals contain gods. Below, four more ovals have gods in them who "stand upright in their coffins in the midst of their decomposition and putrefaction. The Great God calls their souls without seeing them. He knows them by the greatness of their smell and their putrefaction." At left, a mummiform god, his wrappings carefully drawn, has a solar disk inside him. He is flanked by a snake emerging from a pair of arms and a crocodile called Penwenti, rising

RIGHT (NORTH) WALL In the topmost register, at right, a large mummiform figure of the sun god is flanked by deities interred in the "Mound of Darkness." A solar bark sits atop the earth god, a double-headed Aker. Below it, the mummy of the sun god receives rays of light and rejuvenation from the solar disk. It is surrounded by twelve stars and twelve solar disks and four figures of Osiris. At left, twelve goddesses with solar disks on their heads and stars and hieroglyphs for "shadow" at their feet "lead this Great God in the West whose forms are mysterious, toward their hours. They do what they have to do."

In the second register, the "Guardian of the Bodies in the West," wearing horns and feathers on his head, stands between gods and disks, each with three mummiform figures in them. At left, a figure of Osiris is joined "in the land of the soul" by Tefnut, Shu, Khepri, and Nun. Next, a goddess called the Annihilator "comes out of the darkness," her arms encircling a solar disk. Fourteen ram-headed gods and their *bas* turn

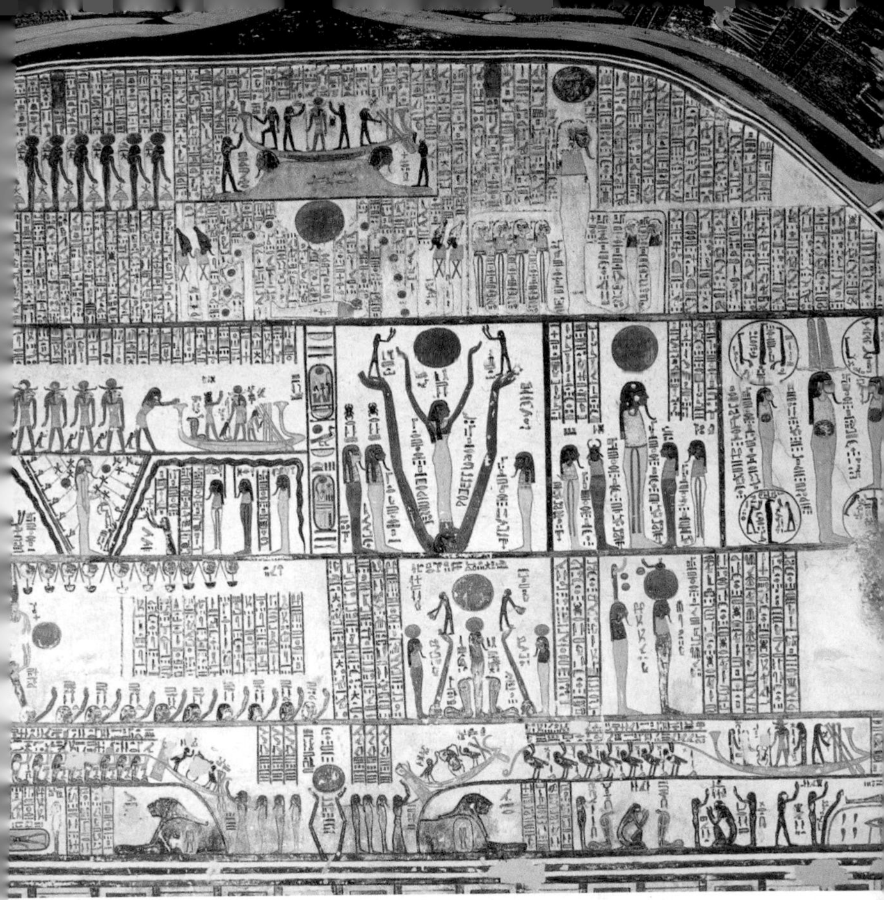

backward toward a solar bark. Below them, an ithyphallic god called "He Who Conceals the Hours" stands in a cavern with a child. Dotted lines, perhaps representing semen, join his phallus to the twelve goddesses representing hours. Around the cavern a great snake encloses several mummiform gods. In this and the two registers below, mounds with heads and arms emerging have female figures lying within.

In the third register, two large figures at right represent mummiform gods, one with a scarab emerging from the sun disk on his head, the other with a female figure. A god wearing a solar disk is next, emerging from the earth between a pair of arms and two cobras. "The Great God passes by the bodies of the Fierce Faces," the text reads, "when he passes by the body of Khepri." The figure is followed by ten heads and arms emerging from the ground. Another ten heads appear in the sky, drawn upside down and carrying the hieroglyph for "shadow."

The lower register depicts the rising and setting of the sun above Aker, the double-headed sphinx representing the earth. The sun is lifted up by a pair of hands and mummies stand by to assist the solar bark on its journey into night (on the right) and day (on the left). They are towed by seven *ba*-birds and fourteen uraei. At right, a mummy lies atop a mound with an eye and hieroglyphs for "flesh" inside. The mound is in "the arms of Geb."

THE CEILING Like the ceilings of corridors D, E, and F, the burial chamber ceiling is also decorated with a figure of Nut and copies of the Book of Day and the Book of Night. The scene is discussed above.

3

KV 6: THE TOMB OF RAMESES IX

THE HISTORY

On the plus side, the tomb of Rameses IX is easily accessible, nearly level, and well decorated. On the minus side, it is probably the most-visited tomb in the Valley of the Kings, crowded, noisy, and equipped with dirty and highly reflective sheets of glass that make it difficult to see the wall decoration. Tour guides like it because it lies near the entrance to the Valley of the Kings and their groups can visit quickly. After midday, however, things calm down and a visit can be very rewarding.

Numerous graffiti carved high up on the walls of KV 6 indicate that it was filled with one or two meters of debris during most of the last three millennia, but it was always partly accessible. The tomb was completely cleared in 1888.

The reign of Rameses IX was a time of economic and political trouble in Egypt and these problems are reflected in the way his tomb was carved and decorated. Rameses IX ruled for eighteen years, but his craftsmen worked only intermittently on the tomb during that time, presumably whenever the palace could afford to pay their wages. This meant that even after eighteen years, the tomb still was only half-finished. It is easy to distinguish which parts were done before the king's death and which after. The former work, in spite of the on-again off-again schedule, was well done, often painstakingly so. By contrast, the later work was hasty, even slapdash. One can see the difference in quality by comparing scenes at the beginning of corridor C with those at the end. At the beginning, chapter 125 of the Book of the Dead is written in thirty columns of finely colored, well-proportioned hieroglyphs. At the end, chapter 126 of the Book of the Dead is written in black ink only and the characters are cursorily drawn.

KV 6 was the last royal tomb to be dug in the Valley of the Kings, and it is interesting to see how it adopted and adapted many elements from earlier tombs in its design and decoration. The tomb has a simple plan, influenced in its early stages by KV 11, the tomb of Rameses III. For example, the pilasters on the side walls of the entrance and the four small side chambers off corridor B were direct borrowings from there. The decoration also was influenced by that in KV 9, the tomb of Rameses VI. The size of the tomb is average for royal tombs in the valley, in spite of its abbreviated plan, but the dimensions of its gates and corridors are the Valley's widest. An ostracon found in the Valley of the Kings and now in the Egyptian Museum, Cairo, gives a red-ink sketch plan of the tomb, perhaps followed by workmen in the course of its digging.

346 DETAIL FROM CORRIDOR D.

347 RAMESES IX DEPICTED ON THE LEFT WALL OF CORRIDOR C.

LEGEND

A *ENTRANCE*
B *FIRST CORRIDOR*
Ba, b, c, d *SIDE CHAMBERS*
C *SECOND CORRIDOR*
D *THIRD CORRIDOR*
E *WELL CHAMBER*
F *PILLARED CHAMBER*
J *BURIAL CHAMBER*

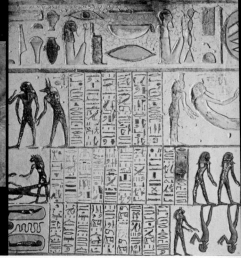

348 DETAIL FROM THE CEILING OF CORRIDOR C.

348-349 THE BOOK OF CAVERNS WITH RAMESES IX OFFERING TO AMEN-RA, FROM THE RIGHT WALL OF CORRIDOR C.

349 CENTER OSTRACON WITH PLAN OF KV 6, NOW IN CAIRO MUSEUM.

VISIT

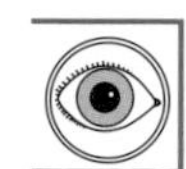

CORRIDOR B The scenes in corridor B offer fine examples of the detail artists could include in their wall paintings. On the left wall, for example, the king stands before Ra-Harakhty and Osiris in an elaborate kiosk. The costumes of all three figures show precise renderings of cloth and beadwork. Equally well done is the band of lion-headed uraei and cartouches running across the top of the wall. To the right, sixty-seven columns of text are part of the Litany of Ra, known in ancient times as The Book of Praying to Ra in the West, Praying to the United One in the West. It is a lengthy hymn of praise to Ra, remarking on his close ties to Osiris. At right, a *Iwnmutef*-priest purifies Osiris with *ankh*-signs as part of the Opening of the Mouth ritual. Here, too, in spite of damage, the hieroglyphs are finely drawn.

On the right wall, the king stands in a shrine offering incense to Amen-Ra-Harakhty and Meretseger. The god has four ram's heads and wears an elaborate crown. The goddess wears a crown indicating that here she is the Goddess of the West. To the left are scenes from the first part of the Book of Caverns, described in detail in the tomb of Rameses VI, KV 9. On the ceiling, huge vultures with outstretched wings alternate with the names and titles of the king. At the end of the corridor, the soffit above the gate shows a solar disk with a ram-headed god, a baboon, and a man kneeling in adoration within it, flanked by figures of the king and a vulture.

CORRIDOR C At far left on the left wall an inscribed door leaf is followed by the figures of fifteen demons shown in thirteen ovals. In the upper

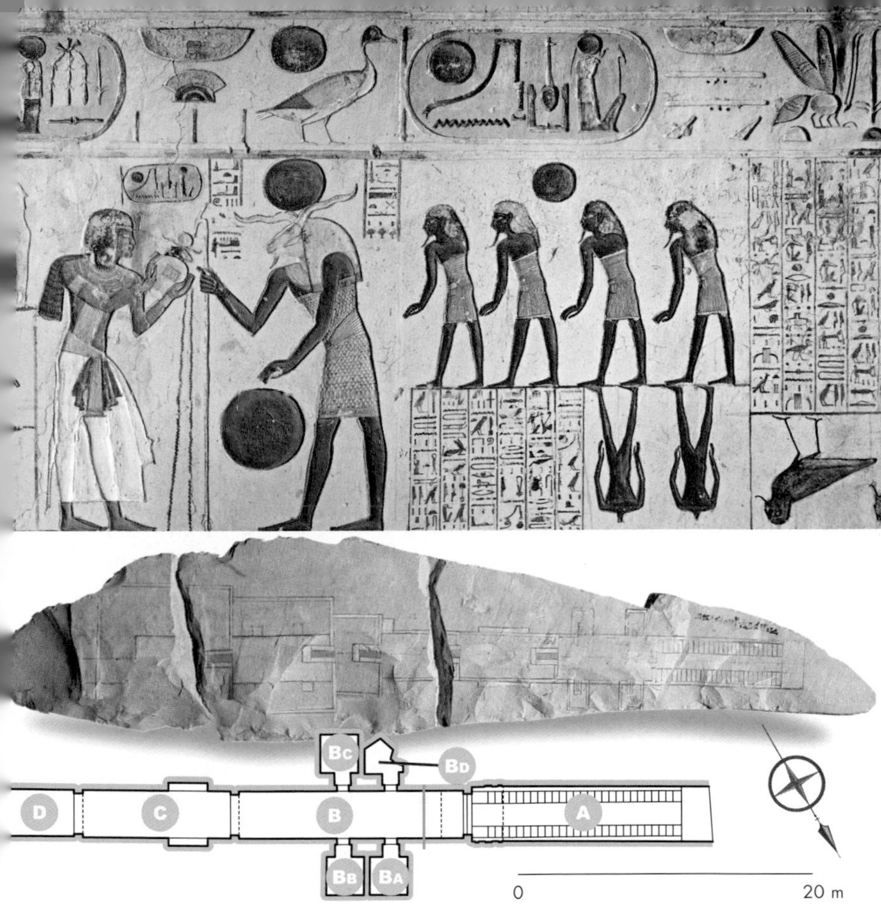

register, scenes from the Litany of Ra are followed by a part of the second hour of the *Imydwat* and, at far right, chapter 126 of the Book of the Dead. The two pools surrounded by baboons and lamps are a vignette associated with that chapter.

In the register below, at left, Rameses IX strides forth into the tomb accompanied by Hathor who holds before her a large stela bearing his names and titles. To their right, chapter 125 of the Book of the Dead is written in thirty columns of text. This is the so-called Negative Confession, in which the king lists sins he did not commit during his lifetime. At the end of the wall, the king stands in adoration before Khonsu-Neferhetep-Shu, the god who wears an elaborately painted kilt.

On the right wall, at right, a single leaf door is guarded by a snake. A ram-headed god looks out over the second hour of the Book of Caverns in the lower register, the third division at the top right of the wall, and the fourth division at the top left. In the upper left section, the king pours a libation for Amen-Ra. The ceiling contains an elaborate set of drawings along the edges that represent Egyptian constellations called the "Unweary Ones," i.e., circumpolar stars that never set. The forward-facing seated figure in the center of a large grid represents a star clock. These scenes, painted in yellow on a blue background, are similar to those found in the tomb of Rameses VI. Above the gate at the end of the chamber, figures of the king, accompanied by family members, pay homage to the solar disk in which a ram-headed deity is accompanied by a baboon and the Eye of Horus.

CORRIDOR D On the left wall, Hours Two and Three of the *Imydwat* appear in an abbreviated version.

The right wall of this chamber is often termed "enigmatic" because its scenes and texts are an amalgamation of several books of the netherworld, often illustrated with unique scenes. At right, the king offers a small figure of Ma'at to Ptah and Ma'at. The costumes are especially well drawn. To their left, a leaning figure of the king as an ithyphallic Osiris is meant to equate the king with the sun god Ra. A solar disk and scarab appear above. A later hieratic graffito has been added at the left of the god. In the upper register, there is no text but only a row of eight human figures, drawn in alternating red and yellow circles. One Egyptologist recently has suggested these are Lords of the Netherworld, meant to represent falling stars. In the middle register, a serpent-shaped solar bark sails across the snake-god Apophis. In front of them, eleven more snakes are struck by single rays of sunlight and rendered impotent. Seven figures, called Those Who Cast Down, pray over pits in which the gods punish evildoers. In the bottom register, four goddesses vanquish serpents while four figures bend backward. These latter figures are apparently related to the infant sun disk. The accompanying text is a variation of chapter 106 of the Book of the Dead.

CHAMBER E Two well-dressed figures of *Iwnmutef*-priests stand on either side of the gate in the rear wall of this chamber. On the left, the priest offers up a bowl before a ram-headed standard; on the right, before an ibis standard, he offers adzes for the Opening of the Mouth ritual.

BURIAL CHAMBER J The left and right walls of the burial chamber contain excerpts from the Book of the Earth (see the similar scenes in KV 9, Rameses VI). The rear wall deals with the journeys, in daytime and nighttime, made by the king and god in solar barks. On the left, the bark is accompanied by six gods of the north; on the right stand eight gods of the south. In the damaged scene below, the king, accompanied by various gods, stands before a large and elaborately decorated shrine. The ceiling is divided in half by figures of the goddess Nut, and the solar disk can be seen coursing through her body during the nighttime. On either side are scenes from the Book of the Day and the Book of the Night.

350 TOP RAMESES IX OFFERING A FIGURE OF MA'AT TO MA'AT AND PTAH, RIGHT WALL OF CORRIDOR D.

350 BOTTOM A LORD OF THE NETHERWORLD, RIGHT WALL OF CORRIDOR D.

351 LEFT THE PILLARED CHAMBER.

351 RIGHT THE BURIAL CHAMBER.

4 THE VALLEY OF THE QUEENS

4

INTRODUCTION

355 AERIAL VIEWS OF THE VALLEY OF THE QUEENS.

The Valley of the Queens, in Arabic *Wadi al-Malakat,* in ancient times was called *Ta Set Neferu,* a phrase that can mean The Place of Beauty and also The Place of Royal Children and Wives. It was used in the New Kingdom as a burial place for several royal wives, princesses, and princes. It is a lovely place, this small, U-shaped *wadi,* curving south and west. Rugged limestone cliffs jut upward, their strata turning and twisting in dramatic contrast to the horizontal beds of other Theban hills. There is a small cave at the base of these cliffs and when it rained, water would pour into it and then flow through the valley. (The watercourse follows the left side of the modern road and footpath.) Some Egyptologists believe it was this feature that caused the valley to be selected for royal burials: the cave represented the womb of Hathor, the celestial cow, and water meant fertility. Burial here would by a physical symbol of rebirth in the afterlife.

The valley's floor rises only slightly and is covered with undulating hillocks into which tomb entrances could easily be dug. About ninety tombs have been located in the valley, some of them simple pit tombs, others with corridors along a straight or L-shaped axis with small side chambers. A few, mostly from the reign of Rameses II, have pillared halls, stairways as well as corridors, and large burial chambers. Those of Dynasty 20 are more like the smaller, late New Kingdom tombs in the Valley of the Kings: nearly-level corridors, with an occasional side chamber, leading to a small, rectangular burial chamber. The three tombs in the Valley of the Queens that are open today are of the latter type. At least ten of the tombs begun in the valley were never finished, probably because poor quality bedrock forced workmen to rethink their plans. That same poor stone meant that heavy layers of plaster had to be applied before walls could be decorated. Some of it fell of its own weight; more was destroyed by occasional flash floods. Well over sixty per cent of the tombs known today are anonymous because such damage has erased evidence of names or titles.

There was continued activity in the valley after the New Kingdom: small tombs continued to be dug, and in the fourth century AD, a Christian monastery called Dayr Rumi was built. Its broken walls can still be seen to the right (west) as one enters the valley from the parking lot.

Excavation of the Valley of the Queens was undertaken by Ernesto Schiaparelli of the Egyptian Museum in Turin between 1903 and 1906. His work was highly successful and most of the named tombs we know today, including the famous tomb of Queen Nefertari, were discovered by him and his staff. More recently, French archaeologists have been working here to clear away the rubble and overburden that covers the limestone bedrock. It is the only part of the Theban Necropolis to be

so thoroughly explored.

Three tombs are currently open in the Valley of the Queens, all from the reign of Rameses III, whose memorial temple lies only a kilometer away, at Madinat Habu. The tombs are similar in content and style, while their simple architecture and decoration offer an interesting contrast to the more complex monuments of that king in the Valley of the Kings—and indeed, to the more heavily-decorated tombs of the officials and courtiers who worked as tutors, wet-nurses, and compatriots.

From 1995 until 2003 a fourth tomb was also open to tourists, that of Queen Nefertari, principal wife of Rameses II. It is considered by many to be the most beautifully painted tomb in all of Egypt. But it is now closed because of concerns for its protection.

LEGEND

QV 1-7	*ANONYMOUS TOMBS, 18TH DYNASTY*
QV 8	*PRINCE HORI AND ANONYMOUS PRINCESS, 18TH DYNASTY*
QV 9-16	*ANONYMOUS TOMBS, 18TH D.*
QV 17	*PRINCESSES MERYTRA (I) AND URMERUTES, 18TH DYNASTY*
QV 18-23	*ANONYMOUS TOMBS, 18TH D.*
QV 24	*ANONYMOUS TOMBS, 20TH D.*
QV 25-29	*ANONYMOUS TOMBS, 18TH D.*
QV 30	*NEBIRY, 18TH DYNASTY*
QV 31	*ANONYMOUS PRINCESS-QUEEN, EARLY 19TH DYNASTY*
QV 32	*ANONYMOUS TOMB, 18TH D.*
QV 33	*PRINCESS-QUEEN TANEDJEMY, EARLY 19TH DYNASTY*
QV 34	*ANONYMOUS PRINCESS-QUEEN, EARLY 19TH DYNASTY*
QV 35	*ANONYMOUS TOMB, 18TH DYNASTY*
QV 36	*ANONYMOUS PRINCESS-QUEEN, EARLY 19TH DYNASTY*
QV 37	*ANONYMOUS TOMB, 18TH DYNASTY*
QV 38	*QUEEN SITRE (GREAT ROYAL WIFE OF RAMESES I), EARLY 19TH DYNASTY*
QV 39	*ANONYMOUS TOMB, 18TH DYNASTY*
QV 40	*ANONYMOUS PRINCESS-QUEEN, EARLY 19TH DYNASTY*
QV 41	*UNFINISHED TOMB, 20TH DYNASTY*
QV 42	*PRINCE PAHERWENEMEF AND MINEFER (SON OF RAMESES III AND WIFE OF RAMESES III), 20TH DYNASTY*
QV 43	*PRINCE SETHHERKHEPSHEF (SON OF RAMESES III), 20TH DYNASTY*
QV 44	*PRINCE KHAEMWASET (SON OF RAMESES III), 20TH DYNASTY*
QV 45	*UNFINISHED TOMB, 20TH DYNASTY*

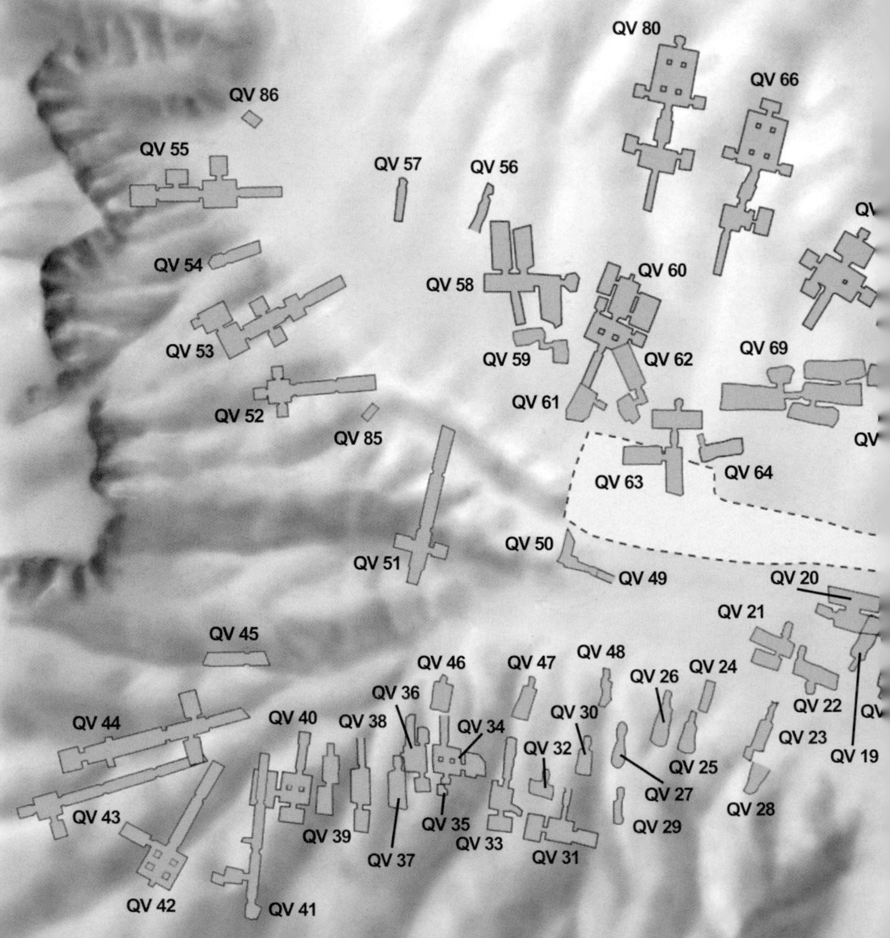

QV 46	*IMHOTEP, VIZIR, 18TH DYNASTY (THUTMES I)*
QV 47	*PRINCESS THUTMES, 18TH DYNASTY*
QV 48	*ANONYMOUS TOMB, 18TH DYNASTY*
QV 49-50	*ANONYMOUS TOMBS, 19TH AND 20TH DYNASTIES*
QV 51	*QUEEN ISIS-TA-HEMDJERET (GREAT ROYAL WIFE OF RAMESES III), 20TH DYNASTY*
QV 52	*QUEEN TYTI (GREAT ROYAL WIFE OF RAMESES III), 20TH DYNASTY*
QV 53	*PRINCE RAMESES-MERYAMEN (SON OF RAMESES III), 20TH DYNASTY*
QV 54	*UNFINISHED TOMB, 20TH DYNASTY*
QV 55	*PRINCE AMENHERKHEPSHEF (SON OF RAMESES III), 20TH DYNASTY*
QV 56	*UNFINISHED TOMB, 19TH DYNASTY*
QV 57	*UNFINISHED TOMB, 19TH DYNASTY*
QV 58	*ANONYMOUS TOMB, 19TH DYNASTY*
QV 59	*ANONYMOUS TOMB., 18TH DYNASTY*
QV 60	*QUEEN NEBETTAWY (DAUGHTER-WIFE OF RAMESES II), 19TH DYNASTY*
QV 61	*ANONYMOUS TOMB, 18TH DYNASTY*
QV 62-65	*ANONYMOUS TOMBS, 18TH DYNASTY*
QV 66	*QUEEN NEFERTARI (GREAT ROYAL WIFE OF RAMESES II), 19TH DYNASTY*
QV 67	*ANONYMOUS TOMB, 18TH DYNASTY*
QV 68	*QUEEN MERYTAMEN (DAUGHTER-WIFE OF RAMESES II), 19TH DYNASTY*
QV 69	*ANONYMOUS TOMB, 18TH DYNASTY*
QV 70	*NEHESY, 18TH DYNASTY*
QV 71	*QUEEN BINT-ANTA (DAUGHTER-WIFE OF RAMESES II), 19TH DYNASTY*
QV 72	*PRINCE BAKI AND PRINCESS HATNEFERET, 18TH DYNASTY*
QV 73	*PRINCESS HENUTTAWY (DAUGHTER-WIFE OF RAMESES II), 19TH DYNASTY*
QV 74	*QUEEN DUATENTIPET (GREAT ROYAL WIFE OF RAMESES IV), 20TH DYNASTY*
QV 75	*QUEEN HENUTMIRE (DAUGHTER-WIFE OF RAMESES II), 19TH DYNASTY*
QV 76	*PRINCESS MERYTRA (II), 18TH DYNASTY*
QV 77-79	*ANONYMOUS TOMBS, 18TH DYNASTY*
QV 80	*QUEEN TUY (GREAT ROYAL WIFE OF SETI I), 19TH DYNASTY*
QV 81	*HEKA-(...), 18TH DYNASTY*
QV 82	*PRINCE MINEMHET AND AMENHETEP, 18TH DYNASTY*
QV 83	*ANONYMOUS TOMB, 18TH DYNASTY*
QV 84-86	*UNFINISHED TOMB, 20TH DYNASTY*
QV 87	*ANONYMOUS TOMB, 18TH DYNASTY*
QV 88	*PRINCE AHMES, 18TH DYNASTY*
QV 89-94	*ANONYMOUS TOMBS, 18TH DYNASTY*
QV 95	*UNFINISHED TOMB, 20TH DYNASTY*

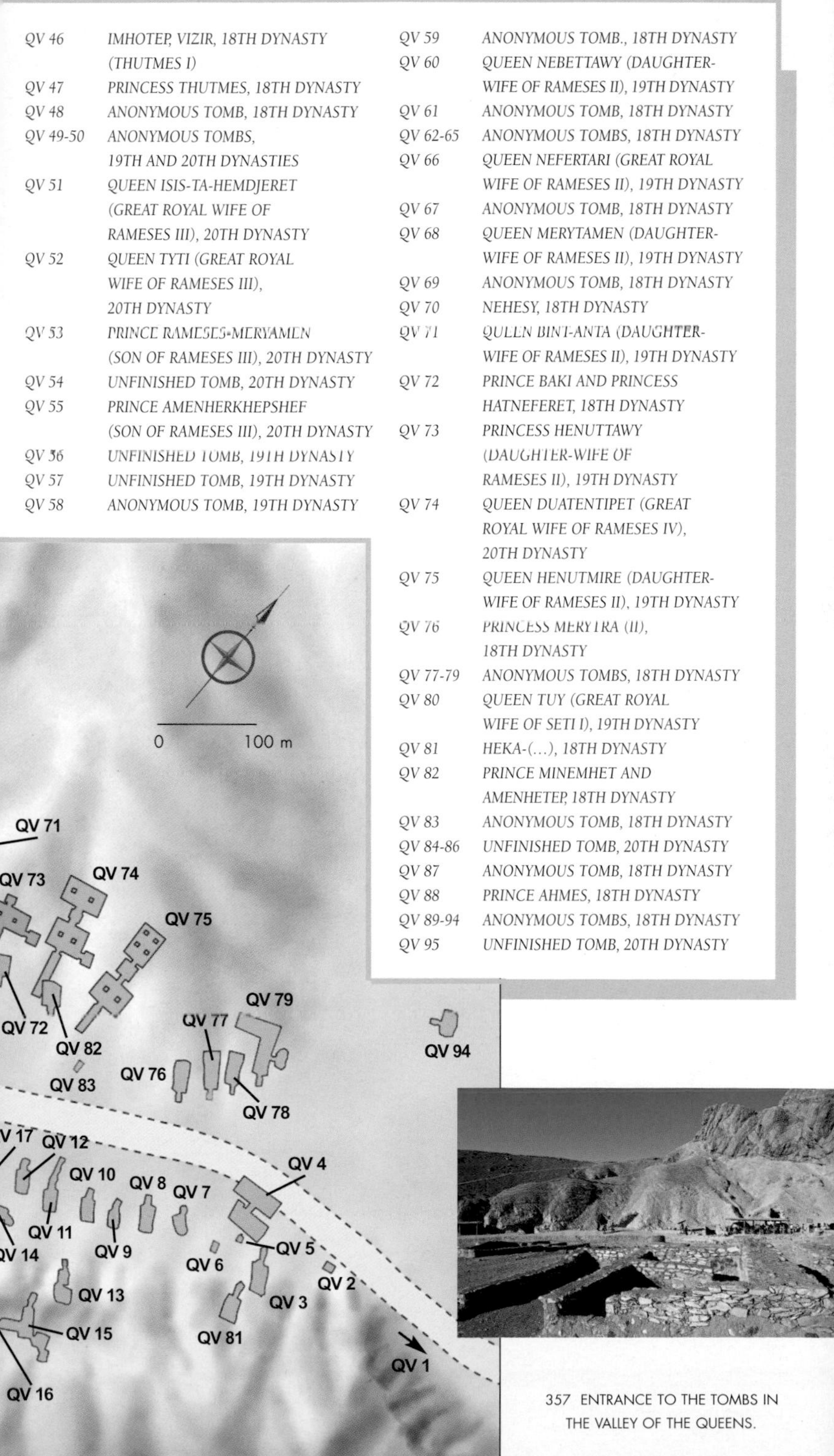

357 ENTRANCE TO THE TOMBS IN THE VALLEY OF THE QUEENS.

QV 44: THE TOMB OF KHAEMWASET

THE HISTORY

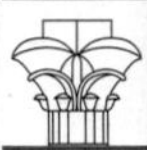

Lying in the southeastern corner of the Valley of the Queens, the tomb of Khaemwaset is very similar to that of his brother or half-brother, Amenherkhepshef (QV 55). Both were sons of Rameses III (and are not to be confused with sons of Rameses II who have the same names.) Khaemwaset was the king's eldest son, and some Egyptologists claim that his mother was Queen Tyti, whose own tomb, QV 52, lies nearby (and is also open to the public). All three tombs were excavated early in the twentieth century by Ernesto Schiaparelli.

Khaemwaset was a *sem* priest and for a time, High Priest of Ptah at Memphis, but little in the decoration of his tomb emphasizes this prestigious role. Instead, like the tomb of Amenherkhepshef, and indeed, like most burials of important royal princes, the decoration showed the king introducing his deceased son to the gods.

Glass panels have been installed in QV 44 that make it difficult to see the walls, but their painted decoration is very good. The scenes do, however, follow some odd Dynasty 20 stylistic conventions: human figures tend to be ill-proportioned and the sons particularly are drawn with impossibly large heads and high foreheads. Figures are drawn against a white or light gray background, and texts are painted over a yellow one. Eyes are painted on the face, not carved, and slope downwards. Ears, on the other hand, are carved and usually pierced. The costumes of deities and the king are drawn with detail that sometimes borders on fussiness. When men are dressed in transparent linen gowns, their skin shows through in an unappealing light pink color, an artistic feature not found in the otherwise similar tomb of Amenherkhepshef.

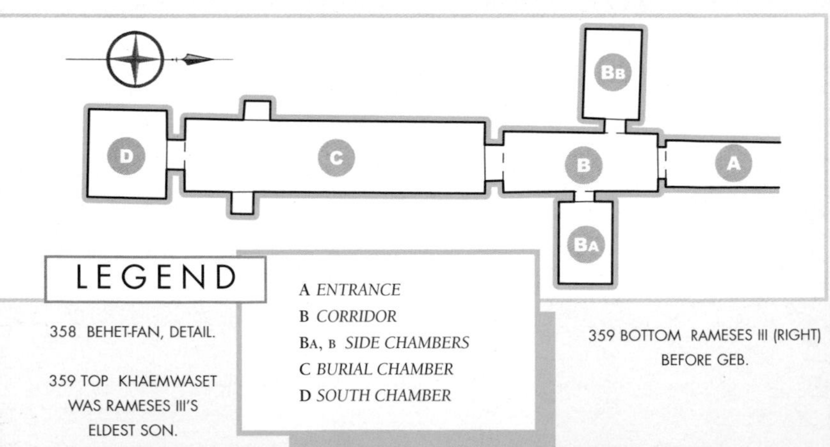

LEGEND

A *ENTRANCE*
B *CORRIDOR*
BA, B *SIDE CHAMBERS*
C *BURIAL CHAMBER*
D *SOUTH CHAMBER*

358 BEHET-FAN, DETAIL.

359 TOP KHAEMWASET WAS RAMESES III'S ELDEST SON.

359 BOTTOM RAMESES III (RIGHT) BEFORE GEB.

VISIT

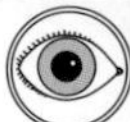

CORRIDOR B The first corridor is entered through a doorway at the base of a gently sloping ramp. Inside, on the front wall, Khaemwaset stands in adoration before the god Ptah, whose figure is housed in a shrine drawn on the left (east) wall. Next on the left wall, Khaemwaset and his father, Rameses III, offer wine to Thoth. The bottom half of the scene has been destroyed. Rameses III holds the hand of Anubis as his son walks behind him in the next scene, and this is followed by the king standing before Ra-Harakhty.

On the opposite side of the corridor, Rameses III stands on the front wall, offering incense to Ptah-Sokar, who is shown around the corner on the right (west) wall. Khaemwaset stands beyond the doorway with his father, offering incense to Geb. Next, the king holds the hand of the god Shu-Ra as Khaemwaset walks behind and finally, father and son offer incense to Atum. The young prince is shown in each scene wearing a different costume, but he always holds the same feathered *khu*-fan and wears the sidelock of a youth.

SIDE-CHAMBER BA

A doorway through the left wall of corridor B leads into a square, low-ceilinged chamber. On the front wall, Neith and Serqet stand on the left side of the door, Isis and Nephthys on the right. On the side walls, Khaemwaset stands before Anubis and, in a second scene, before the Four Sons of Horus and a figure of Serqet (on the left wall) and Neith (on the right).

A double scene on the rear wall shows Neith (on the left) and Isis (on the right) before the god Osiris. Note that in the side chamber Khaemwaset stands alone before deities, whereas in the corridor he is invariably accompanied by his father. It has been suggested that this is because scenes in the corridor are scenes of the son arriving in the Afterlife, still needful of his father's intervention with the deities. Scenes in the side chamber, on the other hand, show the prince after he has been delivered into the Afterlife. He has now joined the deities in the world of the dead and his father has returned to the world of the living.

360-361 RIGHT WALL OF THE CORRIDOR WITH RAMESES III, KHAEMWASET, SHU-RA, RAMESES III, KHAEMWASET AND GEB.

361 TOP KHAEMWASET WITH HANDS RAISED IN ADORATION, SIDE CHAMBER BB.

361 BOTTOM RAMESES III, KHAEMASET AND A GUARDIAN WITH KNIVES.

SIDE-CHAMBER BB On the right side of the corridor, the front wall of another side chamber shows Isis and Nephthys (on the left of the door) and Neith and Serqet (on the right). This is the same scene as in chamber BA. On the left wall, Khaemwaset, again without his father, stands with hands raised in adoration before Hapy, Qebehsenuef, P'at, and Horus-the-Child. On the right wall, he stands before Imsety, Duamutef, Baka, and again, Horus-the-Child. On the rear wall, Isis (at left) and Nephthys (at right) stand before seated figures of Osiris.

CHAMBER C: BURIAL CHAMBER In spite of its corridor-like appearance, this chamber was intended from the outset as Khaemwaset's burial chamber. That is shown by its vaulted ceiling, which is rarely found in tomb chambers that served another purpose. The decoration is taken from chapters 145 and 146 of the Book of the Dead that describe the twenty-one gates through which the deceased must pass on his journey into the afterlife. The scenes in Khaemwaset's burial chamber refer to gates 10, 12, 14, and 16 on the left wall and 9, 11, 13, and 15 on the right. In the tomb of Amenherkhepshef, the references are to gates 5, 6, 7, and 8. Each gate is guarded by a genie. On the left wall, they are *Sekhenur,* whose name means The Great

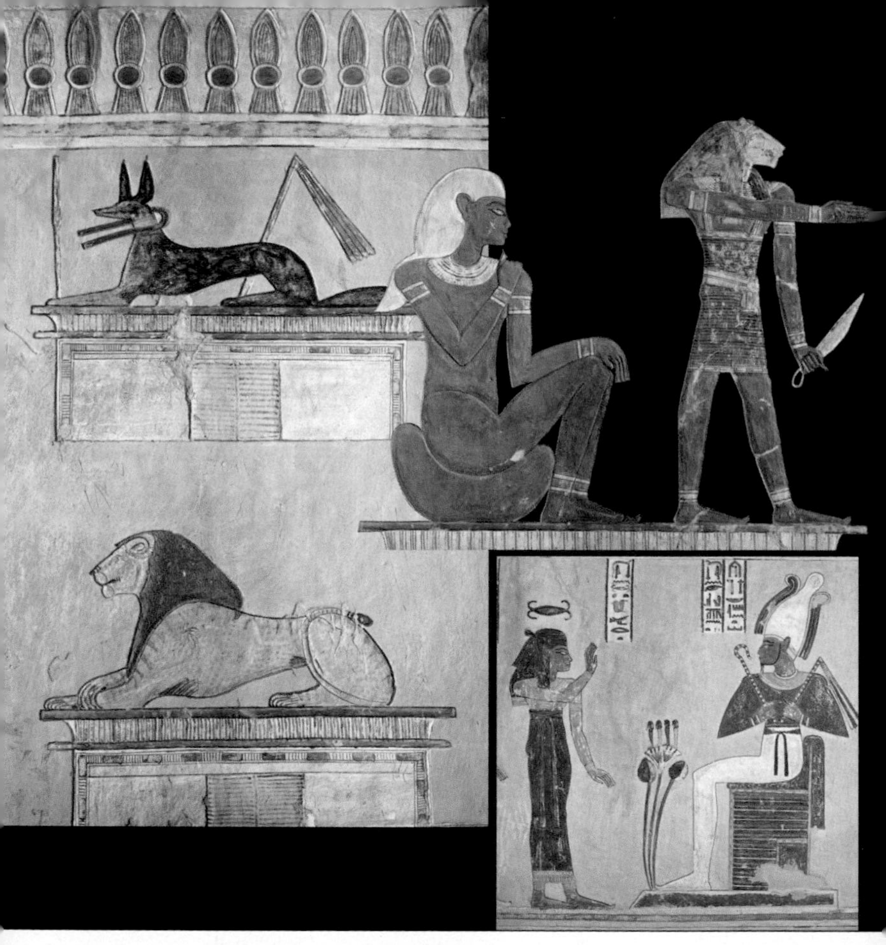

Tightener; *Miu,* The Cat; *Saupen,* The Protector; and one called He Who Imposes Abasement, Provokes Weakness, and Comes Forth as Death. On the right wall, they are *Dendeni,* The Furious; *Pesef-akhu-ef,* He Who Inflames His Brazier; *Hedkiauna;* and Vigilant Face Emerging from the Netherworld. Each guardian carries two knives, but all appear curiously gentle creatures in spite of their sometimes fearsome names. All are similarly dressed.

At the right end of the right wall, Rameses III wears a long, transparent dress, elaborate apron, and blue *khepresh*-crown and stands in a pose of adoration. Behind him stands Khaemwaset, whose name is written in the seven hieroglyphs immediately below the king's cartouche in an intervening column of text. The prince wears an elaborately braided sidelock, a long gown, and a sash with five tassels. He carries an elaborate *behet*-fan, made of ostrich feathers set in gilded wood, a symbol borne by those who were given the prestigious title of Royal Fanbearer.

On the rear wall of the burial chamber, two genii stand on either side of the central doorway. On the left stands the guardian of the sixteenth gate. On the right, stands the guardian of the fifteenth gate, *Nehes-her-per-em-duat*, One Whose Face is Hidden, Descended from the Netherworld. In chapter 146 of the Book of the Dead, the latter genie is described as: "the Terrible One, Lady of Pestilence, who casts away thousands of human souls, who hacks up human dead, who decapitates him who would go out, who creates terror." A pair of side chambers may have been intended off this room but neither was completed.

CHAMBER D *Djed* pillars appear on the thicknesses of the gate leading into this chamber. On the left side of the front wall, the lion-headed Lord of Fear, called *Nebneryu,* stands holding a knife to protect Khaemwaset, who sits on a cushion behind him in the form of *Heryma'at*, He Who Rules over Harmony. On the right side, Anubis sits atop a building symbolizing Khaemwaset's tomb. Below, a lion guards another building. His lazily crossed paws and calm expression give an impression of docility. This amusingly relaxed pose is peculiar to Dynasty 20, and can also to be seen in Amenherkhepshef's tomb, although there, the figure is less well preserved. That here is among the best drawings in either tomb.

On the left wall, Rameses III offers vases to Thoth and Harsiesi. On the right, he stands with incense and a libation before Horus and Shepsi. Figures of the king stand near the corner of each wall. On the rear wall, the king (whose figure is on the side walls) is preceded by Isis and Neith (left) and Nephthys and Serqet (right) standing in adoration before seated figures of Osiris. At the feet of Osiris, flowers grow and Four Sons of Horus emerge from a lotus blossom.

362 LEFT ANUBIS AND A LION SIT ON KHAEMWASET'S TOMB.

362 TOP RIGHT NEBNERYU, LORD OF FEAR, PROTECTS KHAEMWASET.

362 BOTTOM RIGHT NEITH STANDS IN ADORATION OF OSIRIS.

363 RAMESES III OFFERING VASES TO THOTH.

4

QV 52: THE TOMB OF TYTI

Tyti's position in the Rameside royal court is still unclear, but some Egyptologists believe that she was a wife of Rameses III and the mother of Amenherkhepshef (who is buried in nearby QV 55). Her tomb shares common features with his, and also with that of Khaemwaset (QV 44). Her decorative programs are identical in many instances and, as in those tombs, colorfully painted figures are set against a background of white or grey, although in some scenes, the background color changes to near-yellow. An interesting feature is the way in which Tyti is represented: in some scenes she is a young girl, wearing the costume and hair-do of a teenager (on the front wall of chamber D, for example); in other scenes she is a middle-aged woman, dressed more conservatively and with a hint of make-up (corridor B, left wall). The contrast is striking and not common in Egyptian tomb art.

CORRIDOR B On the left wall of this first corridor, beyond a broken figure of a winged Ma'at, Tyti appears in a damaged scene in adoration of Ptah, who is standing in a shrine. To the right, the queen holds two sistra before Ra-Harakhty and stands in adoration before Imsety, Duamutef, and Isis. On the right wall, there is another figure of the winged Ma'at and Tyti adoring Thoth, holding two sistra before Atum, and adoring Hapy, Qebensenuef, and Nephthys.

In the gate leading to chamber C, Neith can be seen on the left thickness, Serqet on the right.

CHAMBER C On the right side of the front wall, Anubis and a very relaxed lion protect Tyti's tomb. On the left side, a lion-headed Nebnery stands before Queen Tyti in the form of a squatting youth, Herima'at. The scenes are the same as those in the tomb of Khaemwaset, but less well preserved.

On the left wall, two baboons and a monkey with a bow stand below several columns of text. Beyond a gate, damaged Hememet genii are shown as a vulture, a hippopotamus, and a frontally drawn human figure, and each holds a pair of knives.

The right wall has badly destroyed figures of guardians flanking the doorway. The anonymous bird-headed genie at the right end of the wall still retains much of its original paint.

Tyti holds sistra before Imsety and Duamutef on the left side of the rear wall. On the right, she holds two rolls of papyrus around which are coiled cobras representing Upper and Lower Egypt, before the gods Hapy and Qebehsenuef. Above them, two boats carry small shrines.

SIDE-CHAMBER CA A gate in chamber C's left wall leads into a low, square side chamber whose side walls show Tyti before the Four Sons of Horus. On the rear wall a few traces remain of a badly destroyed scene of Osiris. The floor of the chamber has collapsed into a passage that leads to the tomb's burial chamber.

SIDE-CHAMBER CB Entered through the right wall of chamber C, a second side chamber is better preserved. On the left wall three demons with the heads of a jackal, a snake, and a crocodile stand near four canopic

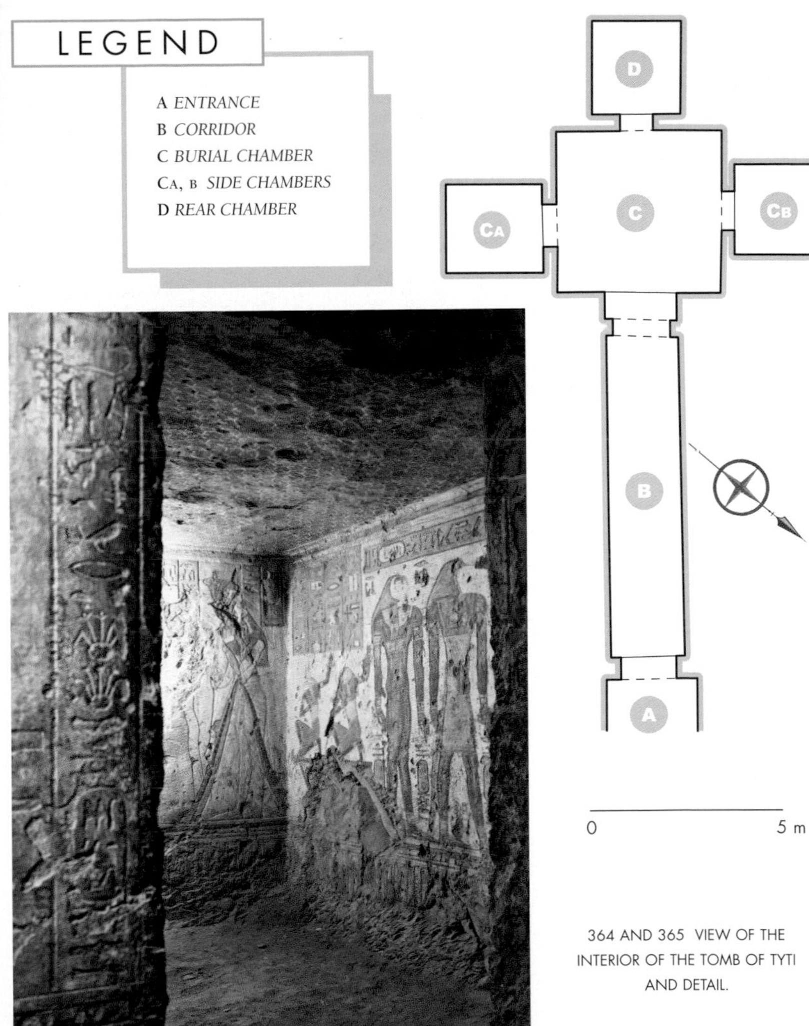

364 AND 365 VIEW OF THE INTERIOR OF THE TOMB OF TYTI AND DETAIL.

chests. The presence of these boxes indicates that the room was used for the storage of the queen's canopic equipment. On the right wall, three more demons stand with the souls of Pe and Nekhen.

The rear wall of this side chamber is especially interesting. At left, the goddess Hathor, depicted as a cow, emerges from a well-painted mountain while at right and now largely gone, Tyti adores a sycomore fig tree in which Hathor resides.

CHAMBER D The rear chamber has well preserved decoration. On the front wall, figures of Tyti stand on either side of the doorway in poses of adoration. On the left wall stand the four Sons of Horus, and in a lower register, before offering tables piled with bread and ewers below, sit mummiform figures of Geb, Nut, Nefertum, and Harhekenu.

The right wall also shows the four sons and the mummiform seated figures of Hu, Sia, Shu, and Tefnut. On the rear wall, Nephthys and Thoth (at left) and Neith and Serqet (at right) pay tribute to enthroned figures of Osiris.

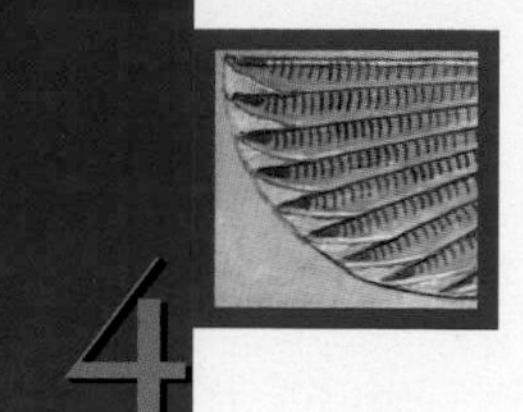

QV 55: THE TOMB OF AMENHERKHEPSHEF

THE HISTORY

Confusingly, Rameses III named several of his sons after sons of Rameses II. The Amenherkhepshef named in QV 55 and the Khaemwaset named in QV 44 are sons of Rameses III and not be confused with the similarly-named sons of Rameses II.

QV 55 is similar to the tomb of Amenherkhepshef's brother or half-brother, Khaemwaset (QV 44). It is a bit smaller, but its decoration is every bit as good, and especially in the detailing of costumes, sometimes exceeds it in quality.

Amenherkhepshef was a prince, an heir to the throne of his father, royal scribe, and Chief of the Charioteers.

Some believe that Tyti, a queen buried in nearby QV 52, was his mother, and that he died young, perhaps while still a teenager. Apparently, he was never actually buried in this tomb. A sarcophagus originally meant for Queen Tausert was re-inscribed for him and was found in KV 13, the tomb of the Chancellor Bay. Amenherkhepshef may finally have been buried there.

The entrance to QV 55, cut at the base of a steep set of stairs, was discovered in 1904 by Ernesto Schiaparelli. It was empty except for a sarcophagus.

The walls were in excellent condition, brightly painted in the style of early Dynasty 20.

366 PROFILE OF AMENHERKHEPSHEF, SON OF RAMESES III AND TYTI.

367 ONE OF THE DIVINITIES PROTECTING RAMESES III AND AMENHERKHEPSHEF.

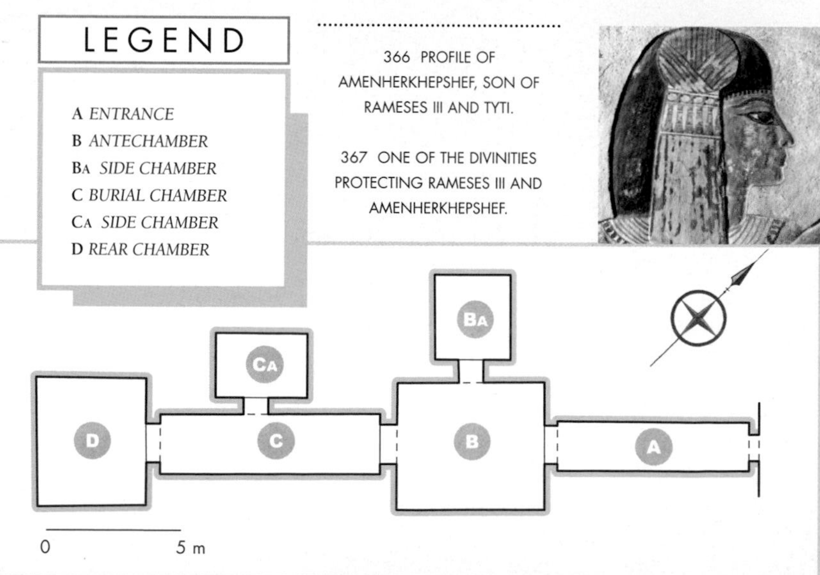

VISIT

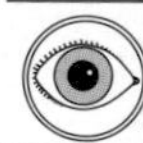

CHAMBER B On the right side of the front wall, a damaged figure of Thoth is followed by Rameses III embraced by Isis. This is a lovely scene: the delicate way in which king and goddess embrace yet do not touch, the elaborate headdress of the goddess, and the apron of the king are masterful touches. Amenherkhepshef also stands on the front wall, facing to the right, carrying a fan. He is following another figure of his father, who stands on the left side wall, censing before the god Ptah. Farther on, father and son are led forward by Ta-Tjenen, then by a canine-headed Duamutef, then a human-headed Imsety, and finally, on the left side of the rear wall, by Isis. The detail in these figures is precise and brightly painted, some of the best work the late New Kingdom has to offer. Look, for example, at the costume of Rameses III, especially in the scene on the rear wall where he and his son stand with Isis, and note his belt buckle, inscribed with the royal name; the elaborate blue and gold (and seemingly unattached) tail he wears; the patterned sleeves that cover his shoulders; the complex yet gracefully draped kilt. Such painting surely must have been done by an artisan who knew well the actual costume. The way in which the hands of the king and Isis are positioned and the modeling of the goddesses' face are equally fine examples of the artist's skill. Amenherkhepshef, too, standing with a feathered fan in his right hand, is well dressed. Here, his skin seen through his transparent skirt is a light shade of brown, not the unpleasant pink color used in similar scenes in the tomb of Khaemwaset. Each figure of king or prince in these scenes wears a different costume; each is elaborately drawn and brightly painted. The head of the prince at the right end of this wall is better proportioned than those farther left.

Scenes on the left front wall of the chamber are now missing. But on the right front wall one can see Amenherkhepshef and his father censing before Shu, and the king led by Qebehsenuef and by Hapy. Finally, on the right rear wall, Amenherkhepshef and Rameses III stand before Hathor in the same pose we saw left of the door. This wall is undecorated.

On the thicknesses of the gate into the next chamber, Isis (on the left) and Nephthys (on the right) face outward and perform an act of purification called "making *nini*." The hieroglyph for "water" is drawn just above each of their outstretched hands.

368-369 RIGHT SIDE OF THE ANTECHAMBER OR CHAMBER B WITH RAMESES III IN FRONT OF PTAH, TA-TJENEN, DUAMUTEF.

369 CENTER LEFT AND BOTTOM DETAILS OF THE ELABORATE DRESSES OF RAMESES III (ABOVE) AND AMENHERKHEPSHEF.

369 CENTER RIGHT RAMESES III EMBRACED BY ISIS.

370 TOP THE PROFILE OF RAMESES III.

370 BOTTOM HATHOR RECEIVES RAMESES III AND AMENHERKHEPSHEF.

371 LEFT PROFILE OF HORUS.

371 RIGHT THE ANTHROPOID SARCHOPHAGUS IN THE REAR CHAMBER D.

CHAMBER C: BURIAL CHAMBER On the front wall, on either side of the gate, Amenherkhepshef is shown as an *Iunmutef* priest, wearing a panther skin with paws and claws but not the panther-headed clasp that is often a part of this costume.

The scenes on the left and right walls are from chapters 145 and 146 of the Book of the Dead. The twenty-one gates through which Rameses III guides his son are described in those chapters, and each is protected by a genie. The accompanying text must be recited by the king and Amenherkhepshef to the genie at the gate in order to pass through. For example, this is what they must say at the seventh gate (the first on the left wall of the chamber): "Make a way for me, for I know you, I know your name and I know the name of the god who guards you. 'Shroud Which Veils the Limp One; Mourner Who Wishes to Hide the Body' is your name. 'Ikenty' is the name of her doorkeeper." These scenes form a companion piece to scenes in the burial chamber of Khaemwaset. Here, the texts refer to gates five through eight, there, they refer to gates nine through sixteen. Some Egyptologists argue that this is evidence that Khaemwaset's tomb was decorated after that of Amenherkhepshef.

A side chamber beyond the right wall of the burial chamber is undecorated.

On the rear wall of the burial chamber, painted above the door, is an especially beautiful scene of two gracefully-coiled serpents, Wadjet and Nekhbet, protectors of the cartouches of Rameses III. Above them is a winged solar disk.

CHAMBER D The walls are undecorated but an unfinished anthropoid coffin sits in the chamber. Originally, it would have been placed in the preceding burial chamber. The mummy of a wrapped human fetus now in a glass case in the corner was found south of the Valley of the Kings by Schiaparelli. It is not from this tomb.

4

QV 66: THE TOMB OF NEFERTARI

THE HISTORY

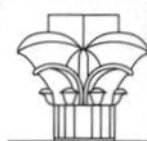

Few royal women in ancient Egypt were more beloved by their husband or played a more active role in his administration than the Great Royal Wife of Rameses II, Queen Nefertari. Married to the young man before he had ascended the throne, she served for twenty-six regnal years as his principal wife, mother of his eldest son, confidant, and colleague. Among her titles and epithets were: Beloved of Mut, King's Great Wife, God's Wife, Mother of the King, Hereditary Noblewoman, and She for Whom the Sun Shines. Other titles such as Mistress of Upper and Lower Egypt and Mistress of the Two Lands were the feminine forms of titles normally reserved for the pharaoh. She was rewarded with her own temple at Abu Simbel and with a tomb in the Valley of the Queens, QV 66. It is a tomb of astonishing beauty.

QV 66 was discovered in 1904 by Ernesto Schiaparelli (1856–1928) and it ranks as one of the great discoveries in Theban archaeology. It was closed to tourists in the 1950s because of concern for its preservation, and from 1988 to 1995 it underwent a major conservation program by the Getty Conservation Institute. The tomb was reopened in 1995 to a limited number of tourists each day but, again, concerns for its safety forced its closure in 2003. Now, only a few small groups willing to pay a very substantial fee will be allowed inside the tomb each year. Even with these restrictions, it is unclear for how long the tomb will survive.

The problem is plaster. KV 66 was cut into a low-lying section of the Valley of the Queens where the bedrock is very friable. Unable to create a smooth surface, ancient artisans were forced to cover the rough-hewn walls with a thick layer of plaster before applying painted decoration. But the weight of this plaster and the tendency for it to separate from the bedrock has caused the plaster to buckle. With no support from the stone behind, the plaster threatens to fall to the floor. The Getty Conservation Institute managed to slow the rate of buckling, but they could not completely stop it. The presence of sweaty tourists in the tomb adversely affects humidity levels and hastens the process of destruction. One can only hope that in the future new conservation techniques will be developed and the serious problems faced by Nefertari's tomb can be halted. Until then, one hopes that it remains closed and is regularly monitored.

372 HATHOR HOLDING NEFERARI'S HAND.

373 NEFERTARI WEARING THE VULTURE HEADDRESS.

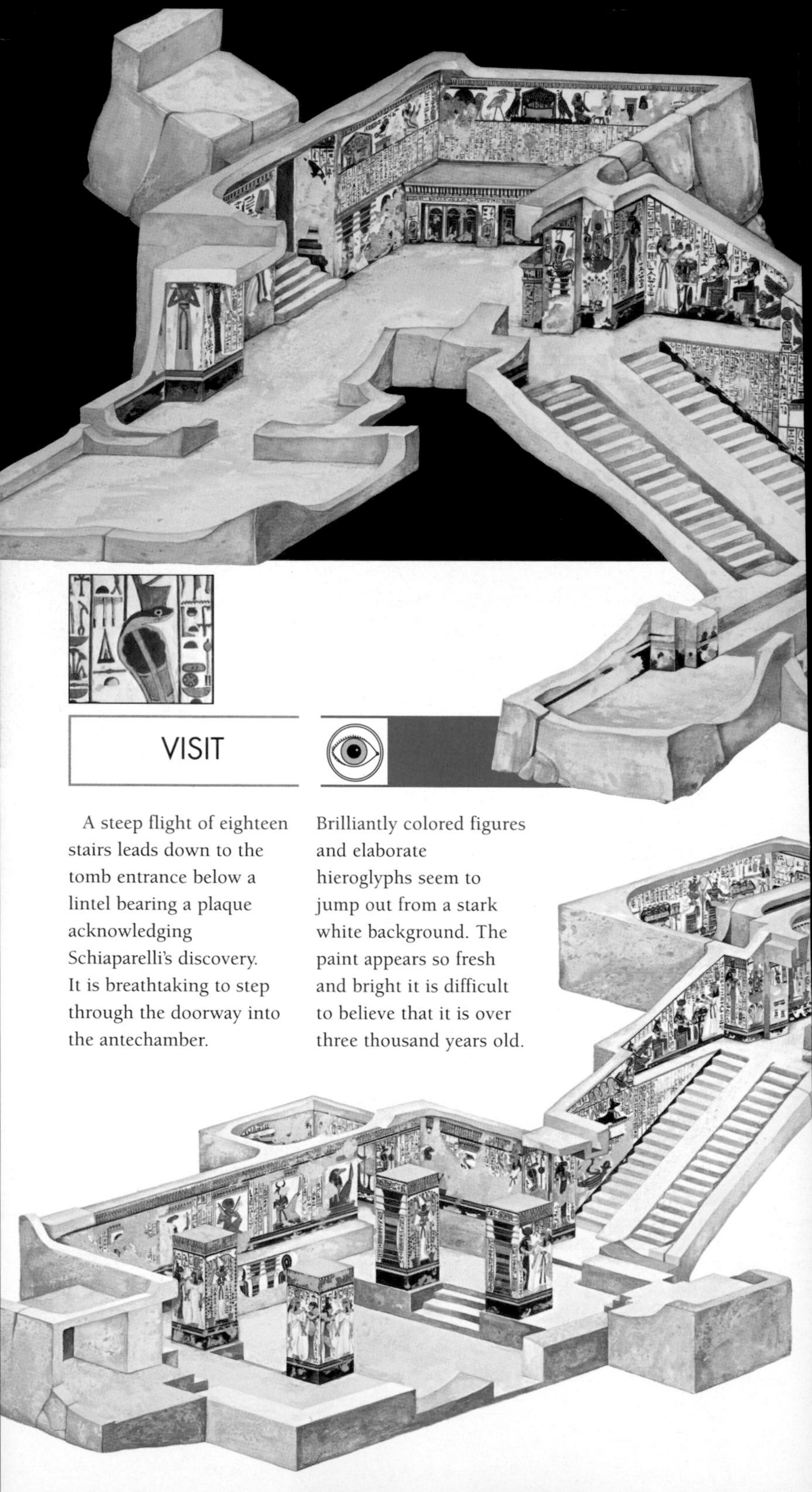

VISIT

A steep flight of eighteen stairs leads down to the tomb entrance below a lintel bearing a plaque acknowledging Schiaparelli's discovery. It is breathtaking to step through the doorway into the antechamber.

Brilliantly colored figures and elaborate hieroglyphs seem to jump out from a stark white background. The paint appears so fresh and bright it is difficult to believe that it is over three thousand years old.

374-375 DRAWINGS OF THE TOMB OF NEFERTARI: WEST SIDE (ABOVE), EAST SIDE (BELOW).

374 CENTER URAEUS FROM THE BURIAL CHAMBER, EAST WALL.

375 TOP MA'AT FROM THE DOOR OF THE BURIAL CHAMBER.

LEGEND

A *ENTRANCE*
B *ANTECHAMBER*
C *VESTIBULE*
D *SIDE CHAMBER*
E *INNER RAMP*
F *BURIAL CHAMBER*
FA, B, C *SIDE CHAMBERS*

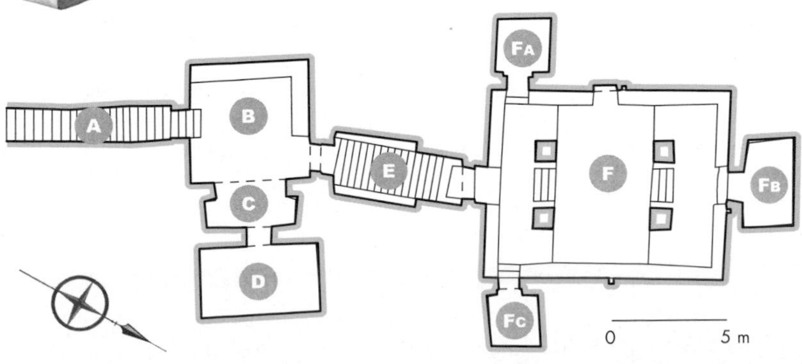

ANTECHAMBER The first scene to be noted is on the soffit of the doorway itself: a golden yellow solar disk rising between two red mountains in the eastern sky, flanked by two falcons wearing the headdresses of Isis and Nephthys. On the thicknesses of the door it is still possible to make out the figure of the Upper Egyptian vulture goddess, Nekhbet, on the left, and the Lower Egyptian cobra goddess, Wadjet, on the right.

On the right side of the antechamber's front wall, above columns of a finely painted hieroglyphic text, a vignette taken from chapter 17 of the Book of the Dead shows Nefertari, wearing an elaborately pleated, almost transparent gown and a tight-fitting vulture headdress. She holds a scepter and sits beneath a woven reed canopy on an elaborately painted chair on a reed mat, playing a game of *Senet*, a game rather like draughts. She must defeat her invisible opponent in this game if she is to gain access to the netherworld. The text reads in part: "Here begins praises and recitations, going in and out of the realm of the dead, having benefit in the beautiful West, being in the suite of Osiris, resting at the food table of Wennefer, going out into the day, taking any shape in which he desires to be, playing at Senet, sitting in a booth, and going forth as a living soul by the Osiris Nefertari after she has died."

Farther right, the *ba*-bird of the queen stands atop her tomb and the queen herself kneels in prayer before the *akeru*, the horizon, defined by two mountains and two lions, shown on the adjacent wall. The painting of the two lions are worth looking at in detail. Rarely are so accurate and appealing drawings of lions to be found in Egyptian art. The delicate whiskers on their chins is a deft touch.

On the antechamber's left wall, to the right of the *akeru*, scenes from chapter 17 of the Book of the Dead continue. The grey heron is a *benu*-bird, a sacred bird of Heliopolis associated with phases of the planet Venus and the soul of Ra. It faces a figure of Nefertari's mummy that lies on a lion-headed bed beneath a canopy walled with elaborately woven and beaded cloth and flanked by falcons whose headdresses identify them as Isis (right) and Nephthys (left). The queen's mummy is wrapped in white linen, bound with red strips, and she wears an elaborate pectoral collar and a bearded mask.

A black-skinned genie of the Nile, called a fecundity figure because of its pendulous breasts and protruding belly, holds a palm branch that symbolizes eternal time. He kneels before figures and a shrine that are now destroyed. A narrow ledge runs along the bottom of this wall and that to the right and is topped with a cavetto cornice. Below are representations of small round-topped shrines, set inside recesses. Several hieratic graffiti of the Ramesside period can be seen on the sides of two of the recesses. They refer to the deliveries of the mud plaster needed by the artisans who worked on the tomb.

376 TOP VIEW OF THE ANTECHAMBER, EAST SIDE.

376 BOTTOM NEFERTARI PLAYING SENET.

377 TOP NEFERTARI'S MUMMY FLANKED BY FALCONS (ISIS AND NEPHTHYS).

377 CENTER AKERU, THE HORIZON WITH ITS LION.

377 BOTTOM THE BA-BIRD OF NEFERTARI.

378 TOP ONE OF THE SONS OF HORUS ABOVE THE DOORWAY.

378 BOTTOM OSIRIS FROM THE ANTECHAMBER.

378-379 VIEW OF THE WEST SIDE OF THE ANTECHAMBER AND PART OF THE VESTIBULE.

Above columns of text and a doorway on the rear wall, two mummiform figures of Ra and Shu face left. To their right, Horus and Nefertari sit on thrones. Facing in the other direction, Horus sits with his four sons before him.

On the right wall of the antechamber, which frames a wide opening into the vestibule, stand figures of Osiris (left), surrounded by text and religious symbols in a curved-top shrine, and flanked by stylized leopard skins attached to inlaid poles. These are fetishes of Anubis. On the right, Anubis stands in an even more detailed shrine. Between them, cobras and blue ostrich feathers alternate on either side of a kneeling genie who touches two ovals each containing a *wedjat*-eye.

On the left side of the front wall, a very elegant figure of Osiris sits and holds a flail and scepter wearing the *atef*-crown. The flail is painted in considerable detail, and the tightly drawn cloth around the god's waist makes a strong contrast to the simple white costume.

Most of the figures of Osiris in QV 66, especially the standing ones, show the god with almost feminine waist and hips. This is probably no accident: Nefertari was to be united with Osiris after her death, and these attributes are meant to suggest that this had already happened. The god sits in an elaborate shrine before figures of the Four Sons of Horus. To their right, Nefertari, equally well dressed, stands in adoration.

380 TOP HORUS WITH NEFERTARI, FROM THE RIGHT SIDE OF THE VESTIBULE.

380 BOTTOM THE SCORPION-HEADED GODDESS SERQET, LEFT SIDE OF THE VESTIBULE.

380-381 VIEW OF THE VESTIBULE.

VESTIBULE On the thicknesses of the wide gate into the vestibule, the goddess Serqet stands on the left with a scorpion on her head, and the goddess Neith stands on the right, wearing her symbol, a shield and arrows. The two deities are identically dressed in elaborate prints; only their headdresses differ. *Djed*-pillars are carved on the pilasters immediately inside the next part of the vestibule.

On the left side wall, Nefertari is led by the goddess Isis before the god Khepri, who sits on the rear wall of the vestibule. Isis is elaborately dressed in a tight-fitting dress and bejeweled with bracelets, arm bands, and tassles. Khepri's beetle-shaped head marks him as a manifestation of the sun god. His elaborate throne, like those on the other side of this wall has a scale-like pattern with the symbol of the unification of Upper and Lower Egypt on the lower back panel.

On the other (right) side of the rear wall, Ra-Harakhty sits beside Hathor-Goddess-of-the-West, preparing to receive the queen. On the right wall, she is led forward by the god Horus-Son-of-Isis, called Horsiesi. Above the doorway, the vulture goddess Nekhbet holds *shen*-glyphs in its paws; its wings are outstretched and covered with elaborately painted feathers.

In all of these scenes, Nefertari presents an especially arresting figure. She has large almond-shaped eyes heavily outlined with eyeliner, full lips, rouged cheeks, and pierced ears with elaborate earrings. In many scenes, she wears the vulture headdress typical of royal mothers. (In ancient Egyptian the vulture was called *mwt*, and those letters also spelled the word "mother.") She is a shapely woman, her figure enhanced by the carefully draped gowns that she wears, the pleats carefully shown in shades of white and grey.

SIDE CHAMBER

Standing figures of the goddess Ma'at appear on the thicknesses of the doorway into the room.

On the right side of the front wall of this 3 by 5 meter (10 by 16 feet) room, Nefertari stands before a table offering the hieroglyphs for "cloth" to the god Ptah. He stands in his small reed shrine with its shutters open. Behind him is a large *djed*-pillar. On the left side wall, chapter 94 of the Book of the Dead tells how the queen asks the god Thoth to "bring me the water-pot and palette from the writing-kit of Thoth, and the mysteries which are in them." Those instruments sit on a tall stand between the queen and the god.

On the rear wall, Nefertari offers a huge pile of food offerings to a seated figure of Osiris and the Four Sons of Horus. The offerings include live cattle, haunches of beef, loaves of bread, baskets of grapes, vegetables, and smoking braziers. At right, another heap of food offerings is made to Atum. Like all the seated gods we have seen, these too sit on elaborately painted thrones.

In the right side of the chamber, the queen stands on the front wall in adoration before seven sacred cows and a bull drawn in two registers on the right side wall. This is a scene from chapter 148 of the Book of the Dead, which gives the cattle such names as the Much Beloved, Red of Hair, and Storm in the Sky That Wafts the God Aloft. The cattle have been deliberately selected for their special markings. Below, in a continuation of this chapter, stand the four steering oars of the four corners of the sky. The queen is especially well dressed in this scene, thin limbs visible through her transparent dress, a large earring emphasized by her well-rouged cheeks. Behind Nefertari, a yellow vertical line separates this scene from that which follows. There, the goddesses Isis (right) and Nephthys (left) stand with a ram-headed god identified in two short columns of text as a fusion of two deities: "It is Ra who sets as Osiris," "It is Osiris who sets as Ra."

382-383 VIEW OF THE LEFT SIDE OF THE SIDE CHAMBER.

383 BOTTOM THE FOUR SONS OF HORUS, FROM THE LEFT SIDE OF THE SIDE CHAMBER.

382 TOP NEPHTHYS AND ISIS FLANK A RAM-HEADED GOD.

382 BOTTOM FOUR OF THE SEVEN SACRED COWS IN THE SIDE CHAMBER.

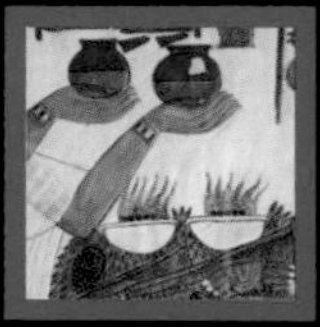

384 TOP LEFT SERQET, FROM THE LINTEL OF THE STAIRCASE DOOR.

384 TOP RIGHT NEFERTARI'S HANDS OFFERING WINE.

INNER RAMP AND STAIRCASE This is a complicated piece of architecture, in which ramp and staircase are surrounded by gates, niches, and walls of different elevations and widths.

Serpents wearing the crowns of Upper or Lower Egypt appear on the left and right thicknesses of the gate. On the next thicknesses, the cartouche of Nefertari is flanked by two cobras. They, and the lilies or papyri below them, symbolize Upper Egypt, on the left, and Lower Egypt, on the right.

On the upper left wall of the corridor, the queen

stands before a well-stocked offering table presenting wine to Isis and Nephthys. If you look closely at the queen's face you can see that a senior artist has whited out paint where a junior artist had sloppily painted outside the outline of her mouth and chin. Such corrections are relatively common in the tomb and are indications of the careful work demanded by the senior artist. Behind the goddesses, Ma'at kneels with her winged arms stretched out protectively. On the upper right wall, this scene is repeated but with the goddesses Hathor ("She Who is Chief in Thebes"), Serqet, and Ma'at before a huge pile of offerings.

On the next section of wall on both sides of the corridor, an elaborately drawn figure of the cobra-goddess Nekhbet is shown with wings protectively stretched toward Nefertari's name. The ring-like hieroglyphs are *shen*-signs symbolizing "eternity." Below the cobra on the left wall the god Anubis lies atop a chapel and, below it, the goddess Isis kneels on the hieroglyph for "gold." The jackal wears a red cloth around its neck and has an elaborate *nekhakha*-flail beside its hind leg. In the accompanying text, the god welcomes Nefertari into the netherworld. On the right wall, a similar welcome is offered by Anubis and Nephthys. The hieroglyphs here, as generally throughout the tomb, are very finely drawn, with much internal detail.

384 BOTTOM WINGED COBRA AND ANUBIS, LEFT WALL OF THE STAIRCASE.

384-385 RIGHT WALL OF THE STAIRCASE, FROM LEFT: MA'AT, SERQET, HATHOR AND NEFERTARI.

BURIAL CHAMBER

This is a large chamber, 10.4 by 8.2 meters (33 by 26 feet). A shelf runs around its four walls, perhaps intended for storing burial equipment. The decoration in this large, pillared hall has two parts: the right half of the room is devoted to chapter 146 of the Book of the Dead; the left half of the room deals with chapter 144. On the right side of the front wall, Nefertari stands before nineteen columns of text from chapter 144, facing three genii who guard the first gate of the netherworld. The first genie, holding a leafy branch, is called He Whose Face is Inverted. He is followed by She with Ears of Fire, and the Shouter. Nefertari speaks to them: "I have paved the way, allow me to cross." On the left side wall of the chamber, beyond a small doorway, the chapter continues and three genii guard the second gate. They are He Who Opens Their Foreheads, Virtuous Face, and the Burner. The third of the five gates mentioned in chapter 144 is guarded by He Who Eats the Excrement of His Hinder Parts, Vigilant, and He Who Curses.

The right side of the burial chamber is decorated with texts from chapter 146 of the Book of the Dead and vignettes show genii who guard the gates in the Field of *Iaru*, the domain of Osiris. One such genie, guarding the fifth gate in the middle of the wall, is the squatting, naked, knife-wielding, youth with an oddly-shaped head called *Henty-reki*, He Who Drives Away the Enemy. On the rear wall, the queen pays homage to seated figures of Osiris, Hathor, and Anubis. In the middle of the left (west) wall, below the ledge, is a small, very plainly inscribed niche that housed the canopic chest and jars of the queen.

The four pillars in the burial chamber display some of the best preserved painting in the tomb. Standing figures of Osiris, painted on the pillar faces closest to the tomb axis, are especially well done, with a complex iconography. *Djed*-pillars face the center of the room, where there is a depression in which the sarcophagus would have been placed. The front of each of the first two pillars show two forms of Horus wearing a panther skin. Other pillar faces are painted with figures of Anubis, Hathor, and Isis standing with Nefertari.

Three side chambers off the burial chamber have lost nearly all decoration and are closed to the public. Throughout the tomb, the ceiling is painted blue and covered with a myriad of five-pointed yellow stars.

386 AND 386-387 VIEWS OF THE BURIAL CHAMBER WITH FOUR DECORATED PILLARS.

387 TOP RIGHT HENTY-REKI, GENIE NAKED AND ARMED WITH KNIFES.

387 BOTTOM LEFT STANDING OSIRIS ON A PILLAR.

387 BOTTOM RIGHT HATHOR STANDING WITH NEFERTARI ON A PILLAR.

5

THE TOMBS OF THE NOBLES

INTRODUCTION

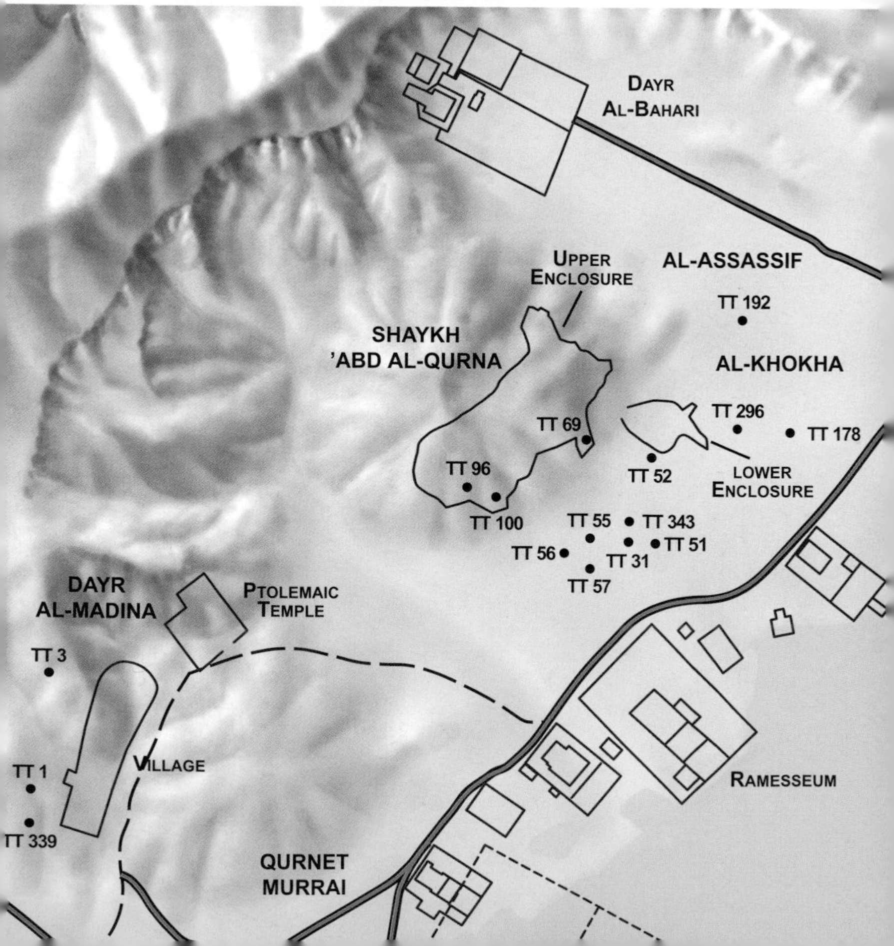

Of the several thousand nobles' tombs identified in the Theban Necropolis, nineteen are today open to the public. They span a period of nearly five hundred years, from the mid-18th Dynasty onward. We have chosen not to describe these tombs in geographical order, as a tour guide might arrange them for a visit, but instead to deal with them in chronological order. The tombs divide themselves chronologically into several distinct stylistic groups, and discussing them in such an order makes it easier to understand the subject matter of their reliefs and paintings, and the details of their iconography. For those who have time, it is recommended that a visit be arranged to at least one tomb from each of the five groups we have identified. That will allow one to trace the changing patterns of Egyptian private mortuary art through the New Kingdom. If time does not permit such a tour, then one should at least visit TT 100: Rekhmire and TT 55: Ramose, the first with superb paintings of daily life, the second with rellief carving of outstanding quality. It is the detail in these tombs' decoration that reward the visitor, and it is much better to explore a few tombs slowly than to hurry through several. The walk from parking areas to the tombs can be equally enjoyable, and one should note the mud-brick houses decorated with *Hajj* paintings that line the footpaths, and the views of the Nile Valley to the east.

TOMBS FROM THE REIGNS OF THUTMES III AND AMENHETEP II

Tombs from the reigns of these two powerful rulers illustrate a transitional period in Egyptian art. Under the reign of king Thutmes III, there was a clear tendency toward archaizing, and human figures are shown in formal Old and Middle Kingdom poses, often arranged in symmetrical groups. Those under the reign of king Amenhetep II, in contrast, are more relaxed, and often highly innovative, the colors subtler, the backgrounds of scenes lighter.

A particularly good example of this transition can be seen in TT 100, the tomb of the vizier of Upper Egypt Rekhmire.

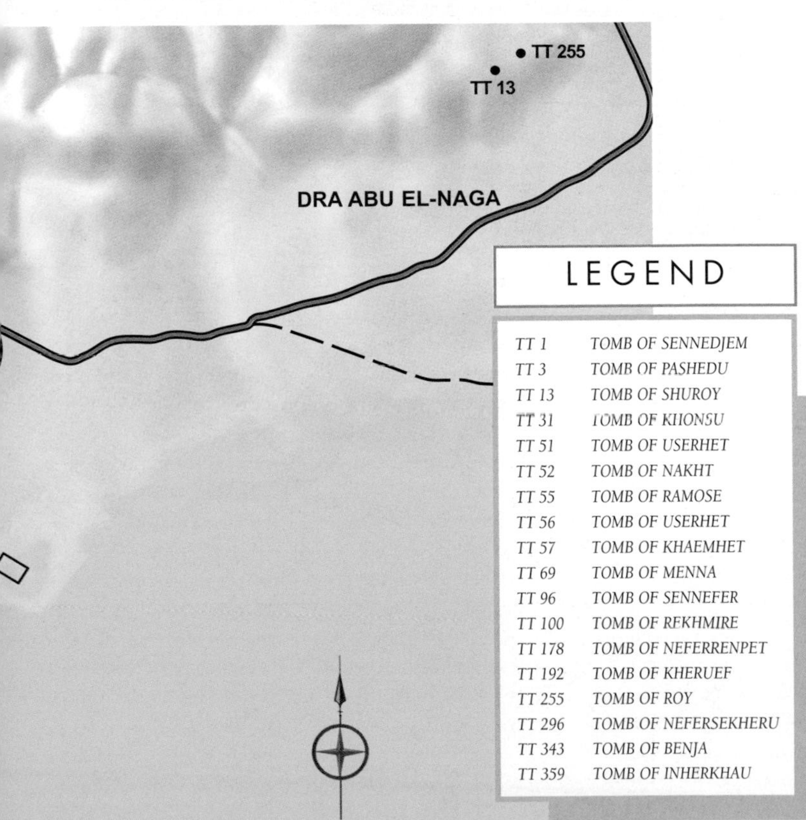

LEGEND

TT 1	*TOMB OF SENNEDJEM*
TT 3	*TOMB OF PASHEDU*
TT 13	*TOMB OF SHUROY*
TT 31	*TOMB OF KHONSU*
TT 51	*TOMB OF USERHET*
TT 52	*TOMB OF NAKHT*
TT 55	*TOMB OF RAMOSE*
TT 56	*TOMB OF USERHET*
TT 57	*TOMB OF KHAEMHET*
TT 69	*TOMB OF MENNA*
TT 96	*TOMB OF SENNEFER*
TT 100	*TOMB OF REKHMIRE*
TT 178	*TOMB OF NEFERRENPET*
TT 192	*TOMB OF KHERUEF*
TT 255	*TOMB OF ROY*
TT 296	*TOMB OF NEFERSEKHERU*
TT 343	*TOMB OF BENJA*
TT 359	*TOMB OF INHERKHAU*

5

TT 100: THE TOMB OF REKHMIRE

THE HISTORY

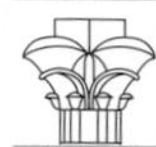

At the top of his career, Rekhmire was Vizier of Upper Egypt, Mayor of Thebes, and possessor of over one hundred other important titles. His great-grandfather, grandfather, and uncle were also viziers, a position second only to pharaoh in prestige and authority. Even though his father never rose above the rank of Priest of Amen, this august lineage helped to ensure his own rapid rise in the bureaucracy. Rekhmire boasted that "there was nothing of which he was ignorant in heaven, on earth, or in any quarter of the underworld." An immodest bit of hyperbole to be sure, but he was one of the best-informed, most powerful men in all Egypt.

Rekhmire held office during the last years of the reign of Thutmes III and the early years of Amenhetep II. These were heady times in Egypt. After Hatshepsut had departed the throne, Thutmes III undertook a series of military campaigns that greatly increased Egypt's power abroad and brought the country a degree of wealth unknown in previous dynasties. The pharaoh launched huge building programs and richly supported the arts and crafts. Egypt continued to thrive under his successor, Amenhetep II, and the great projects continued.

Nearly all these activities were supervised by Rekhmire. He oversaw projects throughout Egypt, managed the vast royal estates, supervised temples, judged court cases, checked irrigation schemes, attended official ceremonies, chaired administrative meetings, managed the civil administration, maintained state security, approved rates of taxation, and collected the taxes. Rekhmire was fully aware of his talents as Egypt's senior administrator, and he proudly and at length quoted his pharaoh's description of the vizier's duties in inscriptions on his own tomb walls:

'Then his majesty said to him: "Look you to this office of vizier. Be vigilant over [everything that] is done in it. Behold, it is the support of the entire land. Behold, as to the vizierate, behold, it is not sweet at all, behold, it is bitter as gall...Behold, it does not mean giving attention (only) to himself and to his officials and councilors, not (yet) making [dependents] out of everybody....Therefore, see to it for yourself that all [things] are done according to that which conforms to law and that all things are done in conformance to the precedent thereof in [setting every man in] his just desserts. Behold, as for the official who is in public view, the (very) winds and waters report all that he does; so, behold, his deeds cannot be unknown...."

Rekhmire describes, with no false modesty, how well he handled this difficult job: "I judged impartially between the pauper and the wealthy. I rescued the weakling from the bully. I warded off the rage of the bad-tempered and I repressed the acts of the covetous. I cooled down the temper of the infuriated. I wiped away tears by satisfying need. I

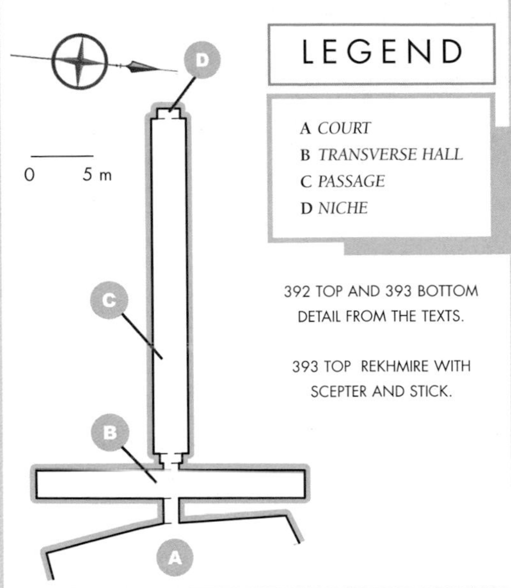

392 TOP AND 393 BOTTOM DETAIL FROM THE TEXTS.

393 TOP REKHMIRE WITH SCEPTER AND STICK.

appointed the son and heir to the position of his father. I gave bread to the hungry, water to the thirsty, meat, beer, and clothing to him who had none. I succored the old man by giving him my staff and caused old women to say, 'What a gracious act!'"

He sounds like the ideal bureaucrat. But later in his career, Rekhmire fell out of favor at court and may even have been stripped of his titles. No offspring are known to have succeeded him to government office, although he had at least five sons and several daughters. There is no evidence that he was ever buried in TT 100, but there are indications that part of the tomb decoration was deliberately mutilated and his name destroyed.

TT 100 was known to most nineteenth century explorers. Some of its scenes were published by Frederic Caillaud in 1831, but the tomb was not cleared until 1889 and not completely published until 1943.

In plan, TT 100 looks like many other cruciform-shaped tombs at Thebes, but in section it is unique. Beyond a standard transverse corridor, an inner room extends nearly 25 meters (82 feet) into the hillside of Shaykh 'Abd al-Qurna. At the entrance, the ceiling is 3 meters (10 feet) high. But the ceiling of the inner room slopes steeply upward, reaching a height of over 8 meters (26 feet) at its western end. The result of this strange design was to give Rekhmire's tomb over 300 square meters (3200 square feet) of wall surface, all of which was decorated with painted scenes of the highest quality. In the transverse hall, the scenes deal with personal and business matters and contain lengthy texts describing the duties of the vizier, the administration of temple holdings, and Rekhmire's activities during the reign of Amenhetep II. The inner room has scenes of arts and crafts, daily life, funeral banquets, and burial rituals. The famed nineteenth century British Egyptologist Sir John Gardner Wilkinson said in 1835 that the paintings of this tomb shed more light on ancient Egyptian culture than any other source known.

VISIT

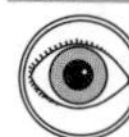

At the **ENTRANCE** to the tomb, prayers to Ra-Harakhty, Amen-Ra, Thoth, Osiris, and other gods are accompanied by Rekhmire's boastful claims of having close relations with each.

On the right half of the front (east) wall of the **TRANSVERSE HALL**, Rekhmire has included texts describing in some detail his duties as vizier. The British Egyptologist Percy Newberry believed that the accompanying scene was meant to show the actual audience hall in which Rekhmire held court, and if you look closely you will see thin columns with palm leaf capitals, walls that define a large chamber, and a raised dais on which Rekhmire sits. Distributed around that chamber are numerous officials and petitioners. The text accompanying the scene goes into considerable detail about Rekhmire's duties, even noting that in the audience hall he has to "sit on a backed chair, a reed mat being on the ground, the chain of office on him, a skin under his back, another under his feet, and a [canopy] of matting over him."

The Duties of the Vizier is one of the most important documents to come down from the New Kingdom, but some Egyptologists wonder what prompted Rekhmire to write it. The British Egyptologist T. G. H. James says, "The very act of composition suggests that all was not well; to find it necessary to set down precepts for action which would have seemed self-evident in happy times, incorporates a kind of condemnation of the moment of composition." He suggests that Rekhmire was being "hypocritical" by including the Duties in his tomb; after all, his fall from grace may well have been the result of official malfeasance.

To the right of the text, tax collectors are at work in Upper Egypt, receiving deliveries of gold rings, cattle, monkeys, grain, honey, pigeons, cloth, and beads. Surprisingly, there are no sheep or pigs, common animals in ancient Egypt. Tax dodgers are led forth by guards armed with heavy sticks. Between them and

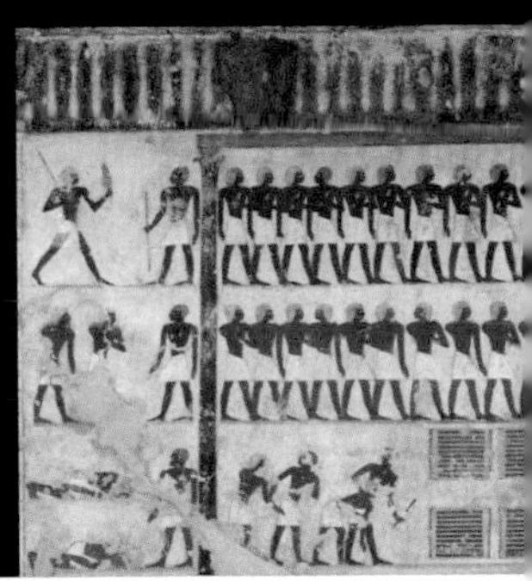

a figure of Rekhmire, four mats lie on the floor of the hall, covered with what Egyptologists believe to be rolls of leather. There are ten rolls on each mat, and some scholars identify them as the forty *sheshemu* or law books that Rekhmire would have consulted when adjudicating legal cases. Others identify the objects as batons, symbols of authority awarded by the vizier to local administrators.

Similar taxation scenes appear on the left (north) half of this front (east) wall, recording deliveries from districts in Middle Egypt. In the center of the wall, Rekhmire inspects rations and furniture to be delivered to the temple of Amen at Karnak. Wooden statues of Thutmes III are shown in the top register, and statues of stone in the register below. The statues include one that stands with ducks hanging from his arm, holding an offering slab, and another with his feet resting on a kneeling Nubian. This latter scene is unique. More than thirty different kinds of temple furnishings are shown at right, including shields, spears, quivers, necklaces, axes, and pots.

394-395 VARIOUS STATUES AND FURNITURE (ABOVE); MEN CARRYING RATIONS AND FURNITURE (BELOW) FOR THE TEMPLE OF AMEN AT KARNAK.

395 TOP TAX DODGERS, FROM THE TRANSVERSE HALL.

395 BOTTOM HARVESTING GRAPES, FROM THE TRANSVERSE HALL.

396 A GIRAFFE AMONG THE TRIBUTE FROM NUBIA.

396-397 FEATHERS, EGGS, IVORY TUSKS, AND MYRRH TREES AMONG THE TRIBUTES.

397 CENTER SYRIAN TRIBUTE INCLUDES A BEAR, AN ELEPHANT AND HORSES.

397 BOTTOM AN ELABORATE HUNTING SCENE.

On the left (south) side of the chamber's rear (west) wall, Rekhmire receives huge quantities of tribute on behalf of the king from various foreign countries, proof that, as the accompanying text states, "Every land is subject to His Majesty."

In the upper register, ostrich feathers and eggs, myrrh trees, ivory tusks, gold, leopards, cheetahs, monkeys, and baboons are brought from the land of Punt, a country on the Red Sea coast in what is now Eritrea.

In the register below, tribute comes from Keftiu, the island of Crete, and includes silver, gold, bronze, and lapis lazuli. Note the dress of the Cretan bearers, who wear phallus sheaths and high-topped laced shoes.

Next come Nubians, bearing ebony, gold, leopard skins, ostrich feathers and eggs, various semi-precious stones, and live animals including hunting dogs, a leopard, a baboon, and an elegant giraffe with a small green monkey climbing on its neck. A small herd of cattle is drawn with strangely deformed horns.

The Retenu from Syria come next, and in the bottom register, Nubian and Syrian captives. At the far left of the Syrian procession, men bring a brown bear and an elephant as part of the tribute. In the bottom register, note the women dressed in elaborate bell-shaped layers of cloth, some with baskets on their backs held in place by a head straps, bearing their young children.

On the right (north) half of the rear (west) wall, men press grapes, gather birds and fish, clean them and preserve them in jars. These are standard scenes, more fully described in the tombs of Menna and Nakht.

To their left is an elaborate hunting scene (see also TT 56: Userhet). Usually the Egyptians indicated chaos, discord, fear, and death by omitting the ground line in scenes and randomly placing the figures. Here, multiple ground lines meander across the surface and figures move in different directions. The result is the same: the scene depicts chaos. Panic-stricken ostriches, gazelle, and antelope try without success to flee the spears and arrows of

Rekhmire. At middle left, a hyena tries to pull an arrow from its chest with its teeth. Blood spurts from a wounded gazelle. Small mammals try to hide themselves beneath desert shrubs. A rabbit, ears flapping, races toward a small bush. But there is no escape.

The hunting ground is encircled by a fence of braided ropes. The animals are trapped, and Rekhmire, as the saying goes, is shooting fish in a barrel. (Such corralled hunts were practiced as recently as the 1930s by Egypt's last king, Farouk.)

In the upper register at right, the dead game lies in a great pile, their numbers tallied by a scribe. The hunt is not sport but provisioning for the afterlife.

The second room is called **THE PASSAGE** and its scenes deal with two broad subjects. On the right (north) wall, Rekhmire treats his activities as vizier and mayor and depicts various stages of his funerary ritual. On the left (south) wall, he illustrates the many workshops that he supervised for the Temple of Amen at Karnak. We will begin with the left wall, rightly considered one of the most important in all Egypt for the study of minor arts and crafts. Because the ceiling rises so dramatically, some registers are nearly impossible to see without ladders or binoculars. But they are of such interest that we will refer to them.

Near the beginning of the left wall, a seated figure of Rekhmire faces the entrance. The scenes he views deal with provisioning the storerooms of the Temple of Amen. In the top register, bags of tiger nuts are dumped in great piles, measured, then ground in a mortar made from the trunk of a tree. Tiger nuts (*Cyperus esculentus*), *wah* in ancient Egyptian, *habb al-'aziz* in modern Arabic, are still eaten in Egypt. They have a sweet flavor tasting like a cross between coconut and almond and are popular on festive days in Luxor, eaten after being soaked in water. After mixing with water, the resulting dough is placed in a three-legged kneading trough to which pastry chefs add fat, then fried in a large pan.

Farther left, men blow smoke into a cylindrical clay beehive and remove the combs of honey. A lone bee hovers forlornly before them. The honey is packed into jars and sealed, and some of it will probably be eaten with the tiger nut cakes. This is one of a few scenes of beekeeping known from dynastic times, although honey was the principal sweetener in ancient Egypt (they had no sugar), and it played a major role in Egyptian cooking and medicine.

In the register below, between the entrances to

vaulted temple storerooms, piles of ostrich feathers, skin shields, elephant tusks, baskets of grapes, sacks of nuts—the goods we saw in the first chamber being received by Rekhmire as taxes from Upper Egyptian districts and as tribute from foreign countries—await inventory. There are some light touches in these otherwise formal scenes: at right, a man strains to carry a huge jug of wine; nearby, monkeys scamper about the piles of *dom*, trying to steal the sweet-tasting fruit.

The flat-topped building at left is called the Double Treasury of Gold and Silver, and piles of precious metals stand ready to be placed inside.

398-399 REKHMIRE SUPERINTENDS THE ACTIVITIES OF CRAFTSMEN AND WORKERS, FROM THE LEFT WALL OF THE PASSAGE.

398 BOTTOM LEFT MEN CARRY HUGE JUGS OF WINE.

398 BOTTOM RIGHT MEN SEALING VASES.

399 BOTTOM VIEW OF THE PASSAGE.

To the right of these activities, other groups of men are engaged in various crafts. Bead makers, leather workers, carpenters, masons, and sculptors work intently to complete projects for the temple. These are some of the most accurate depictions of craftsmen from the New Kingdom and provide unrivalled information on how they made these superb works.

In the uppermost register, a bead maker uses a single bow to power three drills at once, a feat that would have required considerable skill. Behind him, other men string beads into necklaces and collars. Note how their long, curved fingers suggest the delicacy of the work. Farther left, a man with a crank drill hollows out stone vessels.

In the register below, leather workers prepare two different styles of sandals, saddles, ropes, and leather rolls for writing documents. One man stands next to an animal hide stretching or softening leather on the three-legged post. At left, several men stretch a skin, then cut it to the required shape. One man uses his teeth to pull a leather thong through a hole he has punched in the sole of a sandal. Farther left, a skilled worker has cut a piece of leather into a continuous spiral, to make leather strips, perhaps to be used in the rigging of ships.

Below (at right), a craftsman finishes gilding a statue of the king while another inspects the shrine that will house it. The statue is of blackest ebony, and its color indicates its intended association with Osiris. Two men at left sit beside a glue pot heating it on a

small fire. One of them applies adhesive to a piece of veneer. Behind them, a cabinetmaker smoothes the surface of a box with an adze. Note the carpenter's square and the dovetail jig lying next to him. Below, a man saws through a plank that has been lashed vertically to a post; a wedge has been jammed into the cut to prevent the saw from binding. Such techniques are still used today. Here, as elsewhere in this scene, the bare wood is carefully painted to show its grain. A man uses a bow drill to make holes along the edge of a bed through which rope will be passed to weave a mattress. The drill bit, made of bronze, is held in place by a small cup in the man's hand. Next, four men put the finishing touches on a shrine elaborately crafted of fine woods. Nearby, workmen carve chair legs with feet shaped like lion's paws. Other craftsmen cut, drill, saw, and sand pieces of wood. Good quality wood was a scarce and valuable commodity in Egypt—nearly all of it was imported and came only in small sizes—and it took considerable skill to create large objects from many small pieces of ebony, cedar, and other woods.

400-401 ACTIVITIES OF CRAFTSMEN, FROM THE LEFT WALL OF THE PASSAGE.

400 BOTTOM FOUR ARTISANS WORKING ON A SHRINE.

401 TOP A CRAFTSMAN FINISHES GILDING A STATUE; ANOTHER INSPECTS THE SHRINE THAT WILL HOUSE IT.

401 CENTER A BEAD MAKER (RIGHT) AND A MAN STRINGING BEADS INTO NECKLACES.

401 BOTTOM TWO MEN CARVE A CHAIR LEG FOR A FUNERARY BED.

In the next lower register, metalworkers fashion elegant vases and ewers from gold (the yellow rings in this scene), silver (the white rings), and bronze. At right, five rings of gold lie in the balance pan, the precise equivalent of the weight shaped like a bull's head lying in the other pan. Two other weights, one with the shape of a hippopotamus, lie beneath the scale. The top of the balance has the head of the goddess Ma'at on it to ensure honesty and accuracy. The man at right distributes gold and silver to the workmen and keeps track of its precise weight. That weight will later be compared to the weight of the finished products, to help prevent theft. The long-haired man at left, preceded by three workmen, may be the master craftsman who has come to oversee the gold.

At left, a man kneels before an anvil on which he has placed a gold ring. The ring lies beneath a piece of material, probably to keep it from being scratched as the man beats with a hammerstone. Slowly, he will turn the gold ring into a sheet of precious metal thin enough to be shaped into vessels, or beaten further into paper-thin gold leaf. In the two half-registers at the left, men fashion large vessels. Two men at top work with hammers and strange-looking anvils to shape a vessel. Nearby, a fire is used to soften the metal for soldering or chasing. At left, a man with a hollow reed and a pair of tongs holds a piece of gold in an open flame that crackles and spits as he blows air onto it. Below, four men engrave and polish huge gold jars.

Three men carry ingots of Asiatic copper to the workshop. Four hearths are operating there, each fueled with charcoal. At right, a man dumps another basketful of charcoal on the floor,

ready to be shoveled into the hearths. The heat of the fires is made more intense by means of foot-operated bellows made of wood and leather. The men raise the springless bellows by lifting a foot and pulling the cord, then depress it by pushing down with their foot. The reason that four hearths are working simultaneously is because of the size of the object they are making. It is a massive bronze doorway that is to be installed in Luxor Temple. The molten metal must be poured rapidly to prevent a great drop in temperature, and this requires that a supply be available without interruption to be poured quickly into the mold. The mold has seventeen funnel-shaped vents in its top, and two workmen deftly maneuver a large crucible with flexible sticks, pouring molten metal into each vent in turn. It seems almost impossible to believe that so large and heavy an object could be cast as a single piece, and it is true that no such door has ever been found. But there are textual references to doors of this size, and the two completed door leaves standing at the upper left of the scene belie any alternative explanation.

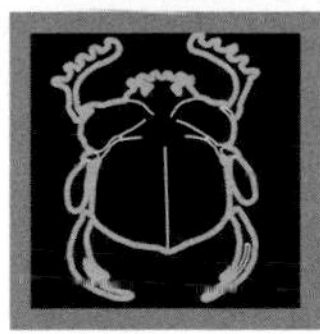

402 TOP TWO METALWORKERS REMOVE A CRUCIBLE FROM THE FIRE.

402 BOTTOM LEFT MEN CARRY COPPER INGOTS.

402 BOTTOM RIGHT AND 403 BOTTOM ARTISANS SHAPE AND DECORATE METAL VESSELS.

403 TOP WORKERS USE BELLOWS TO MAKE A MORE INTENSE FIRE.

404 MEN FILL BASKETS WITH WET MUD, SHAPE BRICKS AND PLACE THEM IN THE SUN TO DRY.

405 TOP TWO MEN FILL JARS WITH WATER FROM A POND.

405 BOTTOM SCULPTORS CARVE COLOSSAL STATUES.

In the next register below, men make bricks for a construction project at the Temple of Amen at Karnak. This is an especially interesting scene: the brick-making methods shown here can be found unchanged in almost any Egyptian village today, and the use of the bricks for building the ramp shown here tells us how the ancient engineers were able to construct huge temples. At left, men fill jars with water from a small tree-lined lake. One man stands to his waist in the water, another dips from the shoreline. The water will be added to mud and wheat chaff by workmen who use an adze and their feet to obtain the proper mixture. Other men fill baskets with the wet mud and carry it to masons who shape the bricks in molds, then place them in the sun to dry. After two days, the finished bricks are then carried to the building site. The text says the building is a sanctuary at Karnak, but we do not know which one.

This scene is one of the best pieces of evidence we have proving that ancient Egyptians used ramps in building constructions. And it shows how huge structures—a hypostyle hall in this case—might have been built. After the floor was laid, the first course of stone for walls or pillars was put in place and the space between the stone blocks filled with mud brick and rubble. A low ramp was built and stones for the second course were then dragged into place atop the first. More brick was added and the ramp was raised. A third course of stone was added, and the ramp raised again. When the building was completed and its roof was in place, the entire structure was packed with mud brick. As the brick was removed, artists stood on the brick, using it as a descending platform, and smoothed and decorated walls and columns from the top down.

The men working in the brickyard are unusual. They are referred to in the accompanying text as "captives," and they appear to be Syrians and Nubians. The Syrians have stubble on their chins and their chests are covered with blond hair, features foreign to Egyptians, who regularly shaved their entire body. A few of the Syrians here are even shown with blue eyes.

At right, ships bring more stone to the building site and men dress it, using strings and pegs to ensure that the blocks are perfectly square. Below, sculptors carve two colossal royal statues from red granite. Men work on scaffolding surrounding the huge statues, and a scribe outlines an inscription on the back of the right hand statue, which will later be carved. A limestone sphinx and an offering table are smoothed and polished, and one workman awkwardly bends down to correct a small imperfection on the table's base.

The remainder of this wall is given over to scenes of Rekhmire's burial ceremonies. The bottom three registers deal with the procession to the tomb and food offerings, watched over by the Mistress of the West. The next three are watched by Anubis and continue the procession. The top three, overseen by Osiris, deal with offerings and purification rituals.

The scenes on the right (north) wall are to be "read" from right to left, bottom to top.

At far right, ships sail toward Thebes, and in the lower register, they moor there. Rekhmire has returned from an audience with his pharaoh, Amenhetep II, and is welcomed home by members of his family.

To the left are Rekhmire's funerary banquets, one for the women of his family, another for the men. The women's banquet is the more interesting, and the artist has shown the guests dressed in tight-fitting robes, elaborately bejeweled and coifed. These are static scenes, formal, unmoving and lacking emotion, with two exceptions. One is the scene of servant girls. Note how their hair coyly falls and hides the girls' faces. The other exception is the girl in the center of the scene who stands with her back to us in a three-quarter view that is unique in Egyptian art. The figure is almost erotic in contrast to the other, formal figures here and is very well done, even though the artist erred in drawing her feet, which cross each other in an anatomically impossible manner. Musicians play stringed instruments, both in the women's hall and in the men's. Butchers prepare meat for the meal and, unusually, care has been taken to show that the cuts of beef are well-marbled.

Farther to the left, a statue of Rekhmire stands in a shrine on a boat towed by priests across a pond in his garden. It is not clear whether the garden is one in this life (in which case the building on the left might be his home) or in the next life (in which case it might be his tomb). The scene is charming in its execution, the trees drawn as if they lie on the ground so that the artist could show them—date and *dom* palms and sycomore figs—in their most recognizable form. Such bird's-eye views are common in Egyptian art. The garden is formally arranged, divided into several nesting rectangles that may indicate terracing. A water carrier stands in the upper right corner, preparing to irrigate the trees. At left, a priest offers up incense beside the pond. This is a funerary scene, perhaps part of the Beautiful Festival of the Valley.

The right (north) wall of the passage nearest the door deals with the Opening of the Mouth ritual.

406-407 REKHMIRE'S FUNERARY BANQUET FOR WOMEN.

406 BOTTOM REKHMIRE'S ATTENDANTS IN THE FUNERARY PROCESSION.

407 BOTTOM SACRIFICING A BULL FOR THE OPENING OF THE MOUTH CEREMONY.

5

TT 96: THE TOMB OF SENNEFER

THE HISTORY

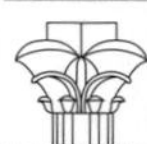

Sennefer was Mayor of Thebes and Overseer of the Garden of Amen during the reign of Amenhetep II. He was one of the most important officials of the court and he came from a wealthy and influential family. Befitting his rank, his tomb is one of the most beautifully decorated in the Theban Necropolis. It is also one of the most unusual. Architecturally, it had two separate components, both of which were decorated. A cruciform-shaped chapel lay beyond a large, level courtyard and was elaborately decorated with wonderful and unique scenes. Unfortunately, the chapel was badly damaged and closed to the public for over a century. It is now used as a storeroom. But in front of the chapel, on the left side of the courtyard, an awkward and steeply-sloping staircase descends through the bedrock to Sennefer's burial chamber. This is one of the few burial chambers in a Theban tomb to be decorated, and the decoration is superb.

Of course, it is the famous ceiling of TT 96 that earned the greatest praise from visitors, who gave it the nickname The Tomb of the Vines. The tomb lies about 100 meters (100 yards) uphill from that of Rekhmire (TT 100), cut into bedrock of very poor quality. It was extremely difficult to create smooth, flat surfaces to paint without resorting to thick layers of plaster. Such heavy plaster could not be applied to the ceiling, so the artist turned a potential problem into an asset, and used the irregular surface to create a grape arbor and a cloth covered gazebo. The rough, undulating surface makes the bunches of grapes seem three-dimensional. A vulture with the *shen*-hieroglyph (meaning "endurance") in its claws flies through the arbor. The effect is remarkable. It is equally so in the paintings of geometric weaving patterns. The painted textiles seem to be loosely hung across the ceiling from poles, and flutter in an imagined gentle breeze.

The burial chamber has not suffered as much as Sennefer's now-inaccessible chapel, but it has deteriorated since it was first seen in the 1820s. The room is small, about 2.5 by 3.5 meters (8 by 11 feet) with a 1.8 meter (6 feet) ceiling. It is awkward for more than four or five tourists at a time, so the Supreme Council of Antiquities has recently installed glass panels to keep tourists from touching the paintings. But the glass is a highly reflective collector of dust that makes the chamber claustrophobic. These annoyances seem minor, however, when one sees the vivid colors of the decorated walls.

Scenes of daily life, usually found in nobles' tombs, decorated the now-closed chapel. The walls of the burial chamber are decorated with funerary scenes. These scenes are special: they give prominence to the women in Sennefer's life and speak of the great affection Sennefer obviously felt for them.

There were several: Senetnefert and Senetnay are both identified as royal wet-nurses. Senetmi, Senetemiah, and Meryt are shown and named, but Egyptologists think it possible that all of these names refer to a single individual, in which case the paintings record the love shared between Sennefer and his wife, who is shown over and over throughout the tomb. Another woman is also mentioned: "his beloved daughter," Muttui; two other daughters are known from other sources.

408 TOP NECKLACE OFFERING TO SENNEFER.

409 SENNEFER'S WIFE MERYT OFFERS HIM A DRINK, BURIAL CHAMBER RIGHT REAR PILLAR.

LEGEND

A *ENTRANCE*
B *ANTECHAMBER*
C *BURIAL CHAMBER*

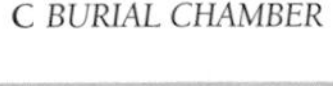

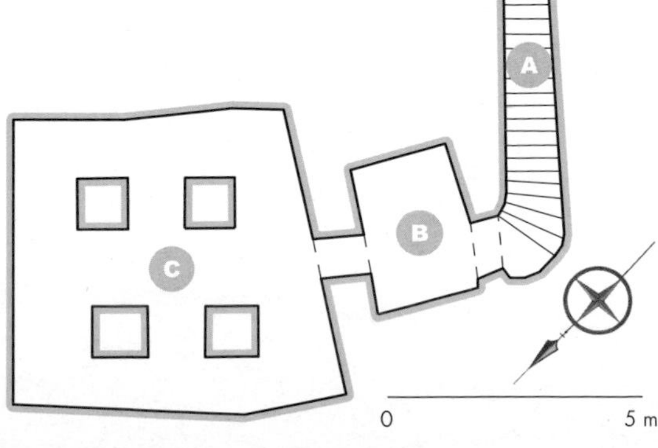

410 TOP VIEW OF THE BURIAL CHAMBER.

410 BOTTOM LEFT SENNEFER'S BOAT PROCESSION TO ABYDOS, FROM THE BURIAL CHAMBER.

410 BOTTOM RIGHT TWO ANUBIS JACKALS, ENTRANCE OF THE BURIAL CHAMBER.

411 TOP DETAIL OF THE DECORATION ON THE CEILING OF THE BURIAL CHAMBER.

VISIT

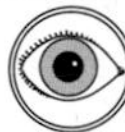

ANTECHAMBER The scenes here were painted by a very talented artist, one of at least two men who worked on the tomb. The artist worked rapidly, with confident strokes, and the figures he drew are attractive and well proportioned. At the bottom of the stairs on the left wall of the antechamber, Muttui offers necklaces (now destroyed) and a heart scarab to the seated figure of Sennefer. Behind her, priests carry offerings of cloth, beef, and incense. Sennefer himself is simply painted, with little detail or modeling, rather like the solid black hieroglyphs above his head.

On the right side of the antechamber, servants carry boxes of funerary equipment to the tomb, including bed, collars, sandals, *shabti*-statues, and a cartonnage head for Sennefer's mummy. Sennefer sits on a chair holding a scepter and staff, wearing earrings and a double heart amulet around his neck. Muttui, called a Chantress of Amen, stands behind him.

BURIAL CHAMBER Above the door into the burial chamber, two Anubis jackals, guardians of the necropolis and the tomb, recline on shrines flanking a bouquet of lotus blossoms. On the right side of the chamber's front wall, Sennefer and Meryt walk toward the doorway, magically leaving the tomb to enjoy the sunshine and "wander the earth." Behind these figures, they are shown seated on a wide bench, formally but affectionately posed, wearing fine linen costumes and elaborate jewelry. On the left side of the front wall, Sennefer's son, wearing the panther skin of a *sem*-priest, prepares burnt offerings for his parents, who sit on chairs at an offering table piled high with foods. The huge quantity of foodstuffs is detailed by a column of text before the son, claiming that Sennefer and wife are being given "a thousand loaves of bread, a thousand jugs of beer, a thousand head of cattle, a thousand fowl, and a thousand of everything good and pure."

The left wall of the chamber is badly damaged. Originally it showed details of Sennefer's funeral procession, including four oxen that pulled a sled carrying his sarcophagus.

412 DETAIL OF THE RIGHT REAR PILLAR.

413 TOP MERYT AND SENNEFER IN FRONT OF AN OFFERING TABLE AND THEIR SON AS SEM-PRIEST.

413 BOTTOM SENNEFER RECEIVES AN OFFERING FROM MERYT.

Servants bring funerary equipment, clothing, symbols of office, and foodstuffs. Cattle and other offerings are shown in the middle register. In the lower register, activities associated with an ancient ceremony, originally performed at the predynastic Delta site of Buto, include dancing and the erection of obelisks. To the right of the men holding the small obelisks, a small figure crouches on an odd-looking stool. This is a *tekenu*, the strange figure also shown in the funeral procession of Ramose. At the far right, Sennefer and his wife stand before an offering table in adoration of the god Osiris. Only the god's headdress remains visible.

On the rear wall of the chamber, three registers of priests stand before Sennefer, who sits at a table heavily laden with food offerings. There is a mirror image of this scene immediately to the right. Beyond it, two registers record the symbolic voyage of Sennefer and Meryt to Abydos. Their statues sit in a shrine on a barge that is towed northward. The return journey to Thebes, shown in the register below, takes advantage of the prevailing winds, and the boat's sails are unfurled.

On the right wall, Sennefer and Meryt sit in a shrine before Osiris and Anubis, gods of the netherworld. Behind the shrine, spell 151 of the Book of the Dead is inscribed in a series of rectangles. The spell is concerned with the embalming of the deceased and the safekeeping of his mummy. In the center of this design, Anubis completes the embalming of Sennefer's mummy. His *ba*, in the form of a bird, stands beneath the embalming bed. Figures of Isis and Nephthys kneel at each end of the scene, their hands resting on the *shen*-sign, a symbol of protection. Figures of the Four Sons of Horus stand at the corners of the inner square. A *djed*-pillar, associated with Osiris and meaning "endurance," stands above the central scene, and below is the Anubis jackal, the god closely allied with the embalmer's arts. Farther right, Sennefer and Meryt are purified with streams of water poured out by a *sem*-priest. The heart amulet worn by Sennefer has the name "Alexander" written on it in hieroglyphs, an addition made by a Greek visitor more than a thousand years after the scene was painted.

THE FOUR PILLARS in the burial chamber are each decorated with scenes of Sennefer and the women in his life. We will "read" them clockwise around each pillar and clockwise around the room.

LEFT FRONT PILLAR: on the front face, Meryt stands with Sennefer, offering incense. On the left face, she offers foodstuffs. On the back, she presents lotus flowers while another female, perhaps a daughter, kneels beside Sennefer, her arm affectionately circling his legs. The right face of the pillar is its most attractive: Sennefer with his wife kneeling at his feet, sits beside a persea tree and an offering table.

LEFT REAR PILLAR: a standing Sennefer receives a lotus flower from his wife, Meryt. On the left face, she presents him with a sistrum. On the back face, she offers incense, and on the right, she and Sennefer sit in chairs before a tree from whose branches emerges the goddess Isis. This is an especially lovely example of a common religious scene. Two Anubis jackals, posed like those above the entrance to the burial chamber, recline above pylons meant to represent Sennefer's tomb.

RIGHT REAR PILLAR: Meryt offers her seated husband a drink. Her left hand delicately touches his thigh. Sennefer holds both a lotus flower and a mandrake, the latter often considered a symbol of love and reproduction. Here, and indeed on most of the pillars where Sennefer and Meryt are depicted, the scenes are filled with such sexual innuendos. On the left face, Meryt presents Sennefer with a necklace and touches the heart amulet that he wears around his neck. On the back face, she offers other necklaces to Sennefer, who grasps her left wrist. On the right face, Sennefer stands on a mound of sand, purified with streams of water poured by four priests. The hieroglyph for "festival" is repeated four times here, once beneath Sennefer's feet, three times above his head.

RIGHT FRONT PILLAR: Meryt presents a drink to Sennefer, their hands affectionately reaching out to each other. On the left face, the couple are again affectionately posed. On the back face, Sennefer sits on a folding stool, receiving pieces of cloth from Meryt. On the right face, Sennefer stands on a mound of sand before a *djed*-pillar with human arms, greeted by four priests.

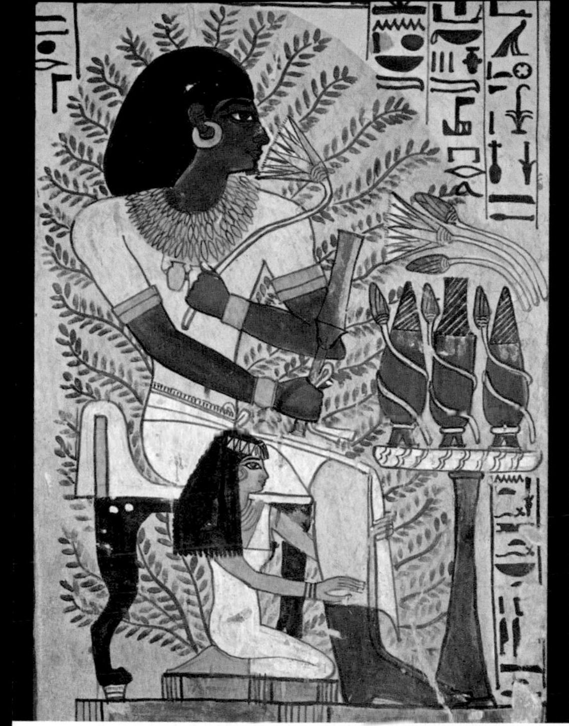

We do not know if Sennefer was actually buried in TT 96. His prestige in the royal court seems to have been so great that possibly he was given permission to be buried in the Valley of the Kings. This is suggested in KV 42, a tomb originally cut for Thutmes II but not used for his burial, by a number of objects inscribed with the names of Sennefer and his wife.

414 LEFT SENNEFER WITH SCEPTER AND STICK.

414 RIGHT MERYT PRESENTS LOTUS FLOWERS TO SENNEFER, AND HIS DAUGHTER KNEELS BESIDE HIM, LEFT FRONT PILLAR.

415 TOP LEFT SENNEFER SITS WITH MERYT UNDER A PERSEA TREE, LEFT FRONT PILLAR.

415 TOP RIGHT SENNEFER PURIFIED BY FOUR PRIESTS, RIGHT REAR PILLAR.

415 BOTTOM LEFT SENNEFER RECEIVES A LOTUS FLOWER FROM MERYT, LEFT REAR PILLAR.

415 BOTTOM RIGHT MERYT OFFERS NECKLACES TO SENNEFER, RIGHT REAR PILLAR.

5

TT 56: THE TOMB OF USERHET

THE HISTORY

The subject matter of the tomb of Userhet is standard, the artist's palette dominated by bland, pastel colors with a heavy emphasis on pink, and many of the walls have been seriously damaged or erased. But there are three scenes that deal with unusual subjects—hunting, barbering, and cattle branding—that are very well drawn and make the tomb well worth a visit.

TT 56 lies near the bottom of the Shaykh 'Abd al-Qurna hill, a few meters south of the tomb of Ramose (TT 55), directly west of that of Khaemhet (TT 57). It has been accessible since at least the early nineteenth century.

The tomb has a typical T-shaped plan, but it was cut 180 degrees from the usual orientation because of problems with local geology. Thus, scenes that normally would appear on a tomb's west wall are here painted on its east. We will refer to the walls as left and right, front and back to minimize confusion.

Userhet held the title of Scribe Who Counts Bread in Upper and Lower Egypt, meaning that he was responsible for inventorying the grain that came to the royal bakeries, tallying the number of loaves they produced, working to minimize theft and waste, and then ensuring that the bread was properly distributed. The position is a good example of New Kingdom Egypt's tightly-organized and micro-managed bureaucracy.

VISIT

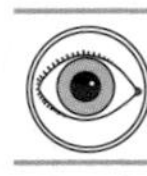

FIRST CHAMBER, RIGHT FRONT WALL Userhet stands with his wife, Mutnefret, and one of their daughters before burnt offerings piled high on four alabaster stands. He pours myrrh onto the offerings to sweeten the smoke that will float heavenward to honor Osiris and Hathor. The offerings are standard ones: loaves of bread, heads of lettuce, vegetables, and cuts of beef. Userhet's brown skin appears pink through the transparent garment he wears over his starched kilt. Behind him, his wife and daughter stand in tight-fitting cloaks, wearing wigs and jewels, offering bouquets of flowers. Several columns of text have apparently been erased or painted over. Early Christian monks drew an elaborate cross over Userhet's body.

To the right, Userhet inspects five registers of cattle and harvest activity. In the upper two registers, cattle are driven forward to be tallied by government scribes as part of an official census. At top, calves jump playfully about in fields of grass and small trees, but in the register below, they have been forced into a more orderly procession so they can be more easily counted. At right, a cow lovingly licks her calf. In the third register, the cattle have been lassoed and their legs tied. Hot irons are used to brand their left shoulder. To their right, two servants prostrate themselves before Userhet, kissing the ground at his feet ready to report the tally.

In the fourth register, nine men carry large baskets of grain under the watchful eye of their supervisors, and again scribes record the quantities being delivered. In the badly damaged lower register, farmhands harvest fields of flax.

LEFT END WALL A false door has been painted to resemble red granite, a material much more valuable than limestone. Above the false door, two couples are seated before great piles of food offerings. Several names are given, but we do not know the relationship of these couples to Userhet or his wife. Left and right of the false door, priests purify Userhet in the

416 A FIGURE OF USERHET.

417 CATTLE DRIVEN TO BE COUNTED, FROM THE FIRST CHAMBER.

LEGEND

A *ENTRANCE*
B *FIRST CHAMBER*
C *LONG HALL*
D *NICHE*

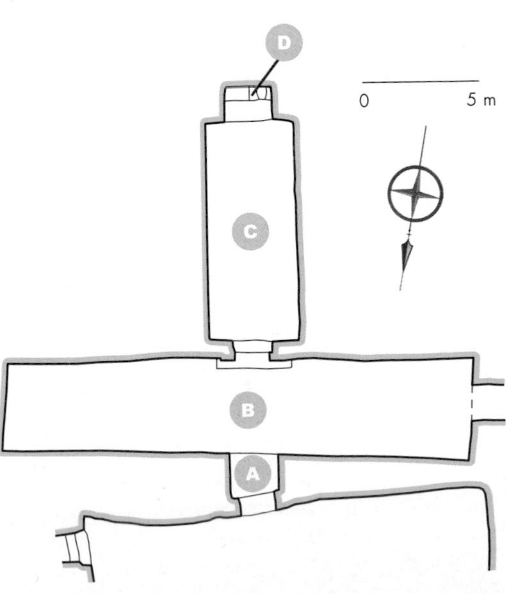

first stages of the Opening of the Mouth ritual.

The left rear wall of this chamber is badly damaged, but next to the doorway Userhet and his wife receive offerings from their children. This is a formal scene, even more rigidly drawn than usual, but a small monkey, eating a fig beneath Mutnefret's chair, adds a lighter touch. Near him sits a finely painted conical basket.

On the right side of the rear wall, soldiers have loaded baskets with quantities of bread for distribution to the troops. Userhet's job required that he oversee these activities. In the upper registers, well-dressed officers inspect their rations of bread, beer, and wine. Some hold lotus flowers to their nose. (Drinking wine and nibbling lotus flowers produced a mild narcotic effect.) Below, ordinary soldiers lug huge baskets of bread to be inspected by an official whose whip suggests that he expects to uncover an occasional irregularity in the quantities.

At left, in the top register, soldiers march across a tree-covered field toward two officers who carry staffs, symbols of their rank. The soldiers hold empty bags in their hands, ready to receive their daily food rations from the storeroom standing beyond the tree at right.

In two registers below, recruits lazily wait their turn for a haircut. Some sit on chairs (like the two men sharing a stool, lower right), while others sit on the ground. Some doze beneath a tree, and all look bored. Two barbers, razors in hand, bowls of water at their feet, shave the heads of each recruit in turn. Real-life scenes like this can still be seen in small, isolated Upper Egyptian villages when an itinerant barber will set up shop in a village and men come for a shave and a haircut, gossiping or discussing football as they wait their turn.

On the right end of the right rear wall, king Amenhetep II sits in an elaborate booth receiving offerings from the deceased Userhet. Here, Userhet is shown with red hair, a feature often associated with the god Seth. It is unusual for a royal figure to be shown with bodyguards, but the bowing men on the end wall at the pharaoh's right may be just that.

On the right end wall is a painted round-topped stela flanked by offering bearers and topped by a winged sun disk and figures of Osiris. No text was written on it. A small niche cut into the base of this wall is now covered by wire mesh. If you have a light, peer inside: the niche is filled with clay bread molds that may have belonged to Userhet himself.

On the left front wall of the transverse hall, Userhet, followed by his wife, again stands before well-drawn piles of food offerings. At left, three women sit with children on their laps—two girls, one boy. The women are the nurses who tended Userhet's children. Two men at right offer them bouquets. Note how the arm of the man at right stretches beyond anatomical possibility to reach past his colleague and present a lotus blossom to the children.

ENTRANCE TO THE LONG HALL The lintel of this elaborate door has a cavetto cornice and below it, scenes of Userhet, Osiris, and Anubis. Columns of text on the two jambs list standard offerings.

LONG HALL, LEFT WALL The hunting scene shown here is the best-painted scene in KV 56. Userhet stands confidently in his chariot, the reins tied around his waist as his two horses race at full gallop across the rough desert surface. Such a pose would have been impossible in real life; certainly, Userhet would have ridden with an experienced charioteer, and even then would probably have had to hold on for dear life. But this is an idealized hunt, where nothing can go wrong, where Userhet can plant his feet, draw his bow, take aim, and kill prey who cannot possibly survive his terrible power.

Such hunting scenes were commonplace in Egyptian tombs from predynastic times onward, but rarely were they drawn with such vivacity, self-assurance and such a minimum of fuss as here. Not a brush stroke is wasted, and the animals' terror, the tautness of their muscles, and the death throes of those hit and bleeding, is palpable. Simply by abandoning the use of a ground line and drawing the animals in scattershot disorder on the wall, the artist has conveyed their fear and the mayhem of death. Actually, the scene is carefully composed: brush strokes, poses, and placement draw the viewer directly into the heart of the action. Rabbits flee, leaping high in the air, their long ears flapping, racing past dazed gazelle with blood gushing from their wounds.

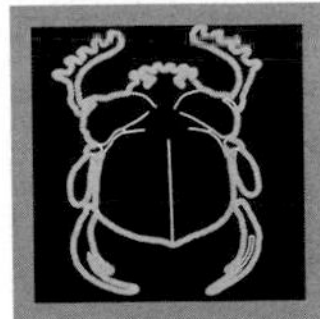

418 HUNTING SCENE WITH USERHET IN HIS CHARIOT, FROM THE LONG HALL.

419 HAIRCUT AND BARBERING SCENE, FROM THE FIRST CHAMBER.

420 TOP NICHE IN THE REAR WALL OF THE LONG HALL WITH STATUES OF MUTNEFRET, USERHET'S WIFE.

420 BOTTOM PRIEST AND OFFERING BEARER IN THE FUNERARY PROCESSION, FROM THE LONG HALL.

421 USERHET ON THE BOAT FISHING, FROM THE LONG HALL.

A fox has impaled itself on a small barbed shrub trying to escape the carnage. Too weak to move, it slowly bleeds to death.

It is difficult to believe that this superb hunting scene was drawn by the same hand that painted the mundane fishing and fowling scene next to it, although apparently that was the case. The fishing scene seems bland, slapdash, and lacking the detail that made similar scenes in the tombs of Menna and Nakht so impressive. Even the early Coptic monks who visited the tomb thought the scene needed improvement: they drew crude four-legged animals on the papyrus skiffs.

Egyptologists who have studied the tomb of Userhet believe that three artists worked here, and the man who painted the scenes on this wall was also responsible for the right rear wall, the right end wall, and the far right front wall of the first chamber. A second artist was responsible for the rest of the first chamber, and a third undertook work on the right wall of the long hall.

There is a nice scene of vintners at work. Men balance themselves by holding onto vines, hanging from a cross bar as they trample grapes in a shallow clay vat. Scribes record the quantities of the vintage dated wine and men work in the arbor filling baskets with bunches of grapes. To their left, three men pull in a bird net beside a papyrus thicket. This is a small and simply done scene, but three ducks standing on a table are drawn with skill and confidence. At far right, Userhet makes offerings to the goddess Renenutet. Beyond her, there was a fishing scene that is now destroyed.

LONG HALL, REAR WALL A small niche was cut in this narrow wall in which seated figures of Userhet and his wife Mutnefret were carved. Today, only her figure remains.

LONG HALL, RIGHT WALL On the long right wall, a series of scenes record the ceremonies held when Userhet died. A shrine that holds Userhet's mummy is pulled by cattle toward his tomb. Priests and offering bearers walk in the procession carrying funerary equipment and offerings. Mourners wail as the shrine passes, but the artist has failed to capture the emotions of these rigidly posed women. In registers below, huge quantities of offerings are depicted in formal rows and in the hands of bearers marching toward the tomb. The scenes are standard ones and not especially well-drawn—the proportions of the figures are wrong, for example—but the drawing of Userhet's lively, prancing horse is a delight. Its curved neck and cropped mane, high tail, and nervous pose give it character. In the lower register, a flotilla of boats makes the pilgrimage to Abydos. Userhet's mummy is in the center boat, towed by four others. Some of the figures in this scene are less formally posed than the figures in pilgrimage scenes in other tombs.

5

TT 343: THE TOMB OF BENJA

THE HISTORY

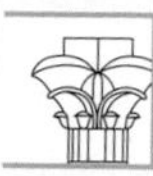

Benja, also called Paheq-amen, was a Boarder in the Royal Nursery and an Overseer of Work and Craftsmen of the Lord of the Two Lands, and Chief Treasurer. He lived during the reign of Thutmes III, a date based on the stylistic elements of his tomb decoration. The cruciform-shaped tomb lies at the bottom of a small pit in Shaykh 'Abd al-Qurna.

VISIT

On the left jamb in the **ENTRANCE**, Benja strides forth from the tomb. His figure is well carved and painted, with elaborate hair, a fine profile, delicate fingers, and a tight-fitting, transparent gown. Many noblemen at Thebes devoted the decoration in their tombs to scenes of arts and crafts, the work they performed during their lifetime, or their religious deeds. There are a few such scenes in Benja's tomb; here the emphasis is on food and drink. Offering tables piled high with meat, fruit, and vegetables, mats covered with jugs of beer and wine, and texts listing foodstuffs cover the walls.

On the right side of the doorway as you face the front wall in the first chamber, one figure of Benja faces left toward three offering tables and mats covered with foodstuffs and containers of salves. Another figure of Benja, this time in his official capacity, faces right before three registers of men who deliver and weigh gold rings, pieces of turquoise and lapis lazuli. Two scribes in the lower register inventory the goods. In the upper register, piles of ivory tusks and ebony logs are stacked beside wooden chests. The stark white background of the scenes in this tomb and the absence of lengthy texts make the decoration seem sparse. At right, on the narrow left wall of the chamber, a false door painted to look like red granite is inscribed with a prayer asking that offerings be made to Benja. On either side, three small registers each show a kneeling figure of Benja holding bread, beer, or foodstuffs.

On the left rear wall of the **FIRST CHAMBER**, Benja's mother and father sit on chairs before a table of offerings. His mother, Tirukak, places her hand on the shoulder of his father Iretnena. Beyond the table, four musicians stand in an upper register playing a flute or clapping hands. Below them, another plays a harp and a second plays a lute. In the register below these scenes, five male guests sit before a small offering table.

To the right, beside the door into the **SECOND CHAMBER**, Benja sits before a table piled high with lettuce, onions, grapes, bread, geese, cow heads, and pottery vessels. An anonymous priest stands before him.

The rear right wall of the chamber shows Benja again seated on a chair before an offering table. Officials in white gowns precede three registers of offering bearers. The bearers wear kilts and carry cattle, amphorae, geese, and vegetables. On the right end wall, a round-topped stela gives an elaborate version of an offering text. Like the false door on the left end wall, figures of Benja kneel on either side holding offerings.

Returning to the front wall, on the left side of the entrance, Benja stands before three offering tables holding two alabaster stands piled with ducks. The texts give his titles and a prayer for offerings to Amen. To the left, his seated figure faces an offering table and three registers of bearers holding geese, lotus flowers, incense, and vessels.

On the left wall of the second chamber a large figure of the Goddess of the West faces three registers showing Benja's funeral. She holds a *was*-scepter and an *ankh*-sign in her hands and has her standard atop her head. In the upper register, a shrine containing Benja's mummy is dragged on a sled by four men toward his tomb (a rectangular building with a cornice.) Women in white dresses stand at each end of the shrine. In the register below, five kilted men walk forward carrying food and jewelry. They are said to be from Pe and Dep, the capital cities of Lower Egypt. The building before them may be a House of Embalming. In the third register, one boat with a shrine, another with a kneeling statue, are traveling to Abydos. Standing atop the shrine is a man with a whip. In the lowest register, the procession returns from Abydos. On the right half, a seated figure of Benja extends his hand toward an offering table and mats piled high with foodstuffs. A table of offerings is written above the destroyed figure of an offering priest.

At the left end of the right wall, Benja sits on a chair holding a piece of cloth, his left hand extended toward a an offering table. To the right is an offering list, and beyond that, three registers of three scenes depicting the Opening of the Mouth ritual. In each of the nine scenes, priests hold various objects such as jars of natron, incense, and jugs of water before the mummy of the deceased. The mummy stands on a small mound of sand representing the site of creation.

In a large niche cut into the rear wall, three seated figures depict (from left to right) Benja's father, Benja himself, and his mother. Their faces have been vandalized.

LEGEND

A *ENTRANCE*
B *FIRST CHAMBER*
C *SECOND CHAMBER*
D *NICHE*

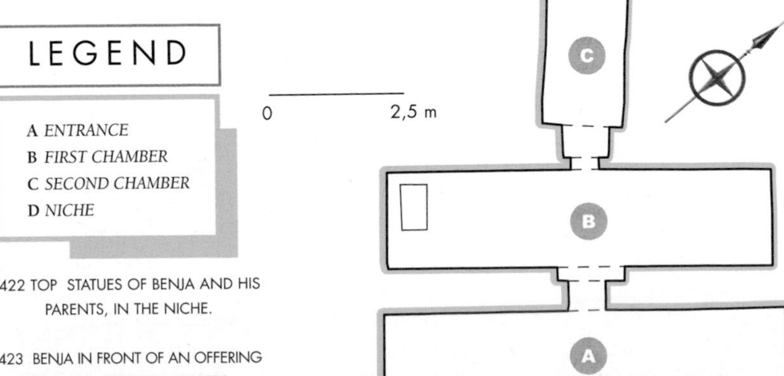

422 TOP STATUES OF BENJA AND HIS PARENTS, IN THE NICHE.

423 BENJA IN FRONT OF AN OFFERING TABLE AND OFFERING BEARERS.

5

INTRODUCTION

PAINTED TOMBS FROM THE LATE REIGN OF THUTMES IV AND EARLY AMENHETEP III

The three tombs from this period currently open to the public–Menna, Nakht, and Thutmes–are among the most interesting nobles' tombs at Thebes and should be a part of any tourist itinerary. The subject-matter of their scenes is standard, but their decoration is innovative and informal, brightly colored and filled with details that are at once amusing and informative. The tombs are cramped, but they each deserve a leisurely visit.

5

TT 69: THE TOMB OF MENNA

THE HISTORY

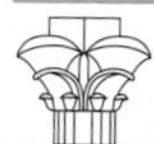

The decoration in the tomb of Menna is a lively mix of the traditional and the innovative. Art historians do not consider the work especially proficient technically, but the tomb's richly detailed and imaginative scenes leave no doubt that the artist was a highly creative man who thoroughly enjoyed himself. He observed the basic requirements of tomb decoration, but he was not afraid to add delicate (and often humorous) touches to otherwise standard scenes. The result transformed what might have been stereotypical, anonymous figures into individuals displaying distinct personalities and visible emotions. Art historians have noted that no two figures in Menna's tomb are drawn in quite the same way. For that matter, neither are any two animals nor any two offerings. Its paintings are very different from the conservative style of the latter part of the reign of Amenhetep III best illustrated by the carved relief in the tombs of Ramose and Kheruef. The informality here, even in scenes of formal subject matter, was copied by other artists of the period, but it was never equaled.

Menna's tomb is small and you may think you can get in and get out quickly, but you should not do so: this is a tomb to be savored. The scenes on the walls are a montage of small vignettes scattered across a large canvas. Each captures a moment of daily life in some of the finest, most creative paintings to be found in the New Kingdom.

Menna was Scribe of the Fields of the Lord of the Two Lands, the overseer of agricultural activities on the extensive royal landholdings, and director of cadastral surveys. His job was an important one, and he proudly devoted much of his tomb's decoration to depicting the activities that occupied much of his professional life.

LEGEND

A *ENTRANCE*
B *TRANSVERSE HALL*
C *INNER CHAMBER*
D *NICHE*

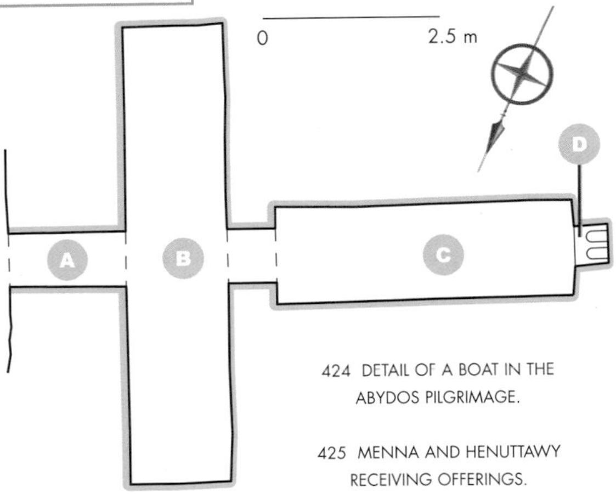

TT 69 is one of a group of tombs that date to the end of the reign of Thutmes IV and the beginning of the reign of Amenhetep III. The group includes the tombs of Nakht and Djehuty-mes, and each exhibits traits common to art of the time of Thutmes IV—thin-limbed female figures, for example—and traits common to the time of Amenhetep III—voluptuous females with narrow waists and long almond-shaped eyes. Each tomb is characterized by lively, imaginative, painted decoration, executed in rich colors with a sure hand—the same hand that may also have decorated WV 22, the royal tomb of Amenhetep III. TT 69 lies on the lower slope of the hill called Shaykh ‘Abd al-Qurna, a short walk uphill from the tomb of Nakht. On the way there, you will pass some of the oldest mudbrick houses in Qurna. One of them is decorated with an early example of Hajj paintings—scenes of folkloric subjects and of the owner's pilgrimage to Mecca—on its front wall.

Menna's is a well-cut cruciform tomb, with an entrance corridor, transverse hall, and inner chamber. This plan is typical of many nobles' tombs at Thebes. Decoration in the transverse hall is devoted to scenes of agricultural activity and funeral banquets. Scenes in the inner chamber deal with funerary rituals and offerings for Menna and his wife Henuttawy.

424 DETAIL OF A BOAT IN THE ABYDOS PILGRIMAGE.

425 MENNA AND HENUTTAWY RECEIVING OFFERINGS.

VISIT

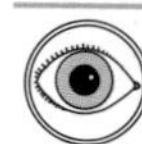

TRANSVERSE HALL, FRONT WALL, RIGHT SIDE On the right (south) side of the front wall of the transverse hall, Menna sits beside the doorway at a table heaped with food offerings. To the right, in the upper register, a servant kisses the feet of his overseer. The artist has confusingly overlapped the two figures, as if he was unsure whether the overseer's left leg should be on this side of the petitioner or on the other. Behind him, men with a knotted rope survey agricultural land. Scribes follow, writing down boundary descriptions, while others calculate the taxes to be levied on each field's harvest. Look at the costumes of these men. The hems of their *jalabiyyas* appear scalloped, probably because they have been tucked into their belts so they will not drag along the ground. This is exactly how modern Upper Egyptian farmers dress for work in their fields.

Instead of simply drawing straight stalks of grain in the background of this scene as most artists would have done, the artist here drew some stalks waving gently in the breeze, others bent and broken by the bureaucrats who trampled through the fields. It is a realistic touch, typical of the imagination that characterizes Menna's tomb.

To the right, a family approaches the tax collectors, either to offer bribes hoping to influence their decisions, or to make an early payment on taxes owing. There was no money in ancient Egypt so payment was made in kind. The man brings a "bride of the corn" or "corn dolly," while the woman carries containers of food. Their son leads a donkey and carries a kid goat in his arms. The late Belgian art historian, Arpag Mekhitarian, described the boy almost in tears, because he is forced to give up his favorite pets to this army of strangers.

To the right, scribes record grain inventories. Menna stands in a kiosk watching the arrival of grain-laden boats at the port of Thebes. A group of men are being flogged in his presence,

probably for failure to pay their taxes. At first glance, the agricultural scenes on this wall appear to be the standard scenes of harvesting, threshing, and winnowing. But they contain wonderful details that surely were taken from real life. Here, a young girl carries water to the men in the field; there, a woman nurses her swaddled infant whose hand tugs at her long hair. Two girls wrestle in the field, perhaps arguing over gleaning rights. A field hand naps beneath a tree in whose branches hangs a waterskin. Beside him, a worker amuses himself by playing a flute. A youth sits on a pile of grain, trying to reckon quantities of wheat by counting on his fingers. A young girl sits on the ground and extends her leg before her friend, who removes a thorn from her foot. A foreman leans on his staff and complains to two men forking grain. They turn and listen to his orders. One of them, a man with a bulbous nose, was described by Mekhitarian as having "an expression of such bovine stupidity that we can understand why his opposite number on the right is watching him with obvious anxiety." Such cameos animate these scenes and give them a degree of liveliness rarely seen in tomb paintings. The artist has imbued the figures with such humanity we can be sure their actions are modeled on real people. They are individuals, not simply generic peasants or officials copied from an artist's handbook of standard scenes.

426-427 MENNA SITS BEFORE OFFERING TABLES AND SERVANTS, RIGHT SIDE OF THE TRANSVERSE HALL.

427 SCENES OF HARVESTING, THRESHING AND WINNOWING.

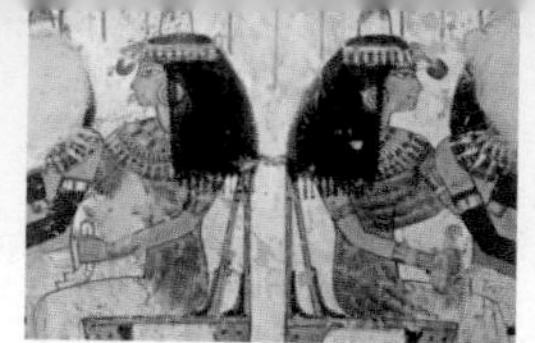

LEFT (SOUTH) END WALL On the left (south) end wall, Menna, his wife, Henuttawy, and two of his sons stand before the enshrined god, Osiris. In the register below, food offerings are being set alight. Yellow flames leap from the tables, the smoke itself an offering to the god. A priest spoons incense into the flames. Such burnt offerings are associated with the important Beautiful Festival of the Valley and figure prominently in New Kingdom tomb scenes.

REAR WALL, LEFT (SOUTH) SIDE This wall has suffered badly and little remains of what originally was a banquet scene. The representations of woven basketry are good examples of the fine quality of painting here.

REAR WALL, RIGHT (NORTH) SIDE In the upper register, Menna and members of his family receive offerings. In the second register, guests sit before huge piles of food offerings. In the two lower registers, bearers bring even more offerings to the banquet, perhaps in celebration of the Beautiful Feast of the Valley.

RIGHT (NORTH) END WALL A stela has been erected within a large shrine. On each side, Menna and his wife raise their hands in adoration. On the stela itself, Anubis, Osiris, the Western Goddess, Hathor, and Ra-Harakhty stand or sit. In the register below, Menna and his wife are seated, and below them stands a row of priests. None of the texts on this wall were ever written, although the column lines were drawn.

FRONT WALL, LEFT (NORTH) HALF Menna and his wife make burnt offerings, while butchers and other kitchen workers prepare still more food for the ceremony. There is an especially charming figure here in the lower register of a servant who carries a young gazelle on his shoulders. It is a fine example of the technical competence of Menna's artist.

428 TOP AND 429 TOP RIGHT END WALL OF THE TRANSVERSE HALL: MENNA AND HIS WIFE RAISE THEIR HANDS IN ADORATION OF A STELA.

428 BOTTOM MENNA AND HIS WIFE RECEIVE OFFERINGS, TRANVERSE HALL, REAR WALL, RIGHT SIDE.

429 BOTTOM LEFT END WALL OF THE TRANVERSE HALL: MENNA, HENUTTAWY AND TWO SONS STAND BEFORE OSIRIS IN A SHRINE.

INNER CHAMBER, LEFT (SOUTH) WALL On the left (south) wall, bearers bring furniture and offerings to Menna's tomb. It is worth comparing this scene to one of identical subject matter in Ramose's tomb. The differences show dramatically how the art style of early Amenhetep III (here) contrasts with that of late Amenhetep III (there). At the far right, Menna stands before a balance on which his heart is being weighed against a figure of Ma'at. Osiris watches as Thoth records the result. The accompanying hieroglyphs were quickly, almost cursively drawn, and painted solid black without internal detail, but they still show a high degree of artistic competence.

REAR (WEST) WALL A niche that once housed a statue of Menna and his wife is flanked by offering bearers.

RIGHT (NORTH) WALL At the front end of the right (north) wall, boats sail to Abydos. The two boats on the right, their sails furled, float northward with the current. The two boats at the left, one a towboat with its sail unfurled, sail upstream with the north wind back to Thebes. A sailor at the bow uses a pole to test the river's depth. Another stands in the rigging, shouting this information to the helmsman. The two boats in the center of the scene carry statues of the deceased Menna and Henuttawy, accompanied by a boat carrying a shrine whose contents are displayed atop it. In most tombs, the pilgrimage to Abydos is drawn in a serious and formal manner, as befits reference to such an important religious event. But even here, Menna's artist could not resist the extra touch: in the boat at left, a sailor nearly falls overboard as he tries to dip water from the Nile.

In scenes below, priests prepare the mummies of Menna and Henuttawy for the Opening of the Mouth ritual and burial.

430-431 AND 430 BOTTOM OFFERING BEARERS FROM THE INNER CHAMBER.

431 CENTER VIEW OF THE INNER CHAMBER WITH A NICHE AT THE END.

431 BOTTOM THE WESTERN GODDESS, IMENTY, FROM THE LEFT WALL OF THE INNER CHAMBER.

The combined scene of fishing and fowling to the left of the boating scene is rightly considered a masterpiece. These are not sporting scenes, but scenes of religious significance, providing food for the tomb owner and his family in the afterlife. Many such scenes are known in Egyptian art. Most of the time, they are rigidly prescribed and lack the dexterous touches that we see here. Menna's artist has used vivid colors; the proportions and poses of the figures are perfectly laid out, while the details of plants and animals are elegant and accurate records of Egypt's natural world.

Look, for example, at the papyrus thicket in the center of the scene. Bird nests are scattered through the thicket, and an ichneumon (an Egyptian mongoose) and a Common Genet focus intently on the eggs they contain. Menna stands on a papyrus skiff, a throwing stick in one hand, a pair of egrets in the other. The egrets perhaps served as decoys. Pintail ducks fly in panic around the thicket, four of them already sent reeling by Menna's throwing sticks. (These are not boomerangs; they do not return.) Two butterflies flutter nearby, oblivious to the confusion. Menna wears a thin gown over his kilt and an elaborate broad collar and bracelets. Behind him stands his wife, far too elaborately dressed for hunting birds in a swamp, a cone of incense on her head, cut papyri draped over her arm. (It is the religious and sexual nature of these marsh scenes that dictated his elaborate costume.) Two equally overdressed daughters stand or kneel behind their mother. The young girl on the skiff, her arms full of lotus flowers and ducks, turns her head and looks back. In contrast to these finely dressed women, a third daughter wears nothing more than a belt and some jewelry.

432-433 THE RIGHT NORTH WALL OF THE INNER CHAMBER WITH SCENES OF PILGRIMAGE TO ABYDOS, PREPARATION OF MUMMIES, OFFERING BEARERS; FISHING AND FOWLING; MENNA AND HIS WIFE RECEIVING OFFERINGS.

432 CENTER AND 433 BOTTOM A DAUGHTER AND THE WIFE OF MENNA.

432 BOTTOM A SAILOR LEANS OUT OF A BOAT DURING THE PILGRIMAGE TO ABYDOS.

434 TOP TWO OF THE FISH (TILAPIA NILOTICA), CAUGHT BY MENNA.

434 BOTTOM DUCKS AND LOTUS BLOSSOMS ON THE NILE.

435 TOP THE PAPYRUS THICKET WITH A GENET AND A BUTTERFLY.

435 BOTTOM FISH AND BIRDS IN THE SHALLOWS OF THE NILE.

She kneels to pluck lotus flowers from the water. She is merely a silhouette here, but her figure is sensuous and elegant, a dramatic contrast to Menna's son farther to the right, whose simply drawn figure and face are flat and lacking in emotion.

In the right half of the scene, Menna, accompanied by family members, spears *Tilapia nilotica*. This fish is frequently shown in tomb paintings, in part because of its habit of holding its fertilized eggs in its mouth until they hatch. Even after birth, the young will swim back into their parent's mouths for safety. The Egyptians saw in this behavior a suggestion of fertility and renewed life. (Of course, the fish are also good eating.) Below the scene flows the Nile, its rippled surface suggested by zigzag lines which form the hieroglyph for water. In the water, several species of fish swim about, and a crocodile holds a huge *Tilapia* in its jaws. Birds wade in the shallows along the shoreline and lotus blossoms grow in profusion.

Note in this scene, and throughout Menna's tomb, that the women are shown with the same skin color as men. Usually—as in the funeral scene in the tomb of Ramose—men have reddish brown skin, women a light yellow, a difference reminiscent of the Victorian sense of beauty: tall, dark, and handsome men, women with creamy complexions never exposed to the sun or wrinkled by labor.

To the right, Menna and his wife receive offerings. Henuttawy's face is painted with great skill. The lines are bold and sure, with the hair simply but elegantly drawn, making a highly effective composition.

The ceiling of the inner chamber is beautifully painted with an elaborate geometric pattern copied from woven mats that perhaps adorned private homes.

5

TT 52: THE TOMB OF NAKHT

THE HISTORY

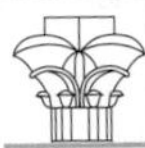

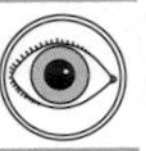

VISIT

Several years ago, in an attempt to protect the decorated walls of Nakht's tomb, the Supreme Council of Antiquities tried to hermetically seal it. They enclosed and covered its entrance court and created a small museum where tourists could read about Nakht while waiting to enter the tomb. There almost always was a wait, because beyond this small room, they built a glass-walled tunnel into the tomb to prevent the hands of tourists from touching the decoration or their breath from affecting its environment. These measures may indeed better protect Nakht's decoration, but they have also made the tomb a claustrophobic and rather unpleasant place to visit. No more than two or three persons at a time can go inside. The corridor is extremely narrow (wheelchairs will not fit); the glass is reflective; and the light is so subdued you can barely see the walls. Having said that, the tomb is worth a visit. Like the tomb of Menna, which was perhaps decorated by the same artists, it contains some unique gems of Egyptian painting.

European explorers found TT 52 in 1889, only a few years after it had been discovered by local villagers, and it was recorded between 1907 and 1910 by Norman de Garis Davies for the Metropolitan Museum of Art. Several objects were found in the debris, including a fine statue of Nakht. The piece was lost in a U-boat attack en route to New York in 1915.

This is a small, cruciform tomb, typical of those cut for middle-level New Kingdom bureaucrats. Nakht was such an official, a scribe and an astronomer in the Temple of Amen at Karnak, who probably was responsible for the scheduling of various cult ceremonies. The scenes in his tomb do not deal with his career, however, but with agriculture and funerary banquets, subjects of importance to his well-being in the afterlife.

There are no royal names in the tomb, but on stylistic grounds TT 52 is almost certainly contemporary with the tomb of Menna, and dates to late in the reign of Thutmes IV and early Amenhetep III.

TRANSVERSE HALL, FRONT WALL, RIGHT (WEST) SIDE On the right (west) side of the front wall, Nakht and his wife, Tawi (who was a chantress in the temple), stand before "offerings of every good and pure thing," including slaughtered cattle and well-painted baskets of grapes. Traces of a sistrum, a musical rattle associated with Hathor, are just visible in his wife's left hand, added almost as an afterthought (for reasons I will mention later). Behind and below them four registers of agricultural scenes are drawn with innovation and style.

The lower register is unusual. Instead of dividing the register in half by means of a straight, horizontal ground line, the artist has painted an undulating strip of land. Some believe this was done to provide more space for the figures; others think that it was the artist's innovative way of injecting greater realism into the scene.

Note how the ground line divides in the left half of the scene to enclose a body of water. Each year in late summer, when the Nile flood receded, it left behind large basins of water in low-lying agricultural land. Those basins covered much of the Nile Valley floor, and in the basins' muddy bottoms the Egyptian peasants sowed their crops. Here, the artist has shown the remains of such a basin, with farmers standing in the surrounding fields, up to their ankles in rich Nile silt. A field hand cuts down tamarisk and mimosa trees at the edge of the cultivation, extending the fields farther into the desert. Another has claimed wild grassland and has begun to cultivate it.

Below the meandering groundline, some men hoe fields while others break up large clods of mud with wooden mallets. Two men plow with cattle. The man on the left is having an easy time of it. But the man on the right is bent nearly double with effort as he forces the plow forward. He is shown partially bald, with unkempt hair, indications perhaps of his low status and the strain of hard work. Sacks of seed-grain sit in the field, and a farmhand has already begun sowing seeds across the muddy landscape.

Above, two girls harvest flax, while beside them farmers pack wheat into a large basket. One man jumps into the air trying to force more grain into the container. A young woman gleans in the fields, while nearby, three officials confer, trying to estimate the expected crop yield.

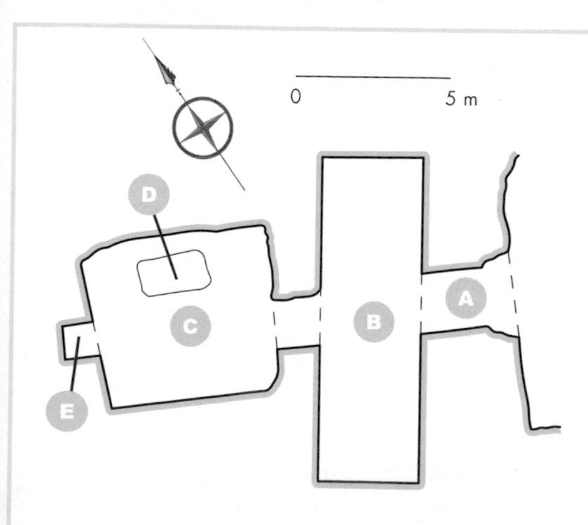

436 A MAN CUTTING TREES.

437 THE EAST END WALL (LEFT) AND THE WEST END WALL (RIGHT) OF THE TRANSVERSE HALL.

LEGEND

A *ENTRANCE*
B *TRANSVERSE HALL*
C *INNER HALL*
D *SHAFT*
E *NICHE*

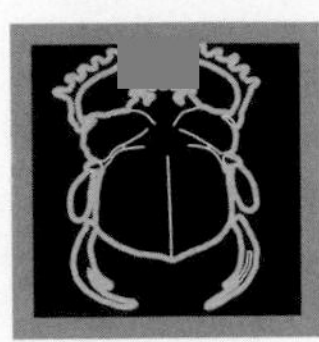

438-439 SIX WOMEN, A SERVANT GIRL, AND A HARPIST, REAR NORTH WALL, LEFT SIDE OF THE TRANSVERSE HALL.

439 BOTTOM WINNOWING SCENE FROM THE FRONT WALL, RIGHT SIDE OF THE TRANSVERSE HALL.

In the top register, Nakht sits in a kiosk, watching winnowers toss grain high into the air. The air is thick with falling grains and blowing chaff. One man carefully sweeps around the pile so not a grain is lost. The strange-looking object between figures at the top of this register is variously described as a symbol of the goddess Renenutet, "Mistress of the Threshing Floor," or a scarecrow or a corn doll (in translation from the Arabic called the "Bride of the Corn"). Below, farmers and scribes use measuring containers to determine the size of the harvest.

The left (west) end wall was completed in elaborate detail. Offering bearers stand beside a false door painted in imitation of costly red granite. Below it, figures of a tree goddess flank huge piles of foodstuffs. On either side, servants bring even more food to the ceremonies.

REAR (NORTH) WALL, LEFT (SOUTH) SIDE

Only a small part of this wall is preserved today, but the scenes that remain are justifiably considered not only the finest in Nakht's tomb but some of the most innovative in Egyptian art. Six elegantly coiffed and dressed women sit on the ground. At right, one woman sniffs a lotus flower and two others pass around pieces of fruit. As they do so, their arms gracefully overlap, creating from the individual figures a unified composition. Behind them, three bare-breasted women clutch unopened lotus flowers. A naked servant girl reaches out to straighten the curls of one of the ladies' hair. These are finely drawn figures, executed by a sure hand and with a minimum of fuss. Some believe that the cones on the women's heads are myrrh pomade; others think that they are cones of perfumed fat that would melt as the party wore on. The yellow color of the women's garments is meant to indicate that they have anointed their body with aromatic oils. In front of them, a harpist plays a six-stringed instrument, his long fingers delicately plucking the strings as he sings. The folds of fat on his abdomen and the creased skin on his neck mark him as a sedentary, overweight man of middle age. His eyes are closed, but whether this means that he is blind or simply concentrating on his music, we do not know. An element of nearly all representations of harpists is the way the sole of one foot is shown in an anatomically impossible position. The outlines of this figure were altered slightly to change the proportions of the harpist's head, neck, and torso.

In the lower register, three beautiful but oddly-proportioned women entertain the banquet guests. One plays a leopard-skin-covered harp,

the other a double flute. Both are clothed and coiffed like the guests. But a third woman, who plays a six-stringed lute, is naked and wears only a beaded belt and necklace. This is unusual, but not unknown. In Egyptian art, nude figures are usually children, but this clearly is an adult woman. Few other nude women found in New Kingdom art are lute players.

The naked musician so bothered Norman de Garis Davies, the English artist and cleric who published this tomb ninety years ago, that he devoted several hundred words trying to explain her. Davies was unwilling to believe that Egyptians could have been guilty of the "gross moral laxity" the naked figure seemed to imply. Two possibilities therefore suggested themselves. The woman was not naked in real life, Davies said, she was only drawn that way here because of misguided artistic license. Or, he said, the woman did perform nude before the guests, but the guests without doubt were all married couples who knew the musician personally and would therefore have found nothing titillating about her nakedness.

The nude dancer's head is turned to the left, and so too is her upper torso. Her breasts therefore are shown frontally. Some art historians have described her pose as a "revolutionary" development in Egyptian art, since frontal drawings of any figure are rare. But interestingly, other figures of naked lute players in Egyptian art are also drawn in this frontal manner.

At right, under Tawi's chair, the family's pet cat hungrily devours a piece of fish. The Egyptians were fond of cats and the realism here is certainly the result of first-hand observation.

440 NAKHT AND TAWI RECEIVING OFFERINGS.

440-441 AND 441 BOTTOM WINE MAKING. BIRDS HUNTING AND MEAT PRESERVATION SCENES (ABOVE); FISHING AND FOWLING SCENE.

REAR (NORTH) WALL, RIGHT (EAST) SIDE

Nakht and members of his family stand in reed skiffs, fishing and fowling. The scene is similar to that in Menna's tomb, but here the work is hasty and less detailed, and the composition rather pedestrian. Compare, for example, the treatment of birds in the two tombs. Here, the birds lack even eyes. The artist posed Nakht's arms as if the nobleman was spearing fish, but he then forgot to draw the spear. The butterflies are crudely drawn, and the water is empty of fish.

The figures of officials here are stiff, almost generic, but the servants and field hands show a much more relaxed treatment, Generally in private tombs, noblemen are more formally posed than, say, cattle herders. Indeed, the farther down the social scale one moves, the more relaxed and experimental the figures, poses, and costumes become, perhaps because the artist felt less constrained by social or religious requirements to idealize.

The scenes below are better executed. Beyond heaps of offerings and four offering bearers, two registers show various stages of winemaking and meat preservation. Both scenes are informative.

In the lower register, adjacent to a papyrus thicket at the Nile's edge—a perfect spot to hunt birds—three men hold a rope tied to a net pegged horizontally about thirty centimeters (more than a foot) above the ground. Bread crumbs have been scattered beneath it. One man's attention has been diverted, but the other two watch a compatriot concealed in the swamp nearby. As soon as enough birds have walked beneath the net, he will give a signal, the rope will be quickly yanked, the net will fall, and the birds will be trapped. The men will then wring the necks of the edible species and take them back to Nakht's estate, where the kitchen staff will preserve them. That work is shown at left. First, a man plucks their feathers, as the fellow here does with unreal daintiness. Another man, seated at a slanted table, cuts the birds open, cleans them, packs them with salt, and hangs them from a rack above his head to dry. Finally, they are packed with more salt in large pots (shown above). Similar netting and preserving techniques are still used in parts of Egypt.

Above, two men pick bunches of grapes in an arbor and put them into small baskets. One of these men, and the fellow at left dipping grape juice from the vat, have light-colored, unkempt hair, and noticeable paunches. This may be meant to tell us something about the men's social status or age.

The grapes are taken to a

crushing floor in Nakht's estate. There, in a large, shallow vat made of white-plastered mud, five men tread the grapes, holding onto ropes to maintain their balance. The grape juice flows out a drain on the right, and then is put into jars, sealed, and allowed to ferment. Four such jars stand above, each with a mud seal that would have been stamped to identify the kind of wine and its vintage.

RIGHT (EAST) END WALL On the right (east) end wall of the chamber, Nakht and Tawi receive more offerings. These scenes were never finished; in fact, many columns prepared for text were left blank. Some Egyptologists believe this is evidence that Nakht's tomb was originally carved and decorated as a generic tomb, a speculative venture by a contractor who would sell it to the highest bidder, or one of several tombs done at the same time to be assigned by the vizier to favored officials. The columns were left blank so that the tomb owner could later decide what personal data he wanted to include on them. (That may be why on the front wall Tawi's sistrum, a symbol of her role as chantress, was added after the scene was completed, when it was finally known who would be buried here.)

FRONT WALL, LEFT (EAST) SIDE The left side of the front (east) wall of the chamber shows Nakht and his wife standing before a great pile of offerings. Behind them, three registers of servants bring even more animals and produce to the scene. Note in the second register how the artist has erroneously painted a "transparent" gazelle through which you can see the servant's legs. The grid system that allowed the artist to more easily and accurately copy scenes from a draughtsman's handbook is visible across the surface of this scene.

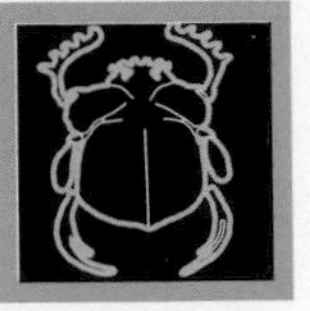

5

INTRODUCTION

RELIEF-DECORATED TOMBS FROM THE LAST DECADE OF AMENHETEP II

For much of early Dynasty 18, Egypt's administrative capital lay in the north, at Memphis. From the reign of Thutmes III onward, however, Thebes played an increasingly prominent role in civil and religious affairs. By the reign of Amenhetep III, Theban fortunes had risen so dramatically that it became a boomtown with a population of nearly 100,000. Programs of construction, artistic projects, and religious ceremonies, already large under the Thutmosids, grew even larger. Officials who would have lived in Memphis earlier in the dynasty now moved south and established their offices at Thebes.

During the last of Amenhetep III's four decades on the throne, Egypt enjoyed peace, increased commercial activity abroad and great wealth at home. Bumper crops were the norm. Temples thrived. A large bureaucracy was needed to administer this bustling society, and today we know the names of over two hundred of Amenhetep III's senior bureaucrats, a near-record number from a single reign.

Many of those officials amassed considerable power and wealth.

At least forty of them built substantial tombs at Thebes. Between regnal years 30 and 38, four officials chose to decorate their tombs in a style that had not been seen before. Their tombs shared several features in common: all were decorated with elegantly-cut raised relief, and their scenes dealt with a limited number of subjects. They had similar floor plans, and were large. In these ways and others, they differed from tombs cut before and after Amenhetep III and from contemporaneous tombs as well. Others were usually painted, not carved, and had more varied subject matter; they showed human figures less rigidly posed and less formally attired. Scholars have described this new style as "ornate" or "highly conservative," even "fussy." Whatever the term, the four tombs show what is arguably the finest relief carving of the New Kingdom. The tombs are: Surero (TT 48), Ramose (TT 55), Khaemhet (TT 57), and Kheruef (TT 192). Three of them are currently open to the public (Surero's is closed), and at least one of them should be on every tourist's "must see" list. Ramose's tomb was probably begun slightly later than Kheruef's, but it will make discussion of the three tombs clearer if we start with TT 55.

443 TOP DETAIL OF RAMOSE'S BANQUET SCENE.

443 BOTTOM PORTRAIT OF VIZIER RAMOSE.

5

TT 55: THE TOMB OF RAMOSE

THE HISTORY

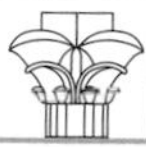

TT 55 is easily reached from a parking lot immediately behind the Ramesseum. One walks from here through a gaggle of schoolgirls selling homemade rag dolls, a herd of baby goats and donkeys, the coffee shop of a kind old man with a fine white beard, and then past an abandoned post office and a workshop selling copies of ancient reliefs, to the edge of a large pit in which the tomb was cut. Ramose was one of the few noblemen with the social and political stature to commission a tomb the size and style of TT 55. It is large, well made, elegantly decorated, and was cut into a hillside in Shaykh 'Abd al-Qurna that boasts unusually fine limestone bedrock. Ramose (his name means 'Ra is born') held some of the country's most prominent positions. He was Hereditary Nobleman, Vizier, Mayor, Superintendent of Royal Works, Judge, Overseer of Priests and Temples. He also bore scores of honorific titles, boasting that he was, among other things, a "doer of truth" and a "hater of deceit." His grandfather was a general in the army, his father the mayor of Memphis and Overseer of the Granaries of Amen, and relatives held high positions in the government. Ramose's tomb was visited in the late nineteenth century, but little of the tomb's decoration was visible because its walls lay buried beneath mounds of dirt and limestone chips. The debris was not cleared until the 1920s. But once the walls were exposed TT 55 immediately gained world-wide attention. Few Theban tombs exhibit so many different and well-executed decorative styles.

You approach TT 55 down a long staircase-ramp combination that leads to an open courtyard. This is the staircase used by ancient priests when they brought Ramose's sarcophagus to the tomb thirty-four hundred years ago. Their procession is shown in one of the tomb's paintings. A narrow doorway in the broad façade at the back of the court leads into the first chamber. The chamber is large, about 26 meters (85 feet) wide and 12 meters (39 feet) deep. Its roof was originally supported by four rows of eight squat columns, but the ceiling collapsed in antiquity and the columns you now see are either the broken originals or modern reconstructions.

The decoration in Ramose's tomb includes none of the scenes of daily life found in the tombs of other nobles from Dynasty 18.

Here, the scenes treat only two subjects: Ramose's funeral, and his relationship with the pharaoh Amenhetep IV. The scenes are masterpieces.

VISIT

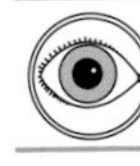

RIGHT (SOUTH) SIDE OF THE FRONT (EAST) WALL Turn left at the bottom of the stairs in the first chamber, then left again toward the front (east) wall of the room. At first you will see little, because the decoration is cut in low relief and diffuse light does not bring out its features. But look more closely and you will be transported back in time to a great funeral banquet for Ramose and his wife. Nearest the doorway, Ramose and Mery-Ptah stand before heaps of food offerings—baskets of grapes and figs, watermelons, haunches of beef, lettuce, onions, fish and fowl, beer and wine. At the right, they sit with relatives—Ramose's parents, his half-brother and nephew, his wife's father and brother—and friends, including the famous and highly important official, Amenhetep son of Hapu. The seated figures are formally, even rigidly posed, like figures in a nineteenth century photograph. But they are carved in perfect proportion and with astonishing attention to detail.

It is this detail that sets the reliefs apart. Each curl of hair, each fold of cloth, each amulet was cut in the limestone with superb

technical skill and keen aesthetic sensibilities. The modeling of the faces and their sensuous lips, the gracefully muscled arms and necks, and the perfectly styled hair offer what one scholar described as "beauty purged of all earthly blemishes." No detail was too small to be labored over. For example, look at the hieroglyphs. In a column of text near the middle of the wall stands a horse, only about five centimeters (two inches) tall. It is a tiny jewel, with perfectly modeled muscles, carefully drawn bridle and trimmed mane, an animal of beauty, power, and grace. Near it, a small basket shows the warp and weft of the woven reeds. An owl, its feathers precisely drawn, stares inscrutably from the wall. One cannot find more meticulous workmanship in Egyptian art.

The reliefs were not painted, perhaps because Ramose died prematurely, but they seem to me even more elegant for that—monochromatic idealizations of Egyptian nobility, perfectly sculpted in flawless limestone. Only the eyes have color. "Blind eyes" some have called them because of their minimalist modeling. But they are prominently outlined in black ink. Eye and eyebrow are placed on the side of the head in the characteristic Egyptian manner that defies anatomical truth but nevertheless achieves artistic clarity. The eye was a potent magical symbol in Egyptian culture, which is why it was singled out for such emphasis.

LEFT (NORTH) SIDE OF THE FRONT (WEST) WALL Left (north) of the doorway are equally fine reliefs, but by different hands, and more figures and heaps of offerings are added to the funerary activities. A figure, perhaps a statue, of Ramose stands in the middle of the wall. Two priests pour streams of purifying water over him. Here, too, Ramose's hair and face are beautifully executed. He wears the simple, unpleated vizier's robe that emphasizes the elaborate necklaces around his neck and the heart-shaped amulet that hangs from a long string of gold beads.

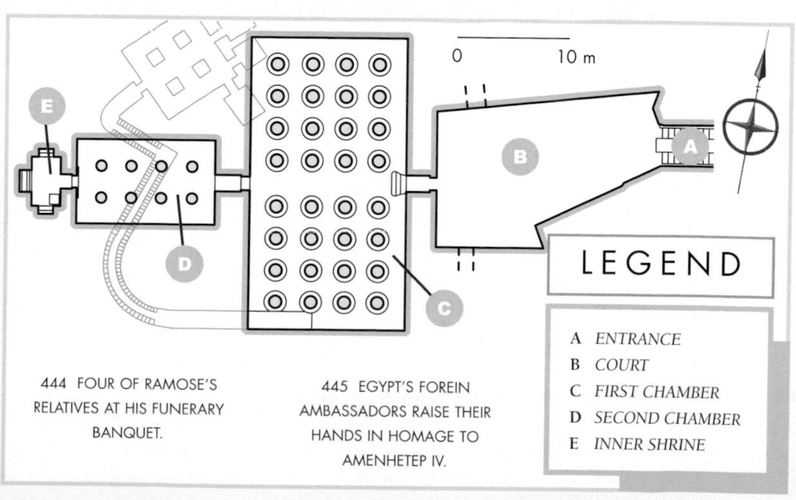

444 FOUR OF RAMOSE'S RELATIVES AT HIS FUNERARY BANQUET.

445 EGYPT'S FOREIN AMBASSADORS RAISE THEIR HANDS IN HOMAGE TO AMENHETEP IV.

446 TOP VIEW OF THE FIRST CHAMBER, WITH RAMOSE'S FUNERAL SCENES.

446 BOTTOM ATTENDANTS CARRYING FURNITURE FOR RAMOSE'S AFTERLIFE.

447 MOURNERS AT RAMOSE'S FUNERAL.

LEFT (SOUTH) WALL

To my mind, the most impressive scenes in TT 55 are those on the left (south) wall showing Ramose's funeral procession. This was the last wall of the tomb to be decorated, and the only one to be painted. The work was done in two stages: the left third of the wall was originally carved, then painted; the remaining two-thirds were painted only, probably so that the tomb decoration could be finished quickly after Ramose's unexpected death. Unlike the formal scenes we have just examined, these are ironically lively scenes of death. Different artists decorated this wall, and they chose a new style anticipating the art of the Amarna period rather than the more conservative style used earlier. One of these new-style artists is shown here, a rare thing in a society whose craftsmen usually remained anonymous. His name is Simut, and he stands far left on the wall, fourth in the line of priests following Ramose's bier.

In the **UPPER REGISTER**, the funeral procession moves toward Ramose's tomb. Appropriately, the scene lies immediately beside a steep ramp that leads beneath the floor to his burial chamber, 16 meters (51 feet) below. In this scene, Ramose's viscera and body have been embalmed and enshrined. They are pulled on sledges, "so that he may have rest and so that his mummy may thrive forever and ever to eternity" the text states. Ahead of them, a large, black lump lies on a small sledge pulled by four men. Exactly what this may be is unclear. It was called the *tekenu* in Egyptian, a word of uncertain meaning. Some believe it is a crouching man wrapped in a black cloth; they point to what could be his feet sticking out the back, and explain that such a figure recalls an earlier time when a servant was killed and buried with his master to attend him in the afterlife. In the New Kingdom, when such ritual murder was no longer practiced, a servant in a shroud was taken to the tomb then set free. It has also been suggested that the sledge is carrying Ramose's placenta, carefully saved since birth and buried with him. As the bier moves toward the tomb, several groups of people walk

beside it. They are shown in the lower register, implying that they stand between us and the bier.

At right, before the entrance to the tomb, mummies of Ramose and Mery-Ptah are purified with water while a second priest censes piles of food offerings. Rows of offering bearers carry foodstuffs, furniture, chairs, caskets, and vessels of metal and clay to be placed in the tomb for use in the afterlife. As groups of mourning women and naked girls watch the procession, they pour dust on their hair, wail, and ululate. Tears and make-up run down their cheeks. Instead of the sure, graceful lines that define the perfectly pressed costumes of others on this wall, the mourners wear dresses that are wrinkled and unkempt.

Ramose's servants file past. Note how their skin color alternates between light brown and dark to make each figure distinct. That is not a feature of the groups of lighter-skinned mourning women, however; their individuality is ensured only by the inked outline of their bodies. A group of well-dressed officials walks behind. Above them, a text proudly states that they are "following in the procession of one who has the approval and love of the Lord of Egypt."

These scenes are among Egypt's most emotive representations. The communal sense of bereavement, together with the individuality of the mourner's emotional responses, captures the personal and social loss felt by Ramose's family and by Egyptian society. But there is also here an upbeat attitude toward death. Look at the men who carry Ramose's bed on their shoulders. One of them is walking too slowly to suit his companion, and in the adjacent text the companion complains, "Get going! Walk faster!" In Upper Egypt today, villagers tell me that, as a good man will surely go to heaven, therefore he will want his funeral cortege to move quickly so he can join God that much sooner. I have often seen processions at Luxor marching quick time to the cemetery. In Ramose's funeral procession, the mourners set a good pace. They know that this good man will soon be welcomed by the gods.

REAR (WEST) WALL

Ramose attained the office of vizier late in the reign of Amenhetep III, but the king with whom he is shown in TT 55 is Amenhetep III's son and successor, Amenhetep IV, later to be called Akhenaten. Amenhetep IV is shown on the rear (west) wall of this chamber, in two contrasting scenes that flank the central doorway. On the left (south) side, Amenhetep IV is shown as an idealized Egyptian pharaoh in traditional royal pose, seated in a kiosk with the goddess Ma'at, wearing conventional royal costume. Before the kiosk, four scenes feature Ramose. In each, he wears a different costume and plays a different bureaucratic role.

To the right (north) of the door, Amenhetep IV has adopted the physical features, but not yet the name, of Akhenaten. He stands in a window of appearance with his wife, Nefertiti. Their pear-shaped bodies, thin limbs, and elongated skulls are dramatically different from the traditional figures to the left of the doorway. The king's elaborately pleated costume sags below his protruding belly, and his lens-shaped navel is prominently drawn. These are early versions of the Amarna style that will characterize royal representations for the remainder of Akhenaten's reign.

Above the pharaoh and his wife, a solar disk sends forth rays of light that end in small hands. Some hands embrace Akhenaten and Nefertiti; others offer them symbols of life and happiness. Before the royal couple stands Ramose, arms in the air in an attitude of jubilation, receiving necklaces and other rewards from his king. Ramose, too, is carved in the Amarna style. The men who dress him bow slightly in a pose peculiar to that art. Further right, Ramose accepts the cheers of crowds of royal subjects as he turns to greet foreign ambassadors. They include four Nubians, two western Asiatics, and a Libyan, each group identifiable by hairstyle, facial features, and dress.

The contrast between the two halves of this rear wall could not be more striking. In the space of only three or four years dramatic changes had taken place in Egyptian art, and this juxtaposition of the two styles shows how remarkable they were, from the outset. It would be fascinating to know how Ramose's career was affected by this "revolution." Was he the consummate bureaucrat, capable of adapting to whatever a new pharaoh might impose? Or were political changes not yet dramatic enough to pose issues other than those of artistic representation? There is no certain evidence that Ramose moved from Thebes to Akhetaten (Tall al-Amarna), Akhenaten's new capital, as did many other court officials. All we can say for certain is that he died early in Amenhetep IV's reign, before the rear wall of TT 55 was completed. No children survived him.

448 RAMOSE'S ATTENDANTS WITH OFFERINGS OF VEGETABLES, FLOWERS AND FOWL.

449 TOP THE GATE FROM THE FIRST TO THE SECOND CHAMBER.

449 BOTTOM LEFT A MEMBER OF RAMOSE'S HOUSEHOLD STAFF.

449 BOTTOM RIGHT A PRIEST BRINGS TWO VASES TO RAMOSE.

5

TT 192: THE TOMB OF KHERUEF

THE HISTORY

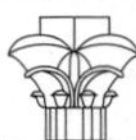

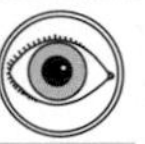

The tomb of Kheruef also boasts the highest quality relief carving. It is of the same date and decorated in the same style as that of Ramose. It is the largest Dynasty 18 noble's tomb to have been cut at Thebes, and confirms that Kheruef was a wealthy and powerful court official. But Kheruef's tomb is seldom visited today; that of Ramose is by far the more popular, to a large extent because it lies on an easily accessible hillside close by the main road. Kheruef's tomb is awkwardly located beside a narrow dirt track that tour buses cannot navigate. Much of it is in poor condition: its roof collapsed in antiquity and parts of the decoration were hacked out after the Amarna Period. The tomb was first visited by Europeans in 1886, and many travelers and scholars since then have described how it has continued to suffer. As recently as the 1940s, thieves hacked out pieces from its walls. However, what remains of the decoration is rightly considered among the finest examples of New Kingdom relief, and the tomb is well worth a visit. Kheruef's tomb, like that of Ramose, is decorated in a conservative style. Kheruef himself acknowledged that there was deliberate archaizing in the selection of scenes and texts, and he proudly states that, "It was His Majesty who did this in accordance with the writings of old. Past generations of people since the time of ancestors had never celebrated such rites..."

TT 192 was cut into the side of a large, irregular pit in the rugged floor of a part of the Theban Necropolis called the 'Assasif. It lies a few hundred meters east of Dayr al-Bahari, near Metropolitan House, the grandly domed mudbrick building that served as headquarters for New York's Metropolitan Museum of Art Egyptian Expedition in the 1920s and 1930s. The tomb can be difficult to find, but there are several guardhouses nearby where you can ask directions. Bring a flashlight with you, as there is no light in the tomb apart from what the guard can reflect inside with a broken mirror.

VISIT

ENTRANCE Originally, a staircase and ramp sloped down to the tomb's entrance on the east side of the open pit. But the staircase has never been excavated, and today you descend modern steps that lead to a short corridor.

Kheruef (who at birth was called Naa) was the son of an army scribe and a chantress in the temple of Amen. By the time he died, shortly after the death of Amenhetep III, he had risen to become Prince, High Official, Overseer of the Palace of the Great Royal Wife Tiy, Royal Scribe, and Seal Bearer of the King in Upper Egypt. His principal responsibility, and certainly the one in which he took most pride, was organizing the king's *Sed*-festivals in regnal years 30 and 37.

The *Sed*-Festival, a ceremony of royal rejuvenation and renewal, was an important milestone in a king's reign. It was a major event that involved thousands of people all over the country. There were scores of religious activities, ceremonies with banquets, music, dancing, processions, and official

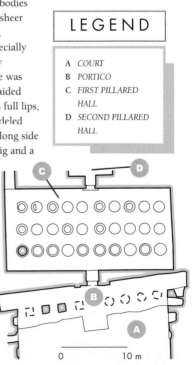

events. Huge buildings were erected for its celebration. For Amenhetep III's year 30 *Sed*-festival, a harbor was dug beside the royal palace in Malqata at the southern end of Thebes. It was one of the largest engineering projects ever undertaken in ancient Egypt, and was further enlarged for the king's later festivals (one in year 34, another in year 37). Over fifteen million cubic meters of silt had to be dug out and carted away. Kheruef was probably in charge of these operations, and he discusses the *Sed*-festivals of years 30 and 37 in his tomb's decoration. A text in the portico describes how Amenhetep III and Queen Tiy were rowed across the harbor during the festival rituals. (No mention is made of the festival held in year 34.)

PORTICO Across the open courtyard lies the entrance to what is today Kheruef's principal tomb chamber. Originally, this was a portico with pillars along its facade, but it was walled up in 1943 to protect the reliefs on its rear (west) wall.

Scenes from the king's year 30 *Sed*-festival cover the left (south) side of this wall, and scenes of the year 37 festival decorate the right (north). Left (south) of the doorway, Amenhetep III, Hathor, and Queen Tiy watch as eight princesses (the texts identify them as foreigners) present vessels of gold and electrum. The beautiful, youthful bodies are visible through sheer dresses, and ankles, abdomens, and especially faces are exquisitely modeled. Great care was taken with their braided hair, their sensuous full lips, and elaborately modeled eyes. Each wears a long side lock over a short wig and a small headdress. There is even more detail here than in the banqueting scenes in Ramose's tomb. The great emphasis given to the long, carefully brushed and meticulously braided hair, by the way, identifies these figures with the goddess Hathor, who was known for her lush, jet-black hair.

LEGEND

A *COURT*
B *PORTICO*
C *FIRST PILLARED HALL*
D *SECOND PILLARED HALL*

450 AMENHETEP III, FROM THE DOORWAY TO THE FIRST PILLARED HALL.

451 LEFT OSIRIS, HATHOR AND MA'AT IN A SHRINE.

451 RIGHT OFFERINGS OF FOOD, FLOWERS AND GOLD.

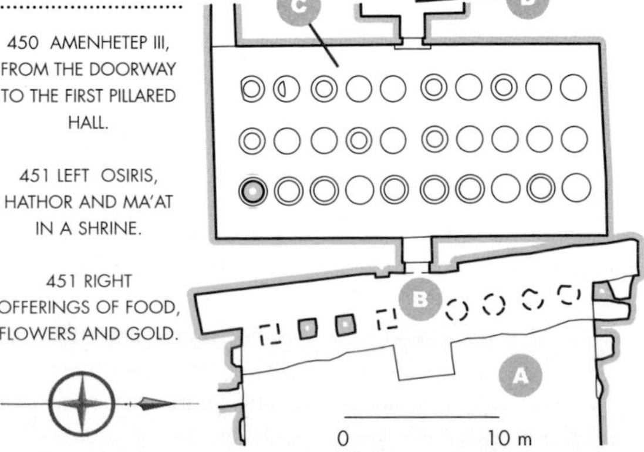

Behind stand more examples of feminine beauty: acrobatic dancers bend low, their long intricately braided hair almost touching the ground as they execute elaborate steps accompanied by flautists, singers and clapping women. Their long fingers curve in a manner that foretells the style of the Amarna Period. Egyptologists and art historians have commented on the stiffness of these dancing figures and their lack of individuality, and it is true that they show a degree of conservatism, in marked contrast to the vibrant, almost erotic figures in the earlier tombs of Menna, Nakht, and, especially Rekhmire.

To the right of the doorway, Amenhetep III and Queen Tiy sit watching the performances of more dancers, this time nearly all male. To the right, in a large upper register, the king helps erect a *djed*-pillar, a potent symbol of royal endurance and resurrection and rebirth of the land. In the register below, men perform a stick dance similar to those performed in Egyptian villages today. In the bottom register, herdsmen lead cattle and donkeys. Some of the men have receding hairlines. Such scenes—herdsmen with unusual features and rows of dancers stylistically reminiscent of the Old Kingdom—are further examples of the archaizing tendencies in Kheruef's tomb.

The doorway in the center of this wall has elaborate raised relief hieroglyphs on its left jamb. Note especially the detailed goose, the figure of the goddess Ma'at, and various snakes and birds. Beyond the door, broken columns are all that remain of the original hall, which apparently collapsed even as the tomb was being cut.

ENTRANCE (AGAIN)

Walk back to the entrance corridor of the tomb. There is a fascinating scene here, but it is badly damaged.

The south wall of the entrance corridor, now on your right, between the doorway to TT 194 and an iron gate, is badly hacked up and covered with a thick layer of soot and grime. The scene here was so badly damaged that, until the 1950s, no one realized it held any interest. However, when the University of Chicago's Epigraphic Survey began to record the decoration in TT 192, their artists and epigraphers spent literally hundreds of hours staring at the remaining traces on this wall. Only a fraction of the original carving was visible, but by observing it in different light and working as much like cryptographers as Egyptologists, the team was able to reconstruct the original. In 1980, the Survey finally produced two drawings. One showed only what was originally visible on the wall. A second showed what they could reconstruct. The differences between the two drawings are a tribute to the patience and skill of the team.

In the scene, Amenhetep IV pays homage to the god Ra-Harakhty. There is a large pile of food offerings before the king, and above it what was once a large, square, now blackened and almost destroyed. It is divided into smaller squares, each measuring about 2 centimeters (1 inch) on a side. There are 13 squares top to bottom, 14 left to right, a total of 182. Each square contains a single hieroglyphic

word, arranged to form two texts, one of which is read in vertical columns from left to right, the other in horizontal lines from top to bottom. For example, the top line of the word square reads: "Adoration of Amen-Ra, the divine god, beloved one...by the Perfect God, Neferkheperura, the Son of Ra, Amenhetep, Ruler of Thebes: Hail to you...". The leftmost column reads: "Adoration of Ra-Harakhty, the good spokesman of the gods, by the Perfect God, the Son of Ra, Amenhetep, Ruler of Thebes: Hail to you..." The texts continue with more effusive praise of king and god.

Puzzle-like "word squares" similar to this have been found in other tombs and in New Kingdom temples. Such cryptographic texts were apparently intended to impress ancient visitors with the mysteries of religion and emphasize the magical powers of the written word.

Much of the damage to TT 192 occurred shortly after the death of Amenhetep IV, when Egyptians sought to erase any memory of him and the changes he wrought in religion and politics. The word square was defaced then, as were references to the king. Figures of Kheruef were also hacked out, perhaps because he was too conspicuously allied with the new pharaoh and his "heretical" beliefs.

There are two other unlit tombs nearby that you can also visit. They are not officially on the list of open tombs, but they are accessible. But take care: both have open shafts, some of them 10 meters (33 feet) deep, that pierce the floors of the pitch black chambers. One slip can mean serious injury. Walk cautiously and always stay with the guard or a companion.

Off the corridor on your left as you enter the courtyard of Kheruef's tomb lies the entrance to TT 194, the Dynasty 19 tomb of Djehuty-em-Heb, an overseer of marsh dwellers and a scribe in the temple of Amen. On the left (east) wall just inside the entrance, he is shown standing in adoration before several gods.

On the right side of the Kheruef corridor lies TT 189, the tomb of Djehuty-Nakht, an overseer of carpenters and goldworkers in the Temple of Amen. The tomb has several damaged but decorated chambers, one of them filled with New Kingdom pottery. This is a labyrinth of cut and broken rooms, and its complex plan and unfinished state give an idea of how ancient quarrymen worked in a necropolis that had become crowded with tombs by the reign of Rameses II, when TT 189 was cut.

452 LEFT DANCERS AT AMENHETEP'S JUBILEE.

452 RIGHT AMENHETEP III AND HIS WIFE TIY WATCHING DANCERS PERFORM.

453 TOP DAUGHTERS OF AMENHETEP III WITH OFFERINGS.

453 BOTTOM A MONKEY AND A CALF AT THE HEAD OF THE DANCERS' REGISTER.

5

TT 57: THE TOMB OF KHAEMHET

THE HISTORY

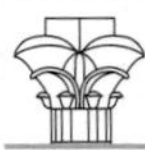

The third of the relief-decorated tombs from late in the reign of Amenhetep III (and early in the reign of Amenhetep IV) was prepared in a style similar to Ramose and Kheruef but the figures are less fussily carved. Of special interest are additions that Khaemhet made to the narrow range of subjects found in other tombs of this period. For example, he added scenes that deal with his career as Overseer of the Granaries of Upper and Lower Egypt, and Royal Scribe. Khaemhet's tomb was discovered in 1842. It had already suffered badly and continued to do so for another century. For many years, locals lived in it and their fires blackened its walls with smoke and soot. Attempts at cleaning were made by Sir Robert Mond in the early 1900s—"scrubbing with soap, water and elbow grease," he boasted—but that did more harm than good and removed whatever paint still remained on the wall. Early Egyptologists made squeezes of the wall relief, damaging them further, and pieces of decorated walls were hacked out in the nineteenth century and shipped to European museums. Nevertheless, the tomb is still worth a visit, both because of the fine quality of its reliefs and the range of its scenes.

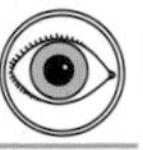

VISIT

The tomb lies on the west side of a small courtyard cut into bedrock 50 meters (150 feet) or so south of the tomb of Ramose, TT 55. Inside the **FIRST CHAMBER**, left (south) of the doorway on the front (east) wall, Khaemhet stands to receive offerings. Farther along, he presents offerings to the Lady of the Granaries, the goddess Renenutet (known to the Greeks as Termuthis), who nurses the young pharaoh. Khaemhet's hair and the collar and necklaces around his neck are meticulously carved. His hands are finely shaped, the nails well manicured. The work is done in the same conservative style as in the

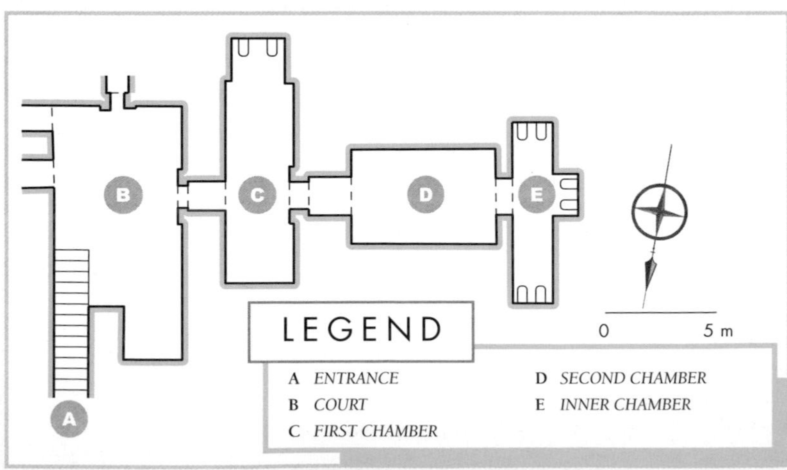

tombs of Ramose and Kheruef, but there is less modeling of facial features and musculature, and in contrast to those other noblemen, the figures of Khaemhet seem soft and less athletic.

Most of this wall has been destroyed, but at the right (south) end, in the lower register, you can still see transport ships unloading wheat at the port of Thebes. Some of the twisted ropes in the rigging are carved in great detail, even showing the knots. The handles of long oars end in finely carved heads of the king. Nearby, longshoremen unload cargo for delivery to temple warehouses and perhaps to the market shown nearby.

454 TOP PROFILE OF KHAEMHET.

455 TOP DOORWAY INTO THE FIRST CHAMBER.

455 BOTTOM THE LADY OF THE GRANARIES NURSES THE YOUNG PHARAOH.

Behind you, at the left (south) end of the rear (west) wall of the chamber, scribes drive bulls to be tallied and presented to Amenhetep III. The animals are extremely fat (note how the skin on the back of their neck lies in folds), their legs unusually short, and they stand just tall enough that their heads reach the waists of the herdsmen. To the right, Khaemhet reports to Amenhetep III on the status of the many projects he was responsible for. Beneath the chairs of the king and his wife are figures of bound Nubian and Asiatic captives. On the other side of the doorway, Khaemhet and his aides stand before Amenhetep III, and in the upper register, the king presents him with a gold necklace.

The most elaborate scenes lie at the left end of the front (east) wall. They are more restrained versions of painted scenes in the tomb of Menna. A comparison between the two will show how greatly conservative decoration late in Amenhetep III's reign differed from the more relaxed style of the first decade of his reign. Here, in six registers, we watch Khaemhet's workmen ploughing, threshing, winnowing, and tabulating the grain harvest. Note the kneeling man in the second register from the bottom, drinking from a water skin tied to the branch of a tree (far left), and the elaborately carved folding stool on which Khaemhet sits (at right). In the third register, a man jumps into the air trying to force more grain into an already full basket. He wears well-made sandals, an unusual touch since everyone else in the scene is barefoot. Left of this vignette, in a half-register, a lone man sits and plays a double flute, his music perhaps intended to spur on the workmen.

In the fourth register, two horses, their bridles carefully carved, are harnessed to chariots. One horse reaches

456 PROFILE OF AMENHEMHET III.

457 TOP LEFT THREE COURTIERS WITH CONES OF UNGUENT ON THEIR HEAD.

457 TOP RIGHT DUCK OFFERING FOR RENENUTET, THE LADY OF THE GRANARIES.

457 BOTTOM FATTED COWS AND OFFERINGS BROUGHT BEFORE KHAEMHET.

down to eat from a bowl of grain, his taut muscles drawn with great accuracy. The horses' manes are carefully clipped, their tails well brushed. The charioteer is asleep, and so is the man at left seated beneath a tree. Four other horses and chariots appear in the fifth register. Scenes such as this first appear in the New Kingdom. The horse and chariot were introduced into Egypt only two centuries earlier, and the animal appeared more often in military scenes on temple walls than in private tombs. Egypt's geographical conditions were such that the horse was used primarily in the desert for military transport, not as a beast of burden in the Nile Valley. In the fifth register, Khaemhet supervises the felling of trees. Trees were a rare and valuable commodity in ancient Egypt, and to harvest one required permission from the highest civil authority, the vizier.

In the upper register, Khaemhet supervises teams of men surveying property boundaries. These often had to be re-checked every year because the annual Nile flood destroyed or moved the markers, and land disputes were among the common legal problems of ancient Egypt. The knotted rope the men carry was used for measuring field dimensions.

The **SECOND CHAMBER** of TT 57 is almost completely destroyed. Originally, several chapters of the Book of the Dead were carved on the walls and in the doorway leading into the next chamber. Such emphasis on religious texts is unusual in a nobleman's tomb.

Three pairs of statues were cut into niches in the **INNER CHAMBER,** one of Khaemhet and his wife, another of Khaemhet and an unknown woman, the third of Khaemhet and the Royal Scribe, Imhotep, a close friend. (Imhotep is also seated with Khaemhet in a fourth statue pair in the tomb's first chamber.)

Copies of a Dynasty 5 offering list were carved beside each of the four statue pairs.

A plaster cast of a relief of Khaemhet has been mounted on the front wall of the inner chamber. The original, cut away in the nineteenth century, is now in the Egyptian Museum, Berlin.

458 TOP KHAEMHET (RIGHT) HOLDING AN OFFERING OF DUCKS, AND SIX REGISTERS OF FIELD WORKERS, FROM THE FIRST CHAMBER.

458 BOTTOM FOUR HORSES HARNESSED TO CHARIOTS, FIRST CHAMBER.

459 TOP LEFT AN OVERSEER GIVES THE TALL TO A SCRIBE, FIRST CHAMBER.

459 CENTER LEFT TWO MEN LOAD A BASKET, FIRST CHAMBER.

459 TOP RIGHT STATUE OF KHAEMHET IN THE INNER CHAMBER.

459 BOTTOM KHAEMHET'S MEN PLOUGHING AND THRESHING, FIRST CHAMBER.

5

INTRODUCTION

TOMBS OF DYNASTIES 19 AND 20

Often regarded as inferior to the tomb paintings earlier in the New Kingdom, Ramesside tombs at Thebes are demeaned for their flat colors and heavily outlined figures. But in fact there is considerable variation in these paintings and some are well-done, with interesting and even amusing features. Scenes of gardens and agricultural activity (as in the tomb of Sennedjem) are lush and filled with detail. Birds and animals are drawn with great regard for accuracy. Yet in these same scenes, human figures can be almost cartoon-like, hastily drawn, with legs far too long for their thin bodies, and costumes and jewelry elaborate to the point of being kitschy. While some scenes show great individuality and imaginativeness, others place such a heavy emphasis upon religious subjects they seem to stifle the artist's willingness to move beyond formal conventions. Both ends of the spectrum can be seen in the Dira' Abu al-Naja tombs of Roy and Shuroy. The former is well-painted, with many fascinating and innovative details. The latter gives the impression of hasty, unimaginative, and even careless work.

5

TT 255: THE TOMB OF ROY

THE HISTORY

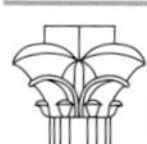

Two tombs on the hill known as Dra' 'Abu al-Naja at the northern end of the Theban Necropolis have recently been opened to the public. Of the two, that of Roy is the most interesting (the other is TT 13: Shuroy). It is a small tomb, only a single chamber that measures 1.85 by 4 meters (6 by 13 feet). Its beautifully painted ceiling, decorated with geometric patterns, is lower than an average person's height, low enough that it is likely to be destroyed by tourists who frequently bang their heads on its plastered surface.

The tomb belonged to Roy, a royal scribe and steward in the estates of king Horemheb and the Temple of Amen, and to his wife Nebtawy. It dates to late Dynasty 18-early Dynasty 19. The decoration treats with Roy's funeral in an informal style that is more reminiscent of rapidly-drawn sketches than the idealized and formal funerary style of, say, Ramose's tomb.

VISIT

461 VIEW OF THE TOMB OF ROY FROM THE ENTRANCE.

LEGEND

A *ENTRANCE*
B *CHAMBER*
C *SHAFT*

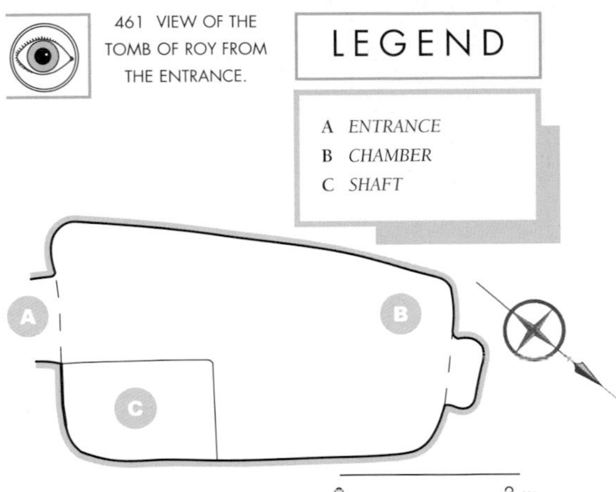

FRONT WALL Four registers are painted on the right side of the front wall. At the top, a servant leads a young cow and brings jars sealed with leaves before Roy and his wife. In the second register, an unusual scene shows two cattle, one white, one brown, passing each other in opposite directions while plowing a field. The cattle themselves are elongated and stick-like, but the composition is imaginative. To their left, a man stands with a child, and above them is a crudely drawn tree, perhaps a sycamore fig, in whose branches a water bottle and a lunch basket have been tied. In the third register, a laborer ploughs a field. Behind him, another man sows seed. Above these figures, a young boy stands next to a tree, apparently drinking from the water bottle. In the bottom register, a foreman in a white gown leans on a staff, supervising a woman and two men harvesting flax. The scene is now largely destroyed.

LEFT WALL In the upper register five scenes from the Book of Gates are painted in a style that contrasts markedly with that in TT 13: Shuroy. At left, the overseer of the royal granary, Amenemope and his wife Tai stand in adoration before a shrine housing Ma'at and Nefertum. To their right, Roy and his wife stand before Hathor and Ra-Harakhty, making food offerings. Next, the deceased couple—she holding a sistrum and a roll of papyrus—stands before the Ennead. Much of this scene has been destroyed. At right, Horus leads Roy and his wife before a balance on which two Ma'at statuettes perfectly balance their two hearts.

Such paired hearts and Ma'at symbols are not unknown, but they are not common. Anubis and Thoth record the favorable judgment. Finally, the couple is presented by Horus-son-of-Isis to the god Osiris, who sits in an elaborately painted naos. Roy is wearing a heart amulet around his neck. Note how the string from which it is suspended has been incorrectly drawn, as if his right arm were caught within it. In front of Osiris stand the four Sons of Horus, emerging from a lotus blossom. Behind the god are two goddesses, probably Isis and Nephthys.

In the lower register, Roy's funeral moves forward. The representations are standard ones, but they are well-painted and the details of the mourners' faces show variety and emotion. It is worth comparing these scenes with the more elaborate funeral procession in TT 55, the tomb of Ramose, which was painted about thirty years earlier. At left, four officials, friends of the deceased, stand with their hands to their mouth. A woman kneels below a casket with the jackal-god Anubis atop it. Eight women, dressed in mourning, precede it. Roy's coffin is pulled on a sledge being censed by Thutmes, Roy's servant, who wears the panther skin of a *sem*-priest. Men drive forward the four cattle that pull the sled. At right, six women and eight men are shown in mourning and they are preceded by a row of officials, now badly destroyed, two of whom make an offering of water. Note that one of the men, clearly the eldest of the group, is shown with white hair. At right, the mummy of Roy stands upright as a priest wearing a mask of Anubis prays for it and Roy's wife kneels, weeping, at its feet. The destination of this procession, Roy's tomb, stands at the far right, a pyramid-topped structure built before the slopes of the Mountain of the West.

Across the top of this wall (and repeated, but without text, on the right wall) runs a frieze of an Anubis-topped chapel, faces of Hathor, double *kheker* friezes, and double columns of text, repeated six times, in very well preserved colors.

462-463 THE LEFT WALL OF THE TOMB OF ROY AND DETAIL.

REAR WALL Much is destroyed here; the painted plaster was applied in a thick coat on rough-cut bedrock and it has fallen to the floor because of its wieght. Scenes of adoration show the deceased before figures of the king's wife, who holds two sistra before the god Osiris. At bottom left, a few traces remain of Hathor as Lady of the Sycamore emerging from her sacred tree before Roy and his *ba*. Above, Roy stands before an offering table piled with various kinds of bread, and Amenhetep I and his mother, Ahmes-Nefertari stand in adoration and offer bouquets before Anubis.

RIGHT WALL At left, Roy and his wife sit and receive offerings from a *sem*-priest. An offering table stands between them. Behind the priest, two female mourners accompany two caskets. Farther right, Roy and his wife again are seated to receive further offerings including a platter covered by a huge and elaborately-made cover of reeds and flowers. Behind, Roy's parents sit in an upper sub-register; other unnamed relatives sit in the lower.

It is interesting that many scenes in this tomb have red-painted columns laid out to receive text but have no text written in them. Some speculate this indicates either that the tomb owner died suddenly before the walls could be completely inscribed, or that tombs such as this were cut and decorated on speculation and the names and titles of their eventual occupants were added later, after the purchase agreement was signed.

At the right end of the wall, Roy sits on a chair with his wife on an elaborate cushion before a priest and two mourners. There is a large hole in the wall here, perhaps where a piece of chert fell from the surrounding limestone or where a wooden beam was installed to help lower a sarcophagus down the shaft in the floor in front of it. Instead of filling in the hole with plaster, the ancient artist covered its surface with a thin plaster on which he then painted bunches of grapes. This is similar to the technique used on the ceiling of TT 96, the tomb of Sennefer.

5

TT 3: THE TOMB OF PASHEDU

THE HISTORY

Of the three tombs at Dayr al-Madina currently open to the public (TT 1: Sennedjem, TT 3: Pashedu, and TT 359: Inherkhau), that of Pashedu is both the most beautifully decorated and the least visited. Tourists are often kept away by their tour guide: the tomb lies about 50 meters (150 feet) up the hill from Dayr al-Madina Village and they are reluctant to spend the extra few minutes needed for the visit. The tomb's entrance is also awkward to navigate: twenty-nine narrow steps descend steeply into the bedrock, leading to a tiny antechamber and a single small vaulted room. Nevertheless, the tomb should be one of the must-see destinations in the Theban Necropolis.

We know little of Pashedu except from the texts in his tomb.

He lived at Dayr al-Madina during the reigns of Sety I and Rameses II and was a Servant in the Place of Truth on the West of Thebes. His specialty was stone masonry, which is to say he was responsible for digging the royal tombs in the Valley of the Kings, overseeing their cutting with chert hand axes to create corridors, chambers, and pillared halls.

Pashedu's tomb was apparently discovered in 1834 during illicit digging by Egyptian army draftees. Shortly thereafter, it was visited by the Scottish artist, Robert Hay, who recorded its decorated walls.

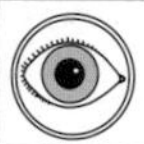

VISIT

The **BURIAL CHAMBER** is entered through a short, vaulted passage at the bottom of the entrance stairs. The side walls of the passage are beautifully painted with Anubis jackals that lie atop large white chapels with cavetto cornices. The jackals have short snouts, a cloth wrapped around their necks, and a flail above their haunches. The background is an elaborate and meticulously painted cloth or mat pattern.

464 TOP PASHEDU'S RELATIVES, TO THE LEFT OF THE ENTRANCE.

464 BOTTOM THE GOD PTAH-SOKAR-OSIRIS IN THE FORM OF A FALCON, ABOVE THE DOORWAY.

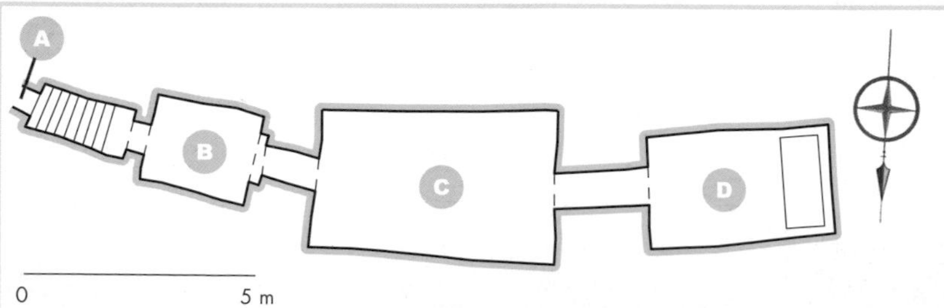

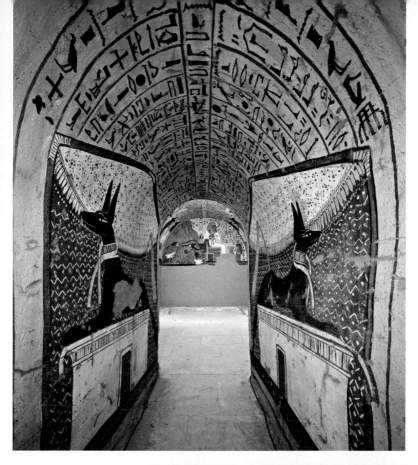

465 TOP DOORWAY INTO THE INNERMOST CHAMBER, WITH TWO ANUBIS FIGURES ON SHRINES.

465 BOTTOM PASHEDU AND HIS DAUGHTER STAND BEFORE RA-HARAKHTY, RIGHT WALL.

LEGEND

- A *ENTRANCE*
- B *FIRST BURIAL CHAMBER*
- C *SECOND BURIAL CHAMBER*
- D *INNERMOST BURIAL CHAMBER*

Above the doorway in the burial chamber, the god Ptah-Sokar-Osiris is shown as a falcon. His elaborately painted wings (of unequal size) stretch out below a *wedjat*-eye and short columns of text. His stylized body, drawn with smoothly curving lines, sits on a simple boat. At right, one of Pashedu's sons, Kaha, kneels before the god. At left, another son, Menna, kneels before gods depicted on the chamber's vaulted ceiling.

On the right side of the door, three registers show various members of Pashedu's family. In the top register, four men and one woman face right in poses of adoration. These are Pashedu's father, Menna, and mother, Huy, a colleague named Nefersekheru, and two sons. Pashedu's father has snow-white hair, an unusual but not unknown feature in tomb paintings of this period. In the middle register, Pashedu's mother- and father-in-law (the parents of his wife, Nedjem-Behdet) stand with four female relatives of the wife's family: three sisters, and at far left, a niece. The parents and a relative are shown with salt-and-pepper hair (perhaps an attempt to show that Nedjem-Behdet's parents were somewhat younger than Pashedu's). In the lower register, five of Pashedu's sons and daughters stand, honoring their parents. All the figures on this wall have white fingernails and wear elaborately pleated costumes, and all but one wear long and elaborately coiffed hair.

In the upper register immediately to the right of the door. a tiny drawing of a tree goddess fills the space beside the vaulted entry passage. It is a delightfully drawn sycamore fig tree standing next to a rectangular pond. In its branches the goddess Nut pours out a libation for Pashedu, and the water can be seen falling onto his body. He kneels at left on the edge of the vault. At the lower right, his wife stands in adoration.

On the chamber's left wall, Pashedu, his wife, son, and granddaughter stand facing a rather squat but nicely detailed Horus falcon. Fifty columns of text, written in black ink, are taken from chapter 78 of the Book of the Dead. This is the Formula for Being Transformed into a Divine Falcon. Note how the long hair of Nedjem-Behdet at the far left end of the wall has spilled over onto the adjacent front wall. She is elegantly decked out in jewelry and fine linen and there is a cone of scented fat on her head. At the far right end of the wall, the couple sits before an offering table in a small boat, with one of their daughters. This scene is repeated on the wall opposite.

466-467 BURIAL CHAMBER LOOKING TOWARD ITS ENTRANCE.

467 TOP PASHEDU, HIS WIFE, SON AND GRANDDAUGHTER.

467 CENTER PASHEDU RECEIVES A LIBATION FROM THE GODDESS NUT.

467 BOTTOM THREE OF PASHEDU'S SONS AND DAUGHTERS FROM THE LEFT WALL.

468 TOP THE REAR WALL WITH OSIRIS ON A THRONE.

468 BOTTOM PASHEDU AND HIS WIFE ON A BOAT OF THE ABYDOS PILGRIMAGE.

469 EIGHT OF THE SIXTEEN DEITIES ON THE CEILING OF THE INNERMOST CHAMBER.

On the rear wall of the chamber, Osiris wears a *nemes*-crown and sits on his throne holding a flail and scepter. Before him, a seated god presents a bowl with burning tapers. Behind, the arms of a *wedjat*-eye also offer up a bowl of tapers, while below it Pashedu kneels in a pose of adoration. His feet are large and crudely drawn. At left, the Horus falcon stands beside the red granite mountain of the west. Note how the falcon's tail has been bent and trimmed down to fit the limited space in the corner. Below this scene and on the side walls, modern mud plaster covers over the original sarcophagus emplacement.

On the right wall, Pashedu, his wife, and daughter Nebnefret sit before four male deities and a *djed*-pillar. The first is the falcon-headed Ra-Harakhty, followed by a human-headed Atum, the scarab-headed Khepri (the morning form of the sun god), and the god Ptah.

Certainly the best-known scene in this tomb—indeed, one of the best-known in Thebes—is that on the left front wall of the chamber. Pashedu kneels and bows down beneath the branches of a *dom*-palm at the edge of a pond. Behind him, twenty-one columns of text, seventeen of them from chapter 62 of the Book of the Dead, the Chapter for Drinking Water in God's Domain, are written in simple fashion. Oddly, they are filled with errors, and this carelessness stands in marked contrast to the beautiful scene before them. This is a wonderful scene, a model of clarity and composition. The palm tree even shows such minute detail as small fibers along its trunk. But look closely at Pashedu: his figure is little more than an oval lump, his torso badly proportioned, with little detail save the fingernails (which are wrongly painted, showing a left hand instead of a right).

The vaulted ceiling has eight deities on each side. On the right: Osiris, Thoth, Hathor, Ra-Harakhty, Neith, Serqet, Anubis, and Wepwawet. On the left: Osiris, Isis, Nut, Nun, Nephthys, Geb, Anubis and Wepwawet. Between the two sides are forty columns of text from chapter 181 of the Book of the Dead, The Chapter of Going into the Tribunal of Osiris and the Gods Who Govern the Netherworld. Here too, there are numerous errors in grammar, spelling, and text.

5

TT 1: THE TOMB OF SENNEDJEM

THE HISTORY

Several architectural and decorative differences set the tombs of the craftsmen and workers who lived in the village of Dayr al-Madina apart from other private tombs at Thebes. The tombs here had forecourts defined by a low mudbrick wall that might enclose a garden and pond. Behind, stood a small pyramid, never more than 10 meters (32 feet) high, that could contain a small chamber or stela niche. (This was the last pyramid to be incorporated into the plan of an Egyptian tomb.)

Tombs at Dayr al-Madina were crowded together on the hillside immediately west of the village. Space was at a premium here, and tombs were used by entire families, not by individuals. Sennedjem's tomb, for example, contained twenty bodies. Successive generations of a family might use a tomb that had been cut decades earlier, and the government might reassign a tomb to another family if the original owners died and left no heirs.

The decoration of tombs at Dayr al-Madina also sets them apart. Here, there are none of the scenes of daily life like those found in the tombs of Rekhmire, Menna, or Nakht. These tombs ignore scenes of funerary ceremonies, banquets, processions, or the Beautiful Festival of the Valley, which figured so prominently in other tombs. Instead, the decorated walls are devoted almost exclusively to texts and scenes from the Book of the Dead, borrowing from the same repertoire of religious scenes that appeared on the walls of royal tombs in the Valley of the Kings. By choosing these scenes, once restricted to royal tombs, the workmen seem to be claiming a special relationship between the royal court, the gods, and themselves.

The decorative style at Dayr al-Madina also followed different rules. Scenes are copies of vignettes from the Book of the Dead. As copies, they are by definition not original and lack the vitality displayed in other private tombs. Nevertheless, their technical quality is impressive. The artists worked quickly and confidently, applying vivid colors against a rich yellow background meant to suggest the color of papyrus. Representations of nature—of trees and shrubs, for example—show considerable attention to detail.

One of the best examples of such Dayr al-Madina painting is that in the tomb of Sennedjem, TT 1, which lies at the top of a flight of modern steps immediately west of his Dayr al-Madina home. Sennedjem's tomb is one of the most interesting and best preserved at Dayr al-Madina. It was found unplundered in 1886, but its objects were shipped off around the world before any proper study was made, and consequently we know little more than that Sennedjem was a senior workman in the village.

470 TOP AND 471 RIGHT DETAIL OF TREES DECORATION IN THE PRINCIPAL CHAMBER OF THE TOMB.

471 LEFT VIEW OF THE LEFT HALF OF THE PRINCIPAL CHAMBER.

VISIT

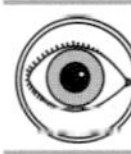

ENTRANCE A pylon and small walled courtyard formed the original entrance to Sennedjem's tomb, and a pyramid stood above the passageway that leads to the principal chamber. Today, the pyramid and courtyard are gone, replaced by a covered rest area. From here, you descend a steep set of badly lit stairs into the hillside to reach the vaulted principal chamber. It is small, only about 3 by 4 meters (9 x 12 feet), and has a low ceiling. The vividness of its colors and the excellent preservation of the walls never fail to astonish visitors.

On the right wall of the gateway into the principal chamber, a solar cat of Heliopolis sits beneath a persea tree and slashes with a large knife at Apophis, an evil serpent who is the enemy of the sun god. Blood gushes from his wounds. On the opposite wall, two seated lions, representing the hills of the western horizon, flank the setting sun. Originally, a beautifully painted wooden door was installed here (it is now in the Egyptian Museum, Cairo), and both it and the door jambs were covered with a copy of Book of the Dead spell 17.

FRONT WALL (RIGHT SIDE) The mummy of Sennedjem lies on a lion-headed bed in an elaborate shrine, flanked by Isis (at the foot of the bed) and Nephthys (at the head). Both are shown as hawks. The brother of these two goddesses was Osiris, and according to New Kingdom theology, Sennedjem would have joined Osiris at death. Thus, by mourning Sennedjem, the two goddesses are also mourning the death of their brother.

LEGEND

A *ENTRANCE*
B *PASSAGE*
C *PRINCIPAL CHAMBER*

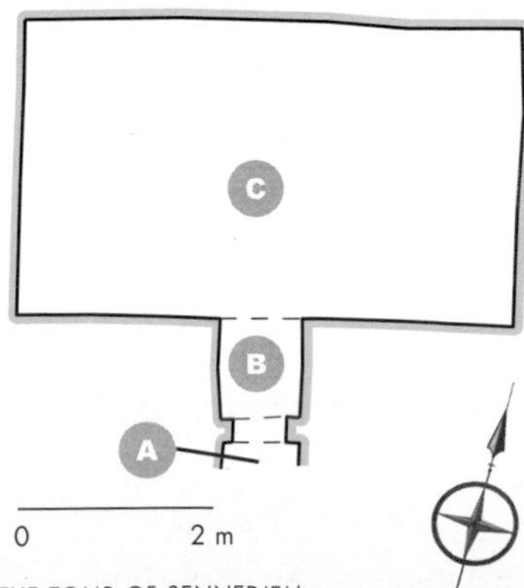

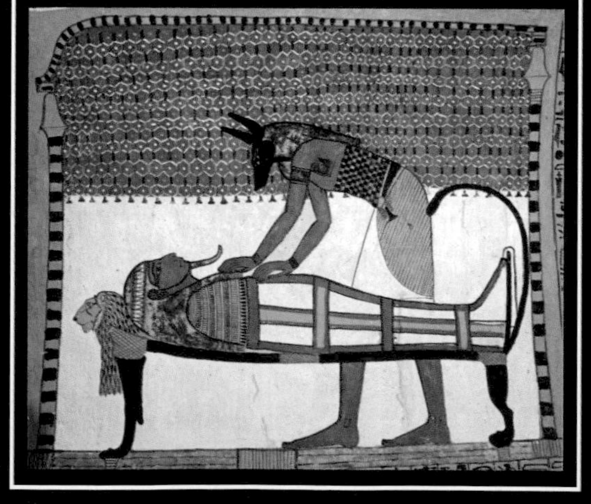

472 TOP THE LEFT WALL OF THE TOMB OF SENNEDJEM.

472 BOTTOM A PRIEST WEARING AN ANUBIS MASK OFFICIATES AT THE MUMMIFICATION OF SENNEDJEM.

473 TOP DETAIL OF THE OFFERING TABLE TO OSIRIS.

473 BOTTOM LEFT OSIRIS IN A SHRINE WITH FLAIL AND SCEPTER.

473 BOTTOM RIGHT A SON OF SENNEDJEM DRESSED AS PRIEST OFFERS WATER TO HIS PARENTS.

In the register below, two couples and another group of three receive offerings. At right, Sennedjem's son, Bunakhtef, wearing the leopard skin of a *sem*-priest, makes offerings to his parents. At left, another priest offers a sail, symbolizing life-renewing air. Farther left, a third priest blesses aromatic cones that sit on the heads of Khabekhnet, Sennedjem's father, and his wives. Children kneel beside the chairs.

LEFT WALL In the upper part of the left end wall, black figures of Anubis, the jackal that guards the necropolis, flank lotus blossoms, symbols of life, and symbols of water. Below, Sennedjem and his wife worship before an elaborate shrine. Inside the shrine, Osiris (first in the top row) and Ra-Harakhty (first in the bottom row) precede eleven other gods of the underworld. The text is from Book of the Dead spell 190 and it will endow Sennedjem with strength and power when he greets these gods.

REAR WALL At the far left, a priest wearing the mask of Anubis completes the mummification of Sennedjem. The mummy lies on a lion-shaped bed that has an elaborate mane and long tail placed within a shrine hung with tasseled cloth. The shrine is surrounded by excerpts from Book of the Dead spell 1, the chapter that was recited as the body was carried to the tomb for burial. At right, a figure of Osiris, holding a flail and scepter, and wearing the *atef*-crown on his head, stands in a shrine equipped with lotus columns and a uraeus frieze. He stands on the hieroglyphic symbol of Ma'at, meaning truth, justice, and order. On either side of his head are *wadjet*-eyes and, below, *imiut*-fetishes. These fetishes are animal skins tied to staffs and wrapped with lotus blossoms symbolizing rejuvenation and life. At right, a kneeling Sennedjem presents food offerings to the god. Another figure of Sennedjem is led forth by Anubis to be presented to Osiris.

RIGHT WALL One of the best-known scenes from the New Kingdom is on the right end wall of this chamber. In four registers, Sennedjem and his wife plough and harvest in the afterlife. This scene is common in Egyptian art—it is a standard vignette that accompanies Book of the Dead spell 110—but never was it so elegantly drawn. At the top of the wall, two baboons worship Ra-Harakhty-Atum, who sails through the underworld. On his bark stands a small shrine representing a temple at the Lower Egyptian religious site of Buto. There is a swallow, the symbol of eternity, and a strange object called a *shemes* combining a harpoon with a knife and a human leg that is said to be the symbol of the followers of Horus. Below, agricultural scenes in the fields of *iaru*, the fields of the blessed, are surrounded by water-filled canals. Sennedjem and his wife kneel on a mound of sand and praise Ra-Harakhty, Osiris, Ptah, and two other gods who represent the Great Ennead. The gods sit on the hieroglyph for Ma'at. Behind them, Sennedjem's son Rahotep kneels in a small bark while another son, Khonsu, performs the Opening of the Mouth ceremony on his father's mummy. Three black ovals on the right of the scene represent a "battle site," an "offering place," and something called "the greatest."

Beneath a narrow, water-filled canal, Sennedjem and his wife Iyneferti harvest a field of grain. The stalks lack the realism seen in the harvest scene in Menna's tomb, but there are some deft touches. For example, Sennedjem holds stalks of wheat in his left hand, and that hand is drawn in ordinary fashion. But his right hand, the hand holding a sickle, is oddly turned. The artist was trying to show Sennedjem holding the sickle horizontally, but the rules of Egyptian art demanded that the sickle be shown in its most recognizable form, which is from the side. Therefore, he has drawn the sickle upright, but twisted the wrist and palm so that it would appear as if Sennedjem were swinging the sickle parallel to the ground. The two lines that form a V on his wrist are tendons that become prominent when his hand is flexed. At right, the deceased kneels on a mat before an offering table laden with food and wine. He sniffs a lotus flower.

Below, Sennedjem pulls green flax stalks, which his wife then ties into bundles. His wife, Iyneferti, walks behind Sennedjem, sowing seed broadcast. Sennedjem is plowing the fields and urging two cows forward with a small flail. In front of the cattle stands a finely drawn sycomore fig tree with branches that extend through the register line into a square with four black ovals like those described above.

Fertility is emphasized in such scenes. In the Book of the Dead, a part of the text accompanying this vignette reads, "I acquire this field of yours which you love, the Lady of Air. I eat and carouse in it. I drink and plow in it. I reap in it, I copulate in it,

474-475 SENNEDJEM AND HIS WIFE PLOUGH AND HARVEST IN THE AFTERLIFE, RIGHT WALL.

475 TOP RIGHT FOUR OF THE TEN GUARDIANS OF THE GATES OF THE AFTERWORLD.

475 CENTER VIEW OF THE RIGHT SIDE OF THE PRINCIPAL CHAMBER.

475 BOTTOM RA-HARAKHTY-ATUM SAILS THROUGH THE UNDERWORLD, RIGHT WALL.

I make love in it, I do not perish in it, for my magic is powerful in it."

Another water-filled canal divides the lower register. In the upper part, dom and date palms alternate with sycomore fig trees, all heavily laden with fruit. Below, cornflowers, mandrake, and red poppies grow along the canal. At right, on a small island, a *djed-tefet* bark (belonging to Ra-Harakhty) has moored in a small inlet.

FRONT WALL (LEFT SIDE) Sennedjem and his wife stand in separate registers and adore figures of the ten guardians of the gates of the underworld. Each guardian sits in a small shrine. Relatives of Sennedjem and his wife bring offerings of flowers and birds. Some of the figures of relatives overlap each other in a confusing, even impossible, manner: look for example, at how the arms and ankles of the two men immediately behind the chairs overlap. Young children, drawn as miniature adults, stand beside their parents' chairs.

CEILING Scenes of formal religious activities were painted on the tomb's vaulted ceiling. Near the door, Sennedjem and wife accept libations of water and loaves of bread from the goddess Nut, whose body emerges from a sycomore fig tree. Scenes of such tree goddesses were very popular in ancient Egypt and a speech by the tree goddess in another Theban tomb tells why: "I am Nut, I have come to you bringing gifts. You sit under me and cool yourself under my branches. I allow you to drink of my milk and to live and take nourishment at my two breasts..." A scene of pharaoh being suckled by a tree goddess can be seen in the tomb of Thutmes III. The sycomore tree bears fig-like fruit which must have small notches cut from it, an arduous process but a necessary one if the figs are to be rid of wasp larvae that render them inedible. Each of the figs on this tree has been notched and is therefore ready to nourish Sennedjem and his wife.

In another scene, Sennedjem stands before the gates of heaven. The door's lower hinges are set in the earth, the upper in the hieroglyphic sign for the sky. Other scenes on the ceiling show the deceased before various gods, adoring and praying. Two sycomore trees stand at the side of one scene, the sun rising between them. These are the "two sycomores of turquoise between which Ra comes forth," and the reborn sun emerges from darkness, riding on the back of a calf.

476-477 THE CEILING OF THE PRINCIPAL CHAMBER OF THE TOMB OF SENNEDJEM.

5

TT 51: THE TOMB OF USERHET

THE HISTORY

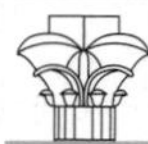

The painted decoration in this small, early 19th Dynasty tomb displays an interesting mix of iconography, some a holdover from the reigns of Amenhetep III and IV, some from the reigns of Rameses I and Sety I. The shaven heads and schematized faces of the men, for example, are Amarnan in outline, their poses typically languid. But there are also Ramesside details, such as the carefully drawn eyebrows, and the ostentatious, even garish costumes and offerings.

Userhet (not to be confused with another Userhet, whose tomb, TT 56, lies nearby) lived during the last years of the reign of Horemheb and Rameses I, and died during the reign of Sety I. He was First Prophet of the Royal *ka* of Thutmes I, an early 18th Dynasty king greatly admired and honored in the later New Kingdom for his close association with the development of the Theban Necropolis, especially the workmen's village at Dayr al-Madina.

TT 51 was one of four Ramesside tombs cut into the faces of a small courtyard low down on the northeastern slope of Shaykh 'Abd al-Qurna. Flooding from occasional rainstorms apparently was a problem here, and the ancient quarrymen constructed a raised sill in the tomb entrance and lowered the floor of the courtyard before it. To the left of the tomb entrance, in the wall of the courtyard, Userhet carved a meter-high limestone stela whose eight lines of text give a standard offering formula and the names of family members.

The plan of Userhet's tomb was meant to be an elaborate one, with a transverse antechamber followed by a four-pillared hall and a corridor that sloped down to the burial chamber. The walls in these spaces were as carefully cut as the poor bedrock allowed, then covered with a heavy layer of white mud plaster made with large quantities of straw chaff (a binding material called *tibn* that is still used in Egypt today). But only the antechamber was decorated, perhaps because of a lack of time. The painted scenes

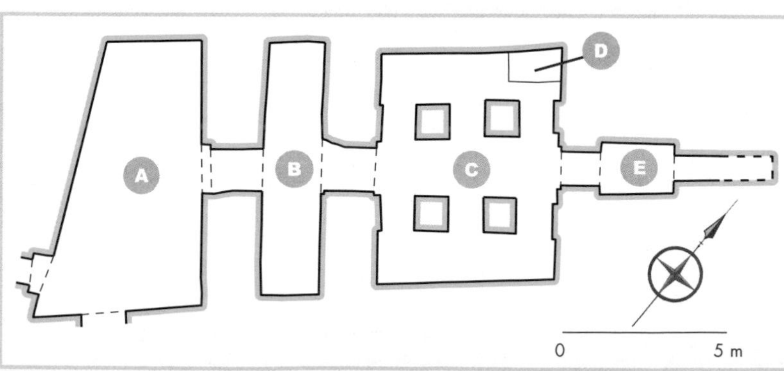

exclusively treat religious themes and funerary rites, not the activities of daily life common in earlier New Kingdom tombs.

The antechamber is a narrow room, 7 meters (18 feet) long but only 1.5 meters (less than 4 feet) wide. Enter the room and turn left to face the wall adjacent to the front door. Here, three registers depict various funerary rites.

478 ONE OF USERHET'S WIVES, FROM THE ANTECHAMBER.

479 LEFT USERHET, HIS WIFE AND HIS MOTHER, FROM THE RIGHT END WALL OF THE ANTECHAMBER.

479 RIGHT THE PILLARED HALL.

LEGEND

A *COURT*
B *ANTECHAMBER*
C *PILLARED CHAMBER*
D *SHAFT*
E *BURIAL CHAMBER*

VISIT

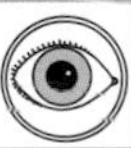

NORTH (FRONT) WALL, EAST HALF Userhet stands in the bottom register before a building (a royal palace, perhaps) in the center of the wall, receiving great heaps of offerings and pieces of jewelry. To the left, his wife also receives gifts. Far left, near the door in a half-register, Userhet's chariot awaits his departure from the ceremonies. His charioteer carries on an animated discussion with the palace gatekeeper.

The middle register is devoted to Userhet's funeral procession. Three cattle pull a sled carrying an elaborate catafalque with his coffin inside, the whole covered with bouquets of flowers. Examples of the funerary furniture destined for the tomb are shown above. At right, seven mourning women pour dirt on their heads, weeping and ululating. Behind them, the mummies of Userhet and his wife stand on a low platform, offered to and prayed over by priests who wear panther skins indicating their rank. Behind the mummies, the deceased is welcomed into the Netherworld by Hathor, who stands before what one Egyptologist called an "absurd" garland-covered pyramid that apparently was meant to represent Userhet's tomb.

In the upper register, Userhet and his wife, Hatshepsut (also called Shepset), are led by Anubis before a beam balance on which their good deeds will be weighed against Ma'at. The goddess Ma'at and the god Thoth flank the scales, and the hippopotamus/ crocodile god Ammet sits nearby, ready to devour those judged to be evil.

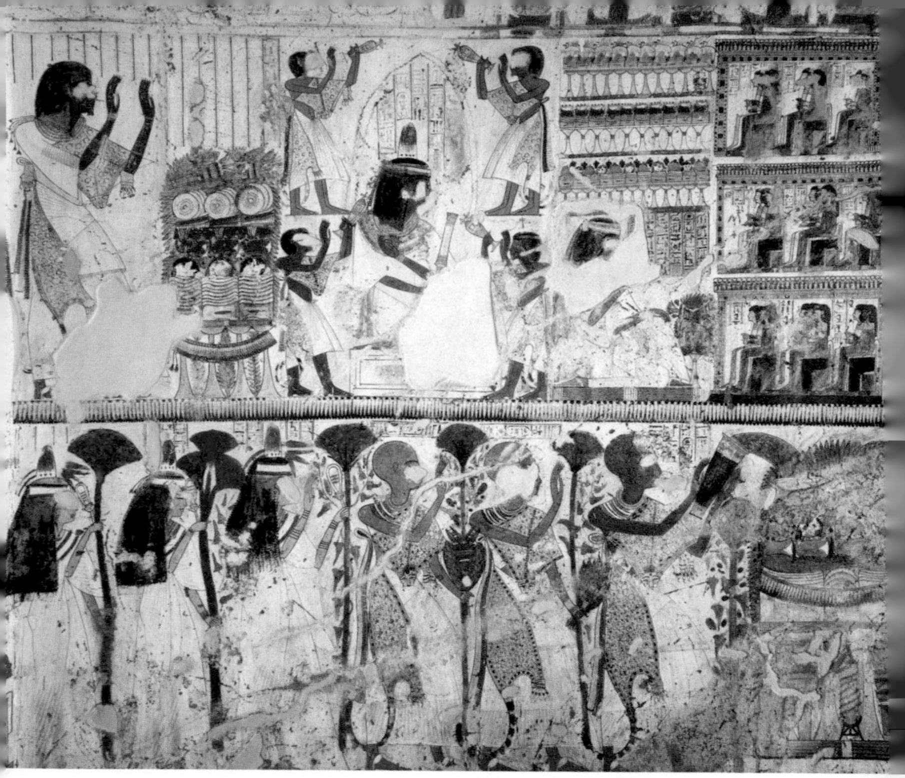

Userhet, of course, passes the test with flying colors, and is shown at right kneeling before Osiris, who sits before a mound of food and floral offerings. The Mistress of the West stands behind him. Norman deGaris Davies, who published the tomb in 1927, considered the workmanship here unforgivably "slovenly." That's an overstatement, but when compared to other scenes in the tomb, it suggests that two artists of very different talent were responsible for various walls.

EAST (LEFT) END WALL The lower register here, although very badly damaged, shows an unusual scene of the tomb-owner and wife seated before a small pond. Userhet hands a fishing pole to his wife, and the couple fish for *int*-fish, a symbol of resurrection. The scene is an example of how richly imbued with religious symbolism even apparently innocuous and homely scenes can be in a funerary context.

In the larger register above, a hawk-headed solar deity, perhaps Montu, receives adoration

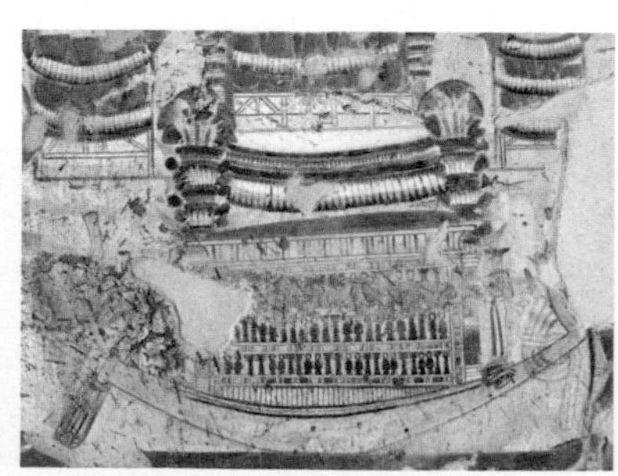

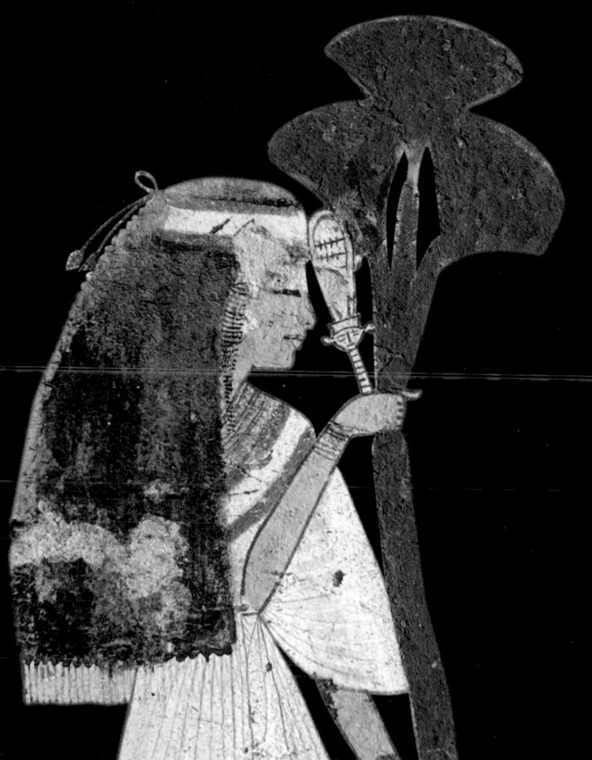

from three males. These men are identified as "The prince, superintendent of the city, the vizier, Imhotep. His beloved son, the high priest of Amen, Hapuseneb. [Userhet's] father, the high priest of Amen, Khonsu-emheb. Their heir, Userhet, called Neferhebef, causes their names to endure."

NORTH (REAR) WALL, EAST HALF Three registers deal with the annual cult ceremony of Thutmes I, held in his West Bank temple under the direction of Userhet. It may have been one of Userhet's most important duties, but the ceremony is shown in a cursory manner. Three registers show the initial preparation of offerings, the procession of the king's statue on land and water, and the return to the temple. In the badly damaged lower register, Userhet sits at left watching as bearers bring forward offerings and equipment for the ceremony. In the middle register at right, an ebony statue of Thutmes I is pulled by priests toward a group of administrators and officials. (The king's name appears in the accompanying cartouches.) The statue is being censed, the pungent smoke fanned toward the king's face. At left, a bark on which the statue has now been placed sails on a rectangular pond that is surrounded by elaborate gardens. In the upper register, the statue is returned to its temple shrine, and the sacred bark is installed on its alabaster stand.

480-481 AND 481 PURIFICATION CEREMONY AND OFFERINGS, FROM THE NORTHEAST WALL OF THE ANTECHAMBER.

480 BOTTOM LEFT THE GODDESS OF THE WEST IN FRONT OF THE MOUND OF THE WESTERN DESERT.

480 BOTTOM RIGHT A BOAT IN THE ABYDOS PROCESSION.

NORTH (REAR) WALL, WEST HALF The two large registers here depict New Year ceremonies intended to ensure the continuation of royal power. Above, Userhet as First Prophet stands before a seated figure of Osiris; below, he stands before Thutmes I. The two registers are very similar in general outline and both are excellent examples of the Egyptians' *horror vacui*. Both at first appear so cluttered and filled with detail that they overwhelm attempts to make sense of their scenes. But it is their rich details and complex iconography that make these registers two of the finest in the tomb. In the top register, Userhet's costume is elaborately drawn. (The empty cartouches on the legs of the animal skin he wears were intended to contain names of Rameses I.) Userhet censes a remarkable table of offerings, piled high with fruits and vegetables, flowers and loaves of bread. At left, a seated Osiris is accompanied by three deities, perhaps Hathor, Ma'at, and Anubis. Behind Userhet stand his wife, his sister, and a son. At right, in two half registers, the deceased couple sit before funerary goods and priests and mourning women who grieve their death and purify the offerings.

The lower register is very similarly laid out, but here, Userhet censes offerings before the pharaoh Thutmes I and his wife, Ahmose-Nefertiry. Again, there is a heavily laden offering table, this time with a brace of large, finely-drawn fowl and a loaf of bread. Behind him stand his mother, Henuttawy, his wife, and a daughter. At right, the upper half register again show the deceased couple, but the lower shows an official called Nebmehyt and his wife. Why this couple should appear here is unclear. (Nebmehyt is also shown on the east wall behind us.)

NORTH (RIGHT) END WALL The most famous scene in TT 51 is this beautiful painting of Userhet, his wife and mother, seated beside a sycomore fig tree. (Unusually, the women's names are written on their arms.) The chairs are of blackest ebony, their costumes brilliant white, in perfect contrast to their vividly-colored pectorals and the green, leafy tree behind. The women's skin–and Userhet's, too–can be seen through their fine, nearly-transparent, carefully-pleated linen. Their eyes are carefully outlined, their cheeks rouged, their hair perfectly braided.

The sycomore fig was a highly important tree in ancient Egypt. It produced a hard, durable wood, six crops of edible fruit annually, and a milky white latex-like sap that was used as a medicament. The tree had close associations with goddesses like Hathor, Nut, and Isis, who were believed to live in its branches. The artist has taken great pains when painting the tree to show that each fig has been notched by hand in order to kill wasps whose eggs prevent the fruit ripening. Note, too, the small birds fluttering among the branches before Userhet's face. The souls of Userhet and his wife appear as human-headed hawks standing on the edge of a T-shaped pond. To its right, the goddess Nut stands beside a rectangular pond, holding forth bowls of sycomore figs and grapes and pouring water from a ewer into cups from which the family members drink.

EAST (RIGHT) WALL, NORTH HALF In the lower register, ceremonies honor the god Montu, with whose temple at Armant, just south of Thebes, Userhet's mother was affiliated. The hawk-headed god wears a solar disk on his head and sits before a standing figure of the goddess Meret-Seger. Before him, Userhet pours libations over a table piled high with offerings. He is followed by two priests, one of whom is identified as Nebmehyt, whom we met in the north corner of the west wall behind us. All three are decked out in elaborate panther skin costumes. They in turn are followed by three women, perhaps wives or priestesses. In the register above, Userhet stands at left, before an offering table, observing various ceremonies. In the center of the wall, Userhet himself is kneeling as eight priests pour purifying water over him. At right, Userhet kneels below (i.e., beside) offerings, and vessels before three shrines house eight deities of the afterlife. Osiris sits at far right in a kiosk attended by Anubis and Thoth.

482-483 USERHET, HIS WIFE, SON AND SISTERS OFFER TO OSIRIS.

483 TOP ANUBIS ON A SHRINE.

483 BOTTOM USERHET AND HIS WIFE SITTING IN FRONT OF A BUNCH OF ONIONS (NOT VISIBLE), SYMBOL OF OSIRIS.

5

TT 31: THE TOMB OF KHONSU

THE HISTORY

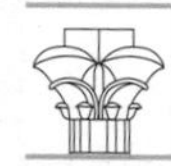

Cut into the side of a small court in Shaykh 'Abd al-Qurna, the tomb of Khonsu dates to the reign of Rameses II. Khonsu was the First Prophet in a temple of Thutmes III and the son of the First Prophet in the memorial temple of Amenhetep III.

VISIT

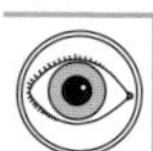

The courtyard in which the tomb was cut is damaged, but broken fragments from the door jambs were reassembled some eighty years ago. They show Khonsu, followed by his mother Tausert, his son, and one of his two wives, walking out of the tomb into the daylight in "adoration of Ra when he arises on the eastern horizon." Khonsu wears a panther skin, the women hold sistra, and his son carries a brace of birds. A frieze of alternating Anubis jackals and *kheker*-ornaments runs across the top of the jamb.

The other side of the door is more heavily damaged, but it showed Khonsu, his mother and son walking into the tomb, i.e. toward the western horizon, in "adoration of Ra when he sets on the western horizon." Mother and son are similarly costumed on both reveals, but Khonsu is shown bald on the north reveal and with a wig on the south. On the ceiling of the doorway, birds in flight are drawn in a very formal style, laid out in ranks and files. (A much more pleasing scene of birds can be seen on the ceiling of the third doorway.)

CHAMBER ONE, SOUTH (FRONT) WALL, LEFT (WEST) HALF In the course of his work as First Prophet, Khonsu was expected to attend annual festivals held at various temples throughout the Theban nome. One festival in which he was a regular participant was that of the war god Montu at his temple in the city of Armant (also called Hermonthis), about 20 kilometers (12 miles) south of Thebes on the west bank of the Nile. One Egyptologist believes that Khonsu was in fact First Prophet of Thutmes III, not at his memorial temple at Thebes, but at that temple's endowment at Armant. The Montu festival forms the subject of most of the reliefs in the west half of the first chamber.

The upper register of the front wall contains very busy scenes of Khonsu and colleagues worshipping the god Montu at his annual festival. Two men stand on the prow of a boat that carries a shrine of Montu. They are identified as brothers, but their relationship to Khonsu is unclear. One is the Vizier of Armant, Usermont, the other a priest of Montu, Huy. With them on the boat stands a shrine containing a model boat resting on a smaller shrine. That shrine houses the statue of Montu. On the bottom right of the larger shrine a small figure of King Rameses II offers to the god. On the prow of the larger boat, Montu wears a sun disk and pectoral collar. The rectangular body of water on which the boat sails is meant to be the Nile, and it is filled with fish. The boats are sailing from Armant to another Montu temple at the town of Tod, a few kilometers north.

The Montu bark is towed by two smaller boats, sailing side by side and tied to the bark with a heavy rope. The design of these boats suggests that they are not the usual towboats, but warships pressed into service for this grand occasion. Two men stand atop the boat cabin, jousting with sticks. In the register above, four priests clad in panther skins cense huge piles of food offerings. The first priest in line is Khonsu's father. To the right, another shrine housing a bark and statue of Montu is censed by Khonsu himself, dressed in an elaborate gown and panther skin and standing beside a pile of food offerings. Below, in a scene topped by a band of lotus blossoms, sit Khonsu and his relatives. At left, Khonsu and his mother sit before an offering table with lit tapers on it being consecrated by a priest. The scene is badly damaged, but four women can be seen standing behind the priest observing the scene. At right, Khonsu sits with his grandmother, mother, and daughter. At left, his son offers a libation.

LEFT (WEST) WALL The scenes in the upper register are a continuation of those on the front wall. Here, both Thutmes III and Rameses II are shown on the sides of the shrine of Montu. Below the outstretched wings of the vulture-goddess Nekhbet, the bark is towed by two vessels. On one of them, two men again joust with sticks. Above one man, who has dropped his stick, a text reads, "It is Amen who gives victory." The boat is thought to be a military transport, not a warship or a towboat. In the small registers above, priests stand on shore ready to greet the vessels on their return from the festival. Khonsu is here too, as are his mother, wife, and daughter. Much of the lower register is missing, but it originally showed an island in a large, square pool on which ceremonies were performed for the mummy of the deceased. At right, family members including a son, Khonsu's mother and sister, and others whose names and titles are missing, partake of a funerary repast.

484 TOP SEM-PRIESTS WITH OFFERINGS.

484 BOTTOM BIRDS IN FLIGHT, DECORATION OF THE CEILING OF THE TOMB.

485 ONE OF THE BARKS DEPICTED ON THE WALLS OF THE FIRST CHAMBER

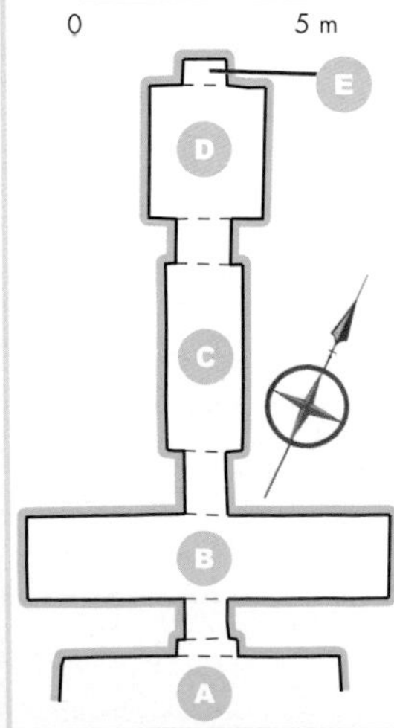

REAR (NORTH) WALL, LEFT (WEST) HALF This too is a continuation of the scenes of the Festival of Montu. The festival has ended and the shrine with the statue of Montu is now being carried back to the temple on the shoulders of eight priests. The High Priest of Montu, Ramose, walks alongside wearing an elaborate costume. The text reads in part, "Welcome! You have come from Tod and are at rest in Armant. All the people stand acclaiming!" At right stand the pylons of a temple of Thutmes III. (Today at Armant one can visit a Ptolemaic temple, but there are also traces of an earlier structure built by Thutmes III and added to by Rameses II.) Farther right, the shrine has been put away and Khonsu pours a libation before its closed doors.

REAR (NORTH) WALL, RIGHT (EAST) HALF Osiris sits in a brightly painted kiosk, his throne and costume painted in overdone color and detail; Anubis stands behind him. Note the traces of a small bird, with human head and hands, drinking water that has spilled from the offering table. This is the *ba*-bird of Khonsu, lapping up water that had been consecrated to Osiris. The priest who offers incense to the god is probably Khonsu himself, and he is accompanied by women and children including his mother, wife, son, and daughter. The boy is shown with impossibly long legs, either an artistic slip or an attempt to depict a gangling adolescent.

THE RIGHT (EAST) WALL is concerned with a ceremony for King Thutmes III. In the upper register at right, a bark carries the shrine and statue of the king, with Khonsu standing on deck making offerings. The bark is towed by a small boat rowed by ten sailors and commanded by Usermont, who also appeared in the Festival of Montu on the front and left walls. The vessels sail on a T-shaped basin, at the end of which (at left) stands Thutmes III's temple. Eight priests welcome the procession with gifts. In the register below, women from the temple act as mourners for the dead king, wailing and pouring dust on their hair.

Below, Khonsu, his wife, son, and daughter, sit in a small arbor or pavilion, watching herdsmen bring cattle, sheep, and goats for inspection from a funerary estate of Thutmes III. Khonsu also held the title of Overseer of Cattle for the temple of Thutmes III. A foreman named Kaka prostrates himself at Khonsu's feet. As Khonsu looks out over the parade, he speaks to one of the herdsmen: "The animals of the god are thriving. Bring this calf to the temple!" The calf in question is hard to see, but it is carried in a rope bag over the shoulder of a herdsmen standing at the far left. He walks beside a tree with a small dog following behind. Most of the animals in this scene are scraggly and poorly drawn. The trees, on the other hand, are attractively done.

FRONT (SOUTH) WALL, LEFT (EAST) SIDE The upper register deals with the Hall of

486 LEFT THE PHARAOH RECEIVING OFFERINGS.

486 RIGHT OSIRIS ON A THRONE RECEIVING OFFERINGS.

487 PRIESTS CARRY THE SACRED BARK IN PROCESSION.

Judgment. Twelve gods, the Council of the Judgment Hall, sit at the top with the god Ra at their head and Khonsu and his mother at the rear. They include Atum, Shu, Tephenis, Montu, Osiris, Harwer, Isis, and Nephthys. Below, Anubis weighs the heart of the deceased on the balance as Thoth looks on and records the result. At left, Horus leads Khonsu and his mother to the shrine of Osiris. The text announces to the god that Khonsu "never wrought wickedness against the great ones in this land...He did what the king desired and that with which the gods are pleased."

In the lower register, we witness the interment of Khonsu and his mother (not his wife, as one might expect). His pyramid-capped tomb, with a columned portico and central pylon, has a painted stela asking visitors to pray for their continued well-being. Khonsu's wife and daughter caress the mummies and two priests conduct the Opening of the Mouth ritual. Six mourning women weep for the deceased. At right, the funeral procession is now partly destroyed and the sarcophagus, on a sled pulled by cattle, has disappeared. But the members of the procession are still visible, and one pours milk on the path to purify it before the sarcophagus passes by. At right, above the procession, two cattle are standing, one with its right leg cut off. The leg is bleeding profusely. Such amputations were apparently a common funeral practice after the Dynasty 18, and in some tombs, a priest is shown performing the operation.

CHAMBER TWO The lintel of the doorway into the second chamber shows Khonsu and his family offering incense and sistra to Osiris, Hathor, and Ra-Harakhty. Only tiny fragments of the decoration are preserved.

CHAMBER THREE The ceiling of the otherwise destroyed doorway is decorated with a superb example of Egyptian painting. The scene shows ducks flying in all directions through the foliage as if they had been startled. Several nests can be seen in the branches. Some have eggs in them and one has two fledglings, their mouths open, tongues sticking out, demanding food. Near the nest sits a larger-than-life locust (there is a second one farther to its left), one of the rare drawings of these insects in Egyptian art. The ducks are well-drawn and particular attention has been paid to their wing feathers.

In the rear wall of the chamber is a large niche. The colors are well preserved and vibrant to the point of being gaudy. On its rear wall, Khonsu, dressed as a priest, offers to Osiris and Anubis. On the left wall, he offers lotus and papyrus flowers to the Dynasty 11 king, Nebhepetra Mentuhetep, who wears the white crown of Upper Egypt. It has been suggested that the king was included here because his memorial temple in the Dayr al-Bahari cirque symbolized the west and was closely identified with the goddess Hathor. Indeed, on the right wall of the niche, Khonsu offers to Hathor.

5

TT 296: THE TOMB OF NEFERSEKHERU

THE HISTORY

Nefersekheru was Scribe of Divine Offerings of All the Gods and an Officer of the Treasury at Thebes during the later years of Rameses II. His tomb lies in a part of the necropolis known as al-Khokha, in the same entrance court as TT 178, the tomb of Neferrenpet, with which it shares many stylistic similarities. Indeed, given their dates and titles, the two men must have known each other and had many activities in common. It is instructive to visit both Nefersekheru's tomb and Neferrenpet's to compare the different ways their artists treated similar subjects. There is a substantial overlap in subject matter, but a marked difference in style. Note the elaborately decorated ceiling in Nefersekheru's tomb. It is rare to find so wide a variety of such finely-done geometric patterns, rarer still to find their colors so well-preserved.

Columns of offering texts flank the tomb's entrance. On the doorjambs, Nefersekheru and one of his wives, Nefertari, stride forward: on the left side they walk out of the tomb toward the rising sun accompanied by texts to Amen. On the right, they walk in, toward the setting sun accompanied by texts to Osiris.

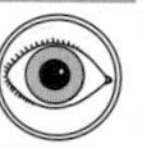

VISIT

FIRST CHAMBER, FRONT (EAST) WALL, RIGHT (SOUTH) HALF
Nefersekheru and Nefertari appear in two very similar scenes on the right (south) side of the first chamber's front (east) wall. At left, nearest the doorway, they stand before a shrine with an open, hinged wooden door. Inside the shrine, two feline-like demons sit with knives in their paws. At right, the couple stands before another shrine, this one holding four demons in human form. These are scenes from chapters of the Book of Gates, in which Nefersekheru and his wife ask the demons' permission to pass through the gates that stand between them and the

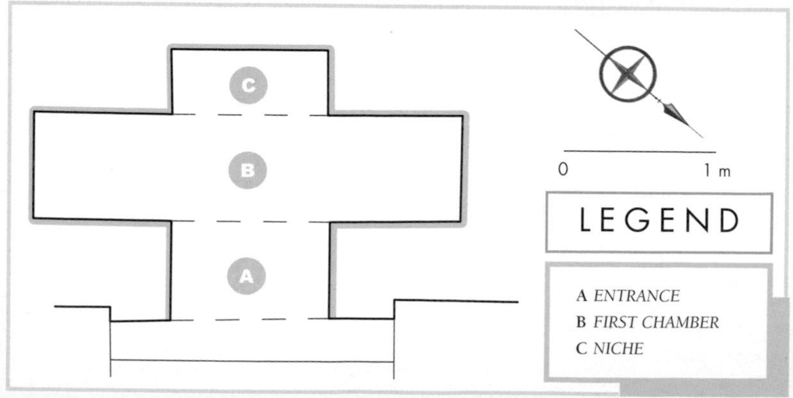

488 DETAIL OF THE CEILING DECORATION OF THE TOMB OF NEFERSEKHERU.

489 NEFERSEKHERU AND HIS WIFE MAKE OFFERINGS.

netherworld. They are granted permission, of course, and in the next scene, the couple stands making offerings. Four tables are piled high with flowers, lettuce, breads, and other foods.

At the right, the jackal-headed god Anubis now leads the couple into the court of Osiris for the ceremony of the Weighing of the Heart, which will determine whether the deceased have behaved well enough in this life to gain admittance to the next. Osiris sits in an elaborately decorated shrine with Isis and Nephthys standing behind him, the four sons of Horus on a lotus blossom in front, watching as Thoth and Horus weigh Nefersekheru's heart against a figure of Ma'at that symbolizes truth, correctness, and justice. Between the deceased and the balance sits a beast called Ammit who combines the fearsome features of a lion, a crocodile, and a hippopotamus. Should the balance not tilt in their favor, Ammit will devour them.

In the register below this, near the door, Nefersekheru and his wife stand beside a T-shaped pool filled with lotus flowers and *Tilapia nilotica*, called *bolti* in modern Egypt. *Tilapia* were especially popular fish in ancient Egypt: they were plentiful, they tasted good, and they carried their young in their mouths and thereby came to be associated with ideas of creation, and their bright colors when breeding reminded Egyptians of the solar deities. The tomb owner and his wife dip into the pool to drink its cool water, some of which falls from their hands. Date palms grow on the shore, laden with fruit and filled with birds' nests. (Compare this with the similar scene in the adjacent tomb of Neferrenpet). The scene is a vignette taken from chapter 62 of the Book of the Dead. It reads in part, "May the cool water of Thoth and the water of Hapi be open for the Lord of the Horizon...the pools of the Field of Reeds serve me, limitless eternity is given to me, for I am he who inherited eternity, to whom everlasting was given."

At right, the couple takes part in a festival for the goddess Bastet, originally celebrated in the Nile Delta city of Bubastis. They sit before a great pile of offerings of sycomore fruit, bread, lettuce, and onions. A naked girl, perhaps their daughter, stands in attendance behind them. A *sem*-priest offers incense and water, and before him another daughter, Isis, kneels in mourning, her hair disheveled, her expression one of great sorrow. To the right, the couple again sits before an offering table receiving water and incense from a *sem*-priest. They are shown yet a third time, seated in a kiosk, playing a game of senet (see also the tomb of Neferrenpet). To their right, the king Amenhetep I and his mother Ahmes-Nefertari, both of them elaborately costumed, sit in a kiosk before a mound of offerings being presented to them by Nefersekheru. (Again, see the similar scene in the tomb of Neferrenpet).

LEFT (SOUTH) WALL Scenes show Nefersekheru and his wife adoring Osiris and Hathor on one side, Anubis and Isis on the other. Between them, a sealed doorway leads into an undecorated room and a passage to the undecorated burial chamber.

REAR (WEST) WALL, CENTER Two scenes of Hathor emerging from the mountain are painted above the central Osiris niche in the rear wall of this chamber. Between the scenes are a *djed*-pillar, Isis knots, *nefer* signs and Eyes of Horus. The niche itself houses a broken statue of Osiris and is flanked by personified *djed*-pillars and figures of Nefersekheru. At the right end of the wall, Osiris sits in an elaborate shrine with Isis and Nephthys behind him.

REAR (WEST) WALL, LEFT (SOUTH) HALF Nefersekheru, dressed in the panther skin of a *sem*-priest, comes with his wife and son before Osiris. He holds a censer and his wife brings a bouquet of papyrus and an instrument used in the cult of Hathor. His son, who is identified as a scribe in the army, carries a duck. Osiris is seated before them in an elaborate but badly damaged shrine with Isis standing behind him. The accompanying text is a hymn to Osiris.

To the right, Nefersekheru and his wife again stand before Osiris who this time is accompanied by Horus (behind him) and Isis (in front). Again, the text is a hymn to Osiris.

In the lower register at left, a *sem*-priest stands before Nefersekheru, his wife, and their daughter, a chantress in the temple of Amen, Heretperi. The priest offers incense and water before small offering tables with loaves of bread. At right, another *sem*-priest stands in front of tables with burning candles and food offerings before Nefersekheru and his wife, who are seated on a low dais.

Farther right, a third *sem*-priest with a censer and a *kebeh*-vessel used for purifying with cool water stands before a harpist. The musician sits cross-legged on the ground, plucking the strings of his harp. While Nefersekheru, his wife, and a young lady listen, three men kneel before offering tables in a small register below the statue niche.

REAR (WEST) WALL, RIGHT (NORTH) HALF Osiris is seated in an elaborately decorated shrine with Isis and Nephthys standing behind him and the Four Sons of Horus on a lotus flower in front. Nefersekheru and his wife, Ma'atmut, stand before the deities in adoration, presenting offerings. The text is a hymn to Osiris.

At right is a complex scene, rich in symbolism, and brightly painted in yellow, pink, red, blue, and black. Nefersekheru stands at left in a pose of adoration, surrounded by nine columns of text with a hymn to the sun god, Ra-Harakhty. In two half-registers at right, the Souls of Buto and Hierakonpolis stand at top, while

Nefersekheru kneels at bottom. The figures are in adoration before the central scene in which a *djed*-pillar with human arms supports an *ankh*-sign with arms that presents the solar disk to the goddess Nut, who reaches out from heaven to receive it. Isis kneels at the right side of the *djed*-pillar, Nephthys at the left. Below each of them stands a *ba*-bird with arms extended in adoration. Behind the figures, the red granite mountain of the west is drawn with undulating lines and small red dots.

RIGHT (NORTH) WALL A seated figure of Nefersekheru is flanked by two of his wives in this large niche. Reclining Anubis-jackals, Hathor-headed columns, and *kheker*-friezes decorate the lintel.

FRONT (EAST) WALL, LEFT (NORTH) HALF On the left (north) side of the entrance, Nefersekheru and his wife stand before a table of offerings and sixty rectangles of text. The texts are parts of Chapter 125 of the Book of the Dead, the so-called Negative Confession, a list of evil deeds the deceased claims he did not commit during his lifetime. He proclaims that he never robbed anyone, never stole food, never cursed a god, never told a lie or gossiped or became impatient, never had sex with a married woman or with a fornicator or in an abnormal manner, never caused terror or became violent or waded in water. The list is a strange and selective one—surely there are many other sins a person would want to deny having committed—and we must assume that behind each entry lies a complicated set of beliefs and allusions. For example, to boast that one has never waded in water may be a convoluted reference to those souls who have died by drowning, their bodies lost, and who therefore required the special intervention of the gods to gain eternal life.

Farther left, Osiris sits in an elaborately decorated shrine with the goddess Ma'at. Before them, Thoth holds an *ankh*-sign and a *was*-scepter in his right hand and a flail in his left. He is about to introduce Nefersekheru, who has successfully passed the Weighing of the Heart ceremony to the Great God.

Below at right, two half-registers show the funeral procession of Nefersekheru. Four men pull a sled holding a box of canopic jars. Before them, men carry a bed and clothing, jugs, and a mummy mask to be placed in the tomb. A cow and her calf are driven forward and women sit on the ground in poses of mourning. In the lower register, the mummy of Nefersekheru, housed in an elaborate shrine, is pulled forward by four cattle. Priests purify it with water and incense. Women mourners stand before the procession, weeping and wailing. Note that one woman, naked to the waist, has her torso drawn frontally, an uncommon occurrence in Egyptian art. At left, priests offer purifying water before a pile of offerings. Behind it, a mourning women kneels before the elaborately wrapped mummy of Nefersekheru which stands, surrounded by flowers, before his pyramid-capped tomb. The goddess Hathor, shown as a cow, emerges from the red granite mountain at the entrance to the netherworld, preparing to greet this new arrival.

In the lower register at right, a tree goddess emerges from a sycomore tree to pour libations for the kneeling figures of Nefersekheru and his wife. They extend their cupped hands to receive the holy water. Behind them, two sons and three daughters kneel and drink of the libation. A *ba*-bird stands at the base of the tree, drinking from its cupped hands.

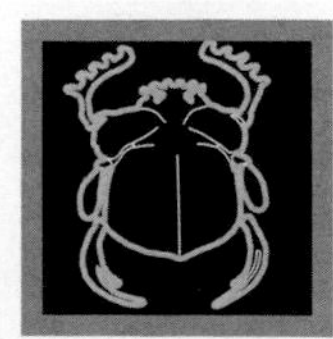

490 OSIRIS AND RA-HARAKHTY SITTING ON THRONES BEFORE OFFERING TABLES.

5

TT 178: THE TOMB OF NEFERRENPET

THE HISTORY

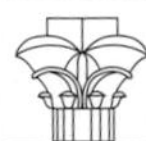

Neferrenpet, also known as Kenro, was a Scribe of the Treasury in the Estate of Amen-Ra during the second half of the reign of Rameses II. His tomb was cut into the wall of a square pit in al-Khokha, a small hillside a few hundred meters west of the memorial temple of Thutmes III.

TT 178 has two small chambers whose walls are decorated with scenes laid out in unusually low registers, some less than 20 centimeters (8 inches) high. Scenes often wrap around corners and continue along several walls. Some begin on the north wall, for example, continue onto the west, and then finish on the south wall. Such wrap-around scenes are not unique in Theban tombs, but they are unusual (TT 31, belonging to Khonsu, offers another example). The workmanship in Neferrenpet's tomb is only fair, hastily-drawn and poorly-proportioned, often lacking detail. That is true of many tombs of Dynasty 19. Neferrenpet's tomb nevertheless is worth visiting because of the ways in which its artists seem to test the limits of Egyptian representation (especially in the second chamber). Minimal attention is paid to detail, and rapidly drawn, cursive lines create almost cartoon-like figures. Non-religious scenes demonstrate a high level of informality both in composition and pose. The tomb is also of interest because of what it tells us about the Treasury of Amen-Ra and because of its emphasis on religious subjects.

VISIT

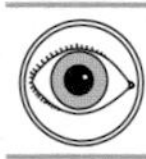

In the entry gate, the Hymn to Atum is carved on the right (west) jamb, the Hymn to Ra on the left (east). On each jamb, a well-carved figure of Neferrenpet, dressed in an elaborate costume with a broad collar and long hair, walks into the tomb (on the right jamb) or out of it (on the left).

FIRST CHAMBER The tops of the walls are decorated with recumbent Anubis jackals that face the tomb entrance and alternate with *kheker*-friezes. Below, two principal registers contain religious scenes. Beneath each register, a line of religious text is written in large and detailed hieroglyphs. These registers are read from the entrance of the tomb on the north wall, across the side wall, and then on the south wall where they end.

LEFT (EAST) HALF OF THE CHAMBER The upper register is divided into several parts, each of which deals with chapter 145 of the Book of the Dead, the chapter that enables the deceased to pass safely through the many locked gates of the underworld. On the front (north) wall, the first scene shows Neferrenpet and his wife, Mutemwia (holding a large floral bouquet), standing before a large portal, called a *sebkhet*. It is topped by a large snake and *djed*-pillars. Isis-knots decorate its sides.

The next scene begins on the front (north) wall and continues onto the left (east). Neferrenpet and Mutemwia stand in adoration before another *sebkhet*. Their costumes are identical to the first scene, but here Neferrenpet carries a pectoral over his arm. The *sebkhet*, placed on a low socle with a *kheker*-frieze on its top, has three demons inside. One has a human head, the second a

492 NEFERRENPET AND HIS WIFE MAKE OFFERINGS.

493 OSIRIS IN A SHRINE OBSERVES THE WEIGHTING OF THE HEART OF THE DECEASED.

lion's, and both hold knives on their knees. The third demon is a recumbent lion with a uraeus on its forehead. Farther right (south) stands an empty portal with Ma'at-feathers on its top. Next, Neferrenpet and Mutemwia again wear the same costumes, she with flowers, he with a pectoral on his arm, and stand in adoration before an empty shrine. To its right, Neferrenpet, with a scribe's palette hanging from his arm, stands before a *sebkhet* topped with Ma'at-feathers. This portal houses four demons holding flails on their knees. Finally, Neferrenpet and wife stand before offerings of meats, geese, vegetables, lettuce, and flowers piled atop four offering stands. Mutemwia holds a head of lettuce and a sistrum. The colors here are especially well preserved and close attention has been paid to fashion. For example, the principal figures are invariably shown with fingernails and toenails delicately painted white.

The final scene in this religious sequence deals with the Weighing of the Heart of the deceased in the Court of Osiris. The scene is formally posed and complex in its iconography, as befits the profound importance of its subject. The Weighing of the Heart is one of ancient Egypt's most recognizable funerary ceremonies and this well-executed scene is typical of Dynasty 19 versions.

The god Anubis, with a human body and the head of a jackal, leads Neferrenpet and wife into the court. Around the corner, on the left rear (south) wall, Horus (on the left) and Thoth weigh the heart of the deceased against the Ma'at-feather. Horus steadies the balance, which is topped by the figure of a baboon and a feather. Thoth holds a scribe's palette, ready to write down the verdict and announce it to Osiris, Isis, and Nephthys, who await the news in an elaborate kiosk. Should the verdict be a bad one and the deceased be found guilty of sin, he will be devoured by a now-defaced demon that originally stood in the corner, just in front of Anubis. This is Ammit, She Who Swallows the Dead, an almost comically grotesque monster with a crocodile's face, a lion's head, and the hindquarters of a hippopotamus.

Before Osiris, small figures of the Four Sons of Horus stand atop a lotus flower. A symbol of Anubis has been placed before the kiosk. Above the balance, four offering tables alternate with seated figures.

LEGEND

A *ENTRANCE*
B *FIRST CHAMBER*
C *SECOND CHAMBER*
D *NICHE*

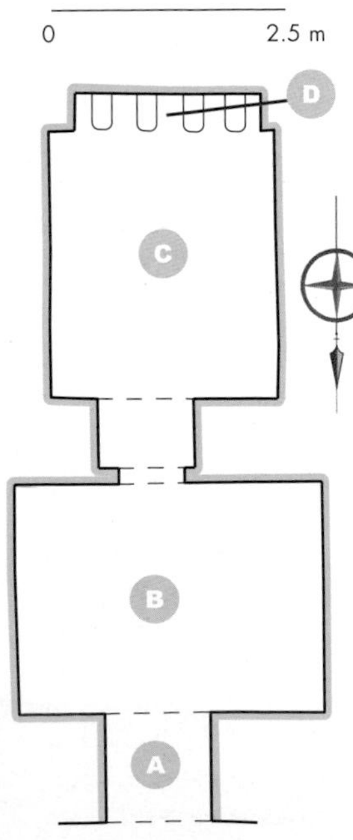

A band of large hieroglyphs, part of the Hymn to Osiris, separates this register from the one below. To follow the lower register, return to the east side of the north wall of the chamber, next to the entrance. In a superbly painted garden scene, Neferrenpet and his wife dip water from a T-shaped pool and drink from their cupped hands. The pool is filled with lotus flowers and fish. Behind it stand three palm trees, heavy with dates and with birds' nests filled with eggs. The transparent gowns of the deceased and his wife, as well as the sensuous curves of their long fingers, are well executed. This scene comes from the vignette that accompanies chapter 62 of the Book of the Dead, a spell for drinking water in the afterlife.

At right, Neferrenpet sits in a delicately carved chair, his feet clad in white sandals resting on a footstool. He holds a scepter and a priest offers him bundles of flowers and baskets of bread.

Around the corner on the left (east) wall, elegantly coiffed and dressed figures of Neferrenpet and Mutemwia sit on chairs placed on a low dais. He holds a scepter and bunches of lettuce and lotuses; she affectionately rests her left hand on his shoulder. The offering table that stood before them has been destroyed, but in a second scene the couple sits before a great heap of foodstuffs including loaves of bread, geese, lettuce, and baskets of dates. A third such scene follows at the right, and here the well-dressed couple watches as Bakenwer, a *sem*-priest clad in the panther skin symbolizing his office, offers incense and pours water over the offerings.

At the end of the wall, a harpist kneels before the kiosk in which Neferrenpet and Mutemwia play a game of *senet*. The scene is from chapter 17 of the Book of the Dead. The deceased is described "going out into the day, taking any shape in which he desires to be, playing at draughts, sitting in a booth, and going forth as a living soul..." Mutemwia gives her husband an affectionate embrace as he daintily balances one of the game pieces on his finger. Beneath Mutemwia's chair, a cat hungrily devours a piece of meat. The animal wears a collar with a string tied to the chair leg.

On the rear (south) wall, Neferrenpet offers incense and libations at an offering table before Amenhetep I and Ahmes-Nefertari. Amenhetep I, the second king of Dynasty 18, and his mother Ahmes-Nefertari were two of the most important figures in New Kingdom Thebes. She was a woman of considerable political power, the first to bear the title God's Wife of Amen, and she served as regent for her son at the start of his reign. The two were said to have founded the workmen's village at Dayr al-Madina, and became the subjects of a major religious cult that survived to the end of the New Kingdom. They extend *ankh*-signs toward the deceased nobleman. In such scenes, Ahmes-Nefertari is usually shown with black skin, meant to symbolize fertility. Here, however, her skin is painted a rather unattractive gray.

The line of hieroglyphs below these scenes contains a prayer for the deceased.

494 NEFERRENPET AND HIS WIFE DRINK (LEFT); THE DECEASED RECEIVES OFFERINGS FROM A PRIEST (RIGHT).

495 NEFERRENPET IN FRONT OF AN OFFERING TABLE, POURING WATER BEFORE THE PHARAOH IN A SHRINE.

RIGHT (WEST) SIDE

Like the left half of the chamber, scenes in the right half also span three walls. Below a *kheker*-frieze and figures of a recumbent Anubis, Neferrenpet stands at the left of the doorway, arms raised in prayer before piles of bread, lettuce, grapes, and vessels set out on mats. The intervening text is a hymn to the sun, and the solar disk, held aloft in the arms of a large *djed*-pillar, is greeted by ten deities standing in two registers all similarly posed and dressed. To their left, the arms of the goddess Nut reach forth from a mountain on the western horizon and grasp the sun disk, preparing to carry it on its nighttime journey through the netherworld. The mountain is painted to suggest red granite, considered more valuable than common limestone or sandstone.

Around the corner on the right (west) wall, the god Thoth sits in a kiosk with the goddess Ma'at standing behind him, facing an offering table piled high with lettuce, lotuses, bread, and meat. Neferrenpet's figure has been almost completely destroyed.

In another kiosk at the left, the goddess Sekhmet stands behind a seated figure of Atum. She wears a sun disk and uraeus on her head; he wears the crown of Upper and Lower Egypt. Next to an elaborate offering table piled high with fruits, vegetables, fowl, and jugs of honey, Neferrenpet and his wife stand in adoration. She holds a lettuce in her right hand.

There is a third offering scene at the left end of the wall, with Isis standing behind a seated Ptah. Unlike the previous two kiosks, which have tent-pole-like columns, this one has *djed*-pillars. Again, Neferrenpet and Mutemwia stand in adoration.

Finally, on the rear (south) wall, the deceased couple offer praise to Ma'at and Ra-Harakhty who stand in a kiosk.

Returning to the front wall, the lower register begins with poorly preserved figures of Neferrenpet and his wife seated beside a sycomore fig tree. To their left, two half-registers that extend across the right half of the chamber show Neferrenpet's funeral procession and the scenes are filled with people who are shown in caricatures of overwhelming grief. A man with a whip drives four cattle pulling a sled that carries the sarcophagus. The mummy of Neferrenpet is elegantly wrapped in fine linen and wears a mask. It is protected by standing figures of the goddesses Isis (at right) and Nephthys. In the register below, nine dignitaries walk beside the sled. The second man in the procession has turned his grief-stricken face to bid a final farewell to Neferrenpet. All the mourners are finely dressed in long gowns and white sandals; each holds a staff. Two of them (the fourth and eighth) are bare-chested, their garments wrapped around their waists. Three men hold their hands to their face, overwhelmed by the death of their beloved master. The names and titles of the first three men in the procession are written beside them. The others are anonymous.

The funeral procession continues onto the left wall. On a second sledge at top left, a boat with a large and elaborate chest holds Neferrenpet's four canopic jars. The jars are protected by standing figures of Isis and Nephthys, and atop the shrine is a recumbent figure of Anubis. Six men pull the sledge and each has a slightly different costume, hairstyle, and pose. At least four men walk ahead carrying boxes of grave goods. In the half-register below, nine women mourners weep and ululate, their hands hiding their faces or pouring dust on their heads. Their breasts are bare and their hair is undone. To their left, five male servants stand between frames covered with flower garlands. Nine mourning women follow a priest and approach a huge pile of bread, meat, and various containers. The priest pours a libation; behind him, a second priest approaches with papyrus and a scribe's palette. Farther left, a *sem*-priest purifies the mummies of Neferrenpet and his wife. The mummies on the rear wall stand on a low mound of sand. Cones of scented fat and lotus flowers sit on their heads and yellow bands of cloth cross their fine linen wrappings. Two female mourners kneel at their feet, overcome with grief.

At left, in the upper scene on a round-topped stela, Neferrenpet stands in veneration before Osiris and Isis. Below, a priest offers incense before an offering table and seated figures of the deceased.

Neferrenpet's tomb is shown at left, an elaborate building with a columned portico, a large entrance gate, and figures of Anubis at the top flanking a small pyramid. This is a typical Ramesside period nobleman's tomb, but there is no archaeological evidence that TT 178 actually looked like it.

The ceiling of this chamber is decorated with four different ornamental designs, two with spiral motifs.

Above the doorway into the second chamber, scenes show the deceased couple venerating Osiris and Isis (on the left) and Ra-Harakhty and Ma'at (on the right). On the ceiling of the entrance a drawing of the *ba*-bird of Mutemwia, shown with a human face, a cone of scented fat and lotus flower on its head, and elaborately painted feathers, is one of the best-executed scenes in the tomb.

SECOND CHAMBER

The extensive use of yellow as a background color on the left (east) side of this room brightens the walls, but the scenes themselves are cluttered, filled with texts, geometric designs, people praying and making offerings, and craftsmen at work. Texts are fitted into every available space, figures are loosely drawn and almost randomly placed, and often there is no ground line. The scenes lack the formal organization characteristic of Egyptian wall paintings.

LEFT (EAST) SIDE

East of the doorway, Neferrenpet stands before an offering table adoring a jackal-headed Anubis. The fringe on his dress is

unusual and finely drawn. The scene continues onto the left (east) wall, where Neferrenpet again adores deities before a table of offerings. This time the gods are Ra-Harakhty and Ma'at, and Neferrenpet is accompanied by his wife Mutemwia and another woman identified only as a "companion." In front of another representation of the couple, a field of text has disappeared, but eight offering tables holding cones and geese are well preserved. To the right, the hippopotamus goddess Taweret (or Ipet), wearing horns and a sun disk, holds an *ankh*-sign.

The scene to the right in the corner of this wall is especially well done. Neferrenpet and Mutemwia stand before an offering table in a pose of veneration. At right, Hathor, Lady of the West, Lady of the Sacred Land, Eye of Ra emerges from a red granite mountain in her customary form as a cow. She wears a *menit* collar around her neck. Above her, the Horus falcon perches on a stand with a Ma'at feather. On the mountainside, a small round-topped stela is painted with a prayer to Osiris.

Between these scenes and those below, a prayer for the dead is written in large hieroglyphs.

In the lower register on the front (north) wall, two crudely drawn scribes of the treasury are dressed in the costume of lector-priests and purify offerings. This is called the *satj*-ritual and is related to the offering scene around the corner on the east wall where the elegantly dressed deceased couple sits before a list of offerings. The list is written in a series of forty-five rectangles, each of which names a different commodity, including water, different kinds of bread, cuts of meat, wine, figs, and the like. For some reason, the list was not completed and many squares were left empty.

Behind the couple, a *sem*-priest purifies offerings piled high on a table before seated figures of Neferrenpet and Mutemwia. At right, another priest holds the *meskhetiu*-tool used in the Opening of the Mouth ceremony. In the corner of the wall, the deceased receives purifying water from another *sem*-priest. In each of these last two scenes, the couple stands on low mounds of sand representing islands of creation. These are very important ceremonies, and the couple wears elaborate costumes and stands in stiff and formal poses. But their bodies have legs that are far too long and thin, unmodeled, and faces that are more caricatures than portraits or idealizations.

496-497 NEFERRENPET AND HIS WIFE BEFORE OSIRIS AND RA-HARAKHTY.

497 TOP POURING LIBATIONS.

497 BOTTOM A SEM-PRIEST PURIFIES NEFERRENPET AND HIS WIFE.

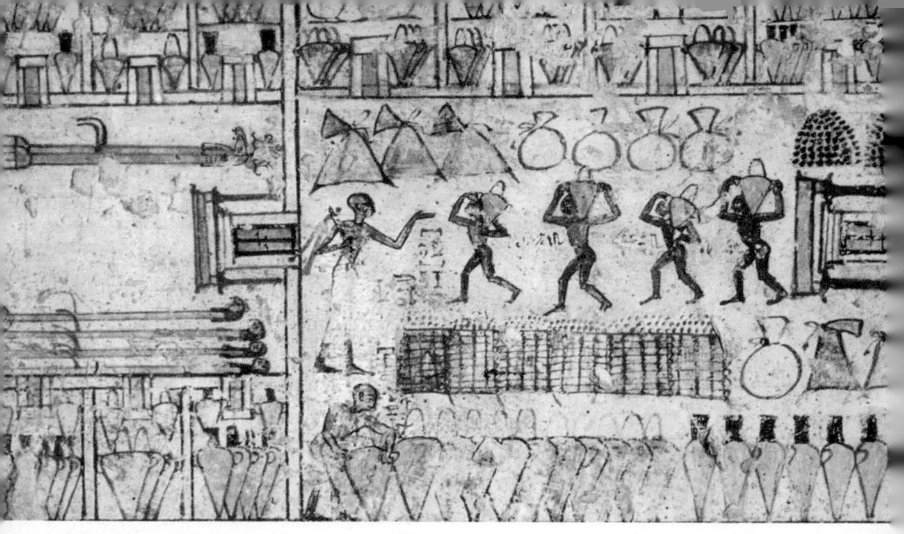

RIGHT (WEST) SIDE

On the west side of the door, the upper register shows the deceased couple looking beyond five columns of text to a richly provisioned offering table. Beyond it, on the west wall, an elaborately outfitted Osiris bark sails on a small rectangle of water. This is a nicely painted scene, complex and filled with religious symbolism. On the boat stands an anthropomorphized *djed*-pillar holding a flail and scepter in its hands, wearing an *atef*-crown and an elaborate costume. The pillar is held by the god Anubis. To the left are the standards of Thoth and Wepwawet, each held in the arms of an anthropomorphic *ankh*-sign or a *was*-scepter. Above the pillar, two falcons hold *shen*-signs in their talons.

Farther left, the couple is shown in different costumes than on the front wall. They look across seven columns of a prayer to Osiris toward offering stands and a shrine. In the shrine, a falcon with a flail and a feathered crown sits on a chest. Another figure of Neferrenpet stands at left before a small offering table, eight columns of text, and a bark carrying Ma'at, Ra, and Osiris. A winged *wedjat*-eye soars above them. Both scenes of barks are references to Book of the Dead chapter 183 that praises Osiris and Wennefer.

Return to the front wall and the lower register that begins there. In contrast to the profoundly religious scenes that we have so far seen in TT 178, this register contains scenes of craftsmen who work in the treasury under Neferrenpet's supervision. These scenes are much less formal than the former, and indeed they seem hastily done and sketch-like. They are interesting because the various activities have been associated with specific rooms and courtyards in the treasury building storerooms. One is looking at the actual activities undertaken in various parts of the treasury and the scenes help us work out the design and functions of building's parts.

Neferrenpet stands with a scribe's brush and palette, recording deliveries to the treasury. In two registers before him, scribes present inventories of the work that is shown at the right end of the wall. In the lower registers, men work with gold bars and copper vessels. One man operates bellows with his feet; another uses tongs to transfer a crucible. In the fourth register, a man blows through a straw to increase the heat in a hearth where metal is being smelted. Above him, a sculptor works on a gold statue lying on a sloping board. To the right, craftsmen use multiple drills to bore holes in beads. Such drills continued to be used in Egyptian craft shops well into the nineteenth century AD.

Behind Neferrenpet stands

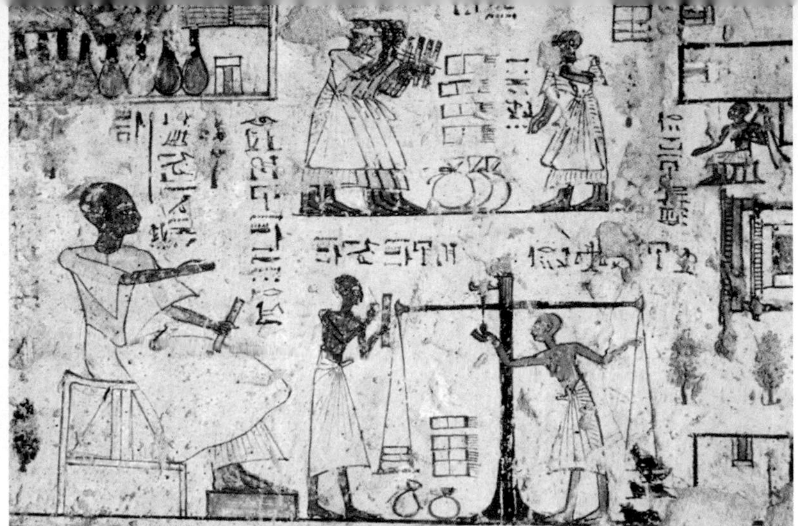

the treasury building itself. Its entrance is a small pylon closed by a double leaf wooden door. The building is drawn in typical Egyptian fashion: an aerial view of the structure is combined with drawings of architectural features and storeroom contents that have been laid on their side to ensure ease of recognition. Like Egyptian drawings of the human figure, this is a physically impossible but immediately intelligible pose. Inside the building, at the top (i.e., to the right of the entrance), the craftsmen Pehemnetjer sits in a small side chamber carving a statue of a nobleman. Before him stand small *shabtis* and a mummy mask. A tree is growing in the building's open courtyard, and at the left of the court (i.e., at the bottom of the scene) an overseer with a whip faces three servants.

The scene continues on the right (west) wall of the chamber. At the right, a doorway leads into the treasury storeroom, guarded by a man holding a whip and sitting on a small stool. There are small rooms to the left and right of the door (i.e., at the top and bottom of the scene) and trees grow in the open yard. Neferrenpet sits at left, holding a palette and watching two men weigh bolts of cloth on a balance. They are using weights shaped like cow heads. Above them, another four men deliver cloth.

Behind Neferrenpet, men deliver goods to the treasury storerooms. Four small rooms at the top (right of the storeroom doorway) contain amphorae. Four men bring sacks, baskets, and pots into the room. To the left, side chambers hold pottery and amphorae. In the central room are piles of rowing oars, some carved with ram heads, others with falcons, perhaps from sacred barges used in temple processions.

The scenes on the rear wall are badly damaged. Four seated figures are carved in a large niche. From the left they are: Neferrenpet's mother Wiai; his father Piai, Neferrenpet; and his wife, Mutemwia.

498 NEFERRENPET STANDS BEFORE THE TREASURY DOOR INSPECTING THE OFFERINGS.

499 TOP NEFERRENPET WITH BRUSH AND PALETTE RECORDS DELIVERIES TO THE TREASURY.

499 BOTTOM A SACRED BARGE TRANSPORTING A DJED PILLAR.

INTRODUCTION

TOMBS OF THE LATE NEW KINGDOM

Private tombs of the late 19th Dynasty and later tend to be small, often cut into areas of poor quality bedrock that earlier craftsmen would have rejected. Decoration in these tombs tends to emphasize religious scenes and texts or representations of the funerary cult. Some of their scenes had formerly been restricted to royal tombs. But in spite of limited subject matter and technical problems, talented artists produced bright and even lively scenes. Two good examples now open to the public are the tombs of Inherkhau and Shuroy.

TT 359: THE TOMB OF INHERKHAU

THE HISTORY

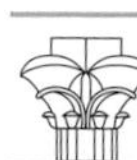

This small Dayr al-Madina tomb is not the best executed at Thebes but it is a beautiful tomb with many interesting and even delightful details. The tomb is an excellent example of Dynasty 20 painting, and one of the very few tombs of that period known from Dayr al-Madina. Inherkhau was a Foreman of the Lord of the Two Lands in the Place of Truth, meaning that he was in charge of workmen in the royal necropolis. He flourished during the reign of Rameses IV and continued working into the reign of Rameses VII some fifteen years later.

It is rare that we know the names of the artisans who decorated Theban tombs. For most of Egyptian history, these talented craftsmen remained anonymous, their works unsigned, their lives unknown. This is not the case with the tomb of Inherkhau. Not only do we know the names of the two artisans who worked here, but we are able to gain a few glimpses into their lives. The two men were brothers, the older named Nebnefer, the younger Hormin, and they were sons of the Chief Draftsman, Hori. Hori was from a distinguished and important family at Dayr al-Madina. His brother was also a man of considerable authority. Their father was permitted to erect a stela for them in the Valley of the Kings, an unusual honor.

We know which brother was responsible for decorating certain scenes in TT 359. Hormin, for example, signed the wonderful painting of the solar cat slaying Apophis on the left (west) wall of the second chamber. Next to it we read: "[This was] made by his brother, the draughtsman of Amen in the Horizon of Eternity, Hormin." On the rear wall of that chamber a scene

is accompanied by this text: "For the *ka* of the Draughtsman in the Place of Truth, Hormin, made by the Draughtsman of Amen in the Place of Truth, Nebnefer."

Perhaps it was while they were working on this tomb that Hormin wrote a letter to his father, Hori. He asked him to "speak with the leaders [of Dayr al-Madina] so that they will call up that servant of yours so that he will give a hand with me in the drawing. I am alone, for my brother [Nebnefer] is ill..."

Hormin's brother, Nebnefer, did very well during the reign of Rameses III, marrying the daughter of a well-off villager and raising three sons. However, early in the reign of Rameses VI, he ran afoul of a scribe of the vizier. He was taken to court and found guilty (but of what we do not know), and sentenced to 100 lashes, ten brandings, and a period of forced labor. One Egyptologist has suggested that such a penalty proves that Nebnefer was a bad man who was punished for more than a single offense. In any case, Nebnefer and his three sons are never heard from again.

A recent comparison of the painting of various scenes in TT 359 concluded that Hormin was a better artist than his brother was. Hormin's style is easy to spot. The faces he draws have a more curving profile and large eyes that slant slightly downwards; the ears are drawn with large tops and small lobes; the figures are high-waisted, and their navels are triangular; Hormin's brush strokes are thinner, and he draws more billowing skirts on the women. This is not to say that either man was a brilliant artist. The figures they drew are monotone, flat, and oddly proportioned, while their hieroglyphs are solid masses lacking detail. It does not help that the scenes they drew were of religious subjects, formal and generic, or that tastes of the time called for large heads and squat bodies. The result is somewhat disconcerting for those who have visited tombs such as those of Ramose or Rekhmire. The scenes in Inherkhau's tomb were done on a light yellow background intended to emulate the color of papyrus, the material on which the Book of the Dead was originally drawn.

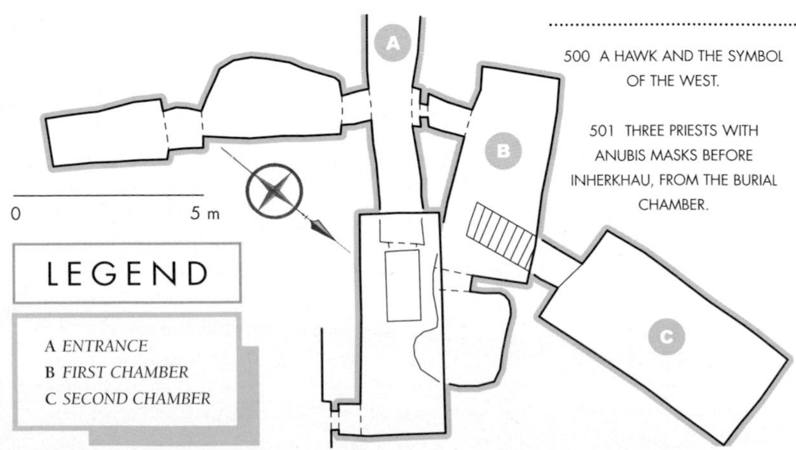

500 A HAWK AND THE SYMBOL OF THE WEST.

501 THREE PRIESTS WITH ANUBIS MASKS BEFORE INHERKHAU, FROM THE BURIAL CHAMBER.

VISIT

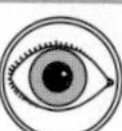

Inherkhau's tomb has two chambers, each 2 by 5 meters (6 by 15 feet). The superstructure is missing. Originally there would have been a courtyard and a small pyramid rising above it. Today, it is fronted by a bookshop and a refreshment stand. Like most tombs at Dayr al-Madina, TT 359 was a family burial site, and Inherkhau was buried here with other members of his family, some of whom were shown on the now-destroyed entrance jambs.

FIRST CHAMBER
Inside the tomb, the texts and decoration are restricted to religious scenes, especially from the Book of Gates. Scenes of daily life, so common in tombs earlier in the New Kingdom, are absent. Many Egyptologists believe this is due to a strong rise in personal piety during the troubled times of the late New Kingdom.

To the left of the entrance, on the side wall of a large niche, a reclining Anubis jackal is painted on a yellow background. On the rear (west) wall of the niche, a few traces remain of a scene in which Inherkhau and his wife kneel before a goddess. The feet of the two worshippers are unusually large. Nine figures who guard the gates of the netherworld sit in a row at the bottom of the wall.

At the left (west) end of the rear (north) wall of the first chamber, Inherkhau and his wife sit and play a board game called *senet*. To the left, the deceased holds a fan and wears a pectoral collar. Figures of the deceased couple at the far right show Inherkhau wearing a linen dress with a panther skin draped over his shoulders, holding out offerings of blue-painted ducks to now-destroyed figures of Osiris and Isis. Inherkhau's panther skin is especially detailed and the head of the animal, which actually was a metal clasp for fastening the panther skin, has finely drawn eyes and whiskers. The standing figure of his wife is destroyed. Other scenes in this register have also been destroyed. In the lower register, two female relatives stand before seated figures of

Inherkhau and his wife. Behind them, three priests, the first wearing the panther skin of a *sem*-priest, walk toward another scene of the couple.

On the left (east) side of the front (south) wall, Inherkhau, in a *sem*-priest's costume, and his wife offer incense to two registers of seated royalty. There are three kings and seven queens in the upper row, and seven kings, one prince, and one queen in the lower. Most are destroyed. All were similarly posed and dressed but bear different cartouches. In the upper row, those that can still be read are Amenhetep I and Ahmes I, the first two kings of Dynasty 18. In the lower row, the kings are Rameses I (Dynasty 19) and Nebhepetre Mentuhetep (of Dynasty 11). The queen with black skin and an elaborate vulture headdress is probably Ahmes-Nefertari, the wife of Ahmes I and mother of Amenhetep I, widely regarded in ancient times as the founder and patron of Dayr al-Madina. Her black skin symbolizes the fertility of the Nile Valley and has nothing to do with her race. The last figure in the lower row, now gone, was an artist named Huy, shown holding a palette. Parts of this wall were the work of Nebnefer.

The ceiling of the first chamber is elaborately painted with spiral designs and bulls' heads (called "bucrania") painted in red and black and drawn in the Minoan style of ancient Crete. There are also eight lovely panels of different geometric patterns, perhaps taken from woven reed matting.

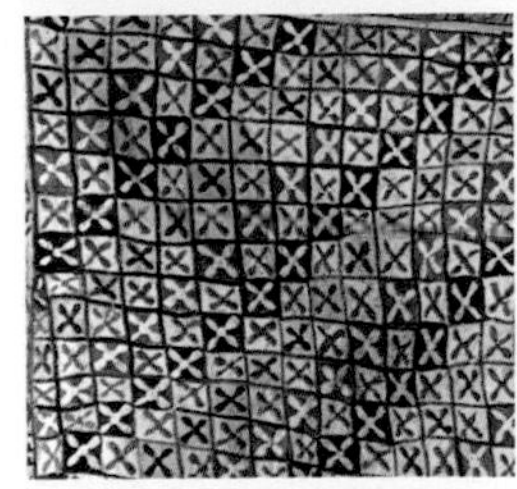

502, 503 CENTER AND BOTTOM THE RICH DECORATION OF THE CEILING OF THE FIRST CHAMBER PRESENTS SPIRAL DESIGNS, BULLS' HEADS, AND GEOMETRIC PATTERNS.

503 TOP VIEW OF THE FIRST CHAMBER OF THE TOMB OF INHERKHAU.

SECOND CHAMBER

Thirty-one scenes from the Book of the Dead are shown in the three registers on the walls of this chamber, fourteen on the right (east), and seventeen on the left (west). Originally, figures of Amenhetep I and Ahmes-Nefertari were painted on either side of the entrance to this chamber, but the figures were removed to Berlin early in the nineteenth century.

At the top left of the left wall, Inherkhau stands facing the entrance and the now-missing figures of Amenhetep I and Ahmes-Nefertari. He holds a staff and an "Isis knot" and stands before a kiosk above which is a sun disk. The scene and accompanying text are from Book of the Dead chapters 44 and 64. At left, the deceased and his wife sit in a boat steered by their son. Most of this wall was the work of Hormin. Nebnefer was responsible only for the right end of the lower register.

The well-drawn scarab beetle attached to a necklace accompanies Book of the Dead chapter 76, intended to "transform you into any shape you desire." Thoth (standing) and Osiris (seated) are being praised in the next scene by Inherkhau and to the right is a copy of Book of the Dead chapter 125, the "Negative Confession". Inherkhau is led toward a fiery lake by an ape-headed god in the next scene, and beyond it two barks sail upon the hieroglyph for "heaven." Four of the ten divisions of the netherworld are represented by cryptic drawings at the end of the wall.

In the middle register on the left wall, at the front of the chamber, Inherkhau kneels before a lotus flower, then again before the jackal-headed Souls of Hierakonpolis. It is unclear exactly what these souls represent, but they seem to have originated in predynastic Egyptian religious practices.

One of the most famous scenes in the tomb shows Inherkhau standing in adoration before a beautifully drawn *benu*-bird, a heron wearing a crown. The bird is nicely proportioned, its feathers finely drawn. To the right, the jackal-headed god Anubis is "returning the heart of the honorary Osiris" to the mummy of Inherkhau in order that he will be able to live again in the netherworld. The device behind the god is a symbol of Osiris and the site of Abydos.

In another well-known scene, the deceased kneels before a highly stylized figure of a falcon. This is one of several scenes in

which Inherkhau is shown with traces of stubble on his face, usually a sign of mourning in ancient Egypt. Like the heron's, the falcon's feathers are also drawn with particular care.

At right, in yet another famous scene, a "solar cat" or "cat of Heliopolis," slays the snake Apophis, the mortal enemy of the sun god. Both animals, and the persea tree behind them, are fanciful but well-executed figures. In the cat's left paw is a knife; its right paw holds down the head of the snake. The hairs on its back are raised in menace and it hisses as it delivers a fatal, bloody blow to the serpent. Note that even the snake hieroglyph in the second column of text above the figure has knives thrust into its twisted coils so that it is rendered harmless. At the end of the wall, a net is attached to a *was*-scepter. A colleague of Inherkhau, the foreman, Nakhtemut, stands below.

504 VIEW OF THE SECOND CHAMBER WITH THREE REGISTERS ON EACH WALL.

505 TOP INHERKHAU PRAISES THOTH AND OSIRIS.

505 BOTTOM LEFT THE CAT OF HELIOPOLIS SLAYS THE SNAKE APOPHIS.

505 BOTTOM RIGHT INHERKHAU AND HIS WIFE ON A BOAT WITH THEIR SONS (ABOVE); A SCARAB ATTACHED TO A NECKLACE (BELOW).

506 LEFT INHERKHAU BEFORE HIS BA-BIRD.

506 RIGHT INHERKHAU AND HIS WIFE BEFORE A HARPIST.

507 TOP INHERKHAU, HIS WIFE AND GRANDCHILDREN RECEIVING OFFERINGS.

The deceased are seated at the far left end of the lower register, receiving incense and water from two of their sons. At right, the couple, wearing rather ludicrous smiles, sits at a table on which stand four lit torches. Here again, Inherkhau is unshaven. He wraps his arm around his wife and lovingly holds her hand. The artist used the wrong skin color for Inherkhau's left arm, making it the same as his wife's, not the same as Inherkhau's right arm and face. Six priests stand before them; the first wears the costume of a *sem*-priest and holds a censer; the others, more plainly dressed, hold metal vessels. They are members of Inherkhau's family: the first are his sons Qenena (a priest), Hormin (a craftsmen), Amenemhab, and Hormes. The others are brothers.

The last scene at the right of this register is a traditional one, but it has some unusual details. The harpist plays a harp with twenty-two strings (although the artist drew thirty-six pegs for the strings). Usually, harpists are shown with their eyes closed to indicate blindness or deep concentration. But this harpist's eyes appear to be open. He sits on a mat, his fingers languidly plucking at the strings. His feet are drawn in an awkward position and, unusually, his mouth is open. Perhaps he is singing. The harpist is corpulent, with rolls of fat on his abdomen and the back of his neck, but his arms are thin. Inherkhau and his wife are smiling, clearly enjoying the music. In spite of their elaborate wigs and costumes, they seem a rather frumpy couple.

On the rear wall, Inherkhau and his son Hormin stand with the god Ptah (on the left); he and another of his sons Qenena, face a well-painted figure of Osiris (on the right). The left (west) half of the wall was the work of Hormin; the right (east) half was done by Nebnefer.

At the beginning of the upper register on the right wall, Inherkhau stands in adoration before a pylon with a human-headed ba-bird on top. The bird's feathers are highly stylized, as are the feathers of the other birds in this tomb, and its face and hands look very similar to those of Inherkhau himself. At left, a second scene shows the deceased before Ptah, the god of craftsmen and therefore one greatly praised in Dayr al-Madina.

The text that follows at left is a copy of Book of the Dead chapter 42, a list of body parts and the deities associated with them. "My hair is Nun," one of the rectangles proclaims, "My face is Ra; my eyes are Hathor; my ears are Wepwawet; my nose is She who presides over her lotus-leaf." The list moves down the body until, "My toes are living uraei; there is no member of mine devoid of a god, and Thoth is the protection of all my flesh."

The figure of a swallow standing atop a red granite mound of creation is a vignette from Book of the Dead chapter 86, a chapter for "being transformed into a swallow," a bird that to the

Egyptians stood for the idea of "wandering."

Inherkhau kneels before the two back-to-back lions of the "horizon." The hieroglyph for that word stands between them, with the sun above it and an *ankh*-sign hanging from the center.

At the right end of the middle register, Hathor strides toward the doorway and the now-missing figure of Ahmes-Nefertari. At left, Inherkhau worships a snake. This vignette is usually accompanied by chapter 87 of the Book of the Dead: "I am a long-lived snake; I pass the night and am reborn every day..." But the text written here has nothing to do with this chapter. Farther left, two jackals stand proudly before a kneeling Inherkhau. These finely drawn animals, with a single piece of cloth encircling their necks, are charged with pulling the solar bark through the night. Next, a priest wearing the mask of a falcon stands before the mummy of Inherkhau holding an adze and performing the Opening of the Mouth ceremony. The hieroglyph for the west stands behind a seated figure of Inherkhau who faces a huge *ka*-symbol.

In the lowest register at right, Inherkhau and his wife sit at a table piled high with offerings. At left, he sits before a low table receiving five couples and a *sem*-priest, but twenty-one names are given in the accompanying text.

One of the most appealing scenes in Inherkhau's tomb is at the left end of this wall. He and his wife sit on a delicately-made chair, surrounded by four grandchildren, all naked, three girls and one boy. (The defacing of the young boy's head occurred only recently, awful proof that better security is needed in Theban tombs.) Each child holds a young bird as an evocation of life. A platter of figs sits on a table before the proud and happy grandparents. Offering bearers approach the group with funerary goods that include a box of *shabtis* and a libation vasel.

507 BOTTOM INHERKHAU IN FRONT OF TWO JACKALS AND THE SNAKE APOPHIS.

5

TT 13: THE TOMB OF SHUROY

THE HISTORY

This small, two-chambered tomb belonged to Shuroy and his wife, Wernefer. Shuroy was the Head of the Brazier Bearers in the temple of Amen at Karnak sometime during Dynasty 19. His tomb is decorated in an informal style; the scenes are rapidly drawn, sometimes only in red ink outline, and they usually (though not always) lack internal details. Colors are soft, almost pastels, applied to a light grey or white background, and there is heavy use of light blue.

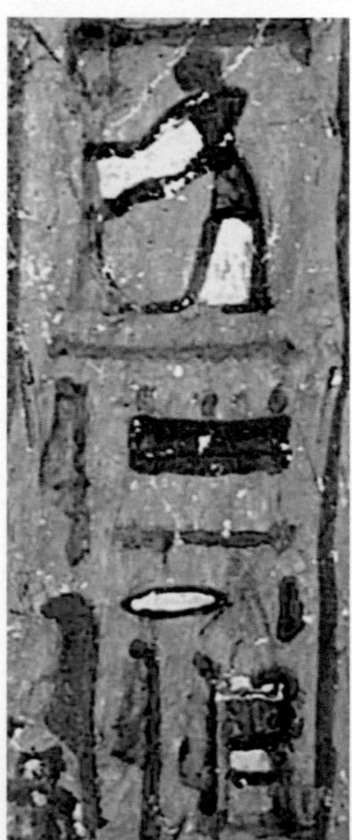

VISIT

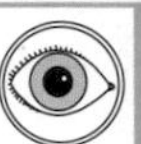

In the **ENTRANCE**, the right thickness of the door shows Shuroy and his wife in a pose of adoration.

CHAMBER 1, LEFT HALF In the upper register, scenes from the Book of Gates show Shuroy and his wife before various deities and guardians of the gates of the netherworld. Near the center of the left wall, the couple face a heavily laden table of offerings. To the right, Ra-Harakhty sits in a kiosk holding an *ankh*-sign and a *was*-scepter, facing left toward a standing figure of the goddess Ma'at. The god's figure is nicely painted, but his arms and legs are disproportionately long and thin, making him appear more a caricature than a formal drawing. In the register below, now mostly destroyed, the couple stand in adoration before various deities and a king and queen. On the left side of the chamber's rear wall, a large *djed*-pillar is clothed in linen and ribbons above a large hieroglyph meaning "the West."

CHAMBER 1, RIGHT HALF On the right side of the rear wall, there is again a *djed*-pillar but below it are variously-shaped loaves of bread and vessels. The front wall and the chamber's right wall continue the Book of Gates and various genii are shown in the same order as on the left wall. Representations of bread loaves are nicely drawn. The small pin pricks painted across the bread's surface are similar to those made by modern Upper Egyptian women when baking at home. They claim that the holes ensure that the loaves bake evenly. In the lower register, Shuroy and his wife are adoring Ma'at and Ra-Harakhty. The ceiling of this chamber is painted with two different geometric patterns.

CHAMBER 2 On the door thicknesses leading into the second chamber, two badly destroyed figures of Shuroy (on the right) and his wife (on the left) were drawn in red ink only.

Four registers cover the long front wall to the right of the door. At the top, twenty-two male offering bearers march forward, nineteen of them carrying large, sloppily painted boxes on their heads, three others with bundles of vegetables. In the second register, Shuroy and male relatives approach a garden. There is a small collection of crudely drawn trees at the right and servants sit beneath them, their head in their hands as if sleeping. In the third register, a funeral procession marches forward with servants bearing foodstuffs, others squatting before baskets of vegetables and, at right, men carrying a yoke on their shoulders to which boxes are attached. A cow walks to the right. In the bottom register, the procession continues. Young, naked girls dance beside their mothers in the center of the register, their hands in the air, knees bent as if jumping or skipping. Male bearers walk toward the mummy of Shuroy, which stands at the right end of the wall. Mourning women kneel at his feet, wailing and pouring dirt on their heads.

On the rear wall, top left, a priest holds instruments to be used in the Opening of the Mouth ritual while a female mourner stands before the mummy. Below, Shuroy kneels and holds braziers before a figure of Hathor, shown as a cow with an elaborate plumed headdress emerging from a mountain.

Inside the central niche in the rear wall, little is preserved except on the right wall where a figure of a squatting man is followed by Shuroy offering braziers, then by his wife and an unidentified male.

To the right of the niche, Thoth leads Shuroy before a seated figure of Osiris, accompanied by Isis and Nephthys. Below, a scene of libation has almost completely disappeared.

The side wall and the left side of the front wall are almost completely gone. Traces can be seen of offering bearers standing before Shuroy and his wife at a banquet scene. The scene continues in the lower register.

The ceiling of the second chamber was decorated with a light yellow and white checkerboard pattern and a series of red and yellow circles arranged in large squares.

508 AND 509 THREE IMAGES SHOWING DIFFERENT STAGES OF THE DECORATION OF THE TOMB OF SHUROY.

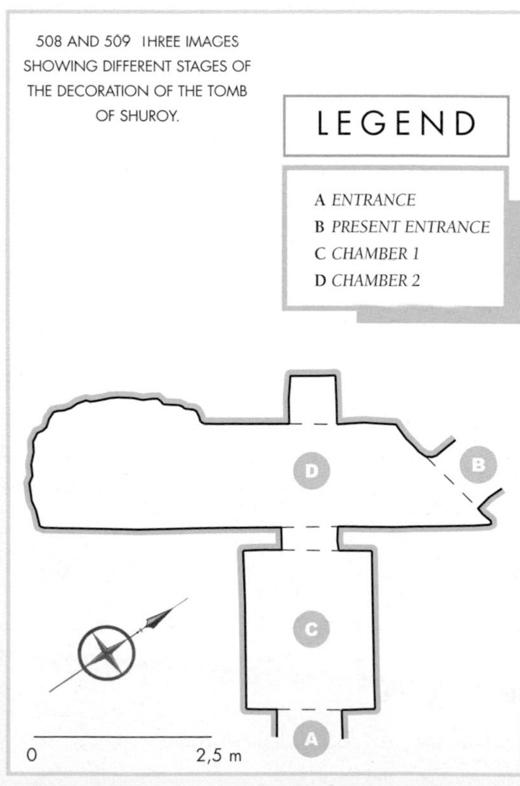

6
TEMPLES OUTSIDE THEBES

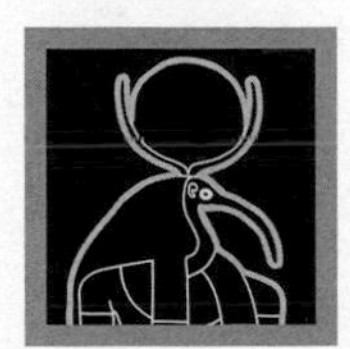

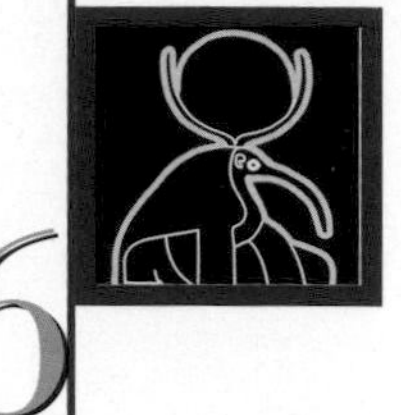

6

INTRODUCTION

512 THE NILE GOD, FROM RELIEFS IN THE TEMPLE OF RAMESES II AT ABYDOS.

Increasingly, tourist itineraries include visits to Upper Egyptian temples outside Thebes. These include Dandara and Abydos, north of Thebes, which can be visited either by car (currently allowed to carry foreigners only in security convoys), and Isna, Edfu, and Kom Ombo, which are usually visited as part of a Nile cruise ship package. The temples are of considerable interest. Abydos boasts some of the finest examples of carved and painted relief from Dynasty 19; Edfu is nearly intact and gives a wonderful feel for Ptolemaic architecture. Getting to these sites is as enjoyable as visiting the temples themselves, especially if one sails to them. The Nile Valley is stunningly beautiful, the river cruise hypnotically restful, and the opportunities for bird- and people-watching are themselves worth the trip.

CAIRO
ABYDOS
DANDARA
THEBES
LUXOR
ISNA
EDFU
KOM OMBO

6

ABYDOS

514 SETY I WITH ISIS, FROM THE ABYDOS TEMPLE.

515 TOP SETY I OFFERING INCENSE AND POURING WATER BEFORE OSIRIS AND HORUS.

515 BOTTOM THE RESURRECTION OF THE DEAD PHARAOH, CHAPEL OF PTAH.

THE HISTORY

For several thousand years, the site of Abydos (the ancient *Abdju*) flourished as a cemetery for the people of Thinis, the capital of Egypt's eighth Upper Egyptian nome. A local deity, Khentyamentiu (the 'Foremost of the Westerners,' meaning the chief one among the dead), had a cult center here during Egypt's first two dynasties. In the Old Kingdom, this god was joined to another underworld deity, Osiris. Osiris came to be seen as the pre-eminent god of the underworld and the personification of Egypt's deceased kings. By the Middle Kingdom, Abydos was described as the burial place of Osiris and many increasingly popular and important religious ceremonies were held there to commemorate his death and rebirth in the afterlife. Pilgrims came in great numbers to make offerings, erect stelae and statues and, if they could afford it, to build a tomb or a cenotaph. The town of Thinis, with which Abydos was associated, has never been located. But Abydos itself is well-known as one of the most extensive and important cemeteries and cult sites of dynastic times.

With good reason, the most famous building at Abydos today is 'The Mansion of Millions of Years of King Menma'atre [Sety I] Who Rests in Abydos.' This temple was begun by Sety I and completed by his son, Rameses II. It is elegantly decorated and uniquely well-preserved, one of the masterpieces of Egyptian art and architecture. Some Egyptologists have claimed that the temple's unusual L-shaped plan was chosen to avoid damaging the Osireion, an ancient, subterranean cenotaph lying immediately behind the temple. But many scholars now believe that the Osireion was also built by Sety I, copying the plans of tombs in the Valley of the Kings. They doubt its reputed Old Kingdom origins.

THE TEMPLE OF SETY I

VISIT

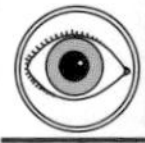

The temple of Sety I lies about 15 kilometers (9 miles) west of the Nile on the edge of the desert, a few meters above the village and fields of al-Balliana. A modern staircase leads to its ruined first pylon and first court. The back of the pylon has fourteen niches built into it that originally held Osiris statues. Fragments of some of them can still be seen here, and three statue heads are on display to the left of the entrance in the first hypostyle hall. A pair of large stone ablution basins used by ancient priests for purification stand in the center of the court. The north and south walls of the court are

decorated with scenes of battles fought in western Asia. Note at the left (east) end of the left (south) wall a soldier emptying a basketful of severed hands before scribes. The hands were hacked from enemy soldiers as a method of tallying the number of dead.

A narrow terrace stretches along the rear (west) wall of the court. In its left rear (southwest) and right rear (northwest) corners, rows of sons and daughters of Rameses II march across the walls. Originally, twenty-seven sons and twenty-nine daughters were shown here, each of them named, and shown in order of their birth.

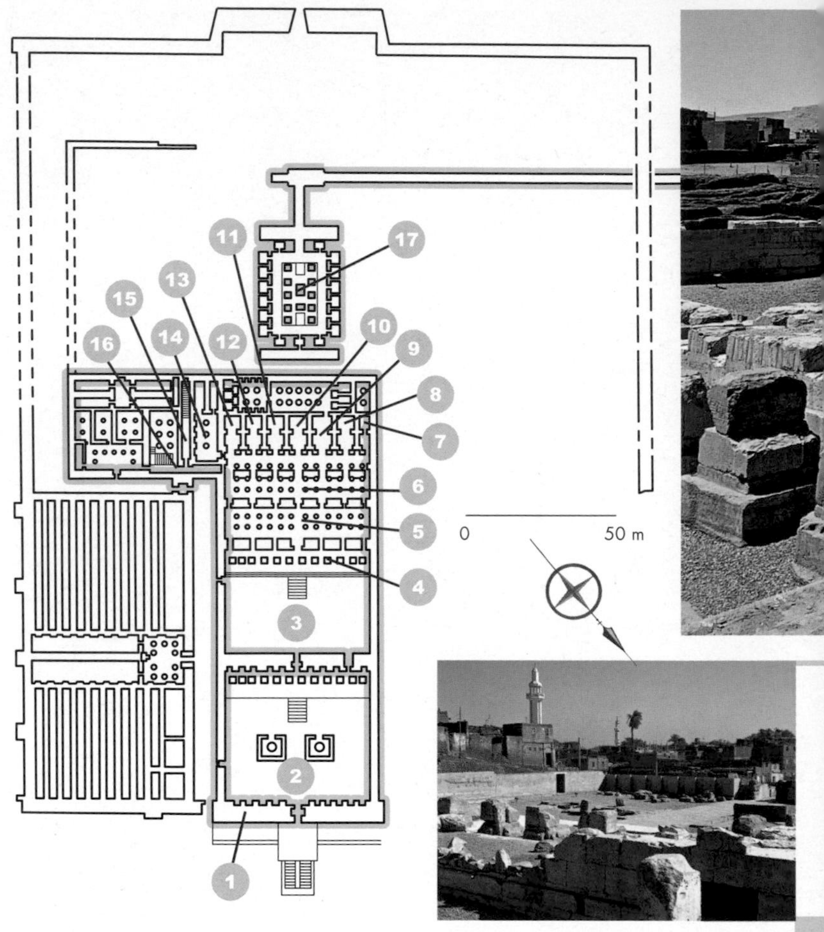

◆ THE SECOND COURT ◆

The Second Court was also the work of Rameses II. At the rear stands a portico, 1.25 meters (nearly 4 feet) high, with a row of twelve pillars across the front. Each pillar is decorated with scenes of Rameses II or Sety I offering to various deities. These are standard scenes, but there is an unusual detail on the right (north) face of the first pillar to the left (south) of the court's main axis. Rameses II wears a long gown that is depicted so sheer that his legs are clearly visible through it. But the gown also overlaps several hieroglyphs carved on the right, and these cannot be seen through the cloth. The rear (west) wall of the portico was originally designed with doors opening between twelve narrow walls. These were filled in, however, to create solid walls on either side of the main gateway and then completely decorated. The colors here are well-preserved, even though the wall has been badly damaged. At the right (north) end, Rameses II stands with Horus and Khnum. To the left, he stands before a persea tree flanked by Thoth and Ptah. Ptah writes the king's name on the leaves of the tree and Thoth carries palm branches that have been notched to indicate the many years the king will hopefully live. Nearer the central gate, the king offers an

LEGEND

1 *FIRST PYLON*
2 *FIRST COURT*
3 *SECOND COURT*
4 *PORTICO*
5 *FIRST HYPOSTYLE HALL*
6 *SECOND HYPOSTYLE HALL*
7 *CHAPEL OF HORUS*
8 *CHAPEL OF ISIS*
9 *CHAPEL OF OSIRIS*
10 *CHAPEL OF AMEN-RA*
11 *CHAPEL OF RA-HARAKHTY*
12 *CHAPEL OF PTAH*
13 *CHAPEL OF THE DEIFIED SETY*
14 *HALL OF NEFERTUM AND PTAH- SOKAR*
15 *CORRIDOR OF THE BULLS*
16 *HALL OF ANCESTORS*
17 *OSIREION*

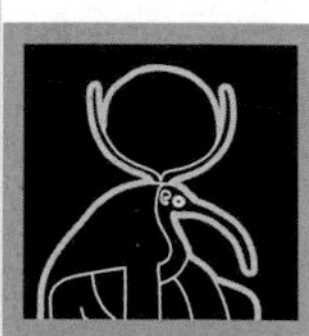

ankh-sign to Osiris, Isis, and Sety I.

South of the central gateway, 116 columns of text describe the youth and early years of the reign of Rameses II. He boasts of having visited Abydos soon after his coronation, and finding his father's temple unfinished, ordering that it be completed. "Now, the Temple of Sety I, its front and its rear were (still) under construction when he entered heaven. There were none who completed its monuments, none who erected its pillars upon its terrace. I being now Lord of the Two Lands, I shall finish them in proper fashion. I will build up the walls in the temple of the one who begot me."

516 CENTER THE FIRST COURT OF THE TEMPLE OF SETY I.

516-517 THE SECOND COURT OF THE TEMPLE AND THE PORTICO.

517 BOTTOM DOORWAY TO THE SECOND COURT.

518 TOP SETY I EMBRACED BY ATUM, RELIEF FROM THE HYPOSTYLE HALL.

518 BOTTOM THE FIRST HYPOSTYLE HALL.

519 PILLARS OF THE PORTICO COVERED WITH RELIEFS DEPICTING SETY I WITH VARIOUS DIVINITIES.

◆ THE FIRST HYPOSTYLE HALL ◆

The First Hypostyle Hall is a huge chamber with two rows of twelve papyriform columns that support an 8 meter (26 foot) high ceiling. The walls are heavily decorated with elaborately carved and painted scenes. (The fluorescent tubes that lie on the floor provide an unsatisfactory light, but even so the fine quality workmanship is obvious.) We will tour the hall starting in its front left (southeast) corner and proceed counterclockwise to the rear left (southwest) corner.

The front (east) wall has three "piers" on each side of the central doorway with large niches between them. At the far right (south), in the upper register, the king pulls the sacred bark of Sokar. Below, he stands before the god Min. On the second pier, the king kneels on symbols of Upper and Lower Egypt and is joined by Anubis and Horus. Below, the king makes offerings to Ptah. On the third pier, the king offers vases to Amen-Ra and, below, receives purification from Atum and Amen-Ra.

On the fourth pier, immediately left (north) of the main doorway, Amen-Ra holds an *ankh*-sign before the king's face and Osiris offers a miniature pavilion, the symbol of the Heb-Sed Festival, and a notched palm branch representing years of long life. The scene below is similar to that on the third pier. On the fifth pier, at the top, the king hoes the earth, preparing the foundations of the new temple, as Osiris watches. Below, the king and the goddess Seshat prepare to drive stakes that will define the temple's plan on the ground. On the sixth pier, the king, dressed in an elaborately painted costume, presents the now-finished temple to Horus. Above, he stands in adoration before the god.

At the right end of the right (north) wall, Thoth and Horus purify the king with *ankh*-signs that flow like water from gold vases. In the center of the wall, below a once-grilled window, the king is led into the temple by Horus and Wepwawet to be greeted by Hathor. The goddesses holds symbols that refer both to water and to obeisance. At left, Rameses II presents to Osiris a papyrus case that holds the deed to the temple. Isis and Horus stand nearby. Above, the king kneels before Thoth, who writes the royal name on the leaves of a persea tree.

At the right (north) end of the rear (west) wall of the hall, Rameses II receives a royal crown from Horus and a uraeus and sistrum from Isis. He is suckled by Isis in the scene above. Farther left, the king receives the symbol of Heb-Sed jubilees from Osiris, Horus, and Isis. Above, the king's name is written on his shoulder by Thoth. Near the main axis of the temple, Rameses II offers small statuettes to Amen-Ra and Mut and above, he burns incense before Amen-Ra and Khonsu. Similar scenes are repeated on the wall immediately left (south) of the main axis. These are followed by further scenes of the king with Mut, Ptah, Sekhmet, and the bark of Sokar. On the left (south) wall of the hall, the birth of Rameses II is shown in a badly damaged scene. He is fashioned on a potter's wheel by Khnum, then cared for by Isis.

◆ THE SECOND HYPOSTYLE HALL ◆

The Second Hypostyle Hall has three rows of twelve columns each, the back row standing on a low raised platform. Behind this row of columns, seven doorways lead into seven chapels. The front (east) wall of the hall shows Rameses II offering to various deities. But the workmanship on this wall, and indeed, in much of the temple, pales in comparison to the reliefs on the right (north) end of this hall. Carved in the reign of Sety I but usurped by Rameses II, these are among the most beautiful reliefs in all of New Kingdom Egypt, and many of them still retain traces of the original paint.

At right, Sety I burns incense and makes libations before Osiris and Horus. The purifying water falls gracefully into three heart-shaped vessels. A superb figure of Horus stands behind them. In the register above, the king kneels, hands in adoration, his body lithe and youthful. In the center of the wall, the king makes offerings before a shrine of Osiris. Farther on, Osiris sits between figures of Ma'at and Renpet, and behind him stand Isis, Imenty, and Nephthys. The goddesses are very finely carved; note especially the details of their hair and dresses. It is also worth pausing to admire the details in the hieroglyphs, the finely-feathered birds, woven baskets, and small, human figures of remarkable grace. Further left, the king offers Ma'at to Osiris, Isis, and Horus, while above, Horus presents symbols of royal office. On the wall that lies opposite the third row of columns, there is an elegantly and elaborately carved *djed*-pillar.

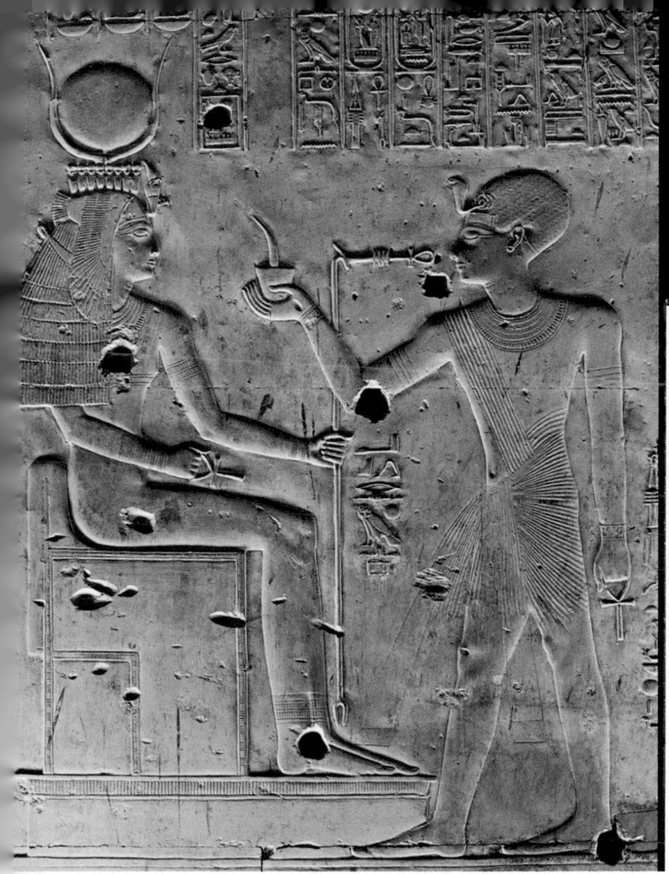

520 TOP VIEW OF THE CORRIDOR LEADING TO THE SEVEN CHAPELS.

520 BOTTOM LEFT HATHOR OFFERING AN ANKH-SIGN TO SETY I.

520 BOTTOM RIGHT SETY I KNEELING BEFORE PTAH IN A SHRINE.

521 SETY I AS A YOUNG MAN OFFERING TO ISIS.

◆ SEVEN CHAPELS ◆

We will describe the seven chapels behind the back wall of the second hypostyle hall from right (north) to left (south). Since the scenes in five of the seven chapels are repetitive, we will describe them in general, reserving more detailed descriptions for scenes in the Osiris Chapel and that of Sety I. From north, the seven chapels are as follows:

1. Chapel of Horus
2. Chapel of Isis
3. Chapel of Osiris (with a complex of other chambers behind it)
4. Chapel of Amen-Ra
5. Chapel of Ra-Harakhty
6. Chapel of Ptah
7. Chapel of the deified Sety I

◆ CHAPELS 1-6 ◆

The chapels have vaulted ceilings recalling the shape of the small reed huts that served as shrines in predynastic times. The last three chapels (numbers 5, 6, and 7) were never painted, in contrast especially to the chapel of Osiris, where the paint is still fresh and bright. On the rear wall of each chapel is an elaborate double false door. On the right (north) wall, the king grasps the two handles of double-leaf doors on the tall, narrow shrine, then censes and adores the deity inside. Farther left, the king stands before an offering table, offering foods and incense before the god's bark, then gives fresh linen robes and ointments to statues of the god or goddess. On the left (south) wall, the king again censes statues of deities and offers clothing and jewelry. Farther left, he presents insignias to the gods and adjusts their crowns. When these ceremonies are completed, the king pours sand from a small bowl onto the floor and departs. The sand will then be swept to erase any footprints, leaving the chapel in pristine condition until the round of ritual feeding, censing, and clothing is repeated.

◆ CHAPEL 3 ◆

Although the scenes on the chapel walls are similar to those in chapels 1–6, the rear wall of the Chapel 3, or Chapel of Osiris, has a real doorway in place of a false door that leads into a chamber with ten columns and well-painted walls. On the front wall, right (south) of the doorway, the king stands before a shrine of Osiris and Isis, and makes offerings of incense, bread, wine, and Ma'at to various deities including Anubis, Heket (a frog goddess), Horus, and a goose-headed Hapy. On the rear (west) wall, the king and Isis erect a *djed*-pillar and dress it in linen garments. At the far right, Sety I raises a very finely carved standard of Abydos, and at left he offers incense to the standard of Thoth, depicted here as an ibis.

At the right (north) end of the columned hall, doors lead into three small sanctuaries dedicated to Horus (with Osiris and Isis), Sety I (with Osiris, Anubis, Isis, Thoth, and Horus-son-of-Isis), and Isis (with Horus). All three are very well decorated, carved with great attention to detail and with much color still preserved. In the Horus sanctuary, Sety offers to the god (right wall), while Isis presents the king to Horus who offers a crook and flail (rear wall). At the right end of the left wall, an unusual scene shows the king scrubbing an offering table and filling an incense burner. The central Sety I sanctuary is decorated with scenes of purification. At right, in the Isis sanctuary, the king makes offerings and receives the symbol of the Heb-Sed Festival.

At the southern end of the columned hall, a doorway leads into a room with four columns and three small sanctuaries beyond its rear wall. In the central sanctuary, Osiris lies on a bier with the king and various deities in attendance. Much in these rooms has been badly damaged.

◆ CHAPEL 7 ◆

Scenes in Chapel 7, or Chapel of the Deified Sety I, are devoted to the celebration of the king's Heb-Sed Festival, his coronation, the recognition of his royal authority by the gods, and the activities of his mortuary cult.

On the right (north) wall, the king is led forward by Montu and Atum and various goddesses to be united with his royal ancestors. The procession is followed by Thoth and the Souls of Nekhen (symbolizing the most ancient rulers of Upper Egypt). In an especially beautiful composition, Sety I is embraced by goddesses of Upper and Lower Egypt, and Horus and Thoth tie together symbols of the Two Lands. On the left (south) wall, Thoth offers to the king, and other deities watch as he is crowned by Horus. The Souls of Pe (ancient rulers of Lower Egypt) and Nekhen are preceded by eight standards, each carried by anthropomorphic *ankh*-signs.

◆ HALL OF NEFERTUM AND PTAH-SOKAR ◆

In the rear left (southwest) corner of the Second Hypostyle Hall, a door leads into a three-columned hall dedicated to two mortuary deities of the Memphite area. Nefertum wears a lotus blossom on his head out of which the sun is said to rise. Ptah-Sokar, a syncretism of two deities, is a god closely associated with the afterlife and with Osiris. The wall adjacent to the door shows Ptah-Sokar offering an *ankh*-sign to the king. The god's titles and forty-three lines of text relate to offerings being made. To the right of the hall are two small shrines. That on the right is dedicated to Ptah-Sokar and shows the king before a list of fifty-two Memphite deities. Below is a scene of the resurrection of Osiris. On the left (south) wall, Osiris lies upon a bier flanked by deities. The left-hand shrine is dedicated to Nefertum and its walls are carved with figures of many other gods as well. The rear (south) wall of the hall has four niches: Atum, Thoth, and Sokar are in the first; Osiris, Min and a third god are in the second.

522 A BEAUTIFULLY CARVED SCENES OF THE KING OFFERING TO HORUS AND RA-HARAKHTY.

523 TOP THE RESURRECTION OF OSIRIS, FLANKED BY HIS SON HORUS AND HIS WIFE ISIS.

523 BOTTOM SETY I, WEARING THE BLUE CROWN, OFFERING A STATUE OF THE GODDESS MA'AT.

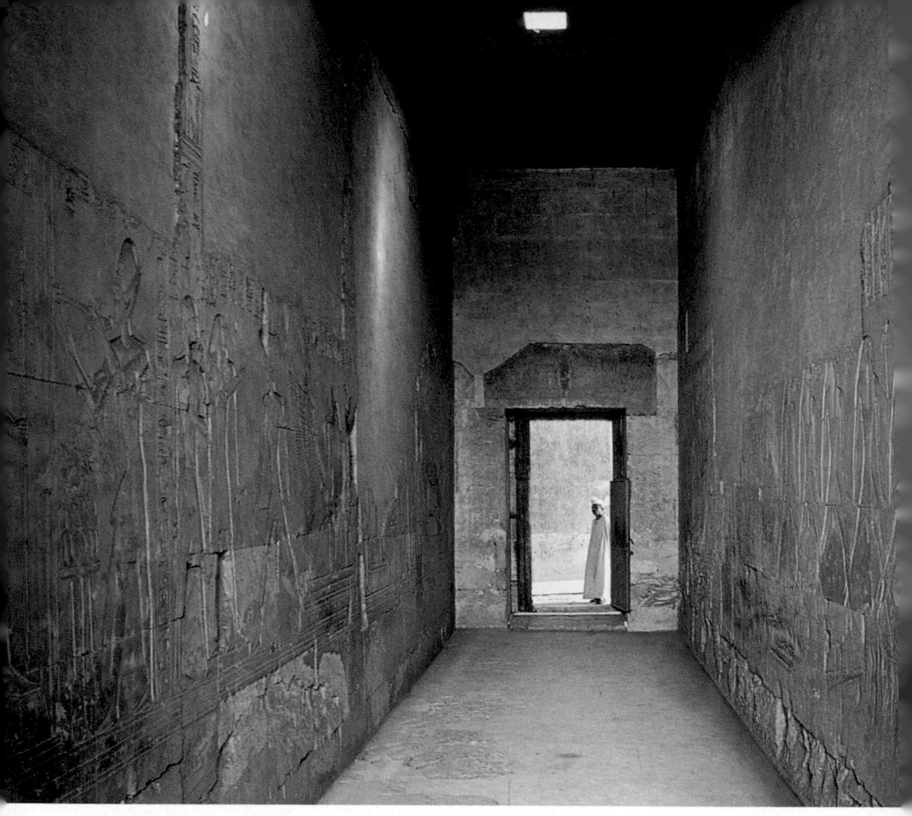

◆ HALL OF ANCESTORS ◆

The entrance to this corridor, also called the Gallery of the Lists, lies immediately left (east) of the Hall of Nefertum and Ptah-Sokar. The left (east) wall of the corridor shows the king offering to many deities, but it is the right (west) wall that visitors come to see. Even better known than the superbly carved walls in the Second Hypostyle Hall, this wall is the most famous at Abydos because of its historical importance and its fine carving. Standing with his father, Sety I, young Prince Rameses (soon to become Rameses II) holds a papyrus bearing the names of his royal predecessors. His father holds incense before the king list (known as the Abydos King List), which is written in a series of rectangles on the wall before them. Beginning with Menes at the top left (traditionally the first king of the First Dynasty), the list names seventy-six kings, ending at the bottom right with Sety I. Minor kings are excluded, as are such female rulers as Hatshepsut and the rulers of the "heretical" Amarna Period, Amenhetep IV/Akhenaten, Smenkhkare, Tutankhamen, and Ay. Thus, Horemheb becomes the immediate successor of Amenhetep III.

Farther south along this corridor, doorways lead into rooms used by priests for the storage of temple equipment and for the preparation of offerings. Immediately beyond the King List, a door cuts through the right (west) wall into a sloping corridor sometimes called the Corridor of the Bulls.

◆ THE CORRIDOR OF THE BULLS ◆

On its walls well-carved scenes show (on the right) Rameses II and his eldest son, Amenherkhepshef, lassoing a bull. Farther west, the king pulls a bark of Sokar. On the left (south) wall, the king drives four calves toward Khonsu and Sety I. To the west, the king and others pull on a bird net, trapping wild ducks and presenting them to Amen-Ra and Mut. Such

scenes are meant to show the king's control over untamed nature. Above, scenes recount the foundation ceremony when the temple was first built.

◆ OSIREION ◆

The Corridor of the Bulls leads out of the temple to the Osireion, a cenotaph of Sety I also regarded as the burial place of the god Osiris. Work on the building was begun by Sety I but it was not completed until seventy years later, by his grandson Merenptah. Modeled on the plan of a New Kingdom royal tomb in the Valley of the Kings, its long L-shaped corridor leads to a subterranean faux burial chamber. Built in a huge pit cut into the desert behind the temple, the structure was then covered over with debris. The burial chamber, a pillared hall measuring 30 by 20 meters (98 by 65 feet), was constructed of red granite. A sarcophagus sat on a low mound in the center of the hall, surrounded by a water-filled channel. The mound represents the primeval island on which creation first took place; the channel represents the ocean in which the island lay. Today, ground water at Abydos has risen and the entire building is flooded year-round. Fish can even be seen swimming in the deep pools that cover the floor. The walls of the original corridor leading down from the surface were decorated with scenes and texts from the Book of Gates. Beyond, after the corridor turns sharply to the left, astronomical scenes and texts from the Book of the Dead can be seen on walls and ceilings. An especially elegant scene of the sky goddess Nut covers the ceiling at the back of the burial chamber. A modern wooden staircase leads down to the center of the structure.

524 VIEW OF THE HALL OF ANCESTORS.

525 TOP DETAIL OF THE KING LIST IN THE HALL OF ANCESTORS.

525 BOTTOM SETY I FOLLOWED BY HIS SON RAMESES II (NOT VISIBLE) OFFERING BIRDS TO AMEN-RA AND MUT.

THE TEMPLE OF RAMESES II

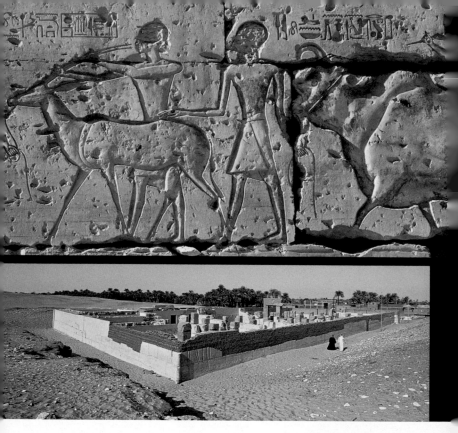

About 300 meters (1000 feet) north of Sety's temple stand the remains of a temple built by Rameses II. Like Sety's Osireion, this too is a cenotaph, but it is modeled on a New Kingdom Theban temple, not on a royal tomb. In spite of its missing roof and upper walls, the standard scenes carved on its walls are of special interest because of their remarkably well-preserved paint. The exterior walls of the temple display an elaborate calendar of festivals on the south wall, and scenes of the battle of Kadesh on the north and west walls. Inside, an open court has Osirid pillars around its perimeter and offering scenes on its walls. West of the courtyard, behind a small portico, four small chapels are dedicated (from right to left) to Rameses II, the Ennead, royal ancestors, and Sety I. Another chapel, for the god Onuris, lies behind them on the right. Around the second of two eight-pillared halls, other chapels, several of them especially well-carved, are dedicated to Osiris, the Theban Triad, Thoth, and Min. The stela at the rear of the temple, placed here only recently, hides the entrance to a chamber housing a large granite statue group of Rameses II, Sety I, Amen, and two goddesses.

526-527 RELIEF FROM THE TEMPLE OF RAMESES II AT ABYDOS OF A PROCESSION FOR A RITUAL SACRIFICE.

526 CENTER VIEW OF THE SMALL TEMPLE OF RAMESES II.

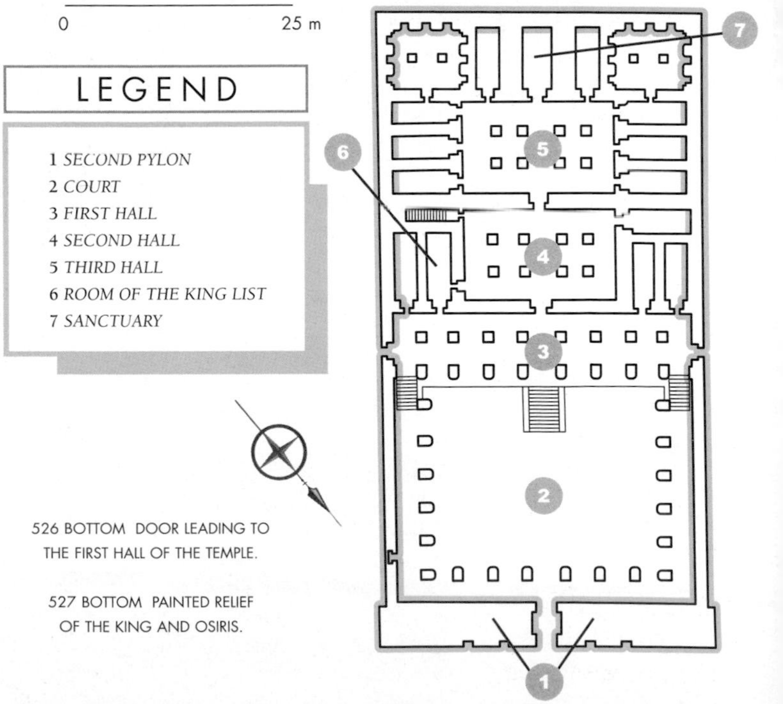

0 25 m

LEGEND

1 *SECOND PYLON*
2 *COURT*
3 *FIRST HALL*
4 *SECOND HALL*
5 *THIRD HALL*
6 *ROOM OF THE KING LIST*
7 *SANCTUARY*

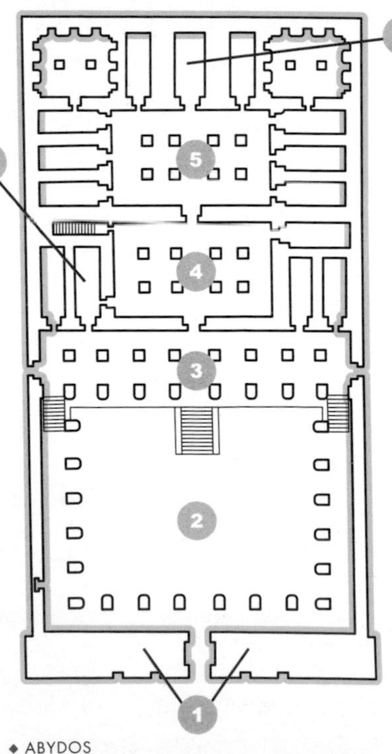

526 BOTTOM DOOR LEADING TO THE FIRST HALL OF THE TEMPLE.

527 BOTTOM PAINTED RELIEF OF THE KING AND OSIRIS.

6

THE TEMPLE OF DANDARA

THE HISTORY

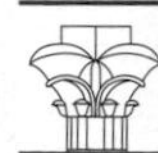

Lying about 70 kilometers (42 miles) north of Luxor, the Ptolemaic temple at Dandara is one of the best-preserved monuments in Egypt and well worth a visit. Several hotels in Luxor offer boat trips to the site, departing early in the morning and returning that evening. The drive from Luxor, in spite of the convoy system imposed by Egyptian security, is pleasant and takes one past several interesting villages. Thirty kilometers (18 miles) north of Luxor on the East Bank lies Qus, ancient Apollinopolis Parva, with a fine twelfth century mosque. Forty-one kilometers (25 miles) north, Qift, ancient Coptos, lies at the mouth of the Wadi Hammamat, one of the principal routes to the Red Sea and to the mines and quarries of the Red Sea Hills. In ancient times, Qift was a major trade center and home to the god Min. In the nineteenth century, it was also home to the Qiftis, archaeological workmen trained by Sir Flinders Petrie to dig Egyptian archaeological sites. Sixty-two kilometers (37 miles) north lies Qena, the governorate capital, and here one crosses a new bridge to the West Bank of the Nile before proceeding another 20 kilometers (12 miles) north to Dandara.

Dandara, the ancient Tantera, called Tentyris by the Greeks, is an extensive site with tombs dating back to the earliest dynasties. It was the capital of Egypt's sixth nome. Its most famous monument is the Temple of Hathor, enclosed within a great mud brick wall, 280 by 290 meters (910 by 943 feet) and 10 meters (33 feet) thick and 10 meters high. The temple is surrounded by a number of other buildings including a Temple of Isis, Ptolemaic and Roman birth houses, a Coptic church, and a sacred lake. Walk through the grand gateway built by Domitian and Trajan in the first century AD into an open yard, past the Roman birth house and Coptic church on the right. The Temple of Hathor sits directly in front of you.

The Temple of Hathor was begun in the first century BC and work continued from 54 to 20 BC. It was built atop the remains of earlier temples, some of which may date as far back as the Old Kingdom, and others erected by Thutmes III and Rameses II and III. The name of Ptolemy XII is found in the rear part of the temple, the first part to be built in the Ptolemaic Period, but many of the cartouches in wall scenes were left blank, apparently because political instability at the time left the artists unsure whose name should be written. Much of the work, however, was undertaken during the twenty-one-year reign of Cleopatra VII. The similarity in the plans of Dandara and Edfu Temples is not coincidental: the former clearly was copied from the latter, although on a smaller scale, and reflects the close relationship between Hathor (worshipped at Isna) and Horus (worshipped at Edfu) and their cults.

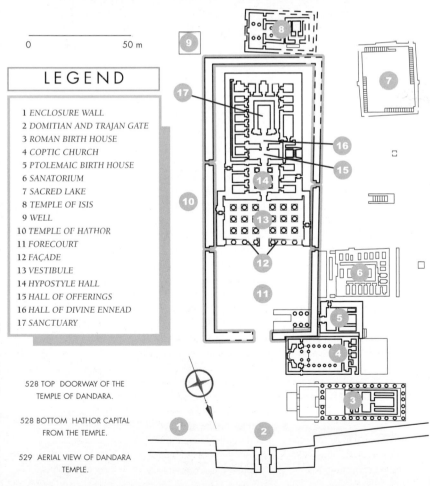

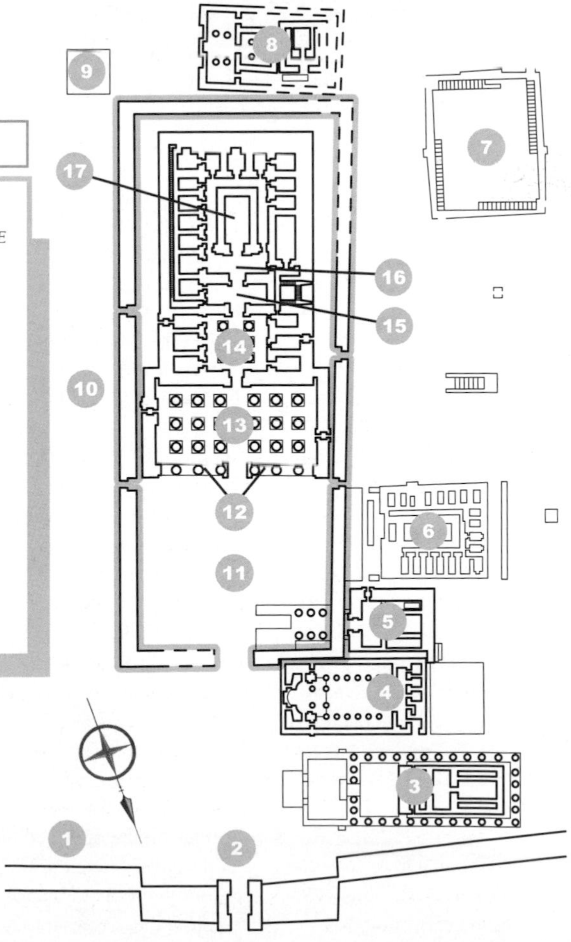

0 50 m

LEGEND

1 *ENCLOSURE WALL*
2 *DOMITIAN AND TRAJAN GATE*
3 *ROMAN BIRTH HOUSE*
4 *COPTIC CHURCH*
5 *PTOLEMAIC BIRTH HOUSE*
6 *SANATORIUM*
7 *SACRED LAKE*
8 *TEMPLE OF ISIS*
9 *WELL*
10 *TEMPLE OF HATHOR*
11 *FORECOURT*
12 *FAÇADE*
13 *VESTIBULE*
14 *HYPOSTYLE HALL*
15 *HALL OF OFFERINGS*
16 *HALL OF DIVINE ENNEAD*
17 *SANCTUARY*

528 TOP DOORWAY OF THE TEMPLE OF DANDARA.

528 BOTTOM HATHOR CAPITAL FROM THE TEMPLE.

529 AERIAL VIEW OF DANDARA TEMPLE.

VISIT

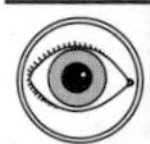

The façade of the temple is impressive: 35 meters (114 feet) wide and 12.5 meters (41 feet) high, with six Hathor-headed columns in the form of musical rattles called sistra, separated by decorated curtain walls and a central doorway. Above, three lines of Greek text, written by Romans in AD 35, proclaim that the temple was "for the Emperor Tiberius Caesar, the new Augustus, son of the divine Augustus, under the prefect Aulus Avillius Flaccus" and others.

◆ VESTIBULE ◆

Inside, eighteen sistra-like columns fill the huge vestibule. Because the temple is so well preserved, with its ceiling still intact, the way in which its chambers are lit is almost exactly as it was in ancient times and the play of light and shade on the columns in the vestibule is a dramatic example of that.

Scenes on the left side of the front wall show the emperor wearing the crown of Lower Egypt, as he leaves the palace to perform temple ceremonies. He is being purified by Horus and Thoth and then crowned by several goddesses. These scenes continue on the right wall of the vestibule, where the king lays out the plan of Dandara Temple and dedicates it to Hathor. On the right side of the front wall, the emperor wears the crown of Upper Egypt and is presented by Montu and Atum to Hathor. The many figures of royalty and deities on the columns, where the king presents offerings to the gods, have been vandalized (probably by Christians who occupied the site) but show clearly the slight corpulence or voluptuousness that is a characteristic of human figures in Ptolemaic art.

530-531 THE FAÇADE OF THE TEMPLE.

531 BOTTOM LEFT VIEW OF THE VESTIBULE.

531 BOTTOM RIGHT RELIEFS OF TIBERIUS CAESAR FROM THE TEMPLE WALLS.

532 VIEW THE CEILING OF THE VESTIBULE AND A DETAIL OF A FALCON.

533 TOP LEFT RELIEF OF THE CEILING WITH THE SKY GODDESS NUT.

533 BOTTOM LEFT ASTRONOMICAL CEILING DECORATED WITH ZODIAC SIGNS.

533 RIGHT REPRESENTATION OF THE GODDESS HATHOR FROM THE ASTRONOMICAL CEILING OF THE VESTIBULE.

The ceiling is elaborately decorated with astronomical scenes including the sky goddess Nut, signs of the zodiac, and decans.

Beyond the vestibule stands a small hypostyle hall with two rows of three columns, called the Hall of Appearances. Unusually, the columns bases are made of granite, while their drums and capitals are of sandstone. On the walls, the king is shown before figures of Hathor, called here the daughter of Ra, Horus, and the child Ihy, also called Harsomtus. Scenes on the walls in the right half of the hall read counterclockwise from the entrance to the rear door. Like those in the vestibule, they deal with the laying out, building, and dedication of the temple to Hathor. Scenes in the left half of the hall read clockwise from the entrance and show the king presenting the temple to Hathor and Horus. On the left side of the rear wall, Ptah presents the king to Hathor and Horus and their son, Harsomtus, who is shaking a sistrum in celebration.

Six small chambers lie around the hypostyle hall, and their purpose can be determined by the scenes on their walls. In each, the king is making offerings to Hathor: silver ornaments in the first chamber on the right, libations of water in the second chamber; incense in the first chamber on the left, and foodstuffs in the second chamber. The two rear chambers were used for storage of temple paraphernalia.

Beyond the hypostyle hall, two antechambers stand one behind the other. The first is called the Hall of Offerings and would have been closed off by a huge double leaf door of wood and metal. Scenes on its walls show the king offering to the gods of Dandara. On either side of the first antechamber, stairways lead up to the roof of the temple, which we describe below.

The second antechamber, the Hall of the Divine Ennead, is surrounded by a series of small rooms that

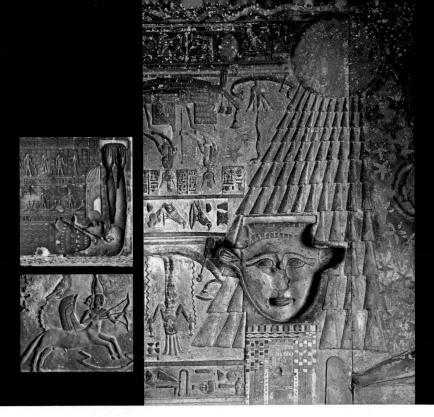

held the clothing and adornment of the gods. The first chamber on the left, for example, is called the Linen Room; that on the right is the Treasury. Walking into the Treasury and turning left takes one into a small court in the rear of which is a staircase leading up to the Pure Chapel, called the *wabet*. It was here that ceremonies joining Hathor and the sun god were conducted on her birthday and on New Year's day. Offerings were made in the small court by priests—these are shown on its walls in remarkable detail—and ceremonies that included processions of gods from Upper Egypt (on the left) and Lower Egypt (on the right) are shown in the *wabet*. The goddess Nut is depicted on the ceiling.

Return to the second antechamber. Eleven other chambers lie around its perimeter and in the center stands a sanctuary, the Great Seat, in which the barks of Hathor, Horus, Harsomtus, and Isis were kept. This is the most sacred part of the temple, accessible only to the king and high priest, and only on a few days each year. At the sides of the sanctuary doors the king offers mirrors to Hathor. Inside, he offers incense before her bark, Horus of Edfu, and Harsomtus. The side chambers were used both as chapels for various gods and as storerooms for temple equipment. In the one directly behind the sanctuary, a gilded 2 meter (6 foot) tall statue of Hathor was housed in a recess high up in the rear (south) wall.

In the floor of the chamber immediately to the right of the Hathor statue room lies the entrance to one of twelve subterranean crypts. These are of interest because of their architecture, but also because their carved and brightly painted walls are still well preserved and depict the various ritual objects stored inside. In one crypt, the Old Kingdom king Pepy I is shown offering a statuette to Hathor.

◆ THE ROOF ◆

The roof of Dandara Temple is a treasure that must be visited. Take the stairs leading from the first vestibule. The stairs on the left side go straight to the roof; those on the right spiral upward. They are the same steps used by ancient priests in the New Year's festival, and the walls of the stairwells are decorated with scenes of the priestly processions, ascending the stairs bearing statues of Hathor for the roof-top ceremonies, or descending after the ceremonies were concluded.

The roof of the temple is built on several levels, depending on the height of the chamber below. In the right rear (southwest) corner stands a small kiosk with twelve Hathor-headed columns around its perimeter. It was built by Ptolemy XII and originally had an unusual vaulted roof made of wood. Toward the front of the temple stand two sanctuaries dedicated to Osiris. Osiris was believed to have been buried at Dandara (among many other places) and celebrations of his death and resurrection were regular events here. The ceiling of one of these sanctuaries was decorated with a beautifully carved oval zodiac. The original was taken to the Louvre in Paris in 1820; a plaster cast has been installed in its place. In an adjacent room, a scene shows Osiris lying on a bed being comforted by Hathor. Isis, in the form of a bird, hovers over him, ready to receive his seed and become pregnant with Horus.

The roofing blocks are crisscrossed with shallow drainage channels designed to capture rain water and direct it to the lion-headed drain spouts placed at intervals at the top of the temple's outer walls. Directly below each drain spout is a vertical column of magical texts down which the water will run, gaining magical

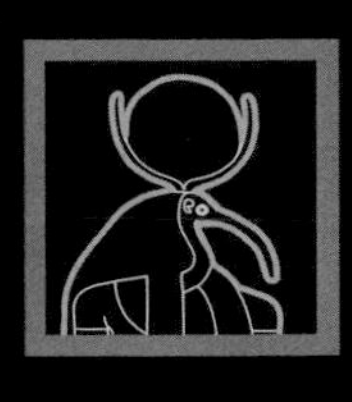

534 AERIAL VIEW OF DANDARA COMPLEX.

535 LEFT THE LION-HEADED DWARF-LIKE GOD BES, FROM THE ROMAN BIRTH-HOUSE.

535 RIGHT HATHOR NOURISHING HER SON HARSOMTUS, RELIEF FROM THE OUTER WALL OF THE TEMPLE.

power from its contact with the potent words.

There are spectacular views of the Dandara complex and the surrounding desert and fields from the roof and a few moments should be spent enjoying them before descending.

The outer faces of the temple walls again show the king laying out the plan of the temple, placing its first stones and dedicating them to Hathor.

◆ OUTSIDE THE TEMPLE ◆

On the rear wall, Cleopatra and her son Caesarion stand in two scenes before Hathor and other deities. Behind the temple stands a small temple of Isis, built from blocks taken by the Emperor Augustus from earlier buildings on the site. A small but attractive tree-filled sacred lake lies nearby.

Returning to the front of the Temple of Hathor, a large Roman birth-house stands left of the main gate in the enclosure wall. Built in the time of Augustus and decorated under Trajan and Hadrian, it was dedicated to Harsomtus, the son of Hathor and Horus. Scenes inside depict the birth of Harsomtus and show figures of the lion-headed dwarf-like god Bes, associated with marriage and childbirth.

Beside the Roman birth-house stand the remains of a Coptic church dating to the fifth century AD. Tradition claims that as many as fifty thousand monks came here annually to celebrate Easter.

Between the church and the temple of Hathor stands another birth-house, begun in the reign of Nectanebo I (of Dynasty 30) and added to throughout the Ptolemaic period. It was abandoned when the forecourt of the temple of Hathor cut through its walls. Scenes depict the birth of Harsomtus. Elsewhere in the enclosure of the Hathor temple stand the remains of several Roman brick buildings and traces of the ancient town.

6

THE TEMPLE OF ISNA

THE HISTORY

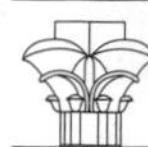

Most visitors to Isna arrive by ship on the cruise between Aswan and Luxor. The town, which lies about 50 kilometers (30 miles) south of Luxor, is an attractive one, filled with many interesting examples of late nineteenth century provincial architecture. Isna has an undeserved reputation as a center of dishonest merchants. In fact, the tourist markets here are clean and pleasant to walk through and the dealers are no different from those at other sites.

The temple at Isna, which was dedicated to ram-headed Khnum and the goddesses Neith and Satet, lies about 200 meters (600 feet) from the boat moorages on the west bank of the Nile. One walks along a street lined with tourist shops, then turns slightly left. Farther left (south), beyond the temple, a fascinating covered market sells local fruits and vegetables, and carpets, dresses, and basketry. Nearby, an old mill still grinds lettuce seed into oil, a concoction considered since dynastic times to be a powerful aphrodisiac. From Late Dynastic times until early in the twentieth century, the town was an important stopping-point on the camel caravan route between the Sudan and Cairo, and on routes to oases in the Western Desert. Today, Isna is famous especially for its superb tomatoes and its woven fabric.

Isna derives its name from the ancient *Ta-senet*, and was known to the Greeks as Latopolis because the Nile perch, *Lates niloticus*, was worshipped here. The town offers an excellent example of archaeological stratigraphy. The temple was begun in the reigns of Ptolemy VI Philometor and Ptolemy VIII Euergetes II, and remained in use through the Roman period. Once abandoned, however, it was buried soon under blowing sand and the accumulated debris of the surrounding town. Today, the temple lies in a pit more than 9 meters (30 feet) deep, dug through fifteen hundred years of rubbish atop which the modern city lies. A long steep staircase, unsuitable for some visitors, leads down to the temple floor. Only a small part of the temple has been exposed, much of it by the Egyptian army, which worked here in the 1840s, and by the Antiquities Service, which worked a few decades later. Further excavation at the site seems unlikely. It would require moving a sizeable part of modern Isna.

536 TOP THE PALMETTE CAPITALS OF THE FAÇADE COLUMNS.

537 TOP OUTSIDE VIEW OF THE VESTIBULE.

536 BOTTOM THE KING BEFORE THE RAM-HEADED GOD KHNUM.

537 BOTTOM THE KING BETWEEN THE GODDESSES NEITH AND SATET.

LEGEND

1 *FAÇADE*
2 *DOORWAY*
3 *VESTIBULE*
4 *VESTIBULE BACK GATE*
5 *BURIED TEMPLE*

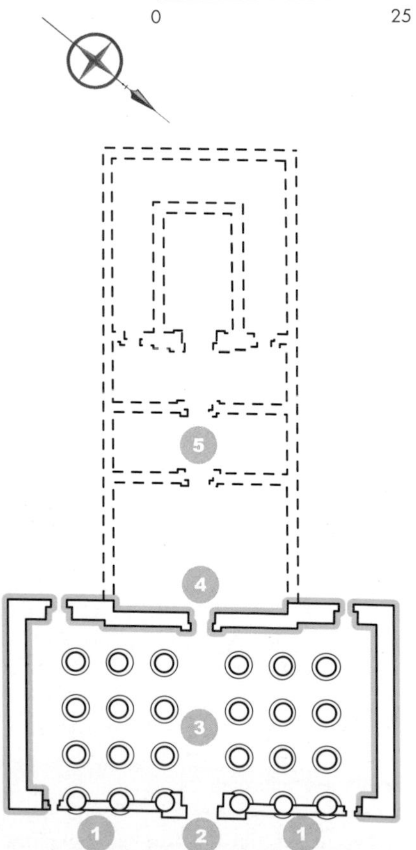

538 A SACRED BOAT WITH A SCARAB INSCRIBED IN A SOLAR DISK, FROM THE VESTIBULE CEILING.

539 TOP THE COLUMNS OF THE VESTIBULE COVERED WITH RELIEFS.

539 BOTTOM THE KING OFFERING TO THOTH AND HARSIESI, RELIEF FROM THE VESTIBULE.

VISIT

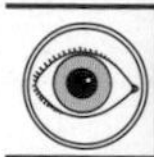

The temple's façade is similar in size and design to that of the Temple of Hathor at Dandara. It stands 37 meters (120 feet) wide, 15 meters (50 feet) high, and consists of six columns separated by curtain walls and a central doorway. At the left end of the façade, the king is purified with water by Thoth and Harsiesi. Between this scene and the main doorway the god Khnum is shown with a potter's wheel on which he is said to have fashioned humankind.

The central doorway leads into a large vestibule filled with eighteen columns arranged in three rows of six each that support a roof decorated with astronomical scenes and, down the main axis, with vultures. The capitals have palmette capitals. If one looks closely, huge locusts can be seen carved on some capitals above the floral motif. Inscriptions on the columns describe some of the ceremonies regularly performed in the temple compound. Some of these texts are cryptographic: one is a hymn to Khnum written with nothing but the figures of rams and crocodiles. Although the vestibule has recently been cleaned of bat droppings and centuries of accumulated filth, the walls still appear dark in the dim light and it takes a moment for one's eyes to adjust to the gloom.

On the walls, emperors dressed as pharaohs make offerings to Isna's local gods. In the lower register on the right (north) side wall, the emperor Commodus stands with the god Khnum in a papyrus thicket on the Nile and pulls on a huge net filled with fish and game birds. This is an especially impressive scene, well carved, with well-proportioned figures. Farther left, the king stands before Khnum and presents to him this very temple. On the left (south) wall, various Roman emperors, including Septimus Severus, Caracalla, Marcus Aurelius, and Geta stand before Khnum. In the left rear (southwest) corner of the vestibule, left of a small doorway, the name of the last emperor to be mentioned in an Egyptian temple, Decius, who ruled from AD 249 to 251, is written in a cartouche. On the rear wall above the door Khnum is shown with several other gods and goddesses.

Outside, the walls of the temple show several scenes of the king—on the left (south) side Titus, on the right Trajan—victorious in battle, and proudly presenting captive enemies to the god. Unfortunately, the walls also display large areas of salt damage caused by the area's rapidly rising ground water.

The vestibule's back gate led to the temple proper, but that is now completely buried beneath debris.

THE TEMPLE OF EDFU

540-541 AERIAL VIEW OF THE TEMPLE OF EDFU, NOW SURROUNDED BY THE CITY.

541 TOP STATUE OF THE GOD HORUS OF BEHDET AT THE ENTRANCE OF THE FIRST PYLON.

THE HISTORY

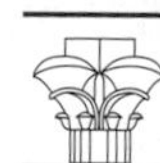

Most temples in Egypt are in a poor state today, and it can take considerable knowledge and imagination to picture what they might have looked like in ancient times. Not so the Temple of Edfu. Most of the paint is gone from its walls, but the building is otherwise in near-perfect condition. For Egyptologists, the content of the temple's reliefs is a rich source of information, showing in detail how the temple and its priesthood functioned and where and when ceremonies were performed inside its many chambers. For tourists it is the sense of mystery and drama the temple offers that are the big rewards. To walk alone through its chambers is to be transported more than two thousand years into the past. Not even Abydos, Madinet Habu, or Dandara offer such an experience, and it is not uncommon that visitors cut short their tour of Edfu because they find its dark and silent interior so evocative of ancient rites that they become unnerved.

Work on Edfu temple was begun in the Ptolemaic period, on 23 August 237 BC, when the first stones of the innermost rooms

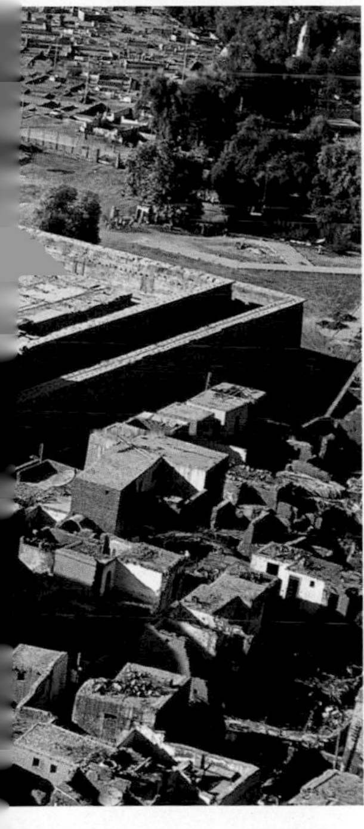

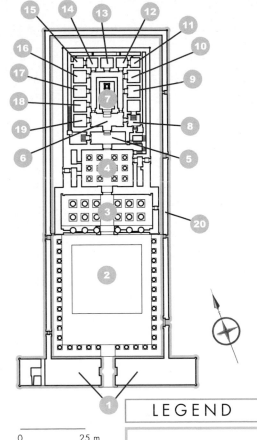

0 25 m

LEGEND

1 *FIRST PYLON*
2 *FORECOURT*
3 *FIRST HYPOSTYLE HALL*
4 *SECOND HYPOSTYLE HALL*
5 *OUTER VESTIBULE*
6 *INNER VESTIBULE*
7 *SANCTUARY*
8 *CHAMBER OF OFFERINGS*
9 *CHAPEL OF THE SPREAD WINGS*
10 *CHAPEL OF THE THRONE OF RA*
11 *CHAMBER OF HATHOR*
12 *CHAMBER OF KHONSU*
13 *CHAMBER OF THE VICTOR*
14 *TOMB OF OSIRIS*
15 *CHAMBER OF THE WEST*
16 *CHAMBER OF OSIRIS*
17 *CHAMBER OF THE THRONE OF THE GODS*
18 *CHAMBER OF THE LINEN*
19 *CHAPEL OF MIN*
20 *OUTER CORRIDOR*

were laid. Construction and decoration were completed 167 years later. The temple was dedicated to the god Horus of Behdet (Behdet was the ancient name of Edfu), a deity worshipped here since predynastic times. The temple is surrounded by the remains of a huge ancient city and necropolis in which archaeologists have found buildings of the Old Kingdom and First Intermediate Period. Adjacent to the temple itself, archaeologists have found traces of its dynastic precursor, a temple built in the Rameside Period.The approach to the temple today requires that visitors enter the site at its rear, then walk around the structure to the first pylon. But that is about to change. A new entrance has been built adjacent to the mammisi about 100 meters south of the temple pylon, and when it is opened, one's first view of the temple will be its imposing façade.

VISIT

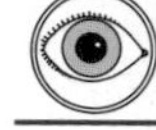

◆ FIRST PYLON ◆

The temple's massive First Pylon stands over 34 meters (110 feet) tall. It lacks a cornice, but includes the customary four niches that held flagstaffs and huge scenes of Ptolemy XIII in a standard pose smiting the enemies of Egypt before Horus.

Two huge statues of Horus as a falcon flank the pylon's gateway. What you see on the two towers of the pylon is a foretaste of what lies inside: walls heavily decorated with relief that impresses more because of its massive scale than carefully-crafted figures.

◆ FORECOURT ◆

Beyond the pylon lies the Forecourt or Court of Offerings, surrounded on three sides by thirty-two columns, each with a different floral capital and decorated with scenes of the king before various temple deities. Behind the columns, reliefs on the front wall of the court show the king before various deities and (at the far left or east end) being presented to Horus of Edfu and Hathor of Dandara. Below, other scenes show statues of these deities sailing between those two sites. These scenes depict the annual Feast of the Beautiful Meeting, when Horus and Hathor visited each other's temples and, after two weeks of ceremonies, were magically united in marriage. Scenes on the right tower are similar to these scenes, but there the king wears the Lower Egyptian crown instead of the Upper Egyptian crown. At the far right, men and women dance and make music. Note that many of the royal cartouches here, and indeed throughout the temple, were deliberately left blank, perhaps in anticipation of a change of ruler. The screen wall at the north end of the court is especially beautiful in early morning sunlight. Its reliefs show Ptolemy VII and Ptolemy X offering to Horus and Hathor.

542 TOP STATUE OF HORUS OF BEHDET IN THE FORECOURT, AT THE ENTRANCE OF THE FIRST HYPOSTYLE HALL.

542 BOTTOM THE COLONNADE OF THE PORTICO IN THE FORECOURT.

◆ THE FIRST HYPOSTYLE HALL ◆

Through the door in its center one enters into the First or Outer Hypostyle Hall, its high ceiling supported by twelve free-standing and six attached columns, each with an elaborate capital. The paint is gone today and the hall may seem rather dim. But in antiquity it must have been bright. Scenes at the right (west) end of the front wall show the king with Horus driving pegs to lay out the temple foundations, and the story of building the temple continues along the left (west) side wall. At the end of that wall, the king offers the building to Horus. The rear (north) wall of the hall also deals with the building of the temple. Two small chambers lie against the screen wall on either side of the hall's main entrance. The chamber on the right (west) is called the Robing Room or the Vestry, where costumes worn by senior priests were kept. Its counterpart on the left (east) is the Library, where papyrus rolls dealing with temple rituals were stored. Two niches in the side walls may have held some of these documents.

542-543 THE INNER WALL OF THE FIRST PYLON AND THE FORECOURT.

543 BOTTOM BOATS SAILING FOR THE FEAST OF THE BEAUTIFUL MEETING, RELIEF FROM THE FORECOURT.

◆ THE SECOND HYPOSTYLE HALL ◆

The Second Hypostyle Hall is the next chamber along the temple axis. It is smaller than the First Hypostyle Hall but its decoration is more dramatic because there is less ambient light, and the shafts of light that pour in through holes in the ceiling act as spotlights that slowly move across the floor and the walls. Twelve columns support the ceiling and the walls are decorated with scenes of the founding of the temple. Doorways in the right and left (east and west) side walls lead into small chambers and to a well beyond the temple ambulatory or to a stairway. The stairway leading from the rear right (northeast) corner of the hall, ascends to the roof. It is now locked about a third of the way to the top, but its lower walls, decorated with processions of priests and gods celebrating a New Year's Festival, are worth a look. There are two chambers on the left (west) side of the hall. The first was used as a storeroom for offerings used in temple rituals. It has a doorway in its rear wall that leads to the temple ambulatory. The second chamber (on the right), is sometimes called the Laboratory, where incense was mixed and stored. The texts on its walls describe how the incense was to be made. One such recipe can be seen at top left on the rear wall.

◆ THE OUTER VESTIBULE OR OFFERING HALL ◆

The Outer Vestibule or Offering Hall, beyond the Second Hypostyle Hall, is a small, rectangular room whose decoration shows the king offering to Horus. Doorways in the right and left (east and west) walls lead to stairs to the roof. They are now closed.

◆ INNER VESTIBULE ◆

An Inner Vestibule, called the Hall of the Repose of the Gods, like most rooms in this part of the temple, was the work of Ptolemy IV Philopater. Here, the king is shown offering and praying before various deities.

◆ THE SANCTUARY ◆

The most sacred part of the temple, the Sanctuary, lies immediately beyond the vestibule. It was here that the divine bark of the god rested on a low platform that stood before a large granite naos that held a statue of Horus. The naos was ordered by Nectanebo I in Dynasty 30, and is one of the oldest parts

544 HATHOR EMBRACES THE KING, RELIEF FROM THE INNER VESTIBULE.

544-545 VIEW OF THE SANCTUARY AND ITS GRANITE NAOS.

545 RIGHT THE GOD ATUM, DETAIL OF RELIEFS FROM THE INNER VESTIBULE.

of the temple still extant. Holes used to hold the double leaf wooden doors that closed the naos can still be seen in the opening. The sanctuary is separated from the rest of the temple by a small ambulatory along which are a series of ten small chapels. These can be accessed from the vestibule. The texts on the sanctuary walls include many of the hymns that would have been sung by priests each morning as they came to awaken the statue of Horus, as well as purify, clothe, and feed him.

◆ CHAMBER OF OFFERINGS ◆

A doorway in the right (east) wall of the vestibule leads into a Chamber of Offerings. Inside, up a flight of six steps, stands a small chapel in which the king and queen offer to Horus and Hathor and to their parents, Ptolemy III and Queen Berenice (left front or southwest corner). Above the doorway of the chapel, seven figures of Hathor beat tambourines.

◆ THE CHAPEL OF THE SPREAD WINGS ◆

Moving counter clockwise around the sanctuary, the next chamber is The Chapel of the Spread Wings, its walls decorated with scenes of those who protect Osiris. One of them is Mehyt, a lion goddess, whose boat can be seen on the left (north) wall.

◆ THE CHAPEL OF THE THRONE OF RA ◆

Next is The Chapel of the Throne of Ra, whose scenes treat the coronation of the king. Note the baboons who greet the sun at dawn on the right (south) wall, and on several walls, the king before persea trees. The third chamber has another chamber opening off of it; the first is dedicated to Khonsu, the second to Hathor.

◆ THE CHAMBER OF THE VICTOR ◆

Beyond the center of the rear wall of the temple is the fourth chamber, The Chamber of the Victor (a reference to Horus), in which a copy of a wooden boat now sits as it would have done in antiquity.

◆ THE TOMB OF OSIRIS ◆

Farther left (west), is another double chamber, The Tomb of Osiris, and farther inside, the Chamber of the West. Around the corner is another Chamber of Osiris, then The Chamber of the Throne of the Gods, the Chamber of the Linen, and finally, the Chapel of Min.

◆ OUTER CORRIDOR ◆

We can now return to the Outer Vestibule or to the First Hypostyle Hall and exit through the right (east) wall into the temple's Outer Corridor or Ambulatory. The walls of this narrow passageway, which surrounds the temple proper, are decorated with scenes of the king smiting Egypt's enemies and scenes of him netting birds and wild game, which some say are representatives of evil. Moving around the back of the temple to the ambulatory's northwest corner, we begin a series of scenes showing the god Horus standing in boats and spearing a tiny hippopotamus or crocodile, the representatives of the evil Seth, whom Horus is set to defeat. Near the southern end of the western wall of the ambulatory, Seth is shown in chains, speared by Horus. Farther on, three men stab a hippopotamus; the god Imhotep reads from a papyrus; and the king feeds a goose that will be sacrificed. Many of the details in these scenes, which together tell the story of The Triumph of Horus, are well-executed, and one can note especially the rigging of the boats and the costumes of the gods. At the end of the ambulatory, just before it narrows, a figure of Seth as a donkey is drawn on the eastern (left) wall.

◆ OUTSIDE THE TEMPLE ◆

About one hundred meters in front of the Temple of Horus stands a smaller building of the same date called the mammisi, a Coptic word meaning a birth-house. Its reliefs tell the story of the wonderful birth of Harsomtus ("Horus the Uniter"), the son of Horus and Hathor. As in parts of the main temple, here too are scenes of the Feast of the Beautiful Meeting, the annual ceremony in which those two deities met and married. There are finely carved details in the scenes here, such as those in agricultural scenes on the north wall, and the figures of a horse and its groom on the east. Some of the scenes still have their original color intact.

Surrounding the main buildings at Edfu are the remains of the ancient town, a deep mound with many meters of highly stratified mud brick and stone buildings that span millennia of occupation. Unfortunately, much of the townsite has been destroyed by modern digging.

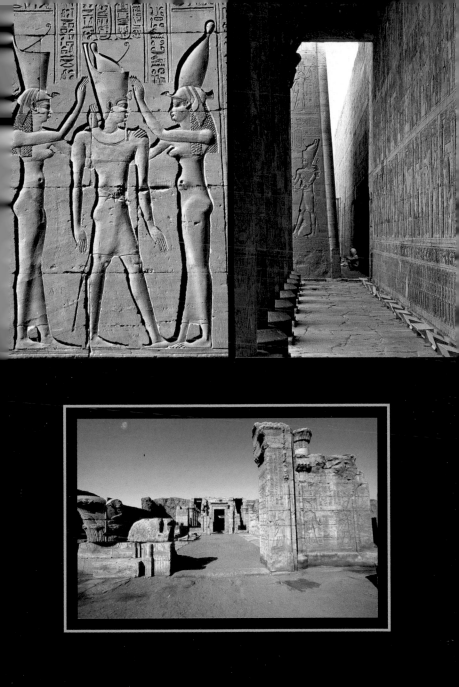

546 VIEW OF THE OUTER CORRIDOR.

547 TOP LEFT THE GODDESSES NEKHBET AND WADJET GIVING THE CROWN OF UPPER AND LOWER EGYPT TO THE KING.

547 TOP RIGHT THE OUTER CORRIDOR SEEN FROM THE PORTICO OF THE FORECOURT.

547 BOTTOM THE MAMMISI.

KOM OMBO

548 TOP DETAIL OF RELIEF WITH SOBEK AND HARWER, THE DIVINITIES TO WHOM THE TEMPLE IS DEDICATED.

548-549 AERIAL VIEW OF THE TEMPLE.

THE HISTORY

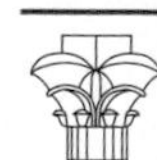

Today, nearly every visitor to Kom Ombo arrives by Nile cruiser from Edfu or from Aswan. Either way, they will have seen or are about to see the largest and best-preserved Ptolemaic temple in Egypt, the temple of Horus at Edfu, and are also likely to visit other Ptolemaic temples, at Philae, Isna, Dandara, and Dayr al-Madina. In comparison to these temples, the reliefs in the temple of Kom Ombo will seem rather mundane. Faces here seem fat and poorly modelled, limbs resemble overstuffed sausages, noses are straight and narrow, bodies seem ill-proportioned. To some extent, these are characteristic features of Ptolemaic art in general. But it is also true that the subject-matter of these reliefs is standard fare, and better examples can be found elsewhere. That

LEGEND

1 *ENCLOSURE WALL*
2 *CHAPEL OF HATHOR*
3 *MAMMISI*
4 *FORECOURT*
5 *FIRST HYPOSTYLE HALL*
6 *SECOND HYPOSTYLE HALL*
7, 8, 9 *VESTIBULES*
10 *SANCTUARY OF HARWER*
11 *SANCTUARY OF SOBEK*

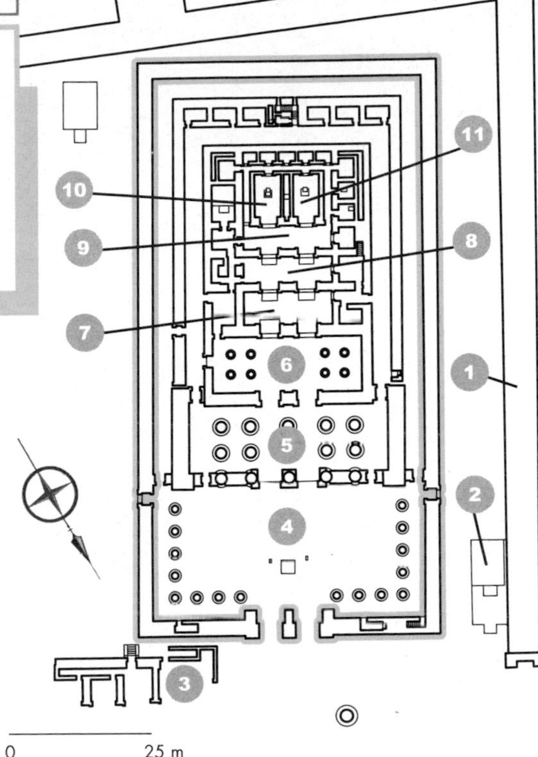

having been said, there is no site that can equal Kom Ombo for its beautiful setting, perched on the edge of the Nile with a commanding view of the intensely blue Nile, emerald fields, and golden desert beyond. When raking sunlight hits the temple's decorated walls, no ancient relief shows to better advantage. Kom Ombo is a site whose proportions and architectural character should be savored.

Kom Ombo, whose name comes from the Coptic *Umbo* and the ancient Egyptian *Nubi*, is a huge village built on the edge of a broad stretch of rich agricultural land. It lies at the start of a road leading to desert gold mines and caravan routes to western oases and the Sudan. Remains of the village can still be seen in the fields to the north and east of the temple. It is said that the Roman army trained the elephants used by its army in North Africa at this site. In the river directly in front of the temple there are several small islands and sandbars visible most of the year. In ancient times these were islands home to large numbers of crocodiles, and the town was closely associated with Sobek, the crocodile god. The temple itself was built during the Ptolemaic reigns of Ptolemy VI through Ptolemy XIII and added to in the Roman period. It has an unusual, bilaterally symmetrical plan: the right (east) half is dedicated to Sobek, the left (west) half to Horus the Elder, called Harwer.

The Nile has migrated eastward during the last fifteen hundred years, and parts of the temple's first pylon and forecourts have been destroyed.

550 LEFT COLONNADE OF THE FIRST HYPOSTYLE HALL.

550 RIGHT RELIEF OF HARWER, HATHOR, AND SOBEK.

551 TOP THE KING OFFERING TO THE GOD HARWER, HORUS THE ELDER.

551 BOTTOM RELIEF DETAIL OF A LION KNEELING BESIDE THE KING'S LEG.

VISIT

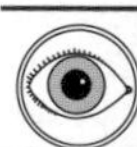

Today, one enters at the southeast corner of a paved forecourt. To the right stands a small chapel of Hathor; across the forecourt, in its southwest corner, are the remains of a mammisi. High up on the left (west) wall of the mammisi a scene of the king standing in a reed skiff and hunting birds in a papyrus thicket is very finely drawn.

Little remains of the temple's ceiling, but as a result the strong sunlight that strikes its walls can dramatically highlight the relief carving, and one should concentrate on those scenes that are well lit. Depending on the time of the day and the season, those will include the left (west) front curtain wall of the First Hypostyle Hall, where Ptolemy XIII receives an *ankh*-sign from Isis, and the left (west) side wall of the hall, with finely modeled but oddly positioned figures of the king and two goddesses before Harwer. Note too, the reliefs on the front (south) wall of the Second Hypostyle Hall and the fascinating offering scene on the left rear wall of that same room.

Two vestibules follow the hypostyle halls and lead to the sanctuaries of the gods, Harwer on the left (west), Sobek on the right (east). They are in poor condition today, but note the narrow hollow in the wall that separates them, access to which is gained through a passageway beneath the floor. Apparently, priests would secretly enter this chamber during religious services and utter oracles or statements on behalf of the gods. Behind the sanctuaries and a series of small rooms, two corridors surround the temple proper. The rear wall of the inner corridor is lined with six chambers and a staircase. The relief in these rooms was left unfinished and offers insight into the techniques used by the ancient artisans who carved and painted the scenes here. In the outer corridor, midway along the rear wall, a set of reliefs is often said to show a collection of ancient surgical instruments. It is more likely, however, that these were tools used in the course of various temple rituals.

Outside, in the large open space to the west of the temple, stands a basin in which young crocodiles were raised by the priests for various ritual purposes. Nearby is a deep well, still filled with water.

GLOSSARY

ABYDOS One of Egypt's holiest and most important religious sites; about 300 kilometers (180 miles) north of Luxor; home and burial place of Osiris and a place of pilgrimage; site of temples built by Sety I, Rameses II; Early Dynastic royal cemetery.
AKER A god of the earth often depicted as two human-headed sphinxes facing away from each other; protector of the king; subject of the Book of the Earth, found in KV 9, the tomb of Rameses V and Rameses VI.
AKH The part of the human soul that continued after death and inhabited the afterlife. (The other parts were the *ba*, *ka*, a person's name, and his shadow.) It is shown as a crested ibis or a mummiform human figure.
AMEN, AMEN-RA Local Theban deity who from the Middle Kingdom became a universal, all-powerful "king of the gods." His name means "the Hidden One," and he was represented in many forms: as a human being with a double plumed headdress, a ram, a goose, or a lion. He was often shown as a composite deity merged with the sun god, Ra. His wife was Mut, his son, Khonsu, and the three of them formed the Theban Triad with major temples at Karnak.
AMENHETEP SON OF HAPU Overseer of works under Amenhetep III, responsible for that king's memorial temple and many other monuments. Highly regarded, after his death he was deified at Thebes as a god of wisdom and medicine.
AMMIT A monster, part lion, part hippopotamus, part crocodile, that devours the unrighteous at the Weighing of the Heart ceremony, depicted in chapter 125 of the Book of the Dead.
ANKH Hieroglyphic word for "life." The glyph is a copy of a sandal strap (or a penis sheath).
ANUBIS God of the dead, associated with mummification, guardian of the necropolis, represented as a black canine, perhaps a jackal or a dog, or as a canine-headed human. He is often shown in scenes of embalming and the preparation of the mummy.
ANUKIS Goddess, daughter of the sun god, associated with the First Cataract of the Nile at Aswan, depicted as a woman holding a papyrus scepter and wearing a tall, plumed crown. At Thebes, she was associated with Hathor.
APIS Sacred bull considered a manifestation of the god Ptah and tied also to the king, Isis, and Osiris. His cult was centered at Memphis.
APOPHIS A snake god considered a principal adversary of the sun god. His attempts to prevent the sun from completing its nightly journey through the Netherworld had to be constantly fought against.
ARCHITRAVE A beam set horizontally to span an open space between two pillars.
ATEF A royal crown consisting of the white crown of Upper Egypt flanked by two feathers and topped by a small disk.
ATEN Solar deity, the physical disk of the sun, which rose to prominence during the reign of Amenhetep IV/Akhenaten.
ATUM Creator god of Heliopolis; father of Shu (air), Tefnut (moisture) and the other deities of the Ennead; depicted as a human being, a lion, a bull, a lizard, or a scarab beetle.
BA, BA-BIRD One of the five parts of the human soul (the others being the *ka*, *akh*, a person's name, and his shadow). The *ba* was the physical manifestation of various gods and a human being's "personality," depicted as a human-headed bird with arms.
BARK A boat that carries a shrine housing a deity or its statue in religious processions.
BARRAGE Nile dam to control irrigation water.
BASALT Black or mottled, very dense, volcanic rock, quarried in the Red Sea Hills and used in ancient Egypt especially for statuary.
BASTET Cat-headed goddess, originally from the Nile Delta, daughter of the sun god and protectress of pregnant women.
BES Lion-headed human dwarf god associated with sexuality and family life.
BIR Arabic word for "well."
BOOK OF CAVERNS A New Kingdom text describing the sun's journey above the caverns of the Netherworld. It emphazises Osiris and Ra and treats them as two parts of a single deity. It discusses the kinds of punishments and rewards awaiting the deceased in the afterlife. A complete copy can be found in the tomb of Rameses V and Rameses VI.
BOOK OF GATES New Kingdom religious text dealing with the journey of the sun through the hours of the night, each hour defined by twelve genie-guarded gates. It was frequently inscribed on royal tomb walls in the Valley of the Kings, most completely in KV 9, the tomb of Rameses V and Rameses VI.
BOOK OF THE DEAD New Kingdom collection of religious "spells," known as the Book of Coming Forth by Day, that deal with funerary ritual, mummification, and the journey of the deceased into the Netherworld. It was excerpted in several Rameside tombs.
BOOK OF THE EARTH Late New Kingdom text describing the sun's nighttime journey. It can be seen in the tombs of Rameses VI, VII, and IX.
BOOK OF THE HEAVENS Late New Kingdom texts, including the Book of the Heavenly Cow, Book of the Day, and Book of the Night, tracing the sun's journey. It is found in the tombs of Rameses IV, VI, and IX.
BUBASTIS Nile Delta town and temple site, home of Bastet, known from the Old Kingdom but flourished especially in Dynasty 22.
BUTO Tell Fara'in, the ancient Pe and Dep, a western Delta site traditionally said to be the predynastic capital of Lower Egypt.
CANOPUS, CANOPIC JARS Sets of four vessels containing the mummified internal organs of the deceased. The lids of these jars were in the shape of the heads of the Four Sons of Horus: human-headed Imsety was used for the mummified liver; ape-headed Hapy housed the lungs; jackal-headed

Duamutef kept the stomach; and falcon-headed Qebehsenuef guarded the intestines. The name is derived from the erroneous belief that these gods were worshipped as manifestations of Osiris by people in the Mediterranean port city of Canopus.
CARTONNAGE Plaster-soaked linen, sometimes painted, shaped into mummy masks, coffins, and other items for burial.
CARTOUCHE The French word for a gun cartridge, used to describe the similarly-shaped oval in which royal names, nomen and prenomen, were written. The shape symbolically offered protection and was used in the New Kingdom as the shape of royal sarcophagi.
CATARACT A stretch of river rapids whose boulders and white waters effectively blocked riverine traffic. The northernmost of the Nile's six cataracts is at Aswan.
CAVETTO CORNICE A quarter-round moulding along the top edge of a wall or above a doorway.
COPTOS The modern Qift, fifty kilometers (thirty miles) north of Luxor, on the West Bank of the Nile near the mouth of the Wadi Hammamat, start of a major route to the Red Sea.
CUBIT A unit of measure equal to 52.4 cm (31 inches), divided into seven palms or 28 digits. Its dimensions varied in later times.
DECAN The thirty-six groups of stars into which the Egyptians divided the night sky and whose appearance on the morning horizon marked the ten-day-long periods into which they divided the year.
DEMOTIC Cursive form of hieroglyphic writing used in papyrus documents from Dynasty 26 through the fifth century AD.
DEP See Buto
***DJED*-PILLAR** Hieroglyph meaning "stability" and associated with Osiris.
DUAMUTEF See Canopic Jars
DUAT The Netherworld.
EDFU Site of a large and well-preserved Ptolemaic temple to Horus, about 100 kilometers (sixty miles) south of Luxor.
EGYPTIAN ALABASTER Calcium carbonate, similar in appearance to true alabaster, and used in Egypt for vessels of various shapes. It was also used to built the shrine of Amenhetep I in the Open-Air Museum at Karnak.
ELEPHANTINE Island in the Nile at Aswan, called Jazirat Aswan, the southern border of ancient Egypt and a significant town from predynastic times onward.
ENNEAD Groups of nine deities, the most significant being that of Atum, his children Shu (air) and Tefnut (moisture), grandchildren Geb (earth) and Nut (sky), and great-grandchildren Osiris, Isis, Seth, Nephthys.
EYE OF HORUS Torn out by Seth, the god's eye was restored by Thoth and came to symbolize good and pleasant things.
FAIENCE Material made from fired quartz, lime, and natron, usually of blue color, used to make jewelry, amulets, small vessels, and architectural inlays.
FAYYUM Large desert depression one hundred kilometers (sixty miles) southwest of Cairo; an important site of agriculture since predynastic times.
FALSE DOOR A symbolic doorway built into the western wall of a tomb or temple through which spirits of the dead could move between this life and the next.
FIELDS OF IARU, FIELDS OF REEDS The domain of Osiris in which the deceased reaped food in the afterlife.
FLAIL Originally perhaps a fly whisk that became, along with the crook, a symbol of kingship.
FOREMOST OF THE WESTERNERS An epithet of Osiris, "westerner" referring to those who are deceased.
FOUNDATION DEPOSIT Miniature vessels, model tools, and other materials placed beneath the foundations of buildings or near the entrances to tombs to magically help maintain the structure for eternity.
GEB God of the earth (see Ennead), often depicted ithyphallically lying beneath his wife, the sky goddess Nut.
GOD'S WIFE OF AMEN From the New Kingdom, the consort of Amen. The union of Amen and the God's Wife was said to give birth symbolically to the reigning king.
HA A minor god, shown in human form, who ruled over the deserts.
HAPY God of the annual Nile inundation, represented as a fecundity figure, a man with sagging breasts and swollen abdomen symbolizing the richness of the Nile's bounty.
HARAKHTY "Horus of the Two Horizons," the Horus of the rising and setting suns whose cult was joined with that of the solar deity, Ra, as Ra-Harakhty.
HATHOR Exceptionally important goddess, much worshipped at Thebes; sky goddess; mother of Horus; wife of Ra; wife or mother of the king; goddess of music, happiness, women, and motherhood; shown as a human female, or as a cow with a solar disk between her horns.
HEKET Goddess depicted as a frog and associated with childbirth.
HELIOPOLIS The On of the Bible, near modern Cairo, site of solar cults such as that of Ra-Harakhty.
HENU The solar bark of Sokar.
HERACLEOPOLIS MAGNA Site in Middle Egypt, Ihnasya al-Madina, from which the Heracleopolitans of the First Intermediate Period challenged the authority of Thebes.
HERMOPOLIS MAGNA Al-Ashmunayn, Middle Egyptian site dedicated to the god Thoth, and together with nearby Tuna al-Jabal, connected with the site of Tall al-Amarna and the reign of Amenhetep IV/Akhenaten.
HIERATIC A cursive form of written Egyptian, used mainly for literary and business documents from the Old Kingdom until Dynasty 26, when it was largely replaced by demotic script.
HIEROGLYPHS Written Egyptian, used mainly for monumental religious and historical inscriptions, deciphered in 1822 by Jean-Francois Champollion. About one thousand different hieroglyphs are known from dynastic times, but that number grew to six thousand during the Ptolemaic Period.
HORUS One of Egypt's earliest and most important gods, depicted as a falcon or a falcon-headed man; god of the sky, god of kingship; son of Isis and Osiris.

HU God of "authoritative utterances," closely associated with the solar god Ra and with Sia, a personification of knowledge.

HYPOSTYLE HALL A columned hall in a temple, symbolizing a papyrus thicket growing around the primeval mound on which creation first took place. The most famous example is that in the Temple of Amen at Karnak.

IBIS A symbol of the god Thoth, the sacred ibis (*Threskiornis aethiopicus*) was raised in great numbers in various temples and the mummified dead birds were buried in huge, labyrinthine catacombs. They are no longer to be seen in Egypt but are plentiful elsewhere.

IMENTET Goddess of the west, a woman wearing the hieroglyph for "west" on her head, considered a variant form of Hathor or Isis.

IMSETY See Canopic Jars.

IMYDWAT The Book of What is in the Netherworld, a New Kingdom text tracing the twelve-hour-long journey of the sun god from sunset through the night sky to sunrise. Copies can be found in several tombs in the Valley of the Kings, including especially attractive versions in the tombs of Thutmes III, Amenhetep II, and Rameses VI.

ISIS Mother of Horus, sister and wife of Osiris; symbolically mother of the king; protector of the dead. She was represented as a human female or as a tree goddess.

KA The life-force of a person, his exact double that survives him at death and to whom offerings are made in the tomb. One of the five elements—*ka, ba, akh*, the name, and the shadow—that constitute the human soul. Written as two arms positioned to form a U.

KHEKER FRIEZE Decorative frieze at the top of walls derived from reed bundles tied off on mud-brick walls.

KHEPRESH The blue crown of the king, a helmet-like headdress made of cloth and dotted with gold.

KHEPRI A creator god represented by a dung-beetle or a beetle-headed man, associated with solar deities and said to roll the sun across the heavens as a dung beetle rolls a ball of dung across the desert.

KHNUM Ram-headed god, associated with the Nile, the annual flood, and original creation. As a creator-god, he was said to have fashioned human beings on a potter's wheel.

KHONSU Son of Amen and Mut, a moon-god, shown as a mummiform male wearing a sidelock indicating youth or as a falcon-headed man. His cult center was at Karnak.

KIOSK A small shrine or processional rest-stop, such as that of Senusret I in Karnak's Open-Air Museum.

LITANY OF RA A New Kingdom text praising the solar deity and revealing his seventy-five different manifestations. The text appears near the entrance of several tombs in the Valley of the Kings, including those of Thutmes III and Rameses IX. Its full title is Book of Praying to Ra in the West.

MA'AT Goddess who personifies justice, truth, order; associated with Osiris. Depicted as a woman, she sometimes has wings as well as arms, with a feather in her hair.

MAFDET A goddess who protects, especially against snakes and scorpions; represented as a mongoose.

MAMMISI A small "birth-house" (the term is a neologism based on Coptic) attached to a temple in which divine births and marriages were celebrated.

MEHEN A coiled snake who protects the solar deity in the Netherworld.

MEMPHIS City located southwest of Cairo near Saqqara, traditionally said to have been the first capital of a united Egypt, and with the rise of Thebes, the country's northern capital and administrative center.

MERETSEGER "She who loves silence," the goddess of al-Qurn, the high point on the Theban Hills above the Valley of the Kings, often represented as a woman with the head of a cobra.

MIN Ithyphallic god of male sexuality, and in the New Kingdom, a creator-god form of Amen concerned with maintaining the potency of the king.

MONTU A falcon-headed war god worshipped initially in the Theban area whose name became part of several Middle Kingdom kings names, as Mentuhetep.

MUT Wife of Amen, mother of Khonsu, part of the Theban Triad, depicted as a woman, sometimes with a lion head, mother of the king and protector of all mothers, associated with the queen.

NAOS The part of a temple in which a statue of the deity or its sacred bark was kept.

NEFERTUM God of the lotus blossom from which the sun god was said to emerge, associated with both Ra and Horus; son of Sekhmet; protector of royal tombs and palaces; shown as a man with a lotus flower on his head.

NEGATIVE CONFESSION The name given to chapter 125 of the Book of the Dead, which lists sins a deceased person proclaims he did not commit during his life.

NEHEBKAU A god in the form of a snake or a man with the head of a snake, beneficent helper of the king, who intercedes on his behalf with the gods.

NEITH A goddess of warriors; mother and creator goddess; associated with funerary customs; depicted as a woman or as a cow.

NEKHBET A vulture goddess originally from Alkab, about eighty kilometers (forty-eight miles) south of Luxor, who with Wadjet, the cobra goddess, represents the king's authority over Upper and Lower Egypt. She is often shown as a vulture with wings outstretched (as in the tomb of Nefertari), or as a woman.

NEKHEN The ancient name of Hierakonpolis, ancient capital city eighty kilometers (forty-eight miles) south of Luxor, across the Nile from Alkab.

NEMES Headcloth of royalty seen, for example, on the statue of Thutmes III in the Luxor Museum.

NEPHTHYS Goddess who protects the dead; wife of Seth; associated with Isis; mother (by Osiris) was Anubis.

NESHMET-BARK The boat in which Osiris traveled during his festival at Abydos.

NOME Greek term for the forty-two provinces into which Egypt was divided, anciently called *sepat*. Twenty-two lay in Upper Egypt, twenty in Lower Egypt. They are named on the shrine of Senusret I in the Open-Air Museum at Karnak.

NUBIA The area south of ancient Egypt, extending south from the First Cataract into the northern Sudan.

NUN The primeval ocean in which original creation took place.
NUT Sky goddess who each evening swallowed the sun and each morning gave birth to it, the subject of many ceiling paintings in royal tombs in the Valley of the Kings. She was depicted in human form.
OGDOAD A group of eight deities. That of Hermopolis consisted of four frog and four snake deities: Nun and Naunet (symbolizing water), Amen and Amaunet (hiddenness), Heh and Hauhet (infinite time and space), and Kek and Kauket (darkness).
OMBITE An epithet of the god Seth, "He of the town of Ombos" in Upper Egypt.
ONURIS The "lord of the lance," a god of war and hunting, depicted as a bearded man carrying a lance or a rope and wearing a large, plumed headdress.
OPENING OF THE MOUTH RITUAL A ritual consisting of seventy-five acts designed to bring the deceased and his statue back to life.
OPET A Theban festival of the New Kingdom held annually in the second month of the inundation when statues of kings and deities were taken from Karnak to Luxor Temple. The procession is depicted on the walls of the processional colonnade of Luxor Temple. Its purpose was to celebrate the sexual union of Amen and the king's mother from which came the royal *ka*.
OSIRIS Important god of death, resurrection, fertility, depicted as a mummy holding a flail and scepter. Called Foremost of the Westerners, his cult center lay at Abydos.
OSTRACON Sherds of pottery or stone inscribed with text or drawings.
OUROBOROS A snake biting its own tail and a reference to endless time and space.
PE See Buto.
PTAH Creator-god of Memphis; husband of Sekhmet; god of craftsmen; often joined with Ptah-tjenen, an earth god, or the mortuary god Sokar. He was represented mummiform, wearing a tight-fitting skull cap, hands protruding from his cloak.
PYLON Greek for "gate," referring to the sloping-sided massive towers and doorway that define the entrance of a temple, said to represent two mountains on the horizon.
QEBEHSENUEF See Canopic Jars.
RA Sun god par excellence; associated with creation, whose cult center was originally at Heliopolis. He is represented as a hawk-headed human, a man with the head of a falcon, a ram, or a scarab, a scarab beetle, a heron, snake, bull, cat, lion, solar disk, and in many other forms. He was sometimes joined with Harakhty, Amen, Horus, Khepri, Atum, and several other gods.
RED CROWN The royal crown of Lower Egypt.
RENENUTET Cobra goddess, often identified with Isis, who served as a protector of the king, pregnant women, and the grain harvest.
SAH Personification of the constellation Orion and of the star Sirius.
SAIS Western Delta town of Sa al-Hajar sacred to the goddess Neith and capital of Egypt during Dynasty 26, the Saite Period.
SATIS, SATET Goddess said to protect Egypt's southern border and to be the source of the Nile, depicted as a woman wearing the White Crown of Upper Egypt with attached plumes or horns.
SCARAB Amulet modeled after the shape of a scarab beetle and associated with Khepri.
SED FESTIVAL, HEB-SED FESTIVAL A ritual of rejuvenation celebrated by a king after thirty years of rule.
SEKHMET Lion goddess; daughter of Ra and consort of Ptah, who bore aggressive female attributes in contrast to the more benign goddess Mut.
SEM-PRIEST A funerary priest who oversaw burial rituals, shown wearing a panther skin.
SERQET, SELKET Scorpion goddess, associated with the protection of royal funerary equipment, especially the sarcophagus and canopic jars, who offered protection from scorpion bites.
SESHAT Goddess of writing, surveying, and the *Sed*-festival, depicted as a woman with a rosette-like headdress.
SETH God of chaos and confusion but also of strength and protection. Iron was called the "bones of Seth." In spite of unpleasant attributes he was highly revered in the New Kingdom (Sety I). He often was shown as a man with a canine-like head, or as a donkey, goat, pig, fish, or other unappealing animal.
SHABTI "The Answerer," a mummiform figurine meant to perform menial tasks on behalf of the deceased in the afterlife and placed in large numbers in most tombs.
SHESMETET A lion goddess, perhaps to be identified with Sekhmet or Bastet.
SHU God of air and sunlight (see Ennead), represented as a man and supporting Nut.
SIA God of intelligence and perception, closely tied to Hu.
SISTRUM Hand-held musical rattle associated with Hathor.
SOBEK Crocodile god, depicted as a crocodile or a man with a crocodile head, associated with protection of the king and with water.
SOKAR Hawk-headed human god of Memphis; linked with Osiris and Ptah as Ptah-Sokar-Osiris, an important funerary deity.
SOLAR BARK Two boats, one for the day and one for the night, which carried the sun through the heavens and the king into the Netherworld.
SONS OF HORUS See Canopic Jars.
SOPDU Falcon god associated with the star Sothis, and a god of the eastern deserts.
STELA An inscribed slab of stone often similar in shape to a modern tombstone and used in a place for funerary offerings.
SYCOMORE *Ficus sycomorus*, the sycomore fig tree, much admired in Egypt for its dense, waterproof wood and prolific, edible figs. The tree was said to be home to several goddesses, including forms of Hathor and Isis. There is a fine drawing of the tree in KV 34.
TALATAT Inscribed sandstone blocks of relatively small size, used by Amenhetep IV/ Akhenaten in temple building. The word comes from the Arabic word for "three," referring to their three-hand breadth size, or may originally have come from the Italian word "agiliata," meaning "cut masonry."
TA-TJENEN A bisexual deity who symbolized the fertility of the Nile Valley after the inundation; the "mother and father" of the gods; and a protector of the deceased king; depicted as a bearded man with a sun disk and horned crown.

TAWERET An apparently pregnant hippopotamus-lion-crocodile composite goddess who protected women during pregnancy and childbirth.

TEFNUT Lion-headed goddess of the atmosphere in the Netherworld with attributes similar to Shu; goddess of the atmosphere in this world.

THOTH, DJEHUTY God of writing, often depicted as a baboon, an ibis, or a man with the head of either. His importance in the royal cult is indicated by the use of his name in royal ones, i.e., Thutmes.

TORUS MOLDING See Cavetto cornice.

TRIAD A group of three, often related, gods, such as the Theban triad of Amen, Mut, and Khonsu.

URAEUS A cobra, identified with the king and with Ra, that often appeared on royal crowns.

VICEROY OF KUSH, KING'S SON OF KUSH New Kingdom administrator of Nubia and a confidant of the king.

VIZIER Directly below the king and the head of the secular administration. The Theban tomb of the vizier Rekhmire offers details of his duties.

WADI An Arabic term referring to a desert stream bed, originally water-cut but now dry except in rare periods of rainfall and flooding.

WAS-SCEPTER A staff topped with a stylized canine head, streamers and feathers, which came to be the emblem of the Theban nome.

WASET The ancient name of Thebes.

WEPWAWET Jackal god whose name means The Opener of the Ways, suggesting that he assisted the king both in battle and entering the afterlife.

WHITE CROWN The royal crown of Upper Egypt.

ESSENTIAL BIBLIOGRAPHY

Arnold, Dieter. *Lexikon der aegyptischen Baukunst*. Bonn, 1994. Published in English as: *The Encyclopaedia of Ancient Egyptian Architecture*. London, 2003.

Assmann, Jan. *Agypten: Theologie und Froemmigkeit einer fruehen Hochkultur.* Berlin, 1984. Published in English as: *The Search for God in Ancient Egypt*. Ithaca, New York, 2001.

Brand, Peter. *The Monuments of Seti I*. Leiden, 2000.

Cerny, Jaroslav. *A Community of Workmen at Thebes in the Ramesside Period*. Cairo, 1973.

Hornung, Erik. *Tal der Konige*. Zurich, 1982. Published in English as: *Valley of the Kings*. New York, 1990.

Hornung, Erik. *The Ancient Egyptian Books of the Afterlife*. Ithaca, New York, 1999.

Kitchen, Kenneth. *Pharaoh Triumphant: The Life and Times of Ramesses II King of Egypt*. Warminster, 1981.

Kozloff, Arielle P. and Betsy Bryan. *Egypt's Dazzling Sun: Amenhotep III and His World*. Cleveland, 1992.

Meskell, Lynn. *Private Life in New Kingdom Egypt*. Princeton, 2002.

Murnane, William J. *United With Eternity: A Concise Guide to the Monuments of Medinet Habu*. Cairo and Chicago, 1980.

Nims, Charles F. *Thebes of the Pharaohs: Pattern for Every City*. London, 1965.

Piankoff, Alexandre. *The Tomb of Ramesses VI*. New York, 1954.

Reeves,C. Nicholas. *The Complete Tutankhamun*. London, 1990.

Riefstahl, Elizabeth. *Thebes in the Time of Amunhotep III*. Norman, Oklahoma, 1964.

Romer, John. *Valley of the Kings*. London, 1981.

Strudwick, Nigel and Helen Strudwick. *Thebes in Egypt*. London, 1994.

Wilkinson, Richard. *The Complete Temples of Ancient Egypt*. London, 2000.

Wilkinson, Richard and C. Nicholas Reeves. *The Complete Valley of the Kings*. London, 1996.

T.G.H. James. *Tutankhamun, the eternal splendour of the boy pharaoh*. Vercelli, 2000.

T.G.H. James. *Ramesses II*. Vercelli, 2002.

Kent R. Weeks. *The valley of the Kings, the tombs and the funerary temples of Thebes west*. Vercelli, 2001.

Alessandro Bongioanni. *Luxor and the Valley of the Kings*. Vercelli, 2004.

Catharine H. Roehrig. *Explorers and artists in the Valley of the Kings*. Vercelli, 2001.

INDEX

nn = dedicated chapter
c = caption

B

C

D

O

P

Q

PHOTOGRAPHIC CREDITS

All photographs are by Araldo De Luca/Archivio White Star except the following:

Archivio Scala: page 27 bottom

Archivio White Star: pages 14-15, 16-17, 18, 20 bottom, 22, 23, 24, 25, 26, 27 top, 28-29 bottom, 29 top, 30-31, 34 right, 34-35, 47 bottom, 54 detail, 57, 58, 161 top, 250-251

Antonio Attini/Archivio White Star: pages 56, 63, 72 top, 75, 80 top, 81 left and right, 82, 84 top and bottom, 86-87, 90 top, 91, 92, 98-99, 103 top, 104 top, 104 bottom, 105, 107, 108 109, 112 right, 113, 128 left, 128 detail, 156 bottom, 157 right, 166 detail, 167, 169, 170 detail, 171, 172 left, 173, 174, 176 detail, 177 top, 182 bottom, 183 detail, 184-185, 186 top, 187 top right, 208 detail, 208, 210 top and bottom, 220-221, 514-515, 520, 521, 522-523, 525 top, 525 bottom, 526-527, 528 detail, 528, 530-531, 531 left, 533, 534-538, 535 top, 538, 539 bottom, 540 detail, 541 left, 542 top, 542-543, 543, 544-545, 546, 547 top right, 550 left and right

Marcello Bertinetti/Archivio White Star: pages 8, 18-19, 20 top, 21, 60-61, 61 detail, 66-67, 72-73, 76 right, 76-77, 77, 78-79, 88, 92 detail, 93, 94-95, 99 bottom, 100-101, 102-103, 106, 106-107, 114-115, 116, 123 bottom, 124, 129, 143, 144-145, 147, 149 bottom, 151, 157 left, 161 bottom, 163 left and right, 166-167, 170-171, 175 top, 177 bottom, 178, 180, 182-183, 184, 187 bottom, 189 top, 193, 195, 197, 202-203, 204-205, 207 bottom left, 208-209, 212, 213 top, 213 bottom, 214, 217, 220, 223, 228-229, 354 detail, 355, 519, 529 top, 532 left and right, 540-541, 548-549

National Library, Florence: pages 22-23

Giovanni Dagli Orti: page 439

Giovanni Dagli Orti/Corbis/ Contrasto: pages 364 detail, 365 left, 419

Francis Dzikowski/Theban Mapping Project: page 246 detail, 247 detail, 284 detail, 286 detail, 294 detail, 295, 296 detail, 297 bottom, 297 top right, 310 detail, 310 bottom, 312 detail, 311 top, 312-313 top, 315 left, 315 right

Eberhard Theim/Lotos Film: pages 437 top left and right, 440

Alfio Garozzo/Archivio White Star: page 49, 61, 70, 72 bottom, 74-75, 78 top and bottom, 80 bottom, 82-83, 83 left and right, 84-85, 90 bottom left, 90 bottom center, 90 bottom right, 96-97, 99 top and detail, 101 top, 114 detail, 115 detail, 115, 118, 120-121, 122-123, 123 top, 124-125, 125, 126-127, 128 right, 130-131, 132-133, 148 detail, 152-153, 156 top, 160, 162, 164 top and bottom, 168 left and right, 172 right, 175 bottom, 180 bottom, 183 top, 183 bottom, 185 top, 185 bottom, 186 bottom left and right, 187 top left, 192 detail, 194 left and right, 196 left and right, 196-197, 198-199, 200-201, 202 bottom left and right, 203, 204, 205 bottom left and right, 206, 207 top, 207 bottom right, 209, 210-211, 214-215, 215, 219, 228 detail, 233 top and bottom, 235 top right, 321, 357, 510, 512, 516 right, 516-517, 517, 518 top, 518 bottom, 524-525, 526 bottom, 527 top, 531 right, 536, 537 top, 537 bottom left, 539 top, 542 bottom, 551

Kenneth Garrett: page 287 top

Abdel Ghaffar Shedid: pages 436 detail, 438-439, 440-441, 441

Griffith Institute/Ashmolean Museum, Oxford: pages 32, 33

J.AND. Livet: pages 492 detail, 493 top, 494, 495, 496-497, 497 top and bottom, 498, 499 top and bottom

Yann Rantier/CNRS: page 285 top

Nicholas Reeves: page 30 top

Alberto Siliotti, Geodia: pages 28-29 top, 29 detail, 422 detail, 423 top, 485 top, 486 left and right, 487

Giulio Veggi/Archivio White Star: pages 3, 43, 47 top, 65, 70-71, 76 left, 101 bottom, 103 bottom, 104-105, 116-117, 154-155, 159, 180 top, 202 top, 526 top, 535 bottom, 547 top left, 547 bottom, 548 detail

Kent Weeks: pages 110, 111 left and right, 112 left, 461 bottom, 462-463, 463, 468

Kent R. Weeks/Theban Mapping Project: page 247 top

Courtesy: Ministry of Cultural Heritage, Museum of Egyptian Antiquities Superintendence, Turin: page 30 bottom

Courtesy of Huguette Hamers: page 488 detail

Courtesy of Thierry Benderitter: page 508 detail, 508 bottom, 509 top

Drawings and maps

Walton Chan/Archivio White Star: pages 69, 119, 150, 166, 170, 179, 189 bottom, 192, 218, 235 bottom, 241, 247 bottom, 248, 255, 258, 268 bottom, 274-275 bottom, 285 bottom, 287 bottom, 289 right, 294-295, 296-297, 298-299, 306 right, 311 bottom, 312-313 bottom, 318-319 top, 348-349 bottom, 358, 365 right, 367 bottom, 375 bottom, 393 top right, 409 bottom, 417 bottom, 423 bottom, 425 bottom, 437 bottom, 445, 451, 454, 461 top, 464 bottom, 471 bottom, 478 bottom, 485 bottom, 488, 493 bottom, 501, 509 bottom, 516 left, 527 bottom, 529 bottom, 537 bottom right, 541 right, 549

Angelo Colombo/Archivio White Star: pages 10-11, 224-225, 234 cartouche, 241 cartouche, 246 cartouche, 248 cartouche, 254 cartouche, 258 cartouche, 268, 272 cartouche, 284 cartouche, 288 cartouche, 294 cartouche, 297 cartouche, 298 cartouche, 304 cartouche, 310 cartouche, 312 cartouche, 316 cartouche, 346 cartouche

Elisabetta Ferrero/Archivio White Star: pages 274-275 top, 318-319 bottom color only, 324 color only, 330 color only, 333 right color only, 335 color only, 339 bottom color only, 374 bottom, 374-375

Oxford Cartographers/ Archivio White Star: pages 232-233 color only, 318-319 bottom lines only, 324 lines only, 330 lines only, 333 right lines only, 335 lines only, 339 bottom lines only, 356-356, 390-391

Elena Tagliabò/Archivio White Star: pages 144 detail, 146

Theban Mapping Project: pages 230-231, 232-233 lines only

All details in black and white are by: Angelo Colombo/Archivio White Star

The publishers would like to thank the following photographers:

Su Bayfield
Huguette Hamers
Thierry Benderitter
Jimmy Dunn

THE AUTHOR

Kent Weeks has conducted archaeological work in Egypt since 1983 and has worked for over thirty years in Thebes and the Valley of the Kings. He is currently Professor of Egyptology at the American University in Cairo and Director of the Theban Mapping Project. Author of over a dozen books and a frequent lecturer and television presenter worldwide, Professor Weeks is the author of over a dozen books among them *The Valley of the Kings* published by White Star Publishers in 2001.

The publishers would like to thank:

His Excellency **Farouk Hosny** - Egyptian Minister of Culture
Zahi Hawass - Secretary General of the Supreme Council of Antiquities and Director of the Giza Pyramids Excavations
Sabry Abd El Aziz Khater - General Director of Antiquities of Luxor and Upper Egypt;
Mohamed A. El-Bialy - General Director of Antiquities of Thebes-West;
Dr Taha Abd Elaleem - President of the Egyptian Information Center;
Apya Shakran - Director General of the Cairo Press Center;
Francesco Zanchi;
A special mention to **Gamal Shafik**, Cairo Press Center and to **Sky Cruise,** Cairo, for their cooperation in the balloon photography.